Last call?

Christians!

Are You Really Serving GOD?

non-Christians!

Have You Checked Out GOD For Yourself?

Pray and think about it!

Seventh Edition

By

John Watobe Hisserv
[John Wants to be His servant]

Edited by

Edward V. Bailey

Published by

B-F Enterprises, Inc.
PO Box 1295
Lakeville, MN 55044-1295

COPYRIGHT INFORMATION

First Edition – Copyright June 24, 1997
Second Edition – completed October 1, 2004
Third Edition – completed July 1, 2005
Fourth Edition – completed February 1, 2006
Fifth Edition – completed April 1, 2006
Sixth Edition – completed April 1, 2007
Seventh Edition – Copyright September 2008

ISBN-13 978-0-9800739-0-4

Library of Congress Control Number: 2008928318

USE-PERMISSIONS

If your beliefs are consistent with all of the essential concepts, facts, and beliefs of Christianity, which are listed in the essay – "What did the author hope to accomplish with this book?", you are hereby granted permission to copy and/or to use any portion of this book in "any noncommercial way" that you feel will glorify God, but you must respect the following "use-permission" conditions. That is, not all of the listed "use-permissions" are transferrable.

If your beliefs are not consistent with all of the essential concepts, facts, and beliefs of Christianity, which are listed in the essay – "What did the author hope to accomplish with this book?", you may not use, modify, reproduce, store in a retrieval system, or transmit in any form or by any means – electronic, mechanical, photocopy, recording, or otherwise – without the written permission of the publisher.

Excerpts from the book – "The Lost Books of the Bible and the Forgotten Books of Eden".
Used under the fair-use policy of being for the purposes of criticism, commentary,
definition, comparison, and/or illustration relative to the position taken by
author John Watobe Hisserv in the applicable essays.

The essay – "What is biblical justice?", is a transcription of several Bible study sessions
conducted by Rev. Eugene Burrell of the Navigators Ministry.
Used by permission of Rev. Eugene Burrell.

The essay – "Does the Bible contradict itself?", is one of three parts
of a web document authored by Dr. Michael J. Bumbulis and two others.
The part used in this book was authored by Dr. Bumbulis.
Used by permission of Dr. Michael J. Bumbulis.

References from the video – "A Question of Origins",
produced by Eternal Productions.
Used by permission of Mr. Jim Tetlow.

References from the "*Easton's Bible Dictionary*", by M. G. Easton.
Used under the public-domain policy.

Comments by Rev. Jack Hayford,
Used under the fair-use policy.

References from the on-line Christian dictionary by Matthew Slick.
(at www.carm.org/dictionary)
Used under this author's intentions to use any profits from this book for the Lord's work.

Comments by Dr. D. James Kennedy.
Used by permission of Coral Ridge Ministries.

Comments by Pastor Alistair Begg.
Used by permission of Pastor Alistair Begg.

Reprints from Pastor Steve King's booklet – "Is the Bible True?".
Used by permission of Pastor Steve King.

Definitions of the words – "Scriptures" and "graphai", from
www.godandscience.org/discovery/chapter1.html.
Used by permission of author Richard Deem.

Paraphrased comments from a
discussion of "the Apocrypha" from www.sacred-texts.com/bib/apo/index.htm.
Used under educational discussion policy, because the web document was not copyrighted
nor was any contact information provided.
Used under the educational-fair-use policy.

Definition of "Vulgate" at www.ntcanon.org/Vulgate.shtml.
Used under the fair-use policy.

Reprint of Q & A from www.studentbodyworld.com.
Used by permission of Ms. Heather Merrill.

Reprint from the web document at www.studentbodyworld.com/Q%20and%20A/
where_did_the_verses_in_the_bible_come_from.htm .
Used by permission of Mr. Jeremy Tullis.

Definitions from "Webster's Revised Unabridged Dictionary [1913], © 1996, 1998 MICRA, Inc.",
Used under the provision that its definitions consist of less than 1% of this book.

Excerpts from the "Ineffabilis Deus", by Pope Pius IX in 1854.
Used under the fair-use policy of being for the purposes of criticism, commentary,
definition, comparison, and/or illustration relative to the position taken
by author John Watobe Hisserv in the applicable essays.

Excerpts from the "*NPNF2-14. The Seven Ecumenical Councils*", by Philip Schaff.
(at http://www.ccel.org/ccel/schaff/npnf214.toc.html)
Used under public-domain policy.

Statements from the Answers In Genesis website,
comments by Mr. Ken Ham of the Answers In Genesis Ministry, &
excerpt from the book – "Millions of Years & the Downfall of the Christian West",
by Terry Mortenson, Ph.D. of the Answers In Genesis Ministry.
Used by permission of the Answers In Genesis Ministry.

DEDICATION

This book is dedicated to my beloved parents.

John Watobe Hisserv

[**John** **Wa**nts **to be** **His serv**ant]

FOREWORD

The Lord works in mysterious ways, His wonders to perform. "My ways are not your ways and My thoughts are not your thoughts", says the Lord (See Isaiah 55:8-9).

In my life as a Christian, I have been ever amazed at the ways the Lord follows, to do His will in the lives of His people, "the ones who believe that He exists and that He rewards those who earnestly and diligently seek Him out". (See Hebrews 11:6.) How He enabled me to review the fourth edition of this book that glorifies Him and defends His presence, is one of the myriads of His ways. Blessed are those who can recognize His presence in their life and give Him all the Glory, for nothing happens accidentally in the life of a person, who loves God, works toward His purpose, and lives by faith in Him. "Her or his steps are directed by the Lord". (See Psalms 37:23.)

While I was partway through my review of the fourth edition of this book, I asked Ed, the publisher of the book, "Ed, how did you get in touch with me?" He replied, "While doing some research for the author, I called your church and asked to talk to someone about the Greek Orthodox Christian view, on several religious issues. They gave me your name and telephone number." I have never met Ed to this day, neither have I met the author. I have been in contact with Ed via telephone and e-mail. Yet, it was the Lord's will for me to review this book, because of the meandering path He led me through, before I found Him. Because of this path, I was able to look at this book, but not from a doctrinal and denominational point of view. Ed entrusted me, by mailing the book in its original form: *a Microsoft Word copy (on a CD) and a printed copy.* I went through it and returned it with a number of suggestions and corrections. Ed told me that he approached me to review the fourth edition of this book, because my review of the previous edition was one of the most thorough. I cannot take credit for that. I love the Lord and I saw the value of the book. He is the One, Who guided me to be as thorough as possible. My second review served, as an attempt to make the book easier to read and to point to areas, where a revision was required, to enable the book to depict correctly the unseen world we live in, the world of the spirits, which any religion is trying to depict and pierce. As a result of this effort, additional changes took place by the author and the publisher. It is the earnest hope of the three of us that this book will enable you to answer some questions you may have, to motivate you to start asking additional questions, and to raise a thirst in you to try to find Him, for there is nothing like Him, if you have Him in your life.

I have been ever amazed, eternally grateful and humbled with His saving action, the power of faith, reliance in Him for everything, how He guides, protects and provides, and the mystery of answered prayer in impossible circumstances in my life and the life of others.

I have been blessed to having started, as a Greek Orthodox by birth and having lived in Greece for nineteen years, the early years of my life, a country immersed in Christian Orthodoxy. I have been blessed to having been exposed through public education in Greece to the New and the Old Testament. In my search for God, after I arrived in the USA, I spent several years in the Episcopal Church and thereafter looked into various ways to find Him, for I was looking for a salvation from problems I was encountering.

I followed all sorts of paths and ended in all sorts of blind alleys. At the end of each search, He guided me back to the Judeo-Christian Holy Scriptures, the Bible, which saved my life. It is through the mystical synergy of God and man that He accomplished the transformation of my mind through His Word, which I accepted by faith. Thus, He led me away from destruction, and to His blessedness. I substituted all the wrong perceptions, attitudes, predispositions, preconceptions with His promises and the way He acts and is, as taken out of His Holy Scriptures, His Word. I put them in my heart.

I can vouch that there is power, mystical power in the Word of God, for I have experienced it. His Word is Truth. A person, who diligently seeks Him, will certainly find Him and will realize, that if they put their trust in the words that He says, what He says are not idle words, but are words of transforming miraculous power. Even though I have never seen Him, I know that He exists. I know that through prayer that was answered in the most impossible way, prayer that only Him and I knew about. I know that He is there, in me, around me, working through me. I know that He is accurately revealed through His Holy Scriptures. I also know through experience that if one follows His voice, as revealed in His Word and in her or his heart, and obeys it, she or he will see great blessings in her or his life.

In the last fifteen years of my sixty-five years of life, I returned to the Greek Orthodox Church. I have been solidly footed in the Eastern Orthodox mystical way of looking at the unseen world of the spirits, God and His energies. It is through His energies that He blesses the life of His people, delivering them from all sorts of bondage and bringing upon them His abundant blessings, due to His great mercy. Yet, I have retained my contact with the Pentecostal and the Charismatic movement, for the Lord works mightily in our days through chosen vessels, whether Orthodox, Pentecostal, Charismatic, etc. He works through whosoever He chooses His miracles and wonders to perform in the life of those who believe in Him, the same way as He did two thousand years ago, when He appeared on earth.

The author, Ed, and I are of different Christian backgrounds. I am Greek Orthodox. They have a Protestant and Catholic background. Yet, all three of us love the Lord and have been united in this project, because of our love for Him. I feel very strongly that there are a huge number of points of faith among Christians with various backgrounds that can be agreed upon. That could happen only through an open mind and lack of denominational indoctrination, under the direction of the Holy Spirit. People of goodwill can discuss, share and with an open mind expand their view of the mystery that is God and His acting among His people. This is the hope that the author, the publisher, and I have in working on this book.

I marvel at the dedication of the author and the amount of work and thought he has put into this book. As he says himself, "this book treats all sorts of subjects that could help the reader to examine their own beliefs on any topic that the book touches. It is a point of contact and the beginning of an exchange of ideas that might lead to spiritual awareness and spiritual growth." I admire the author, for he is tackling subjects that for the most part, I have personally left untouched and accepted by faith. This is especially the case pertaining to what was referred to in Genesis regarding creation, Adam and Eve, Noah and the Ark, the Life of the Patriarchs, etc. I drew from them important lessons that have shaped my life. Yet I concentrated mostly on other aspects of the Divine Revelation that are pertinent to the soul, which the Holy Scriptures are full of, and which have had a tremendous impact in my spiritual development and salvation from bondage. Nevertheless, I love the spirit with which the author approached the whole book, which is "Let us, all Christians, start discussing some fundamental issues and confirm whether we are really serving God."

May this book bless you and may it open new horizons in your spiritual journey. May it answer questions that have been stumbling blocks in your spiritual development. May it enable you to get closer to the Lord through increased knowledge of Him. And may you be set free from all bondage through His Grace. He is willing and able to guide you and enable you to lead a truly blessed life! He will do it if you really thirst for it and obey His voice, no matter what the cost.

Nicolas Criticos
Greek Orthodox Christian
Spring 2006

ACKNOWLEDGMENTS

In composing or gathering the essays in this book, this author was motivated and/or helped, by many individuals. These individuals can be divided into five groups, as follows:

Group-1 consists of Christians, who have directly or indirectly shared their faith and their knowledge with me. Many of the individuals in this group and some of the organizations, which promote their views are listed in the bibliography of this book. Additional comments about some members of this first group are included in the preface.

Group-2 consists of individuals, who asked questions about Christianity or made comments about Christianity in my presence. Their questions and comments caused me to remember statements made, by individuals in the first group. The remembered statements, along with a little pondering and prayer, motivated me to respond to the questions and comments. My responses and further reflections led to many of the essays in this book. Thus, this author can attribute specific essays to the inspiration of questions or comments from specific individuals. For example, several of my nieces and nephews inspired the essay: "What is life all about?" Mr. Ronald W. Brown inspired the two essays: "Did God create man through evolution?" and "Are deathbed conversions to Christianity fair?" *(The essay – "Are deathbed conversions to Christianity fair?", is in a second book: "Last Call!!!")* A co-worker inspired the essay: "Do the four Gospels present in a consistent manner the last words of Christ and the last events, as He died on the cross?" Mr. Robert A. Madoo inspired the four essays: "Is Jesus the only way to God?"; "How should Christians respond to a 'We-don't-know' statement?"; "What is the only meaningful question, about 'God' and 'Christianity'?"; and "Is it proper to use the Bible to prove the Bible?" *(The essay – "Is it proper to use the Bible to prove the Bible?", is in the book: "Last Call!!!")* Mr. John Rickford inspired the essay – "Is evolution a matter of facts or of faith?", which is also in the book: "Last Call!!!"

Group-3 consists of seven individuals, who had a more direct impact on the first two editions of this book. These seven individuals are my mother, two of my sisters, one of my brothers, Mr. George Jones[1], a co-worker (*who did not want her name used here*), and Mr. Edward V. Bailey. My mother read an early draft of the essay: "What is life all about?" Her comments resulted in a major rewrite of that essay. One of my sisters provided some helpful comments about my grammar. Another sister and a brother provided some useful comments on several of the essays. Mr. Jones edited the first two editions of this book. His comments and suggestions also resulted in many rewrites and several new essays. My unnamed co-worker read an early draft of this book, made many helpful suggestions, and inspired several new essays. Mr. Bailey also read many of the essays and provided many helpful comments. But Mr. Bailey's major contributions were to encourage me to write these essays, to agree to publish this book, and to agree to shield my identity, as this was a labor of love, not of glory. To ease the copyright process and shield my identity, Mr. Bailey allowed me to use his name and the name of his company on the copyright documents. Anyway, all of the comments and suggestions made by this group resulted in improvements to this book.

Group-4 consists of more than twenty individuals, who read the second edition of this book looking for grammatical consistency, logical consistency, and biblical consistency. Not all of these individuals agreed with the conclusion of every essay. Consequently, whenever possible, those who disagreed, were asked for the reasons for their disagreement. This author read those reasons and then revised some of the essays in an attempt to address those disagreements. Nevertheless, regardless of whether their disagreements were addressed, all of the individuals in this group provided some valuable comments to this author.

Group-5 consists of a sister, the editor, and Mr. Nicolas Criticos. They read the fourth edition of this book. My sister and the editor found some grammatical and logic errors. Mr. Criticos also found errors, and then he made many very detailed suggestions, about a variety of issues. With the assistance of the editor, Mr. Criticos' suggestions were reviewed and incorporated into the fifth edition of this book, as this author deemed appropriate. The sixth edition resulted from this author's review of the fifth edition. Especially, because of Mr. Criticos' suggestions, this author feels that there was a major improvement in the readability of the fifth and sixth editions of this book.

This opportunity is taken to express my deepest gratitude to everyone in these five groups and to anyone else, who should have been mentioned, but was not.

John Watobe Hisserv
[**John Wa**nts **to be His serv**ant]

TABLE OF CONTENTS

DEDICATION. i

FOREWORD. iii

ACKNOWLEDGMENTS. vii

TABLE OF CONTENTS. ix

PREFACE. xiii

ABBREVIATIONS USED IN THIS BOOK. xvii

DISCLAIMER. xix

Opening prayer. 1

What is life all about?. 3

Does God exist?. 21

What are some names, terms, and phrases, which are useful to a discussion of the formation of the Christian Bible?. 43

What do biblical scholars, Christian historians, and others say, about the formation of the Christian Bible?. 69

Is the Bible the inspired word of God?. 97

Can I prove the credibility of the Bible for myself?. 131

Does the Bible contradict itself?. 135

How is it possible for different believers to get different interpretations of the same verses of the Bible?. 139

Do the four Gospels present in a consistent manner the last words of Christ and the last events, as He died on the cross?. 149

Did Jesus claim to be God and/or the Son of God?. 157

What does the phrase – "ability to sin", mean?
(Is the phrase – "ability to **not** sin", meaningful or is it inappropriate?). 163

What do the three phrases – "knowledge of good and evil",
"knowledge of good", and "knowledge of evil", mean?
and
What is "the age of accountability"?. 171

Is "judgment" one of God's attributes?. 193

Did Jesus, the man, have the "ability to sin"
like Adam and Eve?. 195

Are there unbiblical-heretical
"Jesus Died Spiritually" doctrines and
a biblical "Jesus Died Spiritually" doctrine?. 215

What is the literal and symbolic significance
in the shedding of Jesus' innocent blood?. 243

Is Jesus the only way to God?. 255

Does man have a body, a soul, and a spirit?.. 279

Did Mary also have to be sinless,
since Jesus was born sinless through her?. 295

How do we know that the genealogy of Jesus
in the Gospel of Luke is through Mary?. 323

Did God create man through evolution?. 341

Does the union of a sperm and an egg create human life?. 361

When does human life begin?. 367

Is variety the spice of life?. 379

Is there such a thing, as safe sex?. 385

Should Christians worship God,
under the leadership of a homosexual?. 395

On Judgment Day, how will God probably respond
to nonbelievers, who say,
"They never had a chance to know Him"?. 401

Did God lose ownership of the earth, when Adam sinned,
as some preachers claim?. 407

If God knows where each individual will spend eternity,
then how can each individual have free will?. 411

Who is a "born-again" Christian?.. 417

Are all questions valid and/or contextually appropriate?. 419
Can God make a rock, so large that He cannot handle it?".. 419

Are all statements (*non-questions*)
valid and/or contextually appropriate?. 427

How can I have "free will", if I did not choose to be born?. 429

If God is all-powerful and loving,
then why doesn't He end all evil and human suffering?. 435

If you were going to have a son
and you knew that he would become a mass murderer,
would you still have him?.. 441

How should Christians respond to a
"We-don't-know!" statement?. 447

How should Christians respond to an
"It-is-possible-that-such-and-such-happened" statement?. 449
It is possible that life came here from another planet!.. 450

What is the only meaningful question,
about "God" and "Christianity"?. 455
How could a virgin (*Mary*) conceive a child without sexually knowing a man?. 458
How could men accurately record words, supposedly inspired by God, and
then pass these words accurately down through time?. 458
How could God create man out of nothing?.. 459
Who created God?.. 462
How can there be three Gods (God, the Father, God, the Son, and
God, the Holy Spirit) in One?. 462
What if a believer sins and then dies, before she or he can repent?. 463
How could two of every kind of animal fit on Noah's Ark?. 464

What is biblical justice?. 467

Should Christians be angry with Jews,
because they crucified Jesus?.. 475

What did the author hope to accomplish with this book?.. 477

ENDNOTES. 479

APPENDIX A. 499
Basis for the inclusion of the "Thinking view" and the "Eternal view". 499
Daughters and inheritance custom.. 502
Female circumcisions. 503
The meaning of each of the phrases – "lust of the flesh", "lust of the eyes", and "pride of life". 506
The meaning of the word: "Chastely". 506

BIBLIOGRAPHY. 509

INDEX. 511

PREFACE

As indicated in the acknowledgment, this book is a collection of essays, which resulted from the author's interactions, directly or indirectly, with other individuals – both Christians and non-Christians. Some essays were also influenced by the author's interactions with the things of this world. A complete list of the individuals and/or things, would be impossible. However, the bibliography of this book, does list some of the Christians, and some of the organizations that promote their views. Other than Mr. George Jones and some family members, none of the individuals or organizations listed in the bibliography had any overt part in the preparation of this book. **Therefore, please do not consider the inclusion of any name (*whether an individual or an organization*) anywhere in this book to mean that individual or organization endorses or agrees with any statements made in this book.** Thirteen additional things that you should know about this book are, as follows:

1) An attempt was made to arrange the essays in a sequence that made the most sense logically and biblically. Although many essays stand alone, some essays were written under the assumption that the reader has read the previous essays. Consequently, a sequential-read might be more meaningful than a random-read of the essays.

2) Except for a few comments in each, four essays consist of material authored by others. Two essays – "What are some names, terms, and phrases, which are useful to a discussion of the formation of the Christian Bible?" and "What do biblical scholars, Christian historians, and others say, about the formation of the Christian Bible?", consist mostly of comments extracted from various web documents and/or paraphrased based on several web documents. A third essay – "Does the Bible contradict itself?", is a portion of a web document that is no longer available via the Internet. The fourth essay – "What is biblical Justice?", consists of the transcription of several Bible study sessions that were recorded and then shared with the author. All four essays are included in this book, because they are excellent presentations on related issues. Many of the other essays also include material authored by others, but to a lesser extent. Nevertheless, all of the material authored by others should be indicated, as such.

3) If the author has expressed concepts originated by you, he hopes that you will accept his apology and will allow his use of those concepts. Please note that the author does not claim originality for anything expressed within these pages, because God is the author of everything.

4) Some of the statements expressed herein might represent what some would call – "statements of the obvious". By stating the obvious, the author is not trying to insult anyone's intelligence. He simply feels that it is very important to explicitly state, as much as possible. Explicit statements increase the likelihood that a reader will understand the view of a subject, which the author is taking and why.

5) All of the essays written by the author, are presented from a Christian layman's point of view. He does not claim to be a Bible scholar. The main affirmation made by him is a great love for God.

6) Superscript-numbers indicate footnotes or endnotes. Footnotes are at the bottom of the page under a "**centered three-and-half-inch-two-tone-line**", which serves to separate footnotes and the rest of the material on a given page. Any superscript-number not occurring as a footnote on that particular page is an endnote, which is in a section titled – "Endnotes" near the end of this book. Endnotes were used to identify the source of some excerpts and quotes. Occasionally, some information to be shared seemed too important for either a footnote or an endnote; especially, since too many readers do not even bother reading either footnotes or endnotes. Consequently, often the author inserted comments, at various points in the body of an essay, instead of using footnotes or endnotes. These comments are preceded by the word – "*Comment*", which is underlined. Hopefully, these comments add information, which will increase your understanding of where the author is coming from.

7) The primary reason for this book is that many of the issues, which are addressed, need to be discussed. The discussion could be among Christians only, among non-Christians only, or better yet, between Christians and non-Christians. Whichever it is, we need to talk about these issues. Moreover, we need to turn our focus back to Christ and what He did for us by dying on the cross. The time is short. Yet, many are still not thinking about the reality of accepting Christ, as their Lord and Savior, and then serving Him.

8) A second reason for this book is that some issues are points of contention between Christians. One cause of the contention is that too many Christians simply accept the traditional views of their denomination without getting the facts, without praying for the discernment of the Holy Spirit, and/or without studying the Bible for a biblical confirmation. Therefore, the author's hope is that these essays will push Christians into reassessing the traditional views of their denomination. Furthermore, he hopes that Christians will see that in addition to the Bible, our resources include both Christian and Jewish scholars. But more important, Christians must remember that they have the **Holy Spirit** as a resource. Consequently, it is time for Christians to pray for the discernment of the Holy Spirit, then pull together around the Word of God. Hopefully, this will allow us **to put our focus back on Christ and Christ only!**

> *Comment:* Some Christians say that the only things we need are the Bible and the Holy Spirit. What the author is saying is:
>
> > "Yes! Both the Bible and the discernment of the Holy Spirit, are essential. However, some Christian and Jewish scholars have provided some interesting insights, based on their knowledge of the customs and other

conditions that existed, when both the Old and New Testaments were written."

Some of these insights serve to glorify God even more, because they reveal how God worked things out for His purpose and consistent with His revealed word, the Bible. Two excellent examples are: <u>*first*</u>, the shepherds to whom the angels announced the birth of Jesus, and <u>*second*</u>, the Magi, who brought gifts of gold, myrrh, and frankincense to the infant Jesus. More specifically, some beautiful insights about these two examples were shared by a well-known minister. Paraphrased, this minister shared the following beliefs:

- <u>*First*</u>, after studying Luke 2:8-20 and other literature, this minister believed that the sheep, being tended by the shepherds referenced in those verses, were the sacrificial lambs. This is why the sheep were just outside of the town of Bethlehem. *This information displays God's beauty in that* "**the shepherds of the sacrificial lambs, went to visit the greatest sacrificial lamb of them all, Jesus**."

- <u>*Second*</u>, during a presentation explaining the relationship between Daniel, of the Book of Daniel, and the Magi, this minister said that his studies led him to believe that for some period of Daniel's life, Daniel ruled over the Magi. *This explained how the Magi knew about* "Jesus/<u>the Messiah</u>", also referenced as "Jesus, King of the Jews". *And it adds to the beauty of how God worked things out for His purpose. In addition, the relationship between Daniel and the Magi explains why portions of the first five books of the Bible can be found written in the Babylonian language.*

<u>***Important Note***</u>: While the above comments about biblical scholars are true, a reality of life is that a very large volume of literature has been written, about a large variety of biblical issues: *"the origins and definition of heretical doctrines", "biblical doctrines", "individuals, places, <u>and/or</u> things mentioned in the Bible", "the meaning of specific verses", and so on*. Consequently, an individual could spend her or his entire life just reading this large volume of literature, without ever reading the Bible, itself. Thus, care has to be exercised over those things, which we allow to consume our time. This author strongly recommends that all Christians pray for the discernment of the Holy Spirit and then give reading the sixty-six canonical books of the Bible a high priority.

9) It is not the intent of the author to condemn your faith or beliefs. His intent is to encourage you to examine the "what, why, and how" you believe. Perhaps, such an examination will carry over to how you will serve and honor God, and to the traditions that you will observe. Remember! You are responsible for your own beliefs. It is **your responsibility** to verify that everything you read, whether it was written by the author

or someone else, is consistent with the Word of God. It is also **your responsibility** to verify that everything you hear from any religious leader or anyone else is consistent with the word of God. **You must study the Bible and pray for the discernment of the Holy Spirit**.

10) At the author's discretion, a bold font, an italic font, single underlining, double underlining, and/or indentation were used to emphasize some words, phrases, comments, etc. This practice was even carried to some Bible verses included in a discussion.

11) Please forgive the author for two major violations of the formal rules of grammar and punctuation. ***Violation-1***: The formal rules tell writers to always place most punctuation marks inside of closing quote marks instead of outside. This rule made sense to the author, when the quote marks enclosed a complete grammatical unit like a sentence, a question, or an exclamation. However, it made no sense for a simple phrase or any other incomplete grammatical unit, like a single word. Therefore, generally, the author only complied with this rule, when a complete grammatical unit like a sentence, a question, or possibly an exclamation, was involved. ***Violation-2***: The formal rules do not allow a comma between the subject and the verb. However, for this book, whenever the subject was very complicated, included quote marks, or included apostrophes, a comma was used before the verb. This comma also serves to inform someone reading the essay out loud that the author desires a very short pause before the verb.

12) The essays in this book were developed over a period of more than ten years. With each passing month or two, another essay was born. Consequently, in an effort to get this book to the printer, the decision was made to move some essays, which were originally intended to be included in this book, to a second book titled: "Last Call!!!" Hopefully, this second book will not take another ten years to get to the printer.

13) Originally, an italic font was to be used for words spoken by Jesus in any verse of the Bible, but the author failed to be consistent in this regard and for that he apologizes.

Your comments and suggestions are requested, especially, if you find any errors (*grammatical, logical, biblical, or otherwise*). Letters may be directed to the author through the publisher:

B-F Enterprises, Inc.
PO Box 1295
Lakeville, MN 55044-1295.

Emails may be sent to the author at lastcall@b-fenterprises.com. And please visit the publisher's website at www.b-fenterprises.com.

ABBREVIATIONS USED IN THIS BOOK

- **and**
  to emphasize the joining of two or more similar units.

- **and/or**
  to emphasize the joining of two or more similar units.

- **BCE** or **B.C.E.**
  for "Before the Common Era" or "Before the Christian Era". (*Is equivalent to* BC - "*Before Christ*")

- **CE** or **C.E.**
  for "Common Era", sometimes known, as the "Current Era" or the "Christian Era". (*Is equivalent to* AD - *anno Domini, Latin for "in the year of the Lord"*)

- **Holman Bible Dictionary**
  for Holman Bible Dictionary for Windows – Version 1.0g, which is part of the software package: QuickVerse for Windows Version 3.0h Copyright © 1992-1994 by Craig Rairdin and Parsons Technology, Inc.

- Jesus, **the man**
  for Jesus, **the *Messiah*/the *Anointed One*/the *Christ*/the *Son of God***. (*Note that Jesus was fully God and fully man. However, everything that happened on the cross involved His human nature. And that is what the label – "Jesus, the man", is meant to emphasize.*)

- **KJV** *for* King James Version - an English translation of the Bible.

- **Last Call!!!**
  for The book titled: "Last Call!!!" (*subtitled: "Are You **Still** Serving God?"*)

- **Last Call?**
  for This book (*subtitled: "Are You **Really** Serving God?"*)

- **NASB** *for* New American Standard Bible - an English translation of the Bible.

- **NIV** *for* New International Version - an English translation of the Bible.

- **NRSV** *for* New Revised Standard Version - an English translation of the Bible.

- **NT** or **N. T.**
  for New Testament.

- **OT** or **O. T.**
  for Old Testament.

- **QuickVerse**
  for QuickVerse for Windows Version 3.0h Copyright © 1992-1994 by Craig Rairdin and Parsons Technology, Inc.

- ***Wikipedia***
  for Wikipedia, The Free Encyclopedia at:
  http://en.wikipedia.org/wiki/Main_Page

- ***Wiktionary***
  for Wiktionary, The Open Dictionary
  a Wiki-based Open Content Dictionary at:
  http://en.wiktionary.org/wiki/Wiktionary:Main_Page

- **2003 Grolier Multimedia Encyclopedia**
  for 2003 Grolier Multimedia Encyclopedia - Deluxe Two-Disc Edition 16.00

DISCLAIMER

Statement-1:

Many of those who allowed the use of their material in this book did not review the entire book. Therefore, you should not assume that the use of any name in this book, including Mr. Nicolas Criticos (*author of the Foreword*), means that individual or organization agrees with every word in this book.

Statement-2:

The author presents some "**non-traditional views**" on many topics. But he is not saying that it is his way or no way. Rather he is saying let us review the traditional views on many topics and confirm that those views are really consistent with the Bible.

Statement-3:

Over the years, Christians and non-Christians have tossed words around without taking the time to fully think through the meaning and the implications of some of those words. Thus, the author is also saying, "Especially as Christians, we need to look at some of the words that we are using. We need to make sure that we know what those words mean and then we need to understand the implications of those words."

The English language is a very imprecise language. That is why it has so many modifiers to try to pin down the contextual meaning of some words. For example, the Greek language has four different words for "love" and each word carries a precise connotation of the type of love meant. In English, the one word – "love", would have to have many modifiers and/or additional words to indicate the type of "love" meant in a given context.

With the above comments in mind, please be advised that the author is only human. And while he is supposed to be fluent in English (*really the only language that he knows, besides a few German phrases*), there are places in some essays where He has taken a non-traditional meaning of a word or a phrase. Hopefully, the context should indicate where this was done on purpose.

Opening prayer

This opportunity is taken to offer a short two-part prayer: *First*, may the essays in this book glorify God. *Second*, may God use these essays to draw you closer to Christ.

As you read these essays, if you are a Christian, please pray for the discernment of the Holy Spirit. And this author prays that this book will aid you with your evangelistic efforts. If you are a non-Christian, this author prays that this book will address some of your questions about Christianity.

What is life all about?

Worded one way or another, this question is pondered by most of us. Whether an answer is reached or not, everyone, who seeks an answer, must admit that their potential or actual answer will be shaped, by their view of how all things – *this universe, the earth, all nonliving things, and all living things* – were created. Therefore, in this attempt to answer the topic question, please pretend that we have the resources to collect all of the creation views for our world into one group. This means that we would collect creation views from everyone despite their nationality, their social status, their financial status, their education, their religious belief (*whether they are a Catholic, a Protestant, a Jew, a Muslim, an Atheist, an Agnostic, a Buddhist, a New Ager, or whatever*), where they live, and so on. Then having collected all of the creation views into one group, we would divide this collection into **four-subgroups**, using a ***three-step*** process.

- In the ***first-step***, we would divide all the creation views into the "non-Religious views" or the "Religious views".

  Comment: Dividing all of the creation views into the "non-Religious views" or the "Religious views", means that we must have a definition for each of the two groups. Such definitions are, as follows:

  ✓ "Non-Religious views" is "the label that we would put on the group of creation views, which are defined, as 'creation views based on **something *without* a reason for creation**.'" This "something" includes a force or forces (*cosmic or otherwise*), a condition, or nothing (*even though technically, "nothing" is not a "something"*), as the source of creation.

  ✓ "Religious views" is "the label that we would put on the group of creation views, which are defined, as 'creation views based on **something *with* a reason for creation**.'" This "something" includes a personal or impersonal supreme being, as the source of creation.

  The labels – "non-Religious" and "Religious", are intended to convey this author's belief that when individuals and/or cultures associate "something with a reason for creation", with their existence, they begin some type of worship involving that something.

- In the ***second-step***, we would divide the "Religious views" into the "Christian views" and the "non-Christian views".

- In the ***third-step***, we would divide the "non-Christian views" into the "Jewish/Islamic views" and the "non-Jewish/non-Islamic views".

> Comment: The justification for combining creation views with roots in the Jewish religion (*Judaism*) or the Islamic religion (*Islam*) is:
>
> > "Judaism, Islam, and Christianity are called the 'Abrahamic religions'[1]. However, these three religions differ over things like: the meaning of life, the nature of man, the way to salvation, the nature of eternal life, the nature of God, who Jesus is, and His resurrection. But when the similarities and differences are studied, it becomes apparent that Judaism and Islam are closer to each other, than either is to Christianity."

In summary, for this discussion, all the creation views for this world have been assigned to one of four-subgroups: the "non-Religious views", the "non-Jewish/non-Islamic views", the "Jewish/Islamic views", or the "Christian views". Within man's reasoning capacity, the actual way that this universe was created has to be in one of these four-subgroups. "These four-subgroups are inclusive."[2] Nevertheless, someone might say, "There is no way that you could include the 'Thinking view' in one of the four-subgroups." The "**Thinking view**" revolves around "the logic that perhaps, we only think that we exist." Someone else might say, "There is no way that you could include the 'Eternal view' in one of the four-subgroups." The "**Eternal view**" revolves, around the belief that "this world of ours has always existed." However, this author reasoned that both the "Thinking view" and the "Eternal view" have been included in the four-subgroups. The basis for the inclusion of both the "Thinking view" and the "Eternal view", has been included in Appendix A, in an entry titled: "Basis for the inclusion of the 'Thinking view' and the 'Eternal view'".

Up to this point, except for a sorting definition for the subgroup – "non-Religious views" and the grouping – "Religious views", the four-subgroups have not been explicitly defined. To present more precise definitions of each of the four-subgroups and to address the topic question through these four-subgroups, the rest of this essay is organized in four parts. Part-1 presents a definition of each of the four-subgroups and what that definition implies about an individual's behavior and about what life is all about. Part-2 presents a discussion of some problems that this author noticed with three-subgroups: the "non-Religious views", the "non-Jewish/non-Islamic views",

---

1

Judaism, Islam, and Christianity are called the "Abrahamic religions", because Abraham, who lived around 2000 B.C. and who is mentioned in the Old Testament, is considered the father of all Jews and most Arabs. Sometime after 2000 B.C., Judaism developed around the Jews. Under the inspiration of God, the Jews recorded the Old Testament, which consist of the Torah (*which is the first-five books of the Old Testament and is considered their most sacred text*), the writings, and the prophets. Around two thousand years later, Christianity developed around Jesus, who was Jewish. The sacred text of Christianity is called the Bible. It includes the Jewish Old Testament and the non-Jewish New Testament. Around six hundred years after the start of Christianity, Islam developed among the Arabs. The sacred text of the Islamic religion – the Koran, includes stories and references from the Old Testament.

and the "Jewish/Islamic views". Part-3 presents a discussion of the question – "How does the fourth subgroup – the 'Christian views', solve the problems presented by the other three subgroups?" Part-4 presents some concluding comments.

Part-1: **A definition of each of the four-subgroups and what that definition implies about an individual's behavior and about what life is all about**

Each of the four-subgroups is defined using two or three generalized beliefs for that particular subgroup. However, remember that each of the four-subgroups, is itself a collection of individual views. Thus, the two or three beliefs for a given subgroup must represent a summary of all the individual views collected into that particular subgroup. Although all of the individual views within a subgroup are not totally compatible, the two or three beliefs used to define a subgroup should be acceptable, because the similarities between the incompatible individual views within a subgroup are greater than their differences. Furthermore, whenever possible, the two or three belief statements will reflect the terminology of those who hold some of the individual views within a subgroup. After the generalized beliefs are defined, a brief discussion of the implications of those beliefs on an individual's behavior and on what life is about, is presented. Thus, to facilitate the presentation of the generalized beliefs and their implications, Part-1 is organized in four sections, which is a section for each of the four-subgroups.

Section-1: **The subgroup – "non-Religious views" and its implication**

A definition of the subgroup – "non-Religious views", is based on two beliefs. The *first belief* is that life is the result of the random interaction of cosmic forces.

> *Comment:* The phrase – "cosmic forces", is the label, which some men assigned to unknown entities assumed to have been involved in the creation of our universe, but especially involved in the creation of this planet and life on it. Throughout time, comments have been made about the "cosmic forces" and "creation". Some comments are now presented in web documents. But most of those comments are not supportable from other sources or observations like astronomy and especially astrophysics.

The random interaction of these forces means that we are here by chance. Therefore, the *second belief* is that there is no design or purpose, for our existence.

The implication of these beliefs is that there are no constraints on an individual's behavior, other than those constraints that she or he imposes on herself or himself, for her or his physical and/or emotional welfare. This could imply that life is about living for today. Or more explicitly, life is about getting the most physical and/or emotional enjoyment out of each day, with little regard for the future or others.

Section-2: **The subgroup – "non-Jewish/non-Islamic views" and its implication**

A definition of the subgroup – "non-Jewish/non-Islamic views", is based on three beliefs. The *first belief* is that life is the result of creation, by the interaction of cosmic forces and/or by an impersonal god.

> *Comment:* The inclusion of the "interaction of cosmic forces" in this subgroup – "non-Jewish/non-Islamic views", is done under the assumption that the "cosmic forces" are "something with a reason for creation". In contrast, the inclusion of the "interaction of cosmic forces" in the previous subgroup – "non-Religious views", was done under the assumption that the "cosmic forces" were "something without a reason for creation". In short to be thorough, the "cosmic forces" have been included in both subgroups, because we do not have sufficient information about these forces or more important, about their attributes to know whether or not their attributes allow them to have a reason for creation or not.

The *second belief* is that there is a purpose for each life. This purpose is to learn how to be a better human being. The *third belief* is that, as we learn, we progress through various levels or stages of beings, until we reach the highest level. Once we have obtained the highest level, we will be in harmony with the cosmic forces or an impersonal god.

The implication of these beliefs is that there are constraints on an individual's behavior. These constraints are imposed on an individual, by "her or his non-Jewish/non-Islamic religion", and/or by "her or his perceived relationship to the cosmic forces and/or to an impersonal god". Each individual is in control of her or his own behavior, for her or his cosmic or spiritual welfare. These considerations could imply that life is about living to obtain harmony with the cosmic forces or an impersonal god, by controlling our behavior daily. Or worded differently, life is about living for our future cosmic or spiritual welfare, by controlling our behavior daily.

Section-3: **The subgroup – "Jewish/Islamic views" and its implication**

A definition of the subgroup – "Jewish/Islamic views", is based on two beliefs. The *first belief* is that we are here by the design of God/Allah. Many Jews and Muslims believe that God/Allah created us. They also believe that He had a reason for doing so. Therefore, the *second belief* is that God/Allah has a purpose for each life. This purpose is to love and obey God/Allah. Many Jews and Muslims believe that they show their love for God/Allah by obeying His commandments, "Jewish/Islamic" laws, and "Jewish/Islamic" religious traditions.

> *Comment:* The reference to religious traditions has been included for Jews, because the Bible shows that "Jewish religious traditions" had become a distinct force of its own. Over time, "Jewish religious traditions" facilitated changes in Jewish religious laws, or in the way those laws were observed. Christ pointed this out to the Pharisees in "Matthew 15:1-3"[3]. The reference to religious traditions has

been included for Muslims, because some things done in the name of Allah are inconsistent with the Koran. For example, the Koran indicates that Muhammad was the last prophet. However, there are some Islamic sects that acknowledge the existence of prophets after Muhammad by tradition.

Many Jews and most Muslims do not believe that they can know God/Allah. Nevertheless, a few Jews do believe that knowing God is possible. These Jews believe that such knowledge comes through the Torah and through God's creations (*everything that is*).

The implication of these beliefs is that there are constraints on an individual's behavior. These constraints are imposed on an individual by "God's/Allah's commandments", by "religious laws", and/or by "religious traditions". Each individual is in control of her or his own behavior; however, her or his behavior should reflect her or his observance of God's/Allah's commandments, religious laws, and religious traditions. An individual's behavior seals her or his eternal spiritual welfare. These considerations could imply that life is about living righteously (*obeying religious laws, customs, and traditions*), so that an individual can be with God/Allah through eternity. Or better, life is about living for tomorrow - about living for our future spiritual welfare - by controlling our behavior daily.

Section-4: **The subgroup - "Christian views" and its implication**

A definition of the subgroup - "Christian views", is based on two beliefs. The *first belief* is that we are here, by the design of God. The *second belief* is that God has a purpose, for each life. This purpose is to know, love, and serve Him through Jesus, the only begotten Son of God.

Comment: With regards to the "serve Him" aspect, which was mentioned in the previous sentence, you should note two things: *First*, "'serving God' by man's definition", is "man trying to do something for God". *Second*, "'serving God' by God's definition", is "man putting Jesus, and by that God, first in all that man does - that is, man putting Jesus first in every thought, word, or deed".

The implication of these beliefs is that there are constraints on an individual's behavior. These constraints are imposed on an individual by "her or his belief in God", by "God's commandments", by "the birth, life, death, burial, and bodily resurrection of Jesus", and by "the Bible (*which is the inspired word of God*)". In other words, under this subgroup, an individual's behavior (*an individual's lifestyle*) should reflect her or his love for God. Or worded differently, when an individual accepts the death of Jesus as a penalty payment and as an atoning sacrifice for her or his sins, she or he should invite Jesus to take control of her or his behavior. Then her or his behavior should reflect her or his love for God. This does not mean that this individual will automatically live a sinless life from that invitation, until her or his death. Such individuals are still human. However, it should mean that the individual's behavior moves toward being more Christlike. These considerations could imply that life is about living to know, love, and serve God, by accepting the death of Jesus as a penalty payment and as an atoning sacrifice for our sins and for our future spiritual welfare. It is about living a life that is centered on Jesus, by inviting Jesus to live within us. Accepting Jesus allows Him to send the Holy Spirit to live within us, to help us control our behavior daily. Or more precisely, some would say, "Accepting Jesus, allows Him to send the Holy Spirit to live within us, to help us change our behavior to more Christlike behavior daily."

Part-2: **Some problems with three of the four-subgroups**

Problems that this author noticed with three of the four-subgroups, flow out of the generalized beliefs for each of the three-subgroups: the "non-Religious views", the "non-Jewish/non-Islamic views", and the "Jewish/Islamic views". To discuss these problems, Part-2 is organized in three sections. Section-1 presents a discussion of a problem with the subgroup: "non-Religious views". Section-2 presents a discussion of some problems with the subgroup: "non-Jewish/non-Islamic views". Section-3 presents a discussion of a problem with the subgroup: "Jewish/Islamic views".

> *Comment:* Some people may say that this author is on dangerous ground, because he has setup "three-straw men (*defined the generalized beliefs of the three subgroups*)", in order to knock them down. Such a claim could be countered, by addressing each of the individual creation views within the four-subgroups. However, such a task would require too many resources and then the task would probably end with the same conclusions, which result from the generalized approach used by this author.

Section-1: **The subgroup – "non-Religious views" problem**

A problem with the subgroup – "non-Religious views", is the belief that life was created by the random interaction of an unknown number of "cosmic forces". Most promoters of creation theories like these, want others to pick up creation, from the moment that the "cosmic forces" interacted. This moment is called the "Big Bang" by many people. However, the origins of the forces, which interacted to cause the "Big Bang", are never addressed. If the origins were addressed, then there would be only two options: Option-1 is that "the interacting forces were created by other forces". Option-2 is that "the interacting forces always existed".

If Option-1 – "the interacting forces were created by 'other forces'", is true, we must ask, "What is the origin of the 'other forces'?" This starts an endless string of origin questions that can be reduced to one question: "What is the origin of the very 'first set of forces'?" Either the first set of forces was created or they always existed. Under the "non-Religious views", there is no god (*impersonal or personal*) to create the first forces. And if the first forces were created by "other forces", then the "first forces" could not be the "FIRST FORCES". Therefore, the "first forces", the "other forces", or the "interacting forces", as the case may be, must have always existed and this is covered by Option-2.

If Option-2 – "the forces always existed", is true, the eternal existence of these forces and their chance interaction to create life has, at least, three problematic implications: *Implication-1* is that "there was a change in the relationship between these cosmic forces and this change allowed life to be created." *Implication-2* is that "there was a change from a 'no-interaction/no-man' state (*the state before the 'Big Bang'*) to an 'interaction/man' state (*the state after the 'Big Bang'*)." *Implication-3* is that "'CHANCE' is a valid force in the creation of life". Thus, to present a detailed discussion of each of the previously mentioned implications, the rest of Section-1 is organized into three segments, which are each labeled: "implication".

Implication-1: **There was a change in the relationship between these cosmic forces**

This change had to occur in one of three obvious ways or in an unknown way. The three obvious ways are, as follows – *Way-1*: "one or more of these cosmic forces were in motion and their 'relative locations changed'." *Way-2*: "one or more of these cosmic forces existed in the same space and one or more of their 'compositions changed'." *Way-3*: "there were 'relative location changes' and 'composition changes'." Each of these three ways generates a series of problematic questions. For example,

- *Way-1*: If one or more cosmic forces were in motion and their "relative locations changed", allowing these forces to interact, then several questions arise: *first*, "What put them in motion to begin with?"; *second*, "How were their starting locations and directions determined?"; *third*, "What determined the boundaries in which they existed individually and moved collectively?"; and *fourth*, "What determined that these cosmic forces could interact once their relative locations changed?" (*This last question is especially relevant in, light of the existence of substances in this world that do not interact when mixed.*)

- *Way-2*: If one or more cosmic forces existed in the same space and one or more of their "compositions changed", allowing these forces to interact, then several other questions arise: *first*, "What determined their original (*their beginning*) compositions?"; *second*, "What caused the change in their compositions?"; and *third*, "What determined that these cosmic forces could interact once their relative compositions changed?" (*Again, this last question is especially relevant, in light of the existence of substances in this world that do not interact when mixed.*)

- *Way-3*: If there were one or more "relative location changes" and one or more "composition changes", allowing the forces to interact, the occurrence of both *Way-1* and *Way-2* would be less consistent with a random process, than either way by itself.

Nevertheless, if both Way-1 and Way-2 occurred, both sets of the previously mentioned questions apply, especially, the same fundamental question: "What determined that the cosmic forces could interact once their relative locations and compositions changed?"

As some type of change is required under this implication, if it was not one of the previous three ways, then the change had to occur in some unknown way. Even though this way is unknown, it had to involve some characteristics or aspects of the cosmic forces. Furthermore, the fact that this unknown way involved a change means that questions could be asked about the reasons for the change and what or who established the initial conditions with respect to this unknown way. Thus, an unknown way would generate questions similar to the three obvious ways. Therefore, questions generated, by implied changes in the relationship, between the cosmic forces should make one thing perfectly clear: "It is logically weak to believe in the creation of life, as the result of the chance interaction of cosmic forces."

Implication-2: **There was a change from a "no-interaction/no-man" state to an "interaction/man" state**

Based on observations of our physical world and the observations of modern science, "changes" are based on "rules-or-laws", "action-and-reaction", "cause-and-effect", or "some other ordered transition". However, "rules-or-laws" infer a "rule-or-law" giver – God. "Action-and-reaction" infers an "action-and-reaction" designer – God. "Cause-and-effect" infers a "cause-and-effect" designer – God. "Some other ordered transition" infers a designer – God. Otherwise, random interactions would produce random results, and this is not consistent with observations of our physical world or with the observations of modern science. Current observations of our world reveal an exquisite order and balance, which if shaken, results in disorder and imbalance, so we have to conclude that there is a designer (*a law giver*) behind this exquisite order and balance. The designer is God, Who has established the universe and the laws by which it runs. Therefore, the implied "change" from a "no-interaction/no-man" state to an "interaction/ man" state, is a problem in a framework, without God.

Implication-3: **"CHANCE" is a valid force in the creation of life**

Some people assume that "'*CHANCE*' is a valid force in the creation of life." Since according to evolutionists, the cosmic forces interacted by "chance" to cause life to evolve on this planet. However, logically, because life (*physical life*) does not appear to be eternal, the evolution of life must include the creation of life. Or worded differently, life cannot evolve unless it exists. Thus, again, evolutionists want us to believe that "*CHANCE*" created life. But paraphrasing several Christian philosophers, Christian apologists[2], and Christian leaders, we can say:

2

A paraphrased definition of the word – "apologist", is "someone, who is able to present a formal defense of a concept, a belief, a religion, etc., in any setting, such as in a debate, in writing, in an oral presentation, etc."

"'Chance' is not a 'force'. Thus, 'chance' cannot create anything. 'Chance' is a label placed on a variety of known and unknown factors that produce an event or a result."

Therefore, if evolutionists do not know, how life was created, then they should admit that explicitly, instead of trying to use, the logically invalid label: "*CHANCE*".

Conclusion: *Section-1*: ***The subgroup – "non-Religious views" problem***

Section-1 presented comments, questions and considerations that make it difficult, to accept arguments that life is the result of the "*CHANCE*" interaction of cosmic forces. Therefore, it is hard to believe, the implications of the subgroup – "non-Religious views" that we are here, by "*CHANCE*", and that we are here, without a purpose for existing.

Section-2: **The subgroup – "non-Jewish/non-Islamic views" problems**

Problems with the subgroup – "non-Jewish/non-Islamic views", flow out of the generalized beliefs used to define these views. Two such problems are: *first*, "the creation of life by the interaction of cosmic forces and/or by an impersonal god" and *second*, "the suggestion that the purpose for our life is 'learning to be a better human being'". Thus, Section-2 is organized in two segments. *Segment-1* presents a discussion of "the creation of life by the interaction of cosmic forces and/or by an impersonal god". *Segment-2* presents a discussion of "the suggestion that the purpose for our life is 'learning to be a better human being'".

Segment-1: ***The creation of life, by the interaction of cosmic forces and/or by an impersonal god***

This problem is obviously two separate problems: "the creation of life, by the interaction of cosmic forces" and "the creation of life, by an impersonal god". Thus, *Segment-1* is organized in two subsegments. *Subsegment-1* presents a discussion of "the creation of life, by the interaction of cosmic forces". *Subsegment-2* presents a discussion of "the creation of life, by an impersonal god".

Subsegment-1: **The creation of life, by the interaction of cosmic forces**

Trying to discuss "the creation of life, by the interaction of cosmic forces", is difficult, because we have nothing to provide us with supportable information about these cosmic forces, especially information about their attributes. Thus, we are forced to make assumptions about these forces. Under the subgroup – "non-Religious views", the assumption was that the "cosmic forces" did not have attributes, which would allow these forces to have "a reason for creation". However, to be thorough, here under the subgroup – "non-Jewish/non-Islamic views", the assumption is that the "cosmic forces" <u>have</u> attributes, which would allow these forces to have "a reason for creation". While assuming such attributes does not solve the problem of the origin of these "cosmic forces", it does force "the interaction of the cosmic forces" into "being on purpose" instead of "being by chance". More specifically, we can say this because having "a reason for creation" would mean that the "cosmic forces" interacted on purpose to create life.

With regards to the origin of these "cosmic forces" under the subgroup – "non-Jewish/non-Islamic views", either the "cosmic forces" were created by an impersonal god or these forces always existed. If these "cosmic forces" were created by an "impersonal god", then the discussion shifts to a discussion of the "impersonal god", which is <u>*Subsegment-2*</u>. If these "cosmic forces" always existed, then having "a reason for creation" required that these forces also had godlike attributes (*all-powerful, purposeful, love, justice, mercy, etc.*). But even with both "a reason for creation" and "godlike attributes", these forces did not leave us with any supportable evidence of their existence nor with a knowledge of the reason for our creation. Thus, it seems logically weak to believe that the "cosmic forces" created us.

<u>*Subsegment-2*</u>: <u>**The creation of life, by an impersonal god**</u>

Discussing "the creation of life, by an impersonal god", is not quite as difficult, as discussing "the creation of life, by the interaction of cosmic forces". Because we can make some assumptions based on the meaning of the phrase – "impersonal god", which comes out of the "*implied character*" of the gods worshiped by some of the religions that supplied creation views under the subgroup: "non-Jewish/non-Islamic views". The "*implied character*" of these gods includes their non-intervention or their explicit noninvolvement in the affairs of man or any other living things. The "impersonal god" is "allowing man and other living things to do their own thing, without any explicit or implicit intervention". To counter the existence of an "impersonal god", <u>*logic*</u> and <u>*scientific information*</u> will be used. Such usage might be worded, as follows:

- <u>*Logic*</u> can be used to conclude that if an "impersonal god" does exist, then that "impersonal god" caused our (humans) existence, directly or indirectly, because "something cannot come from nothing, by itself." Our existence includes this planet and this universe. However by default, if this "impersonal god" was involved in our creation, then this god is explicitly involved in the affairs of man. Or from a different view, the statement – "the impersonal god created us or allowed us to be created and then this god is allowing man to do his own things", gives a false impression. Because while the "do our own things" is noninvolvement, the "creating us or allowing us to be created" is involvement no matter how you look at it.

- Current <u>*scientific information*</u> indicates that this planet and this universe, are finely tuned on hundreds, even possibly thousands, of parameters that impact the environment on earth. Thus, together these parameters, allow for the existence of man. A slight change in some of these parameters would cause life, as we know it to cease. Consistent with this information, a well-known evangelist says something to the effect that:

> "The size and the vastness of our universe, is one of the tuning parameters that demonstrates the detail to which 'God' was willing to go in creating an environment for us to live in."

However, where this well-known evangelist used the word – "God", this author would temporarily substitute the phrase – "impersonal god", to be consistent with the implication being discussed. Furthermore, note what the discovery of an increasing number of tuning parameters implies. That is, the more parameters required for the tuning of the environment for life implies more involvement, by the "impersonal god". However, any number of finely tuned parameters required, for the personal survival of man should make it hard, to believe that life was created, by an "impersonal god". Or worded differently, creation by a "personal God" is far more logical.

Segment-2: ***Learning to be a better human being***

The concept of "Learning to be a better human being" raises, at least, two issues: *First*, "this concept implies that 'there is a cosmic or spiritual standard, for human beings.'" *Second*, "this concept implies 'man can learn to conform to a cosmic or spiritual standard.'" Thus, *Segment-2* is organized in two subsegments. *Subsegment-1* presents a discussion of the implication that "there is a cosmic or spiritual standard, for human beings." *Subsegment-2* presents a discussion of the implication that "man can learn to conform to a cosmic or spiritual standard."

Subsegment-1: **A cosmic or spiritual standard for human beings**

The issue – "There is a cosmic or spiritual standard for human beings", has at least, two matters that need to be addressed. *First*, what is a standard? *Second*, do "the realities of life" point to the existence of a cosmic or spiritual standard?

a) What is a standard?

A standard is defined or impacted by, at least, seven factors:

(1) A group of people, things, places, events, and/or processes, which is formed based on some general criteria.

(2) One or more members of the group serve, as a model, for the standard.

(3) The attributes, characteristics, and/or state of the model.

(4) The attributes, characteristics, and/or state of the rest of the group.

(5) The rest of the group is to be compared with the model.

(6) The comparison is based, on some criteria, which may involve the attributes, the characteristics, and/or the desired end-state of the group. If the comparison involves some attributes or some characteristics, then the implication is that the model has those attributes or characteristics, while some non-model members do not. If the comparison involves the end-state, then the implication is that the model represents the desired end-state, while some non-model members do not. (*This factor is really the heart of a standard.*)

(7) If some desired end-results are the objectives of the standard, there are two possible desired end-results:

    (a) The standard allows those members of the group that are, the most similar, to the model to be determined.

    (b) The standard allows the progress of a non-model member, toward the attributes or characteristics of the model or the end-state, as represented by the model, to be determined.

For the cosmic or spiritual standard in this discussion, the seven factors are:

(1) The group is all human beings, based on the general criterion that they are human beings.

(2) The model is that individual, who has learned to be the *best* "better human being".

(3) The state of the model is that of the *best* "better human being".

(4) The state of the rest of the group, is that they are in varying stages of being "*better* human beings", but are less than the *best* "better human being".

(5) The rest of the group of human beings is to be compared with the *best* "better human being".

(6) The comparison is based, on some criteria, which cosmically, spiritually, and/or morally, defines a "better human being". More specifically, these

criteria would probably involve aspects of human behavior, which reflects, one's feeling about the cosmos, one's feeling about the basis of her or his "non-Jewish/non-Islamic" religion, and/or one's feeling about other human beings.

(7) The end-result would be for each individual to become like the *best* "better human being". This means that over an individual's life, she or he would have to be able to determine her or his progress, toward becoming like the *best* "better human being".

b) Do "the realities of life" point to the existence of a cosmic or spiritual standard?

This question is obviously two questions. Thus, we need to separate our discussion of the existence of a standard into a discussion of "the possible existence of a cosmic standard" and a discussion of "the possible existence of a spiritual standard". Such discussions might include the following comments:

✓ The possible existence of a cosmic standard: If there is a cosmic standard for human beings, you would think that the norms for the various religions and cultures on this planet would be more alike. However, reality clearly shows that the norms for the religions and cultures of this world differ greatly. In one culture, people are taught to love their enemies. In another, people are taught to eat their enemies. Thus, simple observations of the cultures on this planet and a review of historical writings, clearly show that there does not seem to be a cosmic standard for human beings. Or more precisely, if there is a cosmic standard, the cosmic forces have done a very poor job of conveying that standard to man, and an even poorer job of motivating man to move toward that standard through some five thousand years of verified human history. Thus, there does not appear to be a cosmic standard.

✓ The possible existence of a spiritual standard: If there is a single spiritual standard for human beings, there should be some similarities in the spiritual beliefs held by the various religions and cultures of this world. While it may be true that some religions and cultures have something akin to the Old Testament Ten Commandments, this may have more to do with the common origin of man than a spiritual standard imposed by the gods of men. Most religions have a spiritual standard for those who choose to believe in that particular religion, but comparatively, the spiritual standards of the religions of this world vary too much. Similarly, most cultures have a spiritual standard based on the prevailing religion for that culture. But again, these religious and cultural spiritual standards vary too much. The wide variances in the spiritual standards of the religions and cultures of this world should make it clear that this world does not have one spiritual standard. There are many spiritual standards. And many spiritual standards mean that it would be very difficult to "learn to be a better human being", because many standards make the model of the *best* "better human being" nearly impossible.

Subsegment-2: **Man can learn to conform to a cosmic or spiritual standard**

The issue – "Man can learn to conform to a cosmic or spiritual standard", has at least, two problems, which we will address, by discussing two things: *first*, the question: "Who will be our standard?" and *second*, the "learning process".

a) Who will be our standard?

"Learning to be a better human being" is a very subjective goal. There are almost six billion humans alive today. Most probably feel that they were born a good human being, whatever their social-economic circumstances. Nevertheless, this does not alter the fact that we have varied moral values, because we develop our values from various conditions and experiences in our life. For example, some "serial killers" claimed or believed that they were acting righteously, by killing homosexuals, homeless people, prostitutes, etc. A better and more recent example of someone executing a moral value, is the pro-lifer, who shot and killed an abortion doctor. Obviously, the pro-lifer thought that he would save the lives of unborn babies, by shooting the doctor. Whether the pro-lifer meant to kill the doctor, only he and God know for sure. Nevertheless, his intentions do not alter the fact that the doctor is dead. Now, the family of the doctor and the families of others killed, by supposedly righteous individuals, probably view the killers, as heartless individuals. Who is right? It is obvious that a consistent standard is needed, if any judging is to be done fairly and accurately or more important, to define a "better human being". Worded differently, to define a "better human being", we need, as our standard, the most morally perfect human being, who has ever lived.

b) The learning process:

The learning process may take either of two forms, for most individuals. The learning may be involuntary or voluntary. For this discussion, "involuntary learning" means "the learning that occurs, when we are unaware that we are learning something". And generally, this is unplanned or unstructured learning. For this discussion, "voluntary learning" means "the learning that is planned or structured". Both forms of learning go on for much of our lives. As babies, there is probably more of the involuntary learning taking place. Then as we age, the learning shifts to the more voluntary form. With the previous comments serving, as an introduction, we will proceed to a discussion of how each type of learning might impact the process of "learning to be a better human being".

- ✓ Involuntary learning: Involuntary learning is ideal for those situations, where someone is modeling the behavior to be learned. Thus, involuntary learning would be ideal for the process of "learning to be a better human being" if, at least, three things could be done. *First*, the right human model would have to be found. *Second*, the model and the students would have to spend time together. *Third*, it would be best to start the process, while the students were very young. But realistically, who has the know-how, which would allow them to find the right human model. And then getting the students and the model together is not necessarily an easy task. Clearly, history shows that getting the right model and students together has not been done in significant numbers to impact this world. After some five thousand years of recorded history, the twentieth century was the bloodiest century ever. Thus, we are obviously not learning to be better human beings in significant numbers to make a difference or to be noticeable.

- ✓ Voluntary learning: Voluntary learning could also be used, in the process of "learning to be a better human being". But the problem is that for the learning to be voluntary, we must be aware of what it is to be learned. This means, at least, three things. *First*, "the process of 'learning to be a better human being'", must be defined in some way. *Second*, the process must be broken down, into manageable pieces. *Third*, the learning evolves, by progressing through the pieces in some sequence. If there are definable pieces or states, one's progress can be determined. Otherwise, progress would be difficult to determine. Nevertheless, even with voluntary learning, we are obviously not learning to be better human beings in significant numbers to make a difference or to be noticeable.

***Conclusion*: Section-2: The subgroup – "non-Jewish/non-Islamic views" problems**

The previous Section-2 comments, questions and considerations, make it difficult to believe the implications of the subgroup: "non-Jewish/non-Islamic views". More precisely, it is difficult to believe the implications that "we are here, because of cosmic forces and/or an impersonal god", and/or that "life is about 'learning to be a better human being'". Once more, if "learning to be a better human being" is what life is all about, then we are in serious trouble, because five thousand years of recorded history, show that men have not learned to be better human beings. And, as previously mentioned, the twentieth century was the bloodiest century to date. More precisely, during the twentieth century more than one hundred million people were killed, as a direct result of immoral political and religious leaders. Clearly, man is not getting better!

Section-3: **The "Jewish/Islamic Religious Views" problem**

A problem with the "Jewish/Islamic Religious views", revolves around the fact that one's eternal spiritual welfare is determined, by one's behavior. More precisely, eternal life is gained, if one's behavior is consistent with God's/Allah's commandments, Jewish/Islamic religious laws, and Jewish/Islamic religious traditions. However, such behavior is contrary, to the natural tendency of most humans. The natural tendency of most of us is to be focused on ourselves. On what we want! On what we need! On what we think! On how we feel! To confirm this, all one has to do is observe the daily activities of most people. But even if one got control of her or his external behavior, an evil thought might race through her or his mind, in the blink of an eye. And an evil thought can be like an evil word or an evil deed. Although, obviously, the consequences of an evil thought are not physical, while the consequences of an evil word might be physical, the consequences of an evil deed are generally physical. Less obvious is the fact that evil thoughts grease the way to evil deeds. Furthermore, evil thoughts sear our conscience just like evil words and evil deeds. But the main reason that an evil thought can be like an evil word or an evil deed, is that the state of the heart is the same for all three. Thus, we need help to always behave in a manner that is consistent, with God's/Allah's commandments, Jewish/Islamic religious laws, and Jewish/Islamic religious traditions. Consequently, if life were only about controlling our behavior, whether thought, word, or deed, we would be in trouble already.

Conclusion: *Section-3*: ***The subgroup "Jewish/Islamic views" problem***

The previous Section-3 comments and considerations, make it difficult to believe the implications of the subgroup – "Jewish/Islamic views", especially since the reality of life is that humans do not keep their focus on God/Allah. Consequently, all of us sin in thought, word, and deed. We also sin by omission when we fail to do what is right. These considerations make it difficult to believe the implication of the subgroup – "Jewish/Islamic views" that life is merely about living a life that is consistent with God's/Allah's commandments, Jewish/Islamic religious laws, and Jewish/Islamic religious traditions. More specifically, most of us would need help to live such a life.

Part-3: **How does the fourth subgroup – the "Christian views", solve the problems presented by the other three subgroups?**

The best way to answer this question is by responding to the four problems presented by the other three-subgroups: the "non-Religious views", the "non-Jewish/non-Islamic views", and the "Jewish/Islamic views". Each problem will be referenced, as part of comments explaining how the subgroup – "Christian views", solves that problem. And, then a fifth problem, which flows from our human nature is presented along with an explanation of how the subgroup – "Christian views", solves that problem, also. Thus, the problems and the explanations are, as follows:

1) The problem of "**how human life was created**" is easily answered. God, who has always existed, created us – created human life. (*If God did not always exist, then whatever created Him would be the most powerful force in the universe. That is, God cannot be God, if He were created. Furthermore, remember that something has to be eternal for anything to exist now, because logically something cannot come from nothing by itself.*)

2) The problem of "**defining a standard, for man**" is answered, by God. He defined the standard, by which we are to live, and presented that standard to us, in the Bible. In the Old Testament, God gave us the Ten Commandments and other principles to live by. In the New Testament, God gave us, Jesus, the man, as a model of the standard. Jesus, the man, kept His focus on God, the Father, by His (Jesus') own free will, and with the help of God, the Holy Spirit. That is why Jesus, the man, was able to live a sinless life.

   Comment: For this essay, the credibility of the Bible is assumed. But the essay – "Is the Bible the inspired word of God?", was written to present information that supports the credibility of the Bible.

3) The question of "**whether the God of the Bible is an impersonal god or a personal God**", is answered, by the Bible. For verses, like Matthew 10:30 and Luke 12:7, clearly show that God is a "personal God". Matthew 10:30 and Luke 12:7 read:

   (Matthew 10:30 NIV) And even the very hairs of your head are all numbered.

   (Luke 12:7 NIV) Indeed, the very hairs of your head are all numbered. Don't be afraid; you are worth more than many sparrows.

   The Book of Genesis also indicates that God is a "personal God", because He walked and talked with Adam. But the Bible also indicates that while God does allow us to exercise our "free will", He has intervened/does intervene in the affairs of man. Two examples are: "the universal flood during the days of Noah (*See Chapter 6 of the Book of Genesis*)" and "the drowning of the Egyptian army, as it was pursuing the Jews (*See Chapter 15 of the Book of Exodus*)".

4) The problems of "**our inability to keep our focus on Jesus**" and of "**our behavior, based on our weak selfish nature**", are answered, when we invite Jesus into our life. Jesus sends the Holy Spirit, to live within us. The Holy Spirit does not force us to do anything. However, He has the power to aid us in keeping our focus on Jesus and in living a more Jesus-centered life.

5) Our "human nature" problem of "**using our five senses in an effort to judge others**",

is answered, by Jesus, the man, when He told us not to judge others.

Comment: It is important to note that there is a difference between "judging a person" and "evaluating a person". A reality of life is:

> "we tend to take on some of the mannerisms, habits, characteristics, etc. of those with whom we associate."

By using the word – "associate", this author means all those individuals, who come within range of our five senses, or more precisely, all those individuals, who come within our "sphere of awareness"[3]. Therefore, it is very important, for us to evaluate the character of our associates. The purpose of this evaluation is to allow us to guard against taking on any unwanted or unGodly characteristics or habits. An evaluation is for our benefit. A judgment is an evaluation that we hold against another individual. A judgment can never be done fairly, because we are unable to obtain all the necessary facts. An evaluation does not have to be fair, because we are not explicitly holding it against the other individual.

Part-4: **Conclusion**

For this author, Part-3 makes it obvious, why the answer to the question – "What is life all about?", is:

"Life is about loving and serving God through His Son, Jesus Christ."

And this answer is shaped, by a "Christian view" of creation, as recorded in the Book of Genesis.

---

3 The phrase – "sphere of awareness", is defined in the essay – "What do the three phrases – 'knowledge of good and evil', 'knowledge of good', and 'knowledge of evil', mean? and What is 'the age of accountability'?"

Does God exist?

This question or any of its variations (*i.e., Does the God of the Christian Bible exist?*), is one of those life impacting questions that many of us ponder. This means that we try to analyze, to define, and/or to interpret, various aspects of our world and our lives, from possibly three viewpoints: a logical viewpoint (*using logical reasoning*), a physical viewpoint (*using nature and/or "human nature"*), and a spiritual viewpoint (*using religious concepts and/or texts – Obviously, for this essay, the "religious concepts and/or text" are "Christian concepts and/or the Bible". However, remember that the "Jewish Old Testament" is part of the "Christian Bible"*)[4]. Hopefully, by using one or more of the previously mentioned three viewpoints, the analyzing, the defining, and/or the interpreting will lead us to a supportable answer for the question: "Does God exist?" However, we must note that sometimes when analyzing, defining, and/or interpreting the things of this world, we rely solely, on our own mind and five senses, or "whatever senses are available, to us individually".

> *Comment:* The phrase – "whatever senses are available, to us individually", serves to acknowledge that some people may have, what is called a "sixth sense", while others may be blind, deaf, and/or experience, some other sense deprivation.

When we use our own minds and senses, there are a lot of things that we should notice. For example,

> "Our daily survival requires that we 'analyze, define, and/or interpret various aspects of this world, as we *react to* or *interact with* those aspects'. As we do this, we should note things about this world and our lives, like this is clearly a 'cause-and-effect' world. We should note our powerlessness, against most forces of nature. And hopefully, we should note the things that we can influence and the things that we cannot influence. Then based on our observations, we might decide on a meaning for life. But more important, we might decide on whether we believe that God does exist or not."

However, using our own mind and senses to analyze, to define, and/or to interpret is probably a rare event for many of us, for most things other than our daily survival. The reason for this is that most of us lack the time, the motivation, and/or the appropriate skills to analyze, to define, and/or to interpret, many things not directly related to our daily survival. Thus, most of the time, we rely on the mind and senses of others. This means that often our final answer to a pondered question will be influenced, by others. And this is okay! But ***care*** needs to be exercised. The point is:

> "If we are going to use the analyses, the definitions, and/or the interpretations of others, then we need to review these 'to confirm' that they make sense logically, physically,

and/or spiritually."

Showing how such a confirmation might be done is the secondary objective of this essay. However, the primary objective is still to develop a supportable answer for the topic question. To accomplish both of these objectives, the rest of this essay is organized in six parts. Part-1 presents a discussion of the topic question, using a "logical viewpoint". Part-2 presents a discussion of the topic question, using a "physical viewpoint". Part-3 presents a discussion of the topic question, using a "spiritual viewpoint". Part-4 presents some concluding comments. Part-5 presents some relevant comments. Part-6 presents five additional presentations relevant to the question: "Does God exist?"

Part-1: **A logical viewpoint**

Using a "logical viewpoint", to ponder the topic question, means discussing an "application of logic" – or more specifically, an "application of logical reasoning", in an attempt to prove the existence of God. To accomplish this task, Part-1 is organized in four sections. Section-1 serves as an introduction. Section-2 presents a discussion of four forms of logical reasoning: *"deductive reasoning", "inductive reasoning", "abductive reasoning", and "retroductive reasoning".* Section-3 presents a discussion of an indirect application of deductive reasoning, to the topic question. Section-4 presents a discussion of the question: "What would be required to prove the existence of God?"

Section-1: **Introduction**

This introduction is begun with definitions of the words – "reasoning" and "logic". Paraphrased consensus definitions are, as follows:

> "Reasoning" is "the process of arriving at inferences (*conclusions*)". "Logic" is "a formal academic discipline that explores the nature and patterns of reasoning".

However, a more complete overview of "logic" is presented with the paraphrased wording:

> "Logic" is "a formal structure under which logical elements – premises, propositions, and statements followed by judgments or conclusions, can be analyzed and manipulated. And then the judgments or conclusions can be declared to be 'valid' or invalid'".

However, the declaration that a judgment or a conclusion is "valid" or "invalid", has more to do with the form (*with the structure*) of the logical presentation, than it does with the truth of the subject of the presentation, especially for inductive reasoning. (*See the discussion under* Section-2.) Consequently, this part of the essay will also discuss whether it is meaningful to attempt to use logic on the information needed to address the question – "Does God exist?" and its related issues. But first, we must note that it is definitely logically meaningless for someone to say,

"There is no God." For such a statement implies that the author of that statement knows everything there is to know about everything. Such a claim from anyone, but a god, is absurd. As we, humans, are not gods, logically, the only way we will know that God exists, is through whatever means He chooses to reveal Himself. Thus, any attempt to prove the existence of God must work through His revelations, which are defined by Christians to be "nature" and "the Bible (*His recorded words*)". "Nature" will also be addressed under a "physical viewpoint". "The Bible" will also be addressed under a "spiritual viewpoint". Here under this "logical viewpoint", we will attempt "an application of logical reasoning" to "nature" and "the Bible". But first, we must develop some understanding of "an application of logical reasoning". Providing and applying that understanding is the purpose of the next three sections - Section-2 through Section-4.

Section-2: **Four forms of "logical reasoning"**

Of the many forms of "logical reasoning", the two best known are "deductive reasoning" and "inductive reasoning". Two other lesser known forms are "abductive reasoning" and "retroductive reasoning". Other forms are defined with respect to various disciplines and/or within various vocations. However, only the four previously named forms will be discussed in this essay. These four are defined in *Wikipedia*, as follows:

- "'Deductive reasoning' is the kind of reasoning where the conclusion is necessitated by previously known premises. If the premises are true then the conclusion must be true. For instance, beginning with the premises 'sharks are fish' and 'all fish have fins', you may conclude that "sharks have fins". This is distinguished from inductive reasoning and abductive reasoning where inferences can be made with some likelihood but never with complete certainty. Deductive reasoning is dependent on its premises. That is, a false premise can possibly lead to a false result, and inconclusive premises will also yield an inconclusive conclusion.

  Examples: Deductive reasoning is the following:

(major premise)	All men are mortal.
(minor premise)	Socrates is a man.
(conclusion)	Therefore, Socrates is mortal.

  (The above formal structure of a "major premise, minor premise, and a conclusion" is also called a "syllogism".)[1] Note that replacing "mortal" with any nonsensical property will not affect the validity of the argument:

(major premise)	All men are purple-skinned.

---

1 This comment was inserted into the definition from the *Wikipedia*, by this author.

(minor premise)	Socrates is a man.
(conclusion)	Therefore, Socrates is purple-skinned.

Intuitively, one might deny the major premise or the conclusion; yet anyone accepting the premises must accept the conclusion.

Popular misuses of the term: It is occasionally taught that deductive reasoning proceeds from the general to the particular, while inductive reasoning proceeds from the particular to the general. This is false - or at least, it is not the way logicians use these terms. There are deductively valid arguments that proceed from the particular to the general (Oscar is grouchy, therefore something is grouchy) and inductive arguments that proceed from the general to the particular (all Rice University students are smart, therefore this particular Rice University student is smart)."[5]

- "'Induction' or 'inductive reasoning', sometimes called 'inductive logic', is the process of reasoning in which the premises of an argument are believed to support the conclusion but do not ensure it. It is used to ascribe properties or relations to types based on tokens (i.e., on one or a small number of observations or experiences); or to formulate laws based on limited observations of recurring phenomenal patterns. Induction is used, for example, in using specific propositions such as:

    This ice is cold.
    A billiard ball moves when struck with a cue.

  ...to infer general propositions such as:

    All ice is cold.
    All billiard balls struck with a cue move."[6]

- "'Abductive reasoning', 'Abduction', or 'inference to the best explanation', is a method of reasoning in which one chooses the hypothesis that would, if true, best explain the relevant evidence. Abductive reasoning starts from a set of accepted facts and infers to their most likely, or best, explanations. The term abduction is also sometimes used to just mean the generation of hypotheses to explain observations or conclusions, but the former definition is more common both in philosophy and computing."[7]

- "'Retroductive reasoning' or 'retroduction' is similar to induction, but it is predicated on known or assumed relationary rules and observations that contain at least one of the predicates or predictors of the rules in question. Another predicate of the relationary rule is then generalized to the observation due to the coincidence of the other predicates in both the observation and the rule. 'Reduction' is commonly applied in police work to determine the initial suspects of a crime via means, motive, and opportunity, and in medical diagnostics via the patient's symptoms and established diagnostic decision trees. However, the most common forms of logic systems built up through **retroductive reasoning** involve or are related to complexity theory."[8]

Definitions aside, a couple of interesting things to note about these forms are: *First*, as "inductive reasoning" is also called "induction" or "inductive logic", "deductive reasoning" is also called "deduction" or "deductive logic". *Second*, in general, the three forms – "deductive reasoning", "inductive reasoning", and "abductive reasoning", serve different objectives. According to an entry titled – "Logical reasoning"[9] in *Wikipedia*, these objectives can be explained in the following way:

Given: preconditions α, postconditions ß, and the rule R_1: α therefore ß. [Where "preconditions α" is "the major and minor premises", "postconditions ß" is "the conclusion or the judgment", and "the rule R_1" equals "a definable relationship between 'α' and 'ß'".][10]

- Deduction means determining ß. It is using the rule and its preconditions to make a conclusion

- Induction means determining R_1. It is learning R_1 after numerous examples of ß and α.

- Abduction means determining α. It is using the postcondition and the rule to assume that the precondition could explain the postcondition ($ß \wedge R_1 \Rightarrow \alpha$).

Section-3: An indirect application of deductive reasoning, to the topic question

To indirectly apply the principles of deductive reasoning to the topic question, we will use a "syllogism". Thus, Section-3 is organized in two segments. *Segment-1* presents a definition of the words: "syllogism" and "premise". *Segment-2* presents an indirect application of deductive reasoning to the topic question.

Segment-1: The words: "syllogism" and "premise"

- A definition of the word – "syllogism", was presented as a comment in the definition for "deductive reasoning". Paraphrased, those comments read:

  A "syllogism" is "the formal structure of 'a major premise', 'a minor premise', and 'a judgment or a conclusion'". For example,

  (major premise) All men are mortal.

(minor premise)	Socrates is a man.
(conclusion)	Therefore, Socrates is mortal.

A "syllogism" is also considered a form of "deductive reasoning".

- A paraphrased definition of the word – "premise", reads:

  A "premise" is "a statement of some type, which serves as the 'major premise – the major statement' or the 'minor premise – the minor statement' of a 'syllogism'". In most "syllogisms", the premises establish a relationship between the subject and the predicate.

Segment-2: **Deductive reasoning and the topic question**

An indirect application of deductive reasoning to the topic question, is begun with a "syllogism" to reflect one aspect of the origin of man. This syllogism reads, as follows:

the major premise is:	*All humans are something.*
the minor premise is:	*Something cannot come from nothing, by itself.*
the conclusion is:	*Therefore, we could not come from nothing, by ourselves.*

A similar syllogism could be used to describe the origin of this world – our environment. We can further argue, regardless of whether you believe in "creation by cosmic forces", "creation by evolution", or "creation by God", logically, the conclusion remains that something had to have always existed. We can further conclude that this eternal something is "what created us or allowed our creation". Otherwise, we have the situation of something coming from nothing, by itself, which is a logical absurdity.

At this stage of our reasoning, we must ask ourselves the question – "Does it make sense for the eternal entity, which is 'what created us or allowed our creation', to have been a mindless, non-purposeful entity, force, or even worse, a substance?" The logical answer should be a clear and resounding, "No!" Thus, logically, God must exist.

Section-4: **What would be required to prove the existence of God?**

To be consistent with our three viewpoints, this question should be more precisely worded, as the following three questions:

1) "What would be required **logically**, to prove the existence of God?"
2) "What would be required **physically**, to prove the existence of God?"
3) "What would be required **spiritually**, to prove the existence of God?"

The last two questions will be addressed in "Part-2: A physical viewpoint" and in "Part-3: A spiritual viewpoint", respectively. As Part-1 is about a "logical viewpoint", in this section, we are only concerned about addressing the more precise question: "What would be required **logically**, to prove the existence of God?"

To logically prove the existence of God, Section-4 will focus on three material things, which are: "the Bible", "the existence of the Jewish people", and "nature". Thus, Section-4 is organized in three segments. *Segment-1* presents reasoning based on "the Bible". *Segment-2* presents reasoning based on "the existence of the Jewish people". *Segment-3* presents reasoning based on "nature".

Segment-1: **The Bible**

Reasoning based on "the Bible", which supports the existence of God, might go as follows:

- "The Bible" serves, as material proof that God does exist, because it contains stories about God's relationship with man and God's revelations to man. Furthermore, "the Bible" begins, with a declaration, which implies that God does exist, because He created.

- When reasoning and logic are applied to "the Bible", it is shown to be a credible document. (*See the essay: "Is the Bible the inspired word of God?"*) Evidence, which supports the credibility of "the Bible", includes "manuscript evidence", "archaeological evidence", "nonbiblical evidence", and "prophetic evidence".

  - ✓ Manuscript evidence: There are ancient copies of most of the books of "the Bible". Many of these copies are in the original biblical languages: Hebrew, Aramaic, and Koine Greek. These ancient copies show that "the Bible" has not significantly changed in more than two thousand years.

  - ✓ Archaeological evidence: Especially during the nineteenth century and the twentieth century, archaeological digs have revealed items, which support what is recorded in "the Bible". For example, an ancient plate from the time of Jesus was found with the name – "Pontius Pilate", on it. The New Testament indicates that Pontius Pilate was the Roman Governor of Judea, who allowed Jesus to be unjustly crucified.

  - ✓ Nonbiblical evidence: Ancient nonbiblical literature written by non-Christians (*both Jews and non-Jews*) references events and individuals, mentioned in "the Bible". The referenced individuals include Jesus Christ. For example, there was a Jewish historian named Flavius Josephus, whose writings are dated around 73 A.D. Josephus wrote about Jewish history and included references about Jesus in his writings. Additional examples were presented by Dr. D. James Kennedy, as part of his CD titled: "Jesus: Fact or Fable?" (*This CD may be purchased from the*

Coral Ridge Ministries [(800) 229-WORD]. The CD is available by itself or as part of an album, which is titled: "Skeptics Answered".) On this particular CD, Dr. Kennedy named two more Jewish writers – in addition to Flavius Josephus, – and, at least, nineteen pagan (*non-Jewish and non-Christian*) writers, who referenced Jesus in their writings. Not all of the references to Jesus were kind. Nevertheless, all of the twenty-two writers mentioned by Dr. Kennedy, accepted Jesus, as a real-historical person.

✓ Prophetic evidence: "The Bible" is filled with prophecies. A major prophecy was fulfilled on May 15, 1948 with the rebirth of the Jewish nation against incredible odds. This rebirth prophecy is referenced by Deuteronomy 30:1-9, Isaiah 11:11-13, and Ezekiel 28:25-26. The prophecy about the "rebirth of the Jewish nation" is discussed in more detail in the essay – "Does the Bible contain prophecies about the rebirth of the Jewish nation in 1948?", which is in the book: "Last Call!!!"

Thus, as mentioned before, when reason and logic are applied to "the Bible", it is shown to be a credible document. Then when a credible document like the sixty-six canonical books of "the Bible" declares the existence of God, we can believe that God does exist.

Segment-2: **The existence of the Jewish people**

Reasoning based on "the existence of the Jewish people", as material proof, which supports the existence of God, might go as follows:

➧ Based on a credible Bible, an overview of God's plan of salvation, which He worked through the Jewish people, was actually revealed in the Garden of Eden. This was even before the Jewish people existed. More specifically, after Adam and Eve sinned, God gave an overview of His redemptive plan in Genesis 3:15. This verse reads:

> (Genesis 3:15 KJV) And I will put enmity between thee and the woman, and between thy seed and her seed; it shall bruise thy head, and thou shalt bruise his heel.

This verse occurred, after the serpent tempted Adam and Eve and they sinned. In Genesis 3:15, God is talking to the serpent, Adam, and Eve. Thus, the phrase – "thy seed", is a reference, to the offspring of the serpent. However, this may be a case of double-meanings. One meaning is probably physical offspring or other serpents. The other meaning is probably spiritual offspring or "human beings, who reject God's plan". The phrase – "her seed", is definitely a reference to a physical offspring (*i.e., to Jesus, the man, who was born of a Jewish virgin*). Then God drove Adam and Eve out of the Garden of Eden, because of their sin. Adam and Eve went from an existence under God's grace in the garden to an existence under God's judgment in the world, where they experienced the trials and tribulations of daily survival. Nevertheless, they had children. Their children had children and so on.

- God chose a descendant of Adam and Eve named, Abram (*later changed to Abraham*) to be the father of the Jewish people through his son, Isaac. Isaac was the father of Jacob, whose name was changed to Israel. Abraham is also considered the father of most of the Arab people through his son, Ishmael. God made a covenant with Abraham "to make him the father of many nations (*actually, this included both sons*)" and "to be the God of his descendants forever (*this only included the descendants of his son, Isaac*)". The Bible contains the details of how God drew Jacob and Jacob's family group of about seventy individuals, into Egypt. Jacob's family group included his twelve sons, his daughter, and their families. Eventually in Egypt, Jacob's descendants were enslaved, for several hundred years. Nevertheless, while they were in Egypt, God grew them into a nation. God also probably guided them in the development of their Hebrew language. (*The Hebrew language is extremely good at describing the plan of God.*) Then, after four hundred years, God guided the Jewish people out of Egypt toward the land that He had promised them, so that they could establish their own nation. On the way, God gave the Jewish People the ten commandments.

- Even before the Jews reached the promised land, they began the process of forming their own nation. As part of this process, God gave the Jewish people many of their social, civil, and religious laws and customs. Many of these modeled the relationship that God wanted with the Jewish people. God told them about the consequences of breaking His laws. Thus, God judged and punished the Jewish people, when they went against His laws and His plans for them.

- The details of God's relationship with the Jewish people were recorded in the Bible. For God inspired them to do the recording. And they recorded, as a prophecy, the rebirth of the Jewish nation on May 15, 1948. In fact, according to Bible scholars, the rebirth of the Jewish nation occurred on the exact day, as prophesied.

<u>The point is</u>:

> "The very existence – the continued existence – of the Jewish people and of the Jewish nation is a testimony to the existence of God. The reason for saying this is, because God chose the Jewish people, as His people, and He promised them a homeland (*the promised land*). Then He preserved the Jewish people through some four thousand years of recorded history through incredible odds, which include several times in history, when many Jews were taken from their promised land and dispersed throughout the world. These incredible odds also include several attempts, by the peoples or leaders of various nations to exterminate the Jewish people. And finally, in May of 1948 against incredible odds, the Jews reestablished their promised homeland, as the Jewish Nation."

Thus, when reason and logic are applied to "the existence of the Jewish people", based on a credible Bible, that existence declares the existence of God.

Segment-3: **Nature**

Based on "nature" - or more precisely, the things of "nature" - as material proof that God does exist, the primary reason, which support the existence of God, is as follows:

- Logically, something cannot come, from nothing, by itself. This means that something had to have always existed. Something had to be eternal. But scientific observations clearly indicate that the living things of "nature" die and decay. Therefore, the living things of "nature" cannot be eternal. And the nonliving things of "nature" exhibit no ability to perform, any creative acts, by themselves. This means that even if the nonliving things of "nature" were eternal, it would be pointless. Thus, the things of nature have to have been created by some other eternal entity. And for this eternal entity not to be God is logically absurd. Furthermore, logically, God could not be God, if He were created - if He were not eternal. Therefore, the existence of the things of "nature" is material proof that God does exist.

> *Comment:* A discussion of how God may have created out of nothing is covered in the sub-essay - "How could God create man out of nothing?", which is part of the essay: "What is the only meaningful question, about 'God' and 'Christianity'?"

Thus, when reason and logic are applied to "nature", it serves as a material proof that God does exist.

But think, about it! To prove God's existence, without appealing to the clear evidence of "the Bible", "the existence of the Jewish people", or "nature", would require that we, as witnesses or observers, be God's equal or His superior. But clearly, being God's equal or His superior contradicts the definition of God. Thus, those individuals crying for empirical evidence to prove God's existence, while rejecting "the Bible", "the existence of the Jewish people", and "nature", as proofs, are deceiving themselves.

Part-2: **A physical viewpoint**

Using a "physical viewpoint", to ponder the topic question, means using "nature" and/or "human nature", to prove the existence of God. To accomplish this task, Part-2 is organized in two sections. Section-1 presents a discussion of the question: "What would be required **physically**, to prove the existence of God?" Section-2 presents a discussion of the question: "How could nature be used to prove the existence of God?"

Section-1: **What would be required *physically*, to prove the existence of God?**

Remember that the word – "physically" is being used in the sense of "using nature or using the things of nature" and/or "using human nature". With one meaning of the phrase – "using human nature" being in the sense of "how does our 'human nature' detect that something is real – that something exists". Obviously, the things of nature are detected with our senses, with or without the aid of any instruments. Thus, a quick response to the question – "What would be required **physically**, to prove the existence of God?", is:

> "For too many individuals, to physically prove the existence of God, they would need to be able to touch Him, to talk to Him, to walk with Him, or more specifically, to interact with Him, using their five senses and their mind. And many would probably ask Him to perform something supernatural to confirm that He is God."

However, being able to perceive God using our five senses, in the same manner that we would perceive another human being, is only possible under His terms. There is a verse in the Bible, which indicates that no man can see God and live. There is another series of verses, which indicate that God spoke directly to the Jewish people, at Mount Sinai. But upon hearing His voice, the Jewish people became so fearful that they asked God through Moses, to never speak directly to them again. Therefore, it is probably safe to say, that generally, we are not able to perceive God, in a comfortable manner, directly through the use of our five senses. However, our senses allow us to perceive the effects of God: "the things of nature". Thus, a second response to the Section-1 question is begun by noting that according to the Book of Genesis, God interacted directly with Adam. Nevertheless, Adam sinned. Now physically, God communicates to us through His creation. More precisely, God left His fingerprints in creation, for us to see. Therefore, a second response to the question – "What would be required **physically**, to prove the existence of God?", is "man using his senses and his skills to examine the things of 'nature', and acknowledging these as God's handiwork (*acknowledging God, as the creator*)".

Section-2: **How could nature be used to prove the existence of God?**

Under a "logical viewpoint", "nature" was addressed with an emphasis on the "very existence of the things of nature". Here under a "physical viewpoint", the focus is on what "nature" reveals when it is examined. Two of many interesting revelations, which support the "physical viewpoint" as evidence of God are, as follows:

> *Findings-1*: A former scientist – and now a well-known evangelist – has concluded that this physical world of ours is finely tuned – conditions are balanced – on more than one hundred factors to support human life. Even the size and mass of the universe are part of this fine tuning. Change any one of these factors by the smallest amount, and life, as we know it, might cease. But the important thing to note is that the probability of more than one hundred factors fine tuning themselves to support life on this planet, by chance is astronomical. Therefore, the mere existence of all these factors alone gives credence

to the existence of a designer (*gives credence to the existence of God*).

Findings-2: The wonderful complexity of "nature" down to and including the molecular level, points to a designer, who had to create many processes and things simultaneously. Such simultaneous creations negate the possibility of creation, by evolution. Thus, the complexity of the things of "nature" gives credence to the existence of a designer (*gives credence to the existence of God*).

In addition to many interesting scientific revelations, the Bible also supports "nature", as an evidence of God's existence. See Romans 1:20. Four translations of this verse read:

(Romans 1:20 KJV) For the invisible things of him from the creation of the world are clearly seen, being understood by the things that are made, even his eternal power and Godhead; so that they are without excuse:

(Romans 1:20 NIV) For since the creation of the world God's invisible qualities--his eternal power and divine nature--have been clearly seen, being understood from what has been made, so that men are without excuse.

(Romans 1:20 NRSV) Ever since the creation of the world his eternal power and divine nature, invisible though they are, have been understood and seen through the things he has made. So they are without excuse;

(Romans 1:20 NASB) For since the creation of the world His invisible attributes, His eternal power and divine nature, have been clearly seen, being understood through what has been made, so that they are without excuse.

Therefore, the answer to the question – "How could nature be used to prove the existence of God?", is "by examining it with an open mind and giving God the credit, as the designer".

Part-3: **A spiritual viewpoint**

Under a "logical viewpoint", "the Bible" was addressed with an emphasis on "its existence and its credibility". Here under a "spiritual viewpoint", the focus is on what "the Bible" reveals, although much of that was also covered under a "logical viewpoint". Nevertheless, to accomplish this task, Part-3 is organized in two sections. Section-1 presents a discussion of the question: "What would be required spiritually, to prove the existence of God?" Section-2 presents a discussion of the question: "How could the Bible be used to prove the existence of God?"

Section-1: **What would be required *spiritually*, to prove the existence of God?**

The implication of this question is "What would it take to prove the existence of God using

Christian concepts and/or the Bible?" Under a "logical viewpoint", "the Bible" was addressed from an "existence-and-credibility" viewpoint and under a "physical viewpoint", "the Bible" was addressed from a "what-does-it-reveal" viewpoint. Here under a "spiritual viewpoint", many of those comments could be repeated. However, a better approach might be to focus on a question, which is applicable to all three viewpoints and which was previously implied with different wording. That question is "Who is the superior, God, or the ones asking about God?" As the answer is obviously God, it should be clear that it is God, Who determines what He will use to reveal Himself to us. But note that Christians believe that God created us with "free will". Thus, whatever God uses to reveal Himself to us, He does not force us to accept. Nevertheless, Christians also believe that God gave us "nature", "the Bible", "the Jewish people", "the Jewish nation", "our consciences", and "Jesus" to reveal His existence. "The Bible", "the Jewish people", "the Jewish nation", and "Jesus" can be considered as spiritual proofs. (*Note that "Jesus" was included in this list even though He is also the only way to God and our free gift of salvation.*) As the other three items are all in the Bible, the answer to the question – "What would it take to prove the existence of God using Christian concepts and/or the Bible?", is "showing that 'the Bible' is a credible document. This would also take care of Christian concepts, because these are based on 'the Bible'."

Section-2: **How could the Bible be used to prove the existence of God?**

This question was actually answered under a "logical viewpoint", under a "physical viewpoint", and the previous Section-1. Thus, this section just serves to provide an opportunity for some summary and relevant comments.

Summary comments are begun with a reminder that "physical realities *(the things of nature)*" can be use to confirm the credibility of the existence of God. And then "logical reasoning" can be use to confirm the credibility of the Bible. Then we note that the stories and words of the Bible clearly reveal God's existence. Thus, both "physical realities *(the things of nature)*" and "logical reasoning" confirm the credibility of the existence of God.

Relevant comments would simply serve to remind you that the Bible states that man has the "light of conscience" and the "light of nature" to prove God's existence. Furthermore, Christians believe that every individual is born with an innate knowledge of God's existence. However, this knowledge is suppressed by many in their desire for the things of this world.

Part-4: **Some concluding comments**

Logically, we examined "nature", "the Bible", "the existence of the Jewish people", and then reason from these that God must exist. Physically, we examined "nature", "the universe", "the Bible", and "the continued existence – the history – of the Jewish people", and then reason from these that God must exist. Spiritually, the stories, which comprise the sixty-six canonical books of the Bible, explicitly indicate the existence of God. Consequently, we conclude from those stories that God must exist. Thus, logically, physically, and spiritually, we can reason or conclude that God must exist. Therefore, we can reason that the answer to the question – "Does God exist?", is "Yes!"

Part-5: **Some relevant comments**

Relevant comments flow out of the fact that too many people say, "The answer to the question 'Does God exist?', is 'No!', because of the existence of 'evil and suffering'." However, if you use the existence of "evil and suffering", as the basis of your denial of the existence of God, you are deceiving yourself. The basis for this statement is the following reasoning:

- God created beings – angels, humans, and whatever – with "free will", which is the "ability or freedom, to make choices, based on one's own wants, needs, lusts, desires, and/or experience".

- The first man, *Adam*, and the first woman, *Eve*, demonstrated their "free will", in the Book of Genesis. They exercised their "free will", by choosing to disobey God (*by choosing to do evil*). Then they suffered the consequences of their evil choice. They were driven out of the Garden of Eden by God. They went from existing under God's grace in the garden to existing under God's judgment in the world. Now, the rest of us suffer from the consequences of the evil choice of Adam and Eve, our own evil choices, and the evil choices of others.

- As we are all the children of Adam and Eve, we were/are/will be born with "free will". This means that each of us can freely choose *good* thoughts, words, and/or deeds, or each of us can freely choose *evil* thoughts, words, and/or deeds. But each choice that we make, has consequences, for each of us, individually, and/or possibly, for others.

- Therefore, "evil and suffering" flow out of each individual's "free will" choices. This means that each individual's life is affected by her or his own "free will" choices and by the "free will" choices of others. But because God gave each individual the "free will" to choose good or evil, it does not mean that He has to protect anyone, from the consequences of her or his evil choices or from the consequences of the evil choices of others.

The point is:

"Either God prevents us from making evil choices, which means no 'free will' or God allows us to exercise our 'free will', which means that we are able to make evil choices. It cannot be both. Besides, with 'free will', men can make good choices, which should mean good consequences. Furthermore, the existence of 'evil and suffering' confirm how perfect (*how complete*) the 'free will' is that God created in us. Therefore, do not deceive yourself. The existence of 'evil and suffering', which flows out of man's 'free will', does not disprove the existence of God, rather 'evil and suffering' support the existence of God."

> Comment: For many of us, the consequences of evil choices put us in a unique situation. While we are *suffering* from the "evil consequences" of our own or of someone else, we want God to intervene. We want God to relieve us from those consequences. While we are *enjoying* the "evil consequences" of our own or of someone else, we want God to mind His own business. We do not want God to relieve us from those immediate consequences.

Part-6: **Five additional presentations**

Five additional presentations, which are relevant to the question – "Does God exist?", are organized, as: *first*, some introductory comments about four classical arguments for the existence of God; *second*, arguments for the existence of God; *third*, some introductory comments about six views of God; *fourth*, a chart presentation of four classical arguments for the existence of God; and *fifth*, a chart presentation of six views of God. In detail, these are, as follows:

1) Four classical arguments for the existence of God:

Over time, several classical arguments for the existence of God have been defined, by various scholars. A summary of four of these classical arguments – in a chart format – was presented on the Internet, several years ago. Now, many arguments are available on the Internet. However, for your convenience, the old summary has been included at the end of this essay. As you review the summary, you will note that it includes the statement:

> "because there will always be skeptics, who demand empirical evidence – evidence that is not available."

The inclusion of the phrase – "evidence that is not available", is very troubling to this author, because there is "empirical evidence" available, by definition. This means that the phrase – "empirical evidence", must be defined. Obviously, the phrase will get its definition from the two words: "empirical" and "evidence". Paraphrased definitions of these two words read:

> "Empirical" means "using our physical senses with or without the aid of instruments to confirm something by observation and/or experimentation".

> "Evidence" means "any thing – an individual, a fact, an object, a process, an act,

etc. - presented in support of a declared statement or presented to aid the formation of a conclusion or judgment about a declared statement".

Based on these two definitions, we can say that "empirical evidence" is:

> "a thing (*or things*) that is (*are*) helpful in forming a conclusion or judgment, because that thing (*or things*) is (*are*) verifiable or provable, by means of observation or experiment".

With this definition in mind, please note that many of the living and nonliving things of nature have been observed and experimented upon. Many of these observations and experiments show a beauty and a design in the things of nature. This is especially true of the living things of nature, which show a very complicated design - down to and including the molecular level - that is too complicated, for either "random chance" or "evolution". An interesting-design example was presented more than ten years ago, on a Public Broadcasting System (PBS) documentary on the "common housefly". During this documentary, scientists discussed experiments, which they had performed on these flies. More specifically, the flies were subjected to various stimuli and objects to see how they would react. Based on the reactions of those flies, it would be very easy to accept the claim that these flies were merely "flying robots" created and designed, by someone with great intelligence. Thus, based on the "observations of", the "examination of", and the "experiments on" the things of nature, a fair inference is that "this universe and the living organisms, it contains, were designed."

In an attempt to disprove the design claims, several experiments to create the components or substances essential for life from nonliving substances have been performed. To date, to the best of this author's knowledge, none of the experiments have been successful without inappropriate procedures.

The supposed problem of "no empirical evidence", is really a false problem, because skeptics refuse to accept the evidence that does exist. Again, this evidence includes "nature", "the Bible", and "the existence of the Jewish people".

2) Arguments for the existence of God

Originally, this author was going to list some of the "arguments for the existence of God". Consequently, the "Google search engine" was used with the phrase: "arguments for the existence of God". This search returned a listing of ninety thousand web documents. Some web documents focused on a single argument, while other presented a number of arguments. Several web documents even presented arguments against the existence of God. (*The book "Last Call!!!" [Subtitled - "Are You Still Serving God?"] will address some of the arguments against the existence of God.*) Here the original intent was to focus only on the "arguments for the existence of God" and then present a paraphrased composite listing of some of those arguments. However, all of that changed during my effort to compile a single list from a review of several web documents, because the web document at:

www.godlessgeeks.com/LINKS/GodProof.htm,

presented three hundred and sixty-one arguments. While it is true that some of the arguments had more than one variation, it is also true that each argument is presented or summarized as a "syllogism", which is a better way. Thus, rather than listing those arguments, this author will simply refer you to the previously mentioned web document.

3) Six spiritual/logical views of the existence of God

Over time, six major spiritual/logical views of the existence of God have developed. These views are presented here in a chart format for your convenience. This chart follows the two charts containing the four classical arguments for the existence of God. The "six-views" summary chart was once available on the Internet.

FOUR CLASSICAL ARGUMENTS FOR THE EXISTENCE OF GOD

Scholars have long searched for an open-and-shut argument for God's existence! Yet arguments alone cannot convince anyone, because there will always be skeptics who demand empirical evidence – evidence that is not available.

Throughout the centuries though, intelligent attempts have been made to form arguments to prove that God is the Creator and Sustainer of this world. Here are four attempts of thinking people to prove God's existence.

Argument from Being

Classical name: Ontological argument
Originated by: Anselm of Canterbury

Main tenet: Anyone who would even consider that God does exist is, in a sense, admitting that there is a God. Here is the logic of that statement. God, by definition, is the greatest being that can be conceived. If He did not exist, He could not be the greatest conceivable being. Therefore, such a being exists. Stated another way, the fact that we have in us the idea of God demands that God is its cause.

Argument from First Cause

Classical name: Cosmological argument
Originated by: Plato and Aristotle

Main tenet: Our world – complex, finite, subject to change, and intelligible – must have had an adequate first cause. Scientists generally agree that our world had a beginning. And that beginning had to be contingent on a thing that was not contingent on anything else for its existence. Therefore, that noncontingent entity had to be infinite, eternal, everlasting, and self-existing. It had to be God.

Continued:

Argument from Design

Classical name: Teleological argument
Originated by: Aquinas and Paley

Main tenet: The purpose and design of the world point to the existence of God. Physicists marvel at the unbelievable complexity of everything they study. Yet, it all fits together in an intricate, workable system. Consider the fragile balance of heat and cold, the delicate mix of oxygen and other gases, the thin curtain that shields us from ultraviolet rays, the complicated relationship of the parts of the ecological system to one another. They point to intelligent design.

Argument from Man

Classical name: Anthropological argument
Originated by: Various thinkers

Main tenet: This argument is based on the nature of the human personality. When we worship, we are able to think abstractly and to project ourselves mentally into the world beyond. We are able to make tough moral decisions that lead to heroic self-sacrificing deeds that could not come from instinct. We admire art, music, and architecture. These unusual qualities of man must be the product of an intelligent, moral, personal Creator.

BELIEVE IT OR NOT - SIX VIEWS

As mankind has struggled to put together his beliefs about God, he has come up with six major viewpoints. Here is a chart of those beliefs.

BELIEF	BASIC TENET	ADVOCATES	THEY SAY
Agnosticism	It is not possible to know whether God exists. We cannot know how the world began.	Thomas Huxley William Spencer	"I don't know if there is a God or not."
Atheism	There is no need for a God. The gods of the Greeks and the God of the Bible are the same.	Madalyn O'Hair Bertrand Russell	"I know there is no God."
Deism	God set the universe in motion and left it to its own results. God no longer interacts with man.	Benjamin Franklin Thomas Jefferson	"The world is like a clock that God wound up once and it is now winding down."
Panentheism	God permeates the universe. All things exist in Him.	Paul Tillich New Age Movement	A panentheist would look at a tree and say, "God is in that tree."
Pantheism	We are all part of God. Everything that exists has God in it.	Spinoza Goethe	A pantheist would look at a tree and say, "That tree is God."
Theism	"There is only one God. And He created the universe."	Christians Jews Muslims	"God is there and He is not silent." - F. Schaeffer

Comment: The above "BELIEVE IT OR NOT - SIX VIEWS" chart is a generalization of the major religious beliefs. Thus, it is not exhaustive. And as previously indicated, this chart is from a web document. For this essay, the wording under the columns labeled – "Basic Tenet" and "Advocates", for the row labeled – "Theism", was changed. The original wording under the "Basic Tenet" column was "There is one God. He created the universe and we can know Him." The underlined wording was inappropriate with the addition of word – "Muslims", under the "advocates" column, because most Muslims do not believe that they can know God. For that matter, not all Jews believe that God is knowable. Thus, the wording – "There is only one God. And He created the universe.", seemed more appropriate, for this discussion. Furthermore, the inclusion of the word – "Muslims", under the "Advocate" column, by this author is not intended to imply that these three religions: Christianity, Judaism, and Islam, are completely compatible. Rather, it serves to simply convey the fact that all three religions endorse "monotheism (*there is only one God*)". The incompatibility of the three religions is highlighted, by the concept of "the Trinity". Christians believe in the Trinity, whereas the Jews and Muslims do not. More precisely, Christians believe that Jesus was the only begotten Son of God and that he is a member of the Trinity: God, the Father, God, the Son, and God, the Holy Spirit. And these three are one God. Jews believe that Jesus was, at best, a righteous man, who committed heresy, by claiming to be coequal with God. Muslims believe that Jesus was a righteous man and a prophet, but not the Son of God. Thus, the more appropriate wording was used for "Theism".

What are some names, terms, and phrases, which are useful to a discussion of the formation of the Christian Bible?

While researching audio, video, and written material on the formation of the Christian Bible, this author repeatedly encountered some of the same names, terms, and phrases, which seemed crucial to any discussion of the Bible, here or elsewhere. Consequently, some of those names, terms, and phrases are defined in this essay, for your convenience. Some terms and/or phrases are not exclusively applicable to the Bible and/or to written material, but as the Bible is the focus of this essay, most of the definitions will be worded, as these apply to the Bible and/or to written material.

The names, terms, and phrases are presented in three sets: *Set-1* provides definitions for some fundamental names and/or terms. *Set-2* provides definitions for some groupings of books, "associated with" and/or "included in" the Old Testament or the New Testament. *Set-3* provides definitions of some important versions and/or translations of the Bible. Within each set, each name, term, or phrase is presented in a bold font. Then following each bold-font name, term, or phrase is, at least, one definition for it. Each definition is preceded, by the symbol ➧. Then each definition is ended with an indication of the source of the definition. However, if the source requires more than a line, it may be given as an endnote.

Some definitions may include unfamiliar names, terms, and/or phrases. Unfortunately, time and space do not allow for every unfamiliar name, term, and/or phrase to be defined here. When appropriate, some comments have been included to share interesting information. The sets are, as follows:

Set-1: **Some fundamental names and terms**

Some of the fundamental names and terms in this set facilitate the definitions of names, terms, and phrases in the other two sets. The names and terms are, as follows:

Aramaic

➧ is "a 'Semitic language'[11] with a 3,000-year history. It has been the language of administration of empires and the language of divine worship. It is the original language of large sections of the biblical books of Daniel and Ezra, and is the main language of the Talmud. Aramaic was the native language of Jesus. '*Modern Aramaic*' is spoken today as a first language by numerous, scattered communities, most significantly by Assyrians.

The language is considered to be endangered."[12]

The "Aramaic" used in the Bible is more specifically referred to as "*Biblical Aramaic*" to distinguish it from "*modern Aramaic*" and other "*Aramaic*" dialects. Furthermore, note that because "Aramaic" is more than 3,000-years old, it has gone through many changes – many dialects. *(Source: A paraphrased consensus)*

"'Aramaic' only accounts for about ten chapters of the whole Bible. 'Biblical Aramaic' is closely related to Hebrew (*perhaps a bit like Spanish and Portuguese*), and they are written with the same alphabet.

During the eighth century BCE, Aramaic became the lingua franca of the Near East. Before that period, it had been the native language of the Aramaean city-states to the east. In 701 BCE, King Hezekiah of Judah negotiated with King Sennacherib of Assyria, as his army besieged Jerusalem. The account in 2 Kings 18:26 sets the meeting of the ambassadors of both camps just outside the city walls. Hezekiah's envoys pleaded that the Assyrians make terms in Aramaic so that the people listening could not understand. Thus, Aramaic had become the language of international dialogue, but not of the common people. In 586 BCE, King Nebuchadnezzar II of Babylon destroyed Jerusalem and exiled many of the people of Judah to the east. Aramaic became the language of necessity for the exiles, and after the Persian Empire's capture of Babylon, it became the language of culture and learning. King Darius I declared that Aramaic was to be the official language of the western half of his empire in 500 BCE, and it is this Imperial Aramaic language that forms the basis of 'Biblical Aramaic'."[13]

To this point only general references to the location of "Aramaic" words in the Bible, have been given. However, several reference sources were more specific, by indicating that "Aramaic" words occurred in Ezra 4:8-6:18, Ezra 7:12-26, and Daniel 2:4-7:28. One source also indicated two other things: *first*, "*Aramaic*" also occurs in Genesis 31:47 and Jeremiah 10:11 and *second*, because Aramaic was the language of Jesus and His disciples, some "*Aramaic*" occurs in the "New Testament" in Matthew 27:46, Mark 5:41, Mark 7:34, Mark 14:36, Mark 15:34, Romans 3:15, 1 Corinthians 16:22, and Galatians 4:6. *(Source: A paraphrased consensus)*

Autograph

- is a term used to reference an original writing of a biblical document. The original manuscript written. The autographs would be the actual, original written documents from which copies are made. (Source: "autograph" by Matthew Slick, http://www.carm.org/dictionary/dic_a-b.htm#Autograph)

Bible

- is "the English form of the Greek name 'Biblia', meaning 'books', the name which in the fifth century began to be given to the entire collection of sacred books, *called*[1] the '**Library of Divine Revelation**'. The name 'Bible' was adopted by Wickliffe[14], and came gradually into use in our English language. The Bible consists of sixty-six different books, composed by many different writers, in three different languages, under different circumstances; writers of almost every social rank, statesmen and peasants, kings, herdsmen, fishermen, priests, tax-gatherers, tentmakers; educated and uneducated, Jews and Gentiles; most of them unknown to each other, and writing at various periods during the space of about sixteen hundred years: and yet, after all, it is only one book dealing with only one subject in its numberless aspects and relations, the subject of man's redemption. It is divided into the Old Testament, containing thirty-nine books, and the New Testament, containing twenty-seven books. The names given to the Old in the writings of the New are 'the scriptures' (Matthew 21:42), 'scripture' (2 Peter 1:20), 'the holy scriptures' (Romans 1:2), 'the law' (John 12:34), 'the law of Moses, the prophets, and the psalms' (Luke 24:44), 'the law and the prophets' (Matthew 5:17), 'the old covenant' (2 Corinthians 3:14, R.V.). There is a break of four hundred years between the Old Testament and the New Testament."[15]

Book

- is a term used to refer to a unit or single collection of writings, which are part of the Bible. The term – "book", is also used for writings, which are not included in the Bible. *(Source: A paraphrased consensus)*

Canon

- is derived from a Hebrew and Greek word denoting a reed or cane. Hence it means something straight, or something to keep straight; and it also means a rule, or something ruled or measured. It came to be applied to the Scriptures, to denote that they contained the authoritative rule of faith and practice, the standard of doctrine and duty. A book is said to be of canonical authority, when it has a right to take a place with the other books which contain a revelation of the Divine will. Such a right does not arise from any ecclesiastical authority, but from the evidence of the inspired authorship of the book. The canonical (i.e., the inspired) books of the Old and New Testaments, are a complete rule, and the only rule, of faith and practice. They contain the whole supernatural revelation of God to men. (Source: "*Easton's Bible Dictionary*", by M. G. Easton)

---

[1] The word – "called", was inserted into the definition by this author.

Canonicity

- is the process by which men apply a standard – tests – to a book "**to recognize**" whether that book belongs in the "Old Testament canon", in the "New Testament canon", or in neither, because that book "was" or "was not" inspired by God, as defined by the tests. *(Source: A paraphrased consensus)*

Codex

- is an early book form made from papyri leaves cut, folded, and sewn together in the middle to make a book. First used in the 2nd century (A.D.). (Source: "codex" by Matthew Slick, http://www.carm.org/dictionary/dic_c-d.htm#Codex)

  Comment: Obviously, associating the term – "Codex", with another name is intended to mean that a copy of the named book is of the codex form and material. Many codices (*which is the plural form of the term "codex"*) were preserved, by various denominations or religious groups. Examples of codex books are the "Aleppo Codex" (See www.bible-researcher.com/aleppo.html) and the "Codex Vaticanus (B)" (See www.bible-researcher.com/codex-b.html).

Copy

- is a term used to refer to all or some portion of a unit or single collection of writings, which is not an "Autograph" (*is not an original*). A copy is like the original, but it is not the original. The source for a copy is the original or another copy. *(Source: A paraphrased consensus)*

Deuterocanonical

- is a derivation of the Greek word – "deutero", which means "second" and the English word – "canonical", which comes from the English word: "canon". The word – "canon", is derived from the Greek word – "kanon", which means "rod" or "rule". Thus, the two words – "deutero" and "canonical", combine to form the word – "deuterocanonical", which has come to mean "second canon" or "books added to the canon". This term is used by Catholics to refer to the additional verses and books in the Old Testament of the "Catholic Bible" over and above the verses and books that make up the thirty-nine canonical books of the Old Testament of the "Protestant Bible". (*The New Testament is the same in both Bibles.*) Protestants appear to use the phrase – "**Old Testament Apocrypha**" to refer to the "deuterocanonical" verses and books, and to several other books, which are not in either the "Catholic Bible" or the "Protestant Bible". See the entry for the "**Catholic Bible**" in *Set-3* for more comments about the additional verses and books in the Old

Testament of the "Catholic Bible". (*Source: A paraphrased consensus*)

Epistle

- is a synonym for the word – "letter". (*Source: A paraphrased consensus*)

- is a term that "refers to written correspondence. The majority of the canonical writings of the New Testament are epistolary in nature. The New Testament includes letters written by Paul, James, Peter, John, and Jude. The author of the Epistle to the Hebrews is unidentified. See Letters." (Source: "Holman Bible Dictionary")

Extant

- is an adjective meaning "surviving" or "still existing". It is used to refer to all or some portion of a unit or single collection of writings, which has "survived" or "still exist", as either an "**autograph**" or a "**copy**". (*Source: A paraphrased consensus*)

Greek

- is the original language of most of the "New Testament". But the "Greek" of the "New Testament" is more specifically called "*Koine Greek*". (*Source: A paraphrased consensus*)

  "'*Koine Greek*' is the more universal offspring of '*Attic Greek*', which persisted until the 4th century BCE, when it was replaced by '*Koine Greek*'."[16] According to Dr. D. James Kennedy, "*Modern Greek*" is a simplified subset of "*Koine Greek*". The word – "Koine" is Greek for "common", which is intended to indicate that it was the common language of the period 300 B.C. to about 300 A.D. See the article on "*Koine Greek*" in "Wikipedia".

Hebrew

- is interchangeable with the word – "Jewish" in many uses. The difference is whether whatever is being qualified with either word, is being associated more with the people (*Jewish*) or with their language (*Hebrew*). (*Source: The author's understanding*)

- is the original language of most of the "Old Testament". But the "Hebrew" of the "Old Testament" is more specifically called "*Classical Hebrew*".

  "'*Classical Hebrew*' is specifically the dialect of '*Biblical Hebrew*' that scholars believe flourished around the 6th century B.C.E., before the Babylonian exile. The '*Biblical Hebrew*' text contained nothing but consonants and spaces and this is still the case with Torah scrolls that are used in synagogues. A system of writing vowels called niqqud, (*from the root word meaning 'points' or 'dots'*) developed around the 5th Century CE. It is used today in printed Bibles and some other religious books and also in poetry, children's literature, and texts for beginning students of Hebrew. Most '*modern Hebrew*' texts contain only consonant letters, spaces and western-style punctuation and to facilitate reading without vowels 'mater lectionis'[17] are often inserted into words, which would be written without them in a text with full niqqud. The niqqud system is sometimes used when it is necessary to avoid certain ambiguities of meaning — such as when context is insufficient to distinguish between two identically spelled words — and in the transliteration of foreign names."[18]

Note that "*Classical Hebrew*" and/or "*Biblical Hebrew*" are different from "*modern Hebrew*", in several ways (*i.e., symbols that are no longer used, the way some words are pronounced*). An article, which is titled "Hebrew language", in "*Wikipedia*" presents an extensive discussion of the "Hebrew language". This article implies that while both "*Classical Hebrew*" and "*Biblical Hebrew*" are considered "Semitic languages", a few people hold the position that the "*modern Hebrew*" dialect has more of a European - (*especially, Germanic*) - than Semitic sound. (*Source: A paraphrased consensus*)

Despite the Hebrew dialect used for religious texts before 585 B.C., those religious texts generally used the "Paleo-Hebrew alphabet"[19]. The web document at: www.hebrewold testament.com, shows a "Parallel Hebrew Old Testament" from a modern Hebrew version, a Paleo-Hebrew version, a Hebrew transliteration, the Latin Vulgate, and eight English translations of the Old Testament. (*Source: A paraphrased consensus*)

Letter

- is "A written message sent as a means of communication between persons separated by distance. Letters in the Bible consist of two categories: (1) letters mentioned and sometimes found in Bible books and (2) books of the Bible that are themselves letters." (Source: "Holman Bible Dictionary")

MSS., MSS, mss., mss

- are abbreviations for the word - "Manuscripts". (*Source: A paraphrased consensus*)

Nestorius

- became the Patriarch of Constantinople, around 428 A.D. His name is important, because of references to the "Nestorian Church" and the "Nestorian Bible". He viewed Mary, as the "Mother of Christ" and not the "Mother of God". And he viewed Jesus as having two natures, which many in the Christian community of that period took to mean that Jesus was two persons. His view of Christ was the reason for the "the Council of Ephesus" in 431 A.D. Because of the council, his followers, who were called - "Nestorians", and the

"Assyrian Church of the East" (*which traces itself back to the Apostle Thomas and which supported Nestorius*), split from the rest of the Christian Church under what is called the "Nestorian Schism". Then because the "Assyrian Church of the East" had supported the Nestorians, the rest of the church began calling the "Assyrian Church of the East" by the name the "Nestorian Church". Thus, the two names – the "Assyrian Church of the East" and the "Nestorian Church" – were interchangeable from that point in history to about 1975, when the leaders of the modern "Assyrian Church of the East" began a move to dissociate the two names. Now, members of the modern "Assyrian Church of the East" do not like being called the "Nestorian Church" and call their version of the Bible – the "Peshitta Bible", not the "Nestorian Bible". (*Source: A paraphrased consensus*)

Pentateuch

- is from the Greek "penta", ("five") and teuchos, ("a tool"). It refers to the first five books of the Bible known as Genesis, Exodus, Leviticus, Numbers, and Deuteronomy. All five were authored by Moses and are also known as "the Law". (Source: "Pentateuch" by Matthew Slick, http://www.carm.org/dictionary/dic_p-r.htm#_1_32)

Protocanonical

- is use to reference "those books of the Old Testament, which were coextensive with the 'Hebrew Bible' and which have always been considered canonical, by almost all Christians throughout history. The term '*protocanonical*' is often used to contrast these books to the 'deuterocanonical books' or 'apocrypha', which were sometimes doubted in the early church."[20]

Scriptures

- is the English word used as a translation of the Greek word – "*graphai*", which can also be translated as "writings". (Source: www.godandscience.org/discovery/chapter1.html)

> *Comment:* The entry titled – "Scriptures" in the "Easton's Bible Dictionary", by M. G. Easton, reads – "Invariably in the New Testament, [the word – 'scriptures'][2] denotes that definite collection of sacred books, regarded as given by inspiration of God, which we usually call the Old Testament (2 Timothy 3:15, 16; John 20:9; Galatians 3:22; 2 Peter 1:20). It was God's purpose thus to perpetuate his revealed will. From time to time he raised up men to commit to writing in an infallible record the revelation he gave. The 'Scripture', or collection of sacred writings, was thus enlarged from

---

2 The wording – "the word – 'scriptures'", was inserted into the definition by this author.

time to time as God saw necessary. We have now a completed 'Scripture', consisting of the Old and New Testaments. The Old Testament canon in the time of our Lord was precisely the same as that which we now possess under that name. He placed the seal of his own authority on this collection of writings, as all equally given by inspiration (Matthew 5:17; 7:12; 22:40; Luke 16:29, 31)."

Syriac

- is more correctly rendered "Aramaic", including both the Syriac and the Chaldee languages. In the Old Testament, 2 Kings 18:26; Ezra 4:7; and Daniel 2:4 use Syriac words. In the New Testament there are several Syriac words, such as "Eloi, Eloi, lama sabachthani?" (Mark 15:34; Matthew 27:46 gives the Hebrew form, "Eli, Eli"), "Raca" (Matthew 5:22), "Ephphatha" (Mark 7:34), "Maran-atha" (1 Corinthians 16:22). (Source: "*Easton's Bible Dictionary*", by M. G. Easton)

- is the literary dialect of "Aramaic". *(Source: A paraphrased consensus)*

Testament

- is a derivation of the Latin word testamentum, which was used in Jerome's Vulgate to translate the Hebrew word b'rith, covenant. The Greek equivalent is diatheke, which also means covenant. The word has come to be used in describing the two main divisions of the Bible: The Old Testament and The New Testament. It should be understood then, that the Bible is generally to be looked at as a covenant between God and man. (Source: "Testament" by Matthew Slick, http://www.carm.org/dictionary/dic_t.htm#_1_172)

- occurs twelve times in the New Testament (Hebrews 9:15, etc.) as the rendering of the Greek "diatheke", which is twenty times rendered "covenant" in the Authorized Version, and always so in the Revised Version. The Vulgate translates incorrectly by testamentum, whence the names "Old" and "New Testament", by which we now designate the two sections into which the Bible is divided. (Source: "*Easton's Bible Dictionary*", by M. G. Easton)

Torah

- is the most important document in Judaism, revered as the inspired word of God, traditionally said to have been revealed to Moses. The word Torah means "teaching," "instruction," "scribe", or "law" in Hebrew. It is also known as the Five Books of Moses, the Law of Moses (Torat Moshe) or Sefer Torah (which refers to the scroll cases in which the books were kept), in Greek called Pentateuch ("five rolls or cases").

Other names current in Judaism include "*Hamisha Humshei Torah* ('[the] five fifths/parts [of the] Torah')" or simply the "Humash ('fifth')". A "Sefer Torah" is a formal written scroll of the five books, written by a Torah scribe under exceptionally strict requirements. The term is sometimes also used in the general sense to also include both Judaism's written law and oral law, encompassing the entire spectrum of authoritative Jewish religious teachings throughout history, including the Mishnah, the Talmud, the Midrash, and more.

The five books, their names and pronunciations in the original Hebrew, are as follows:

- ✓ Genesis (בראשית, Bereshit: "In the beginning...")
- ✓ Exodus (שמות, Shemot: "Names")
- ✓ Leviticus (ויקרא, Vayyiqra: "And he called...")
- ✓ Numbers (במדבר, "Bamidbar"[3]: "In the desert...")
- ✓ Deuteronomy (דברים, Devarim: "Words", "Discourses", or "Things")

The Hebrew names are taken from initial words within the first verse of each book. See, for example, Genesis 1:1. These books describe the creation of the Universe and its history, and it describes in particular the special covenant between God and the people of Israel.

Jews have revered the Torah through the ages, as have Samaritans and Christians. It is traditionally accepted as the literal word of God as told to Moses. For many, it is neither exactly history, nor theology, nor a legal and ritual guide, but something beyond all three. It is the primary guide to the relationship between God and man, and the whole meaning and purpose of that relationship, a living document that unfolds over generations and millennia.

(Source: Torah. (2007, November 14). In *Wikipedia, The Free Encyclopedia*. Retrieved 19:57, November 14, 2007, from http://en.wikipedia.org/w/index.php?title=Torah&oldid= 171346859)

Translation

- is the result of taking a source Bible or Bibles in one or more languages and creating a copy by translating the source language or languages into a different (*target*) language. There are, at least, two types of translations: "word-for-word" and "thought-for-thought". Then to further complicate things, the "thought-for-thought" type can occur by applying a translation method, which has two extremes. At one extreme, the "thought-for-thought"

---

3 Spelled "Bammidbar" by some reference sources.

translators focus on each unit of thought in the source document (*or documents*) and try to convey the meaning of that unit, as accurately as possible with less concern for readability in the target language. At the other extreme, the "thought-for-thought" translators focus on larger groups of thoughts and try to make those groups as easy to read in the target language as possible with less concern for the exact meaning in the source language(s). Some web documents indicate that "the latter extreme turns the results into what could be called 'paraphrasing', which is more of a commentary than a translation." Furthermore, the two types of translations automatically imply a third type, which would be some combination of the two. More specifically, someone could translate some portions of a document, as the "word-for-word" type, and other portions of the same document, as the "thought-for-thought" type. *(Source: A paraphrased consensus)*

Version

- is a term applied to a particular translation of the holy Scriptures in a given language, or to all the translations in that particular language. *(Source: A paraphrased consensus)*

  Comment: Some people use the terms – "translation" and "version", as synonyms. By the literal definition of the word – "synonyms", this is okay, because these two words mean about the same thing.

Set-2: **Some groupings of books**

Several web documents indicate that by 300 A.D., early Christian scholars and theologians may have defined three-primary groupings of books: "Homologoumena", "Antilegomena", and "Notha". These were mainly applicable to the books associated with the "New Testament", because many of those Christian scholars and theologians took the position that the "Old Testament canon" was settled before the birth of Jesus or better, by the testimony of Jesus and His Apostles. Nevertheless, some groupings, which are associated with the "Old Testament" and/or the "New Testament", are defined, as follows:

Antilegomena

- is spelled "**antilogomena**" by some sources. "It is used to reference certain books of the New Testament which were for a time not universally received, but which are now considered canonical. These are the Epistle to the Hebrews, the Epistles of James and Jude, the second Epistle of Peter, the second and third Epistles of John, and the Revelation. All of the undisputed books are grouped under the term the '**Homologoumena**'." (Source: "Webster's Revised Unabridged Dictionary [1913]", © 1996, 1998 MICRA, Inc.)

Apocrypha

- means hidden. It is used in a general sense to describe a list of books written by Jews between 300 and 100 B.C. More specifically, it is used of the seven additional books accepted by the Catholic church as being inspired. The entire list of books of the apocrypha are: 1 Esdras, 2 Esdras, Tobit, Judith, the Rest of Esther, the Wisdom of Solomon, Sirach, (also titled Ecclesiasticus), Baruch, The Letter of Jeremiah, Song of the Three Young Men, Susanna, Bel and the Dragon, The Additions to Daniel, The Prayer of Manasseh, and 1 and 2 Maccabees. The books accepted as inspired and included in the Catholic Bible are Tobit, Judith, 1 and 2 Maccabees, Wisdom of Solomon, Sirach (also known as Ecclesiasticus), and Baruch. The Jews never recognized these books as being canonical (inspired). There is no record that Jesus or the apostles ever quoted from the apocryphal books. The Septuagint (LXX) includes the books, not as scripture, but as part of the translation of the Hebrew manuscripts as a whole. (Source: "Apocrypha" by Matthew Slick, http://www.carm.org/dictionary/dic_a-b.htm#Apocrypha)

  Comment: As indicated by the entry for the term – "Deuterocanonical", Catholics and Protestants use the term – "Apocrypha" differently.

- means "hidden" or "spurious". It is a name associated with two groups of books. One group is associated with the "Old Testament" and is called "**Old Testament Apocrypha**". The other group is associated with the "New Testament" and is called "**New Testament Apocrypha**". *(Source: A paraphrased consensus)*

  Comment: With regards to the Old Testament, an entry in *Wikipedia* titled – "Biblical apocrypha"[21], states: "In Greek circles, however, these books are not traditionally called *Apocrypha*, but "***Anagignoskomena*** *(which means 'things that are read')*", and are integrated into the Old Testament."

Biblical canon

- is "a list of Biblical books which establishes the set of books which are considered to be authoritative as scripture by a particular Jewish or Christian community. These lists, or *canons*, have been developed through debate and agreement by the religious authorities of those faiths. Believers consider these *canonical* books to be inspired by God or to express the authoritative history of the relationship between God and his people. Although the canons are in agreement regarding most of the books of the Bible, there is variation regarding some books. Texts excluded from a particular canon are considered apocryphal; however, many disputed works considered 'apocryphal' by some Churches are considered 'deuterocanonical', or 'fully canonical', by others. There are differences between the Jewish and Christian canons, and between the canons of different Christian denominations. The differing criteria and processes of canonization dictate what the communities regard as the inspired books.

Some canons are considered '*closed (i.e. additional books cannot be added)*'. By contrast, an '*open*' canon would allow additional books, should they meet the criteria. The closure of the canon reflects a belief that public revelation has ended and thus the inspired texts may be gathered into a complete and authoritative canon."[22]

> Comment: The previous definition explicitly indicates that the process of recognizing some books, as inspired by God results in a "**list of those books**". The definition also indicates that different list, by different groups (*cultural, religious, or otherwise*), means that the process of recognizing books inspired by God was applied differently, by some groups. But a different list implies a basis or reason for the differences. These reasons and differences need to be noted. Furthermore, using a word or a phrase to qualify the word – "Canon" (*to form phrases like – "Biblical Canon", "Ordinary Jewish Canon", "Jewish Canon", "Roman Catholic and Orthodox Canon", "New Testament Canon", "Old Testament Canon", etc.*), indicates a reference to a specific list or collection of books and the justification for that list or collection. But we must also note that in some cases a list contains a subset of the books in another list. The obvious example of this would be that a *"New Testament Canon"* and a *"Old Testament Canon"* could be subsets of a *"Biblical Canon"*. To confirm this, one would only need to compare the list of books referenced by each canon.

Homologomena

- are those books of the New Testament, which were acknowledged as canonical by the early church; – distinguished from antilegomena. (Source: "Webster's Revised Unabridged Dictionary [1913]", © 1996, 1998 MICRA, Inc.)

> Comment: Books included under this grouping were the four gospels, Acts, Paul's epistles, 1 Peter, and 1 John. *(Source: A paraphrased consensus)*

New Testament Apocrypha

- is a group of books associated with the "New Testament", based on the supposed writer of the material and/or the subject matter. The list of books in this group does not appear to be consistent across reference sources. However, the web document at:

  www.comparative-religion.com/christianity/apocrypha/

  may present the most extensive list of "New Testament Apocrypha", available via the

Internet. This particular web document also provides a link to whatever text is available for a particular writing. *(Source: A paraphrased consensus)*

New Testament Canon

- was formed gradually under divine guidance. The different books as they were written came into the possession of the Christian associations which began to be formed soon after the day of Pentecost; and thus slowly the canon increased till all the books were gathered together into one collection containing the whole of the twenty-seven New Testament inspired books. Historical evidence shows that from about the middle of the second century this New Testament collection was substantially such as we now possess. Each book contained in it is proved to have, on its own ground, a right to its place; and thus the whole is of divine authority. (Source: "*Easton's Bible Dictionary*", by M. G. Easton)

Notha

- is the name given to a group of books (*associated with the New Testament*), which claimed to be inspired. But these books were authored by individuals, who wrote under an Apostle's name and/or who falsely claimed to be an Apostle. Generally, these books were considered false, because they contradicted previously accepted apostolic books. However, some people considered some of these books useful, even though they were not inspired. *(Source: A paraphrased consensus)*

Old Testament Apocrypha

- is the name given to certain ancient books which found a place in the LXX and Latin Vulgate versions of the Old Testament, and were appended to all the great translations made from them in the sixteenth century, but which have no claim to be regarded as, in any sense, parts of the inspired Word because:

  (1.) They are not once quoted by the New Testament writers, who frequently quote from the LXX. Our Lord and his apostles confirmed by their authority the ordinary Jewish canon, which was the same in all respects as we now have it.

  (2.) These books were written not in Hebrew, but in Greek, and during the "period of silence", from the time of Malachi[23], after which oracles and direct revelations from God ceased till the Christian era.

  (3.) The contents of the books themselves show that they were no part of Scripture. The Old Testament Apocrypha consists of fourteen books, the

chief of which are the Books of the Maccabees (q.v.)[4], the Books of Esdras, the Book of Wisdom, the Book of Baruch, the Book of Esther, Ecclesiasticus, Tobit, Judith, etc. The New Testament Apocrypha consists of a very extensive literature, which bears distinct evidences of its non-apostolic origin, and is utterly unworthy of regard.

(Source: "Easton's Bible Dictionary", by M. G. Easton)

Comment: The above entry from the "Easton's Bible Dictionary" indicates that the "Book of Esther" is an "Old Testament Apocrypha". However, the wording should have more precisely indicated that the apocryphal verses are those extra verses not occurring in the "Book of Esther" in the "Protestant Bible", when compared with the "Book of Esther" in the "Catholic Bible".

Comment: One web document indicated that "*Most of the Old Testament Apocrypha are accepted by the Catholic Church, while all of the New Testament Apocrypha are rejected by all.*" However, several other web documents indicate that – "The 'Ethiopian Bible' may have from sixty-six to eighty-one books, depending on the reference source for the information." If the sixty-six-books version of the "Ethiopian Bible" is true, it would probably be like the "Protestant Bible". However, if the eighty-one-books version is true, it must consist of "Old Testament Apocrypha", "Pseudepigrapha", and/or "New Testament Apocrypha".

- is used in a general sense to describe a list of books written by Jews between 300 and 100 B.C. More specifically, it is used of the seven additional books accepted by the Catholic church as being inspired. The entire list of books of the "Old Testament"[5] apocrypha are: "1 Esdras", "2 Esdras", "Tobit", "Judith", "the rest of Esther", "the Wisdom of Solomon", "Sirach (also titled Ecclesiasticus)", "Baruch", "The Letter of Jeremiah", "Song of the Three Young Men", "Susanna", "Bel and the Dragon", "The additions to Daniel", "The Prayer of Manasseh", and "1 and 2 Maccabees". The books accepted as inspired and included in the Catholic Bible are: "Tobit", "Judith", "1 and 2 Maccabees", "Wisdom of Solomon", "Sirach

---

4

Quod vide, Latin phrase meaning "which see". Used in books, etc, to make reference to other material. (Source: "q.v." In *Wiktionary, The Open Dictionary*. Retrieved 22:08, November 12, 2007, from http://en.wiktionary.org/w/index.php?title=qv&oldid=3121707)

5

The phrase – "Old Testament", was inserted by this author.

(also known as Ecclesiasticus)", and "Baruch"[6]. The Jews never recognized these books as being canonical (inspired). There is no record that Jesus or the apostles ever quoted from the apocryphal books. The Septuagint (LXX) includes the books, not as scripture, but as part of the translation of the Hebrew manuscripts as a whole. (Source: "Apocrypha" by Matthew Slick, http://www.carm.org/dictionary/dic_a-b.htm# Apocrypha)

- is certain writings which are received by some Christians as an authentic part of the Holy Scriptures, but are rejected by others. Fourteen such writings, or books, formed part of the Septuagint, but not of the Hebrew canon recognized by the Jews of Palestine. The "Council of Trent"[24] included all but three of these in the canon of inspired books having equal authority. The German and English Reformers grouped them in their Bibles under the title Apocrypha, as not having dogmatic authority, but being profitable for instruction. The Apocrypha is now commonly omitted from the King James's Bible. (Source: "Webster's Revised Unabridged Dictionary [1913]", © 1996, 1998 MICRA, Inc.)

Old Testament Canon

- is witnessed to by the New Testament writers. Their evidence is conclusive. The quotations in the New from the Old are very numerous, and the references are much more numerous. These quotations and references by our Lord and the apostles most clearly imply the existence at that time of a well-known and publicly acknowledged collection of Hebrew writings under the designation of "The Scriptures"; "The Law and the Prophets and the Psalms"; "Moses and the Prophets", etc. The appeals to these books, moreover, show that they were regarded as of divine authority, finally deciding all questions of which they treat; and that the whole collection so recognized consisted only of the thirty-nine books which we now posses. Thus they endorse as genuine and authentic the canon of the Jewish Scriptures. The Septuagint Version (q.v.) also contained every book we now have in the Old Testament Scriptures. As to the time at which the Old Testament canon was closed, there are many considerations which point to that of Ezra and Nehemiah, immediately after the return from Babylonian exile. (Source: "*Easton's Bible Dictionary*", by M. G. Easton)

Pseudepigrapha

- is spelled "**pseudopigrapha**" by some sources. "It is from Ancient Greek *pseudes* = 'false', *epigraphe* = 'inscription'). Pseudopigrapha are falsely attributed works, texts whose claimed authorship is unfounded; a work, simply, 'whose real author attributed it

---

6 For the "Catholic Bible", the "Book of Baruch" includes the "Letter of Jeremiah", as the last - as the sixth - chapter of Baruch.

to a figure of the past.'[1] For instance, few Hebrew scholars would ascribe the Book of Enoch to the prophet Enoch, and few liberal Christian scholars would insist today that the Third Epistle of John was written by John the Evangelist,[2] or that the Second Epistle of Peter was written by Saint Peter[3] Nevertheless, in some cases, especially for books belonging to a religious canon, the question of whether a text is pseudepigraphical or not elicits sensations of loyalty and can become a matter of heavy dispute. The authenticity or value of the work itself, which is a separate question for experienced readers, often becomes sentimentally entangled in the association. Though the inherent value of the text may not be called into question, the weight of a revered or even apostolic author lends authority to a text: in Antiquity pseudepigraphy was 'an accepted and honored custom practiced by students/admirers of a revered figure'.[4] This is the essential motivation for pseudepigraphy in the first place.

In Biblical studies, the Pseudepigrapha are Jewish religious works written c 200 BC to 200 AD, not all of which are literally pseudepigraphical.[5] They are distinguished from the Apocrypha, the fourteen books that appear in the Septuagint and Vulgate but not in the Hebrew Bible or in Protestant Bibles.[5]"[25]

(*The superscript numbers enclosed in brackets in the source comments above are the source footnotes, which are presented in the indicated endnote.*)

> *Comment*: An article in the "Holman Bible Dictionary", which was authored by Clayton Harrop and is titled – "PSEUDEPIGRAPHA", indicates that there are, at least, fifty-two books in this group. And the most important and representative books, which show the significance of the Pseudepigrapha in understanding the background of the New Testament, are: "First Enoch", "Second Enoch", "Second Baruch", "The Sibylline Oracles", "The Testament of Moses (sometimes called the Assumption of Moses)", "The Testaments of the Twelve Patriarchs", "The Book of Jubilees", "The Psalms of Solomon", "Third Maccabees", "Fourth Maccabees", "The Life of Adam and Eve", and "The Letter of Aristeas". The article presents an overview of each of these representative books.

Set-3: **Some important versions and/or translations of the Bible**

Through the years, there have been many important versions and/or translations of the Bible. Some of these are, as follows:

Catholic Bible

- includes the same canonical verses in the sixty-six books of the "Protestant Bible", plus some additional verses, which are included in the "Old Testament" of the "Catholic Bible". More specifically, these additional verses are in the "Book of Esther" and the "Book of Daniel" and seven additional books: "Tobit", "Judith", "1 Maccabees", "2 Maccabees", "Wisdom of Solomon *(also called 'Wisdom')*", "Ecclesiasticus *(also called 'Sirach')*", and "Baruch and Letter of Jeremiah"[7]. Thus, the "Catholic Bible" consist of seventy-three books. Catholics use the term – "Deuterocanonical", which means "second canon" or "books added to the canon" to refer to the additional verses and books. Protestants use the phrase – "Old Testament Apocrypha", to refer to these same additional verses and books in the Catholic Bible and to several books, which are not in either Bible. But note. By using the term – "Deuterocanonical" and the phrase – "Old Testament Apocrypha", both Catholics and Protestants are tacitly admitting that the additional verses and books are not on the same authoritative level as the verses and books, which comprise the "Protestant Bible". *(Source: A paraphrased consensus)*

Greek Old Testament

- is also called the "Septuagint" or the "LXX". It is a translation of the "Hebrew Old Testament" into Greek, which took place in stages from 250 B.C. to 150 B.C. This translation includes the "Old Testament Apocrypha", in a separate section. But it is difficult to tell exactly, when and why the "Old Testament Apocrypha" was included. *(Source: A paraphrased consensus)*

Hebrew Old Testament

- is a phrase that must be used with care, because someone might think that there is a "Hebrew New Testament". And that is not the intent of the phrase. The intent was to indicate that the entire "Hebrew Bible" is almost the same, as the "Protestant Old Testament", but the "Hebrew Bible" is obviously mostly in the Hebrew language, thus the phrase: "Hebrew Old Testament". Even though the "Hebrew Old Testament" is the source of the thirty-nine books of the Protestant "Old Testament", there are differences between the two. In fact, there are, at least, five differences:

  ✓ *Difference-1*: The books are arranged in a different order. The different order comes from changes in how a particular book is classified. For instance, in the "Protestant Old Testament", Daniel is grouped, with the "Prophets", and Ruth is grouped, with the "historical writings". In the "Hebrew Bible", Daniel and Ruth are grouped with other books, under the classification of "Writings".

---

7 Here "Baruch" and the "Letter of Jeremiah", are being counted as one book. Some reference sources consider "Baruch" as a book and the "Letter of Jeremiah" as a separate book.

- ✓ *Difference-2*: In the "Protestant Old Testament", Kings, Chronicles, and Samuel were each divided into two books. In the "Hebrew Bible", the books of Kings, Chronicles, and Samuel are each one book.

- ✓ *Difference-3*: In the "Protestant Old Testament", the Book of Ezra and the Book of Nehemiah are separate books. In the "Hebrew Bible", these two books are one-book called the Book of "Ezra-Nehemiah".

- ✓ *Difference-4*: In the "Protestant Old Testament", the books of the twelve minor prophets are twelve separate books. In the "Hebrew Bible", these twelve books are counted as one book.

- ✓ *Difference-5*: Not all of the verse numbers match. A web document titled - "Hebrew and English Verse Differences" at:

  www.lebtahor.com/ScribalChanges/hebengverse.htm

  presents a list of Hebrew and English verse differences. It also gives a brief explanation of why many of the differences may have occurred.

The "Hebrew Old Testament" is also called the "Hebrew Bible", "Jewish Bible", "Jewish Old Testament", or the "Tanakh". The "Hebrew Old Testament" does not include any of the "Old Testament Apocrypha". *(Source: A paraphrased consensus)*

Hebrew Text

- is the label given to versions of the "Hebrew Bible" written in the Hebrew language over the years. The "Massoretic Text" is probably the best known of these versions. The versions may differ slightly from one another, because of things like verse numbers and the Hebrew characters used. *(Source: A paraphrased consensus)*

  Comment: Some reference sources use the spelling - "Masoretic", while other sources use the spelling - "Massoretic". In this book, the spelling used by the source is the spelling that will be used, with the paraphrased or quoted comments.

Jewish Bible

- is also called the "Jewish Old Testament", the "Hebrew Old Testament", the "Hebrew Bible", and the "Tanakh". *(Source: A paraphrased consensus)*

Jewish Canon

- is the Jewish list of the books of the "Jewish Old Testament". However, the number of books in this canon differs at "a count of twenty-two" or at "a count of twenty-four", according to the reference source and according to the period of history involved. Currently, the count is twenty-four books. However, all reference sources agree that the contents of the Jewish Bible did not change, only the way that the books were grouped and counted changed. For instance, in the writings of Flavius Josephus, he indicates that there were twenty-two books in the Jewish canon. Some scholars, who have studied the writings of Josephus, indicate that his writings imply that for the twenty-two book count. The book of Ruth was attached to the Book of Judges and the Book of Lamentations (*also called the "Book of Lamentations of Jeremiah"*) was attached to the Book of Jeremiah. But a quick search of the books written by Josephus by this author was unsuccessful at confirming this. On a speculative basis, this author favors the belief that the two books of Samuel and the two books of Kings existed as four parts of a book named – "Kingdoms (or Reigns)", so at sometime in the past the four parts of the Book of "Kingdoms" could have been counted as one book. Similarly, the Books of Ezra, Nehemiah, 1 Chronicles, and 2 Chronicles may have been one-book. Remember that "Chronicles, Ezra, and Nehemiah covered consecutive periods of Jewish history"[26]. Furthermore, when the current "twenty-four-book count" for the "Jewish canon" (*the "Jewish Old Testament"*) is compared with the thirty-nine-book count of the "Protestant Old Testament", we note that:

  - ✓ the two books of Samuel and the two books of Kings are each counted as one book,
  - ✓ the two books of Ezra and Nehemiah are counted as one book, and
  - ✓ the two books – 1 Chronicles and 2 Chronicles – are counted as one book.

Thus, the speculative combination of books would yield a twenty-two-book count. Another reason for this author favoring this speculative basis is that the Books of Ruth and Lamentations were among the five books: "The Song of Songs (also called Canticles)", "Ruth", "Lamentations", "Ecclesiastes", and "Esther", which were read on five special occasions in the Synagogues. This practice would seem to be a good reason for the Jews keeping these books separate and distinct. Thus, as previously mentioned, there is a chart at the end of the essay titled – "What do biblical scholars, Christian historians, and others say, about the formation of the Christian Bible?" This chart lists the books in the "Jewish Bible", the "Septuagint", the "Catholic Old Testament", and the "Protestant Old Testament". However, it has two columns for the "Jewish Bible", because one column reflects this author speculative twenty-two-book count for the "Jewish Bible" and the other column shows the current twenty-four-book count. (*Source: author's speculation and a paraphrase consensus*)

Latin Vulgate

- is "an early 5th century version of the Bible in Latin which is largely the result of the labors of Jerome, who was commissioned by Pope Damasus I in 382 to make a revision of the 'old Latin' translations. Its Old Testament is the first Latin version translated directly from the Hebrew Tanakh rather than from the Greek Septuagint. It became the definitive and officially promulgated Latin version of the Bible of the Roman Catholic Church and ultimately took the name *versio vulgata*, which means simply 'the published translation'. There are 76 books in the Clementine edition of the Vulgate Bible: 46 in the Old Testament, 27 in the New Testament, and 3 in the Apocrypha."[27]

  Comment: Vulgate is from the Latin "editio vulgata" meaning "common version". (Source: www.ntcanon.org/Vulgate.shtml)

  Comment: According to several web documents, the phrase - "Old Latin", is used to indicate translations of the Bible in Latin that existed before Jerome's "Latin Vulgate", more than the phrase is intended to indicate a different (*earlier*) version of the Latin language. However, the online version of "The Catholic Encyclopedia", has an entry titled - "Ecclesiastical Latin", which implies that Jerome wrote the "Latin Vulgate" in "Ecclesiastical Latin", rather than "Classical Latin". (*See the web document at: www.newadvent.org/cathen/09019a.htm*). (Source: *A paraphrased consensus*)

  Comment: Several reference sources indicated that Jerome may have begun his translation efforts as early as 383 C.E. (*a discussion of "CE" follows*) and finished around 405 C.E. However, most of the reference sources about Jerome and the "Latin Vulgate" that were reviewed by this author, were very confusing, because most indicated that Jerome translated from the Hebrew Tanakh. If this were true, then we would have to ask why his Latin translation includes seven books from the Septuagint, which are not in the Tanakh? Furthermore, several reference sources indicated that the directive of Pope Damasus I to Jerome may have been for a revision of the Old Latin versions using the Greek. Consequently, this author does not understand what most of the reference sources mean when they say that Jerome translated from the Tanakh. (*Source: The author's understanding*)

  Comment: "The Common Era (**CE**), sometimes known as the **Current Era** or less often referred to as the **Christian Era**, is the period of measured time beginning with the year 1 (*the traditional birth date of Jesus*) to the present. The notations **CE** and **BCE** (**Before the Common Era** or **Before the Christian Era**) are alternative notations for **AD** (*anno Domini, Latin* *for 'in the year of the Lord'*) and **BC** (Before Christ), respectively. They may also be written C.E. and B.C.E. Although the term common era was first used by some Christians, it is now the term preferred by some as a religiously-neutral alternative. Others criticize it as an unnecessary euphemism or an attempt at political correctness, pointing out that the pivotal year 1 still centers on the supposed date of Jesus' birth."[28]

LXX

- is also called the "Greek Old Testament" or the "Septuagint". The label – "LXX" was derived from the fact that seventy-two Jewish translators worked on the translation of the "Hebrew Bible" into Greek. One web document indicated that "LXX" was the nearest whole number to seventy-two. The web document at: www.kalvesmaki.com/LXX/, presents a detailed discussion of the "Septuagint". The discussion includes comments about the differences between the "LXX" and the "Masoretic Text". *(Source: A paraphrased consensus)*

Massoretic text (MT)

- is spelled "**masoretic**" by some sources. "The masoretic text is the Hebrew text of the Jewish Bible (Tanakh). It defines not just the books of the Jewish canon, but also the precise letter-text of the biblical books in Judaism, as well as their vocalization and accentuation for both public reading and private study. The MT is also widely used as the basis for translations of the Old Testament in Protestant Bibles, and in recent decades also for Catholic Bibles.

  The MT was primarily copied, edited and distributed by a group of Jews known as the Masoretes between the seventh and tenth centuries CE. Though the consonants differ little from the text generally accepted in the early second century (and also differ little from some Qumran texts that are even older), it has numerous differences of both greater and lesser significance when compared to (extant 4th century) manuscripts of the Septuagint, a Greek translation (made in the 3rd to 2nd centuries BCE) of the Hebrew Scriptures that was in popular use in Egypt and Palestine and that is often quoted in the Christian New Testament.

  The Hebrew word *'mesorah'* refers to the transmission of a tradition. In a very broad sense it can refer to the entire chain of Jewish tradition (see Oral law), but in reference to the masoretic text the word mesorah has a very specific meaning: the diacritic markings of the text of the Hebrew Bible and concise marginal notes in manuscripts (and later printings) of the Hebrew Bible which note textual details, usually about the precise spelling of words.

The oldest manuscripts containing substantial parts of the Masoretic Text known to still exist date from approximately the ninth century CE,[1] and the Aleppo Codex (the oldest complete copy of the Masoretic Text in one manuscript) dates from the tenth century."[29]

(The superscript number enclosed in brackets in the source comments above is a source footnote, which is presented in the indicated endnote.)

Nestorian Bible

- is the name that several reference sources give to one of the early versions of the "Syriac Bible". Some might think that this Bible is associated with the "Nestorian Church", which is an inappropriate reference to the "Assyrian Church of the East". However, a member of the modern "Assyrian Church of the East" said, "The title – the 'Nestorian Bible' is inappropriate, as far as the 'Assyrian Church of the East' is concerned. Their Bible is called – the 'Peshitta Bible'. Furthermore, the title – the 'Syriac Bible' is like saying the 'Hebrew Bible', because like Hebrew, Syriac is the language." *(Source: A paraphrased consensus)*

Orthodox Bible

- is the name given to various versions of the Christian Bible, which have been formed in the "Oriental Orthodox Church" and in the "Eastern Christian Church". The "Oriental Orthodox Church" split from the main branch of the Christian Church in 451 A.D. This split was labeled the "Oriental Orthodox Schism". *(Currently, the "Oriental Orthodox Church" includes the "Coptic[8] Orthodox Church of Alexandria", the "Syriac Orthodox Church", the "Armenian Apostolic Church", the "Ethiopian Orthodox Tewahedo[9] Church", the "Malankara Orthodox Syrian Church", and the "Eritrean Orthodox Tewahedo Church".)* Then in 1054 A.D., the main branch of the Christian Church split into the "Eastern Christian Church" and the "Western Christian Church". This split was labeled the "Great Schism" or the "East-West Schism". The "Western Christian Church" was based in Rome and used Latin

---

8

The word – "Coptic", literally means "Egyptian Christian". The individual is called a "Copt". Most "Copts" are members of the "Coptic Orthodox Church", the "Coptic Catholic Church", or the "Coptic Protestant Church". (Source: Copt. [2008, March 25]. In *Wikipedia, The Free Encyclopedia*. Retrieved 18:09, April 3, 2008, from http://en.wikipedia.org/w/index.php?title=Copt&oldid=200869661)

9

The word – "Tewahedo", is spelled – "Tewahido", by some sources. It is from the "Ge'ez" language (*which is an ancient south Semitic language that developed in what is now Eritrea and northern Ethiopia*). This word means "being made one" or "unified". Thus, it serves to reference the belief of "Oriental Orthodox Christians" that "Christ had one unique nature that was a union of His divine nature and His human nature." (Paraphrased source: Ethiopian Orthodox Tewahedo Church. [2008, March 22]. In *Wikipedia, The Free Encyclopedia*. Retrieved 18:03, April 3, 2008, from http://en.wikipedia.org/w/index.php?title=Ethiopian_Orthodox_Tewahedo_Church&oldid=200177198)

for its versions of the Bible. The "Eastern Christian Church" was based in Constantinople and used Greek for its versions of the Bible. The "Western Church" developed into the Catholic Church and later many other denominations (*i.e., Lutheran, Baptist, and Protestant*). The "Eastern Church" developed into the "Eastern Orthodox Church", and then later on a regional basis instead of a denominational basis, it developed into churches like "the Greek Orthodox Church", "the Russian Orthodox Church", "the Romanian Orthodox Church", "the Bulgarian Orthodox Church", "the Church of Alexandria", "the Church of Jerusalem", and "the Orthodox Church in America". Then these regional churches defined, which non-canonical books would be included with the sixty-six canonical books in its version of the "Orthodox Bible". Similarly, the various "Oriental Orthodox Churches" decided on their version of the Bible. This means that some of these churches may have included "Old Testament Apocrypha", "Pseudepigrapha", and "New Testament Apocrypha" in their version of the "Orthodox Bible". Therefore, a given "Orthodox Bible" might consist of from sixty-six to eighty-one books, depending on the church it belongs to. (*Source: The author's understanding*)

Peshitta

- is used to refer to a "common Syriac version of the Scriptures. The Old Testament was likely translated between 100 and 300 A.D. The New Testament translation dates from before 400 A.D. The Peshitta lacked those books rejected by the Syriac-speaking churches (2 Peter; 2 and 3 John; Jude; Revelation)." (Source: "Holman Bible Dictionary")

  Comment: The "Old Testament" of the "Peshitta Bible" contains some "Old Testament Apocrypha" and "Pseudepigrapha".

Peshitto

- is the name given to a westernized version of the "Peshitta". Per a web document and a member of the "Assyrian Church of the East", the "Peshitto" includes "2 Peter"; "2 John", "3 John", "Jude", and "Revelation", whereas the "Peshitta" does not. The "Peshitto Bible" may be similar to the "Protestant Bible". *(Source: A paraphrased consensus)* One reference source was more specific by indicating that "the 'Peshitto' was the name given to the first major translation of the Hebrew Old Testament into Syriac, sometime before the 3rd century, with the twenty-seven canonical books of the New Testament being added in the 5th century."[30]

  Comment: As previously mentioned, whenever the "Peshitta Bible" was formed, its Old Testament included "Old Testament Apocrypha" and "Pseudepigrapha". Furthermore, the impression that this author received from several reference sources, was the difference between the "Peshitto" and the "Peshitta" may be that when the translators were creating the

"Peshitta", they used the "Septuagint", instead of "Hebrew Text".

Protestant Bible

- contains only the verses, which comprise what the "Western Christian Church" calls "the sixty-six canonical books of the Bible". The New Testament of the "Protestant Bible" is the same as the "Catholic Bible". However, the "Old Testament" of the two Bibles differ, as indicated under the entry for the "**Catholic Bible**". *(Source: A paraphrased consensus)*

Septuagint

- is also called the "LXX" or the "Greek Old Testament". *(Source: A paraphrased consensus)*

  Comment: There is a very interesting discussion of the Septuagint at www.kalvesmaki.com/LXX/.

Syriac Bible

- contained all the canonical books, along with some apocryphal books (called the Peshitto, i.e., simple translation, and not a paraphrase), was made early in the second century, and is therefore the first Christian translation of the Old Testament. It was made directly from the original, and not from the LXX. Version. The New Testament was also translated from Greek into Syriac about the same time. It is noticeable that this version does not contain the Second and Third Epistles of John, 2 Peter, Jude, and the Apocalypse. These were, however, translated subsequently and placed in the version. (Source: "*Easton's Bible Dictionary*", by M. G. Easton)

Tanakh

- is an English transliteration of the Hebrew word – תנ"ך, for the "Hebrew Bible". It is also spelled – "Tanach", "Tenakh", or "Tenak", by other sources. Nevertheless, the letters TNK (***TaNaKh***) are an acronym for the three parts of the "Hebrew Bible":

  - The "T" is for "Torah (tor-AH)" or "The Law", which is also called the "Pentateuch *(which is Greek for 'five books' or 'five scrolls')*".

  - The "N" is for "Nebiim (neh-veh-EEM)" or "The Prophets".

- The "K" is for "Ketubim[10] (keh-tu-VEEM)" or "The Writings (*or* **Hagiographa**)[11]".

(Source: A paraphrased consensus)

Note: *A list of the books in each of the three parts of the "Hebrew Bible" is shown in a chart at the end of the essay titled – "What do biblical scholars, Christian historians, and others say, about the formation of the Christian Bible?"*

Targum

- is "an Aramaic translation of the "Hebrew Bible (Tanakh)" written or compiled in Palestine or in Babylonia from the Second Temple period until the early Middle Ages (late first millennium). Targum also means translation or interpretation. In Arabic Targem (verb) means to translate or interpret. (Mutargem = Translator/Interpreter).

  Aramaic was the dominant language or lingua franca for hundreds of years in the major Jewish communities of the Palestine and Babylonia. To facilitate the study of Tanakh and make its public reading understood, authoritative translations were required. As translations, the targumim largely reflect rabbinic (i.e. midrashic) interpretation of the Tanakh, and are notable for eschewing anthropomorphisms in favor of allegorical readings.[1] (Rambam, for one, notes this often in The Guide.) This is true both for those targumim that are fairly literal, as well as for those which contain a great many midrashic expansions."[31] (*See the source for the complete discussion.*)

  (The superscript number enclosed in brackets in the source comments above is a source footnote, which is presented in the indicated endnote.)

  Comment: A web document at www.newadvent.org/cathen/14454b.htm, also presents a detailed discussion of the word – "Targum".

10

"Ketubim" is an English "transliteration (*which is the spelling of a word using the alphabet of another language*)" of the Hebrew word – כתובים. Other sources use the spelling – "ketuvim", "kethubim", "kethuvim", or "kethubhim".

11

The Hebrew word – כתובים (*ketuvim*) means "writings". In English translations of the Hebrew Bible, this section is usually entitled "Writings" or "Hagiographa". (Source: "Ketuvim". [2007, December 24]. In *Wikipedia, The Free Encyclopedia*. Retrieved 16:04, January 10, 2008, from http://en.wikipedia.org/w/index.php?title=Ketuvim&oldid=179907202) Note that "Hagiographa" is the English transliteration of a late Latin word, which is the plural of the late Greek word – "Hagiographos".

Hopefully, some of the names, terms, and phrases, which were presented in this essay, will be of some use to you, during some of your future religious activities.

What do biblical scholars, Christian historians, and others say, about the formation of the Christian Bible?

Before addressing the topic question, two issues need to be expressed explicitly:

- *Issue-1*: Some so-called "mature Christians" may feel that this essay and several others discuss issues that are not important to "their" faith in Christ. That feeling is okay! However, remember! Mature Christians – No! All Christians – are not Christians for themselves. Rather, all Christians are Christians, so that God will have people to use to draw others to Christ. And remember that a "Christian" is "a follower of Christ". Or more specifically, a "Christian" is "someone, who has accepted Christ, as their Lord and Savior". Also remember that the phrases – "mature Christian" and "immature Christian", have nothing to do, with the length of time that someone has been a Christian. Rather, these phrases reference a Christian's "spiritual and biblical" state. That is, a "mature Christian" is "a Christian, who desires the word – the Bible – and is as familiar with the word, as their time and circumstance permit; who is strong in her or his faith in Christ; who has a strong trust in the working of the Holy Spirit, in people's lives; who may have witnessed the working of the Holy Spirit in the lives of others; who may have experienced the working of the Holy Spirit in her or his own life; who has a good discernment of good and evil; and who is becoming Christlike". An "immature Christian" is "a Christian, who has not yet obtained many of the characteristics of a mature Christian". Despite the availability of mature Christians and immature Christians, the reality of life is that God could even use non-Christians to draw others to Christ. But this author believes that God prefers to use Christians, because using non-Christians may involve circumstances that are emotionally and physically harsher on the individual being drawn to Christ. Nevertheless, the point is:

> "**Most of the issues discussed in this book are things that all Christians should be aware of.**"

This awareness is really crucial when Christians (*especially, mature Christians*), encounter non-Christians tossing issues like those discussed, in this book, at others (*especially, immature Christians*). This author has seen and fully understands, what can happen to immature Christians left in the hands of some knowledgeable non-Christians. An immature Christian could be caught off guard (*could have their faith shaken*), by a non-Christian simply saying, "You, Christians, cannot even agree on the books for your Christian Bible. For example, look at how the Bibles used by Catholic Christians, Protestant Christians, Greek Orthodox Christians, Ethiopian Orthodox Christians, and several over Orthodox Christian churches differ." (*For some differences, see the essay – "What are some names, terms, and phrases, which are useful to a discussion of the formation* of the Christian Bible?") Thus, "It is important for all Christians 'to know that different Christian denominations, churches, and/or groups may use slightly different variations of the Old Testament and the New Testament' and 'to know why this is so'. Similarly, **there are other issues that all Christians should be aware of. And presenting some of those issues is one of the objectives of this book.**"

- *Issue-2*: This essay presents some comments on two themes: *first*, "literally, what is the Christian Bible?" and *second*, "how the Christian Bible was formed, according to biblical scholars, Christian historians, and others." **This essay does implicitly, accept the sixty-six books of the Protestant Bible, as the "inspired word of God"**, without explicitly trying to prove it. Proving the credibility of the Bible is the goal of the essay – "Is the Bible the inspired word of God?", which presents some comments, on two themes: *first*, the "credibility of the Bible" and *second*, "whether the Bible is the inspired word of God".

With the previous two issues in mind, this essay will address the topic question, using a seven-step approach. Step-1 presents a discussion of the question: "Literally, what is the Christian Bible?" Step-2 presents the web addresses of web documents, which list some books from possibly the "*Old Testament*" period *(from creation to about 400 B.C.)*" and the "*between the Old Testament and New Testament*" period *(from around 400 B.C. to about 32 A.D.)*. Step-3 presents the web addresses of web documents, which list some books from the "*New Testament*" period *(from around 32 A.D. to about 120 A.D. or possibly 200 A.D. [depending on the date that a particular reference source assigned to a book])*. Step-4 addresses the question: "On what basis were some books included, in the 'Old and New Testaments', and other books excluded?" Step-5 addresses the question: "When were the chapters and verse designations added to the 'Old and New Testaments'?" Step-6 presents a conclusion. Step-7 presents some relevant comments.

> *Comment:* As a visual aid, three-horizontal separators are used to indicate specific units, within this essay and book. These separators are, as follows: *first*, a "margin-to-margin-double-line" separator is used to separate the steps; *second*, a "margin-to-margin-single-line" separator is used to separate subdivisions of a step, such as parts, sections, segments, subsegments, direct quotes, reprints, and some comments by this author; and *third*, a "centered-thick-three-and-half-inch-two-tone-line" separator is used to separate footnotes from the rest of the material, on that particular page. Any superscript number that does not point to a footnote on that particular page, points to an endnote, which is near the end of this book.

Step-1: Literally, what is the Christian Bible?

Literally, the "Christian Bible" is "a collection of various kinds of literature on a wide variety of topics, grouped into books written over fifteen hundred years by, at least, thirty-nine known and unknown authors". Christians understand that God inspired this literature, which includes histories, poems, songs, prophecies, genealogies, wise teachings, laws, parables, love stories, dramas (*murders, adulteries, etc.*), and apocalypses. Because God wanted to confirm Himself to us and because God wanted to share with us, His thoughts about topics, which include creation, sin, salvation, heaven, hell, Satan (*or the Devil*), His relationship with man, His redemption plan for man, Jesus, our eternal destiny (*in heaven or in hell*), and medical procedures (*i.e., circumcisions on the eighth day [see Leviticus 12:3] and the isolation of individuals with Leprosy [see Leviticus 13:45-46]*).

The books of the Bible are grouped into two major divisions called the "Old Testament" and the "New Testament". These two divisions are tied to the phrases – "Old Covenant" and "New Covenant", because the word – "testament" comes from a Latin word, which was the translation of a Hebrew word, which meant "covenant". Thus, the "Old Testament" is about the "Old Covenant" that God had with His people – the Jews – through the "Law". And the "New Testament" is about the "New Covenant" that God has with believers[1] – Jews and non-Jews – through "Jesus".

Unfortunately and currently, the Christian church has what we will call – "four-major variations of the 'Christian Bible'". These variations were formed over the years in four branches of the early Christian Church. These branches are the "Assyrian Church of the East", the "Oriental Orthodox Church", the "Western Christian Church", and the "Eastern Christian Church". These four branches are discussed in more detail in Part-1, which is labeled – "Some background information", and in Part-2, which is labeled – "Comparisons and other information". In this paragraph only their names are used. Now, returning to the four-major variations, one variation formed in the "Assyrian Church of the East" and is called the "Peshitta Bible". Two variations formed in the "Western Christian Church". The first of these two variations was formed as the "Catholic Bible". Then later the second one formed as the "Protestant Bible". The fourth variation formed in the "Oriental Orthodox Church" and the "Eastern Christian Church". Their Bible is called the "Orthodox Bible". However, the "Orthodox Bible" has several of what we will call – "subvariations". Most of these "subvariations", include all sixty-six canonical books of the "Protestant Bible". However, most also include some of the "Old Testament Apocrypha", "Pseudepigrapha", and/or some of the "New Testament Apocrypha". That is why a given "Orthodox Bible" may consist of from sixty-six to eighty-one books, depending on the church to which it belongs.

As previously indicated, to present some background, comparative, and other information, the rest of Step-1 is divided into two parts. Part-1 presents some background information. Part-2 presents some comparisons and other information about the four-major variations of the Christian Bible.

---

1 Those who have accepted Jesus as their Lord and Savior.

Part-1: **Some background information**

According to several web documents and several entries in "*Wikipedia*", the early Christian Church may have suffered as many as seventeen schisms from its beginning through 1054 A.D. There were also schisms after 1054 A.D., but those schisms are not the focus of this discussion. Schisms occurred when some believers split from the rest of the Christian Church, a local church, or regional church. These splits occurred for either of two reasons: "believers rejected the teachings and/or interpretations of their leadership and/or a specific council" or "the leadership of the church or a specific council rejected the teachings and/or interpretations of a specific individual, group, local church or churches, and/or a regional church or churches".

Although there may have been, at least, one council of church leaders before 100 A.D., most occurred after 320 A.D. The later councils were gatherings of the Bishops of the Christian Church. They gathered to issue administrative procedures, set doctrine, fight what they viewed as heresies, etc. Thus, according to "*Wikipedia*", councils were involved in two of three notable schisms prior to 1055 A.D. These three notable schisms occurred in 431 A.D., 451 A.D., and 1054 A.D.

In 431 A.D., the schism called the "Nestorian Schism" occurred, because "the Council of Ephesus" condemned the beliefs of the Nestorians (*named after Nestorius, who was the Patriarch of Constantinople*). Many members of this council, which was a gathering of some two hundred Bishops, believed that Nestorius was promoting the belief that "Jesus is two persons rather than He has two natures." However one web document indicated that Nestorius clearly believed that Jesus was one person, so it is possible that the members of the council misunderstood Nestorius. Nevertheless, because this council rejected the Nestorians, who were supported by the "Assyrian Church of the East". The Nestorians and the "Assyrian Church of the East" split from the rest of the Christian Church. The "Assyrian Church of the East" is sometimes incorrectly referred to as the "Nestorian Church". It may also be referred to as the "Syrian Church" or the "Persian Church".

> *Comment*: Paraphrased, several web documents and entries in *Wikipedia* indicate that from the 7th through the 10th century, the Nestorians and/or possibly members of the "Assyrian Church of the East" were effective missionaries, reaching from Persia into India, China, and possibly even Japan. However, starting in possibly the 12th century through the 20th century, the Nestorians and/or the "Assyrian Church of the East" were almost persecuted into extinction by the Muslims, the Hindus, the Chinese, the Turks, and the Kurds. During their persecutions, the Nestorians and/or the "Assyrian Church of the East" lost some of their ancient religious documents.

In 451 A.D., the schism called the "Oriental Orthodox Schism" occurred, because some believers refused to accept the teaching of "The Council of Chalcedon". The main emphasis of the teaching was about the relationship of the "Divine Nature" of Christ to His "human nature". Thus, these believers split into the "Oriental Orthodox Church". (*The "Oriental Orthodox Church" includes the "Coptic Orthodox Church of Alexandria", the "Syriac Orthodox Church", the "Armenian Apostolic Church", the "Ethiopian Orthodox Tewahedo Church", the "Malankara Orthodox Syrian Church", and the "Eritrean Orthodox Tewahedo Church"*).

In 1054 A.D., the schism called the "East-West Schism (*also called the Great Schism*)" occurred when what was left of the main branch of the Christian Church "officially split" into the "Western Christian Church" and the "Eastern Christian Church". The Western Church was based in Rome and used Latin as the language for its version of the Christian Bible. The Eastern Church was based in Constantinople and used Greek as the language for its version of the Christian Bible. The phrase – "officially split", was used, because several web documents indicate that the split had been developing from possibly as early as 293 A.D., but was not official until around 1054 A.D. Between 285 and 293 A.D., Emperor Diocletian divided the then Roman Empire into East (*which was a Greek-based culture*) and West (*which was a Latin-based culture*) for administrative reasons and to provide a line of succession for each portion. Then around 313 A.D., Constantine (*who had become the Emperor of the western empire in 312 A.D.*) and Licinius (*who was the Emperor of the eastern empire*) issued the "Edict of Milan", which (*by removing all penalties for being a Christian*) legally stopped the persecution of Christians. However, some reference sources indicate that in 311 A.D., the persecution had already been officially stopped (*at least, in the eastern empire*) by Galerius (*who was one of the Emperors of the eastern empire before Licinius*). Nevertheless, after the formal split of the Christian Church, the Western Church developed into the Catholic Church – *more specifically, the Roman Catholic Church* – and then later other denominations (*Lutheran, Protestant, Baptist, and so on*) split from the Catholic Church or from other denominations, which had previously split from the Catholic Church. At first, the Eastern Church developed into the Eastern Orthodox Church and then later it reorganized on more of a regional basis than a denominational basis. Now, the Eastern Orthodox Church includes the Greek Orthodox Church, the Russian Orthodox Church, the Romanian Orthodox Church, the Bulgarian Orthodox Church, the Church of Alexandria, the Church of Jerusalem, and the Orthodox Church in America.

Obviously, at this point in time, there are eastern churches (*Greek Orthodox, Russian Orthodox, Romanian Orthodox, etc.*) in the west, oriental churches (*Coptic Orthodox, Ethiopian Orthodox, etc.*) in the west, and western churches (*Catholic, Protestant, etc.*) in the east.

(*The previous background comments are paraphrased, based on several web documents and on several entries in Wikipedia.*)

Part-2: **Comparisons and other information**

To form some comparative and other information for this essay, this author used web documents and hard copies of some Bibles. Some of the web documents included downloadable files of various versions of these Bibles. The hard copies used were, as follows:

For the "**Catholic Bible**":	"THE CATHOLIC BIBLE" - "PERSONAL STUDY EDITION" - "NEW AMERICAN BIBLE", published by Oxford University Press.
For the "**Jewish Bible**":	"TANAKH - THE HOLY SCRIPTURES" [The New JPS (*Jewish Publication Society*) Translation According to the Traditional Hebrew Text].
For the "**Orthodox Bible**":	"THE ORTHODOX STUDY BIBLE", published by Thomas Nelson.
For the "**Peshitta Bible**"[32]:	"HOLY BIBLE FROM THE ANCIENT EASTERN TEXT", George M. Lamsa's translation from the Aramaic of the Peshitta.
For the "**Protestant Bible**":	The "UNIVERSITY EDITION OF THE BIBLE" - (NIV), published by the International Bible Society.
For the "**Septuagint**":	"THE SEPTUAGINT WITH APOCRYPHA: GREEK AND ENGLISH", by Sir Lancelot C.L. Brenton, published by Hendrickson Publishers.

The comparative and other information developed from various web documents, on-line versions of the various Bibles, and the hard copies, serve as the basis for some additional comments. These comments are presented in nineteen groups, as follows:

- [01]: The Old Testaments of the four-major variations of the "Christian Bible" - *the "Peshitta Bible", the "Orthodox Bible", the "Catholic Bible", and the "Protestant Bible"* - appear to include all thirty-nine books of what the Western Christian Church calls the canonical books of the Old Testament. However, the "Peshitta Bible", the "Orthodox Bible", and the "Catholic Bible", include some additional verses and/or additional books, in their version of the Old Testament.

- [02]: The New Testaments of three of the four-major variations of the "Christian Bible" - *the "Orthodox Bible", the "Catholic Bible", and the "Protestant Bible"* - appear to include all twenty-seven books of what the Western Christian Church calls the canonical books of the New Testament. However, the "Peshitta Bible", only includes twenty-two of the twenty-seven canonical books, whereas, some "Orthodox Bibles", include some additional verses and/or additional books in their version of the New Testament.

- [03]: Currently, there appears to be only one version (*i.e., there are no subvariations*) of each the "Catholic Bible" and the "Protestant Bible". However, there appears to be two versions of the "Peshitta Bible" – a westernized version (*the newer version*) and an easternized version (*the older and possibly, the original version*). As for the "Orthodox Bible", there are many versions, which have various books from among the "Old Testament Apocrypha", "Pseudepigrapha", and/or "New Testament Apocrypha".

- [04]: The older-easternized version of the "Peshitta Bible" appears to be the official Bible of the "Assyrian Church of the East". The New Testament of the easternized version has only twenty-two of the twenty-seven canonical books of the New Testament of the "Protestant Bible". The excluded books are: 2 Peter, 2 John, 3 John, Jude, and Revelation. The Old Testament of the easternized version has more than thirty-nine books. The westernized version appears somewhat similar to the "Protestant Bible". Some people may call this westernized version of the "Peshitta Bible", the "Peshitto Bible" to distinguish it from the easternized version of the "Peshitta Bible".

- [05]: Even though the thirty-nine-canonical books of the "Protestant–Old Testament", are based on the "Jewish Bible", there are some differences in the way that the verses are grouped into chapters. More specifically, there are some verse differences involving both the numbering of the verses and the text of the verses, between the "Jewish Bible" and the Old Testament of the "Protestant Bible". See the web document at: www.lebtahor.com/ScribalChanges/hebengverse.htm.

- [06]: As previously implied, the "Catholic Bible" contains the same verses as the "Protestant Bible". But the "Catholic Bible" also contains some additional verses, which are in two books (*Esther and Daniel*), and which form seven additional books, which are "Tobit", "Judith", "1 Maccabees", "2 Maccabees", "Wisdom of Solomon [*Wisdom*]", "Ecclesiasticus [*Sirach*]", and "Baruch and Letter of Jeremiah". Obviously, this means that there are seventy-three books in the "Catholic Bible", with forty-six of these books being grouped, as the Old Testament and the remaining twenty-seven books being grouped, as the New Testament.

- [07]: Catholics use the label – "deuterocanonical", to refer to the additional verses and books in their Bible when compared to the Protestant Bible. Whereas, Protestants use the label – "Old Testament Apocrypha", to refer to those same additional verses and books in the "Catholic Bible" and to several books, which are in neither Bible. By using these two labels, both Protestants and Catholics are tacitly admitting that the additional verses and books in the "Catholic Bible" do not have the same authoritative value, as the verses in the sixty-six canonical books that makeup the "Protestant Bible".

- [08]: In the "Protestant Bible", the "Book of Esther" has ten chapters. When compared with the "Protestant Bible", the "Catholic Bible", the "Book of Esther" has one-hundred-

and-seven additional verses, which are grouped in six chapters. These additional chapters are labeled – "chapter A through chapter F". With the understanding that chapters referenced with a number are from the "Protestant Bible" and chapters referenced with a letter are from the "Catholic Bible", to convert a Protestant version of the "Book of Esther" to a Catholic version, "Chapter A" would be inserted before "chapter 1" and would serve as a prologue. "Chapter B" would be inserted in between "chapter 3 verses 13 and 14" (*as Chapter B, so no renumbering is required of Chapter 3*). "Chapters C and D" would be inserted after "chapter 4". However, verse 4:17 appears to have been moved inside of "Chapter C" (*before the first verse of "Chapter C"*). "Chapter E" would be inserted between "chapter 8 verses 12 and 13" (*as Chapter E, so no renumbering is required of Chapter 8*). "Chapter F" would be inserted after "chapter 10" and would serve as the Epilogue. In passing this author noted that a copy of the "Douay Old Testament" had most of the same additional verses for the "Book of Esther", but these were placed after what would be "chapter 10 verse 3" of the Protestant version of Esther, as chapters 11 through 16. The "Douay Old Testament" also appeared to have some additional verses after verse 10:3, besides chapters 11 through 16. However, the additional verses in chapters 11 to 16, are arranged differently from the additional verses in Chapters A through F. Furthermore, there appears to be some verses in the "Douay Old Testament", which are not in the current version of the "Catholic Bible".

- [09]: When compared to the "Protestant Bible", the "Book of Daniel" in the "Catholic Bible", has some extra verses, which consist of three books from the special section of the Septuagint containing the "Old Testament Apocrypha". These three books are inserted into the "Book of Daniel", as follows: the "Book of Susana" was inserted as Daniel "chapter 13", the "Book of Bel and the Dragon" was inserted as "chapter 14", and the "Song of the Three Children (*also called 'Song of the Three Holy Children' or 'Song of the Young Men'*)", was inserted in Daniel "chapter 3" between verses 23 and 24. Actually, the inserted verses were renumbered as verses 24 to 90. The original verse 24 was renumbered as verse 91. This renumbering caused some other differences between the Catholic and Protestant versions of the "Book of Daniel". Namely, the Protestant verses 3:24 through 3:30 and verses 4:1 through 4:3 were renumbered as Daniel 3:91 through 3:100, in the "Catholic Bible". Thus, the Protestant verse 4:4, becomes the Catholic verse 4:1. Obviously, this means that the numbering for the rest of chapter 4 differs between the two Bibles.

- [10]: As previously mentioned, there appears to be several versions of the "Orthodox Bible". Nevertheless, most versions contain the same verses as the "Protestant Bible". But most also contain additional verses and/or books. There are additional verses in three books (*Psalms, Esther and Daniel*), and a few Orthodox churches may add verses to "2 Chronicles", by appending the "Prayer of Manasseh" to it. Those churches, which do not append the "Prayer of Manasseh" to Chronicles, may add the "Prayer of Manasseh" by including the "Book of Odes[2]", which includes the "Prayer of Manasseh", as one of fourteen odes. Then many "Orthodox Bibles" generally add, at least, ten books to the thirty-nine canonical books of the "Old Testament". These ten books are: "2 Esdra", "Tobit", "Judith", "1 Maccabees", "2 Maccabees", "3 Maccabees", "Wisdom (Wisdom of Solomon)", "Sirach (Ecclesiasticus)", "Baruch", and the "Letter of Jeremiah". Some Orthodox Churches also add the "4 Maccabees", "Psalms of Solomon", and/or "1 Esdra".

- [11]: For the "Orthodox Bible", the additional verses in Psalms consist of the addition of another song – the one-hundred-and-fifty-first song – called the "Psalms of David". Although the placement of the additional verses within the respective books may differ, the additional verses to the "Books of Ester and Daniel", are similar to those of the "Catholic Bible". Generally, for both the "Orthodox Bible" and the "Catholic Bible", the "Prayer of Azariah" is added to the "Book of Daniel", as part of the "Song of the Young Men", which is referenced by several other names (*i.e., "Song of the three Holy Children"*).

- [12]: What the Western Christian Church calls – the "thirty-nine-canonical books" in the "Old Testament" of the "Peshitta Bible", the "Orthodox Bible", the "Catholic Bible", and the "Protestant Bible", cover the God-man relationship during the "*Old Testament*" period *(from creation to about 400 B.C.)*. The "Old Testament" says, "Jesus, the Messiah, is coming to reestablish man's existence under God's grace (*i.e., is coming to redeem all, who accept His gift of salvation*)."

- [13]: The "Jewish Bible" has "three major divisions: Law, Prophets (*Former and Latter*), and Writings. The Law (Genesis--Deuteronomy) begins with the creation of the world and concludes as Israel is about to enter the Promised Land. The Prophets--Joshua, Judges, Samuel, Kings, Isaiah, Jeremiah, Ezekiel, and the Twelve Minor Prophets--continue with the nation in the land of Palestine until the Exile and includes prophetic messages delivered to the nation. The Writings (all other books) contain the account of the return from Exile, collected wisdom literature from throughout the nation's history, and selected stories about God's leading in individual lives."[33]

- [14]: Some words and/or verses in the "Jewish Bible" – the source for the "Protestant Bible" – were written in "*Aramaic*", which some people more specifically label as "*Biblical Aramaic*" to distinguish it from "*modern Aramaic*" and other "*Aramaic*" dialects. However, most of the books of the "Old Testament", were written in what is called "*Classical Hebrew*".

---

2 The word – "Odes", is the plural form of the word – "Ode", which is from classical Greek meaning a song with a specific structure. See the entry for "Ode" in *Wikipedia* – (Ode. [2008, March 17]. In *Wikipedia, The Free Encyclopedia*. Retrieved 01:08, March 24, 2008, from en.wikipedia.org/w/index.php?title=Ode& oldid= 198747837).

➧ [15]: According to historians and scholars, the thirty-nine books of the Protestant "Old Testament" were twenty-two books in the original version of the "Jewish Bible". However, sometime in the 1st century or the 2nd century, the twenty-two books of the "Jewish Bible" were re-divided into twenty-four books. See the web document at: askelm.com/ restoring/res003.htm. Although the ancient-twenty-two-book "Jewish canon" contains the same verses as the current-thirty-nine-book "Protestant Old Testament canon", some non-critical verses, which are in the "Jewish Bible", are not in the "Protestant Old Testament". Furthermore, there does not seem to be an agreement on how the thirty-nine books of the "Protestant Old Testament canon" or the twenty-four books of the current "Jewish canon" were combined to make the twenty-two-book count. The previously referenced web document expressed the belief that the twenty-four-book count resulted from the single book of Joshua being divided into two books, and the single Book of Kingdoms being divided into one book called Samuel and a second book called Kings. Several other web documents expressed the belief that for the twenty-two-book count, the Book of Ruth was attached to the Book of Judges and the Book of Lamentations (*also called the "Book of Lamentations of Jeremiah"*) was attached to the Book of Jeremiah. The comments about the books of Ruth, Judges, Lamentations, and Jeremiah are attributed to Flavius Josephus. Therefore, this author tried to confirm Josephus as the source, by searching downloaded text files of most of the books written by him. However, this search did not find any statements "tying the Book of Ruth to the Book of Judges" nor any statements "tying the Book of Lamentations to the Book of Jeremiah".

➧ [16]: In general, the books of the New Testament of the "Orthodox Bibles", the "Protestant Bible", and the "Catholic Bible", cover the God-man relationship from the "*New Testament*" period (*from around 32 A.D. to about 120 A.D.*) through the "*after the New Testament*" period (*from about 120 A.D. to the 'SECOND COMING' of Christ*). The New Testament says, "Jesus, the Messiah, came to reestablish man's existence under God's grace (*i.e., He came to redeem all, who accept His gift of salvation*) and He will come a second time at the end of this age, as a Judge."

➧ [17]: The twenty-seven books of the "Protestant New Testament" are "attributed to at least eight different writers. Four accounts of Jesus' life – [*the Gospels of "Matthew, Mark, Luke, and John"*][3] – are at the core. The first three Gospels (*called 'Synoptic'*) are very similar in content and order. The fourth Gospel has a completely different perspective. A history of selected events in the early church (*Acts*) is followed by twenty letters to churches and individuals and one apocalypse. The letters deal mainly with the interpretation of God's act of salvation in Jesus Christ. Matters of discipline, proper Christian behavior, and church polity[34] also are included. The apocalypse is a coded message of hope to the

---

3 The names of the four gospels were added by this author.

church of the first century which has been reinterpreted by each succeeding generation of Christians for their own situations."[35]

- [18]: Originally, the "New Testament" books were written in "*Koine Greek*". "'*Koine Greek*' is the more universal offspring of '*Attic Greek*', which persisted until the 4th century BCE, when it was replaced by '*Koine Greek*'."[36] According to Dr. D. James Kennedy, "*Modern Greek*" is a simplified subset of "*Koine Greek*". The word – "Koine" is Greek for "common", which is intended to indicate that it was the common language of the period 300 B.C. to about 300 A.D. See the article on "*Koine Greek*" in "Wikipedia". However, as previously mentioned, because Jesus and His disciples spoke "*Aramaic*", the "New Testament" contains some "*Aramaic*" words.

- [19]: A web document at: www.bible-researcher.com/barker1.html, presents "pertinent data on the New Testament Books". This data includes a list showing the name of the book, the name of the author, the year or period during which the book may have been written, and the place where it may have been written. However, other web documents do not agree with the indicated date that some books were supposedly written.

Except for space, there are other things, which could have been mentioned here.

Step-2: A list of some books from possibly the *"Old Testament"* period and the "between the Old Testament and New Testament" period

Originally, Step-2 was to present a list of some books (*some writings*) from the indicated periods, which were not included in the "Old Testament". However, while doing research via the Internet, this author encountered several web documents that did indeed provide such a list of books. But the names of the books in the various list were too inconsistent to allow this author to form a single list. Part of the difference may have been the language on which a list was based. More specifically, the same book may exist in Greek, Hebrew, Latin, and/or so on. Thus, a book would have a title in Greek, Hebrew, Latin, and/or so on. Then when each title is translated into English, they may appear slightly different, because of the source language. In addition, a book might have a formal name and an informal name or it might have a short name and a long name. For example, with regards to the "New Testament" in English, the "Gospel of Luke" is called "Luke", "The Book of Luke", "The Gospel according to Luke", "The Gospel of Luke", and "The Gospel of Saint Luke", by various reference sources. Therefore, because of the differences, this author decided to simply provide the web addresses of several web documents that presented a list of such books. Three such websites are:

- ✓ www.deliriumsrealm.com/delirium/articles/articleview.asp?ID=36
- ✓ bible1.crosswalk.com/History/BC/Apocrypha/ApocryphaBookList.html

✓ members.aol.com/twarren13/apoc.html

The existence of books that were not included in the "Old Testament", does not detract from the credibility or the authenticity of those books, which were included. The credibility and/or authenticity issues will be discussed in Step-4. Nevertheless, the purpose of indicating the existence of such lists, is that Christians need to be aware of the existence of books, which were not included with the thirty-nine books that makeup the "Protestant Old Testament". This awareness will lessen the chance of Christians being blind-sided by hostile non-Christians. The specific details regarding these books are not as important, as just knowing that such books exist.

Step-3: A list of some books, which were written during the "*New Testament*" period to possibly 400 A.D.

Originally, Step-3 was to present a list of some books from perhaps "32 A.D. through possibly '200 A.D.'[4]", which were not included in the "New Testament". However, again, while doing research via the Internet, this author encountered several web documents that did indeed provide a list of such books. But the lists of books were too numerous and too variant for this author to form a single list. Nevertheless, two websites that provided a list of such books are:

✓ www.earlychristianwritings.com/

✓ www.ntcanon.org/writings.shtml

The existence of books that were not included in the "New Testament", does not detract from the credibility or the authenticity of those books, which were included. The credibility and/or authenticity issues will be discussed in Step-4. Nevertheless, the purpose of indicating the existence of such lists, is that Christians need to be aware of the existence of books, which were not included with the twenty-seven books that makeup the "Protestant New Testament". This awareness will prevent Christians from being blind-sided by hostile non-Christians, with regards to this issue. Furthermore, it is important to note that some Christian apologists say,

> "Other books may have been created in an attempt to destroy Christianity. Or other writings may have been created in an attempt to sow confusion within Christianity."

Step-4: On what basis were some books included, in the "Old and New Testaments", and other books excluded?

---

[4] The date "200 A.D.", reflects the fact that the dates assigned to some books vary among reference sources.

This question has two answers. A primary answer, which is independent of and supersedes the second answer, revolves around "*the actions of God*". The second answer revolves around "*the actions of men*". More specifically:

- ***The actions of God***: Although God inspired all of the books of the Bible – both the Old Testament and the New Testament, His actions appeared to be more overt, than just simple inspiration, with regards to the formation of the Old Testament. This may be true, for possibly three reasons: *first*, "during the 'Old Testament' period, God was choosing, guiding, protecting, judging, punishing, and/or confirming His chosen people and chosen individuals (*prophets, judges, kings, leaders, the generational line to Jesus, etc.*)", *second*, "God was modeling the relationship that He wanted with His chosen people", and *third*, "God was unveiling and laying the groundwork for the fulfilment of His redemption plan for man".

  Comment: Several well-known evangelists promote the belief that "The writers of the canonical books were not inspired. **The canonical books were inspired**." These evangelist claim support for their belief from the fact that some canonical writers wrote other material that did not become part of Bible Canon and/or wrote something that was disputed by another canonical writer. They also claim some support from the fact that not everything said by Jesus was recorded in the Bible.

- ***The actions of men***: Men have a tendency to try to confirm things, by applying a standard to them – by testing them – and/or by using the testimony of others.

As previously mentioned, "*the actions of God*" were slightly different for the two Testaments. And there was a slight difference in the tests defined by "*the actions of men*". Thus, discussing the two Testaments separately is a better approach. To facilitate this approach, the Step-4 question is reworded, as the two questions:

✓ "On what basis were some books included,
in the '**Old** Testament', and other books excluded?"

✓ "On what basis were some books included,
in the '**New** Testament', and other books excluded?"

To address these two questions, the rest of Step-4 is organized in two parts. Part-1 addresses the question: "On what basis were some books included, in the '**Old** Testament', and other books excluded?" Part-2 addresses the question: "On what basis were some books included, in the '**New** Testament', and other books excluded?"

Part-1: **On what basis were some books included, in the "Old Testament", and other books excluded?**

As previously mentioned, the two answers to this question revolve around "*the actions of God*" and "*the actions of men*". Thus, Part-1 is organized in three sections. Section-1 presents comments about "*the actions of God*". Section-2 presents comments about "*the actions of men*". *Section-3* presents some concluding comments.

Section-1: **The actions of God**

Explicitly and implicitly, "*the actions of God*" are reflected in the thirty-nine books, which make up the "Protestant Old Testament". More specifically, these books show that God, the Father, was overtly involved in the process of choosing, confirming, inspiring, guiding, judging, and protecting His chosen people, prophets, judges, leaders, and others. Actually, this was true, even before the chosen people - the Jewish people - came into existence. In fact, it was true from the creation of man through about four hundred years before the birth of Christ. But more to the point, many of the chosen prophets, judges, leaders, and others, were the writers of a book and/or the main character of a book of the "Protestant Old Testament". Consequently, the books are filled with phrases, which reflect the writer's and/or the main characters relationship to God, the Father. That is, the books include phrases like:

- ✓ "Thus saith God" *(which occurs 2 times in 2 verses of the* KJV *Old Testament),*
- ✓ "saith the Lord" *(which occurs 841 times in 802 verses of the* KJV *Old Testament),*
- ✓ "Thus saith the Lord" *(which occurs 415 times in 413 verses of the* KJV *Old Testament* [this represents a subset of the previous phrase]),
- ✓ "The Lord said" *(which occurs 203 times in 203 verses of the* KJV Old Testament),
- ✓ "The Lord spake" *(which occurs 143 times in 143 verses of the* KJV Old Testament), and
- ✓ "Thus speaketh the Lord" *(which occurs 6 times in 6 verses of the* KJV *Old Testament).*

Other phrases indicate the accomplishment of miraculous deeds and/or the fulfilment of prophecies, according to the will of God. Thus, to reiterate and summarize, the point is:

> "God, the Father, chose the main characters and/or writers of the thirty-nine books of the "Protestant Old Testament". Most of these characters and/or writers were chosen for His special purposes or chosen to be prophets, judges, and/or leaders *(of families, tribes, the Jewish people, and/or the Jewish nation)*. After having been chosen by God, He guided, protected, judged, punished, and/or inspired them. God also confirmed many of them

to the Jewish people, by allowing them to accomplish miraculous deeds and/or to present prophecies, which were fulfilled. For example sometimes, God confirmed His chosen 'Old Testament' prophets, by giving them short-term information: 'a task, a prediction, a warning that the people need to do this, a warning that the people need to stop doing this, etc. and then a result or consequence. When the thing happened as the prophet indicated, that particular prophet was confirmed to the Jewish people and/or to other nations. Generally, after a short-term confirmation, God gave that particular prophet, more crucial long-term information to be shared with the people. Thus, when God chose and confirmed, His prophets, judges, leaders, and others, God was confirming the related books. Some people seem to believe that God had completed His confirmation of the thirty-nine books of the 'Old Testament' just before the start of His four-hundred years of silence, around 400 B.C. Or worded differently, God had closed the 'Old Testament Canon' by 400 B.C. with His last prophet Malachi."

Section-2: **The actions of men**

As mentioned previously, "*the actions of men*" occurs in two major ways: "applying a test" and "presenting the testimony of others". Thus, Section-2 is organized in two segments. *Segment-1* presents a discussion of tests applied to the actual and/or potential books of the Old Testament. *Segment-2* presents a discussion of the testimonies of others.

Segment-1: **The application of tests**

Various past Jewish and/or Christian leaders, scholars, and theologians developed tests that many have labeled: "tests of canonicity". Based on a review of some thirty web documents, which discussed "the Canonicity of the 'Old Testament'", these tests focus on two to six issues that had to be satisfied, for an Old Testament book to be acknowledged or recognized by man, as inspired by God. A paraphrased-consensus of the "tests of canonicity for the 'Old Testament'", might read as follows:

Old Testament – tests of Canonicity

Tests applied by those seeking to recognize a book, as inspired by God, were as follows:

Authoritative Test: Does the book display the authority and/or power of God, through the words, events, or deeds that it recorded?

Authorship Test: Was the book written and/or endorsed by one, who was recognized and/or confirmed, as a servant of God?

Authentic Test: Does the book have any provable errors? Is the book consistent with the other accepted books?

Power Test:	Do the words of the book display the life-changing power of God? Do the words of the book edify, build-up, and/or bless the reader?
Receptive Test:	Has the book been received as inspired by God, by people in the past? Was the book read at religious gatherings in the past?

Segment-2: **The testimonies of others**

Presenting "the testimonies of others" is a way that men attempt to add to the credibility of something. Those testimonies that were/are closer to an event, or to the creation of something, like a document, are considered better testimonies, than those occurring later. The thirty-plus web comments reviewed by this author on this topic, indicated that there is a considerable amount of historical testimony to show that the books, which make up our Old Testament (*and not the Apocrypha*) are indeed to be regarded as Scripture, by Jews, Jesus, His Apostles, and other early Christians prior to 120 A.D. Examples of this historical testimony include: "the testimony of the Septuagint", "the testimony of the New Testament", and "the testimony of Flavius Josephus". More specifically:

- The testimony of the Septuagint (*which is a translation of the "Jewish Bible" into Greek that took place in stages from 250 B.C. to 150 B.C.*) is that even though the Septuagint includes the "Old Testament Apocrypha" (*in a section by itself*), scholars believe it was the "Old Testament scriptures" of the "*New Testament*" period. Furthermore, according to several web documents, the consensus is that the Septuagint was the source of the "Old Testament" quotes in the "New Testament", but none of those quotes were from the Apocrypha section.

- The testimony of the New Testament is mainly the words and quotes of Jesus and His Apostles. More specifically, Jesus acknowledged the "Old Testament" canon by referring to one or more parts - the Law, the Prophets, and the writings - of the "Hebrew Bible". For example, in Luke 24:44, Jesus references all three. In the KJV, Luke 24:44 reads:

  > (Luke 24:44 KJV) And he said unto them, *These are the words which I spake unto you, while I was yet with you, that all things must be fulfilled, which were written in the law of Moses, and in the prophets, and in the psalms, concerning me.*

  Jesus references Genesis in Matthew 19:4. In the KJV, this verse reads:

  > (Matthew 19:4 KJV) And he answered and said unto them, *Have ye not read, that he which made them at the beginning made them male and female,*

  While talking to a Pharisee and perhaps, some lawyers, Jesus acknowledged prophets and apostles with words recorded in Luke 11:46-52. In the NIV, these verses read:

> Luke 11:[46]Jesus replied, "*And you experts in the law, woe to you, because you load people down with burdens they can hardly carry, and you yourselves will not lift one finger to help them.* [47]*"Woe to you, because you build tombs for the prophets, and it was your forefathers who killed them.* [48]*So you testify that you approve of what your forefathers did; they killed the prophets, and you build their tombs.* [49]*Because of this, God in his wisdom said, 'I will send them prophets and apostles, some of whom they will kill and others they will persecute.'* [50]*Therefore this generation will be held responsible for the blood of all the prophets that has been shed since the beginning of the world,* [51]*from the blood of Abel to the blood of Zechariah, who was killed between the altar and the sanctuary. Yes, I tell you, this generation will be held responsible for it all.* [52]*"Woe to you experts in the law, because you have taken away the key to knowledge. You yourselves have not entered, and you have hindered those who were entering."*

- The testimony of "Flavius Josephus"[5], (*who was a Jewish general defeated by a Roman Legion, which crushed a Jewish revolt in 70 A.D.*) is through his writings as a Jewish historian. More specifically, he lived from 37 A.D. to around 100 A.D. After his defeat, he became a historian and writer. His writings include a history of the Jews and a defense of Judaism. His two books in defense of Judaism are titled – "Contra Apion I" and "Contra Apion II" (*or Against Apion I and Against Apion II*). According to several entries in Wikipedia, "**Apion**" was a writer, who lived from around 20 B.C. to around 45 A.D. Apion apparently wrote some unflattering literatures about the Jews and Judaism, so Josephus wrote two books in defense of Judaism and against what Apion wrote. In defending Judaism, Josephus referenced the three parts of the Hebrew Bible: the Law, the Prophets, and the Writings. He also mentioned that the Hebrew Bible consisted of twenty-two books. (*The comparison chart and notes at the end of this essay give the twenty-four books Jewish canon in one column and this author's speculative twenty-two book Jewish canon in a second column.*)

The books of the "Old Testament" fulfilled the "tests of canonicity". And once more, those books indicate that God was more obvious in letting the world know, who His chosen leaders, judges, and prophets were. For example:

- ***Among the chosen leaders***, there was Moses, who warned the Egyptian Pharaoh to let the Jewish people go and then warned the Pharaoh of God's ten plagues, because Pharaoh would not let the Jews leave Egypt.

---

[5] One reference source also indicated that Josephus may have been a priest.

- ***Among the chosen judges***, there was Samson, who slew more than a thousand Philistine soldiers with the jaw bone of a donkey.

- ***Among the prophets***, there was Jonah, who was swallowed by a big fish and taken to the land where God had asked him to go to warn the people to repent.

Thus, clearly, God validated many of His chosen leaders, judges, prophets, and others through impossible and unlikely events and/or deeds. And as previously mentioned, while God was validating His chosen leaders, judges, prophets, and others through impossible and unlikely events and/or deeds, He was also validating the books of the "Old Testament", which recorded those impossible and unlikely events.

Section-3 **Some concluding comments**

As previously mentioned, God closed the "Old Testament Canon" with His last prophet, Malachi around the fourth century B.C. Nevertheless, because other books, which some people considered useful, were written after Malachi, the "tests of canonicity" were performed and the "testimonies of men" were documented to recognize God's canon. These tests and testimonies were complete by the end of the first century A.D. Thus, Part-1 can be summarized by saying:

> "'*The actions of God*' defined the books of the Old Testament and then '*the actions of men*' – the 'tests of canonicity' and the 'testimonies of men' – looked backwards to ***RECOGNIZE*** what God did."

Although the four so-called main branches of the Christian Church – the "Assyrian Church of the East", the "Oriental Orthodox Church", the "Western Christian Church", and the "Eastern Christian Church" – may have a different number of books in their Old Testament, the thirty-nine canonical books of the "Protestant Bible" represent the common core. Other books from the period of silence (*after the prophet Malachi*), were included in the Old Testament of some Churches, because that book or those books were considered useful for other reasons. For example, the Catholic Church references the additional books in its Old Testament, as support for their "concept of purgatory" and their practice of "praying to saints, to and/or for the dead, and to Mary".

Part-2: **On what basis were some books included, in the "New Testament", and other books excluded?**

Similar to the Old Testament, this question has two answers. One answer revolves around "*the actions of God*". The other answer revolves around "*the actions of men*". Thus, Part-2 is organized in three sections. Section-1 presents comments about "*the actions of God*". Section-2 presents comments about "*the actions of men*". Section-3 presents some concluding comments.

Section-1: **The actions of God**

Explicitly and implicitly, "*the actions of God*" are reflected in the twenty-seven books of the Protestant New Testament, but not to the same extent, as in the Old Testament. Nevertheless, the twenty-seven books do show that God was overtly involved in the activities of His chosen people and His only begotten son, Jesus, the Messiah – Jesus, the man. These books show that God chose the Virgin Mary to be the Mother of Jesus, the man. And God planned things such that Jesus, the man, would be crucified as a penalty and as an atonement for our sins. However, unlike the books of the Old Testament, the New Testament books do not have as many phrases and statements, which reflect God's actions and/or someone's relationship with God. This situation is reflected in the counts for the following phrases and statements:

✓ "saith the Lord" (*which occurs 13 times in 13 verses of the* KJV *New Testament*).

✓ "The Lord said" (*which occurs 16 times in 16 verses of the* KJV *New Testament*).

✓ "The Lord spake" (*which occurs 1 time in 1 verse of the* KJV *New Testament*).

✓ "Angel said" (*which occurs 9 times in 9 verses of the* KJV *New Testament*).

Despite a lower count of the occurrences of the previously indicated phrases when compared to the Old Testament, verses containing such phrases still indicate an involvement by God. But what is more important, God's relationship with His chosen people – (*i.e., the Jews, Joseph, Mary, Jesus, and so on*) is also supported by many other verses. (*I.e., Matthew 11:27, Matthew 16:13-18, Matthew 16:16-17, Matthew 18:19, Matthew 20:23, Matthew 26:63-66, Matthew 27:43, Matthew 27:46, Mark 8:29, Mark 14:61-63, Luke 2:49, Luke 4:43, Luke 9:20, Luke 22:42, Luke 22:66-71, John 3:35, John 4:25-26, John 5:19, John 5:20, John 5:37, John 6:46, John 6:57, John 8:42, John 8:50-59, John 10:17, John 10:30, John 10:36, John 12:49, John 14:9, John 14:28, John 17:21, John 17:25, John 19:6-7, John 20:17, John 20:21, and Revelation 3:12 – This list is not exhaustive.*) In fact, the New Testament includes verses, which indicate that God, the Father, sent God, the Son, in the form of a human, named Jesus, to fulfill His redemption plan for man. As part of that plan, Jesus selected twelve men to be His Apostles. Some of these twelve Apostles wrote many of the books of the New Testament.

Section-2: **The actions of men**

As mentioned previously, "*the actions of men*" occurs in two major ways: "applying tests" and "presenting the testimony of others". Thus, Section-2 is organized in two segments. *Segment-1* presents a discussion of tests applied to the actual and/or potential books of the New Testament. *Segment-2* presents a discussion of the testimonies of others.

Segment-1: **The application of tests**

Again, the application of tests means that a standard was developed. The "tests of canonicity" for the "New Testament" books are the same as those for the "Old Testament", except the phrase – "servant of God", is replaced by the word – "Apostle". Thus, the "tests of canonicity" for the "New Testament" might read, as follows:

New Testament – tests of canonicity

Tests applied by those seeking to recognize a book, as inspired by God, were as follows:

Authoritative Test: Does the book display the authority and/or power of God, through the words, events, or deeds that it recorded?

Authorship Test: Was the book written and/or endorsed by one, who was recognized and/or confirmed, as an Apostle of Jesus?

Authentic Test: Does the book have any provable errors? Is the book consistent with the other accepted books?

Power Test: Do the words of the book display the life-changing power of God? Do the words of the book edify, build-up, and/or bless the reader?

Receptive Test: Has the book been received as inspired by God, by people in the past? Was the book read at religious gatherings in the past?

Segment-2: **The testimonies of others**

As mentioned previously, presenting "the testimonies of others" is a way that men attempt to add to the credibility of something. However, most of "the testimonies of others", which are related to the New Testament, are about the individuals and/or events, which were recorded in the books of the New Testament, rather than the books of the New Testaments. Thus, with respect to the New Testament, "the testimonies of others" do not appear to exist to the same extent, as "the testimonies of others", with respect to the books of the Old Testament. However, when "the testimonies of others" confirm the individuals and/or events mentioned and/or recorded by the books of the "New Testament", then those books are confirmed.

Section-3: **Some concluding comments**

God was still involved in the formation of the "New Testament Canon", but not to the same extent as with the "Old Testament Canon". And the 'testimonies of men' had a slightly different focus. While the focus for the "Old Testament" was the books themselves, the focus for the "New Testament" was Christ, Himself. Thus, the "tests of canonicity" had a larger role than the "Testimonies of men", as far as the "New Testament" was concerned. Thus, Part-2 can be summarized by saying:

> "'*The actions of God*' defined the books of the New Testament and then '*the actions of men*' – the 'tests of canonicity' – looked backwards to ***RECOGNIZE*** what God did."

Although the four so-called main branches of the Christian Church – the "Assyrian Church of the East", the "Oriental Orthodox Church", the "Western Christian Church", and the "Eastern Christian Church" – may have a different number of books in their New Testament, twenty-two of the twenty-seven canonical books of the "Protestant Bible" represent the common core. The "Assyrian Church of the East", is the only branch at the twenty-two-book count. This count excludes the five books: 2 Peter, 2 John, 3 John, Jude, and Revelation. Most of the other churches have the twenty-seven-book count. However, some "Oriental Orthodox Churches", may add some of the New Testament Apocrypha to the twenty-seven canonical books to form their New Testament. Nevertheless, the thing to note is that there is a common core of twenty-two books. And there are reasons for the differences. For example, one reference source implied that the reason for the twenty-two-book count for the "Assyrian Church of the East", is that even though this church traces its roots back to one of the Apostles, their canon may have been formed before they had a full knowledge of the five excluded books. Remember that in ancient times, communicating was not as easy as it is today.

Step-5: When were the chapters and verse designations added to the "Old and New Testaments"?

The Step-5 question was researched, using web documents. This research left this author with three impressions:

- *Impression-1*: As man developed different media to transmit the written word on, the method of separating the words and the different books of the Bible changed.

- *Impression-2*: Men divided the written word into verses and sections to make it easier to use and/or to reference.

- *Impression-3*: The rules for separating the written-units (*thoughts, phrases, clauses, sentences, etc.*) of a document, may vary depending on the language used.

More specifically, three web documents, which support some of the three impressions and/or which answer the Step-5 question, were at:

- ✓ www.ccel.org/e/easton/ebd/ebd/T0000500.html#T0000580. (*Is **web-document-1***)
- ✓ www.studentbodyworld.com/Q%20and%20A/ where_did_the_verses_in_the_bible_come_from.htm. (*Is **web-document-2***)
- ✓ www.fuller.edu/ministry/berean/chs_vss.htm. (*Is **web-document-3***)

A summary and excerpt from each web documents is separated by a margin-to-margin line. These excerpts read, as follows:

Web-document-1 is an on-line version of the "*Easton's Bible Dictionary*", by M. G. Easton, which is in the "Public Domain". Nevertheless, as part of the definition for the term – "Bible", a brief response to the Step-5 question is presented. The portion of the definition, which is relevant to this essay, reads:

> The division of the Bible into chapters and verses is altogether of human invention, designed to facilitate reference to it. The ancient Jews divided the Old Testament into certain sections for use in the synagogue service, and then at a later period, in the ninth century A.D., into verses. Our modern system of chapters for all the books of the Bible was introduced by Cardinal Hugo about the middle of the thirteenth century (he died 1263 A.D.). The system of verses for the New Testament was introduced by Stephens in 1551 A.D., and generally adopted, although neither Tyndale's nor Coverdale's English translation of the Bible has verses. The division is not always wisely made, yet it is very useful.

Web-document-2 also presented a brief response to the Step-5 question and a link to the third web document for more details. This second web document reads:

> The books of the Old and New Testament were NOT written with chapters and verses. These were added later. The Bible was divided into chapters by Stephen Langton (who later became Archbishop of Canterbury) early in the 1200s. Robert Stephanus, a book printer from Paris, is credited with dividing those chapters into verses in 1551. The first complete printed Bible using the chapter and verse divisions was the Geneva Bible of 1560. For more details about versification, see web document at www.fuller.edu/ministry/berean/chs_vss.htm (*The third web document for this Step-5 response*).

Web-document-3 presented a more detailed response to the Step-5 question. This web document was titled: "Bible Chapter and Verse Divisions--Late Comers" and was authored by Dr. Daniel P. Fuller. Including Dr. Fuller's footnotes (*which have been converted to endnotes for this essay*), the web document reads:

Parchment or papyrus were difficult to come by as materials upon which to write, and thus in many ancient texts of both the Greek New Testament and Hebrew Old Testament there is the space-saving device of *scriptio continua*, that is, continued writing in which there are not even spaces between words or sentences. Of course, we do not possess any of the original autographs of the biblical books, but it is safe to infer from the evidence of the most ancient extant manuscripts that the autographs likewise contained little if any punctuation. Even question marks were not used commonly in Greek manuscripts until the ninth century A.D.[37]

With the passage of time, however, the need arose in connection with biblical texts to delimit the sections that were about the size of large paragraphs, both because of the necessity to be able readily to locate a passage in the text and because of the desirability to have units of this magnitude stand out clearly. Thus in the Old Testament, even as far back as the time of Qumran[38], the text was divided into sections called *parashoth*. Larger sections were denoted by beginning a new line or by omitting an entire line, and smaller sections were denoted by leaving a gap within a line. Such sectioning, historically related to the practice evident in the Qumran texts but not identical with it, continued on in the Masoretic texts and is present in our Hebrew Bibles today. A *samech* (the Hebrew "s") between sentences indicates a paragraph break of smaller degree, while a *pe* (the Hebrew "p") between the ending of a sentence on one line and the beginning of a new sentence on another indicates a larger break.

Verse divisions within these *parashoth* came in during the Mishnaic period (c. A.D. 200) when it was necessary to intersperse the Hebrew reading with an Aramaic translation so the hearers could understand. The amount of Hebrew that was read before the translation was given in Aramaic became the verse divisions in the Old Testament, and around A.D. 500 these were signified by the *soph pasuq* (:) that still appear in the Hebrew text.[39]

Divisions of paragraph magnitude were also the first punctuation marks that came into the New Testament texts. The earliest such divisions were the *kephalaia* indicated in the Nestle text by a single number in italics in the inner margin. Smaller divisions are indicated by a large Roman script number in the inner margin. A good bit of the function of these early textual divisions was for reference rather than for giving the author's units of composition, and their use has not been carried over into our modern versions.

The present chapter divisions in our Bibles were invented in 1205 by Stephen Langton, a professor in Paris (he later became Archbishop of Canterbury), who put these into a Vulgate edition of the Bible. These chapter divisions were first used by the Jews in 1330 for the Hebrew Old Testament in a manuscript and for a printed edition in 1516. This system of chapter divisions likewise came into the Greek manuscripts of the New Testament in the 1400s.

It was Robert Stephanus, a Parisian book printer, whose versification of the Bible has prevailed to the present. He took over the verse divisions already indicated in the Hebrew Bible by the *soph pasuq* and assigned numbers to them within the chapter divisions already assigned by Stephan Langton. While riding on horseback from Paris to Lyons he affixed his own verse divisions to the New Testament and numbered them within Langton's chapter divisions. Consequently the quality of his work was not the best. Von Soden complained,

> "The verse divisions of Stephanus which he, according to an incidental remark by his son, made during a trip from Paris to Lyons, frequently do not do service to the sense of the text. There is no consistent method at work in this system. The verses sometimes coincide with a single sentence, and sometimes they include several sentences; sometimes a single sentence is divided into two verses, with the result that the reader is led to consider the second verse while forgetting the point of view of the first verse. Especially objectionable is the way in which words introducing a direct quotation sometimes belong to the preceding verse and sometimes to the verse in which the quotation is found."[40]

But through Stephanus the versification of the Old Testament found its way into the Hebrew Bible printed first in 1571. Then Theodor Beza's use of Stephanus' verse and chapter divisions in his edition of the textus receptus of the New Testament (1565) assured them the permanence that they enjoy in our Bibles today.[41]

From this brief survey of the history of the Bible's chapter and verse divisions it is very apparent that these are nothing more than a handy method of reference. They do not necessarily represent those units of composition present in the author's mind as he strove to impart his thoughts. It is utterly impractical, however, to think of expunging them from our Bibles. As von Soden says,

> There is no doubt that the chapter divisions which we have inherited from Langton leave much to be desired. These divisions do not rest upon a comprehension of the literary structure of the Biblical books. . . But it is utterly impractical today to think of trying to correct this system of chapter divisions. From practical considerations, this system must be kept as the means for designating individual passages. All that we can do is to realize that this system falls far short of doing justice to the inherent units of Scripture. Therefore, if future editions want to aid rather than hinder a reader's understanding of the New Testament, it should be realized that the time is ripe to cause both the verse and chapter divisions to disappear from the text and to be put on the margin in as

> inconspicuous a place as possible. Every effort must be made to print the text in a way which makes it possible for the units which the author himself had in mind to become apparent.[42]

The Nestle edition of the Greek New Testament does as von Soden recommended and places the chapter and verse divisions on the margin. So does the text of Tasker[43]. The Greek text put forward by the American Bible Society for use in Bible translation keeps these references within the text[44], but possibly this would be more helpful to Bible translators. It is unfortunate that the Biblia Hebraica of Kittel has both chapter and verse divisions in the text. But whatever the text that is being used, the advice of A. T. Robertson should be followed: "The first step in interpretation is to ignore the modern chapters and verses."[45]

But what of the punctuation marks, inserted by more recent editors as an attempt to delimit the author's own units of thought? Indeed, the interpreter should acquaint himself with the system of punctuation used in these texts, and he or she should seek to discern the reasons why the various editors divided the texts as they did. No two editors, however, agree fully on where these units begin and end, and this means that the interpreter himself must make the final decision as to the all-important matter of the delimitation of the larger and smaller literary units.

The three web documents answered the Step-5 question better and more completely than this author could.

Step-6: A conclusion

This essay served to present comments by biblical scholars, Christian historians, and others about the formation of the Christian Bible. Hopefully, these comments have presented some useful and interesting information about the Christian Bible. However, we must also remember that Satan and various individuals through the ages tried to discredit the Christian Religion and especially, the Christian Bible. Thus, it is very easy to understand the existence of many books other than those, which make up the sixty-six canonical-books of the "Protestant Bible". But keep in mind that the existence of those other books does not negate the existence of the genuine. Furthermore, those who ask, "How could men record the word of God without messing it up?", should note that men explicitly tried, and continue to try, to mess up the Bible, to challenge its credibility, and/or to sow confusion among Christians. While God used more explicit methods to indicate His chosen leaders, judges, and prophets, during Old Testament times, it was, and continues to be, easy for men to create some misinformation about both the Old Testament and the New Testament.

> *Comment:* And speaking of misinformation, while researching some topics via the Internet, it became clear that there is "good information (*correct information*)" and "bad information (*incorrect information, misleading information, and/or incomplete information*)" in cyberspace, so one must exercise care. And hopefully, this author used and/or referenced only the "good information".

However, this author believes that God knew men's hearts, so He fills the canonical books with His wonders to such an extent that it is easier to spot the books, which are frauds and counterfeits.

Many biblical scholars and historians have full confidence in the credibility of the sixty-six books, which comprise the "Protestant Bible (*Old and New Testament*)". But please note that a logical review of the evidence, also supports such confidence. Nevertheless, it must be emphasized that different denominations apply the tests of canonicity differently and end up with possibly additional and/or different books in their version of the Bible. In fact in ancient times, the Samaritans only accepted the first five books of the "Jewish Bible". Nevertheless, sometimes other denominations like the Catholics admit that the additional verses and/or books do not have the same authoritative value as the sixty-six canonical books. Furthermore, when there are differences, most denominations present the basis for the differences. This provides all Christians with a way to discuss the differences. But, more important, the basis provides us with information that will allow us to protect ourselves from hostile non-Christian attacks around the differences.

Step-7: Some relevant comments

Implicitly, this essay attempted to also address the issue of different "books" in different versions of the Christian Bible, like the "Catholic Bible" versus the "Protestant Bible". Consistent with this effort, the web document, which was once at:

✓ www.studentbodyworld.com/Q%20and%20A/The%20Bible/do_some_bibles_have_different_books.htm

presented a relevant question and then an appropriate answer for the question. The portion of the web document, relevant to this essay, reads:

Question: I was getting friendship quotes online and I came across some that said they were from the Bible, but from a book called Sirach or something like that. I asked my neighbor and she said that it was in the Catholic Bible. Why doesn't my Bible have that book? How did those books get in their Bible and are those books "God's Word?"

Answer: Great question! I'll do my best to make the answer brief (might be hard!) The last prophet of the Old Testament was Malachi, around 400 BC. According to Jews, this was the end of the prophetic period in which God was speaking through his prophets, to His people, providing them the words of Scripture. Certainly God was still at work after 400 BC, but the Scriptures were "closed" until God took the next great move in his plan of salvation. No more books would be added until that happened. However, during this time from 400 BC, to the time of the writing of the New Testament (starting 40 AD) there were many historical books written by Jews. 1 and 2 Maccabees is a good example. These books are called "intertestamental" or "between the testaments". These books are often called the Apocrypha. These books have always been valued by the Jews, but never looked upon as Holy Scripture, and are NOT included in the Hebrew Bible. Around 250 BC, Alexander the Great was ruling the ancient world, and he decided that he wanted to build a library. He heard that the Jews had marvelous history books, and he sent a team of scholars to Jerusalem to translate these history books into Greek. They did so, and when they asked for the "history books", they received ALL the history books, the Holy Old Testament books, as well as the others that came later. It made no difference to them. These books, including the Apocrypha, were translated into Greek, and that translation was called the Septuagint. Greek became the major language of the ancient world, and the Septuagint was often used as the Bible that many would read from in the early church. Soon Christianity became the official religion of the Roman Empire, and the emperor decided that he wanted a Bible in Latin. So he commissioned Jerome to translate the Bible into Latin. So Jerome went and got the Greek New Testament (it was written in Greek) and the GREEK Old Testament (the Septuagint, which included the NON Holy Books). He then translated all of them into Latin, and the translation was called the Vulgate. Jerome, later realized his error, as he checked to see that none of the Jewish Bibles contained the Apocrypha, he then went to the emperor, but it was too late...the books were included. The Vulgate and the Roman Catholic church have been together ever since. This was one of the objections that Martin Luther had at the reformation, that some books were included that were not from the revelation of God. This is why these books are not in most Bibles, and why they are not in Bibles used by Protestants. While there are not many major problems or weird things in these books, there are the vague ideas of purgatory, prayer for the dead, saint worship, and salvation through works. It is important to note that the New Testament writers quote the Old Testament 295 times, but never from the Apocrypha with divine authority. I would suggest basic reasons to reject the books of the Apocrypha as God's Word:

1. They do not claim to be God's word as other canonical books do.
2. They were not regarded as God's words by the Jewish people from whom they originated.
3. They were not considered to be scripture by Jesus or other New Testament authors.
4. They contain teaching inconsistent with other scripture.

[End of the web document]

Comparison of the Jewish Bible, the Orthodox Old Testament, the Catholic Old Testament, and the Protestant Old Testament

HEBREW BIBLE / TANAK [Jewish Bible]					OLD TESTAMENT [Orthodox Bible (OB)]		OLD TESTAMENT [Catholic Bible (CB)]		OLD TESTAMENT [Protestant Bible (PB)]	
Type	Sub-Type	Book #**	Book #	Name	Book #	Name	Book #	Name	Book #	Name
Law		1	1	Genesis	1	Genesis	1	Genesis	1	Genesis
Law		2	2	Exodus	2	Exodus	2	Exodus	2	Exodus
Law		3	3	Leviticus	3	Leviticus	3	Leviticus	3	Leviticus
Law		4	4	Numbers	4	Numbers	4	Numbers	4	Numbers
Law		5	5	Deuteronomy	5	Deuteronomy	5	Deuteronomy	5	Deuteronomy
Prophets	Former Prophets	6	6	Joshua	6	Joshua (= Josue)	6	Joshua	6	Joshua
Prophets	Former Prophets	7	7	Judges	7	Judges	7	Judges	7	Judges
Prophets	Former Prophets	8	8	Samuel (1 Samuel)	8	Ruth	8	Ruth	8	Ruth
Prophets	Former Prophets			Samuel (2 Samuel)	9	1 Kingdoms (= 1 Samuel)	9	1 Samuel	9	1 Samuel
Prophets	Former Prophets		9	Kings (1 Kings)	10	2 Kingdoms (= 2 Samuel)	10	2 Samuel	10	2 Samuel
Prophets	Former Prophets			Kings (2 Kings)	11	3 Kingdoms (= 1 Kings)	11	1 Kings	11	1 Kings
Prophets	Latter Prophets	9	10	Isaiah	12	4 Kingdoms (= 2 Kings)	12	2 Kings	12	2 Kings
Prophets	Latter Prophets	10	11	Jeremiah	13	1 Paralipomenon (= 1 Chronicles)	13	1 Chronicles	13	1 Chronicles
Prophets	Latter Prophets	11	12	Ezekiel	14	2 Paralipomenon (= 2 Chronicles) and Prayer of Manasseh	14	2 Chronicles	14	2 Chronicles
Prophets	Book of the Twelve:	12	13	Hosea	15	1 Ezra (= 1 Esdras)	15	Ezra	15	Ezra
Prophets	Book of the Twelve:			Joel	16	2 Ezra (= Erza / 2 Esdras)	16	Nehemiah	16	Nehemiah
Prophets	Book of the Twelve:			Amos	17	Nehemiah	17	Tobit	17	Esther
Prophets	Book of the Twelve:			Obadiah	18	Tobit (= Tobias)	18	Judith	18	Job
Prophets	Book of the Twelve:			Jonah	19	Judith	19	Esther and Additions	19	Psalms (150 Songs)
Prophets	Book of the Twelve:			Micah	20	Esther and Additions	20	1 Maccabees	20	Proverbs
Prophets	Book of the Twelve:			Nahum	21	1 Maccabees	21	2 Maccabees	21	Ecclesiastes
Prophets	Book of the Twelve:			Habakkuk	22	2 Maccabees	22	Job	22	Song of Songs (= Song of Solomon)
Prophets	Book of the Twelve:			Zephaniah	23	3 Maccabees	23	Psalms (150 Songs)	23	Isaiah
Prophets	Book of the Twelve:			Haggai	24	Psalms (151 songs) (151 th song = Psalms of David)	24	Proverbs	24	Jeremiah
Prophets	Book of the Twelve:			Zechariah	25	Job	25	Ecclesiastes	25	Lamentations
Prophets	Book of the Twelve:			Malachi	26	Proverbs of Solomon (= Proverbs)	26	Song of Songs (= Song of Solomon)	26	Ezekiel
Writings		13	14	Psalms (150 songs)	27	Ecclesiastes	27	Wisdom (= Wisdom of Solomon)	27	Daniel
Writings		14	15	Proverbs	28	Song of Solomon (= Song of Songs)	28	Sirach (= Ecclesiasticus)	28	Hosea
Writings		15	16	Job	29	Wisdom of Solomon (= Wisdom)	29	Isaiah	29	Joel
Writings		16	17	The Song of Songs	30	Sirach (= Wisdom of Sirach) and (= Ecclesiasticus)	30	Jeremiah (= Jeremias)	30	Amos
Writings		17	18	Ruth	31	Hosea (= Osee)	31	Lamentations	31	Obadiah
Writings		18	19	Lamentations	32	Amos	32	Baruch (Chapter 6 = Letter of Jeremiah)	32	Jonah
Writings		19	20	Ecclesiastes	33	Micah (= Micheas)	33	Ezekiel	33	Micah
Writings		20	21	Esther	34	Joel	34	Daniel and note # 1	34	Nahum
Writings		21	22	Daniel	35	Obadiah (= Abdias)	35	Hosea	35	Habakkuk
Writings		22	23	Ezra -	36	Jonah (= Jonas)	36	Joel	36	Zephaniah
Writings				Nehemiah	37	Nahum	37	Amos	37	Haggai
Writings			24	Chronicles (1 Chronicles)	38	Habakkuk (= Habacuc)	38	Obadiah	38	Zechariah
Writings				Chronicles (2 Chronicles)	39	Zephaniah (= Zacharias)	39	Jonah	39	Malachi
					40	Haggai	40	Micah		
					41	Zechariah	41	Nahum		
		99	99	= one book in the Hebrew Bible	42	Malachi (= Malachias)	42	Habakkuk		
					43	Isaiah (= Isaias)	43	Zephaniah		
					44	Jeremiah	44	Haggai		
					45	Baruch	45	Zechariah		
					46	Lamentations (= Lamentations of Jeremiah)	46	Malachi		
					47	Letter of Jeremiah (= Epistle of Jeremiah)				
					48	Ezekiel (= Ezechiel)				
					49	Daniel and note # 1				
					50	4 Maccabees not included in all OB's				
					51	Psalms of Solomon not included in all OB's				

** Author's speculation about the original organization of the Jewish Bible.

Legend for **Catholic Bible** Column

Book names in shaded cells with border are the Apocryphal books in the Catholic Bible.

Note # 1 - Additions

- Susanna
- Song of the Young Men
- Bel and the Dragon

Is the Bible the inspired word of God?

Many of the first essays written for this book assumed a "yes-answer" to the question: "Is the Bible the inspired word of God?" However, none of those essays devoted an explicit effort to showing why a "yes-answer" is more appropriate than a "no-answer". There were brief comments on the credibility of the Bible, here and there. But a more comprehensive effort was lacking. Therefore, this essay serves, as that more comprehensive effort. To ease the process of putting this essay together, some of the brief comments on the credibility of the Bible from other essays are also presented in this essay. Some comments are even presented in more detail. Nevertheless, none of the essays, which supplied comments for this essay were changed.

The wide variety of issues that need to be discussed to address the question - "Is the Bible the inspired word of God?", seemed to best fit an outline format. Thus, this essay is structured to fit the following outline:

Is the Bible the inspired word of God?

I. What does the phrase - "the inspired word of God", mean?
II. Evidence that supports the credibility of the Bible.
  A. Manuscript evidence.
  B. Archaeological evidence.
  C. Prophetic evidence.
    1. Bible critics claim "Bible prophecies are actually historical recordings."
    2. Bible critics claim "Bible prophecies were self-fulfilling."
    3. Many Bible prophecies have a beauty about them.
  D. Statistical evidence.
  E. The evidence of lives changed, by the influence of those who accept the Bible.
    1. The story of Mr. Stephen Morin, by Mrs. Margy Mayfield.
    2. The story of Mr. Tom Papania, by Mr. Papania.
  F. The evidence of lives changed, by the influence of the Bible alone.
    1. Two stories from Pastor Steve King's booklet - "Is the Bible True?"
      a. The story of a South-American bandit in the early 1900's.
      b. The story of an Eskimo.
    2. The story of a well-known Christian evangelist.
III. What the Bible says about itself?
  A. through F.
IV. Some general comments about the Bible.
  A. through P.
V. Scientific concepts referenced in the Bible.

A. through E.
VI. Conclusion and summary.

Now, the above outline will be filled in to add credibility to the Bible being the inspired word of God:

Is the Bible the inspired word of God?

Throughout time, people have asked questions like: "Is the Bible the inspired word of God?", "Did God inspire men to write the Bible?", and/or "How could men write the Bible and not mess it up?" But the real question these people are asking is "What evidence is there that the Bible is the inspired word of God?" This essay is an attempt to address all these questions.

I. What does the phrase – "the inspired word of God", mean?

This question had to be addressed, by this author in order to decide, whether to use the title: "Is the Bible the word of God?" or the title: "Is the Bible the *inspired* word of God?" That is, the need for a title for this essay forced thoughts, about the implications of each of the two phrases: "word of God" and "inspired word of God". Obviously, the common wording – "word of God", means "the source of the words is God." The addition of the word – "inspired", does not change the source. The purpose of the word – "inspired", is to convey a sense of how the "word of God" got into the minds and hearts of possibly two groups of individuals:

✓ One group consists of individuals, who were the subjects of various books of the Bible, or who were participants in events, recorded in the various books.

✓ The other group consists of the writers of the various books of the Bible. These individuals may have been the original authors of the stories and facts recorded in the Bible. Or the stories and/or facts may have been passed to them, by someone else (*including possibly God*).

Some individuals may have been in both groups. Nevertheless, the Bible recorded things that tell us how the "word of God" got into the minds and hearts of some individuals, in the two groups mentioned. In fact, Numbers 12:4-5 indicates that God was speaking directly to Moses, Aaron (Moses' brother), and Miriam (Moses' sister) about how He communicates with us. In the NIV, these verses read:

> Numbers 12:[4]At once the LORD said to Moses, Aaron and Miriam, "Come out to the Tent
> of Meeting, all three of you." So the three of them came out. [5]Then the LORD came
> down in a pillar of cloud; he stood at the entrance to the Tent and summoned Aaron and
> Miriam. When both of them stepped forward, [6]he said, "Listen to my words: 'When a
> prophet of the LORD is among you, I reveal myself to him in visions, I speak to him in

dreams. [7]But this is not true of my servant Moses; he is faithful in all my house. [8]With him I speak face to face, clearly and not in riddles; he sees the form of the LORD. Why then were you not afraid to speak against my servant Moses?'"

Eight examples, which reinforce Numbers 12:4-8 and show additional ways that God communicated with various individuals are, as follows:

✓ *Example-1*: Again, some individuals like Adam, Eve, and Moses had direct conversations with God. With regard to Adam and Eve, see Genesis 3:16-17. In the NIV, these verses read:

> Genesis 3:[16]To the woman he said, "I will greatly increase your pains in childbearing; with pain you will give birth to children. Your desire will be for your husband, and he will rule over you." [17]To Adam he said, "Because you listened to your wife and ate from the tree about which I commanded you, 'You must not eat of it,' Cursed is the ground because of you; through painful toil you will eat of it all the days of your life.

The pronoun "I" in Genesis 3:16-17 is God referring to Himself. Thus, God is speaking to Adam and Eve. And Adam and Eve probably shared stories of their interactions with God, with their descendants.

✓ *Example-2*: As previously mentioned, Moses had direct conversations with God. See Exodus 3:4-6, which references a direct conversation. In the NIV, these verses read:

> Exodus 3:[4]When the LORD saw that he had gone over to look, God called to him from within the bush, "Moses! Moses!" And Moses said, "Here I am." [5]"Do not come any closer," God said. "Take off your sandals, for the place where you are standing is holy ground." [6]Then he said, "I am the God of your father, the God of Abraham, the God of Isaac and the God of Jacob." At this, Moses hid his face, because he was afraid to look at God.

Moses is believed to be the writer and/or collector of the first five books of the Bible.

✓ *Example-3*: Jeremiah, a prophet of God, had direct and indirect conversations with God. See Jeremiah 1:1-10, which references a direct conversation. In the NIV, these verses read:

> Jeremiah 1:[1]The words of Jeremiah son of Hilkiah, one of the priests at Anathoth in the territory of Benjamin. [2]The word of the LORD came to him in the thirteenth year of the reign of Josiah son of Amon king of Judah, [3]and through the reign of Jehoiakim son of Josiah king of Judah, down to the fifth month of the eleventh year of Zedekiah son of Josiah king of Judah, when the people of Jerusalem went into exile. [4]The word

of the LORD came to me, saying, [5]"Before I formed you in the womb I knew you, before you were born I set you apart; I appointed you as a prophet to the nations." [6]"Ah, Sovereign LORD," I said, "I do not know how to speak; I am only a child." [7]But the LORD said to me, "Do not say, 'I am only a child.' You must go to everyone I send you to and say whatever I command you. [8]Do not be afraid of them, for I am with you and will rescue you," declares the LORD. [9]Then the LORD reached out his hand and touched my mouth and said to me, "Now, I have put my words in your mouth. [10]See, today I appoint you over nations and kingdoms to uproot and tear down, to destroy and overthrow, to build and to plant."

Jeremiah, a prophet of God, is believed to be the author of the Book of Jeremiah.

✓ *Example-4*: Several individuals, including Joseph, the legal father of Jesus, had dreams in which God or angels talked to them. See Matthew 2:13-15. In the NIV, these verses read:

> Matthew 2:[13]When they had gone, an angel of the Lord appeared to Joseph in a dream. "Get up," he said, "take the child and his mother and escape to Egypt. Stay there until I tell you, for Herod is going to search for the child to kill him." [14]So he got up, took the child and his mother during the night and left for Egypt, [15]where he stayed until the death of Herod. And so was fulfilled what the Lord had said through the prophet: "Out of Egypt I called my son."

Joseph may have shared this information with his legal son, Jesus, who may have shared it with Matthew. Obviously, Matthew is the writer of the Book of Matthew.

✓ *Example-5*: Some individuals, including Mary, the birth Mother of Jesus, had encounters with angels while they were awake. See Luke 1:26-28. In the NIV, these verses read:

> Luke 1:[26]In the sixth month, God sent the angel Gabriel to Nazareth, a town in Galilee, [27]to a virgin pledged to be married to a man named Joseph, a descendant of David. The virgin's name was Mary. [28]The angel went to her and said, "Greetings, you who are highly favored! The Lord is with you."

Many scholars believe that Mary was a primary source for Luke, who wrote the Book of Luke.

✓ *Example-6*: Some individuals, like Samuel, heard the voice of God. See "1 Samuel 3:1-18". (*The verses 1 Samuel 3:1-18 are listed in the Endnote*[46] *to save space here.*)

✓ *Example-7*: There were a few occasions where the "word of God" came through an unlikely source, like a donkey. See Numbers 22:27 - 31. In the NIV, these verses read:

Numbers 22:[27]When the donkey saw the angel of the LORD, she lay down under Balaam, and he was angry and beat her with his staff. [28]Then the LORD opened the donkey's mouth, and she said to Balaam, "What have I done to you to make you beat me these three times?" [29]Balaam answered the donkey, "You have made a fool of me! If I had a sword in my hand, I would kill you right now." [30]The donkey said to Balaam, "Am I not your own donkey, which you have always ridden, to this day? Have I been in the habit of doing this to you?" "No," he said. [31]Then the LORD opened Balaam's eyes, and he saw the angel of the LORD standing in the road with his sword drawn. So he bowed low and fell facedown.

✓ *Example-8*: The Holy Spirit helped some individuals, like some of the writers of the New Testament, remember things about the life of Jesus and/or about other important people, events, and/or issues. See John 14:23-26. In the NIV, these verses read:

John 14:[23]Jesus replied, "If anyone loves me, he will obey my teaching. My Father will love him, and we will come to him and make our home with him. [24]He who does not love me will not obey my teaching. These words you hear are not my own; they belong to the Father who sent me. [25]"All this I have spoken while still with you. [26]But the Counselor, the Holy Spirit, whom the Father will send in my name, will teach you all things and will remind you of everything I have said to you.

As the previous eight examples include more indirect, than direct, communications of the "word of God", it is probably appropriate to say, "The indirect communications of God through angels, dreams, visions, and inspirations occurred more often than direct communications."

A web document indicated that the word – "inspired" means "to breathe into". Thus, the phrase – "the inspired word of God", would take on the meaning "the breathed into word of God". This meaning and the connotations of the word – "inspired" also fit the indirect communications more than the direct communication, from God to man. Therefore, the title – "Is the Bible the *inspired* word of God?", is more appropriate for this essay. This position implies that the answer to the question – "What does the phrase – 'the inspired word of God', mean?", is:

"One-way communications from God to man via angels, dreams, visions, and inspirations".

II. Evidence that supports the credibility of the Bible.

Evidence that supports the credibility of the Bible (*and thus, supports the claim that the Bible is the inspired word of God*), comes from various sources. There is manuscript evidence, archaeological evidence, prophetic evidence, statistical evidence, the evidence of lives changed by the influence of those who accept the Bible, and the evidence of lives changed by the influence of the Bible alone.

A. Manuscript evidence.

Bible scholars say, "There are more ancient copies of manuscripts for various books of the Bible than any other ancient document. These copies include books from both the Old and the New Testaments and are from various points in history. But the most important thing is that these copies support the accuracy of the contents of the Hebrew and Greek versions of the Bible, today." Paraphrased, several web documents present facts like:

> "The works of Plato were written down nineteen hundred years after his death, and only twenty-two antique copies have survived. Homer's Odyssey was written down six hundred years after his death, and sixty antique copies have survived. Parts of the New Testament were written down within four years of the death of Christ, and more than twenty-four thousand antique copies have survived."

Another fact of interest was posted on the Internet. Paraphrased, it read:

> "With respect to antique copies, there are some ancient clay fragments representing some of the Apocryphal books, other literature, and all the books of the Hebrew Bible (*the Old Testament*), except the Book of Esther. These ancient fragments are called the "Dead Sea Scrolls" and were discovered in caves in the Judean Desert (*a region of southern Israel and southwest Jordan*) starting in 1947. Scholars have dated these fragments to the period 300 B.C. to 68 A.D. But the important thing to note is that there are no substantive differences, between the material in the "Dead Sea Scrolls" and a modern copy of the Hebrew Bible."

<u>The point (for Manuscript evidence)</u>: As implied previously, when ancient copies of the Bible are compared with modern copies, there are no substantive differences. Or more precisely, there are no doctrinal differences. This proves that the passage of more than two thousand years has not corrupted the Hebrew version of the Old Testament and the Greek version of the New Testament. This also adds credibility to the Bible being the inspired word of God.

B. Archaeological evidence.

Bible scholars say, "Many historical and geographical statements in the Bible, have been validated by archaeological finds, especially during the twentieth century and the latter half of the nineteenth century." For instance, archeologists have found inscriptions that reference Pontius Pilate. Until these inscriptions were found, supposedly, there were no secular references to Pontius Pilate. Thus, many Bible critics claimed that he was a myth. A similar situation occurred with a reference to the "House of David". Until some inscriptions were found that referenced the "House of David", many Bible critics claimed that King David was just a myth.

The point (for Archaeological evidence): In the land of the Old Testament, every new turn of the archeologist's shovel adds new support for the historical credibility of the Bible. And even more important, archeologists have found nothing to explicitly discredit the Bible. This also adds credibility to the Bible being the inspired word of God.

C. Prophetic evidence.

Bible scholars say, "Most of the prophecies recorded in the Bible are about Jesus, the Jewish people, and the Jewish nation." Furthermore, there are more prophecies recorded in the Old Testament, than in the New Testament. Most prophecies were recorded in such a manner that we know, who the prophet was. To confirm most true prophets to the people, God gave those prophets short-range prophecies. When the short-range prophecies came to pass, the prophets were confirmed. Then God would give a true prophet, a more substantial, and possibly further into the future, prophecy. When the short-range prophecy did not come to pass, a prophet was declared to be a false prophet. To reduce the occurrence of false prophets, God set a standard of death for false prophets. In the Old Testament, this standard is set in Deuteronomy 18:15-22. In the NIV, these verses read:

> Deuteronomy 18:15The LORD your God will raise up for you a prophet like me from
> among your own brothers. You must listen to him. 16For this is what you asked of the
> LORD your God at Horeb on the day of the assembly when you said, "Let us not hear
> the voice of the LORD our God nor see this great fire anymore, or we will die." 17The
> LORD said to me: "What they say is good. 18I will raise up for them a prophet like you
> from among their brothers; I will put my words in his mouth, and he will tell them
> everything I command him. 19If anyone does not listen to my words that the prophet
> speaks in my name, I myself will call him to account. 20But a prophet who presumes
> to speak in my name anything I have not commanded him to say, or a prophet who
> speaks in the name of other gods, must be put to death." 21You may say to yourselves,
> "How can we know when a message has not been spoken by the LORD?" 22If what
> a prophet proclaims in the name of the LORD does not take place or come true, that
> is a message the LORD has not spoken. That prophet has spoken presumptuously. Do
> not be afraid of him.

In the New Testament, the destruction of false prophets seems to be reconfirmed, by 2 Peter 2:1. In the NIV, this verse reads:

> 2 Peter 2:1But there were also false prophets among the people, just as there will be false teachers among you. They will secretly introduce destructive heresies, even denying the sovereign Lord who bought them--bringing swift destruction on themselves.

However, some true prophets were also killed, because the Jewish people, or the Jewish leadership did not want to hear the warning(s) or message(s) that these prophets were trying to proclaim.

Most of the prophecies listed in the Bible have already come true, but a few have yet to be fulfilled. However, before closing this discussion of prophecies, we will address two accusations made about prophecies. These accusations are:

- Item-II.C.1 – Bible critics claim: "Bible prophecies are actually historical recordings."

- Item-II.C.2 – Bible critics claim: "Bible prophecies were self-fulfilling."

Then we will conclude our discussion of prophecies with Item-II.C.3, which is a discussion of the fact that "Many Bible prophecies have a beauty about them."

1. Bible critics claim: "Bible prophecies are actually historical recordings."

Saying that "Bible prophecies are actually historical recordings" is easy. The question is: "Is this statement true?" Or better, "Is there any evidence to support this statement?" If this statement is true, then it would have required a major conspiracy, by many different Jews and/or non-Jews over many centuries for, at least, two reasons:

✓ *Reason-1*: It would have required Jews, because they recorded these prophecies.

✓ *Reason-2*: It would have required some non-Jews, along with the Jews, because they were part of the process of fulfilling some prophecies.

One way to counter those making this "historical recordings" accusation, is to remind them of the two primary functions of Bible prophecies:

✓ *Function-1*: Bible prophecies were intended to confirm God, specifically, to the Jews, and generally, to the rest of the world.

✓ *Function-2*: Bible prophecies served to provide guidance and warnings to the Jews, and even to some non-Jews.

Thus, based on the two primary purposes of prophecies, would it make sense for the Jews to knowingly perpetuate a conspiracy, around prophecies, and yet not reject God? Yes! The Jews did reject Christ, but that rejection was consistent with prophecies. Therefore, the acceptance of God, by the Jews, confirms the credibility of Bible prophecies. A more specific counter to the "historical recordings" claim is presented, by the essay – "Does the Bible contain prophecies about the rebirth of the Jewish nation in 1948?", in the book: "Last Call!!!"

2. Bible critics claim "Bible prophecies were self-fulfilling."

Saying that "Bible prophecies were self-fulfilling", is also easy. And this accusation might be valid, if a prophecy was made about a small group of individuals, involved only this group, and was fulfilled only through the efforts of the members of this group, without the aid or interference of others. However, even when Bible prophecies involved a single individual, the fulfillment of that particular prophecy usually involved many unrelated individuals. Sometimes many of these unrelated individuals were not Jews. In addition, all prophecies were not favorable to the health and welfare of those who were the subjects of the prophecy. For example, before 33 A.D., Jesus prophesied the total destruction of Jerusalem. This was fulfilled in 70 A.D., when Titus, a Roman general, destroyed Jerusalem and killed or enslaved more than an estimated one million Jews. Thus, the self-fulfilling accusation is invalid. And here again, an excellent counter to the self-fulfilling accusation is the essay – "Does the Bible contain prophecies about the rebirth of the Jewish nation in 1948?"

3. Many Bible prophecies have a beauty about them.

Many Bible prophecies have a beauty about them, because they are fulfilled on more than one level, fulfilled in more than one way, fulfilled in a seemly impossible way, or fulfilled at precisely the predicted time, against seemingly impossible odds. Four examples are:

✓ *Example-1*: Bible scholars say, "The virgin birth of Jesus was prophesied, by Genesis 3:15." In the KJV, Genesis 3:15 reads:

> And I will put enmity between thee and the woman, and between thy seed and her seed; it shall bruise thy head, and thou shalt bruise his heel.

More precisely, it is the phrase – "her seed", which implies the virgin birth, because traditionally, the seed was understood to be from the male. Thus, a "virgin birth" was an impossibility to the Jews and to Bible critics. However, to God, all things that are consistent with His nature, are possible.

✓ *Example-2*: Several Bible prophecies said that Christ would be from the line of King David. Traditionally, the Jews traced their lineage through the father. But Jesus was born of a virgin, which meant that He did not have an earthly father. However, Joseph was declared to be His legal father. Thus, legally, Jesus was from the line of David and Bathsheba through their son, Solomon.

For Jesus to be from the line of David, by blood, then Mary (*His birth mother*) would also have to be of the line of David. Some Bible scholars accept the Gospel of Luke, as an indication that Mary was from the line of David and Bathsheba through their son, Nathan. This is discussed in greater detail in the essay: "How do we know that the genealogy of Jesus in the Gospel of Luke is through Mary?"

If Mary was also from the line of King David, it would mean that the lineage prophecies were fulfilled three ways: by the word of God, by Jewish law, and by blood. Fulfillment, by the word of God, was through Mary. Fulfillment, by Jewish law, was through Joseph. Fulfillment, by blood, was also through Mary.

✓ *Example-3*: The Bible prophesied that Jesus would die for the sins of man. Specifically, Christ died in place of Barabbas. Generally, Christ died in place of every human being throughout time. Thus, these prophecies were fulfilled on two levels: "specifically" and "generally". Furthermore, these prophecies were fulfilled in two ways: "spiritually" and "physically", because Christ died spiritually, as the penalty payment for our sins, and then He died physically, as the atoning sacrifice for our sins. See the essay: "What is the literal and symbolic significance in the shedding of Jesus' innocent blood?"

✓ *Example-4*: According to Dr. David Moore of the "Moore on Life" radio program (*which now may only be available over the Internet*), the prophecies about the reestablishment of Israel as a nation on May 15, 1948 occurred to the day according to Bible prophecies. All of Dr. Moore's comments on this issue are given in his audio tape: "God's Plan for the Planets – Living in Light of Christ's Return". Here, the point is:

> "If you reviewed the prevailing political, religious, social, and military trends, at that point in history (*around 1948*), the prophecies about the rebirth of the Jewish Nation were fulfilled, against seemly impossible odds. And the fulfillment occurred, at precisely the predicted time."

The point (for Prophetic evidence): God used Bible prophecies "to confirm Himself to the Jews and to the world", "to provide guidance to both Jews and non-Jews", and/or "to warn both Jews and non-Jews, about their conduct". God used Jews and non-Jews, alike to accomplish those things that were prophesied. Once more, most of the prophecies were about Jesus, the Jews, and the Jewish nation. Thus, after several attempts to exterminate the Jews, their continued existence, their continued belief in the God of the Old Testament, and the rebirth of the Jewish nation, add to the credibility of Bible prophecies. Which also adds credibility to the Bible being the inspired word of God.

<u>Comment</u>: The prophecies about the rebirth of the Jewish nation, which occurred on May 15, 1948, are prophecies that anyone can confirm for them self, with very little research. Simply find a copy of the Bible published, before 1948 and confirm that the prophecies are in that copy.

D. Statistical evidence.

When the military, political, social, moral, and religious conditions, at the time a prophecy was given, are compared with the same conditions, at the time of the fulfillment of that prophecy, statistically, most often the fulfillment happened against incredible odds. That is, generally, the conditions, at both ends: "the prophesying-end" and "the fulfilling-end", were such that any fulfillment would have seemed almost impossible. Look at the many prophecies concerning Christ. The statistical probability of one person fulfilling all of the Old Testament prophecies, about the Messiah, is astronomical. Thus, statistics support Christ being, who He claimed to be, the Messiah. Look at the prophecies concerning the rebirth of the Jewish nation. These prophecies were fulfilled on May 15, 1948, to the day according to the prophecies studied, by scholars, like Dr. David Moore of the "Moore on Life" radio program. Listen to Dr. Moore's audio tape: "God's Plan for the Planets – Living in Light of Christ's Return". And see the essay – "<u>Does the Bible contain prophecies about the rebirth of the Jewish nation in 1948?</u>", in the book: "<u>Last Call!!!</u>" Once more, the military, political, social, moral, and religious conditions, existing in 1948 meant that the Jewish Nation was reborn against incredible odds. More precisely, the conditions meant that the rebirth prophecies were fulfilled against incredible odds.

<u>The point (for Statistical evidence)</u>: The Statistical evidence is that "The fulfillment of Biblical prophecies far exceeds the probability of such fulfillment." This adds credibility to the Bible being the inspired word of God.

E. The evidence of lives changed, by the influence of those who accept the Bible.

This evidence was dramatized, in 1997, by two heartwarming stories broadcast by WAVA, a Christian FM radio station, in Arlington, Virginia. The broadcast was part of the Focus on the Family radio program. Both stories are worth your time and may still be available on audiotapes or on a CD from Focus on the Family for a nominal fee. [*The toll-free telephone number for Focus on the Family is (800) 232-6459.*] One story is titled: "Spiritual Warfare: The Story of Stephen Morin, by Mrs. Margy Mayfield". The other story is titled: "From Mafia to Ministry, by Mr. Tom Papania". A brief-paraphrased summary of each story follows:

1. The story of Mr. Stephen Morin, by Mrs. Margy Mayfield.

This story is the testimony of Mrs. Mayfield, a Christian, and her encounter with Mr. Morin. At the time of their encounter, Mr. Morin was on the run from the law, after committing a murder. Law enforcement agencies from several states, were seeking Mr. Morin for several rapes and several other murders. When Mr. Morin encountered Mrs. Mayfield, he abducted her along with her vehicle. Because Mrs. Mayfield accepted the Bible, as the word of God, she put her trust for her safety in the hands of God and focused on her Christian duty of witnessing to others. Thus, Mrs. Mayfield used Bible verses and concepts to witness to Mr. Morin, during their time together. God used Mrs. Mayfield to get Mr. Morin to accept Jesus, as his Lord and Savior. Mrs. Mayfield also shared how Mr. Morin was later captured, tried, and sentenced to be executed. But while Mr. Morin was waiting for his execution, he brought others to Christ, because his life had been changed, by his encounter with Mrs. Mayfield.

2. **The story of Mr. Tom Papania, by Mr. Papania**.

This story is the testimony of Mr. Tom Papania, who became a Christian. When Mr. Papania was a teenager, he embraced his heritage, as the grandson of a Mafia leader. This Mafia heritage had been rejected, by Mr. Papania's father. However, Mr. Papania's acceptance of his heritage allowed him to live the Mafia lifestyle for a while. Then God used a Christian minister to witness to Mr. Papania. Because of the witness of this minister, Mr. Papania's life was changed and he accepted Jesus, as his Lord and Savior. Mr. Papania also shared how, after he became a Christian, God worked in his life to save him from an unjust prison term, when he was accused and tried for something that he had not done.

The point (for lives changed, by the influence of those who accept the Bible): Both Mrs. Mayfield, who witnessed to Mr. Morin, and the Christian minister, who witnessed to Mr. Papania, accepted the Bible, as the word of God. Thus, God used the witness and conduct of both Mrs. Mayfield and the Christian minister to change the lives of both, Mr. Morin and Mr. Papania, respectively. Stories like these add credibility to the Bible being the inspired word of God.

F. The evidence of lives changed, by the influence of the Bible alone.

This evidence was also dramatized, in 1997, by two interesting stories. These stories were broadcast by WAVA, a FM radio station, in Arlington, Virginia. One story was the spiritual quest and personal testimony of a fairly well known Christian evangelist. The other story was that of a bandit. This bandit's story was part of a sermon, by Pastor Steve King, the senior pastor of Cherrydale Baptist Church, of Arlington, Virginia. This bandit's story was also included with another story in a booklet titled "Is the Bible True?", which was authored by Pastor King. The two stories from Pastor King and a brief-paraphrased summary of the story of the evangelist follow:

1. The two stories from Pastor Steve King's booklet.

"One of my (*Pastor King's*) seminary professors, Dr. Donald Launstein, had a hobby of collecting and documenting stories from missionaries. To qualify for his collection, the stories had to fit these criteria: (1) it must be documented; and (2) the stories were to be of people whose lives were transformed through reading the Bible with no human messenger involved. The professor fascinated us with many amazing stories. I remember two that impressed me." (*Source: Pastor King's booklet "Is the Bible True?"*)

a. The story of a South-American bandit in the early 1900's.

"The bandit lived in the wilderness and waited for travelers to come through so he could kill and rob them. One day a preacher passed through and the bandit killed him and found in his pocket a little book, the New Testament. The bandit enjoyed the book because he could tear the pages out and use them to roll his cigarettes and smoke every night. Each night he would sit by the campfire, pull out another page, and smoke it. One night he was bored and decided to read the book. He soon stopped his nightly ritual of burning its pages and instead eagerly read them. He believed the Bible's message, repented of his sins and became a preacher of the Gospel of Christ'." (*Source: Pastor King's Class Notes from Dr. Donald Launstein; Western Baptist Seminary, 1976.*)

b. The story of an Eskimo.

"This Eskimo lived in the north, far away from civilization. Once a year, he would come into town to get supplies. On one visit he met a man selling Bibles. Somebody said to him, 'Don't buy that book. It's the devil's book.' This provoked the Eskimo, so he bought one. He took the Bible home with him. He told his Eskimo wife not to bother him as he was reading this book to find out if it was God's book or the devil's. He read through the whole Bible in one sitting. When he was finished, he said to his wife. 'I think it's God's book, not the devil's. I'm going to read it again.' He read through the whole Bible again and embraced Christ as his Savior and Lord. He began to teach the Scriptures to his family and community. Years went by and when missionaries finally reached his area, they found a growing thriving church where Jesus Christ was honored and the Scriptures taught!" (*Source: Pastor King's Class Notes from Dr. Donald Launstein; Western Baptist Seminary, 1976.*)

2. The story of a well-known Christian evangelist.

(In the original version of this essay, the conversion testimony of a fairly well known

Christian evangelist was presented here. However, the ministry of that leader would not grant this author permission to use that testimony. Thus, this portion of the essay was rewritten, under the "fair-use" policy.) "The story of a well-known Christian evangelist" would have demonstrated a crucial point, which is "this leader saw God in nature." Because this leader saw God in nature, he decided to read the sacred documents of most of the major religions of this world, to see if these sacred documents displayed the same God. As this leader read the sacred documents, he looked for inconsistencies and inaccuracies. He found inconsistencies and inaccuracies in all the sacred documents, except the Jewish Bible and the Christian Bible. Based on his findings, he felt that he saw the God of nature in the Christian Bible. Therefore, he accepted Jesus, as his Lord and Savior.

The point (for lives changed by the influence of the Bible alone): Lives are changed, by the influence of the Bible alone. More precisely, some individuals have read the Bible for themselves, accepted Jesus, as their Lord and Savior, and then allowed God, the Holy Spirit, to change their lives. Thus, lives changed by a reading of the Bible adds credibility to the Bible being the inspired word of God.

Comment: Lives are changed, by the influence of the Bible alone and by the influence of those who accept the Bible. But the issue of changed lives needs to be discussed in more detail, because some people will say, "Both Islam and Judaism change lives. Or for that matter, many, who believed in communism changed their life, because of it." Consequently, we need to ask, "How are the 'changed lives' of Christians different from the 'changed lives' of those in other religions or ' isms'?" Here, the premise is:

> "A strong belief in anything can change one's life. Or more precisely, a strong belief in anything can change the focus of one's life."

Now, the difference between the "changed lives" due to "other beliefs" and/or "isms" and the "changed lives" due to an acceptance of Christianity is significant. Due to "other beliefs" or "isms", lives are changed to accomplish a goal or an objective. That is, an individual will change the focus of her or his life, by performing works to accomplish or obtain a specific goal. Due to Christianity, lives are changed, due to a change of focus, from the individual to Christ. Thus, lives are changed in response to what Christ has already done for us. The life change is the result of the believer turning his or her life over to Christ. More precisely, the believer puts her or his trust in Christ and then begins to depend on the Holy Spirit for guidance. Therefore, any works performed, by a believer are not to accomplish or obtain a goal, but merely to reflect the believer's love for God.

III. What the Bible says about itself.

"What the Bible says about itself" can be demonstrated, by listing verses, which make statements about the Bible, the purpose of the Bible, and its source, and/or by referencing wording used in the Bible and the source of those words. Such verses and words are as follows.

A. In 2 Timothy 3:16-17, the Bible states that it was inspired, by God. In the NIV, these verses read:

> 2 Timothy 3:[16]All Scripture is God-breathed and is useful for teaching, rebuking, correcting and training in righteousness, [17]so that the man of God may be thoroughly equipped for every good work.

B. Twenty-four of the thirty-nine books of the King James Version of the Old Testament contain the phrase – "saith the Lord", in eight hundred and two verses. This phrase indicates the writer of the book is recording something said, by the Lord.

C. Twenty-one of the thirty-nine books of the King James Version of the Old Testament contain the phrase – "the Lord said", in two hundred and three verses. This phrase also indicates the writer of the book is recording something said, by the Lord.

D. Ten of the thirty-nine books of the King James Version of the Old Testament contain the phrase – "God said", in forty-five verses. This is another phrase, which indicates that the writer of the book is recording something said, by the Lord.

E. Some of the thirty-nine writers of the Bible explicitly confirm their inspiration and the truthfulness of their words. For example, in Galatians 1:20, Paul confirms the truthfulness of his words. Two translations of Galatians 1:20 read:

> (Galatians 1:20 NIV) I assure you before God that what I am writing you is no lie.
>
> (Galatians 1:20 KJV) Now the things which I write unto you, behold, before God, I lie not.

F. In rejecting the Bible, some non-Christians say, "The Bible does not include some important things that Jesus could have talked about, because if Jesus was God, He knew everything. And if Jesus knew everything, why did He not tell us about this or that?" The Apostle John answers this via the verse John 21:25. In the KJV, this verse reads:

> John 21:[25]And there are also many other things which Jesus did, the which, if they should be written every one, I suppose that even the world itself could not contain the books that should be written. Amen.

Clearly, the Bible contains only the highlights of what the Holy Spirit inspired in the writers of the various books of the Bible. Remember the main emphases of the Bible are "God's relationship to man" and "His redemptive plan for man".

Comment: People, who focus on "What the Bible does not say", without learning "What the Bible does say", are unfair to themselves. They are like a hungry man, who will not eat a plate of spaghetti, because he is focused on the fact that it is not a bowl of chili.

IV. Some general comments about the Bible.

"Some general comments about the Bible", follow. As you read, you might notice that some comments represent an issue, which has already been presented, but with different wording. Different wording is okay, because hopefully, the new wording provides a different view with different insights. Some general comments follow, as Item-IV.A through Item-IV.P.

A. Some Christian Apologists say, "The Bible is sixty-six love letters written from God to His people." More specifically, "The Bible is sixty-six love letters written from God to those who accept Jesus and His finished work on the cross."

B. Jesus did not do or say anything by accident. Every deed and every word recorded in the Bible models a lifestyle, or conveys a message to us, if we are paying attention. Jesus, with His words and deeds, modeled God's love for us, and He modeled the way God wants us to live.

C. During a Christian radio program, paraphrased, one of the participants said something to the effect that "The Bible was written **TO** the people of ancient times, but written **FOR** Christians today." However, a well-known minister prefers the wording: "The Bible was written **FOR** believers to preach **TO** the world."

D. Some religious leaders say that the Bible is like an owner's manual. God created us. Then He tells us in His owner's manual (*in the Bible*) the best life style for us to follow in the environment that He created for us. The essence of the owner's manual analogy is highlighted, by four notable examples from the Old Testament of the Bible. These are:

1. Dietary laws.
2. Sabbath rest (*Seventh day of rest*).
3. Child rearing.
4. Circumcision on the eighth day of the male's life.

Modern scientific studies: medical, psychological, and so forth, confirm the wisdom in God's owner's manual, the Bible. More precisely, these studies show that if one follows the instructions given in the Bible for all four examples, then one should experience optimum physical and mental health. If the instructions involving the four examples stated were not provided by God, then humans would have had to develop these instructions on a trial and error basis over time. Such a development on a trial and error basis is hard to believe, because of the very nature of the four examples. Some benefits show up in a long life and are very subtle. These benefits imply that someone really understands the human physiological and psychological makeup.

Comment: With regards to dietary laws, there is an excellent book: "What the Bible Says About Healthy Living", by Dr. Rex Russell, M.D.

E. A contrast to the owner's manual analogy is provided by "female circumcisions", which is the label given to "the process of removing part of the female's genitals"[47]. Unlike male circumcision, female circumcision is not mentioned in the Bible. Nevertheless, female circumcisions are performed in some African, Middle Eastern, and Asian cultures. Female circumcisions supposedly have a cultural and traditional value. But generally, these circumcisions can be both psychologically and physiologically detrimental to women. More precisely, female circumcisions can be especially detrimental to female sexual satisfaction.

F. Some people accuse God of being a "cosmic kill joy", when in reality, He has only tried to tell us the best way to live for our own health, safety, and happiness. He has used the Bible to convey the best way for us to live.

G. To maximize your enjoyment and understanding of a novel, you must understand the setting for that novel. You must also develop a sense of the character (*the attributes, traits, or abilities*) of all the important individuals in the novel. Obviously, your sense of the character of the individuals in the novel is developed, as you read about how those individuals interact with one another. More precisely, your sense of the character of the individuals is developed from the actions and words of those individuals. For the Bible, besides praying to the Holy Spirit for discernment, you must understand what type of literature – a parable, a history, a poem, etc., a given set of verses of the Bible represents. Then the same things that apply to understanding a novel, also apply to understanding the Bible. That is, when you read the Bible, you need to understand the setting for whichever verses you are reading and you must develop a sense of the character of those individuals in those verses. This includes developing a sense of the character of God, based on the actions and words attributed to God. However, you must realize that the Bible can only give us a glimpse of the character of God.

Like the author of a novel weaves patterns into her or his story, God wove patterns into the Bible. Therefore, when you read the Bible, you should try to see the patterns woven into its verses. Whether you believe the patterns or the Bible, in general, is a side issue. Here, the main issue is:

"The patterns reflect the relationship that God intended, between Himself and man, and the relationship that God intended between men."

The central patterns are: "God is love", "God is just", "God is merciful", "Man is sinful", "God hates sin", "God wants us to treat each other with love", and "God loves us, so much that He gave His only begotten Son for our redemption." If you do not see these patterns, then it is hard to understand how you could truly claim to have read the Bible. In fact, if you do not see any patterns, this author would say, "You have not read the Bible. You have merely looked at its words, because you did not take the time to analyze those words and to understand what was being said, and why. In short, you have not taken the time to understand the character of God, as revealed in the Bible."

H. In summarizing the previous comments with more detailed comments, one could say, "When the Bible is read with an eye toward seeing the patterns woven into its verses, it displays historical, life, and prophecy patterns."

1. Historical Patterns (*The label – "Historical" is used, because these patterns are reflected in verses from the Book of Genesis, which covers creation, through the Book of Revelation, which covers the end of the Age, or more precisely, because these patterns reflect God's relationship with man, God's attitude toward man, and God's desire for man, throughout history.*)

a. God created – the universe and man.
b. God creates – opportunities for us to know Him and for us to know and accept Christ.
c. God chooses – for His purposes: His chosen people, various non-Jewish nations, and various Jewish and/or non-Jewish individuals.
d. God loves – man and His chosen people.
e. God hates – sin and rebellion.
f. God judges – man and His chosen people.

2. Life Patterns (*The label – "Life" is used, because these patterns are reflected in verses, which indicate how we are to live.*).

a. How man should live (Owners' manuals for humans).
(e.g., dietary laws, Sabbath rest, child rearing, male circumcisions, etc.)
b. How man should relate to his fellow man.
(1) Man is to hate sin, but love the sinner.
(2) Man is to love his neighbor, as himself.

3. Prophetic Patterns (*The label – "Prophetic" is used, because these patterns are reflected in many prophecies contained in the Bible.*).

a. Old Testament prophecies indicated the coming of Christ, as part of God's redemption plan.
b. Old Testament prophecies indicated many things about the birth, life, death, burial, and resurrection of Christ.
c. New Testament prophecies indicate the return of Christ, at the end of this age.
d. Old and New Testament prophecies, indicated many things, which did/will happen to the Jewish nation.

Please note that the previous comments about the historical, life, and prophecy patterns are representative, not exhaustive. Nevertheless, again, patterns like those previously mentioned, are modeled repeatedly in the Bible.

I. On many occasions in the Old Testament, God modeled "**on a short-term basis**", what He was going to do "**on a long-term basis**".

On a short-term basis, God established many of the Jewish civil, social, moral, religious, and ceremonial laws. Most of these laws were related to the thoughts, words, and deeds of individuals and/or defined the relationships between God and man, between men, and/or between man and other creatures. Obviously, the civil laws defined relationships between people as they went about the business of living, under their government. The social laws defined relationships between people as they interacted with one another on a social level. The moral laws defined relationships between God and people, relationships between people, and/or relationship between people and other creatures. The religious laws defined relationships between God and people. The ceremonial laws defined how the chosen people were to honor and to worship God. Some laws fit in more than one category of law. In addition to establishing many of the Jewish laws, God also established many of the penalties or consequences of breaking these laws. He also established atonement procedures for both the civil and religious offenses:

- For the civil offenses, there was the concept of "the kinsman-redeemer". Under this concept, a kinsman could recover property lost, by a blood relative.

- For the religious offenses, there was the concept of "an atoning sacrifice, by the shedding of innocent blood, of especially, an unblemished lamb". Under this concept, an individual's sins were covered "on a short-term basis".

In summary, "on a short-term basis", God established many concepts, which modeled the relationship of the Jews with each other and with Him.

On a long-term basis, God used variations of the concepts established "on a short-term basis", as part of His eternal plan to redeem man. For instance, in regards to the redemption of man:

God told Abraham, the father of the Jews, to sacrifice his son, Isaac. Abraham trusted God and began to carry out God's orders. But God stopped him and provided a ram for the sacrifice that Abraham was to offer. This ram sacrifice was a short-term sacrifice. Then God told Abraham that He (God) would provide His own, Son as a long-term sacrifice (*as an eternal sacrifice*). Thus, this long-term sacrifice is what allows men to be reestablished under God's grace, through His son, Jesus Christ. And that is love. More specifically, God established Jesus, as the only way to Him (God), under the concepts of "the kinsman-redeemer" and of "a blood sacrifice as an atoning sacrifice for sin". Once more,

- Under the civil law, Jesus was born of a Jewish virgin and became our human "kinsman". Then He lived a sinless life and was crucified for our sins. Thus, He became our "redeemer". This made Jesus our "kinsman-redeemer".

- Under the religious laws, because Jesus lived a sinless life, He became an unblemished sacrificial lamb, who shed His innocent blood for our sins – who serves as an atoning sacrifice for our sins.

In summary "on a long-term basis", Jesus was born of a Jewish virgin and became our "kinsman", then He died spiritually and physically to become our "redeemer". This made Jesus our kinsman-redeemer, who paid our sin debt in full, spiritually and physically.

J. The comments under Item-H included the phrases: "on a short-term basis" and "on a long-term basis". These phrases can be considered paired phrases. Such "paired phrases/words" and/or "multi-phrases/words" occurred or were modeled, by several biblical events or situations. Before referencing a specific event, note that other paired phrases/words are: "'physically' and 'spiritually'", and "'generally' and 'specifically'". Sometimes, there may be more than just two phrases or words. The three phrases – "'by God's word', 'by Jewish Law', and 'by blood'", are an example of this situation. Now, an event, which displays paired phrases/words is the crucifixion of Christ. More precisely, one member of a paired phrase/word occurs in each of the following two comments:

- According to "Roman Law" and then "specifically", "physically", and "immediately", Christ was crucified for (*in place of*) one man, Barabbas.

- According to "the word of God" and then "generally", "spiritually", and "eternally", Christ was crucified for the sins of all men.

K. In researching the name – "Barabbas" in the "Holman Bible Dictionary (*a component of the Parson Technology QuickVerse software package*)", an article titled – "Barabbas", indicated that "Barabbas" was named "Jesus Barabbas". This entry reads, as follows:

BARABBAS (Buh rab' buhs) A murderer and insurrectionist held in custody at the time of the trial of Jesus (Mark 15:17). All four Gospels record that when Pilate offered to release Jesus, the assembled crowd demanded the release of Barabbas instead. Pilate gave in to the demand, ordered Jesus crucified, and set Barabbas free. Nothing is known of his subsequent history.

According to Origen[48], supported by a relatively small number of late manuscripts at Matthew 27:16, **Barabbas was named "Jesus Barabbas."** Though not well attested, the reading is possible. If it is correct, Pilate's question to the crowd in Matthew 27:17 would have added poignancy.

Matthew 27:16-17 are included here for your convenience. In the KJV, these verses read.

Matthew 27:[16]And they had then a notable prisoner, called Barabbas. [17]Therefore when they were gathered together, Pilate said unto them, Whom will ye that I release unto you? Barabbas, or Jesus which is called Christ?

Note. For Matthew 27:16-17 above, the KJV (King James Version) does not reference the name – "Jesus" with the name – "Barabbas". However, below are the same verses from the NRSV (New Revised Standard Version). These verses do reference the name – "Jesus" with the name – "Barabbas". Thus, in the NRSV, Matthew 27:16-17 read:

Matthew 27:[16]At that time they had a notorious prisoner, called **Jesus** Barabbas. [17]So after they had gathered, Pilate said to them, "Whom do you want me to release for you, **Jesus** Barabbas or Jesus who is called the Messiah?"

Barabbas also having the name – "Jesus" adds a touch of symmetry and beauty to the events involving him and Jesus, the Messiah.

L. When reading the Bible, many Christian apologists say,

"We must interpret the Bible in the manner (*in the sense*) that it is written. Pronouns should be interpreted as pronouns. Nouns should be interpreted as nouns. Poems should be interpreted as poetry, figurative language as such, literal language as such, and so on."

The point is: "Context is everything."

M. Before we read the Bible, we are supposed to pray for the discernment of the Holy Spirit. If this is done, then it would seem that the actual words used in whatever translation is being read, should become less important, because the Holy Spirit will convey to us what He wants us to know.

N. Over time, the Bible has been translated into many languages. Some languages like English have more than one translation. Some English translations are good and some are not so good. Some are "thought-for-thought" translations. Others are "word-for-word" translations. Some translations were done with a specific objective in mind. For example, there is a translation that was specifically designed for women and there is the translation used by the Mormon Church. However, regardless of the language, in light of the various translations and the specific objectives, which produced a given translation, confusion has arisen/will arise, because of the different wording used in the various translations. To clear up such confusion, we should refer to and/or check the Bible in its original languages. We should check the "Hebrew/Aramaic" Old Testament and the "Koine Greek" New Testament, to get a better sense of what was meant. Furthermore, understanding the political and social customs of both Old Testament times and New Testament times, is also useful. An English example of an improved understanding is Exodus 20:13, which reads: "Thou shall not kill", in the King James Version of the Bible. After some reflection on the original language, scholars began saying that a more precise translation is "Thou shall not murder". The use of the word – "murder", is intended to convey a prohibition against the taking of innocent lives. Because, clearly, God is not against the taking of life for what He considered just reasons, since the Bible recorded God's instructions to the Jews to stone to death specific groups of individuals for specific reasons. For example, the Jews were to stone to death children, who curse their parents. See Exodus 21:17 and Leviticus 20:9. These verses read:

> (Exodus 21:17 NIV) "Anyone who curses his father or mother must be put to death.
>
> (Leviticus 20:9 NIV) "'If anyone curses his father or mother, he must be put to death. He has cursed his father or his mother, and his blood will be on his own head.

Another example is one of several occasions, where God instructed the Jews to kill the men, women, children, and animals of unGodly nations. See 1 Samuel 15:3. Two translations of this verse read:

> (1 Samuel 15:3 KJV) Now go and smite Amalek, and utterly destroy all that they have, and spare them not; but slay both man and woman, infant and suckling, ox and sheep, camel and ass.
>
> (1 Samuel 15:3 NIV) Now go, attack the Amalekites and totally destroy everything that belongs to them. Do not spare them; put to death men and women, children and infants, cattle and sheep, camels and donkeys.'"

The point is:

"Clearly, as written in the original languages, the Bible was inspired. The same cannot be said of translations. That is why the Bible in its original languages needs to be reviewed and checked, whenever we find a problem in a translation or between translations."

O. The Bible recorded the fact that the Jews were chosen by God. But it also recorded how God used both Jews and non-Jews to accomplish His purposes. God used non-Jews to enforce His judgments upon the Jewish people when they turned their backs on Him. Originally, the Jews were to be the priests to the non-Jewish world. And thus, the whole world was to be blessed through the Jews. See Genesis 12:3 which reads:

(Genesis 12:3 NIV) I will bless those who bless you, and whoever curses you I will curse; and all peoples on earth will be blessed through you."

But actually, in spite of the disobedience of the Jewish people, the rest of the world was still blessed, because of them, since Jesus was born a Jew. And Jesus offers the gift of salvation to all, Jews and non-Jews, who accept His gift.

P. Christian scholars like Dr. D. James Kennedy of the Coral Ridge Ministries, remind us that the Bible is very unique in that it recorded the warts (*the evil deeds*) and the good deeds, of those mentioned. Most historical writings were sanitized. That is, the warts were not recorded, by those who wrote the writings or by those for whom the writings were written. Thus, the warts add credibility to the Bible.

V. Scientific principles referenced in the Bible.

Some scientific principles referenced in the Bible have been noticed over the years, especially during the twentieth century. These references are presented to counter those individuals, who feel that the Bible is not scientific or that Jesus could have said something about scientific things. However, everyone, who feels that Jesus could have said more about scientific things, must answer the question: "What purpose would have been served, if Jesus had shared modern day phenomenons like electricity, automobiles, etc. with those of His time?" To share any scientific things, Jesus would have used terms that were in use at that time. And that would have been a waste of His time and energy. Some of the same people, who feel Jesus could have said more about scientific things, also feel that ancient cultures did not have the scientific knowledge we have now. However, some scholars believe that some Egyptian hieroglyphics show something like an electric generator being used. For your convenience, some scientific principles or modern objects referenced in the Bible are presented here in five parts based on five sources: *Source-1* (*Item-V.A*), Eternal Productions; *Source-2* (*Item-V.B*), some principles of modern physics; *Source-3* (*Item-V.C*), some paraphrases of statements this author believes were made by author Hal Lindsey; *Source-4* (*Item-V.D*), the testimony of a well-known evangelist; and *Source-5* (*Item-V.E*), statements by author Bob Fraley's in his book: "God Reveals the identity of the 'Beast'".

A. Eternal Productions produces many excellent resources. However, two of those resources specifically fit this essay. These two resources are the booklet – "101 Scientific Facts & Foreknowledge" and the video – "A Question of Origins". As the title of the booklet indicates, it presents 101 scientific facts and foreknowledge indicated in the Bible. This booklet may still be available from Eternal Productions via their toll-free telephone number (877) 370-7770 or via their website at www.eternal-productions.org. This booklet is also viewable on the Internet at – www.eternal-productions.org/101science.html. The neat thing about the on-line version of the booklet is that under each of the 101 scientific facts and foreknowledge listed, there are links to other web resources to facilitate a more detailed study of that particular fact or foreknowledge. But here, only eight-Biblical-scientific principles presented in the video – "A Question of Origins", are listed. The eight principles are:

1. **Atomic Fusion in 2 Peter 3:10.** From four translations, this verse reads, as follows:

   (2 Peter 3:10 KJV) But the day of the Lord will come as a thief in the night; in the which the heavens shall pass away with a great noise, and the elements shall melt with fervent heat, the earth also and the works that are therein shall be burned up.

   (2 Peter 3:10 NIV) But the day of the Lord will come like a thief. The heavens will disappear with a roar; the elements will be destroyed by fire, and the earth and everything in it will be laid bare.

   (2 Peter 3:10 NRSV) But the day of the Lord will come like a thief, and then the heavens will pass away with a loud noise, and the elements will be dissolved with fire, and the earth and everything that is done on it will be disclosed.

   (2 Peter 3:10 NASB) But the day of the Lord will come like a thief, in which the heavens will pass away with a roar and the elements will be destroyed with intense heat, and the earth and its works will be burned up.

2. **Ocean Currents in Psalms 8:8 and Isaiah 43:16.** From four translations, these verses read, as follows:

   (Psalms 8:8 KJV) The fowl of the air, and the fish of the sea, and whatsoever passeth through the paths of the seas.

   (Psalms 8:8 NIV) the birds of the air, and the fish of the sea, all that swim the paths of the seas.

   (Psalms 8:8 NRSV) the birds of the air, and the fish of the sea, whatever passes along the paths of the seas.

(Psalms 8:8 NASB) The birds of the heavens, and the fish of the sea, Whatever passes through the paths of the seas.

(Isaiah 43:16 KJV) Thus saith the LORD, which maketh a way in the sea, and a path in the mighty waters;

(Isaiah 43:16 NIV) This is what the LORD says-- he who made a way through the sea, a path through the mighty waters,

(Isaiah 43:16 NRSV) Thus says the LORD, who makes a way in the sea, a path in the mighty waters,

(Isaiah 43:16 NASB) Thus says the LORD, Who makes a way through the sea And a path through the mighty waters,

3. **Hydrologic Cycles in Job 36:27 and Amos 9:6.** From four translations, these verses read, as follows:

   (Job 36:27 KJV) For he maketh small the drops of water: they pour down rain according to the vapour thereof:

   (Job 36:27 NIV) "He draws up the drops of water, which distill as rain to the streams;

   (Job 36:27 NRSV) For he draws up the drops of water; he distills his mist in rain,

   (Job 36:27 NASB) "For He draws up the drops of water, They distill rain from the mist,

---

(Amos 9:6 KJV) It is he that buildeth his stories in the heaven, and hath founded his troop in the earth; he that calleth for the waters of the sea, and poureth them out upon the face of the earth: The LORD is his name.

(Amos 9:6 NIV) he who builds his lofty palace in the heavens and sets its foundation on the earth, who calls for the waters of the sea and pours them out over the face of the land-- the LORD is his name.

(Amos 9:6 NRSV) who builds his upper chambers in the heavens, and founds his vault upon the earth; who calls for the waters of the sea, and pours them out upon the surface of the earth-- the LORD is his name.

(Amos 9:6 NASB) The One who builds His upper chambers in the heavens, And has founded His vaulted dome over the earth, He who calls for the waters of the sea And pours them out on the face of the earth, The LORD is His name.

4. **Jet Streams in Ecclesiastes 1:6-7.** From four translations, these verses read, as follows:

(Ecclesiastes 1:6 KJV) The wind goeth toward the south, and turneth about unto the north; it whirleth about continually, and the wind returneth again according to his circuits.

(Ecclesiastes 1:7 KJV) All the rivers run into the sea; yet the sea is not full; unto the place from whence the rivers come, thither they return again.

(Ecclesiastes 1:6 NIV) The wind blows to the south and turns to the north; round and round it goes, ever returning on its course.

(Ecclesiastes 1:7 NIV) All streams flow into the sea, yet the sea is never full. To the place the streams come from, there they return again.

(Ecclesiastes 1:6 NRSV) The wind blows to the south, and goes around to the north; round and round goes the wind, and on its circuits the wind returns.

(Ecclesiastes 1:7 NRSV) All streams run to the sea, but the sea is not full; to the place where the streams flow, there they continue to flow.

(Ecclesiastes 1:6 NASB) Blowing toward the south, Then turning toward the north, The wind continues swirling along; And on its circular courses the wind returns.

(Ecclesiastes 1:7 NASB) All the rivers flow into the sea, Yet the sea is not full. To the place where the rivers flow, There they flow again.

5. **"The Earth is floating in space" in Job 25:7.** From four translations, Job 25:7 reads, as follows:

(Job 26:7 KJV) He stretcheth out the north over the empty place, and hangeth the earth upon nothing.

(Job 26:7 NIV) He spreads out the northern skies over empty space; he suspends the earth over nothing.

(Job 26:7 NRSV) He stretches out Zaphon over the void, and hangs the earth upon nothing.

(Job 26:7 NASB) "He stretches out the north over empty space, And hangs the earth on nothing.

6. **"Matter is composed of things that we cannot see" in Hebrew 11:3.** From four translations, Hebrew 11:3 reads, as follows:

(Hebrews 11:3 KJV) Through faith we understand that the worlds were framed by the word of God, so that things which are seen were not made of things which do appear.

(Hebrews 11:3 NIV) By faith we understand that the universe was formed at God's command, so that what is seen was not made out of what was visible.

(Hebrews 11:3 NRSV) By faith we understand that the worlds were prepared by the word of God, so that what is seen was made from things that are not visible.

(Hebrews 11:3 NASB) By faith we understand that the worlds were prepared by the word of God, so that what is seen was not made out of things which are visible.

7. **Dinosaurs in Job 40:15-23 and Psalms 74:14.** In the NIV, these verses read:

Job 40:[15] "Look at the behemoth, which I made along with you and which feeds on grass like an ox. [16]What strength he has in his loins, what power in the muscles of his belly! [17]His tail sways like a cedar; the sinews of his thighs are close-knit. [18]His bones are tubes of bronze, his limbs like rods of iron. [19]He ranks first among the works of God, yet his Maker can approach him with his sword. [20]The hills bring him their produce, and all the wild animals play nearby. [21]Under the lotus plants he lies, hidden among the reeds in the marsh. [22]The lotuses conceal him in their shadow; the poplars by the stream surround him. [23]When the river rages, he is not alarmed; he is secure, though the Jordan should surge against his mouth.

(Psalms 74:14 NIV) It was you who crushed the heads of Leviathan and gave him as food to the creatures of the desert.

8. **Innumerable Stars in Jeremiah 33:22.** From four translations, Jeremiah 33:22 reads, as follows:

(Jeremiah 33:22 KJV) As the host of heaven cannot be numbered, neither the sand of the sea measured: so will I multiply the seed of David my servant, and the Levites that minister unto me.

(Jeremiah 33:22 NIV) I will make the descendants of David my servant and the Levites who minister before me as countless as the stars of the sky and as measureless as the sand on the seashore.'"

(Jeremiah 33:22 NRSV) Just as the host of heaven cannot be numbered and the sands of the sea cannot be measured, so I will increase the offspring of my servant David, and the Levites who minister to me.

(Jeremiah 33:22 NASB) 'As the host of heaven cannot be counted, and the sand of the sea cannot be measured, so I will multiply the descendants of David My servant and the Levites who minister to Me.'"

B. This author recalls reading that when scientists examine some physical relationships on a molecular level under the principles of modern physics, they cannot understand "how some things hold together". Some Bible scholars feel the appropriate answer to how some things are held together is Colossians 1:15-17. Four translations of these verses are, as follows:

In the KJV, Colossians 1:15-17 reads:

Colossians 1:15Who is the image of the invisible God, the firstborn of every creature:
16For by him were all things created, that are in heaven, and that are in earth, visible and invisible, whether they be thrones, or dominions, or principalities, or powers: all things were created by him, and for him: 17And he is before all things, and <u>by him all things consist</u>.

In the NIV, Colossians 1:15-17 reads:

Colossians 1:15He is the image of the invisible God, the firstborn over all creation.
16For by him all things were created: things in heaven and on earth, visible and invisible, whether thrones or powers or rulers or authorities; all things were created by him and for him. 17He is before all things, and <u>in him all things hold together</u>.

In the NRSV, Colossians 1:15-17 reads:

Colossians 1:15He is the image of the invisible God, the firstborn of all creation; 16for in him all things in heaven and on earth were created, things visible and invisible, whether thrones or dominions or rulers or powers--all things have been created through him and for him. 17He himself is before all things, and <u>in him all things hold together</u>.

In the NASB, Colossians 1:15-17 reads:

> Colossians 1:[15]And He is the image of the invisible God, the first-born of all creation. [16]For by Him all things were created, both in the heavens and on earth, visible and invisible, whether thrones or dominions or rulers or authorities-- all things have been created by Him and for Him. [17]And He is before all things, and in Him all things hold together.

C. This author believes that either in one of his books or in a presentation, author Hal Lindsey said that something like a "helicopter" is referenced in Revelation 9:7-10. These verses read:

(Revelation 9:7 KJV) And the shapes of the locusts were like unto horses prepared unto battle; and on their heads were as it were crowns like gold, and their faces were as the faces of men.

(Revelation 9:8 KJV) And they had hair as the hair of women, and their teeth were as the teeth of lions.

(Revelation 9:9 KJV) And they had breastplates, as it were breastplates of iron; and the sound of their wings was as the sound of chariots of many horses running to battle.

(Revelation 9:10 KJV) And they had tails like unto scorpions, and there were stings in their tails: and their power was to hurt men five months.

Paraphrasing:

Revelation 9:7 indicates some type of flying object, which is used in battle. When John looked at the front of this object, it appeared to have the face of a man. Some people say that some helicopters do have face-like features.

Revelation 9:8 indicates rotating helicopter blades, which John referenced as hair. That is, John knows that there is something there, but it is not solid. It is fine. He can see through it. The reference to "teeth of Lions" could be machine guns, or it could be Lion's teeth painted on the sides of the helicopters.

Revelation 9:9 indicates armor on the helicopter and the sound of the rotating helicopter blades.

Revelation 9:10 indicates some type of chemical dispenser possibly mounted on the tail of the helicopter.

Remember: "The Bible was written over a period of more than fifteen hundred years using three languages. The writers were inspired to include those issues and events that conveyed issues important to God, not necessarily those important to modern man. However, note that Revelation was written to address the future. The referenced future is the last days before the second coming of Jesus."

D. A well-known evangelist has given his testimony about how he became a Christian on several occasions. Some of those presentations were recorded. In one of his presentations, he mentioned three scientific principles that are referenced in the Bible. These three are, as follows:

1. "**The Earth is spherical**" is referenced in Isaiah 40:22. From four translations, this verse reads, as follows:

   (Isaiah 40:22 KJV) It is he that sitteth upon the <u>circle of the earth</u>, and the inhabitants thereof are as grasshoppers; that stretcheth out the heavens as a curtain, and spreadeth them out as a tent to dwell in:

   (Isaiah 40:22 NIV) He sits enthroned above the <u>circle of the earth</u>, and its people are like grasshoppers. He stretches out the heavens like a canopy, and spreads them out like a tent to live in.

   (Isaiah 40:22 NASB) It is He who sits above the vault of the earth, And its inhabitants are like grasshoppers, Who stretches out the heavens like a curtain And spreads them out like a tent to dwell in.

   (Isaiah 40:22 NRSV) It is he who sits above the <u>circle of the earth</u>, and its inhabitants are like grasshoppers; who stretches out the heavens like a curtain, and spreads them like a tent to live in;

2. The phrase - "**The stars exceeding the billions**", is referenced in Jeremiah 33:22, which has already been listed under the previous outline <u>Item-V.A.8</u>. Thus, Jeremiah 33.22 will not be repeated here.

3. "**The gravitationally bound Pleiades star cluster**" is referenced in Job 38:31. This verse reads, as follows:

   (Job 38:31 NIV) "Can you bind the beautiful Pleiades? Can you loose the cords of Orion?

   The well-known evangelist indicated it was only in the past century that science was able to confirm that the stars in the Pleiades star cluster were gravitationally bound.

<u>Comment:</u> The Pleiades is a gravitationally bound cluster of stars in the constellation of Taurus. It is also known as "Messier 45" or simply "M45". This star cluster consist of from two hundred and fifty to five hundred thousand stars. With the naked eye only 6 of these stars can be seen. Now, as this author understands it, the phrase – "gravitationally bound cluster of stars", means the stars move more "<u>as a unit</u>" than "<u>as individual stars</u>". *(Source: Paraphrased consensus)*

E. This item uses reprints from the book – "<u>God Reveals The Identity Of The Beast</u>", by Mr. Bob Fraley, copyrighted in 1978 by Crane Publishing. These reprints are included by the permission of Christian Life Outreach; 6438 East Jenan Drive; Scottsdale, AZ 85254. In Mr. Bob Fraley's book – "<u>God Reveals the identity of the 'Beast'</u>", he shares his interpretation of scriptures, including some from the Book of Revelation. Here, we are interested in his interpretation of Revelation 13:11. Mr. Fraley feels that this verse is a reference to "**electricity**". Revelation 13:11 reads, as follows:

> (Revelation 13:11 NIV) Then I saw another beast, coming out of the earth. He had two horns like a lamb, but he spoke like a dragon.

Mr. Fraley feels that the "**two horns**" are the "positive" and "negative" charges of electricity. More precisely, on pages 112 through 113 of his book, Mr. Fraley writes:

POWER SOURCE REVEALED

The Lord gave the meaning on John's prophetic statement in Revelation 13:11 very clearly. The Holy Spirit taught me how the meaning revealed in this verse very closely resembles His methods. These two horns like a lamb, or these two power sources John saw Satan using in our society to teach and deceive the saints in their involvement with the standards of the world, are the positive and negative power charges of electricity that make possible the use of electrical power in the field of electronics. It is this power source which appears like a lamb (harmless) that is now able to teach, influence, mold and greatly control our conscience and develop our attitudes in the ways of the world. This may be hard for some to accept but I know in time this truth will be confirmed in our hearts because of the strong confirmation the Spirit of God has given me.

Is there anything intrinsically wrong with electricity? Of course not. Electricity is a part of God's creation. It can be used for many wonderful purposes. But we also know that Satan uses all that he can from God's creation for evil purposes in this world. Satan uses electricity just as he used an object from God's creation in the Garden of Eden to tempt Adam and Eve to become independent. The same is true in Revelation 13:11 as John prophetically describes what he saw to be the teaching power source of "the second beast" or "the false spiritual influence" coming from the world and attacking the saints.

It might help us to understand the reason why John described the false teaching power source of electricity as he did, and why Satan has used this power source the way he has, if we examine the resemblance between the operation of the spirit and electricity. Our spirit is power which is breathed into us from God. It is an invisible power force which gives us power for life. It denotes action. Likewise, the Holy Spirit of God which comes and dwells in us when we are reborn spiritually is also an invisible power force. He is the source of power which enables us to live a holy life. He motivates the holy activities and attitudes of our lives as we yield to His control.

This is the end of Mr. Fraley's comments on the "two horns". However, a second example of the Bible referencing modern processes or principles, according to Mr. Fraley follows. In this second presentation, Mr. Fraley makes some very interesting statements about the influence of television on our children. Now more than thirty-nine years later, the truth of his statements should be obvious. Anyway, on page 115 of his book, Mr. Fraley writes:

The National Commission on the Causes and Prevention of Violence reported the following in October of 1969: "The preponderance of the available evidence strongly suggests that violence in TV programs can and does have adverse effects upon audiences." This report explains how powerful television is in the learning processes of children. Television is teaching moral and social values about violence which are inconsistent with the standards of a civilized society. Please note: this report compares the commission's findings with the norm for what is considered to be a civilized society. The norm for a society which claims to follow biblical standards should be much higher.

This report reveals how violence is promoted on television as an acceptable standard of achieving ends and handling difficult situations. Even more devastating is the fact that TV, with its accessibility, now has a much greater influence on standards and the general teaching of children than a child's own parents. The report comments: "The TV set is never too busy to talk to them, and it never has to brush them aside while it does household chores. Unlike their preoccupied parents, TV seems to want their attention at any time and goes to considerable lengths to attract it. Indeed, parents too often use the TV set as an abdication of their parental responsibility to instill proper values into their children."

Paul A. Witty of Northwestern University has commented on this subject, stating that "Children gradually come to accept violence, hate, and destruction as normal ways of life. Their sensitivity to human suffering gradually becomes affronted by frequent exposure to anti-social behavior" Notice how Satan is using this teaching weapon to destroy the characteristic of love, which is the very nature of God.

The truly sad part about the influence of television on our children is that some people back in 1969 recognized the harmful influence of television on our children. More than thirty-nine years later, nothing has been done yet to correct this situation.

VI. Conclusion.

To all who seek, there is enough evidence to support the claim of the Bible that it is the "inspired word of God". This evidence supports the claim beyond a reasonable shadow of a doubt. And by far the strongest evidence for "the existence of God" is "the existence of the Jewish people". The strongest evidences for "the credibility of Bible prophecies" are "the continued existence of the Jewish people" and "the reestablishment of the Jewish nation". However, evidence aside, the Bible is either true, or not true. If the Bible is not true, then God cannot hold us accountable, and the Bible does not deserve our time and attention. On the other hand, if the Bible is true, then God can hold us accountable, and the Bible does deserve both our time and attention. For our eternal destiny is at stake. In summary, the answer to the question – "Is the Bible the inspired word of God?", is "Yes!", because there is evidence, which supports the claim that the Bible is the inspired word of God.

In closing, if you have read the Bible, then you should have noticed that the Bible recorded unflattering events or situations that a human author probably would have omitted. That is, the Bible recorded unflattering events and situations that non-Christians have used to imply that God is not loving. More precisely, four unflattering events and situations recorded in the Bible are:

1) God caused a universal flood, which killed all humans (*men, women, children, babies*), except Noah and his family. (*See the Book of Genesis.*)

2) God told the Jews to put to death lawbreakers among themselves (*See the Book of Leviticus and Book of Numbers.)* and to put to death the men, women, children, babies, and sometime, even the animals of some specific non-Jewish tribes and/or non-Jewish people groups (*See the Book of Numbers and the Book of Deuteronomy.*).

3) King David, a biblical hero, ordering the death of Uriah, the husband of Bathsheba. This occurring after King David had committed adultery with Bathsheba and she became pregnant. (*See the Book of Second Samuel.*)

4) The Apostle Thomas doubting the resurrection of Jesus. (*See the Book of John.*)

Thus, again, the unflattering events and situations add credibility to the Bible being the inspired word of God. Yes! **The Bible is the inspired word of God**. For God inspired men to record those things, which He wanted us to know (***warts and all***) and to do.

Can I prove the credibility of the Bible for myself?

The essay – "Is the Bible the inspired word of God?", references some resources, which prove the credibility of the Bible. Those resources included manuscript evidence, archaeological evidence, prophetic evidence, statistical evidence, and the evidence of changed lives. That essay shows, how an analysis of the evidence proves the credibility of the Bible beyond a reasonable shadow of a doubt. Still, someone might ask, "Can I prove the credibility of the Bible for myself?" This question has two possible responses: "a short response" and "a long response". "A short response", would be a simple "yes", "no", or "maybe", based on the knowledge of the responder. "A long response", would be a more involved reply, which might indicate why the responder considered a "yes", "no", or "maybe" answer appropriate. More specifically, if the answer was "yes", the responder might indicate how a "yes-answer" could be accomplished. If the answer was "no", the responder might indicate why the task indicated by the question could not be accomplished. If the answer was "maybe", the responder might indicate why that seemed like the appropriate response.

This essay serves to promote a "yes-answer" through "a long response", which presents a discussion of the topic: "Proving the credibility of a document like the Bible for yourself". This essay promotes a "yes-answer", because proving the credibility of the Bible for themselves is what several well-known religious leaders did. Some of these leaders incorporated their effort into their testimony (*into their story of how they found Christ, as their Lord and Savior*). A few of them even had their testimony recorded using a written format and/or using an audio format. One such audio testimony, started with a particular religious leader explaining that before he became a Christian, he saw God in nature. Based on this observation, he decided to check the sacred documents of all the major religions of this world, *for the God that he saw in nature*. Thus, he began reading those sacred documents. While he read, he looked for inconsistencies and inaccuracies, whether these were logical, physical, spiritual, and/or scientific. He found inconsistencies and inaccuracies in all of the sacred documents, except the sixty-six canonical books of the Protestant Bible (*which also includes the Jewish Bible*). In the Protestant Bible, he found things that he did not understand, but no inconsistencies or inaccuracies. The lack of inconsistencies or inaccuracies in the Protestant Bible was one of two proofs for him that the Protestant Bible is a credible document. The other proof was his belief that the same God, whom he saw in nature, was revealed in the Protestant Bible. These two proofs caused this leader to accept Christ, as his Lord and Savior. Originally, a transcription of this leader's audio testimony formed the heart of this essay. However, circumstances beyond this author's control, forced this essay to be rewritten with only paraphrased and/or "fair-use" references to this particular religious leader.

To accomplish the task of addressing the topic question, this essay is organized in two parts: "a long response" and "a conclusion". Part-1 presents "a long response" through a discussion of the topic: "Proving the credibility of a document like the Bible for yourself". Part-2 presents some concluding comments.

Part-1: **Proving the credibility of a document like the Bible for yourself**

You prove the credibility of the Bible like you would any document. More precisely, there are a series of things that you would do. Some of these things are, as follows:

1. Researching the author, if possible. This includes:

    a. Finding background information, about the author and her or his character.

    b. Determining the purpose for the document. (*Why did the author write this document?*)

    c. Determining the target audience for the document. (*Whom did the author have in mind, as the document was being written?*)

    d. Determining the writing style, used to create the document. (*Is the document a historical document, poetry, a novel, a technical document, or something else?*)

    e. Depending on the style, determining the culture and background from which the author wrote. (*This will provide insight into the meaning of some words and phrases. Recall that the meaning of a word or a phrase is dynamic – is changeable with time.*)

2. Reading the document. However, you must read the document with an open mind. And if possible, try to read the document in its original language, because some translations are not true to the original language.

3. Analyzing the document, as you read it. Depending on the style, this includes:

    a. Looking for patterns (*the how, what, when, why, and where things occurred*).

    b. Trying to develop, a sense of the character (*the attributes, traits, and/or abilities*) of those entities (*individuals, deities, and so on*), who may be portrayed in the document.

    c. Looking for inconsistencies, whether these are logical, physical, spiritual, and/or scientific. If you read a translation and find any inconsistencies, then you should check the document in its original language, to confirm whether the same inconsistencies are in the original language. (*Some inconsistencies can develop, because of the translation process.*)

d. Looking for inaccuracies, whether these are logical, physical, spiritual, and/or scientific. If you read a translation and find any inaccuracies, then you should check the document in its original language, to confirm whether the same inaccuracies are in the original language. (*Some inaccuracies can develop, because of the translation process.*)

e. Looking for things that are testable. If you find things that are testable, then you should try to confirm and/or to test those things through other references and/or through the most appropriate method.

f. Looking for information that is historic. If you find historic information, then you should check other documents for the same or similar information. But note that the occurrence of the same information in other documents, does not necessarily mean that the author's information is correct or true. Such occurrences only increases the probability that the author's information, is correct or true.

g. Looking for prophetic statements. If you find prophetic statements, then you should check to see if any of the prophetic statements were fulfilled and in the manner indicated by the document.

h. Looking for other copies of the document, and comparing them; especially, if it is an ancient document. Check to see, if and how the various copies of the document vary. Analyze any variations to determine the impact of the variance, on the purpose and meaning of the document.

4. Evaluating your findings, based on issues like those above, and any other available evidence. (*Note that if many individuals are assessing the same document and its supporting evidence, and if each individual can suppress her or his preconceived notions and prejudices, they should all reach similar conclusions about the credibility of that document.*)

Part-2: **Some concluding comments**

Many people do not believe that the Bible is a credible document. Thus, these people do not believe the claims of the Bible or of Christianity. However, too many of these people simply parrot the disbelief statements of others, without doing their own research or without reading the Bible for themselves. But by not reading the Bible, these people are really being unfair to themselves. In fairness to themselves, this author would challenge all unbelievers to do: their own study, their own reading, and their own credibility-check. An unbeliever could start by reading one of the following three translations of the Bible: a King James Version (KJV), a New International Version (NIV), or a New American Standard Bible (NASB). But the selected translation should be read like a novel or a history book would be read. The reader should look for the character (*the attributes, traits, and/or abilities*) of those entities (*individuals, deities, and so on*), who are portrayed in the verses of the Bible. The reader should try to see how those entities interact, while checking for patterns in the events, which happened, or in any recorded relationships between the entities in the verses. And even though the reader may be an unbeliever, she or he could say, "God, if You exist, reveal Yourself to me through Your word (*through the Bible*)."

Anyone, who reads the Bible with an open mind, should notice that it is no ordinary book. For the Bible contains stories about its heroes, that reveal everything "warts and all". The Bible also contains prophecies that were beneficial and not beneficial to the chosen people of God (*to the Jewish people, who were the recorders of the prophecies*). Thus, if you read the Bible and review the evidence, you may surprise yourself and prove the credibility of the Bible for yourself. But whether you do your own reading and research or not, the answer to the question – "Can I prove the credibility of the Bible for myself?", is "Yes!" Once more, this "yes-answer" flows out of the fact that many individuals have already performed their own credibility-check. In fact, Christian history is filled with stories of individuals, who set out to disprove the Bible, for themselves and ended up accepting Christ, as their Lord and Savior. A couple of recent – twentieth century – examples of this situation are: Evangelist and author: Josh McDowell and evangelist, preacher, and author: Lee Strobel.

Does the Bible contradict itself?

Many non-Christians and perhaps, even a few Christians, believe the claim that "The Bible contradicts itself". Those who hold this belief can be divided into two groups. One group consists of those who have never read the Bible. These individuals are simply parroting the contradictory claim without referencing any specific Bible verses. The second group consists of those who may have read some, or all, of the Bible. Many of these individuals reference specific Bible verses that they claim are contradictory. But saying that something is contradictory, does not make it so. Thus, we must ask, "Does the Bible contradict itself?" To answer this question, this short essay will share part of what was once a "web document"[49]. The web document was organized in three parts. The first part served as an introduction. The second part served to classify one-hundred-and-forty-three purported contradictions in the Bible. The third part listed each of the purported contradictions and followed each listing with a brief explanation to disarm the contradiction raised. This essay uses the material presented in the second part of that web document. In that part, one of the three authors of the disarming explanations, Dr. Michael J. Bumbulis, noted that the one-hundred-and-forty-three contradictions could be classified by the erroneous assumptions or methodologies used to define the contradictions. This author considers Dr. Bumbulis' discussion and classifications among the best general counters to claims of contradictions within the Bible. Dr. Bumbulis' classifications are quoted from the second part of the web document and his part is titled: "The Contradictions".

The Contradictions
by Dr. Michael J. Bumbulis

I have noticed that the supposed 143 contradictions can in essence be classified according to the erroneous assumptions or methodologies that they employ.

1. A popular mistake is to take things out of context. It is easy to make contradictions, when there are no contradictions, by violating the context of the passage(s) in question.

   More significant, though less mentioned, is violating the context of belief. Christian understanding is a synthesis of many beliefs, and Biblical teachings are often interpreted through this background belief, which has been synthesized. Such a synthesis may include other facts, not directly related to the contradiction in question, but nevertheless, relevant. When the critic proposes a contradiction, he ought to do so from within the context of this background belief. By failing to do this, he merely imposes alien concepts, as if they belong. This error is common, when the critic tries to cite contradictions related to doctrine or beliefs about the character of

God. For example, most Christians believe in the Trinity. One could argue about this concept elsewhere, but trying to impose contradictions by ignoring Trinitarian belief, violates the context provided by the Christian's background belief.

Or consider a mundane example. Say that Joe is recorded as saying that Sam is not his son. But elsewhere, he is recorded as saying that Sam is his son. An obvious contradiction, right? But what if one's background belief about Joe and Sam includes the belief that Sam is Joe's adopted son? By ignoring the context this belief provides, one perceives contradictions where there are none.

2. The critic assumes that the Biblical accounts are exhaustive in all details and intended to be precise. This is rarely the case. As such, the critic builds on a faulty assumption and perceives contradictions where there are none.

   This is related to the context problem. Let's say that the only records of Joe speaking about Sam are the two cases where he affirms and denies that Sam is his son. Certainly Joe said many other things in his life, but they were not recorded - including the fact that he adopted a boy and named him Sam.

   Another real-life case concerns a newspaper report which lists the time of birth of twin babies. The first was born at 1:40 A.M., and second was born at 1:10 A.M. If this account did not have the added detail that the birth occurred during the night in which Daylight Savings ended, it would APPEAR to be a real contradiction/error. But it was not. You have to know the whole story.

   Since the accounts in the Bible are rarely intended as exhaustive and precise descriptions, it would seem prudent to see if differing accounts complement, rather than contradict.

3. The critic seems to assume that the Bible is written in one genre - a literal and descriptive account. While the Bible does indeed contain literal and descriptive accounts (which, of course, are not exhaustive in all detail), it also contains many other styles of composition: the Proverbs list "rules of thumb," the Psalms communicate through poetry, many teachings/prophecies are in the form of hyperbole and metaphor, parables contain deeper messages, etc. Since the Bible is actually many books of different genres, the critic's assumption leads her astray if it is used to see contradictions.

4. This point is related to the one above, namely, the contradictions are often contradictions as a function of a particular interpretation. This is clear when one reads how the author of the list presents the biblical teachings in contrast to the actual verses he/she cites. Thus, the contradiction would exist only if the correct interpretation is applied by the author, and this is often not the case (or at least, it is

often not clear if this is the case).

For example, in many situations, the critic uses particular incidents or rules of thumb and interprets these as absolute principles.

5. Sometimes the critic equivocates. He/she uses the same sense of a word in two sets of verses, when sometimes it is the case that the word has two meanings. For example, peace could mean lack of war or it can mean an internal sense of tranquility.

6. The critic often reads contradictions into the accounts. This is often a function of all of the points listed above, but sometimes it is due to plain ignorance. In other cases, it is due to the fact that aspects of Hebrews idiom are not always captured in English translations.

7. The critic assumes that the believer in Biblical Inerrancy also believes that copyists could make no mistake. I have found not many believers in inerrancy to hold to this position. It is their belief that the original documents were without error, and were copied as faithfully as humanly possible. Thus, copyist errors are of little concern (and are unlikely to result in significant changes).

8. Finally, the critic engages in black and white either/or thinking when a both/and approach seems to be called for. This can be tricky, so let me set up my case by using one of the supposed contradictions cited:

   (Proverbs 26:4 NIV) Do not answer a fool according to his folly, or you will be like him yourself.

   (Proverbs 26:5 NIV) Answer a fool according to his folly, or he will be wise in his own eyes.

   The first thing to note is these seemingly contradictory teachings are right next to each other. Could the writer of Proverbs be so stupid as to not notice this? I hardly think so. In fact, I think it is very illuminating that these teachings are closely tied. They highlight the fact that biblical admonitions need not fall under the "either/or" criteria, but can be more properly understood in term of "both/and." In fact, I have often found these two teachings from Proverbs quite useful. In debating various non-Christians, I often encounter foolish responses and name-calling. I can either choose not to respond or ignore the foolishness and get to the point of contention. At such times, I follow Proverbs 26:4. In other instances, I mirror the foolishness of my antagonist in the hopes that he/she can perceive the folly of their approach when I employ it. At such times, I follow Proverbs 26:5. The key is knowing when to use which approach, and in such instances, I try to allow the Spirit to guide me.

"I *(Dr. Bumbulis)* encourage the reader to keep these points in mind when you are dealing with any purported contradictions"[50].

by Michael J. Bumbulis (mjb10@po.CWRU.Edu)

(Note. Neither the purported contradictions nor most of the disarming arguments have been included in this book. As the website may no longer be available, you will have to contact Dr. Bumbulis for more information. Possibly, the easiest way is through the publisher of this book, because the referenced email address for Dr. Bumbulis is no longer valid.)

Conclusion

As Dr. Bumbulis has very clearly stated, when examined in the appropriate light, contradictory claims can be disarmed. This author is not aware of any supposed contradictory verses, which cannot be disarmed (*which cannot be explained*), by biblical scholars. Thus, the answer to the topic question – "Does the Bible contradict itself?", is "No!" This "No!" answer is specifically with respect to the Bible in its original languages: Hebrew, Aramaic, and Koine Greek. Some translations have problems due to the fundamental differences between languages and the translation process.

How is it possible for different believers to get different interpretations of the same verses of the Bible?

A fact of Christian history is that different individuals have gotten different interpretations of the same verses of the Bible. And this situation will probably continue until the "second coming of Christ at the end of this age". However, the fact that different nonbelievers get different interpretations is not surprising, because the Bible was not written to nonbelievers. Some scholars say, "The Bible was written TO the people of ancient times, but written FOR Christians today." Others prefer the wording: "The Bible was written FOR believers to preach TO the world." And a few prefer the wording: "The Bible is sixty-six love letters written TO believers." Thus, at first glance, it might seem a little surprising and confusing that believers can get different interpretations.

Throughout history, one consequence of believers getting different interpretations is the formation of churches, denominations, groups, sects, etc., around those different interpretations. When searching for examples of this situation, we note that in 1054 A.D., the separation of what was left of the main branch of the "Christian Church" into the "Western Christian Church" and the "Eastern Christian Church", had doctrinal, theological, linguistic (*Latin versus Greek*), and political (*who was the head of the Christian Church*) overtones, so it will not be used as an example. Several better examples for the "Christian Church", are the separation of the "Assyrian Church of the East" in 431 A.D. from the main branch of the church and then the separation of the "Oriental Orthodox Church" in 451 A.D. from what was left of the main branch. These two separations were over a Biblical understanding of the nature of Christ. Then a 16th century example of a separation within the "Western Christian Church", is the formation of the Lutheran denomination, which was the result of Martin Luther's disagreement with the Roman Catholic Church, over the biblical interpretations of "salvation" and "penitence". Other divisions could be mentioned, but the point is:

> "the divisions within Christianity caused by different interpretations, have even been noticed by nonbelievers."

This is why both nonbelievers and believers ask, "How is it possible for different believers to get different interpretations of the same verses of the Bible?" To provide some reasons, which answer the topic question, this author remembered reasons proposed, by a variety of sources, over the years. All of these sources were encountered too far in the past for this author to identify. Nevertheless, the remembered reasons appeared to fall into two groups. One group of reasons involves the attributes, knowledge, and ways of believers. The second group of reasons involves the apparent attributes, knowledge, and ways of God. Thus, this essay is organized in four parts. Part-1 presents some reasons, which involve believers. While a bit presumptuous, Part-2 presents some reasons, which involve God. Part-3 presents a critique of the topic question. Part-4 presents a conclusion.

Part-1: **Some reasons, which involve believers**

Believers may get different interpretations for the following reasons:

1) Believers are human. And most forget to pray for the discernment of the Holy Spirit before reading the Bible.

2) Believers are human. Therefore, each believer comes to the Bible with her or his own experiences, wants, needs, values, beliefs, emotions, gender, culture, view of God, and so on.

3) Believers are human. And human nature says, "Take the path of least resistance." Thus, it has become far too easy for too many believers to ask someone else about the Bible, rather than praying for the discernment of the Holy Spirit and reading the Bible for themselves. Of course, asking someone else for their interpretation is okay, if you are going to analyze their interpretation and then confirm that it is consistent with the Bible. However, if you take someone else's interpretation without analyzing it or without checking its biblical consistency, that may create a problem or spread a misinterpretation.

4) Some believers do not have a complete understanding of the political climate, the Jewish customs, and/or the Jewish traditions that existed when both the Old and New Testaments were written. However, even with such an understanding, care must be used in how that understanding is applied to an interpretation of some verses.

5) Sometimes, believers do not have a good overview of a given book of the Bible. This includes believers failing to understand "to whom" the writer of a given book was writing and "why". Examples of this situation are the four writers of the four gospels – the Gospels of Matthew, Mark, Luke, and John, in the New Testament. Some believers fail to understand the "to whom" and the "why" for the four gospels are, as follows:

Matthew	*wrote to the*	**Jews**	to present **Jesus, as King of the Jews**.
Mark	*wrote to the*	**Romans**	to present **Jesus, as a servant of God**.
Luke	*wrote to the*	**Greeks**	to present **Jesus, as the Son of Man**.
John	*wrote to the*	**Church**	to present **Jesus, as the Son of God**.

6) Some believers do not understand the writing styles used in the Bible. For example, one writing style was the practice of repeating things up to three times for emphasis.

7) Many believers do not have a working knowledge of the original languages of the Bible: "Hebrew and Aramaic *(for the Old Testament)*" and "Koine (*Common*) Greek *(for the New Testament)*". Consequently, most believers are forced to read a translation of the Bible.

A paraphrased, a radio evangelist said, "All translations of the Bible are really interpretations." This means that most believers are forced to read someone else's interpretation of the Bible. Now, God did inspire the original writers. However, based on some translations that exist today, it should be clear that God did not inspire all of the translators. For example, there is a translation in which all of the male pronouns were removed, ignoring the fact that references to some male pronouns were understood to include females. Another example is the translation used by Mormons. Their translation uses wording that implies that Jesus was one of many gods. Consequently, believers have to be careful of which translation they read. In addition, note that publishing anything these days is, extremely easy.

8) Too many believers forget that most languages change with time. In fact with the passage of time, some words have taken on a totally opposite meaning from their original use. The word – "bad", is a modern example of a word taking on the opposite meaning. Furthermore, as Mr. Ken Ham of the Answers In Genesis Ministry reminded viewers of his "Creation Mini-series" videos, "Most words have more than one meaning. And the meaning which is applicable is usually determined by the context that the word is used in." Thus, the context and the meaning of a word at the time the translation was written are crucial. An English example of this is Exodus 20:13. In the King James Version (KJV), Exodus 20:13 reads:

> Thou shalt not kill.

While in the New International Version (NIV), Exodus 20:13 reads:

> "You shall not murder.

The KJV is a translation of the Bible from the seventeenth century. The NIV is a translation from the nineteenth century. Like most modern translations of the Bible, the NIV uses the word – "murder", in place of the word – "kill", because the word – "murder", carries the connotation of taking the life of the innocent.

9) Some believers do not read the Bible in the sense that it was written. That is, literal statements should be taken literally; symbolic statements should be taken symbolically; poems should be taken, as poetry; historical statements, as history, and so on.

10) Many believers are really introduced to the Bible through a specific Christian denomination or a specific religious group, which may have its own traditional interpretations of the Bible. Then most believers rarely question or examine the traditional interpretations of their own denomination or own religious group.

11) Some believers might have a specific agenda that requires them to take a specific interpretation in order to be consistent with that agenda. Similarly, some translations are written with a specific agenda in mind. For example, within the past twenty years or so, translations have been written specifically for women, for Black Americans, for Native Americans, and for isolated non-English cultures around the world. In fairness, the agenda for many of the previously mentioned translations is "converting members of that particular group to Christianity". However, the problem is that sometimes with this agenda in mind, the message of the Bible is softened to make it more palatable. And this softening can lead to different interpretations compared with other translations.

12) Some believers may have an incomplete feel for the character of God, as revealed by the Bible taken as a whole. Thus, not understanding the character of God, causes some to take an inappropriate interpretation of various verses. Believers need to get a feel for the whole Bible, before trying to understand a specific verse. With that hopefully, the believer will come to the understanding that one verse cannot contradict the Bible, as a whole. Thus, if a believer feels that some verse does contradict the Bible, as a whole, then there is definitely a misinterpretation going on. And the Bible in the original languages should have the final impact on the interpretation.

13) Different interpretations in different believers also flow out of the use of different references to interpret some verses. With respect to this reason, some Bible scholars say one thing, but practice another. More specifically, some Bible scholars say, "Whenever possible, the Bible should be allowed to interpret itself." What this statement means is that often one part of the Bible can be used to interpret another part instead of using nonbiblical information or sources like Jewish customs or Jewish traditions. One example of this reason flows out of Matthew 12:40. In the NIV, this verse reads, as follows:

> *For as Jonah was three days and three nights in the belly of a huge fish, so the Son of Man will be three days and three nights in the heart of the earth.*

These are the words of Jesus. And most scholars interpret this to be a reference by Jesus that after His death on the cross, "He would be in the heart of the earth (*He would be in a tomb*), for three days and three nights."[51] However, too many Bible scholars claim a Friday crucifixion, which does not allow "three days and three nights" between the crucifixion of Jesus and His resurrection on Sunday morning. To support their claim, these Bible scholars reference the Jewish custom of counting as a whole day any portion of the day. On the other hand, these scholars could allow the Bible to interpret itself by using John 11:9. In the NIV, this verse reads:

> Jesus answered, *"Are there not twelve hours of daylight? A man who walks by day will not stumble, for he sees by this world's light.*

Thus, if one uses Jesus' definition of a day, then He could not have been crucified on a Friday. Nevertheless, the point is:

> "Different interpretations are caused, by some believers referencing nonbiblical sources, customs, or traditions to interpret some verses, while other believers reference other parts of the Bible." *(See the essay: "Which day of the week was Jesus crucified on? And why does it matter?" in the book: "Last Call!!!")*

14) A believer may have part of the truth, but not necessarily the whole truth. And unfortunately, such a believer may share their "part of the truth" with someone else, as if it were the "whole truth".

15) It does seem like God may allow a believer to receive what they need spiritually from a given verse. Thus, again, the believer could have part of the truth, but not necessarily the whole truth. A radio evangelist put this in terms of three blind men and an elephant. Paraphrased, the radio evangelist said, "Three blind men are trying to explain an elephant. The first blind man has the elephant by its trunk. The second blind man has the elephant by its tail. And the third blind man has the elephant by one of its legs. Obviously, each blind man has a different perception of the elephant (*each man has part of the truth*), but not the whole truth."

There are probably more reasons why believers develop different interpretations of the same verses of the Bible. However, the fifteen reasons listed previously are those that this author is aware of based on statements by others. Nevertheless, when the listed reasons are analyzed, we should note one obvious implication, which is "not all differing interpretations are correct." A less obvious implication is "not all differing interpretations are incorrect, because sometimes each interpretation is true, but each is only part of the whole truth." The reason for explicitly addressing this less obvious implication is to prevent some readers from getting the impression that "reading the Bible is like taking an inkblot test – the Rorschach test – given by psychiatrists." Recall that during an inkblot test, what the patient sees, is dependent upon her or his mental state and experiences. Now, it is true that an individual's mental state and experiences could impact the way that they interpret the Bible, if that individual fails to pray for the discernment of the Holy Spirit. But this does not alter the fact that the Bible is a dynamic book. And individual verses may give a reader what she or he needs, to come to a knowledge of God. And yes! The same verse may be interpreted differently by different individuals. But again, not all differing interpretations are invalid or untrue. However, even though individual verses may be interpreted differently by various believers, the Bible, as a whole has only one message. That message is:

> "God, who is full of grace, mercy, and justice, loves us, and sent His only Son, Jesus, to redeem us."

In spite of having only one message, whether a believer is planning to read the whole Bible or individual verses, she or he should always pray for the discernment of God, the Holy Spirit. It is the Holy Spirit's job to move each believer to an appropriate interpretation of the Bible.

Part-2: **Some reasons, which involve God**

The Bible implies that God understands all of His created beings, and He knows what He is trying to accomplish in each of us and through each of us. Although it is a bit presumptuous, this author would guess that some reasons that God might allow different interpretations are to provide Himself with an opportunity to display His wisdom and His understanding of us. More specifically, some reasons that God might allow different interpretations are, as follows:

1) God knows that if we understand that there is the possibility of getting an incorrect or incomplete interpretation of the Bible, then each time before reading the Bible, we will be motivated to pray for the discernment of the Holy Spirit.

2) God wants to draw us back to the Bible. Therefore, He allowed enough ambiguity about the Bible in each believer's mind to ensure that would happen. Again, God wants each believer to depend on the Holy Spirit for her or his understanding of the Bible.

3) God knew that if one person read and completely understood the Bible, others would seek this individual, instead of praying for the discernment of the Holy Spirit, and reading the whole Bible for themselves. This individual, who understood the Bible, would become our spiritual leader. And eventually, we might put our copy of the Bible on a shelf, because we would simply direct our biblical questions to this individual and listen to her or his interpretation. Even if this individual constantly reminded everyone to verify her or his interpretations for themselves and they did, this individual's practice of sharing her or his interpretation of the Bible would still be a problem. More precisely, the problem is the whole focus is pulled off Christ and onto this individual, who supposedly understood the Bible. The climax of this problem would come, when those seeking answers from this individual would put her or him on a pedestal. On the

other hand, if this individual did not manage to remind everyone to verify her or his interpretation for themselves, then the focus would most definitely be pulled from Christ. The point is:

> "By allowing different interpretations, God is lessening the opportunity for too many of us to look to one individual for our interpretations."

4) Similar to an individual, God knew that if any group or religious denomination claimed a total understanding of the Bible, it would draw followers. More specifically, individuals would be drawn to that group or religious denomination, instead of those individuals turning to the Holy Spirit for the discernment of the Bible.

5) God inspired the writers of the Bible to compose it in such a "dynamic manner", that each time a given believer reads the same verses, the believer could see something different. Thus, the phrase – "dynamic manner", is intended to convey the sense of multiple meanings and/or multiple levels. More precisely, the phrase – "dynamic manner", is intended to convey the fact that many events and/or things recorded in the verses of the Bible convey "meanings on more than one level", "meanings that are true in more than one way", "meanings that are fulfilled in more than one way", and/or "meaning that are partially fulfilled, at some point in time, awaiting to be completely fulfilled at a later time". For instance, the events and/or things of a verse could be fulfilled in a "specific way" and a "general way". An example of this is the crucifixion of Jesus. Specifically and according to Roman law/tradition, Jesus was crucified in place of Barabbas. Generally and according to the word of God, Jesus was crucified for the sins of all men. On the other hand, the events and/or things of a verse could be fulfilled in a "spiritual way" and a "physical way". The crucifixion of Jesus also serves, as an example of this situation, because on the cross, Jesus died "spiritually" and then He died "physically". His spiritual death caused Him to go from an existence under God's grace to an existence under God's judgment, because that is the penalty for our sins. His physical death served as an atoning sacrifice for our sins and served to provide the way for us to reestablish our existence under God's grace. (*See the essay: "What is the literal and symbolic significance in the shedding of Jesus' innocent blood?"*) The point is:

> "An event, a thing, and/or a fulfilment might occur on multiple levels and/or in multiple ways. These multiple levels and multiple ways easily lend themselves to different interpretations."

In summary, you could say, "There is so much meaning packed into some verses of the Bible that more than one reading is required to move a believer toward a complete understanding of those verses."

6) The previous reason could also be worded as follows: "The insight and information gleaned from the Bible come from different views of the same verses. With each reading, God sheds a little more light in a believer's spirit and as we gain more light, we conform more and more to the image of Christ. Getting us to conform to the image of Christ is what the Holy Spirit is all about. Thus, this is also why we should be praying for the discernment of the Holy Spirit before we attempt to read the Bible." The point is:

> "That the different views of the same verses also lend themselves to different interpretations of those same verses."

God knows everything. This author does not. Thus, the six reasons listed above may or may not be appropriate. But they are definitely not the only reasons why God might permit different interpretations in different believers.

Part-3: **A critique of the topic question**

The previously stated twenty-one reasons serve to remind us that getting an incorrect and/or incomplete interpretation of a Bible verse is possible. Thus, while believers need to read the Bible as often as possible, believers must form habits that lessen their possibility of getting an incorrect and/or incomplete interpretation. The most important habit is praying for the discernment of God, the Holy Spirit. The reason for saying this is that God is not going to excuse us for our action, or lack of action, because our action or lack of action was based on someone else's interpretation of the Bible. Ultimately, each believer's understanding of the Bible is her or his own responsibility. But this does not mean that believers should not listen to someone else's interpretation of a verse. Discussing the meaning of specific verses can be helpful. Some brilliant individuals have devoted their entire life to the study of the Bible. Some of these studies reveal some interesting interpretations. However, whenever a believer encounters someone else's interpretation of a given verse, the believer should read that verse for herself or himself, pray for the discernment of the Holy Spirit, and confirm her or his reading is consistent with the other person's interpretation. If a believer's interpretation is different from others, then the believer needs to review the differences and pray for discernment to understand why. And even if a believer is just reading the Bible for herself or himself, she or he must still pray for the discernment of the Holy Spirit.

Additional reasons for praying for the discernment of the Holy Spirit involve two human conditions. *Condition-1*: We lose our focus on things very easily. *Condition-2*: We have a God-shaped vacuum in us that makes us want to worship something. That something can be God, another god, another human, some thing, or our self. To expand upon these two conditions, the following comments are presented.

- *Condition-1*: The loss of our focus. Reading the Bible could help believers keep their focus on Jesus and His finished work on the cross. However, too many believers let their focus get distracted by the habits, beliefs, and traditions of their denomination. They forget that denominations are the creations of man, not God.

- *Condition-2*: Our desire to worship something. Reading the Bible helps believers remember that we should be worshiping God – (*and only God*). However, from God's standpoint, He has always known that we have a worship problem. That is why this author believes that God:

  1) Hid Moses' body from the rest of the Jewish people. Consequently, the Jews could not enshrine Moses' body and possibly, stop all efforts to get into the promised land, or even worse, enshrine his body in the promised land,

  2) Has made it difficult for us to get back to Noah's Ark,

  3) Has hidden the Ark of the Covenant from us,

  4) Has hidden knowledge of the ancestors of the sisters and brothers of Jesus,

  among many other things.

Part-4: **Conclusion**

Each believer must always ask herself or himself, "Is my interpretation of a specific verse or verses consistent with the whole Bible?" In addition, when reviewing another believer's interpretation, each believer must remember that the Bible is read by individuals, who come from different backgrounds. Obviously, one's background is a combination of her or his experiences, wants, needs, values, beliefs, emotions, gender, culture, view of God, and so on. These factors can have some influence on how a specific verse of the Bible is interpreted. That is why each believer must pray for the discernment of the Holy Spirit. With that discernment, the interpretations of different believers should start to be more consistent, particularly for, what Bible scholars call the "clear and plain" verses. Nevertheless, based on reasons, which involve believers and on reasons, which involve God, two answers are proposed for the question: "How is it possible for different believers to get different interpretations of the same verses of the Bible?" These two proposed answers are, as follows:

- Based on reasons, which involve believers, *Proposed-answer-1* is "Believers are human beings from different backgrounds. Thus, different believers may get interpretations based on their own background, they may get 'correct and/or incorrect' interpretations, and/or they may get 'complete and/or partial' interpretations."

- Based on reasons, which involve God, *Proposed-answer-2* is "God allows different interpretations according to His will and for His purposes."

However, remember that no interpretation of a given verse or verses should contradict the Bible, as a whole!!

Do the four Gospels present in a consistent manner the last words of Christ and the last events, as He died on the cross?

During a cordial discussion about Christianity, a friend said, "In college, he read the Bible, as part of a literary class." Based on this reading, he felt that the four gospels - the Gospels of Matthew, Mark, Luke, and John - were inconsistent. Then in spite of his inconsistency claim, this friend questioned the need for all four gospels. Thus, this friend raised two issues: *first*, the inconsistency of the four gospels, and *second*, the need for all four gospels. To discuss these two issues, this author has chosen to combine some overview comments with a brief look at some selected verses, as representative of each of the four gospels. The overview comments about each of the four gospels are paraphrases from several religious leaders. The selected verses focus on the most recognizable event, which is common to all four gospels, that event is the crucifixion of Christ. Thus, the selected verses focus on some of the last words of Christ and some of the last events, as He died on the cross, as given in the four gospels. This author used the question - "Do the four Gospels present in a consistent manner the last words of Christ and the last events, as He died on the cross?", to summarize all of the preceding comments and to label this essay. Furthermore, focusing on this question allowed this essay to be organized in four-parts. Part-1 presents verses selected from each of the four gospels. Part-2 presents some words and events from the selected verses of Part-1 and a possible sequence of those words and events. Part-3 presents some concluding comments. Part-4 presents a table (*the format*) of the possible sequence of "the last words of Christ and the last events, as He died on the cross", as given in the four gospels.

Part-1: **Verses from each of the four gospels**

Each of the four gospels has verses, which reference some of "the last words of Christ and the last events, as He died on the cross". Some of those verses are listed here with some words underlined, for emphasis. In the NIV, these verses are, as follows:

As written by Matthew

27:45 From the sixth hour until the ninth hour darkness came over all the land.

27:46 About the ninth hour Jesus cried out in a loud voice, "*Eloi, Eloi, lama sabachthani?*" - which means, "My God, my God, why have you forsaken me?"

27:47 When some of those standing there heard this, they said, "He's calling Elijah."

27:48 Immediately one of them ran and got a sponge. He filled it with wine vinegar, put it on a stick, and offered it to Jesus to drink.

27:49 The rest said, "Now leave him alone. Let's see if Elijah comes to save him."

27:50 And when Jesus had cried out again in a loud voice, he gave up his spirit.

As written by Mark

15:33 At the sixth hour darkness came over the whole land until the ninth hour.

15:34 And at the ninth hour Jesus cried out in a loud voice, *"Eloi, Eloi, lama sabachthani?"* – which means, "My God, my God, why have you forsaken me?"

15:35 When some of those standing near heard this, they said, "Listen, he's calling Elijah."

15:36 One man ran, filled a sponge with wine vinegar, put it on a stick, and offered it to Jesus to drink. "Now leave him alone. Let's see if Elijah comes to take him down," he said.

15:37 With a loud cry, Jesus breathed his last.

As written by Luke

23:34 Jesus said, *"Father, forgive them, for they do not know what they are doing."* And they divided up his clothes by casting lots.

23:35 The people stood watching, and the rulers even sneered at him. They said, "He saved others; let him save himself if he is the Christ of God, the Chosen One."

23:36 The soldiers also came up and mocked him. They offered him wine vinegar

23:37 and said, "If you are the king of the Jews, save yourself."

23:38 There was a written notice above him, which read: THIS IS THE KING OF THE JEWS.

23:39 One of the criminals who hung there hurled insults at him: "Aren't you the Christ? Save yourself and us!"

23:40 But the other criminal rebuked him. "Don't you fear God," he said, "since you are under the same sentence?

23:41 We are punished justly, for we are getting what our deeds deserve. But this man has done nothing wrong."

23:42 Then he said, "Jesus, remember me when you come into your kingdom."

23:43 Jesus answered him, *"I tell you the truth, today you will be with me in paradise."*

23:44 It was now about the sixth hour, and darkness came over the whole land until the ninth hour,

23:45 for the sun stopped shining. And the curtain of the temple was torn in two.

23:46 Jesus called out with a loud voice, *"Father, into your hands I commit my spirit."* When he had said this, he breathed his last.

As written by John

19:26 When Jesus saw his mother there, and the disciple whom he loved standing nearby, he said to his mother, *"Dear woman, here is your son,"*

19:27 and to the disciple, *"Here is your mother."* From that time on, this disciple took her into his home.

19:28 Later, knowing that all was now completed, and so that the Scripture would be fulfilled, Jesus said, *"I am thirsty."*

19:29 A jar of wine vinegar was there, so they soaked a sponge in it, put the sponge on a stalk of the hyssop plant, and lifted it to Jesus' lips.

19:30 When he had received the drink, Jesus said, *"It is finished."* With that, he bowed his head and gave up his spirit.

Part-2: **Some words and events from the selected verses of Part-1 and a possible sequence of those words and events**

Some of the events in the selected verses were underlined in Part-1. Those events and any associated words allow Part-2 to be organized, as eight comments. The first-six comments serve, as a setup for the seventh comment, which presents a possible sequence of some of the events and any associated words from Part-1. The seventh comment is also presented in a table format, as Part-4. That table is labeled: "Last Words and Events Table". Then the eighth comment is presented, as a relevant comment. The eight comments are, as follows:

1) To ease this discussion and to make labeling the events and any associated words, the abbreviations – Mw, Mk, Le, and Jn, are used for the Gospel names: Matthew, Mark, Luke, and John, respectively.

2) Some of the last words of Christ will be labeled, as follows:

a) The label – "Mw/Mk Loud-cry-1"	*will be*	for the words – "Eloi, Eloi, lama sabachthani?", as recorded by Matthew and Mark.
b) The label – "Mw Loud-cry-2"	*will be*	for some words, which were not given, as recorded by Matthew. Thus, the phrase – "words not given", will be used.
c) The label – "Mk Loud-cry-3"	*will be*	for some words, which were not given, as recorded by Mark. Thus, the phrase – "words not given", will be used.
d) The label - "Le Said-1"	*will be*	for the words – "Father, forgive them, for they do not know what they are doing", as recorded by Luke.
e) The label – "Le Loud-cry-4"	*will be*	for the words – "Father, into your hands I commit my spirit", as recorded by Luke.
f) The label – "Jn Said-2"	*will be*	for the words – "I am thirsty", as recorded by John.
g) The label – "Jn Said-3"	*will be*	for the words – "It is finished", as recorded by John.

5) Jesus was being crucified, which is a slow death by strangulation, as His muscle tone was lost and His body parts fell out of place due to gravity. With the decline of His muscle tone, He had to push up on His heels to allow His chest cavity to expand and take in air. This effort would have been very painful and noticeable

to all the bystanders. Thus, the last attempt that Christ made to breathe should have been a very noticeable and distinct event. Consequently, it is not difficult to accept the statement - "He breathed His last", as a literal statement.

4) In John 10:17 and 18, Jesus said that no one would take His life. John 10:17-18 read:

> (John 10:17 NIV) The reason my Father loves me is that I lay down my life--only to take it up again.
>
> (John 10:18 NIV) No one takes it from me, but I lay it down of my own accord. I have authority to lay it down and authority to take it up again. This command I received from my Father."

These verses tell us that Jesus would "willingly" give up His life. This is consistent with the statement - "He gave up his spirit", which also implies a willful act. Thus, it is not difficult to accept the statement - "He gave up his spirit", as a literal statement.

5) The four gospel writers: Matthew, Mark, Luke, and John, did not mention all of the same words or events related to the crucifixion of Jesus. However, this is not surprising, since each writer emphasized those words or events, which he considered important to his presentation. Each writer presented a different view of Jesus. The presentations according to some apologists could be characterized, as follows:

Matthew	*presented*	**Jesus,**	**as King of the Jews**.
Mark	*presented*	**Jesus,**	**as a servant of God**.
Luke	*presented*	**Jesus,**	**as the Son of Man**.
John	*presented*	**Jesus,**	**as the Son of God**.

Each of the four writers directed his presentation to a different audience. According to Pastor Jack Hayford of Living Way Ministries, the audiences could be characterized, as follows:

Matthew	*wrote to the*	**Jews**.
Mark	*wrote to the*	**Romans**.
Luke	*wrote to the*	**Greeks**.
John	*wrote to the*	**World**.

With respect to John's gospel, Dr. Merrill F. Unger prefers the wording:

"**John** *wrote to the* **Church**".

(See page 467 of Dr. Unger's book: "Unger's Bible Handbook".)

8) In the same way that Luke did not mention "Mw/Mk Loud-cry-1" or "Offered wine vinegar" and John did not mention "Mw/Mk Loud-cry-1", Matthew, Mark, and Luke may have chosen not to explicitly mention "Jn Said-2" or "Jn Said-3". However, "Mw Loud-cry-2" could be "Mk Loud-cry-3", "Le Loud-cry-4", or "Jn Said-3". "Mk Loud-cry-3" could be "Mw Loud-cry-2", "Le Loud-cry-4", or "Jn Said-3".

9) Exact words are given for "Mw/Mk Loud-cry-1", "Le Loud-cry-4", "Jn Said-2", and "Jn Said-3". While no exact words are given for "Mw Loud-cry-2" and "Mk Loud-cry-3". Nothing occurring in the four gospels precludes the following sequence of events: "Le Said-1", "Mw/Mk Loud-cry-1", "Jn Said-2", "Offered wine vinegar", "Mw Loud-cry-2" (equal to "Mk Loud-cry-3" and "Le Loud-cry-4"), "Jn Said-3", "Breathed last", and finally "Gave up His spirit". This is the order presented in the "Part-4: Last Words and Events table".

10) Nothing occurring in the four gospels specifically declares that these are the final words of Jesus. The sequence of events may imply this. However, there is no such explicit declaration. There can be MANY FINAL WORDS, as the number of words in "FINAL WORDS" is relative. On the other hand, there is only "ONE FINAL WORD".

Part-3: **Conclusion**

The four gospels written by Matthew, Mark, Luke, and John, present information about the life of Christ. This information includes some of the last words said by Christ and some of the last events, before His death on the cross. However, according to biblical scholars, the four gospels were written to present four different views of Christ to four different audiences. Thus, four gospels are appropriate. In fact, the four different views of Christ to four different audiences", mean that the question about the "consistency" of the four gospels is inappropriate. Worded differently, whether one is talking about each of the four gospels, as a whole, or talking just about some of the last words of Christ, and some of the last events, as Christ died on the cross, there is nothing explicitly or implicitly inconsistent about the four presentations. Therefore, the answer to the question – "Do the four Gospels present in a consistent manner the last words of Christ and the last events, as He died on the cross?", is "Yes!"

Part-4: **Last Words and Events Table**

Writer	Event 1	Event 2	Event 3	Event 4	Event 5	Event 6	Event 7	Event 8
Matthew		Mw/Mk Loud-cry-1 ("Eloi, Eloi, lama sabachthani?")		Offered wine vinegar	Mw Loud-cry-2 ("words not given")			Gave up His spirit
Mark		Mw/Mk Loud-cry-1 ("Eloi, Eloi, lama sabachthani?")		Offered wine vinegar	Mk Loud-cry-3 ("words not given")		Breathed His Last	
Luke	Le Said-1 ("Father, forgive them . . . are doing.")			Offered wine vinegar	Le Loud-cry-4 ("Father, into your hands I commit my spirit.")		Breathed His Last	
John			Jn Said-2 ("I am thirsty.")	Offered wine vinegar		Jn Said-3 ("It is finished.")		Gave up His spirit

Did Jesus claim to be God and/or the Son of God?

Some people, mostly non-Christians, believe that "Jesus never claimed to be God and/or the Son of God." Exactly how this belief originated is unclear. However, those who hold this belief must not have read the Bible for themselves. For clearly, the Bible contains verses that show Jesus did claim to be God and/or the Son of God. Thus, to explicitly answer the question – "Did Jesus claim to be God and/or the Son of God?", this essay is organized in three parts. Part-1 presents some Bible verses that show Jesus did claim to be God and/or the Son of God. Part-2 presents some concluding comments. Part-3 presents some relevant comments.

Part-1: **Bible verses**

Implicitly or explicitly, Bible verses that show Jesus did claim to be God and/or the Son of God, include Matthew 16:13-18, Matthew 26:63-66, Matthew 27:43, Mark 14:61-63, Luke 22:66-71, John 8:50-59, John 19:6-7, John 6:46, John 14:9, John 10:30, and John 10:36. After some comments to provide the setting for each verse or set of verses, the verse or verses will be presented.

---

1) Matthew 16:13-18 is a conversation between Jesus and the disciples about who He was. In the NIV, Matthew 16:13-18 read:

> Matthew 16:[13]When Jesus came to the region of Caesarea Philippi, he asked his disciples, "Who do people say the Son of Man is?" [14]They replied, "Some say John the Baptist; others say Elijah; and still others, Jeremiah or one of the prophets." [15]"But what about you?" he asked. "Who do you say I am?" [16]Simon Peter answered, "You are the Christ, the Son of the living God." [17]Jesus replied, "Blessed are you, Simon son of Jonah, for this was not revealed to you by man, but by my Father in heaven. [18]And I tell you that you are Peter, and on this rock I will build my church, and the gates of Hades will not overcome it.

2) Matthew 26:63-66 is an incident where the Jews set about to kill Jesus, because He claimed to be equal to God. In the NIV, Matthew 26:63-66 read:

> Matthew 26:[63]But Jesus remained silent. The high priest said to him, "I charge you under oath by the living God: Tell us if you are the Christ, the Son of God." [64]"Yes, it is as you say," Jesus replied. "But I say to all of you: In the future you will see the Son of Man sitting at the right hand of the Mighty One and coming on the clouds of heaven." [65]Then the high priest tore his clothes and said, "He has spoken blasphemy! Why do we need any more witnesses? Look, now you have

heard the blasphemy. [66]What do you think?" "He is worthy of death," they answered.

3) Matthew 27:43 is set at the cross, as Jesus is being crucified. In the prior verses, we are told that some, who were passing by the crucifixion, began hurling insults and shaking their heads, at Jesus. Then the chief priests, the teachers of the law, and the elders also began to mock Jesus, by repeating, some comments that Jesus had made about Himself. Matthew 27:43 contains one of those comments. In the NIV, Matthew 27:43 reads:

> Matthew 27:[43]He trusts in God. Let God rescue him now if he wants him, for he said, 'I am the Son of God.'"

4) Mark 14:61-63 occurs after Jesus has been arrested and taken before the "high priest", all the "chief priests", the "elders", and the "teachers of the law". This group is questioning Jesus in an attempt to find a reason to have Him crucified. During this questioning, Jesus responds to a question from the high priest. Mark 14:61-63 represents the exchange between the high priest and Jesus. In the NIV, Mark 14:61-63 read:

> Mark 14:[61]But Jesus remained silent and gave no answer. Again the high priest asked him, "Are you the Christ, the Son of the Blessed One?" [62]"I am," said Jesus. "And you will see the Son of Man sitting at the right hand of the Mighty One and coming on the clouds of heaven." [63]The high priest tore his clothes. "Why do we need any more witnesses?" he asked.

5) Luke 22:66-71 is an incident during one of the several trials that Jesus endured, before His crucifixion. In this particular incident, one of Jesus' prosecutors asked Him about His relationship to God. Jesus' response was recorded in Luke 22:66-71. In the NIV, these verses read:

> Luke 22:[66]At daybreak the council of the elders of the people, both the chief priests and teachers of the law, met together, and Jesus was led before them. [67]"If you are the Christ, " they said, "tell us." Jesus answered, "If I tell you, you will not believe me, [68]and if I asked you, you would not answer. [69]But from now on, the Son of Man will be seated at the right hand of the mighty God." [70]They all asked, "Are you then the Son of God?" He replied, "You are right in saying I am." [71]Then they said, "Why do we need any more testimony? We have heard it from his own lips."

6) John 8:50-59 is another incident where Jesus claimed to be God. This claim occurred while Jesus was conversing with and teaching those in the Temple. In the NIV, John 8:50-59 read:

> John 8:[50]I am not seeking glory for myself; but there is one who seeks it, and he

is the judge. [51]I tell you the truth, if anyone keeps my word, he will never see
death." [52]At this the Jews exclaimed, "Now we know that you are
demon-possessed! Abraham died and so did the prophets, yet you say that if
anyone keeps your word, he will never taste death. [53]Are you greater than our
father Abraham? He died, and so did the prophets. Who do you think you are?"
[54]Jesus replied, "If I glorify myself, my glory means nothing. My Father, whom
you claim as your God, is the one who glorifies me. [55]Though you do not know
him, I know him. If I said I did not, I would be a liar like you, but I do know him
and keep his word. [56]Your father Abraham rejoiced at the thought of seeing my
day; he saw it and was glad." [57]"You are not yet fifty years old," the Jews said to
him, "and you have seen Abraham!" [58]"I tell you the truth," Jesus answered,
"before Abraham was born, I am!" [59]At this, they picked up stones to stone him,
but Jesus hid himself, slipping away from the temple grounds.

John 8:59 indicates that the Jews picked up stones to throw at Jesus, because of His use of the phrase – "I am", in John 8:58. From this reaction of the Jews, we know that they knew that Jesus was making Himself equal to God, the Father. Because God, the Father, had used the phrase – "I am", when Moses asked, "Whom, should he (Moses) say sent him (Moses)?" Reference "Exodus 3:13-15". In the NIV, these verses read:

Exodus 3:[13]Moses said to God, "Suppose I go to the Israelites and say to them, 'The
God of your fathers has sent me to you,' and they ask me, 'What is his name?'
Then what shall I tell them?" [14]God said to Moses, "I AM WHO I AM. This is what
you are to say to the Israelites: 'I AM has sent me to you.'" [15]God also said to
Moses, "Say to the Israelites, 'The LORD, the God of your fathers–the God of
Abraham, the God of Isaac and the God of Jacob–has sent me to you.' This is my
name forever, the name by which I am to be remembered from generation to
generation.

7) John 18:26 through John 19:16 present another incident in which the Jews confirm that they understood Jesus was claiming to be the Son of God. In this incident, Pilate has had Jesus flogged. Then some of Pilate's soldiers made a crown from thorns and placed it on Jesus' head. These soldiers also placed a purple robe on Jesus. Then Pilate had Jesus brought back in front of a crowd of Jews, which included the chief priests and other officials. The chief priests and other officials verbally responded to the reappearance of Jesus. Finally, they convinced Pilate to let Jesus be crucified. The part of this incident that we are the most interested in was recorded in John 19:6-7. In the NIV, these verses read:

John 19:[6]As soon as the chief priests and their officials saw him, they shouted,
"Crucify! Crucify!" But Pilate answered, "You take him and crucify him. As for me,
I find no basis for a charge against him." [7]The Jews insisted, "We have a law, and
according to that law he must die, because he claimed to be the Son of God."

8) On several occasions, people asked Jesus to show them God, the Father, two of Jesus' responses were recorded in John 6:46 and John 14:9. In the NIV, these verses read:

John 6:[46]No one has seen the Father except the one who is from God; only he has seen the Father.

John 14:[9]Jesus answered: "Don't you know me, Philip, even after I have been among you such a long time? Anyone who has seen me has seen the Father. How can you say, 'Show us the Father'?

9) In John 10:30, the Bible recorded that Jesus equated Himself with God. In the NIV, John 10:30 reads:

John 10:[30]I and the Father are one."

10) Clearly, John 10:36 recorded that Jesus claimed to be the Son of God. In the NIV, John 10:36 reads:

John 10:[36]what about the one whom the Father set apart as his very own and sent into the world? Why then do you accuse me of blasphemy because I said, 'I am God's Son'?

Part-2: **Conclusion**

Clearly, the Bible did record Jesus' claims to be "God" and/or "the Son of God". It also recorded these claims, as the reason the Jews wanted Him crucified. Thus, the answer to the topic question – "Did Jesus claim to be God and/or the Son of God?", is "Yes!"

Part-3: **Some relevant comments**

Comments are presented, here in three groups, as follows:

Group-1: It is interesting to note that 2 Corinthians 4:4 indicates, why unbelievers do not believe in the deity of Jesus. This verse reads:

(2 Corinthians 4:4 NIV) The god of this age has blinded the minds of unbelievers, so that they cannot see the light of the gospel of the glory of Christ, who is the image of God.

Group-2: C. S. Lewis authored the book: "Mere Christianity", which may have been published by the MacMillan Publishing Company in 1943. However, my copy is the Harper Collins Edition 2001. On page 52 of this edition, Mr. Lewis said,

> "A man who was merely a man and said the sort of things Jesus said would not be a great moral teacher. He would either be a lunatic—on a level with the man who says he is a poached egg—or else he would be the Devil of Hell. You must make your choice. Either this man was, and is, the Son of God: or else a madman or something worse. You can shut Him up for a fool, you can spit at Him and kill Him as a demon; or you can fall at His feet and call Him Lord and God. But let us not come with any patronising nonsense about His being a great human teacher. He has not left that open to us. He did not intend to."

Other scholars have paraphrased the above quote by saying, "Based on the words and events attributed to Jesus, we must conclude that either 'Jesus was a liar', 'Jesus was a lunatic', or 'Jesus is God, <u>the Son</u>.' We have no other choices."

<u>Group-3</u>: Those who say, "**Jesus never claimed to be the 'Messiah'**", should read Matthew 16:16, Mark 8:29, Luke 9:20, and John 4:25-26. The setting for Mark 8:29 and Luke 9:20, is the same as for the previously mentioned Matthew 16:13-18, which is item-1 of <u>Part-1</u>. More specifically, that setting was that Jesus asked His disciples, "Who do the people say I am?" After His disciples responded, He asked them, "Who do you say I am?" Peter's response is given in Matthew 16:16, Mark 8:29, and Luke 9:20. Once more, Matthew 16:16 has already been presented, as part of item-1 of <u>Part-1</u>. As for Mark 8:29 and Luke 9:20, in the NIV, Jesus' question and Peter's response read, as follows:

> (Mark 8:29 NIV) "But what about you?" he asked. "Who do you say I am?" Peter answered, "You are the Christ."

> (Luke 9:20 NIV) "But what about you?" he asked. "Who do you say I am?" Peter answered, "The Christ of God."

After hearing Peter's response, Jesus did not say no you are wrong. Rather, He told them to not tell anyone. Now, the setting for John 4:25-26 is, as follows:

> "Jesus and some of His disciples were on their way to Galilee. They had to travel through Samaria. Near a town called Sychar, Jesus rested by a well, while His disciples went into the town to buy food. A Samaritan woman came out to draw water from the well. Jesus asked her for a drink of water. This began a conversation between Jesus and this Samaritan woman."

The important part of their conversation was recorded in John 4:25-26. In the KJV and the NIV, these verses read, as follows:

(John 4:25 KJV) The woman saith unto him, I know that **Messias** cometh, which is called Christ: when he is come, he will tell us all things.

(John 4:26 KJV) **Jesus saith unto her, I that speak unto thee am he**.

(John 4:25 NIV) The woman said, "I know that **Messiah**" (called **Christ**) "is coming. When he comes, he will explain everything to us."

(John 4:26 NIV) Then **Jesus declared, "I who speak to you am he."**

Thus, clearly, Jesus knew that He was also the "**Messiah**". In an article in the "Holman Bible Dictionary", author Ralph P. Martin defines the term "Messiah", as follows:

> MESSIAH (Mehs si' uh) Transliteration of Hebrew word meaning, "anointed one" that was translated into Greek as "Christos". See Christ, Christology. Since apostolic times the name "Christ" has become the proper name of Jesus, the Person whom Christians recognize as the God-given Redeemer of Israel and the church's Lord. "Christ" or "Messiah" is therefore a name admirably suited to express both the church's link with Israel through the Old Testament and the faith that sees in Jesus Christ the worldwide scope of the salvation in Him.

What does the phrase – "ability to sin", mean?

(Is the phrase – "ability to **not** sin", meaningful or is it inappropriate?)

These two questions flowed out of two situations:

- *Situation-1*: The phrase – "ability to sin", is used in several essays including the essay: "Did Jesus, the man, have the 'ability to sin' like Adam and Eve?" Most of the other essays, which use the phrase – "ability to sin", were written before this essay and did not provide an explicit meaning for this phrase. Some people might say, "The phrase – 'ability to sin', defines itself." However, this author feels that a couple of very subtle issues are associated with this phrase. These issues need to be dealt with. And the best way is, by developing an explicit definition of the phrase: "ability to sin".

- *Situation-2*: While researching the phrase – "ability to sin" on the Internet, this author came across several web documents, which used both the phrase: "ability to sin" and the phrase: "ability to **not** sin". This author also heard a radio evangelist use both phrases. Thus, it became obvious that not only was an explicit definition needed for the phrase – "ability to sin", but an explicit definition was needed for the phrase: "ability to **not** sin".

To address these two situations via the two topic questions, this essay is organized in four parts. Part-1 presents some introductory comments and definitions. Part-2 presents a discussion of the two phrases: "ability to sin" and "ability to **not** sin". Part-3 presents a discussion of the question: "How does one know that she or he has the ability to do something?" Part-4 presents some concluding comments.

Part-1: **Some introductory comments and definitions**

To present some introductory comments and definitions, Part-1 is organized in five sections. Section-1 presents the introductory comments. Section-2 presents a definition of the word: "ability". Section-3 presents a definition of the word: "sin". Section-4 presents a definition of the phrase: "to sin". Section-5 presents definitions of the two phrases: "ability to sin" and "ability to **not** sin".

Section-1: **Introductory comments**

Several web documents and a radio evangelist used the two phrases – "ability to sin" and "ability to **not** sin", by stating that:

"Adam and Eve were created with both the 'ability to sin' and the 'ability to **not** sin'. However, when Adam and Eve chose to sin, they lost the 'ability to **not** sin'. Therefore, they were left with only the 'ability to sin', which they passed on to the rest of us."

Some additional comments about the radio evangelist's use of the two phrases, are presented in Part-2. Meanwhile, we must note that the fact that someone – scholar, radio evangelist, author, or whomever – uses the phrase – "ability to **not** sin", does not automatically mean that the phrase is appropriate. Determining the appropriateness of this phrase is one of the objectives of this essay. As previously indicated, other objectives include defining the two phrases: "ability to sin" and "ability to **not** sin". Once more to move toward these objectives, Section-2 through Section-5 of Part-1, serve to define the crucial words – "ability" and "sin", and to define the three phrases: "to sin", "ability to sin", and "ability to **not** sin".

Section-2: **A definition of the word: "ability"**

The word – "ability", is defined by *Wiktionary*, as follows:

> "The quality or state of being able; power to perform, whether physical, moral, intellectual, conventional, or legal; capacity; skill or competence in doing; sufficiency of strength, skill, resources, etc.; – in the *plural*, faculty, talent."[52]

To personalize the previous definition, our working definition of the word – "ability" will be:

> "An individual has the necessary physical, mental, and spiritual attributes that would allow that individual to do something".

Section-3: **A definition of the word: "sin"**

The word – "sin", is defined by author Billy E. Simmons in the "Holman Bible Dictionary", as follows:

> "Sin" is "actions by which humans rebel against God, miss His purpose for their life, and surrender to the power of evil rather than to God."

Consistent with this definition, many Christians define "sin" as "missing the mark". However, this definition and author Simmons' definition define "sin", as "a result". This author prefers to define the word – "sin", as it relates directly to God. Such a definition might read, as follows:

> "Sin" is "a freewill thought, word, and/or deed, which is contrary to God's will".

This definition defines "sin" as "an event" and will be used, as the working definition of the word – "sin", for this essay and book.

Section-4: **A definition of the phrase: "to sin"**

The phrase – "to sin", is defined as the action form of our working definition of the word – "sin", from Section-3. Thus, the phrase – "to sin", is defined, as follows:

> "To sin" is "to freely choose a thought, word, and/or deed, which is contrary to God's will".

However, this definition is really only appropriate for "sins of commission (*sins, which occur, because we do unGodly things – here, the emphasis is on 'doing the unGodly things'*)". A slightly different variation of this definition is needed for "sins of omission (*sins, which occur, because we fail to do Godly things – here, the emphasis is on 'not doing Godly things, when such things are needed or are appropriate.*)". This variation is defined, as follows:

> "To sin" is "to freely fail to choose a thought, word, and/or deed, which is not contrary to God's will, when such a thought, word, and/or deed are/is needed or are/is appropriate".

With regards to both variations of the definitions of the phrase – "To sin", the "choosing" or the "failing to choose" might be done in "ignorance (*unintentional*)" or might be done with "forethought (*intentional*)". Thus, both variations could more precisely be worded, as follows:

- "To sin" is "to freely choose – *in ignorance or with forethought* – a thought, word, and/or deed, which is contrary to God's will".

- "To sin" is "to freely fail to choose – *in ignorance or with forethought* – a thought, word, and/or deed, which is not contrary to God's will, when such a thought, word, and/or deed are/is needed or are/is appropriate".

These two variations will be the working definitions of the phrase – "to sin", for this essay and book.

Section-5: **A definition of the phrases: "ability to sin" and "ability to not sin"**

Based on Section-2 through Section-4, a clearer sense of the meaning of the two phrases – "ability to sin" and "ability to **not** sin", is indicated by replacing the phrases – "to sin" and "to **not** sin", in each phrase with an appropriate variation of the definition of the phrase: "to sin". Furthermore, for this essay and book, the phrases – "to **not** sin" and "**not** to sin", will be treated as equals (*as synonyms*). Therefore, the phrases – "ability to **not** sin" and "ability **not** to sin", will be treated as equals (*as synonyms*). Thus,

- "ability to sin" *becomes* "ability to **freely** choose – *in ignorance or with forethought* – a thought, word, and/or deed, which is contrary to God's will" *and* "ability to **freely** fail to choose – *in ignorance or with forethought* – a thought, word, and/or deed, which is not contrary to God's will, when such a thought, word, and/or deed are/is needed or are/is appropriate".

- "ability to **not** sin" *becomes* "ability to **not freely** choose – *in ignorance or with forethought* – a thought, word, and/or deed, which is contrary to God's will"

and "ability to **not freely** fail to choose – *in ignorance or with forethought* – a thought, word, and/or deed, which is not contrary to God's will, when such a thought, word, and/or deed are/is needed or are/is appropriate".

Then by inserting the definition of the word – "ability" from Section-2, into the two previous statements,

- "ability to sin" *becomes* "an individual has the necessary physical, mental, and spiritual attributes that would allow that individual to **freely** choose – *in ignorance or with forethought* – a thought, word, and/or deed, which is contrary to God's will"

and "an individual has the necessary physical, mental, and spiritual attributes that would allow that individual to **freely** fail to choose – *in ignorance or with forethought* – a thought, word, and/or deed, which is not contrary to God's will, when such a thought, word, and/or deed are/is needed or are/is appropriate".

- "ability to **not** sin" *becomes* "an individual has the necessary physical, mental, and spiritual attributes that would allow that individual to **not freely** choose – *in ignorance or with forethought* – a thought, word, and/or deed, which is contrary to God's will"

and "an individual has the necessary physical, mental, and spiritual attributes that would allow that individual to **not freely** fail to choose – *in ignorance or with forethought* – a thought, word, and/or deed, which is not contrary to God's will, when such a thought, word, and/or deed are/is needed or are/is appropriate".

The two latter statements will be the working definitions of the phrases – "ability to sin" and "ability to **not** sin", for this essay and book.

Part-2: **The phrases: "ability to sin" and "ability to not sin"**

As previously mentioned, during a recent radio program, the phrases – "ability to sin" and "ability to **not** sin", were discussed by a radio evangelist. This evangelist also indicated that in the past, religious scholars explained the capacity for "being a sinner" and for "being sinless", using the two phrases: "ability to sin" and "ability to **not** sin". However, this author has a problem with using these two phrases to explain anything, because the two phrases – "ability to sin" and "ability to **not** sin", were not defined, by the radio evangelist. Whether the radio evangelist and past religious scholars would agree with the definitions of these two phrases in Part-1/Section-5, is unknown to this author. But this author would say that they must be using different definitions, because of the implications of their usage, which is that the "ability to **not** sin" was a one-time event (*i.e., once Adam and Eve sinned, the "ability to **not** sin" was lost forever in time*). For this author, another issue is "How would this radio evangelist and past religious scholars relate the two phrases to the concept of 'free will'?" Nevertheless, it is possible that this author has misunderstood the use of the two phrases. However, if it is true that the intended use by the radio evangelist and past scholars requires wording like the following:

> "Adam and Eve were created or began their existence with both the 'ability to sin' and the 'ability to **not** sin'. But they lost the 'ability to **not** sin', when they exercised their 'ability to sin' by choosing to sin."

Then this author has a problem with this intended use of especially the phrase: "ability to **not** sin". The reasoning for this could go, as follows:

- The Bible indicates that Adam and Eve were created with "free will", which is the "ability to make choices, based on one's own wants, needs, and/or desires".

- However, "free will" can be defined with words similar to those used to define the phrase: "ability to sin". Such a definition might read, as follows:

  "Free will" is "the ability to freely choose a thought, a word, or a deed".

  Comment: Implicit in this definition is the fact that an individual can only choose from what she or he perceives as the available choices.

- The concept of "sin" requires the existence of "free will" and the existence of "good (*Godly*) and evil (*unGodly*) choices", because "to sin" means "to 'freely choose' an 'evil choice' instead of a 'good choice'". (*Obviously, the words – "Godly" and "unGodly", serve to emphasize that "good choices" are consisted with God's will and "evil choices" are not.*)

- The concept of "free will", can exist without or with the concept of "sin" *(which includes the "ability to sin")*. But as previously indicated, the concept of "sin" cannot exist without the concept of "free will". More specifically, one could have "free will", but there only be Godly choices available, which was the case for Adam and Eve, before the tempting by Satan. That is, Adam and Eve had the "free will" to select fruits to eat from the many allowable trees, and to observe God's request not to eat the fruit from the forbidden tree.

- The previous point could be worded differently as: "While the phrases – 'ability to sin' and 'ability to **not** sin', are only meaningful in the context of 'free will' and 'good and evil choices', we note that Adam and Eve began their existence with 'free will' and many 'good choices', which were to eat any of the allowable fruits and '*not to eat the forbidden fruit*'. Then when Satan tempted them, they gained the knowledge of an 'evil choice', which was '*to eat the forbidden fruit*'. Consequently, the phrases – 'ability to sin' and 'ability to **not** sin', would only be meaningful once Satan told Adam and Eve that they could eat some of the fruit of the tree of the knowledge of good and evil. In fact, for Adam and Eve when Satan told them that they could eat the forbidden fruit, it was probably like what some comedians call an '*Ah-moment*', which is that moment when someone realizes that **something can be done** or that **there is another way to do something**."

Based on the previous reasoning and everything else presented to this point, this author would have no problem with the phrase: "ability to sin". As long as it is understood, the phrase – "ability to sin", is only meaningful in the context of "free will" and "good and evil" choices. However, the phrase – "ability to **not** sin", seems inappropriate for, at least, three reasons:

- *Reason-1*: The expanded definition of the phrase – "ability to **not** sin", from Part-1/Section-5 contains the phrases – "to **not** freely choose" and "to **not** freely fail to choose". Both of these phrases imply a "robotic" situation, not a "freewill" situation.

  Comment: A proofreader responded to *Reason-1*, with the comment that there is clearly a difference between the phrase: "to **not** freely choose" and the phrase: "to freely **not** choose". For this author's response, see endnote[53].

- *Reason-2*: The use of the two phrases by a radio evangelist and some scholars implies that Adam and Eve were created with both the "ability to sin" and "ability to **not** sin". If this was true, the implication is that it would be like Adam and Eve being created with two switches: an "ability-to-sin" switch and an "ability-to-**not**-sin" switch. To begin with, both were in the "on" position. Then when Adam and Eve sinned the "ability-to-**not**-sin" switch would have changed to the "off" position. Thus, the implication is that the "ability to **not** sin" was lost forever. However, a reality of the Christian life is, as follows:

  "While all humans, except Adam, Eve, and Jesus, were/are/will be born sinners, with the aid of God, the Holy Spirit, there are moments, when many individuals are able "to not exercise their 'ability to sin'". These are moments, when individuals flee from temptation. Thus, while some might say that 'not exercising the ability to sin', is not the same, as the 'ability to **not** sin', this author would say that the effects or the results are the same – at least for that moment."

Thus, if the "ability to **not** sin", is a valid ability, then along with the "ability to sin", it would be an ongoing ability, experienced, by many. Actually, the "ability to **not** sin", could only be a valid ability in the sense of "not exercising one's 'ability to sin'".

- *Reason-3*: Another way to word *Reason-2* is "The two phrases are not opposites like 'on' and 'off'. We can say this because the 'ability to sin' allows for those instances 'when an individual sins' and 'when an individual does **not** sin' – (*this latter situation is just an individual not exercising her or his 'ability to sin'*). However, the way that past scholars and the radio evangelist used the phrase – 'ability to **not** sin', this phrase does not allow for those instances 'when an individual sins'. As used by the radio evangelist, this phrase only allows for 'not sinning'. And that is why the two phrases are not opposites. Therefore, because the phrase – 'ability to sin' covers both the 'sinning' and the 'not sinning', the phrase – 'ability to **not** sin', is not needed and only unnecessarily complicates a discussion of the 'ability to sin'."

In summary, with regards to the phrases – "ability to sin" and "ability to **not** sin", this author would summarize Part-2, as follows:

- "Adam and Eve were created with 'free will'. They were not created with either the 'ability to sin' or the 'ability to **not** sin'. They gained the 'ability to sin', after God and Satan presented them with a good choice and an evil choice."

- "By definition, the phrase – 'ability to **not** sin', is inappropriate under the existence of the concept of 'free will', because it implies a robotic situation (*a non-freewill situation*)."

Part-3: **How does one know that she or he has the ability to do something?**

This question is important to any discussion of the phrase: "ability to sin". And it seems to have two answers:

- *Answer-1*: One way to know that you have an ability is "to exercise" or "to display" that ability or the fruits of it.

  Comment: With regards to "the ability to sin", *Answer-1* is represented, by "Adam and Eve", because they exercised their "ability to sin" by sinning. More specifically, God gave Adam and Eve a Godly choice, which was to eat any fruit except the forbidden fruit, and then later, Satan gave them an unGodly choice, which was eating some of the forbidden fruit. Then Adam and Eve chose to exercise their "ability to sin", by exercising the unGodly choice.

- *Answer-2*: Another way to know that you have an ability is by a comparison with someone, who displays that ability. The comparison would only need to show that you possess the same or similar, physical, mental, and spiritual attributes, as someone, who has displayed the ability. For example, every driver should be aware of the fact that they have the "ability to kill someone with their automobile", because other drivers have already done so. Or perhaps a better example is that most females beyond puberty, believe that they have the "ability to have a baby", because they are a female.

  Comment: With regards to "the ability to sin", *Answer-2* is represented, by Jesus, the man, when He is compared with "Adam and Eve", who exercised their "ability to sin" by sinning. More specifically, Adam and Eve, were *created "sinless" and with "free will"*. Jesus, the man, was *born "sinless" and with "free will"*. Clearly, Adam, Eve, and Jesus, the man, were all fully human. Adam and Eve exercised their "ability to sin" by sinning. Thus, a comparison with Adam and Eve would indicate that Jesus, the man, had the "ability to sin". But note that having the "ability to sin" or to do anything, especially under this comparison mode, does not mean that the individual has to exercise or to display that ability.

Part-4: **Some concluding comments**

As mentioned before, this essay served to provide this author with an opportunity to review, to present, and to discuss some subtle issues, with regards to the phrase: "ability to sin". In the process, the two phrases – "ability to sin" and "ability to **not** sin", were defined. This essay also served to propose that both phrases were only relevant in the context of "free will" and "good and evil choices". More specifically, the proposal is that while "Adam and Eve were created with 'free will', they were not created with either the 'ability to sin' or the 'ability to **not** sin', because 'sin' is only relevant in the context of 'free will' and 'good and evil choices'. And they did not have both choices to begin with."

Thus, once more, the question – "What does the phrase – 'ability to sin', mean?" was answered by defining that phrase. Then the answer to the question – "Is the phrase – 'ability to **not** sin', meaningful or is it inappropriate?", was determined to be that "the phrase is inappropriate", because it is incompatible with the concept of "free will".

What do the three phrases – "knowledge of good and evil", "knowledge of good", and "knowledge of evil", mean?

and

What is "the age of accountability"?

These two questions flowed out of two situations:

- *Situation-1*: The three phrases – "knowledge of good and evil", "knowledge of good", and "knowledge of evil", are used in several essays in this book. Those essays provide only a superficial meaning for the three phrases, if any meaning is presented at all. This fact was mentioned by a proofreader of the fourth edition of this book. This particular proofreader also presented a strong argument against the implied meanings of the three phrases, especially as presented in a previous version of the essay: "Did Jesus, the man, have the 'ability to sin' like Adam and Eve?" The proofreader's argument made this author pray and ponder about the implied meanings of the three phrases.

- *Situation-2*: While reasoning through meanings for each of the three phrases, the logical and biblical credibility of the concept of "the age of accountability" – also called "the age of reason" – was noticed. Thus, developing a meaning for the concept of "the age of accountability" became apparent.

To address these two situations via the two topic questions, this essay is organized in seven parts. Part-1 presents definitions of some words and phrases, which are relevant to a discussion of the topic questions. Part-2 presents a discussion of the meaning of the phrase: "knowledge of good and evil". Part-3 presents a discussion of the meaning of the phrase: "knowledge of good". Part-4 presents a discussion of the meaning of the phrase: "knowledge of evil". Part-5 presents a discussion of the meaning of the concept: "the age of accountability". Part-6 presents some concluding comments. Part-7 presents some relevant comments.

Part-1: **Some relevant definitions**

Definitions, which are relevant to a discussion of the topic questions, are presented in six sections. Section-1 begins the process of defining the words: "good" and "evil". Section-2 presents a definition of the word: "awareness". Section-3 presents a definition of the phrase: "sphere of awareness". Section-4 presents a definition of the word: "focus". Section-5 presents definitions of the phrases – "outward focus" and "inward focus" and completes the process of defining the words: "good" and "evil". Section-6 presents definitions of the phrases: "a reactive mode" and "an interactive mode".

Section-1: **The words: "good" and "evil"**

Most Christians would probably agree that the word – "good" takes its definition from the attributes of God and/or God, Himself, because God is the "ultimate good". And the word – "evil" is the antonym (*opposite in meaning*) of the word: "good". Thus, Satan, who is God's opposite with regards to the attribute "good", is the "ultimate evil". However, not all dictionaries relate the word – "good" to the attributes of God. In fact, one dictionary indicates that both the words – "evil" and "sin" are antonyms for the word – "good". This author disagrees with that indication, because there is a difference between "evil" and "sin". One difference is recognizable from the definition of the word – "sin" in the essay: "*What does the phrase – 'ability to sin', mean? (Is the phrase – 'ability to not sin', meaningful or is it inappropriate?)*" That definition reads:

"Sin" is "a freewill thought, word, and/or deed, which is contrary to God's will".

Based on this definition, the word – "sin" is only indirectly defined by the attributes of God, while the word – "good" is directly defined by the attributes of God and the word – "evil" would be the opposite of "good". Thus, the words – "good" and "evil" are qualities, while the word – "sin" is not a quality. "Sin" is an event. Or worded differently, for the word – "good" to be the antonym of the word – "sin", we would have to use a definition like:

"Good" is "a freewill thought, word, and/or deed, which is not contrary to God's will".

Basically, this would be defining the word – "good" as an event, not a quality.

Even though the basic definitions of the words – "good" and "evil", are best defined in terms of God and Satan, another aspect, which is important to the definitions of these two words, is an individual's focus. Either an individual is "focused on God" or an individual is "focused on herself or himself". Consequently, the working definitions of the words – "good" and "evil" for this essay and book, will be explicitly presented in Part-1/Section-5 (*titled: The phrases – "outward focus" and "inward focus" and the words: "good" and "evil"*).

Section-2: **The word: "awareness"**

A definition of the word – "awareness", flows from the reality that most people are born with "a brain", "a mind", and "five senses: 'hearing', 'smelling', 'seeing', 'tasting', 'touching'[54]". However, due to birth defects, some individuals are born with some kind of brain damage (*which impacts their mind*) and/or with some degree of disability with one or more of their five senses. Some individuals are also born with what some call – "a sixth sense", which is "the ability to perceive information about something, some individual, and/or whatever, with a sense other than the five previously mentioned".

To provide a sense of how the "brain" and "mind" might be related, there is a neat computer analogy, which comes to mind, because of Dr. Walter Martin, who was the founder of the Christian Research Institute and the "Bible Answerman" radio program. On Dr. Martin's audiotape – "Evil and Human Suffering"[1], he explains "God's sovereignty" and"our 'free will'" using a computer analogy. This explanation is the best explanation of "God's sovereignty" and "our 'free will'" that this author has ever heard. Nevertheless, a similar computer analogy can be use to explain the relationship between our "brain" and our "mind". Such an explanation might read, as follows:

- Our "brain" is like a living computer stored in our head. More specifically, our "brain" is like the central processor (*for processing input via a computer program*) and the memory chips (*for the storage of instructions, data, etc.*) of a computer. Thus, for most of us, this living computer is wired to all of our senses, in order to receive signals from those senses. This living computer is also wired to most of the other components (*muscles, organs, etc.*) of our "body" in order to receive and to transmit signals to those components.

- Our "mind" is like a computer program running in the living computer. This computer program interprets signals from our senses and from the other components of our body. As this computer program interprets those signals, it determines – *it computes* – an emotional and/or unemotional response (*"thought(s)", "word(s)", and/or "deed(s) [an action, which is reactive or interactive]"*) for each signal. Then it transmits the required signals to the various components of the body in its effort to accomplish its determined response. This computer program also stores information in the memory chips. Some information is "feedback" from the various components of the body. This "feedback" information can then be used by the "mind" to analyze past "stimulus-response" situations, in order to possibly modify present and/or future "stimulus-response" situations.

As babies, our "feedback" database used by our mind is not that extensive. Thus, babies begin to perceive the world around them using their senses, but they react in more of a "reactive mode" than an "interactive mode". (*These modes will be discussed in greater detail later in this essay.*) However, as we grow toward adulthood, our "feedback" database expands and our "minds" may start overriding our senses and/or modifying how our senses perceive something or someone. Therefore, for this essay and book, the word – "awareness" will be defined, as follows:

> "Awareness" is "our mind sensing the physical, logical, spiritual, and/or emotional characteristics of something or something's, which could be beings, things, concepts, events, processes, etc., and/or any combination of these."

Thus, that something can be concrete (*like the material things of this world*) and/or abstract (*like love, hate, jealousy, etc.*).

---

[1] Dr. Martin has gone home to be with the Lord. But he left us with some excellent audiotapes. Some of these audiotapes might be available via website www.waltermartin.org.

Section-3: **The phrase: "sphere of awareness"**

A definition of the phrase – "sphere of awareness", is derived from the fact that there is a range, within which each of our senses functions. For instance, we see as far as environmental circumstances and the condition of our eyes allow. We hear those sounds that are within our audio frequency range and that enters our ears and/or that cause our bodies to vibrate, from whatever distance. We taste whatever we put in our mouth and/or put our tongue on. We smell odors, aromas, and/or fragrance that enter our noses from close up and/or from miles away. Under normal circumstances, we can touch – can feel – most things or people that are within the length of our arms and/or in direct contact with our body. Thus, the collective ranges of our senses, is our "sphere of awareness". Furthermore, each individual's "sphere of awareness" is not only influenced by "her or his senses", but it is also influenced by where the individual is in terms of "her or his development from a baby into an adult", by "her or his mind", and/or by "her or his circumstances (*environment, culture, health, family situation, religious beliefs, gender, and so on*)".

In passing, we also need to remember that God created each of us with "free will". Thus, each individual is born with some degree of "free will" within her or his "sphere of awareness". However, once more, her or his "free will" is influenced by "her or his senses" and where the individual is in terms of "her or his development from a baby into an adult", "her or his mind", and/or "her or his circumstances". That is, each individual is able to make "free will" choices – to make "good or evil" choices – based on "her or his senses" and where the individual is in terms of "her or his development from a baby into an adult", on "her or his mind", and/or on "her or his circumstances". Furthermore, God created human babies such that they need the most and among the longest care, when compared with the babies of other species. Nevertheless like the babies of other species, human babies begin life merely reacting to the basic needs of food, water, and comfort and to the basic need to release internal waste. Or worded differently, human babies do not appear to be fully aware of everything and/or every individual in their environment, but they merely react more obviously to some things and/or some individuals more than to others in their immediate environment, because of their basic needs. Therefore at first, a new born baby may appear to be focused on herself or himself, because its "sphere of awareness" is empty. She or he is merely "reacting" to its immediate environment and those in it, because of her or his basic needs. However normally, as a baby grows into adulthood, her or his "sphere of awareness" will expand. Generally, the first expansion might be the inclusion of itself to some extent. The next expansion would probably include, whoever is feeding her or him, on an ongoing basis. Another expansion would probably include those with whom she or he has an ongoing contact with, which could possibly be other family members. Thus in time, her or his sphere will expand to include more and more of those individuals within range of her or his senses. Furthermore with time, she or he will begin to "interact" with those things and individuals within her or his "sphere of awareness", instead of merely "reacting". Consequently, for this essay and book, the definition of the phrase – "sphere of awareness", will be, as follows:

An individual's "sphere of awareness" is "the 'extent' of those beings, things, concepts, events, process, and/or any combination of these, perceived directly or indirectly by her or his senses."

This "extent" may be expanded or influenced by where the individual is in terms of "her or his development from a baby into an adult", by "her or his mind", and/or by "her or his circumstances (*environment, culture, health, family situation, religious beliefs, gender, and so on*)". However, please note that this definition is not meant to imply that everything, which is in the individual's "sphere of awareness", whether living or nonliving things, is noticed. It only means that those unnoticed living and/or nonliving things could be noticed if those things were the objects of an individual's focus.

Section-4: **The word: "focus"**

A definition of the word – "focus" flows from the fact that normally our senses – especially, sight – are "directed at" and/or are "detecting" one or more specific things and/or one or more specific individuals. Thus, this essay and book will use one of the definitions of the word – "focus", from *Wiktionary*. That definition reads, as follows:

"Focus" is "a concentration of attention."

Section-5: **The phrases – "outward focus" and "inward focus" and the words: "good" and "evil"**

The definitions of the words – "good" and "evil" must be preceded by the definitions of the phrases: "outward focus" and "inward focus". The definitions of these two phrases flow from the observation that God appears to have designed man, such that man has a bend toward an "inward focus". Because as individuals grow from babies to adults, that growth process reinforces the tendency of each individual to feel that the world revolves around them. The development of this feeling should be obvious, when you note that each individual uses their own senses to define their "sphere of awareness". God probably created Adam and Eve as adults, so they missed this feeling. Nevertheless, the bend of this growth process is probably why God designed the family, such that one of the primary jobs of an individual's parents is to teach her or him that the world does not revolve around her or him. Another important job of an individual's parents is to teach her or him to submit to authority. This submission includes the parents' authority, God's authority, and the authority of the civil leaders. With these comments in mind, to present definitions of the phrases – "outward focus" and "inward focus", and to complete the process of defining the words – "good" and "evil", Section-5 is organized in three segments. *Segment-1* presents a definition of the phrase: "an outward focus". *Segment-2* presents a definition of the phrase: "an inward focus". *Segment-3* completes the process of defining the words: "good" and "evil".

Segment-1: **An outward focus**

For this essay and book, an "outward focus" is defined, as follows:

An "outward focus" is defined as those times "when an individual is focused outward *'away from herself or himself'.*"

That is, an individual's mind has her or his "focus and senses" directed outward to interpret the living and/or nonliving things in the individual's "sphere of awareness", without regards to any personal benefit from those perceptions. More specifically, an individual's mind has her or his "focus and senses" directed outward for any hint of God. Thus, under an "outward focus", the phrase – "the knowledge of good and evil", can be replaced with the phrase – "the knowledge of God and Satan", because "God is the ultimate good" and "Satan is the ultimate evil."

With regards to Adam, the Bible indicates that Adam had "knowledge of God", because he walked and talked with God. Eve also had a "knowledge of God", because the Bible indicates that she knew about not eating the fruit from the tree of the knowledge of good and evil. We also know that Adam and Eve had "knowledge of Satan", because Satan, who was in the form of a serpent, tempted Eve. Then Satan tempted Adam through Eve. Satan's tempting caused Adam and Eve to change their focus from being outward *"on God"* to being inward *"on themselves"*.

In passing, it is interesting to note that Satan talked Adam and Eve into sinning against God – into disobeying God's only request to them. But Satan only suggested that they would be "like God, 'knowing good and evil'". More specifically, there is no hint that Satan suggested they would become God's equal in every way. However, "before Adam and Eve sinned" and "without enticement from anyone else", Satan rebelled against God and wanted to be God's equal or superior. This is another justification for labeling Satan, the "ultimate evil".

Segment-2: **An inward focus**

For this essay and book, an "inward focus" is defined, as follows:

An "inward focus" is defined as those times "when an individual is focused inward *'on herself or himself'.*"

That is, an individual's mind has her or his "focus and senses" directed outward to interpret the living and/or nonliving things in the individual's "sphere of awareness", for any hint of personal benefits from those perceptions. More specifically, an individual's mind has her or his "focus and senses" directed outward for any hint of anything, which might satisfy "'the lust of the flesh', 'the lust of the eyes', and/or 'the pride of life'"[2]. This means that an individual is noticing those things, which are good choices (Godly choices), and those things, which are evil choices

---

[2] See entry titled – "The meaning of each of the phrases – 'lust of the flesh', 'lust of the eyes', and 'pride of life'" in Appendix A.

(unGodly choices). Thus, under an "inward focus", the phrase – "the knowledge of good and evil", can be replaced with the phrase – "the knowledge of Godly choices and unGodly choices", because when an individual is focused inward, that individual has the "free will" to choose good or evil thoughts, words, and/or deeds.

With regards to Adam, the Bible indicates that Adam and Eve began their existence under God's grace in the Garden of Eden. At first, Adam and Eve were focused on God, not on themselves – they were focused outward. They only knew that which was consistent with God's will. Even when God told Adam that he could eat any fruit in the garden except the fruit of the "tree of the 'knowledge of good and evil'", Adam and Eve only knew that which was consistent with God's will. But the important thing here, is to note that God told Adam about a "good choice", which was *"to eat any fruit except the forbidden fruit"*. Then Satan came along. And he tempted Eve. He told her about an "evil choice", which was *"to eat the forbidden fruit"*. When Eve and Adam, succumbed to Satan's tempting, they chose the "evil choice" and ate of the forbidden fruit. They chose to sin and their sinning meant that they had changed their focus from God to themselves. In other words, Adam and Eve changed their focus from being outward (*on God*) to being inward (*on themselves*). This is confirmed by Adam and Eve realizing that they were naked. God showed His unhappiness with the sin of Adam and Eve by removing them from an existence under His grace in the Garden of Eden, to an existence under His judgment in the world. In the world, Eve suffered the pains of child birth and Adam suffered the toil of getting their daily bread.

Segment-3: **The words: "good" and "evil"**

Definitions of the words – "good" and "evil", are formed around "God and Satan" and around "the focus of each individual". Thus, as previously indicated, we can say, "When an individual is focused outward, the 'knowledge of good and evil' is about 'God and Satan'. When an individual is focused inward, the 'knowledge of good and evil' is about 'Godly choices and unGodly choices'." Therefore, we can define the words – "good" and "evil", as follows:

"If an individual is focused outward,

'good' **is** **'God'** and **'evil'** **is** **'Satan'**.

If an individual is focused inward,

'good' **is** **'Godly choices'** and **'evil'** **is** **'unGodly choices'**."

Section-6: **The phrases: "a reactive mode" and "an interactive mode"**

Definitions of the phrases – "a reactive mode" and "an interactive mode", flow from the observation that God created the living things of this world such that most newborns of all species enter their environment in "a reactive mode". For humans as we grow and gain in experience and knowledge, our mode begins to include "an interactive mode". In fact, as we mature, our minds allow us to "react" and/or "interact" with the things or people within our "sphere of awareness". In time, the way that we "interact with" or "react to" something can be changed by our mind's perception of something else. This includes our mind's ability, at times, to override our senses or to modify the perception of our senses. With these comments in mind and to present a definition of the phrases – "reactive mode" and "interactive mode", Section-6 is organized in two segments. *Segment-1* presents a definition of the phrase: "a reactive mode". *Segment-2* presents a definition of the phrase: "an interactive mode".

Segment-1: **A reactive mode**

The definition of a "reactive mode" is defined, as follows:

> A "reactive mode" *is* "the reaction mode under which an individual merely 'reacts' to those beings, things, concepts, events, and/or processes in her or his 'sphere of awareness'."

Under this "reaction mode", the reaction to those beings, things, concepts, events, and/or processes in her or his "sphere of awareness" is not selective. That is, there may be multiple beings, things, concepts, events, and/or processes in her or his "sphere of awareness", but her or his attention is generally directed at only one being, thing, and/or process at a time, because "of her or his basic needs" and/or because "that being, thing, and/or process drew her or his focus".

Segment-2: **An interactive mode**

The definition of an "interactive mode" is defined, as follows:

> An "interactive mode" *is* "the reaction mode under which an individual 'interacts' with those beings, things, concepts, events, and/or processes in her or his 'sphere of awareness'".

Under this "interaction mode", the reaction to those beings, things, concepts, events, and/or processes in her or his "sphere of awareness" may be selective and/or may be influenced by her or his mind.

Part-2: **The meaning of the phrase: "knowledge of good and evil"**

The phrase – "knowledge of good and evil", is used in Genesis 2:9 and Genesis 2:17. Genesis 2:9 reads:

> (Genesis 2:9 NIV) And the LORD God made all kinds of trees grow out of the ground--trees that were pleasing to the eye and good for food. In the middle of the garden were the tree of life and the tree of the knowledge of good and evil.

And Genesis 2:17 reads:

(Genesis 2:17 NIV) but you must not eat from the tree of the knowledge of good and evil, for when you eat of it you will surely die."

Based on Genesis 2:9 and Genesis 2:17, the phrase – "knowledge of good and evil", is being used as part of the name for a particular tree in the Garden of Eden. This raises the question: "Why did God name this particular tree the 'tree of the knowledge of good and evil'?" An answer can be derived from the Bible, by noting two things:

- *First*, God named individuals, events, places, and/or things to convey a specific meaning or for a specific reason. More specifically, individuals were named to reflect their character, to reflect what God would accomplish through their life, and/or to reflect something else that God intended. For example, God told Moses that He (God) was to be referenced by the name: "I AM". Events, places, and/or things were named to reflect their use or to memorialize how God used those events, places, and/or things, as He dealt with people, especially, His chosen people.

- *Second*, God directly or indirectly "told certain Jews" or "inspired certain Jews" to use specific names for their children, events, places, and/or things. The names conveyed God's intent, specific meanings, and/or memorialized something for that generation and/or for future generations. For example, God sent an angel to tell Mary that she was "with child" and that she should name the child, Jesus, because He would save His people from their sins.

Therefore, a name was more than just a simple label. Once more, in many incidences, a name conveyed God's actual and/or intended use for an individual, event, place, and/or thing. Consequently, we can assume that when God named a particular tree, the "tree of the knowledge of good and evil", He was telling us that particular tree would be involved in Adam and Eve displaying the fact that they had gained the "knowledge of good and evil".

To develop a Biblical sense of the meaning of the phrase – "knowledge of good and evil", three things will be discussed: *first*, two possible meanings of the phrase: "knowledge of good and evil"; *second*, the question: "How does an individual's focus relate to the phrase: 'knowledge of good and evil'?"; and *third*, the question: "When did Adam and Eve gain the 'knowledge of good and evil'?" To discuss these three things, the rest of Part-2 is organized in three sections. Section-1 presents two possible meanings of the phrase: "knowledge of good and evil". Section-2 presents a discussion of the question: "How does an individual's focus relate to the phrase: 'knowledge of good and evil'?" Section-3 presents a discussion of the question: "When did Adam and Eve gain the 'knowledge of good and evil'?"

Section-1: **Two possible meanings of the phrase: "knowledge of good and evil"**

The phrase – "the knowledge of good and evil" has, at least, two possible meanings: "a literal meaning (*a direct meaning*)" and "an interpreted meaning (*an indirect meaning*)". The literal meaning results from taking the words of the phrase at face value. Thus, this meaning is "knowing good and evil". The interpreted meaning results from developing an interpretation of the phrase. Thus, this meaning is "knowing the difference between good and evil". However, these two meanings are really the flip-sides of the same coin, because in order for an individual to know the "difference" between good and evil, that individual must "know what good is" and "know what evil is". The phrases – "know what good is" and "know what evil is", can be reworded as the phrases: *"knowledge of good"* and *"knowledge of evil"*. Furthermore, modern English grammar allows the formation of the two phrases – *"knowledge of good"* and *"knowledge of evil"*, from the phrase – "knowledge of good and evil", because of the conjunction: "and". Whether biblical Hebrew (*classical Hebrew*) allows, the same formation is unknown to this author. However, for the two phrases – *"knowledge of good"* and *"knowledge of evil"*, to convey the previously mentioned direct meaning of the phrase – "the knowledge of good and evil", the two phrases must be used together, in the form: "*'knowledge of good'* and *'knowledge of evil'*".

Section-2: **How does an individual's focus relate to the phrase: "knowledge of good and evil"?**

This question flows out of the fact that for each individual, there are two ways "to focus her or his attention". There are two ways "to focus her or his five senses" and/or "to focus her or his mind": an "outward focus (*a non-personalizing process*)" and an "inward focus (*a personalizing process*)". Actually, this question was answered by Part-1/Section-4 and by Part-1/Section-5. To summarize that answer, we can say, "When an individual is focused outward, the 'knowledge of good and evil' is 'about God and Satan'. When an individual is focused inward, the 'knowledge of good and evil' is about 'Godly choices and unGodly choices'."

Section-3: **When did Adam and Eve gain the "knowledge of good and evil"?**

Based on tradition, most Christians would probably answer this question, as follows:

- *First*, Adam and Eve exercised their 'right to choose' – exercised their right to eat or to not eat, some of the fruit of the "tree of the 'knowledge of good and evil'".

- *Second*, as they chose to eat, it was the physical act of eating some of the fruit that gave them the 'knowledge of good and evil'.

However, this author would like to propose something else and to suggest some symmetry between Adam and Jesus, the man. Thus, this author proposes that:

"The physical act of eating some of the fruit, confirmed that Adam and Eve had gained the 'knowledge of good and evil'. And their sudden awareness that they were naked, also confirmed that they had gained the 'knowledge of good and evil'. But the 'knowledge of good and evil', had to come before their decision to eat. Adam and Eve had to have the 'knowledge of good and evil', at the moments that they were separately 'evaluating their *good and evil* choices' – at those moments that they were separately 'deciding whether to *eat or not eat*', because it would have been at those moments (*first, Eve, and then Adam*) that their focuses shifted from God to themselves."

In addition, as previously mentioned, the Bible seems to imply that the "*knowledge of good*" and "*knowledge of evil*", were "not gained at the same time", as far as Adam and Eve were concerned. This "not gained at the same times" is confirmed by the following Biblical facts and implications about Adam and Eve:

- *Adam and Eve were created "sinless" (and Jesus, the man was born "sinless"). Thus, they began their existence without the "knowledge of good and evil".* For Adam and Eve, beginning their existence without the "knowledge of good and evil", would seem consistent with the existence of the "tree of the 'knowledge of good and evil'".

- *God told Adam that he could eat any fruit in the garden except the fruit of the "tree of the 'knowledge of good and evil'".* Thus, this author would propose that this is the moment, when Adam gained the "knowledge of good", as focused inward, *whether he realized it or not*.

- *The Bible does not explicitly indicate how Eve gained the knowledge that she and Adam could eat any fruit in the garden except the fruit of the "tree of the 'knowledge of good and evil'". However, the Bible does explicitly indicate that Eve knew.* (See Genesis 3:2-3.)[55] Thus, this author would propose that whenever Eve gained the knowledge that she and Adam could eat any fruit except the fruit from the "tree of the 'knowledge of good and evil'", is when she gained the "knowledge of good", as focused inward, *whether she realized it or not.*

- *Satan tempted Eve by suggesting some possible benefits from eating some of the fruit of the "tree of the 'knowledge of good and evil'", contrary to God's will. Eve succumbed to Satan's tempting and ate some of the forbidden fruit. After eating some of the fruit, Eve tempted Adam by giving him some. Then Adam also ate some of the fruit.* Thus, this author would propose that Eve gained the "knowledge of evil", as focused inward, when Satan tempted her. And because Adam was with her during her tempting by Satan, he gained the "knowledge of evil", as focused inward, at the same time. (*It does not matter whether Adam and Eve realized that they were gaining the "knowledge of evil" or not. The most crucial aspect of their situation was that they both knew that God did not want them to eat of the fruit of the tree of the knowledge of good and evil.*)

Thus, in summary, based on this author's reasoning and on the Book of Genesis:

"Adam gained the 'knowledge of good', first, as God told him that he could eat any fruit in the garden except the forbidden fruit. Sometime later, Eve gained the 'knowledge of good'. Then as Satan tempted Eve – as Satan told Eve to eat the forbidden fruit, Adam and Eve gained the 'knowledge of evil', before they sinned – before they ate the forbidden fruit."

Now, because God appears to love symmetry, this author would suggest two conditions, with regards to Jesus, the man:

- *Condition-1*: Jesus, the man, might have gained the "knowledge of good", as He learned the Law and the Old Testament, because He was focused on God, the Father – (*because He [Jesus] was focused outward*), *whether He realized it or not.*

- *Condition-2*: Jesus, the man, most likely gained the "knowledge of evil", during the tempting by Satan. Satan tried to get Jesus, the man, to focus on Himself – (*to focus inward*), *whether He realized it or not.*

  Comment: Having the "knowledge of evil – knowing what evil is", does not automatically make an individual a sinner. (*See the meaning of the phrase – "knowledge of evil", in Part-4 of this essay.*)

Both these conditions maintain some symmetry, between Adam and Jesus, the man.

Part-3: **The meaning of the phrase: "knowledge of good"**

As briefly indicated in Part-1/Section-5/*Segment-3* – biblically, the phrase – "knowledge of good", appears to have several possible meanings, which can be presented in two groups, based on an "outward focus" or an "inward focus". These groups are, as follows:

- *Group-1*: For an individual, "who is focused outward *(on God)*", the meaning of the phrase – "knowledge of good", is:

  - ✓ a "knowledge of God".

- *Group-2*: For an individual, "who is focused inward (*on herself or himself*)", the meaning of the phrase – "knowledge of good", is:

  - ✓ a "knowledge of Godly choices".

Part-4: **The meaning of the phrase: "knowledge of evil"**

As briefly indicated in Part-1/Section-5/*Segment-3* – biblically, the phrase – "knowledge of evil", appears to have several possible meanings, which can be presented in two groups, based on an "outward focus" or an "inward focus". These groups are, as follows:

- *Group-1*: For an individual, "who is focused outward *(on God)*", the meaning of the phrase – "knowledge of evil", is:

    - ✓ a "knowledge of Satan".
    - ✓ a "knowledge of the unGodly".

- *Group-2*: For an individual, "who is focused inward *(on herself or himself)*", the meaning of the phrase – "knowledge of evil", is:

    - ✓ a "knowledge of unGodly choices".
    - ✓ a "knowledge of choices that seem to promise the possibility of satisfying 'the lust of the flesh', 'the lust of the eyes', and/or 'the pride of life'"[3].

An implication of the previous Group-2 meanings is that "perhaps an individual does not gain the 'knowledge of evil' until either of two events occurs." These are, as follows:

- *Event-1*: An individual "personalizes" her or his life, based on her or his wants, needs, and/or desires, with a deliberate disregard for the wants, needs, and/or desires of others, but without being enticed by someone else. Such an individual is focused on herself or himself to the deliberate exclusion of others, especially God.

- *Event-2*: An individual is being enticed by someone else to "personalize" her or his life, based on her or his wants, needs, and/or desires, with the enticer hoping that the individual will deliberately disregard the wants, needs, and/or desires of others, especially God.

    Comment: *Event-2* is applicable to Jesus, the man, or for that matter to anyone, who appears to live a life, which is dedicated to the welfare of others. But, more comments about Jesus, the man, and this issue are presented later in this essay.

This concept of "personalizing one's life" generates, at least, two questions:

- *Question-1*: Aren't most of our lives "personalized" from our birth? *(Aren't most individuals*

---

3 See entry titled – "The meaning of each of the phrases – 'lust of the flesh', 'lust of the eyes', and 'pride of life'" in Appendix A.

focused on themselves from birth?)

- *Question-2*: How was this concept of "personalizing one's life", reflected in the lives of Adam, Eve, and Jesus, the man?

To address these two questions, the rest of Part-4 is organized in three sections. Section-1 presents a discussion of the question: "Aren't most of our lives personalized from our birth? (*Aren't most individuals focused on themselves from birth?*)" Section-2 presents a discussion of the question: "How was this concept of 'personalizing one's life", reflected in the lives of Adam and Eve?" Section-3 presents a discussion of the question: "How was this concept of 'personalizing one's life", reflected in the life of Jesus, the man?"

Section-1: **Aren't most of our lives personalized from our birth? *(Aren't most individuals focused on themselves from birth?)***

These questions were implicitly answered by Part-1/Section-2 through Part-1/Section-6. Nevertheless, these questions will be explicitly answered here for emphasis. These questions flow out of the fact that most people appear to grow toward adulthood feeling that the world revolves around them. This feeling appears to be especially true in western cultures. However, this feeling is a natural consequence of the way that God designed mankind, because human babies are born needing the most care and among the longest care of any species. Thus, many babies grow into young children feeling that each of them is the center of attention. Then add to this situation the fact that each individual, regardless of age, is generally perceiving her or his "sphere of awareness" through "her or his own senses". And, it should be easy to see why these conditions lend themselves to each individual feeling that the world revolves around her or him. And why these conditions lend themselves to each individual appearing to be focused on herself or himself. But if this is all that an individual knows, then it is probably not fair to accuse the individual of being focused on herself or himself from birth. More specifically, it is probably not fair to accuse someone of being focused on herself or himself until that individual has passed "the age of accountability". Because only when each individual has passed "the age of accountability" will they have truly personalized their life. (*See Part-5 for the meaning of the* phrase: *"the age of accountability".*)

Section-2: **How was this concept of "personalizing one's life", reflected in the lives of Adam and Eve?**

This question is answered by the Bible and was emphasized in "a sermon by Dr. Dick L. Temple of the Bethel Christian Center"[56]. The Bible indicates that Satan got Eve to sin, by stressing what eating the fruit of the tree of the knowledge of good and evil, would do **for her**. That is, it would allow her to be like God, knowing good and evil. Then, after Eve ate, she gave some of the forbidden fruit to Adam to eat. Thus, to sin, both Adam and Eve had to change their focus from God to themselves. The fact that Adam and Eve completed their "personalization of life", is confirmed by their realizing that they were naked.

In Dr. Temple's sermon, he noted that the temptations, which especially Eve gave in to, could be summarized, as follows: *first*, "Eve saw that the tree was good for fruit. This was the lust of the flesh."; *second*, "The fruit was pleasant to her eyes. This was the lust of the eyes."; and *third*, "She saw that it was a tree to make one wise. This was the pride of life."

Section-3: **How was this concept of 'personalizing one's life', reflected in the life of Jesus, the man?**

This question is also answered by the Bible and was also emphasized in a sermon by Dr. Dick L. Temple of the Bethel Christian Center. The Bible indicates that Jesus, the man, never sinned and always had His focus on God, the Father. However, someone might try to use a portion of Matthew 26:39 to imply that Jesus, the man, personalized life and that He focused on Himself. More precisely, this implication might be taken from the wording: "My Father, if it is possible, may this cup be taken from me", in Matthew 26:39. The counter to such an implication is the remainder of Matthew 26:39. More precisely, it is the wording: "Yet not as I will, but as you will." Clearly, this wording indicates that Jesus, the man, did not complete His "personalization of life". Thus, He never sinned. Jesus, the man, kept His focus on God, the Father. Furthermore, the fact that Jesus, the man, had His focus on God, the Father – had submitted His will to God's will, is confirmed, by one of His last statements, as He was dying on the cross. This statement was recorded by Luke 23:46. This verse reads:

> (Luke 23:46 NIV) Jesus called out with a loud voice, "Father, into your hands I commit my spirit." When he had said this, he breathed his last.

In Dr. Temple's sermon, he noted that the temptations, which Jesus did not give in to, could be summarized, as follows: *first*, "Turn the stones into bread. This was the lust of the flesh."; *second*, "Offered Him all the kingdoms. This was the lust of the eyes."; and *third*, "Told Him to jump off the pinnacle of the temple and the angels would come to his rescue. This was the pride of life."

Part-5: **The meaning of the phrase: "the age of accountability"**

Some Christians believe in a concept called: "the age of accountability". This belief is only implicitly supported by the Bible. Nevertheless, you could ask, "What does the phrase – 'the age of accountability', mean?" To answer this question, Part-5 is organized in three sections. Section-1 presents some introductory comments about the concept of "the age of accountability". Section-2 presents some Bible verses, which provide some implicit support for the concept of "the age of accountability". Section-3 presents a critique of "the age of accountability".

Section-1: **Some introductory comments about the concept of "the age of accountability"**

The concept of "the age of accountability", probably developed, as Christians tried to reconcile three things: *first*, "the deaths of members of a specific group of individuals"; *second*, "salvation"; and *third*, "a just and merciful God". More precisely, Christians wanted to reconcile "the deaths of those who had not lived long enough to understand and then to accept or to reject Christ, as their Lord and Savior", with "salvation" and "a just and merciful God". The need for this reconciliation caused some Christians to probably reason, as follows:

- Adam and Eve sinned, by eating some of the fruit of "the tree of the 'knowledge of good and evil'". When they sinned, they lost their existence under God's grace, because God banished them from the Garden of Eden. Thus, they went from existing under God's grace in the Garden of Eden to existing under God's judgment in the world.

- Because all members of subsequent generations, except Jesus, the man, were in Adam's loins when he and Eve sinned, all those members were/are/will be born sinners - were/are/will be born with Adam's sin-nature.

- Because of sin and its penalty (*which is being separated from God's grace and which is an existence under God's judgment*), God established a temporary redemption-plan through animal sacrifices. This temporary redemption-plan served, as a model for His eternal redemption plan through the finished work of Jesus, the man, on the cross. Note that the finished work of Jesus, the man, on the cross, was His spiritual and physical deaths. His spiritual death (*which caused His separation from God's grace*) served, as the penalty for our sins. And then His physical death served, as the atoning sacrifice for our sins. After His deaths, He was buried. Then God resurrected Jesus to confirmed to the world that Jesus' finished work on the cross was accepted. Thus, God provided Jesus, the man, as the only way to Him (God).

- However, for those individuals, who did not have the "light of Jesus" to draw them to God, God also provided the "light of our conscience" and the "light of nature" to steer individuals toward the "light of Jesus", since Jesus, the man, is the only way to Him (God).

- Jesus, the man - the Christ - offers the free gift of salvation to those who believe in and accept His finished work on the cross.

- If an individual did not/does not/will not accept the spiritual death and the physical death of Jesus, as the penalty payment and as the atoning sacrifice for her or his sins, then someone else would have to pay the penalty for her or his sins and then that someone else would have to also serve, as the atoning sacrifice for her or his sins. However, this atoning sacrifice has to be without a blemish - has to be sinless. But there has only been one "sinless" human being, and He was Jesus. Therefore, to obtain salvation, an individual must accept the deaths of Jesus, the man, as the penalty for her or his sins and as the atoning sacrifice for her or his sins.

- There appears to be a group of humans, who do not have an opportunity to consciously accept or reject, Christ, as their Lord and Savior. This group includes, the following individuals:

  - ✓ Those born mentally impaired or who become mentally impaired before they gain the "'knowledge of good' and the 'knowledge of evil', and thus the 'ability to sin'" – "(*before they reach the age of accountability*)".

    Comment: For a definition and discussion of the phrase – "ability to sin", see the essay – "What does the phrase – 'ability to sin', mean? (Is the phrase – 'ability to **not** sin', meaningful or is it inappropriate?)"

  - ✓ Babies, who die before they are born.

  - ✓ Babies and other young individuals, who die before they gain the "'knowledge of good' and the 'knowledge of evil', and thus the 'ability to sin'" – "(*before they reach the age of accountability*)".

- In addition to lacking an opportunity to gain the "light of Jesus", the members of the previously referenced group also lack the ability or the time to experience the "light of their conscience" and/or the "light of nature". Consequently, many Christians feel that a just and merciful God, has incorporated some type of consideration for this group, in His plan of redemption.

Thus, such reasoning lends itself to the existence of the concept of "the age of accountability".

Section-2: **Biblical support for "the age of accountability"**

Implicit support for the concept of "the age of accountability", is provided by Numbers 14:28-30, Numbers 32:5-13, and 2 Samuel 12:13-23. Thus, Section-2 is organized in three segments. *Segment-1* presents a discussion of Numbers 14:28-34. *Segment-2* presents a discussion of Numbers 32:5-13. *Segment-3* presents a discussion of 2 Samuel 12:13-23.

Segment-1: **Numbers 14:28-34**

Bible scholars say that the bible records only one instance of God dividing His chosen people by age. This one instance was recorded by Numbers 14:28-34.

Background: After more than four hundred years of slavery in Egypt, Moses has led the chosen people out of Egypt toward the land promised to them by God. At the border of the promised land, twelve men, one from each tribe, were chosen to go into the promised land, as spies. Ten of the twelve spies came back with negative reports, which indicated that the people living in the promised land were too strong to be conquered. These negative reports spread among the rest of the Jewish people to the extent that the people began to grumble against God. This angered God, because the people were not trusting Him to keep His promise. Thus, He divided the people into two groups: "one group consisted of all those younger than twenty" and "the other group consisted of those twenty and older". God also included in the former group (*the "those younger than twenty" group*), those who expressed a trust in Him, namely, Caleb and Joshua, the two spies, who brought back positive reports. Then God told His chosen people that everyone in the "twenty years and older" group, who had grumbled against Him would not go into the promised land. They would die in the desert. The verses, which refer to this instance, are Numbers 14:28-34. In the NIV, these read:

> Numbers 14:[28]So tell them, 'As surely as I live, declares the LORD, I will do to you the very things I heard you say: [29]In this desert your bodies will fall--every one of you twenty years old or more who was counted in the census and who has grumbled against me. [30]Not one of you will enter the land I swore with uplifted hand to make your home, except Caleb son of Jephunneh and Joshua son of Nun. [31]As for your children that you said would be taken as plunder, I will bring them in to enjoy the land you have rejected. [32]But you--your bodies will fall in this desert. [33]Your children will be shepherds here for forty years, suffering for your unfaithfulness, until the last of your bodies lies in the desert. [34]For forty years--one year for each of the forty days you explored the land--you will suffer for your sins and know what it is like to have me against you.'

Segment-2: **Numbers 32:5-13**

Numbers 32:5-13 represent a look at the events of Numbers 14:28-34, forty years later. As previously mentioned, Numbers 14:28-34 records the only instance of God dividing His chosen people by age.

Background: After the deaths of those twenty and older in the desert over about a forty-year period, Moses led the chosen people back toward the land promised to them by God. Just before the Jews reached the Jordan River, they fought and conquered several tribes. Then as they prepared to cross the Jordan River, into the promised land, two of the twelve tribes (of *the chosen people*) – the Reubenites and the Gadites, decided that they liked the land that they were on. Thus, these two tribes did not want to go any further (*did not want to cross the Jordan River*). This is when Moses reminded these two tribes of the judgment of God, forty years earlier on those who did not exhibit faith in Him. The verses, which refer to this instance, are Numbers 32:5-13. In the NIV, these verses read:

> Numbers 32:[5]If we have found favor in your eyes," they said, "let this land be

> given to your servants as our possession. Do not make us cross the Jordan."
> [6]Moses said to the Gadites and Reubenites, "Shall your countrymen go to war
> while you sit here? [7]Why do you discourage the Israelites from going over into
> the land the LORD has given them? [8]This is what your fathers did when I sent
> them from Kadesh Barnea to look over the land. [9]After they went up to the Valley
> of Eshcol and viewed the land, they discouraged the Israelites from entering the
> land the LORD had given them. [10]The Lord's anger was aroused that day and he
> swore this oath: [11]'Because they have not followed me wholeheartedly, not one of
> the men twenty years old or more who came up out of Egypt will see the land I
> promised on oath to Abraham, Isaac and Jacob--[12]not one except Caleb son of
> Jephunneh the Kenizzite and Joshua son of Nun, for they followed the LORD
> wholeheartedly.' [13]The Lord's anger burned against Israel and he made them
> wander in the desert forty years, until the whole generation of those who had
> done evil in his sight was gone.

Segment-3: **2 Samuel 12:13-23**

Bible scholars say that 2 Samuel 12:13-23 implies a heavenly destiny for babies, who die before they are born and for the young, who die.

Background: King David had an adulterous affair with Bathsheba. She became pregnant, because of the affair. Uriah, her husband, was off fighting with the Jewish army. King David had Uriah killed to prevent him from discovering King David's affair with Bathsheba. Then King David married Bathsheba. However, the child, who was conceived as a result of their adulterous affair, became sick soon after birth and eventually died. But while the child was still alive, King David fasted and prayed for the infant's recovery. After the infant died, King David told his servants that the infant could not come back to him, but he would go to the infant. The verses, which refer to this instance, are 2 Samuel 12:13-23. In the NIV, these verses read:

> 2 Samuel 12:[13]Then David said to Nathan, "I have sinned against the LORD."
> Nathan replied, "The LORD has taken away your sin. You are not going to die.
> [14]But because by doing this you have made the enemies of the LORD show utter
> contempt, the son born to you will die." [15]After Nathan had gone home, the LORD
> struck the child that Uriah's wife had borne to David, and he became ill. [16]David
> pleaded with God for the child. He fasted and went into his house and spent the
> nights lying on the ground. [17]The elders of his household stood beside him to get
> him up from the ground, but he refused, and he would not eat any food with
> them. [18]On the seventh day the child died. David's servants were afraid to tell
> him that the child was dead, for they thought, "While the child was still living, we
> spoke to David but he would not listen to us. How can we tell him the child is
> dead? He may do something desperate." [19]David noticed that his servants were
> whispering among themselves and he realized the child was dead. "Is the child

dead?" he asked. "Yes," they replied, "he is dead." [20]Then David got up from the ground. After he had washed, put on lotions and changed his clothes, he went into the house of the LORD and worshiped. Then he went to his own house, and at his request they served him food, and he ate. [21]His servants asked him, "Why are you acting this way? While the child was alive, you fasted and wept, but now that the child is dead, you get up and eat!" [22]He answered, "While the child was still alive, I fasted and wept. I thought, 'Who knows? The LORD may be gracious to me and let the child live.' [23]<u>But now that he is dead, why should I fast? Can I bring him back again? I will go to him, but he will not return to me</u>."

<u>Section-3</u>: **A critique of "the age of accountability"**

"The age of accountability" could very well be a given "physical age" like a "nineteen-year-old" to be consistent with Numbers 14:28-34. But whether it is tied to a specific age or not, the implication of such a concept is that there is a point in each individual's life where God begins to hold her or him accountable for her or his thoughts, words, and deeds. Such an age is not hard to believe, because it is exactly what our U.S. legal system does. Depending on the crime, if you are younger than eighteen and commit a crime, in many cases, the legal system tries to give you a break, because of your age. However, if you are eighteen or older, the system will probably try to throw the book at you. But even with the U.S. legal system as a supporting example, this author believes that for the event recorded by Numbers 14:28-34, a specific physical age was appropriate, because God was dealing with a large number of people at the same time. However when it comes to individuals, "the age of accountability" is probably related to the spiritual state of an individual's mind and conscience. More precisely, it might be that moment in an individual's life:

- ✓ when she or he has gained the "knowledge of good and evil" (*i.e., has gained the knowledge of "good choices [Godly choices]" versus "evil choices [unGodly choices]*)",

- ✓ when she or he realizes or personalizes those "good choices (*Godly choices*)" versus "evil choices (*unGodly choices*)", and

- ✓ when she or he understands that "she or he has the free will to choose 'good choices (*Godly choices*)' over 'evil choices (*unGodly choices*)'."

Under this reasoning, an individual reaching "the age of accountability", would be akin to Adam and Eve gaining the "knowledge of good and evil" and thus the "ability to sin". Therefore, this author would make two proposals:

- ➧ *<u>Proposal-1</u>*: The concept of "the age of accountability", seems to be consistent with each individual, who lives long enough to realize or personalize their "Godly choices" <u>and/or</u> their "unGodly choices". Such individuals would have gained the "knowledge of good and evil", and thus, the "ability to sin" – to sin more with foreknowledge and planning, than unintentional. Now, some individuals may freely choose to focus on themselves and live totally evil lives. However, most probably flip back and forth between being good at some times and being evil at other times, with fewer individuals choosing to freely focus on God and trying to live Godly lives. And still fewer individuals choosing to accept Jesus as their Lord and Savior.

- Proposal-2: God's plan of redemption does include:

  - ✓ Those born mentally impaired or who become mentally impaired before they gain the "'knowledge of good and evil', and thus the 'ability to sin'" – "(*before they reach the age of accountability*)".

  - ✓ Babies, who die before they are born.

  - ✓ Babies and other young individuals, who die before they gain the "'knowledge of good and evil', and thus the 'ability to sin'" – "(*before they reach the age of accountability*)".

These individuals are included in the redemption plan of God, which is through Christ only, by way of the "innate knowledge of God" that each of us has at the beginning of our existence. More specifically, this author would propose that at some point in each individual's existence, their soul and spirit have to be united with their body. This author is not going to pretend to know when this happens, only that it has to occur. And probably at this same moment, each individual receives their "innate knowledge of God". This "innate knowledge of God" may be related to an individual's "spirit", while an individual's "conscience", may be related to her or his soul. Nevertheless, if an individual survives to birth, then from birth as the individual grows, this "innate knowledge of God" probably diminishes due to the distractions of daily survival. This knowledge probably only remains strong in those individuals, who willingly seek God or who are mentored by other Godly individuals. If an individual dies before the age of accountability, then her or his "innate knowledge of God" ties her or him to Christ as the only way to God. Thus, these individuals would be saved. This same situation probably applies to those who develop mental disabilities before reaching the age of accountability.

Part-6: **Concluding comments**

This essay presented a meaning for each of the three phrases – "knowledge of good and evil", "knowledge of good", and "knowledge of evil" and presented a meaning for the concept of "the age of accountability". This essay also implied that with regards to Adam and Eve, the points at which they gained the "knowledge of good" and the "knowledge of evil", are easily recognized. But it is more difficult to recognize, when Jesus, the man, gained the "knowledge of good" and the "knowledge of evil". Nevertheless, based on the symmetry that God appears to love, Jesus, the man, had to gain the "knowledge of good" and the "knowledge of evil", after His birth, because He was born "sinless". As previously proposed, Jesus, the man, might have gained the "knowledge of good", as He learned the Law and the Old Testament, because He was focused on God – because He was focused outward. And He most likely gained the "knowledge of evil", during the tempting by Satan, because Satan tried to get Him to focus on Himself – to focus inward.

Part-7: **Some relevant comments**

Two groups of relevant comments are, as follows:

- *Group-1*: A proofreader suggested that Jesus, the man, had to have the "knowledge of good and evil" even before His ministry started, because He knew the Law and the Old Testament. And we know the Old Testament contains references to the evil done by Adam, Eve, the people of Noah's day, King David, and many others. This proofreader also suggested that we can learn from the evil committed by others. While it might be true that a few individuals might learn from the evil committed by others, clearly the realities of life show that most people do not. Otherwise, evil would end. (*Or a better example: STD's would disappear.*) Thus, this author would propose that "the 'knowledge of the evil committed by others', is not the same as the 'knowledge of evil'. The 'knowledge of the evil committed by others' is about the evil choices (*unGodly choices*) made by others. The 'knowledge of evil', is about the evil choices (*unGodly choices*) available to you and/or chosen by you." This author would also propose that you cannot use your own experiences as a basis for understanding this issue, because you were born a sinner. Jesus, the man, was born sinless. Nevertheless, one thing is certain, if Jesus, the man, did not have a "knowledge of evil" before His tempting by Satan, He had that knowledge afterward. Once more, there is a big difference between reading about the sins of others in the Old Testament and being tempted by Satan. In the latter case, evil would have become more real – more personal – to Jesus, the man.

- *Group-2*: Being presented with "good and evil choices" allows each individual to complete the process of personalizing life. Again, that personalization occurs, when the "knowledge of good" and the "knowledge of the 'Lust of the flesh', the 'Lust of the eyes', and the 'pride of life'"[4], becomes real for an individual – becomes "**personal**" for an individual.

---

4 See entry titled – "The meaning of each of the phrases – 'lust of the flesh', 'lust of the eyes', and 'pride of life'" in Appendix A.

Is "judgment" one of God's attributes?

The phrase – "God's judgment", is used in no less than nine essays in this book. In this phrase, the word – "judgment", is used as one of God's attributes. However, the topic question flows out of the belief of some Christians that "justice", not "judgment", is one of God's attributes. This belief worried this author to the point where an Internet search was performed, using the phrase: "attributes of God". The purpose of this search was to see what others say about the "attributes of God". A quick read of several web documents, which addressed the "attributes of God", produced two observations and two inspirations. The two observations are:

- *Observation-1*: Several web documents listed what they felt were the "attributes of God".

- *Observation-2*: Not all of the web documents presented the same number of attributes. Neither did all of these web documents use the same names for the various "attributes of God".

The two inspirations are:

- *Inspiration-1*: The "attributes of God" are uncountable. Some are unnameable and others are undefinable.

- *Inspiration-2*: One or more of the "attributes of God" could be displayed at any given instance in time and/or in the Bible. Such displays might allow a different name – (*but more specifically, a single name*) – to represent that particular combination of the "attributes of God". For example, "God's judgment" could be a combination of "His justice", "His knowledge", "His will", "His Holiness", and/or "His power".

Therefore, this author is comfortable using the word – "judgment", as one of God's attributes.

Did Jesus, the man, have the "ability to sin" like Adam and Eve?

Comment: This essay addresses the topic question from a "biblical viewpoint". Whereas, the essay – "What does the phrase – 'ability to sin', mean? (Is the phrase – 'ability to **not** sin', meaningful or is it inappropriate?)", served two purposes: *first*, it addressed the topic question from a "logical viewpoint". And, *second*, it defined the phrase: "ability to sin".

Many individuals – probably more Christians than non-Christians – have pondered some variation of the topic question. However, of all the variations, this variation seemed like the best, because its wording references two crucial issues: *first*, the "nature of Jesus" (*because of the* phrase – *Jesus, the man*) and *second*, the comparison indicated, by the phrase: "like Adam and Eve". These two crucial issues and the process of developing an answer for the topic question, allows this essay to be organized around an eight-step approach. Step-1 begins a discussion of the crucial issue represented by the phrase: "nature of Jesus". Step-2 presents a discussion about the "nature of Jesus" and His "ability to sin". Step-3 begins a discussion of the crucial issue represented by the phrase: "like Adam and Eve". Step-4 presents a discussion of the "like Adam and Eve" issue via the question: "Whom should Jesus be compared with regarding the 'ability to sin'?" Step-5 presents a discussion of the words – "innocent", "sinless", and "tempted", along with the phrase: "without the knowledge of good and evil". Step-6 presents a discussion of the question: "How did the words – 'innocent', 'sinless', and 'tempted' and the phrase – 'without the knowledge of good and evil', apply to Adam, Eve, and Jesus, the man?" Step-7 presents some concluding comments. Step-8 presents some relevant comments.

Step-1: **The phrase: "nature of Jesus"**

The crucial issue represented by the phrase – "nature of Jesus", is that "the Bible indicates that Jesus has two "natures"[57]: the 'nature of God' and the 'nature of man'". That is, Jesus is fully God and Jesus is fully human. Or a more complete wording would be something like, the following:

"Jesus *is* God, the Son [a member of the Trinity],
and
Jesus *is* a man [the *Messiah*/the *Anointed One*/the *Christ*/the *Son of God*]."

- His "nature of God" is indicated by John 1:1 and John 1:14. These verses read:

(John 1:1 NIV) In the beginning was the Word, and the Word was with God, and the Word was God.

(John 1:14 NIV) The Word became flesh and made his dwelling among us. We have seen his glory, the glory of the One and Only, who came from the Father, full of grace and truth.

- His "nature of a man" is confirmed by the virgin birth of Jesus. Reference Luke 1:30-35. In the NIV, these verses read:

Luke 1:[30]But the angel said to her, "Do not be afraid, Mary, you have found favor
with God. [31]You will be with child and give birth to a son, and you are to give him
the name Jesus. [32]He will be great and will be called the Son of the Most High.
The Lord God will give him the throne of his father David, [33]and he will reign over
the house of Jacob forever; his kingdom will never end." [34]"How will this be,"
Mary asked the angel, "since I am a virgin?" [35]The angel answered, "The Holy
Spirit will come upon you, and the power of the Most High will overshadow you.
So the holy one to be born will be called the Son of God.

Step-2: **The "nature of Jesus" and His "ability to sin"**

Because the Bible indicates that "Jesus has two-natures – the 'nature of God *(Jesus, God, the Son)*' and the 'nature of man *(Jesus, the man)*'", both of His natures have to be examined, to see how each might impact His "ability to sin". After such an examination, we note that the "ability to sin" is only relevant to Jesus, the man, and not to Jesus, God, the Son, for at least, five reasons:

- *Reason-1*: Being that Jesus, God, the Son is a member of the Trinity, "sin" would not be relevant to Him, because by definition "sin" is "a freewill thought, word, and/or deed, which is contrary to God's will"[58]. In other words, since Jesus, God, the Son is God, there is no way for Him to rebel against Himself. Or worded differently, since Jesus, God, the Son is God, He could never do anything contrary to His will. Thus, the "ability to sin", would only be relevant to Jesus, the man.

- *Reason-2*: When discussing "Jesus, God, the Son, and sin", some non-Christians might try to say, "You Christians believe in a Triune God ('God, the Father', 'God, the Son', and 'God, the Holy Spirit'). Consequently, would it not be possible for one member of the Trinity to disobey another member of the Trinity?" One biblical response to anyone saying anything like that is – "The Bible clearly indicates that the members of the Trinity are of one mind and are working toward one objective, the redemption of man, so the concepts of disobeying or sinning are not logically and spiritually applicable to any of the three members of the Trinity. Thus, the 'ability to sin' would not be logically or spiritually relevant to Jesus, God, the Son."

- *Reason-3*: Jesus, God, the Son willingly veiled His deity to take on the human form of Jesus, the man, via the Jewish virgin, Mary. With His God-nature veiled, then the "ability to sin" would only be relevant to Jesus, the man.

- *Reason-4*: Jesus, the man, is fully human. And all humans have the "ability to sin", because we were born with "free will". Then recall that the "ability to sin" was defined in the essay: "What does the phrase – 'ability to sin', mean? (Is the phrase – 'ability to not sin', meaningful or is it inappropriate?)". For "*sins of commission*", the "ability to sin" was defined, as follows:

  > "An individual has the necessary physical, mental, and spiritual attributes that would allow that individual to **freely** choose – *in ignorance or with forethought* – a thought, word, and/or deed, which is contrary to God's will".

  For "*sins of omission*", the "ability to sin" was defined, as follows:

  > "An individual has the necessary physical, mental, and spiritual attributes that would allow that individual to **freely** fail to choose – *in ignorance or with forethought* – a thought, word, and/or deed, which is not contrary to God's will, when such a thought, word, and/or deed is needed or is appropriate".

  Furthermore in that same essay, it was determined that a comparison with Adam and Eve indicated that Jesus, the man, had the "ability to sin", but that did not mean that He did sin.

- *Reason-5*: The redemptive work on the cross was explicitly through Jesus, the man, not through Jesus, God, the Son. That redemptive work required a spiritual death (*which was a separation from God's grace*) and a physical death (*which was the shedding of innocent blood*), neither of which are relevant to Jesus, God, the Son. However, both deaths were relevant to Jesus, the man, along with the "ability to sin".

Thus, based on reasons like the previous five, it is logically and spiritually inappropriate to talk about "Jesus, God, the Son having the 'ability to sin'". And even though the Bible does not explicitly indicate whether Jesus, the man, "*could* or *could not*" have sinned, it does explicitly indicate that Jesus, the man, "did not sin". However, the fact that "Jesus, the man, did not sin" does not automatically mean that Jesus, the man, did not have the "ability to sin". "To sin" – "to deliberately disobey the known will of God" – requires, at least, two conditions:

- *Condition-1*: The individual must have the "ability to sin", which includes having "free will" and having "evil choices" available.

- *Condition-2*: The individual must be focused on herself or himself, which includes the individual having a desire or lust for an "evil choice".

As a human, Jesus, the man, was born with "free will". However, Jesus, the man, was focused on God, the Father, not on Himself. Consequently, He never had the "desire to sin", even though, "UNGODLY choices" were presented to Him, especially, by Satan. Therefore, even though Jesus, the man, never sinned, the "ability to sin" is still relevant to His nature, as Jesus, the man. Worded differently, logically and spiritually, the "ability to sin" is relevant to Jesus, the man and not to Jesus, God, the Son.

Step-3: **The phrase: "like Adam and Eve"**

The crucial issue represented by the phrase – "like Adam and Eve", is "confirming whom Jesus should be compared with regarding the 'ability to sin'". The obvious options are comparing Jesus to: "all other humans *(including Adam and Eve)*", "all other humans *(except Adam and Eve)*", or "Adam and Eve only". By using the Bible, the correct option is determined to be "Adam and Eve only". As this step only served to introduce this issue, the details and the reasoning used to arrive at this correct option are presented in Step-4.

Step-4: **Whom should Jesus be compared with regarding the "ability to sin"?**

Based on Step-2, a more precise wording of the Step-4 question is: "Whom should Jesus, the man, be compared with regarding the 'ability to sin'?" This more precise wording also implies that the "whom" of our comparison should be "other humans".

> *Comment:* Considering "other humans" sounds like the obvious answer to the Step-4 question. And, it is the answer! However, note that if Jesus, God, the Son, had to be considered with Jesus, the man, then the comparison would have to include "spirit beings" in addition to "human beings". As the Step-2 presentation indicated why the "ability to sin" was not applicable to Jesus, God, the Son, Jesus, God, the Son, does not have to be considered with Jesus, the man. Therefore, other "spirit beings" do not have to be considered, in the comparison question for this step.

While ignoring "spirit beings", a grouping of "other humans" would include: "those who have lived", "those who are living", and "those who will live". This group can be divided into two subgroups, based on information recorded in the Bible. However, to facilitate a comparison, a third subgroup, which consist of only Jesus, the man, will be established. But the subgroup consisting of Jesus, the man, will be placed between the other two. More specifically, the three subgroups are defined, as follows: *Subgroup-1* is "Adam and Eve only", *Subgroup-2* is "Jesus, the man, only", and *Subgroup-3* is "all other humans (*all humans, except Adam, Eve, and Jesus, the* man)". Actually, the same three subgroups can be formed using two different criteria: "how created" and "spiritual". More specifically, each subgroup can be summarized within each criterion, as follows:

- Under the "how created" criterion:

  Subgroup-1: "Adam and Eve"

  - were created directly by God. God created Adam from the dust of the ground. God created Eve from one of Adam's ribs.

  Subgroup-2: "Jesus, the man"

  - was created directly and indirectly, by God. Jesus, the man, was created directly, when God, the Holy Spirit, overshadowed a Jewish virgin named, Mary, and afterward, she was found to be pregnant (*See Luke 1:35.*). Jesus, the man, was created indirectly, through the birth process, when the Virgin Mary gave birth to Him nine months, after the overshadowing of God, the Holy Spirit.

  Subgroup-3: "All other humans"

  - were/are/will be created indirectly by God, through the birth process.

- Under the "spiritual" criterion:

  Subgroup-1: "Adam and Eve"

  - began their earthly existence "under God's grace" – "spiritually alive".
  - were created with "free will".
  - were created "sinless".
  - were created with an outward focus (*on God*), but developed an inward focus (*on themselves*) upon being tempted by Satan. Their inward focus aided their ability and their desire to sin.
  - freely chose to sin.
  - were banished from the Garden of Eden, because of their sin. That is, Adam and Eve went from existing under God's grace in the garden to existing under God's judgment in the world.
  - ended their earthly existence "spiritual alive" or "spiritually dead". It all depends on whether they were looking forward to the cross or not.

  Subgroup-2: "Jesus, the man"

- began His earthly existence "under God's grace" – "spiritually alive".
- was created with "free will".
- was created "sinless" and He remained "sinless", until God, the Father, laid our sins in His (Jesus') spiritual account.
- was created with an outward focus (*on God*) and by keeping His focus on God, Jesus was able to remain "sinless".
- went from existing under God's grace to existing under God's judgment, when God laid our sins in His (Jesus') spiritual account. That is, Jesus paid the penalty for our sins.
- went from existing under God's judgment, because of His (Jesus') spiritual death, to existing under God's grace, because of His atoning sacrifice – because of His physical death on the cross.

Subgroup-3: "All other humans"

- began/begin/will begin their earthly existence: "under God's judgment" – "spiritually dead".
- were/are/will be born with "free will".
- were/are/will be born with a "sin-nature".
- were/are/will be born with inward focus (*on themselves*).
- ended/end/will end their earthly existence in either of two ways, which depend on whether an individual did accept/accepts/will accept the finished work of Jesus, on her or his behalf.

  ✓ Those who did accept/accept/will accept the finished work of Jesus, ended/end/will end their earthly existence "under God's grace" – "spiritually alive".

  ✓ Those who did not accept/do not accept/will not accept the finished work of Jesus, ended/end/will end their earthly existence "under God's judgment" – "spiritually dead".

The information indicated under both criteria is explicitly or implicitly, based on the Bible. Thus, this summary shows that biblically, it is more appropriate to use "Adam and Eve only" in a comparison with "Jesus, the man", for two reasons: *first*, because God was more involved in the creation of Adam, Eve, and Jesus, the man, than He was for the rest of us and *second*, because those three began life in the same "spiritual" condition. More precisely, Adam, Eve, and Jesus, the man, were created more directly than the rest of us and began their existence as "sinless" individuals, "under God's grace" ("*spiritually alive*"). Because of Adam's sin, the rest of us began/begin/will begin our existence as "sinners" and "under God's judgment" ("*spiritually dead*"). Then we end our existence either "under God's grace" ("*spiritually alive*") or "under His judgment" ("*spiritually dead*"), depending on whether we "accept" or "reject" the finished work of Jesus, the man, on our behalf.

Step-5: The words: "innocent", "sinless", and "tempted", and the phrase: "without the knowledge of good and evil"

To discuss the words – "innocent", "sinless", and "tempted", and the phrase – "without the knowledge of good and evil", Step-5 is organized in two parts. Part-1 presents a discussion of the words: "innocent" and "sinless", and of the phrase: "without the knowledge of good and evil". Part-2 presents a discussion of the word: "tempted".

Part-1: The words: "innocent" and "sinless", and the phrase: "without the knowledge of good and evil"

The Book of Genesis implies that Adam and Eve were created "innocent" ("sinless") and were created "without the knowledge of good and evil". The Bible uses the word – "innocent", as a synonym for the word – "sinless", which obviously means "without sin". The word – "sin", means "some created being – [an angel or a human – a spiritual being or a physical being] – has deliberately *'thought something', 'said something'*, or *'performed some deed'*, that is contrary to the will of God". Thus, the issues become: "How do we know that Adam and Eve were created 'innocent' ('sinless')?" and "How do we know that Adam and Eve were created 'without the knowledge of good and evil'?". To discuss these two questions, Part-1 is organized in two sections. Section-1 presents a discussion of the question: "How do we know that Adam and Eve were created 'innocent' ('sinless')?" Section-2 presents a discussion of the question: "How do we know that Adam and Eve were created 'without the knowledge of good and evil'?"

Section-1: How do we know that Adam and Eve were created "innocent" ("sinless")?

We know that Adam and Eve were created "innocent" ("sinless"), because the Book of Genesis records their first sin, which was disobeying God by eating some of the forbidden fruit. Their sin was also confirmed by God when He drove Adam and Eve out of their garden paradise, as punishment for their sin. To repeat and to summarize, the Bible explicitly and implicitly indicates several facts:

- ✓ *Fact-1*: God created Adam and Eve.
- ✓ *Fact-2*: God told Adam not to eat the forbidden fruit, but Eve knew too.
- ✓ *Fact-3*: Adam and Eve committed their first sin, by eating some of the forbidden fruit.
- ✓ *Fact-4*: God drove Adam and Eve out of the Garden of Eden, as a punishment for their first sin.

Therefore, implicitly, Adam and Eve had to be created "innocent" ("sinless").

Section-2: **How do we know that Adam and Eve were created "without the knowledge of good and evil"?**

The fact that Adam and Eve were created "without the knowledge of good and evil", seems to be implicit in several verses in the Bible. Some of these verses record God's instructions directly to Adam and indirectly to Eve. One of God's instructions was: "You may eat of any fruit in the garden, except the fruit from the 'tree of the knowledge of good and evil'". Thus, an obvious question is "When did Adam and Eve gain the knowledge of good and evil?" As mentioned before in another essay, traditionally, most Christians would probably say,

- "*First*, Adam and Eve exercised their 'right to choose' – exercised their right to eat or to not eat.

- *Second*, as they chose to eat, it was the physical act of eating some of the fruit that gave them the 'knowledge of good and evil'."

But this author would like to propose something else. This author would like to propose that:

> "The physical act of eating some of the fruit only confirmed that Adam and Eve had gained the 'knowledge of good and evil'. And their sudden awareness that they were naked, also confirmed that they had gained the 'knowledge of good and evil'. But the 'knowledge of good and evil' had to come before the decision to eat. Adam and Eve had to have the 'knowledge of good and evil' at the moments that they were separately 'evaluating their *good and evil* choices', because it would have been at those moments (*first, Eve, and then Adam*) that their focuses shifted from God to themselves."

To support this timing, see the essay: "What do the three phrases – 'Knowledge of good and evil', 'Knowledge of good' and 'Knowledge of evil', mean? (What is 'the age of accountability'?)" However, here, for your convenience, a summary of that essay is presented, with the following comments:

God created Adam and Eve. When God told Adam (*directly*) and Eve (*probably indirectly*) that they could eat the fruit of any tree except the tree of the knowledge of good and evil, He was giving them "good choices", which is the same as giving them the "knowledge of good". At that moment, this author believes that Adam and Eve had no thought that they could actually eat the forbidden fruit. Later Satan told Eve that it was okay to eat of the fruit on the "tree of the knowledge of good and evil". That she would gain the knowledge of good and evil like God, if she ate some of the fruit. When Satan told Eve and Adam (*Adam was probably near Eve as Satan was talking to her.*) that it was okay to eat the forbidden fruit, he was giving them an "evil choice", which is the same as giving them the "knowledge of evil".

> *Comment*: Adam and Eve may not have fully realized that they were gaining the "knowledge of good" and the "knowledge of evil", as God and later Satan spoke to them about the forbidden fruit. Nevertheless, their realization does not alter the fact that is what happened.

Then having "good and evil choices" and "free will", Adam and Eve had to evaluate "the good" versus "the evil" – prior to exercising their "right to choose", prior to not eating or to eating any of the forbidden fruit. Adam and Eve had to decide whether to trust God or to trust Satan. Adam and Eve exercised their "right to choose" by choosing to eat some of the forbidden fruit, and thus, they sinned against God. Therefore, as previously mentioned, for this essay, the point is:

> "Adam and Eve gained the 'knowledge of good and evil' sometime after their creation by God, but just prior to their actual sinning."

Part-2: **The word: "tempted"**

The word – "tempted" and its variations, are best defined biblically, by looking at examples of "tempting's" in the Bible. The two best known "tempting's" in the Bible are the tempting of "Adam and Eve" and the tempting of "Jesus, the man". Choosing between these two examples is easy, because "Adam and Eve" succumbed to their tempting, while "Jesus, the man" did not. In addition, there are more verses about the tempting of "Jesus, the man". Thus, obviously the tempting of Jesus, the man is the better of the two "tempting's". To examine the tempting of Jesus, the man, Part-2 is organized in two sections. Section-1 presents some Bible verses, which refer to the tempting of Jesus, the man. Section-2 presents a discussion of the question: "What does it mean to be 'tempted'?"

Section-1: **The tempting of Jesus, the man**

Several books of the Bible contain verses, which refer to the tempting of Jesus, the man, by Satan. For example, see Matthew 4:1-11. In the NIV, these verses read:

> Matthew 4:1 Then Jesus was led by the Spirit into the desert to be tempted by the devil.
> 2 After fasting forty days and forty nights, he was hungry. 3 The tempter came to him and
> said, "If you are the Son of God, tell these stones to become bread." 4 Jesus answered, "*It
> is written: 'Man does not live on bread alone, but on every word that comes from the mouth of
> God.'*" 5 Then the devil took him to the holy city and had him stand on the highest point
> of the temple. 6 "If you are the Son of God," he said, "throw yourself down. For it is
> written: 'He will command his angels concerning you, and they will lift you up in their
> hands, so that you will not strike your foot against a stone.'" 7 Jesus answered him, "*It is*

also written: 'Do not put the Lord your God to the test.'" [8]Again, the devil took him to a very high mountain and showed him all the kingdoms of the world and their splendor. [9]"All this I will give you," he said, "if you will bow down and worship me." [10]Jesus said to him, *"Away from me, Satan! For it is written: 'Worship the Lord your God, and serve him only.'"*
[11]Then the devil left him, and angels came and attended him.

The tempting of Jesus, the man, is also mentioned in Hebrews 2:18 and Hebrews 4:15. In the NIV, these verses read:

Hebrews 2:[18]Because he himself suffered when he was tempted, he is able to help those who are being tempted.

Hebrews 4:[15]For we do not have a high priest who is unable to sympathize with our weaknesses, but we have one who has been tempted in every way, just as we are—yet was without sin.

Matthew 4:1-11 and Hebrews 4:15, indicate that Jesus, the man, was tempted, but He did not give in to the temptation – He did not choose to sin. Thus, when you read about the tempting of Jesus, the man, and everything that happened to Him, it should become obvious that there is a difference, between "being tempted" and "sinning". The difference may become even more obvious, after you read about the tempting of Adam and Eve, which led to their "sinning". (*See Genesis 3:1-24.*)

Section-2: **What does it mean to be "tempted"?**

To address this question, Section-2 is organized in three segments. *Segment-1* presents verses, which explicitly "define" the word – "tempted", along with some more verses concerning the tempting of Jesus, the man. *Segment-2* presents a definition of the word – "tempted", from the "Holman Bible Dictionary". *Segment-3* presents a working definition of the word – "tempted", for this essay, and this book, based on the first two segments.

Segment-1: **A biblical definition**

A biblical definition of the word – "tempted", is presented in James 1:13-15. Four different translations of James 1:13-15 read:

(James 1:13-15 KJV) James 1:[13]Let no man say when he is tempted, I am tempted of God: for God cannot be tempted with evil, neither tempteth he any man: [14]But every man is tempted, when he is drawn away of his own lust, and enticed. [15]Then when lust hath conceived, it bringeth forth sin: and sin, when it is finished, bringeth forth death.

(James 1:13-15 NIV) James 1:[13]When tempted, no one should say, "God is tempting me."

For God cannot be tempted by evil, nor does he tempt anyone; [14]but each one is tempted when, by his own evil desire, he is dragged away and enticed. [15]Then, after desire has conceived, it gives birth to sin; and sin, when it is full-grown, gives birth to death.

(James 1:13-15 NASB) James 1:[13]Let no one say when he is tempted, "I am being tempted by God"; for God cannot be tempted by evil, and He Himself does not tempt anyone.
[14]But each one is tempted when he is carried away and enticed by his own lust. [15]Then when lust has conceived, it gives birth to sin; and when sin is accomplished, it brings forth death.

(James 1:13-15 NRSV) James 1:[13]No one, when tempted, should say, "I am being tempted by God"; for God cannot be tempted by evil and he himself tempts no one. [14]But one is tempted by one's own desire, being lured and enticed by it; [15]then, when that desire has conceived, it gives birth to sin, and that sin, when it is fully grown, gives birth to death.

These four translations of James 1:13-15, appear to be saying that the biblical sense of the word – "tempted", is "to try to draw away and to encourage to go against the will of God through our own desires and lust". These translations used the words: "desire", "lust", "enticed", and "lure". Therefore, to facilitate this discussion, we will look in *Wiktionary*, for a definition of these four words:

- "'Desire', as a *noun*: 1. Someone or something wished for. 2. Strong attraction, particularly romantic. 3. The feeling of desire. 'Desire', as a *verb*: 1. More formal or stronger word for want. 2. Another word for want, connoting emotion."[59]

- "'Lust', as a *noun*: 1. Strong desire, especially of a sexual nature. 'Lust', as a *verb*: 1. To very strongly desire. 2. To want to have sexual intercourse with."[60]

- "'Entice', is a *verb*: 1. (*transitive*) To lure; to attract by arousing desire or hope."[61]

- "'Lure', as a *noun*: 1. Something that tempts or attracts, especially one with a promise of reward or pleasure. 'Lure', as a *verb*: 1. To attract by temptation etc.; to entice."[62]

Providing these four definitions serves to add more depth, to our biblical sense of the word: "tempted".

Segment-2: **The "Holman Bible Dictionary" definition**

The word – "tempted" is defined in the "Holman Bible Dictionary" with a five-paragraph entry titled – "Temptation", by author H. Page Lee. A shortened version of the first paragraph of this entry reads:

TEMPTATION: Used in KJV to refer to testing, trying, and enticing to evil. When the KJV was translated in 1611, "temptation" meant all of these, but the word has narrowed in meaning in modern times. Modern translations use "testing," "proving," "trying," and "tempting."

Segment-3: **A working definition**

A working definition of the word – "tempted", will be derived from definitions found in the Bible and the "Holman Bible Dictionary". These definitions indicate that the word – "tempted", conveys the meaning of "testing", "trying", and "enticing to evil". Using these meanings, a working definition of the word – "tempted", can be derived from the following statement:

> "Individuals are 'tempted' when they are pushed into 'the position of having to evaluate good and evil choices, prior to exercising their 'right to choose' – prior to selecting one of the choices'."

This statement is consistent with the word – "testing", because in order to test someone, you have to push them into the position of "evaluating choices" prior to their choosing one. Consequently, the phrase – "pushed into the position of having to evaluate good and evil choices, prior to exercising one's 'right to choose' – prior to selecting one of the choices", will be our working definition of the word: "tempted".

Step-6: **How did the words – "innocent", "sinless", and "tempted", and the phrase – "without the knowledge of good and evil", apply to Adam, Eve, and Jesus, the man?**

This question will be addressed by listing conditions relevant to the lives of Eve, Adam, and Jesus, the man, around two major points in their lives. One point is around their creation, by God. The other point is around their tempting, by Satan. After the two lists have been presented, their similarities will be discussed. To accomplish these tasks, this step is organized in three parts. Part-1 presents a list of conditions relevant to the lives of Adam and Eve, around the two points mentioned. Part-2 presents a list of conditions relevant to the life of Jesus, the man, around the two points mentioned. Part-3 discusses the similarities between the two lists of conditions.

> *Comment:* Note two things: *First*, some of what follows has been stated before in other essays and in this essay, but that is okay, because we need to examine, as much as possible from as many angles as possible. *Second*, both Part-1 and Part-2 of this Step-6 discussion, reference the words: "innocent", "sinless", and "tempted", and the phrase: "without the 'knowledge of good and evil'". [*These words and this phrase are discussed in detail in the essays: "What does the phrase – 'ability to sin', mean? (Is the phrase – 'ability to not sin', meaningful, or is it inappropriate?)"* and

"What do the three phrases – 'knowledge of good and evil', 'knowledge of good', and 'knowledge of evil', mean? (What is 'the age of accountability'?)"]

Part-1: **Conditions involving the lives of Adam and Eve**

A list of conditions relevant to the lives of Adam and Eve, around their creation by God and around their tempting by Satan, are explicitly or implicitly, based on the Bible, but specific verse designations will not be given. The conditions are, as follows:

✓ Adam and Eve were created by God.
✓ Adam and Eve were created "innocent" (*"sinless"*).
✓ Adam and Eve were created "without the 'knowledge of good and evil'".
✓ Adam and Eve gained the "knowledge of good", when God told them about the fruits that they could and could not eat.
✓ Adam and Eve gained the "knowledge of evil", when Satan tempted them – when Satan told them that they could eat the forbidden fruit.
✓ Adam and Eve had to "evaluate their good and evil choices".
✓ Adam and Eve exercised their "right to choose".
✓ Adam and Eve chose "evil".
✓ Adam and Eve chose to "disobey" God – they chose to "do things their own way".
✓ Adam and Eve shifted "their focuses from God to themselves".
✓ Adam and Eve lost their "innocent" (*"sinless"*) condition, because they chose evil.
✓ Adam and Eve became "sinners".
✓ Adam and Eve gained "self-awareness".

Part-2: **Conditions involving the life of Jesus, the man**

A list of conditions relevant to the life of Jesus, the man, around His creation by God and around His tempting by Satan, is based on the Bible. And note that the things that Satan tried to tempt Jesus with were meaningless to Jesus, God, the Son, who created everything. That is how we know that it was Jesus, the man, whom Satan was tempting. Anyway, the relevant conditions are, as follows:

✓ Jesus, the man, was created by God, the Holy Spirit, through the virgin, Mary.
✓ Jesus, the man, was created "innocent" (*"sinless"*).
✓ Jesus, the man, was created "without the 'knowledge of good and evil'".
✓ Jesus, the man, gained the "knowledge of good", because He was focused on God.
✓ Jesus, the man, gained the "knowledge of evil", when Satan tempted Him.
✓ Jesus, the man, had to "evaluate his good and evil choices".
✓ Jesus, the man, exercised his "right to choose".

✓ Jesus, the man, chose "good".
✓ Jesus, the man, chose to "obey" God – He chose to "do things God's way".
✓ Jesus, the man, kept "His focus on God".
✓ Jesus, the man, kept his "sinless" condition, because He chose not to sin,
✓ Jesus, the man, remained "innocent" (*"sinless"*).
✓ Jesus, the man, might have gained some "self-awareness"[63], because of Satan's tempting. But it was not total, because His focus was still on God.

Part-3: **The similarities between the two lists of conditions**

Many similarities between the two lists of conditions are obvious. However, the most important similarity is the fact that Adam, Eve, and Jesus, the man, were created "sinless". This is the main condition that distinguishes these three from all other human beings, who have lived, are living, or will live. And this condition is the main justification for comparing Jesus, the man, with Adam and Eve, with regards to the "ability to sin". The essay – "What does the phrase – 'ability to sin', mean? (Is the phrase – 'ability to not sin', meaningful or is it inappropriate?)", presents a more detailed comparison and a logical justification for the comparison of Jesus, the man, with Adam and Eve, with regards to the "ability to sin".

Step-7: **Conclusion**

Jesus has two natures: "God – (*Jesus is God, the Son.*)" and "man – (*Jesus is a man.*)". Having two natures means that Jesus is "fully God" and Jesus is "fully man". The "fully man" nature had to be just like Adam and Eve, because all three were created "innocent". Otherwise, the "fully man" nature of Jesus could not be "fully man". To be "fully man" means that Jesus, the man, had "free will" like Adam and Eve. He had the "right to freely choose" like Adam and Eve. And it is the "right to freely choose" that gives man the "ability to sin", when presented with Godly choices and unGodly choices, because "sin" is "choosing the unGodly choice". Yes! Jesus, the man had the "right to choose". But when He exercised His "right to choose", He chose to obey God. Therefore, Jesus, the man, remained "sinless" unlike Adam and Eve, who chose to disobey God and thus, became sinners. Thus, once more, although Jesus, the man, never sinned, the answer to the question – "Did Jesus, the man, have the "ability to sin" like Adam and Eve?", is "Yes!"

This author may not fully understand how God worked it out. But this author is sure that Jesus, the man, had to have the "ability to sin". For it is meaningless, to applaud someone for not doing those things that they are incapable of. For example, it is meaningless to applaud an unmarried man, because "he" does not get pregnant and give birth to a baby. Likewise, it would be meaningless to applaud Jesus, the man, for not sinning, if He was incapable of sinning. Now, some people say that God allowed the tempting of Jesus, the man, (*See Matthew 4:1-11*), to prove to us that "Jesus, the man, could not sin." But such arguments are logically weakened, by the occurrence of actions in the Bible, where God asked someone to do something and that individual chose not to do it. The primary example of this is the sinning of Adam and Eve. Thus, at best, it can be said, that the verses - Matthew 4:1-11 were placed in the Bible, by God, to SHOW that "Jesus, the man, DID not sin, not that Jesus, the man, could not sin." Thus, once more, the answer to the question - "Did Jesus, the man, have the 'ability to sin' like Adam and Eve?", is "Yes!"

Step-8: **Some relevant comments**

Comments are presented to tie up four "loose ends", to share relevant comments by three different radio ministers, and to present two final comments by this author. Thus, Step-8 is organized in six parts. Part-1 presents the first "loose end", which revolves around the reference to the phrase - "knowledge of good and evil" in Genesis 3:5-8. Part-2 presents a second "loose end", which revolves around Genesis 2:9 and Genesis 3:22. Part-3 presents a third "loose end", which revolves around an argument used to support the position that Jesus, the man, *could not sin*. Part-4 presents a fourth "loose end", which revolves around ten arguments used to support the position that Jesus, the man, *had the "ability to sin"*. Part-5 presents some paraphrased comments by three radio ministers. Part-6 presents some final comments.

Part-1: **The phrase - "knowledge of good and evil" in Genesis 3:5-8**

In the NIV, the Genesis 3:5-8 read:

> Genesis 3:[5]"For God knows that when you eat of it your eyes will be opened, and you will be like God, knowing good and evil." [6]When the woman saw that the fruit of the tree was good for food and pleasing to the eye, and also desirable for gaining wisdom, she took some and ate it. She also gave some to her husband, who was with her, and he ate it. [7]Then the eyes of both of them were opened, and they realized they were naked; so they sewed fig leaves together and made coverings for themselves. [8]Then the man and his wife heard the sound of the LORD God as he was walking in the garden in the cool of the day, and they hid from the LORD God among the trees of the garden.

The two crucial verses are Genesis 3:5 and Genesis 3:7:

Genesis 3:5 could be understood to mean: "Adam and Eve would gain the 'knowledge of good and evil', when they ate the fruit." But Satan is a liar and a deceiver. Satan's goal was to get Adam and Eve focused on themselves and on the forbidden fruit, so that they would eat some. And the wording of Genesis 3:5 is consistent with Satan's goal. Thus, it is not necessarily true that Adam and Eve actually gained the "knowledge of good and evil", when they ate the forbidden fruit. From previous comments, you already know that this author believes that Adam and Eve had gained the "knowledge of good and evil", before they ate the forbidden fruit. Actually, they had to gain the "knowledge of good and evil", before they "decided" to eat the forbidden fruit. But for sure, eating some of the forbidden fruit confirmed that Adam and Eve had gained the "knowledge of good and evil".

In the NIV, Genesis 3:7 uses the wording: "the eyes of both of them were opened, and they realized they were naked." Consequently, Genesis 3:7 could be understood to mean: "eating the forbidden fruit did open the eyes of Adam and Eve." But that is okay, because Genesis 3:7 indicates that "their eyes were opened and *they realized that they were naked*", not that "their eyes were opened and *they knew good and evil*." Thus, the question becomes: "Is there a relationship between '*Adam and Eve realizing that they were naked*' and '*Adam and Eve knowing good and evil*'?" Surely, the wording – "*they realized they were naked*", confirms that Adam and Eve had shifted their focuses from being on God to being on themselves. Therefore, someone might say, "When Adam and Eve had their focuses on God, that was consistent with God's plan for them – that was 'good'. When Adam and Eve shifted their focuses to themselves, this shift was contrary to God's plan for them – that was 'evil'. Thus, realizing that they were naked confirmed their 'knowledge of good and evil'." But such reasoning might be somewhat of a stretch. Shifting one's focus is "doing" (*is a mental action*). But shifting one's focus is not "knowing". Having a reason for the shift is "knowing". Nevertheless, this author still holds to the position that Adam and Eve had to have the "knowledge of good and evil" before exercising their right to choose "good" or "evil".

Part-2: **Genesis 2:9 and Genesis 3:22**

Genesis 2:9 establishes the existence of the "tree of 'life'" and the existence of the "tree of the 'knowledge of good and evil'". In the NIV, Genesis 2:9 reads:

> Genesis 2:[9]And the LORD God made all kinds of trees grow out of the ground--trees that were pleasing to the eye and good for food. In the middle of the garden were the tree of life and the tree of the knowledge of good and evil.

But the potential problem is Genesis 3:22. In the NIV, Genesis 3:22 reads:

> Genesis 3:[22]And the LORD God said, "The man has now become like one of us, knowing good and evil. He must not be allowed to reach out his hand and take also from the tree of life and eat, and live forever."

The amount of figurative or literal language in this verse is unknown to this author. Thus, the sentence – "He must not be allowed to reach out his hand and take also from the tree of life and eat, and live forever", is a potential problem in that someone could try to use it to support the "eat and gain the knowledge of good and evil" position that this essay and the previous loose end discussion were trying to dispute. However, there appears to be a line of reasoning that can be use to counter the ability of someone to use this verse to support the "eat and gain the knowledge of good and evil" position. This reasoning might go, as follows:

Eating and gaining the "knowledge of good and evil" is a matter of the "body" and the "soul (*which is our mind, heart, and emotions*)". Eating and gaining "eternal life" are matters of the "body" and the "spirit (*which may be our connection to God*)". Thus, the two acts involve different aspects of our beings. But the reality of the relevant verses may be that God presented an overview of both situations with the simplest language possible, without providing the details. And presumptuous or not, those details are what this author was proposing in an effort to understand, what was involved in the sinning of Adam and Eve.

> *Comment:* A radio evangelist made the observation that "God did not deny Adam and Eve access to the fruit of the 'tree of life' until after they sinned. Therefore, instead of eating the fruit of the 'tree of the knowledge of good and evil', Adam and Eve could have eaten the fruit of the 'tree of life' and lived forever."

Part-3: **An argument against Jesus, the man, being able to sin**

Probably, the most often used argument *against* Jesus, the man, being able to sin, is worded, as follows:

> "Jesus is forever the God-man. If He could have sinned in the past, then He could sin in the future, in eternity."

There appear to be two good counters to this argument. These are, as follows:

- *Counter-1*: The sin issue was dealt with by the spiritual death and the physical death of Jesus, the man, on the cross. Thus, there can be no such thing, as sinning in eternity. More precisely, the ability of Jesus, the man, to sin is only meaningful before His deaths on the cross. Furthermore, God raised Jesus, the man, from the dead to show His (God's) acceptance of the finished work of Jesus, the man, on the cross. And God raised Jesus, the man, with His eternal (*glorified*) body. Thus, at that point, the "sin" issue was dealt with on an eternal basis.

- *Counter-2*: Once Jesus, the man, died spiritually and physically on the cross and was resurrected with His glorified body by God, there was no longer a need for Him to veil His deity from His human nature. Once His deity was unveiled, there would be no reason for His human nature to want to sin against His divine nature.

Part-4: **Arguments for Jesus, the man, having the "ability to sin"**

Ten arguments *for* Jesus, the man, having the "ability to sin", are, as follows:

- Satan and his demons knew who and what Jesus, the man, is. Satan tempted Jesus, the man. Therefore, Satan must have believed that Jesus, the man, could sin. Otherwise, if Jesus, the man, could not sin, then Satan has to be the dumbest entity, that ever existed inside and outside of time.

- Satan tempted Jesus, the man, by giving Him choices that were not consistent with God's way of doing things. Obviously, Jesus, the man, evaluated Satan's choices and determined that those choices were inappropriate, because He responded to Satan's choices by stating God's choices from the Bible. Thus, Jesus, the man, was exercising His "free will" – His "right of choice" – in choosing God's way.

- Jesus, the man, is called the "last Adam" in the Bible and is called the "second Adam" by many Christians. If Jesus, the man, did not have the "ability to sin", then it is not appropriate to call Him, the "last Adam" or the "second Adam", because His human nature would be different from that of the "first Adam".

- Jesus, the man, was born "innocent" – was born "sinless" and "without the 'knowledge of good and evil'" – like the first Adam, who obviously had the "ability to sin". However, while the first Adam did sin, Jesus, the man, did not sin. Nevertheless, Jesus, the man, also had to have the "ability to sin". Such an ability would increase the symmetry between Jesus, the man, and Adam.

- For God to send One, Who did not have the "ability to sin", seems inconsistent with the character of God. God sending One, Who could not sin, is like God sending a "robot". And how could such a "robot" serve, as a valid model for the rest of us, who can and do sin?

- If Jesus, the man, the "last Adam", could not sin, then God, the Father, was unfair to the "first Adam".

- If Jesus, the man, could not sin, then He could not have been "fully human". If Jesus, the man, was "fully human", then He had to have "free will" and He had to have the "ability to sin". You cannot have it both ways. It must be either "Jesus was fully human and He had 'free will' and the 'ability to sin'" or "Jesus was not fully human and He did not have 'free will' nor the 'ability to sin'".

- If God, the Father, could keep the "last Adam" from sinning by some methodology other than freewill choices, then He could have kept the "first Adam" from sinning using the same methodology. However, in creating us, God gave us the "free will" to choose. Choice is a central theme of creation, for both angels and man. Consequently, under Satan's leadership, one-third of the angels rebelled against God by choice. And the first man, Adam, and the first woman, Eve, sinned against God by choice. Therefore, why would God, the Father, not allow the "last Adam" – Jesus, the man, to have the "right of choice"? To say, "the 'last Adam' did not have the 'free will' to choose", is inconsistent with the way God created man, as revealed in the Bible.

- If Jesus, the man, could not sin, then God played a trick on man. And if God was not going to allow Jesus, the man, to have the "ability to sin", then why didn't God just stop Adam and Eve from sinning? He would have saved Himself and us a lot of pain and suffering.

- Despite whether Jesus, the man, could sin or could not sin, the reality of His life is that He did not sin, because He kept His focus on God. And God provided Him and us with the means to resist all temptations. This is confirmed by 1 Corinthians 10:13. In the NIV, this verse reads:

> 1 Corinthians 10:[13]No temptation has seized you except what is common to man. And God is faithful; he will not let you be tempted beyond what you can bear. But when you are tempted, he will also provide a way out so that you can stand up under it.

But remember that while God provides us with a way to stand up under any tempting, He does not force us to accept the way.

Part-5: **Comments by three radio ministers**

Some interesting insights on the issue of "testing" were aired during three different Christian radio programs:

Program-1: During a broadcast of the daily radio program – "Truths for Life", Pastor Alistair Begg compared "testing by God" and "tempting by Satan", by saying, "Testing by God is a setup for you to pass. Tempting by Satan is a setup for you to fail."

Program-2: Another radio minister compared "testing by God" and "tempting by Satan" using the comments: "God does things to draw us to Him. Satan does things to draw us away from God."

Program-3: A third radio minister made comments to the effect that "God knows the past, present, and future. Thus, testing is for the benefit of the individual being tested."

Part-6: **Some final comments**

Final comments are presented in two groups, as follows:

- *Group-1*: It is important to remember that there is a difference between "being tempted" and "sinning". "Being tempted" is 'being pushed into the position of having to evaluate choices prior to exercising your *right to choose* – prior *to selecting one of the choices*'. Or more precisely, 'being tempted" is "being pushed into the position of having to choose *good* or *evil* – of having to choose *Godly choices* or *unGodly choices*. Whereas, "sinning" is "choosing evil" – "choosing the unGodly choices".

- *Group-2*: By using the phrase – "Jesus, the man", this essay did explicitly indicate that it was the human nature of Jesus that Satan tempted. This is confirmed by noting the three things that Satan referenced, during his tempting of Jesus, the man. These three things were recorded in Matthew 4:3, 4:6, and 4:9. These verses read, as follows:

> (Matthew 4:3 NIV) The tempter came to him and said, "If you are the Son of God, tell these stones to become bread."
>
> (Matthew 4:6 NIV) "If you are the Son of God," he said, "throw yourself down. For it is written: 'He will command his angels concerning you, and they will lift you up in their hands, so that you will not strike your foot against a stone.'"
>
> (Matthew 4:8 NIV) Again, the devil took him to a very high mountain and showed him all the kingdoms of the world and their splendor.
> (Matthew 4:9 NIV) "All this I will give you," he said, "if you will bow down and worship me."

An excellent sermon on "temptation", "the tempting of Eve", and "the tempting of Jesus" was presented by Dr. Dick L. Temple of the Bethel Christian Center. Dr. Temple's sermon was titled – "WHAT YOU NEED TO KNOW ABOUT TEMPTATION". A PDF version of the sermon is available at: www.bethelchristian center.org/sermon_notes/temptation/734dt01_temptation.pdf. For this essay, only the three comments, which relate each of the three tempting's of Jesus to one of the three categories of temptation – the "lust of the flesh", the "lust of the eyes", and the "pride of life" – are presented. More specifically, Dr. Temple said:

> "The 'lust of the flesh' was 'Turn the stones into bread'. The 'lust of the eyes' was 'Offered Him all the kingdoms'. The 'pride of life' was 'Told Him to jump off the pinnacle of the temple and the angels would come to his rescue'."

Are there unbiblical-heretical "Jesus Died Spiritually" doctrines and a biblical "Jesus Died Spiritually" doctrine?

Comment: It is important that you continue reading to understand what the phrase – "Jesus Died Spiritually" means, because it does not literally mean that the "Spirit of Jesus Died." More specifically, the phrase – "Spirit of Jesus Died", does not convey an appropriate-Christian representation of the situation indicated by the phrase: "Jesus Died Spiritually." An analogy is noted by examining the phrase – "He died physically", where the "He" is "any man". Obviously, this phrase could literally mean that "the body of a man died." However, the phrase – "the body of a man died", does not convey an appropriate-Christian representation of the situation. A more precise-Christian representation of the situation would be to say that the phrase – "He died physically", means that "a man's soul and spirit were separated from his body". Thus, a more precise-Christian representation of the phrase – "Jesus Died Spiritually", is given later in this essay.

The question – "Are there unbiblical-heretical 'Jesus Died Spiritually' doctrines and a biblical 'Jesus Died Spiritually' doctrine?", was formed to allow this author to address, resolve, and respond to two apparently-contradictory situations.

- *Situation-1*: While researching issues that are discussed in this book, this author came across several web documents, which promote the claim that it is heresy to say, "Jesus died spiritually, on the cross."

- *Situation-2*: While composing the essay – "What is the literal and symbolic significance in the shedding of Jesus' innocent blood?", this author was convinced that "Jesus, the man, had to die spiritually on the cross, as the penalty for our sins. Furthermore, this spiritual death had to occur before His physical death (*on the cross*), which was the atoning sacrifice for our sins."

Thus, the fundamental questions become "Did Jesus, the man, die spiritually, on the cross or not?" and "Is it unbiblical and/or heretical to believe in the spiritual death of Jesus, the man?" The latter unbiblical-heretical question is a bit touchy for this author, because all of the "Jesus Died Spiritually" doctrines that have been encountered by this author, are clearly unbiblical and heretical, because the promoters of "unbiblical-heretical Jesus Died Spiritually" doctrines try to use the Bible to support their position. Therefore, the words – "unbiblical-heretical", are intended to emphasize two things: *First*, their attempts are logically invalid and biblically inappropriate, because they use unclear verses, as support, while they ignore clear verses, which contradict the "underlying implication" of the "unbiblical-heretical Jesus Died Spiritually" doctrines. And, *second*, their attempts are contrary to the essential beliefs of Christianity. Thus, the word – "unbiblical" represents the "contrary to the Bible" aspect and the word – "heretical" represents the "contrary to the essential beliefs of Christianity" aspect.

Unbiblical-heretical "Jesus Died Spiritually" doctrines, are discussed in many web documents. Four such web documents are at the following web addresses:

- ✓ www.discernment.org/jesus.htm.
- ✓ www.deceptioninthechurch.com/word-faith2.html.
- ✓ frontpage.kconline.com/faithassembly/jdsfirstpart.htm.
- ✓ www.afcministry.com/Was_Jesus_separated_from_the_Father.htm.

Many of these web documents present the "underlying implication" of unbiblical-heretical "Jesus Died Spiritually" doctrines and the "common components" of such doctrines. Some web documents even explain why most "Jesus Died Spiritually" doctrines are unbiblical and/or heretical. However, the existence of unbiblical-heretical "Jesus Died Spiritually" doctrines, does not negate the existence of a biblical "Jesus Died Spiritually" doctrine. Thus, the tasks for this essay are:

1) Presenting the "underlying implication" and the "common components" of unbiblical-heretical "Jesus Died Spiritually" doctrines,

2) Presenting some comments explaining, why most of the "common components" of the unbiblical-heretical "Jesus Died Spiritually" doctrines, are unbiblical and/or heretical,

and then,

3) Presenting a biblical "Jesus Died Spiritually" doctrine, by defining its "underlying implication", and its "components",

4) Presenting support for the "underlying implication", and the "components" of a biblical "Jesus Died Spiritually" doctrine.

To accomplish these four tasks, the rest of this essay is organized in six parts. Part-1 presents the "underlying implication" and the "common components" of unbiblical-heretical "Jesus Died

Spiritually" doctrines. Part-2 presents some comments explaining, why most of the "common components" of the unbiblical-heretical "Jesus Died Spiritually" doctrines, are unbiblical and/or heretical. Part-3 defines the "underlying implication" and the "components" of a biblical "Jesus Died Spiritually" doctrine. Part-4 presents support for the "underlying implication", and the "components" of a biblical "Jesus Died Spiritually" doctrine. Part-5 presents some concluding comments. Part-6 presents a final comment about this essay.

Part-1: **The "underlying implication" and the "common components" of unbiblical-heretical "Jesus Died Spiritually" doctrines**

Because there are more than two variations of the unbiblical-heretical "Jesus Died Spiritually" doctrine, it is easier to define them in terms of an "underlying implication" and the "common components". The "underlying implication" and the "common components" are two separate issues. Thus, Part-1 is organized in two sections. Section-1 presents the "underlying implication" of unbiblical-heretical "Jesus Died Spiritually" doctrines. Section-2 presents most of the "common components" of unbiblical-heretical "Jesus Died Spiritually" doctrines.

Section-1: **The "underlying implication"**

The "underlying implication" of unbiblical-heretical "Jesus Died Spiritually" doctrines is:

"Jesus finished His redemptive work in Hell, *not on the cross*."

Because these doctrines indicate that Jesus finished His redemptive work in Hell, most promoters of unbiblical-heretical "Jesus Died Spiritually" doctrines include a "War in Hell/War in the Pit" scenario and/or a "Jesus was tormented in Hell/Jesus suffered in Hell" scenario in their doctrine. Based on several web documents, a paraphrased unbiblical-heretical "Jesus died spiritually" doctrine might read, as follows:

"Jesus was nailed to the cross. There He became sin when He yielded himself to Satan and took on the evil nature of Satan. He became one in nature with the Adversary. That is, when Jesus took on the diabolical nature of Satan, Jesus became the Serpent lifted up. See John 3:14. At this point, Jesus was a 'lost' man, crying, 'My God, my God, why hast thou forsaken me?' He had now died spiritually. Then Jesus died physically (*His second death*). Upon His physical death, His spirit was taken into the pit of Hell, where He was chained with the fetters of sin, disease, and with all the evil of Satan. Satan stood before the choir of Hell directing the demonic hosts, who gleefully chorused: 'We have won; we have conquered the Son of God!' There followed a gala celebration in the Pit, by Satan and his demons, because Satan believed that he had triumphed over God. However, what Satan did not know was that Jesus, when He became sin and took on Satan's evil nature, was acting as a substitute for sinners by identifying as a lost man with them. Jesus was, therefore, abandoned by God, Who was no longer His Father, inasmuch as Satan was now

His master. Jesus suffered agonies beyond description in the Pit for three days as all the hosts of Hell were upon Him. Then suddenly – Jesus was justified! From His throne in heaven, Almighty God arose, put His hands to his mouth and screamed: 'It is finished, it is enough!' Jesus was now born again and made spiritually alive once more. Hell itself was shaken, as Jesus shook off His chains of sin, sickness, and evil. Then Jesus walked over to Satan, grabbed him and threw him to the ground. As Satan cowered and trembled on the floor of the Pit, Jesus put His foot on top of Satan and took the keys of death, Hell, and the grave from him. At that moment, God, the Holy Spirit, kicked open the gates of Hell and raised Jesus from death. After being raised, Jesus ascended to God, the Father, and announced: 'I have paid the price; the prison is now open.' It was 'a-born-again' man, Who defeated Satan. Jesus is the firstborn from the spiritually dead. Thus, it was when Jesus was made alive down in the Pit that the believer was also made alive. The Church had its origin in the Pit of Hell, when Jesus was begotten from the dead as the 'firstborn among many brethren'."

The above scenario is characteristic of unbiblical-heretical "Jesus Died Spiritually" doctrines and includes most of the "common components" of such doctrines.

Section-2: **The "common components" of the unbiblical-heretical "Jesus Died Spiritually" doctrines**

Using the same or slightly different wording, than that used in the presentation of Section-1, a list of "common components" might read, as follows:

1) On the cross, Jesus became sin.

2) Because Jesus became sin, He was separated from God.

3) Because Jesus became sin, He took on Satan's sin-nature.

4) Being separated from God means that Jesus died spiritually on the cross.

5) Since Jesus died spiritually on the cross, He had to be reborn in Hell.

6) Jesus died physically and then spent three days in Hell, where He was tormented by Satan and his demons (*Satan's demons*).

7) Satan and his demons rejoiced at the arrival of Jesus in Hell, because they assumed that Jesus had been defeated.

8) However, after three days, God, the Father, found a loophole that "allowed Him and Jesus to defeat Satan and his demons", that "allowed Jesus to be freed from Hell", and most

importantly that "allowed Jesus to finish His redemptive work".

As mentioned before, some unbiblical-heretical "Jesus Died Spiritually" doctrines might use different wording and/or even a different number of components than the previous eight summarized components. However, the "underlying implication" is the same, regardless of either condition.

Part-2: **Some comments that explain why most of the "common components" of unbiblical-heretical "Jesus Died Spiritually" doctrines are unbiblical and/or heretical**

These comments are presented in the following format: *First*, each of the eight "common components" from Part-1/Section-2, is listed. *Second*, immediately following each listing are comments, which explain why that particular component might be considered unbiblical and/or heretical, by many Christians. These comments are enclosed between double bold-typed brackets. Thus, the presentation is, as follows:

1) On the cross, Jesus became sin.

[[*Is unbiblical and/or heretical because*: The statement - "Jesus became sin", is sloppy and incomplete English. What does it mean for "Jesus to become sin"? There are two approaches to addressing this question. One approach would replace the word - "sin", in the statement - "Jesus became sin", with its meaning to see if the resulting statement makes sense. Another approach - possibly a better approach - is to present a web document at web address:

"http://kingdomready.org/blog/2006/11/27/sin-or-sin-offering/".

This web document was authored by Pastor Vince Finnegan of the Living Hope Community Church in Latham, New York, and reads:

Sin or Sin-Offering
November 27th, 2006 by Vince

What do you think? Did Jesus become sin on the cross?

> 2 Corinthians 5:21 states "He made Him who knew no sin to be sin on our behalf, so that we might become the righteousness of God in Him."

Yet there are so many verses that state Jesus was innocent and sinless (Matthew 27:4; Luke 23:47; John 8:46; 1 Peter 1:19; 2:22). How could he become sin?

> Various interpretations have been put forward to understand this: 1) Christ was made a sinner, 2) Christ was made a sin-offering, and 3) Christ was made to bear the consequences of our sins. One popular teaching is because Jesus became sin, God forsook him on the cross which is why Jesus uttered, "My God, my God why have You forsaken me?" However, Psalm 22 contradicts this reasoning since this is the Scripture Jesus is quoting while he was on the cross.
>
> A major part of the Old Covenant was the sacrificial offering that provides a type for the sacrifice of Jesus. The Greek word *hamartia*, translated sin in 2 Corinthians 5:21, is never translated sin-offering in the New Testament however, it is translated sin-offering in Leviticus 4:24 and 5:12 (LXX). It seems consistent with the whole Bible that Jesus was the sin-offering and not that he became sin. How could a sinless person become sin? How could innocent blood be shed on the cross if Jesus became sin?

This web document reminded the reader that "***A major part of the Old Covenant was the 'sacrificial offering' that provides a type for the sacrifice of Jesus.***" Thus, "Jesus becoming a sin-offering", would be a more appropriate interpretation, than "Jesus became sin." Furthermore, this particular web document also indicated that "*the Greek word – 'hamartia', translated as the word – 'sin', in 2 Corinthians 5:21, is never translated 'sin-offering' in the New Testament.* And this last statement seems to be true for most English translations except the NIV, because it does translate this Greek word as "sin-offering" in Romans 8:3 and Hebrews 13:11. (*More comments on this are presented later under this component.*)

Since languages change over time and since the LXX, also called the "Septuagint" and the "Greek Old Testament", is a translation of the "Hebrew Old Testament" into Greek from 250-150 B.C., it could be that the Greek word – "hamartia", had one meaning around the period 250-150 B.C., and another meaning around the time that 2 Corinthians was written and afterward. The word – "afterward", is included, because three other translations – the NIV, the NASB, and the NRSV – also use similar wording – "to be sin" – for 2 Corinthians 5:21, as the KJV. Also note that translations are not inerrant, but the Bible in its original languages is.

In concluding this discussion of the phrase – "Jesus became sin", it is interesting to note two things. *First*, in the Old Testament of the NIV translation, the phrase – "sin-offering" occurs one-hundred and nine times in one-hundred verses. In the New Testament of the NIV translation, the phrase – "sin-offering" occurs two times in two verses – (Romans 8:3 and Hebrews 13:11). Thus, again as indicated by Pastor Vince Finnegan, the concept of "a sin-offering" is well established, especially in the Old Testament. And then note that the use of the phrase in Romans 8:3 is with regards to Jesus, the man. Romans 8:3 reads:

(Romans 8:3 NIV) For what the law was powerless to do in that it was weakened by the sinful nature, God did by sending his own Son in the likeness of sinful man to be a sin offering. And so he condemned sin in sinful man,

Second, in another essay, the word – "sin" was defined as "an event", which was simply the occurrence of "a freewill thought, word, and/or deed, which is contrary to God's will". This definition implies that the statement – "Jesus became sin", would mean that "He became an event." While one could consider something happening to an individual, an event, literally, the statement – "Jesus became 'a freewill thought, word, and/or deed, which is contrary to God's will'", makes no sense. Thus for this author, the statement – "Jesus became sin", has to be an inappropriate translation. The statement – "Jesus became a sin-offering" makes more sense.**]]**

2) Because Jesus became sin, He was separated from God.

[[*Is unbiblical and/or heretical because*: Of the ambiguity of the statement – "He was 'separated' from God." Note that the statement – "Jesus became Sin", was dealt with under the first component. Therefore only the statement – "He was separated from God", has to be examined here with the focus on the meaning of the word – "separated". Clearly, this word has to be clarified, because two or more things can only be separated, if they are related to each other – are associated – in some way or in some fashion. That is, the two or more things would have to be related or associated by "time", by "location", by "substance", by some "attribute of one or more of the things", or by some "characteristic of one or more of the things", then these things could be separated. Thus, there are, at least, three thoughts on "Jesus being separated from God". These are, as follows:

- *Thought-1*: There should be no doubt that there is no way for Jesus, God the Son, to be separated from God, the Father, and God, the Holy Spirit, because They are One. And even though Jesus has two natures: "God" and "man". His "God-nature" was veiled and the redemptive work on the cross involved only His "man-nature (*His human nature*)". Thus, the issue of a separation has to be about "God" and "Jesus, the man".

- *Thought-2*: Being "separated from God" cannot be an issue of "time", because God and Jesus, the man, are being referenced, in the same moment that Jesus is on the cross. Besides, although God works in time, He also exist outside of time. Being "separated from God" cannot be an issue of "location", because God is omnipresent, which means "there is no place that God is not." Being "separated from God" cannot be an issue of "substance", because the redemptive work on the cross involved Jesus, the man. Once more, Jesus' "God-nature" was veiled. And spiritual and physical death are not relevant to Jesus, God the Son. More specifically, being "separated from God" cannot be an issue of "substance", because God and Jesus, the man, are not of the same "substance". God is spirit and Jesus, the man, is a human being. Thus, a "separation" based on "substance" is meaningless. Therefore by a process of elimination, the being "separated from God" has to be an issue of the "attributes of God and/or of man". Then because God is the One, who designed the "redemption plan for man", it is more logical that being "separated from God" has to be an issue of His attributes (*the attributes of God*), rather than the "attributes of man". This means that when we speak of being "separated from God", such a "separation", has to involve "someone being separated from the presence of one of God's attributes, but placed in the presence of another of God's attributes." For example, men, angels, and other creatures will exist eternally in heaven, under God's grace – (*grace is obviously one of God's attributes*). Or they will exist eternally in the "Lake of Fire" or "Hell", under God's judgment – (*judgment is one of His attributes, which flows from a combination of some of His other attributes, like His justice, His knowledge, His will, and His power*). If the meaning – "separated from God's grace" is accepted as the meaning of the phrase – "separated from God", then as far as this author is concerned, the statement – "He was 'separated' from God", would not be unbiblical nor heretical. But lacking any clarification, the statement – "He was 'separated' from God", would have to be considered, at best, incomplete, and at worse, unbiblical and heretical.

- *Thought-3*: Being "separated from God" is taken by some opponents of "Jesus Died Spiritually" doctrines to mean "a separation of the 'God-nature of Jesus' from 'God'". However, this meaning is "biblically inappropriate" and "illogical", because the work on the cross involved Jesus, the man, not Jesus, God, the Son. Nevertheless, again, most opponents of "Jesus Died Spiritually" doctrines reject such doctrines, based on their belief that it would be impossible for there to be any type of separation between "God, the Father" and "God, the Son". This impossibility is held by most Christians, including this author. However, this author would base his rejection of the "'God-nature of Jesus' being separated from 'God'" on the fact that the redemptive work on the cross involved only Jesus, the man and not Jesus, God, the Son. Otherwise, there would have been no reason for Jesus, God, the Son, to also become Jesus, the man.**]]**

3) Because Jesus became sin, He took on Satan's sin-nature.

[[*Is unbiblical and/or heretical because*: Of reasoning, which focuses on the statement – "He took on Satan's sin-nature." (*Again note that the statement – "Because Jesus became sin", has already been dealt with.*) Such reasoning might go, as follows:

- *Reason-1*: The statement – "He took on Satan's sin-nature", is meaningless, as Jesus, the man, is dying on the cross. Such an assessment is based on the meaning of the wording – "sin-nature", which could simply mean "one has a tendency toward freely choosing a thought, a word, and/or a deed that are contrary to God's will" – nothing more or nothing less. If such a meaning is valid, then Jesus, the man, taking on Satan's "sin-nature", is meaningless in a situation, where He (*Jesus, the man*) does not have an opportunity to display the tendency. That is, if Jesus, the man, does not have an opportunity to sin, how could it be confirmed that He took on Satan's sin-nature. Furthermore, even as our substitute, Jesus, the man, taking on Satan's "sin-nature", is meaningless, because the penalty that Jesus, the man, paid was for our "sins", not our "sin-nature". Yes! Our "sins" are the result of our "sin-nature". But "sin" and "sin-nature" are two different things. "Sin-nature" is a "probably will do" issue, whereas "sin" is a "did/done" issue. Thus, God laid our "sins" in the "spiritual account" of Jesus, the man, not our "sin-nature". The point is:

> "However God accomplished the assignment of our sins to our substitute, who is Jesus, the man, is probably beyond our comprehension. But based on the nature of God, we know that He worked it out such that it was consistent with His attributes and His word."

Speaking of God's word (*the Bible*), there is no explicit indication in the Bible that while Jesus, the man, was being crucified, He took on Satan's sin-nature.

➧ *Reason-2*: The redemptive process was designed by God, to redeem man, and not Satan nor his demons. Therefore, if Jesus, the man, had to take on someone's sin-nature, that sin-nature should be Adam's, since Adam represented all of us when he sinned, because all of us (*except Jesus, the man*) were in his loins (*in his DNA*). Therefore, biblically and logically, there is no reason for Jesus, the man, to take on Satan's sin-nature.

Reason-3: A variation of *Reason-2* is worded around the belief that there is a difference between the "sin-nature of Satan" (*the "sin-nature that formed in Satan, as he rebelled against God"*) and the "sin-nature of Adam" (*the "sin-nature that formed in Adam, as he sinned against God"*). The difference is probably a matter of focus, intensity, or degrees. Nevertheless, support for this reason seems to flow from two facts:

✓ *Fact-1*: Satan rebelled against God. This rebellion was of his own "free will" without any enticement from any other source. Furthermore, Satan rebelled, because he wanted to be greater than God. And, Satan talked another third of the angels into joining him in his rebellion against God.

✓ *Fact-2*: Adam sinned against God. This sin was of his own "free will", but it was with the enticement of Satan and Eve. Adam was not trying to be greater than God. He might have been trying to be like God, knowing good and evil, but not greater than God. That is, one of the enticements of Satan was that Adam and Eve would be like God, knowing good and evil.

Based on these two facts, this author would reason that "Satan's sin-nature" is more evil than "Adam's sin-nature", if it is "spiritually correct to make such a comparison". Thus, once more, being that Jesus was paying the penalty and atonement for the sins of man, if Jesus took on anyone's "sin-nature", it would seem more appropriate for that to be "Adam's sin-nature" not "Satan's sin-nature".**]]**

4) Being separated from God means that Jesus died spiritually on the cross.

[[<u>*This is not unbiblical nor heretical*</u>: As long as you understand, that the phrase – "separated from God", is not like being somewhere that God is not. Rather, as indicated under the second component, the phrase – "separated from God", means "a separation from His grace", not from His presence, because God is omnipresent, which means being present everywhere at the same time. This meaning of the phrase – "separated from God", is supported by three events: <u>*first*</u>, "*What God said to Adam, before he sinned*"; <u>*second*</u>, "*What God said to Adam and Eve, after they sinned*"; and <u>*third*</u>, "*What God did to Adam and Eve, after they sinned*". More specifically:

- "<u>*What God said to Adam, before he sinned*</u>", was recorded in Genesis 2:17. Four translations of Genesis 2:17 read, as follows:

  (Genesis 2:17 KJV) But of the tree of the knowledge of good and evil, thou shalt not eat of it: <u>for in the day that thou eatest thereof thou shalt surely die</u>.

  (Genesis 2:17 NIV) but you must not eat from the tree of the knowledge of good and evil, <u>for when you eat of it you will surely die</u>."

  (Genesis 2:17 NASB) but from the tree of the knowledge of good and evil you shall not eat, <u>for in the day that you eat from it you shall surely die</u>."

  (Genesis 2:17 NRSV) but of the tree of the knowledge of good and evil you shall not eat, <u>for in the day that you eat of it you shall die</u>."

  Note that while the NIV translation used the word – "when", the other three translations used the phrase: "in the day". Thus, we can assume that the original language references wording that is consistent with the word – "when" and the phrase: "in the day". If this is true, then God told Adam that he (*Adam*) would die sometime, relatively soon, after he ate some of the forbidden fruit.

- "*What God said to Adam and Eve, after they sinned*", was recorded in Genesis 3:15-24. In the NIV, these verses read:

  Genesis 3:[15]And I will put enmity between you and the woman, and between your offspring and hers; he will crush your head, and you will strike his heel." [16]To the woman he said, "I will greatly increase your pains in childbearing; with pain you will give birth to children. Your desire will be for your husband, and he will rule over you." [17]To Adam he said, "Because you listened to your wife and ate from the tree about which I commanded you, 'You must not eat of it,' "Cursed is the ground because of you; through painful toil you will eat of it all the days of your life. [18]It will produce thorns and thistles for you, and you will eat the plants of the field. [19]By the sweat of your brow you will eat your food until you return to the ground, since from it you were taken; for dust you are and to dust you will return."

- "*What God did to Adam and Eve, after they sinned*", was put them out of the "Garden of Eden". See Genesis 3:20-24. In the NIV, these verses read:

  Genesis 3:[20]Adam named his wife Eve, because she would become the mother of all the living. [21]The LORD God made garments of skin for Adam and his wife and clothed them. [22]And the LORD God said, "The man has now become like one of us, knowing good and evil. He must not be allowed to reach out his hand and take also from the tree of life and eat, and live forever." [23]So the LORD God banished him from the Garden of Eden to work the ground from which he had been taken. [24]After he drove the man out, he placed on the east side of the Garden of Eden cherubim and a flaming sword flashing back and forth to guard the way to the tree of life.

By summarizing the previous three events and by using Genesis 5:5, a line of reasoning is presented, which serves two functions. *First*, it serves as explicit support for the meaning of the phrase – "separated from God" to be "being separated from His grace". And, *second*, it serves as implicit support for the point that the use of the phrase – "separated from God", is sloppy and incomplete grammar. A summary of the previous three events is:

✏ "*What God said to Adam, before he sinned*": "for when you eat of it you will surely die."

✏ "*What God said to Adam, after he sinned*": "By the sweat of your brow you will eat your food until you return to the ground."

✏ "*What God did to Adam, after he sinned*": "the LORD God banished him from the Garden of Eden to work the ground from which he had been taken."

In the NIV, Genesis 5:5 reads, as follows:

✏ "Altogether, Adam lived 930 years, and then he died."

The line of reasoning begins with taking the word – "die", in Genesis 2:17, to mean "spiritual death", not "physical death". This conclusion is supported by four facts:

✓ *Fact-1*: The death implied in Genesis 2:17, had to happen soon, after Adam sinned.

✓ *Fact-2*: The phrase – "until you return to the ground" in Genesis 3:19, is "physical death".

✓ *Fact-3*: Adam lived nine hundred and thirty years, after he and Eve sinned.

✓ *Fact-4*: The statement – "Altogether, Adam lived 930 years, and then he died", is a reference to the 'physical death' of Adam.

Worded differently, we can reason that:

"Because Adam and Eve sinned, God put them out of the 'Garden of Eden'. That is, Adam and Eve went:

from	existing	***under God's grace***,	in the Garden of Eden
to	existing	***under God's judgment***,	in the world."

Thus, "Adam and Eve died spiritually", in that "they were separated from God's grace." Then based on what happened to Adam and Eve, this author would propose that:

➧ "Men, angels, and other creatures
will exist eternally ***under God's grace***, in "Heaven",

or

- "Men, angels, and other creatures
  will exist eternally ***under God's judgment***, in the "Lake of Fire" or "Hell".

To summarize, the point is:

> "The phrases – 'being separated from God' and 'separated from God', are 'sloppy English phrases' and 'biblically inappropriate', without more words to qualify or clarify them. However, if the meaning of the phrase – "being separated from God", is accepted as "being separated from God's grace", then we can say, "Jesus died spiritually on the cross." And this would be consistent with the Book of Genesis. Furthermore, with that acceptance the fourth component would not be unbiblical nor heretical."]]

Comment: Some Christians feel that in is inappropriate to associate the word – "grace", with Adam and Eve. This feeling is based on their belief that "grace" only began with the new covenant and Christ. However, anyone holding this belief must consider two facts:

✓ *Fact-1*: While it is true that "grace" is a central component of the new covenant and the redemptive work of Christ, "grace" is one of the attributes of God. And, God is unchanging. Therefore, God's "grace" has always existed, whether it was displayed or not. This view is confirmed by Christian authors like author A. W. Tozer. See Chapter 19 (*titled: The Grace of God*) of his book: "Knowledge of the Holy".

✓ *Fact-2*: God did display His "grace", with Adam and Eve. In fact, God showed them "mercy" and "grace". God's "mercy" was shown, because He did not destroy them immediately after they sinned. God's "grace" was shown, because He provided a way – (*by looking forward to the cross and the finished work of Christ*) – for them to return to an existence under His grace.

---

5) Since Jesus died spiritually on the cross, He had to be reborn in Hell.

[[*Is unbiblical and/or heretical because*: Of the statement – "He had to be reborn in Hell." The statement – "Jesus died spiritually on the cross", is acceptable and biblical, as far as this author is concerned. However, the need for "Jesus, the man, to be reborn in Hell", is biblically and logically inappropriate, for three reasons, which are, as follows:

➧ *Reason-1*: Biblically, the need for "Jesus, the man, to be reborn in Hell", is inappropriate, because the proponents of unbiblical-heretical "Jesus Died Spiritually" doctrines forget that the "penalty for sin is death", but this death is "spiritual death", which is "a separation from God's grace". "The penalty for sin" is not a visit to Hell, nor is it suffering in Hell. Romans 6:23 seems to support this position. In the NIV, this verse reads, as follows:

> Romans 6:[23]For the wages of sin is death, but the gift of God is eternal life in Christ Jesus our Lord.

Thus, based on Romans 6:23, we can reason that the indicated "death" is the opposite of an "eternal life in Christ Jesus". And then based on other references in the Bible, we can equate the "opposite of an 'eternal life in Christ Jesus'" to the "Second Death", which is "the eternal separation from God's grace".

➧ *Reason-2*: Logically, the need for "Jesus, the man, to be reborn in Hell", is inappropriate, because after the "penalty for our sins" was paid *(after Jesus, the man, "died spiritually", on the cross)*, He "died physically", on the cross. His "physical death" served as the sacrificial shedding of His innocent blood, which was required, as "an atoning sacrifice for our sins". Thus, while proponents of unbiblical-heretical "Jesus Died Spiritually" doctrines, stress the "spiritual death" of Jesus, on the cross, they are obviously ignoring the purpose of His "spiritual death". Then they compound the issue by ignoring the purpose of His "physical death", on the cross. By ignoring the purposes of His "spiritual and physical deaths", proponents can say that the rebirth of Jesus, the man, in Hell, satisfied the "penalty aspect" of sin. To which we could respond by asking, "When and how was the 'atonement aspect' of sin satisfied?", since Jesus, the man, had to be physically dead to go to Hell. In addition, the "penalty aspect" of sin would have to be fulfilled before the "atonement aspect". And again, the "atonement aspect" would require the shedding of His blood, which is His physical death. Thus, unless this author is missing something, proponents of unbiblical-heretical "Jesus Died Spiritually" doctrines, are trapped in an absurd situation, by ignoring the purposes of the "spiritual and physical deaths of Jesus, on the cross".

➧ *Reason-3*: Biblically and logically, for Christians, the word – "reborn", usually carries the meaning of "the spiritual rebirth of an individual, because of the reestablishment of her or his spiritual connection to God, through her or his acceptance of the free gift of salvation, which is offered by Jesus Christ". However, this author prefers the definition: "'reborn' is 'the spiritual rebirth of an individual, which occurs when an individual *returns to* an existence under God's grace *from* an existence under God's judgment. That return is based on the individual's acceptance of the free gift of salvation, which is offered by Jesus

Christ'". However, if proponents of "Jesus Died Spiritually" doctrines want to indicate that "Jesus had to be 'reborn' in Hell", then this "reborn" has to be carrying a different meaning, because it is Christ, who is being reborn. Did Christ save Himself in Hell? To this author, such a condition creates a "biblical and logical" problem for proponents of these doctrines. That is, to this author, biblically and logically, it is very simple:

✓ "*First*, when God placed our sins in the 'spiritual account' of Jesus, the man, He 'died spiritually', on the cross to pay the penalty for those sins. More specifically, when God placed our sins in the 'spiritual account' of Jesus, the man, He went from existing under God's grace to existing under God's judgment, as a penalty for our sins. Remember Jesus, the man, was born of a virgin. Therefore, He was born under God's grace. He lived a sinless life. Therefore, He remained under God's grace until, our sins were placed in His 'spiritual account'.

✓ *Second*, Jesus, the man, 'died physically', on the cross. The 'physical death' of Jesus, the man, served as an atoning sacrifice for our sins and was the basis for His rebirth (*was the basis for His return to an existence under God's grace*). Therefore, there was no need for Jesus, the man, to go to Hell to be reborn."]]

6) Jesus died physically and then spent three days in Hell, where He was tormented by Satan and his demons (*Satan's demons*).

[[*Is unbiblical and/or heretical because*: Of four considerations. These are, as follows:

- *Consideration-1*: Similar to the animal sacrificial offerings, the "physical death" of "Jesus, the man", who is the Christ (*the innocent sacrificial lamb of God*), served, as the "atoning sacrifice for our sins", not the "penalty for our sins". Recall that animal sacrifices served, as a temporary atonement; whereas the "physical death" of "Jesus, the man" served, as an eternal atonement. It was the "spiritual death" of Jesus that served, as the "penalty for our sins", not going to Hell nor suffering in Hell. Once more, the point is:

  "the 'penalty for sin' is 'spiritual death', nothing more and nothing less. And 'spiritual death' is 'being separated from God's grace and being under God's judgment'. (*Remember Jesus, the man, was born innocent – sinless. Therefore, He was born under God's grace and was only separated from that grace, when God placed our sins in the spiritual account of Jesus, the man.*)"

- *Consideration-2*: If Jesus, the man, went anywhere, after His physical death on the cross, He went to "Abraham's bosom", which is a euphemism for the "abode of the righteous dead", because that is where Abraham was with the rest of the righteous dead. In "Abraham's bosom", Jesus announced the completion of His redemptive work on the cross. Then He led the righteous dead into the presence of God, the Father, in "Paradise". Support for His ending in "Paradise" is provided by His statement to one of the thieves being crucified with Him. When this thief expressed a confession of faith in Him (Jesus, the man), Jesus told this thief that he (*the thief*) would be with Him (*Jesus, the man*) in "Paradise" that very day. This was recorded in Luke 23:39-43. In the NIV, these verses read:

> Luke 23:[39] One of the criminals who hung there hurled insults at him: "Aren't you the Christ? Save yourself and us!" [40]But the other criminal rebuked him. "Don't you fear God," he said, "since you are under the same sentence? [41]We are punished justly, for we are getting what our deeds deserve. But this man has done nothing wrong." [42]Then he said, "Jesus, remember me when you come into your kingdom." [43]Jesus answered him, "I tell you the truth, today you will be with me in paradise."

The word – "Paradise", only occurs two other times in the NIV. These other occurrences are in 2 Corinthians 12:4 and Revelation 2:7. In the NIV, these verses read:

> (2 Corinthians 12:4 NIV) was caught up to paradise. He heard inexpressible things, things that man is not permitted to tell.

> (Revelation 2:7 NIV) He who has an ear, let him hear what the Spirit says to the churches. To him who overcomes, I will give the right to eat from the tree of life, which is in the paradise of God.

Based on the reference to the "tree of life" in Revelation 2:7, "Paradise" and "Abraham's bosom" are two different places. A sense of "Abraham's bosom" is derived from the parable of "the rich man and Lazarus" recorded in Luke 16:19-31. In the KJV, these verses read:

> Luke 16:[19]There was a certain rich man, which was clothed in purple and fine linen, and fared sumptuously every day. [20]And there was a certain beggar named Lazarus, which was laid at his gate, full of sores, [21]And desiring to be fed with the crumbs which fell from the rich man's table: moreover the dogs came and licked his sores. [22]And it came to pass, that the beggar died, and was carried by the angels into Abraham's bosom: the rich man also died, and was buried; [23]And in hell he lift up his eyes, being in torments, and seeth Abraham afar off, and Lazarus in his bosom. [24]And he cried and said, Father Abraham, have mercy on me, and send Lazarus,

that he may dip the tip of his finger in water, and cool my tongue; for I am
tormented in this flame. [25]But Abraham said, Son, remember that thou in
thy lifetime receivedst thy good things, and likewise Lazarus evil things:
but now he is comforted, and thou art tormented. [26]And beside all this,
between us and you there is a great gulf fixed: so that they which would
pass from hence to you cannot; neither can they pass to us, that would
come from thence. [27]Then he said, I pray thee therefore, father, that thou
wouldest send him to my father's house: [28]For I have five brethren; that
he may testify unto them, lest they also come into this place of torment.
[29]Abraham saith unto him, They have Moses and the prophets; let them
hear them. [30]And he said, Nay, father Abraham: but if one went unto
them from the dead, they will repent. [31]And he said unto him, If they hear
not Moses and the prophets, neither will they be persuaded, though one
rose from the dead.

From Luke 16:26 above, we are told that there was a "great gulf" between the "the abode of the righteous dead (*where Abraham and the beggar were*)" and "the abode of the UNrighteous dead (*where the Rich man was*)".

- *Consideration-3*: The statement – "He (*Jesus*) was tormented by Satan and his demons (*Satan's demons*)", implies that Satan and his demons, rule Hell or have some control in Hell. However, there is no biblical support for such an implication. The Bible does imply that "Satan was created by God", that "Satan rebelled against God", and that "God created the 'Lake of Fire', as the eternal abode of Satan and His demons." More precisely, the "Lake of Fire" is where Satan and his demons will be condemned for all of eternity, along with those who reject the free gift of salvation offered by Jesus, the man. Or worded another way, the "Lake of Fire" is where Satan and his demons will exist eternally under God's judgment along with those who reject the free gift of salvation offered by Jesus, the man.

  Comment: Recently a radio evangelist said, "If Satan ruled or controlled Hell, then it would not be a place of punishment for him." Furthermore, as previously mentioned, Hell is the abode of the UNrighteous dead, and the Bible indicates that it is a place of torment.

- *Consideration-4*: Some opponents of "Jesus Died Spiritually" doctrines, try to use Luke 23:46 to imply that Jesus, the man, did not go to Hell. This verse reads:

  (Luke 23:46 NIV) Jesus called out with a loud voice, "Father, into your hands I commit my spirit." When he had said this, he breathed his last.

This author totally agrees with the position that Jesus, the man, did not go to "Hell". As previously indicated, this author believes that Jesus, the man, went to "Abraham's bosom (*a euphemism for the 'abode of the righteous dead, before the cross'*)". But here, the issue is that Luke 23:46 merely indicates Jesus, the man, placed His care in the hands of God, the Father. There is no mention of a destination. Thus, this verse cannot be used to say that Jesus, the man, went or did not go anywhere. However, this verse can be used to say that Jesus, the man, submitted His will to the will of God, the Father, until the end of His (*Jesus'*) physical life.**]]**

7) Satan and his demons rejoiced at the arrival of Jesus in Hell, because they assumed that Jesus had been defeated.

[[*Is unbiblical and/or heretical because*: The phrase – "arrival of Jesus in Hell", implies that Jesus went to Hell. Thus, some of the comments made under the previous sixth component could be repeated here to emphasize that Jesus, the man, did not go to Hell, which is "the abode of the UNrighteous dead". He went to "the abode of the righteous dead", which was separated from Hell, by a wide gulf. And He went there to preach the "good news" of His finished work on the cross.**]]**

8) However, after three days, God, the Father, found a loophole that "allowed Him and Jesus to defeat Satan and his demons", that "allowed Jesus to be freed from Hell", and most important that "allowed Jesus to finish His redemptive work".

[[*Is unbiblical and/or heretical because*: Of two implications:

Implication-1: "Jesus, the man, went to Hell upon His physical death." This implication was refuted by the discussion for the sixth component.

Implication-2: "The redemptive work of Jesus was completed in Hell, not on the cross." Clearly, such an implication is a contradiction of Jesus' statement – "It is finished", just before His "physical death" on the cross. See John 19:30. This verse reads:

> (John 19:30 NIV) When he had received the drink, Jesus said, "It is finished." With that, he bowed his head and gave up his spirit.

Some support for John 19:30 indicating that the "penalty payment" aspect of the redemptive work of Jesus, the man, was finished, is provided by Matthew 27:46 and Mark 15:34. These verses read:

> (Matthew 27:46 NIV) About the ninth hour Jesus cried out in a loud voice, "Eloi, Eloi, lama sabachthani?"--which means, "My God, my God, why have you forsaken me?"

(Mark 15:34 NIV) And at the ninth hour Jesus cried out in a loud voice, "Eloi, Eloi, lama sabachthani?"--which means, "My God, my God, why have you forsaken me?"

These two verses could be taken, as the way that Jesus, the man, chose to tell us two things had happened. *First*, God, the Father, had placed our sins in His *(Jesus')* "spiritual account". *Second*, as a result of those sins, He *(Jesus, the Christ [Jesus, the man])* was "separated from God's grace", which means that He paid the penalty for our sins. The two verses would be consistent with someone, who had been focused on God, noticing the transition from existing under God's grace to existing under God's judgment. But once more, the point is:

> "Based on the Bible, the 'penalty for sin' is 'spiritual death', not suffering in Hell."

Comment: Please note that while proponents of unbiblical-heretical "Jesus Died Spiritually" doctrines, provide a detailed account of the activities and treatment of Jesus, the man, in Hell, they are very vague about the "loophole *(the 'reason')*", which allowed God to free Jesus, the man, from Hell and by that caused His rebirth spiritually.**]]**

Hopefully, this Part-2 discussion has provided you with an explanation of why most of the "common components" of unbiblical-heretical "Jesus Died Spiritually" doctrines are unbiblical and/or heretical.

Part-3: **The "underlying implication" and the "components" of a biblical "Jesus Died Spiritually" doctrine**

Since the "underlying implication" and the "components" of a biblical "Jesus Died Spiritually" doctrine, are two separate issues, Part-3 is organized in two sections. Section-1 presents the "underlying implication" of a biblical "Jesus Died Spiritually" doctrine. Section-2 presents the "components" of a biblical "Jesus Died Spiritually" doctrine.

Section-1: **The underlying implication**

The "underlying implication" of a biblical "Jesus Died Spiritually" doctrine is:

> "Jesus finished His redemptive work, on the cross, and not anywhere else."

This implication revolves around the belief that Jesus, the man, died "spiritually", on the cross, as the "penalty for our sins". Then He died "physically", on the cross, as "an atoning sacrifice for our sins". His "penalty payment" and His "atoning sacrifice" were all that God required from Jesus for the redemption of man. *(Our requirement is accepting Jesus' "penalty payment" and "atoning sacrifice" on our behalf. That is, our requirement is accepting the gift of salvation offered by the redemptive work of Jesus, on the cross.)*

Section-2: **Components**

The essential components of a biblical "Jesus Died Spiritually" doctrine, are as follows:

1) The penalty for sin is death. But this is "spiritual death", which is "a separation from God's grace". In other words, "spiritual death" is "a transition from an existence under God's grace to an existence under God's judgment". Thus, being "spiritually dead", means that "an individual is existing under God's judgment, instead of under His grace." Because of Adam's sin, all humans – except Jesus, the man – were/are/will be born "spiritually dead" (*"i.e., were/are/will be born under God's judgment"*).

2) Jesus, the man, was born of a Jewish virgin, named Mary. Thus, He was born without the stain of the original sin of Adam. More specifically, He was born "sinless". And then He kept His focus on God, which means that He remained "sinless" throughout His life.

3) While Jesus, the man, was on the cross, God, the Father, laid our sins in Jesus' "spiritual account". When this occurred, Jesus, the man, went from existing under God's grace to existing under God's judgment.

4) Jesus, the man, sensed His separation from God's grace, that is why He cried out, "Eloi, Eloi, lama sabachthani?", which means: "My God, my God, why have you forsaken me?"

5) Under God's judgment, the atoning sacrifice for sin is the shedding of innocent blood. This is physical death. Thus, after the "spiritual death" of Jesus, the man, as a "penalty payment" for our sins, He experienced "physical death", which served as the "atoning sacrifice" for our sins.

6) Because the "physical death" of Jesus, the man, served as the "atoning sacrifice" for our sins, His "physical death" reestablished His existence under God's grace. He was "spiritually reborn".

7) When we accept both the "spiritual death" of Jesus, the man, as the penalty for our sins, and His "physical death", as an "atoning sacrifice" for our sins, we are "spiritually reborn". More specifically, such an acceptance means that we return to an existence under God's grace from an existence under God's judgment.

8) After the "physical death" of Jesus, the man, He went to "Abraham's bosom", which was the "abode of the righteous dead" (*before the cross*). There Jesus, the man, preached the good news of His finished work for the redemption of man. Then He led those in the "abode of the righteous dead" into the presence of God, the Father, in "Paradise".

9) Three days after Jesus, the man, died spiritually and physically on the cross, and was buried, God, the Father, resurrected Him bodily to show the world that He (God, the Father) accepted the finished work of Jesus, the man, on the cross. And the Bible indicates that the resurrected-Jesus appeared to more than five hundred individuals.

These nine components may not be all the components that could be defined, but these are the ones that seemed the most essential.

Part-4: Support for the "underlying implication", and the "components" of a biblical "Jesus Died Spiritually" doctrine

A wide variety of issues and biblical references provide support for a biblical "Jesus Died Spiritually" doctrine. To present some of these issues and references, Part-4 is organized, as four presentations. *Presentation-1* is based on a summarization of the Bible. *Presentation-2* is based on the story of Adam and Eve in the Book of Genesis. *Presentation-3* is based on the two natures of Jesus, as revealed by the Bible. *Presentation-4* is based on the presence of God, as revealed by the Bible. These four presentations contain some comments, which have been presented before with the same wording or with different wording. Nevertheless, these presentations support a biblical "Jesus Died Spiritually" doctrine.

Presentation-1: A summarization of the Bible

A summarization of the Bible with regards to the "penalty for sin" and the "atonement for sin", should yield something like the following comments:

In time, there is a *"penalty for sin"* and an *"atonement for sin"*.

✓ *Under* the law,
the Old covenant, the *"penalty for most intentional sins"* is the "physical death" of the sinner,
and
the *"atonement for most unintentional sins"* is the "physical death" of sacrificial animals.

✓ *Under* grace,
the New covenant, the *"penalty for sin"* is the "spiritual death" of Jesus, the man,
and
the *"atonement for sin"* is the "physical death" of God's sacrificial lamb, Who is Jesus, the man.

In eternity, there is no *"penalty for sin"*. Nor is there an *"atonement for sin"*. There is only the consequence of *"not having paid the penalty in time"* or *"having paid the penalty in time"*. Here, the phrase – *"not having paid the penalty in time"*, is being used as a euphemism for the phrase – "not accepting the free gift of salvation offered by the finished work of Jesus, the man, on the cross", while the phrase – *"having paid the penalty in time"*, is being used as a euphemism for the phrase: "accepting the free gift of salvation offered by the finished work of Jesus, the man, on the cross". Thus, to summarize, we have:

✓ The consequence of *not having* paid the penalty is –

✎ eternal *death*.
✎ eternal *separation* from God's grace.
✎ eternal *existence* under God's judgment.

✓ The consequence of *having* paid the penalty is –

✎ eternal *life*.
✎ eternal *separation* from God's judgment.
✎ eternal *existence* under God's grace.

This summary is also the "underlying implication" of the other three presentations that follow. Nevertheless, "based on a summarization of the Bible", saying that "Jesus, the man, died spiritually" is not unbiblical. Nor is it heresy.

Presentation-2: **The story of Adam and Eve in the Book of Genesis**

The story of Adam and Eve could be presented here in either of two formats: "an overview" and "a detailed view". Because "a detailed view" would require too much space, here, only the overview format is presented. Besides, you can read the details for yourself, by reading the Book of Genesis. Therefore, "an overview" is, as follows:

✓ God created Adam, from the dust of the ground.
✓ God created Eve, from one of Adam's ribs.
✓ God created Adam and Eve sinless and without the knowledge of good and evil.
✓ God created the Garden of Eden, for Adam to take care of.
✓ God told Adam that he could eat any fruit in the garden, except the fruit from the "tree of the 'knowledge of good and evil'".
✓ God told Adam that he would die, if he ate of the fruit from the "tree of the 'knowledge of good and evil'".

- ✓ Eve also knew that she and Adam were not to eat of the fruit from the "tree of the 'knowledge of good and evil'".
- ✓ Eve was tempted by the serpent, and chose to sin, by eating fruit from the "tree of the 'knowledge of good and evil'".
- ✓ Eve gave some of the forbidden fruit to Adam and he also chose to sin by eating it.

- ✓ When God discovered that Adam and Eve sinned and why,
  He cursed the serpent,
  He put a judgment of pain from childbirth, on Eve,
  He put a judgment of pain from the toil of obtaining their daily bread, on Adam, and then
  He put Adam and Eve out of the Garden of Eden.

- ✓ Thus, Adam and Eve went:

from	*existing under*	**God's grace**,	*in the garden,*
to	*existing under*	**God's judgment**,	*in the world.*

The shift of Adam and Eve from an "existence under God's grace" to an "existence under God's judgment", was "**SPIRITUAL DEATH**", because of *their sin*. Similarly, when God assigned our sins to the "spiritual account" of Jesus, the man, biblically, Jesus, the man, would have experienced "**SPIRITUAL DEATH**", because of *our sins*. (*Remember Jesus, the man, was born and remained "sinless" until this point in time. Consequently, before this point in time, He was existing under God's grace.*) Therefore, based on the story of Adam and Eve in the Book of Genesis, saying that "Jesus, the man, died spiritually" is not unbiblical. Nor is it heresy.

Presentation-3: **The two natures of Jesus**

The Bible indicates that Jesus is eternally Jesus, God, the Son, a member of the Trinity. This was His first nature. However, He took on a second nature, when He took on human form via a virgin birth. Thus, He also became Jesus, the man – became "the Christ". More specifically, He became our "Kinsman-Redeemer". Having two natures meant that Jesus was "fully God" and "fully human". With respect to these two natures of Jesus, hopefully, it is obvious that everything that happened on the cross happened to Jesus, the man, because "physical death" and "spiritual death" are meaningless and illogical, when we are talking about Jesus, God, the Son. Obviously, "physical death" is meaningless, because Jesus, God, the Son, is immortal and "spiritual death", which is a separation between man and God's grace, is meaningless, because God and Jesus, God, the Son, are one. Thus, "spiritual death" and "physical death" are only meaningful to Jesus, the man. Therefore, based on the two natures of Jesus, saying that "Jesus, the man, died spiritually" is not unbiblical. Nor is it heresy.

A side issue regarding the two natures of Jesus is that too many Christians believe that Jesus was not the Christ until His baptism by John, the Baptist. Christians, who hold this belief, are in all branches of the Christian church – the "Assyrian Church of the East", the "Oriental Orthodox Church", the "Western Christian Church", and the "Eastern Christian Church". Thus, this belief has also become a point of contention between Christians. This belief will be addressed in detail in the essay – "When did Jesus become the Christ?" This essay will be in a second book titled – "Last Call!!!". Here, we note that those, who believe that "Jesus was not the Christ until His baptism by John, the Baptist", have not thought through its implications. Nor have they thought through the Biblical problems that it generates.

Presentation-4: **The presence of God**

Bible scholars indicate that one of the many attributes of God is that He is "omnipresent", which means being present everywhere at the same time. This also means that "there is no place that God is not." The "omnipresence of God", is why the phrase – "separated from God", or any of its variations, must be used with care and complete qualification. That is, when the "definition of the word – 'omnipresent'", as it relates to God, is used with regards to men, angels, and other creatures, it should be clear that there is nowhere where men, angels, or other creatures, can exist without the presence of God. This means – "that in time and in eternity, men, angels, and other creatures, will either exist under God's presence, as represented by His grace, or exist under God's presence, as represented by His judgment." And here it is important to note that it is "SIN" and "our rejection or acceptable of the finished work of Jesus" that determines whether we exist under God's grace or His judgment. Thus, it should be obvious to all that when God placed our sins in the spiritual account of Jesus, the man, He had to die spiritually – He had to be separated from God's grace at that instance. Therefore, based on the presence of God, saying that "Jesus, the man, died spiritually" is not unbiblical. Nor is it heresy. That is, based on the presence of God, saying that "Jesus, the man, went from an existence under God's grace to an existence under God's judgment (*however brief*), because of our sins is not unbiblical. Neither is it heresy.

Another way to form this presentation, based on the presence of God, is through a definition of the six phrases – "spiritual death", "spiritually dead", "spiritual rebirth", "spiritually alive", "being born physically", and "being reborn spiritually", as these are defined in terms of one's relationship to the presence of two of God's attributes: "grace" and "judgment". As these definitions are applied *in time* (*as oppose to in eternity*), they might read, as follows:

- "Spiritual death" *means* "leaving an existence under God's grace, and beginning an existence under God's judgment".
- "Spiritually dead" *means* "existing under God's judgment, not His grace".
- "Spiritual rebirth" *means* "returning to an existence under God's grace and

leaving an existence under God's judgment, because an individual accepts the finished work of Jesus, the man, on the cross, on her or his behalf".

- "Spiritually alive" *means* "existing under God's grace, not His judgment".
- "Being born physically" *means* "entering an existence under God's judgment, because of Adam's sin".
- "Being reborn spiritually" *means* "entering an existence under God's grace and leaving an existence under God's judgment, because an individual accepts the finished work of Jesus, the man, on the cross, on her or his behalf".

Therefore,

"based on the presence of God",

"the definitions of the six phrases",

and

"the requirement that Jesus, the man, had to experience the 'penalty for our sins', which is 'spiritual death'",

it is not unbiblical nor heresy to say that "Jesus, the man, experienced 'spiritual death', on the cross", prior to "His experiencing 'physical death', on the cross."

Part-5: **Some concluding comments**

As mentioned before, too many Christians interpret the "physical death" of Jesus, the man, on the cross, as both the "penalty for our sins" and as the "atoning sacrifice for our sins". These Christians ignore the fact that only the "atonement for our sins" required the "physical death" of Jesus, the man. That is, the "penalty for our sins" is "spiritual death" not "physical death". God kept it simple, but man with his sin-nature (*with his "pride of life"*), complicates things by over analyzing them. Or more precisely, man complicates things by trying to out think God. God says, "It is white." But man says, "No! It can't be. It is gray." God says, "It is black." But man says, "No! It can't be. It is gray." God says, "This is how it happened." And then He has it recorded in the Bible. Man reads the Bible and then says, "God did not mean that. He meant this." As previously mentioned, this habit flows out of man's sin-nature. More specifically, it flows out of, individuals taking pride in themselves, in their churches, in their denominations, in their traditions, and so on, instead of taking pride in God's word (*instead of taking pride in the Bible*).

People! We serve a good God, who keeps things direct and simple, because He knows that He is dealing with simple man. Thus, His redemptive plan is simple and might be summarized, as follows:

[[When our sins were placed in the "spiritual account" of Jesus, the man, He had to die spiritually, as the penalty for our sins. He had to be separated from God's grace, because of our sins. And He paid the penalty for the sins of those who believe in Him, and those who do not believe in Him. This must be true for the latter group, because someone cannot reject something that is not offered (*someone cannot reject something that is not done for them*). Furthermore, Jesus, the man, crying out, "Eloi, Eloi, lama sabachthani?", which means, "My God, my God, why have you forsaken me?", was His way of informing us of His "spiritual death". However, this cry also allowed Jesus to fulfill the scriptures. Reference Luke 24:44-47. In the KJV, these verses read:

> Luke 24:[44]And he said unto them, *These are the words which I spake unto you, while I was yet with you, that all things must be fulfilled, which were written in the law of Moses, and in the prophets, and in the psalms, concerning me.* [45]Then opened he their understanding, that they might understand the scriptures, [46]And said unto them, *Thus it is written, and thus it behoved Christ to suffer, and to rise from the dead the third day:* [47]*And that repentance and remission of sins should be preached in his name among all nations, beginning at Jerusalem.*

When Jesus used the phrase – "*in the psalms*" in Luke 24:44, it was probably a reference to Psalms 22:1, which some scholars say prophesied his use of the words – "'Eloi, Eloi, lama sabachthani?". This verse reads:

> (Psalms 22:1 NIV) For the director of music. To the tune of "The Doe of the Morning." A psalm of David. My God, my God, why have you forsaken me? Why are you so far from saving me, so far from the words of my groaning?

Then after the "spiritual death" of Jesus, He had to experience "physical death", as "an atoning sacrifice for our sins".**]]**

Therefore, saying that "Jesus, the man, died spiritually", is logical and it is consistent with the Bible. More specifically, saying that "Jesus, the man, died spiritually", is not heresy. Thus, the answer to the question – "Are there unbiblical-heretical 'Jesus Died Spiritually' doctrines and a biblical 'Jesus Died Spiritually' doctrine?", is "Yes!"

This essay can be summarized by saying, "Christ was born to be our substitute. As our substitute, He had to suffer everything that we would have suffered, because of our sins, including being separated from God's grace and existing under God's judgment – however brief that was for Christ. Our substitute had to experience 'spiritual death', as the 'penalty for our sins' and 'physical death', as the 'atoning sacrifice for our sins'."

Part-6: **A final comment about this essay**

Part-3, Part-4, and Part-5 of this essay discuss some of the same issues and topics that are covered in the essay – "What is the literal and symbolic significance in the shedding of Jesus' innocent blood?" However, the difference is the perspective and the objective of each essay. Obviously, the objective of this essay was to confirm the existence of a biblical "Jesus Died Spiritually" Doctrine. The objective of the essay – "What is the literal and symbolic significance in the shedding of Jesus' innocent blood?", is to examine the "spiritual and physical" deaths of Jesus, the man.

What is the literal and symbolic significance in the shedding of Jesus' innocent blood?

Most Christians have heard references to some variation of the Christian concept: "Jesus shed His innocent blood for the 'sins' of all men." Some Christians even understand that the word – "sins", means "all the sins of each man except the one 'unpardonable sin'". "The 'unpardonable sin' is also referenced by the phrases: 'the sin of unbelief' and 'the sin of the blasphemy of the Holy Spirit'."[1] But note that the "unpardonable sin" is such, because a sinner will not accept the pardon (*which is the gift of salvation*) offered by the finished work of Jesus – (*offered by the deaths and resurrection of Jesus*). And "not accepting the gift of salvation" means that none of that particular individual's sins are covered by the finished work of Jesus on the cross. Nevertheless, most Christians do understand that "Jesus shed His innocent blood for 'their sins'." But many of these same Christians have not pondered the full significance of the shedding of Jesus' innocent blood. Too many Christians have never asked, "What is the literal and symbolic significance in the shedding of Jesus' innocent blood?" At this point, some might say, "Why is this an issue?" This author would respond, "It is an issue for, at least, three reasons:

- *Reason-1*: Most Christians understand that the phrase – 'Jesus shed His innocent blood', means 'Jesus died'. However, too many Christians have not really thought through 'what Jesus did on the cross and its purposes'.

- *Reason-2*: Too many Christians have not learned 'to appreciate the wonder' in the shedding of Jesus' innocent blood. The wonder comes out by noting 'how God fulfilled His words on the themes implied, by the verses of the Bible', in more than one way and/or on more than one level, in many instances.'

- *Reason-3*: Too many Christians are focused only on the fact that Jesus had to satisfy the 'penalty for our sins'. These Christians seem to ignore the fact that Jesus also had to satisfy the 'atonement for our sins'. More specifically, too many Christians seem to associate the physical death of Jesus with the 'penalty for our sins', rather than the 'atonement for our sins'. These Christians do not fully understand 'how the deaths of Jesus – *His spiritual death and His physical death* – satisfied the "penalty for our sins" and

---

1 The different names reflect the way that a "*rejection of Jesus is displayed*", by an individual. More specifically, a rejection of Jesus' finished work – *the free gift of salvation* – is the "unpardonable sin". A rejection of any variation of the belief that Jesus can save is "the sin of unbelief". A rejection, which includes unkind remarks about God, the Holy Spirit, is "the sin of the blasphemy of the Holy Spirit", since one of the main purposes of God, the Holy Spirit, is to attest to the free gift of salvation offered by Jesus, the man.

the "atonement for our sins". But more important, these Christians do not understand that the shedding of His innocent blood – *His physical death* – satisfied only the atonement.'"

These three reasons allow us to focus on three biblical themes, which are:

1) The wages of sin is death (*which Christians understand to mean "the penalty for sin is death"*).

2) The atonement for sin is the shedding of innocent blood.

3) Jesus, God, the Son (*God's only begotten Son*), would take on human form and then suffer and die to redeem man.

Thus, the three reasons and the three themes, will be addressed in this attempt to answer the topic question – "What is the literal and symbolic significance in the shedding of Jesus' innocent blood?" To develop an answer, the rest of this essay is organized in six parts. Part-1 presents some bible verses, which support the three themes. Part-2 presents definitions of the words: "penalty", "atonement", and "innocent". Part-3 presents a discussion of the question: "Why was Jesus, the man, called the 'innocent lamb of God'?" Part-4 presents a critique of the topic question. Part-5 presents some concluding comments. Part-6 presents two relevant comments.

Part-1: **Some Bible verses, which support the three themes**

The previously mentioned three themes are supported by various Bible verses. Where the word – "support", is intended to mean that the verse or verses either explicitly or implicitly indicate the existence of the theme. However, to get a full understanding of the context of the verse or verses presented in this part of the essay, you really need to read the surrounding verses, because context is everything. However, to save space in this essay, only the most appropriate verses are presented. And whenever more than four or five consecutive verses are included, a more condensed presentation of those verses is used. At this author's discretion, underlining is used in some verses to emphasize some words. And an italic font is used for words attributed to Jesus. To further shorten this presentation, rather than providing four translations (*i.e., KJV, NIV, NASB, and NRSV*) of each verse or set of verses, only the translation, which uses wording that best supports a theme, is presented. The themes and supporting verses are, as follows:

1) The wages of sin is death (*which Christians understand to mean "the penalty for sin is death"*).

(Proverbs 10:16 NIV) The wages of the righteous bring them life, but the income of the wicked brings them punishment.

(Romans 6:23 NIV) For the wages of sin is death, but the gift of God is eternal life in Christ Jesus our Lord.

2) The atonement for sin is the shedding of innocent blood.

(Exodus 30:10 NIV) Once a year Aaron shall make atonement on its horns. This annual atonement must be made with the blood of the atoning sin offering for the generations to come. It is most holy to the LORD."

(Leviticus 17:11 NIV) For the life of a creature is in the blood, and I have given it to you to make atonement for yourselves on the altar; it is the blood that makes atonement for one's life.

(Numbers 6:14 NIV) There he is to present his offerings to the LORD: a year-old male lamb without defect for a burnt offering, a year-old ewe lamb without defect for a sin offering, a ram without defect for a fellowship offering,

(Numbers 15:25 NIV) The priest is to make atonement for the whole Israelite community, and they will be forgiven, for it was not intentional and they have brought to the LORD for their wrong an offering made by fire and a sin offering.

(Numbers 29:5 NIV) Include one male goat as a sin offering to make atonement for you.

(Matthew 27:4 NIV) "I have sinned," he said, "for I have betrayed innocent blood." "What is that to us?" they replied. "That's your responsibility."

> *Comment:* Matthew 27:4 recorded the words of Judas to all the chief Priests and the elders of the people, about Jesus. This verse is included to indicate that Judas understood that Jesus was innocent. Remember that even though Judas betrayed Jesus, Judas was still one of the original twelve Apostles.

3) Jesus, God, the Son (*God's only begotten Son*), would take on human form and then suffer and die to redeem man.

- (*God's only begotten Son*):

(Luke 1:35 NIV) The angel answered, "The Holy Spirit will come upon you, and the power of the Most High will overshadow you. So the holy one to be born will be called the Son of God.

(Romans 8:3 NIV) For what the law was powerless to do in that it was weakened by the sinful nature, God did by sending his own Son in the likeness of sinful man to be a sin offering. And so he condemned sin in sinful man,

(Hebrews 9:12 KJV) Neither by the blood of goats and calves, but by his own blood he entered in once into the holy place, having obtained eternal redemption for us.

(1 John 4:14 NIV) And we have seen and testify that the Father has sent his Son to be the Savior of the world.

- Take on human form:

(Matthew 1:21 NIV) She will give birth to a son, and you are to give him the name Jesus, because he will save his people from their sins."

(Luke 1:35 NIV) The angel answered, "The Holy Spirit will come upon you, and the power of the Most High will overshadow you. So the holy one to be born will be called the Son of God.

- Suffer and die to redeem man:

(Luke 24:41-47 KJV) Luke 24:[41]And while they yet believed not for joy, and wondered, he said unto them, *Have ye here any meat?* [42]And they gave him a piece of a broiled fish, and of an honeycomb. [43]And he took it, and did eat before them. [44]And he said unto them, *These are the words which I spake unto you, while I was yet with you, that all things must be fulfilled, which were written in the law of Moses, and in the prophets, and in the psalms, concerning me.* [45]Then opened he their understanding, that they might understand the scriptures, [46]And said unto them, *Thus it is written, and thus it behoved Christ to suffer, and to rise from the dead the third day:* [47]*And that repentance and remission of sins should be preached in his name among all nations, beginning at Jerusalem.*

(1 John 2:2 NIV) He is the atoning sacrifice for our sins, and not only for ours but also for the sins of the whole world.

> *Comment:* It is important to note the phrase – "for the sins of the whole world", in 1 John 2:2. For clearly, John is indicating that Jesus's atoning sacrifice covers the sins of believers and of unbelievers, but because God, the Father, said, "the only way to Him was through Jesus", the sin covering offered, by the finish work of Jesus, is only good for those who willingly accept it (*for those who believe that Jesus died for them*).

Part-2: **Definitions of the words: "penalty", "atonement", and "innocent"**

Paraphrased definitions of the words – "penalty", "atonement", and "innocent", are derived from several formal and informal definitions. These definitions are, as follows:

- A paraphrased definition for the word – "penalty":

  A "penalty" is "one or more acts applied to a law breaker, by those with the power and/or the authority to enforce the application". The "penalty" might be a civil penalty, a social penalty, a religious penalty, or some combination of the three. Thus, worded differently, a "penalty" is "the defined consequence of breaking a civil, social, or religious law". Usually, civil laws define the relationship, between a government and its citizens, and possibly the relationship, between the citizens, as defined by the government. Social laws define the relationships, between the citizens of a given society, on a formal basis, whereas, social traditions define the relationships, between the citizens of a given society, on an informal basis. Religious laws define the relationship, between the citizens of a given society and their god(s), and possibly the relationship, between the citizens, as influenced by their god(s).

- A paraphrased definition for the word – "atonement":

  An "atonement" is "one or more acts performed, by a law breaker, or by those with the power and/or the authority to perform the act(s), on behalf of a law breaker, to compensate the individual(s) injured, by the law breaker or to restore something disturbed, by the law breaker." The atoning act(s) must be acceptable to the individual(s) injured, by the law breaker. Otherwise, the "atonement" is not valid (*which means that the "atonement" is not an "atonement"*).

- A paraphrased definition for the word – "innocent":

  The nonreligious sense of the word – "innocent", is that "something is missing". This "something that is missing" is "knowledge of some kind" or "behavior of some type". Both the "knowledge of some kind" and the "behavior of some type" are generally, but not always, understood to be of an evil nature. In Christianity, the word – "innocent", is treated, as a synonym for the word: "sinless".

Part-3: **Why was Jesus, the man, called the "innocent lamb of God"?**

Jesus, the man, was called "innocent", because He was free from sin. That is, He was born sinless and remained sinless until God, the Father, placed **our sins** in Jesus' spiritual account.

Now, the question becomes: "How did Jesus, the man, (*a human*), *become* and *remain* 'sinless'?"

> *Comment:* The use of the phrase – "Jesus, the man", serves to emphasize that Jesus has two natures – "God" and "man" and that this discussion involves His human nature – Jesus, the man [the *Messiah*/the *Anointed One*/the *Christ*/the *Son of God*] and our kinsman-redeemer, who went to the cross, died spiritually and physically, was buried, and then was resurrected by God, the Father.

The question – "How did Jesus, the man (*a human*), *become* and *remain* 'sinless'?", is obviously two questions: "How did Jesus, the man, *become* 'sinless'?" and "How did Jesus, the man, *remain* 'sinless'?" To address these two questions, the rest of Part-3 is organized in three sections. Section-1 presents a discussion of the question: "How did Jesus, the man, *become* 'sinless'?" Section-2 presents a discussion of the question: "How did Jesus, the man, *remain* 'sinless'?" Section-3 presents some concluding comments about the question: "Why was Jesus, the man, called the 'innocent lamb of God'?"

Section-1: **How did Jesus, the man, *become* "sinless"?**

This question is answered by the Bible, which indicates that the answer is "Jesus, the man, was born of a virgin." The supporting background for this is, as follows:

> After choosing the Jews, growing them into a nation in Egypt, and then delivering them out of Egypt, God established civil, social, moral, and religious laws for them. Under these laws, the family lineage was traced through the male members of the family. Furthermore, the family inheritance was passed through the male members of the family. However, if there were no male members to receive the inheritance, God gave the Jews a custom, which some have labeled: the "daughter and inheritance" custom, to take care of this circumstance. This particular custom simply allowed an inheritance to be passed to daughters. But the daughters had to marry within their own tribe, to keep the inheritance within that tribe. Nevertheless, the sinful nature of Adam was understood to be passed, by the man. That is, the sin-nature of Adam was "passed from the father to his children"[64]. Since Jesus, the man, was born of a virgin, He did not have a human father. Thus, the sin-nature of Adam was not passed to Jesus, the man. The birth of Jesus, the man, to a virgin is recorded by Matthew 1:18 and Luke 1:35. These verses read:
>
> > (Matthew 1:18 NIV) This is how the birth of Jesus Christ came about: His mother Mary was pledged to be married to Joseph, but before they came together, she was found to be "with child" through the Holy Spirit.
> >
> > ---
> >
> > (Luke 1:35 NIV) The angel answered, "The Holy Spirit will come upon you, and the power of the Most High will overshadow you. So the holy one to be born will

be called the Son of God.

> *Comment:* The wording – "the Most High will overshadow you", should not be taken to mean that the Holy Spirit had intercourse with Mary. The Holy Spirit is God, and as such, He would not need, such a process to ensure that a virgin conceived a child.

Section-2: **How did Jesus, the man, *remain* "sinless"?**

This question is also answered by the Bible, which indicates that the answer is "Jesus, the man, lived a life that was focused on God." Several verses in John 5 support this answer. Some of these verses are:

(John 5:19 NIV) Jesus gave them this answer: *"I tell you the truth, the Son can do nothing by himself; he can do only what he sees his Father doing, because whatever the Father does the Son also does.*

(John 5:20 NIV) *For the Father loves the Son and shows him all he does. Yes, to your amazement he will show him even greater things than these.*

(John 6:38 NIV) *For I have come down from heaven not to do my will but to do the will of him who sent me.*

Section-3: **Some concluding comments about the question: "Why was Jesus, the man, called the 'innocent lamb of God'?"**

Generally, we sin, because we are focused on ourselves (*on our needs, our wants, our desires, our lust, etc.*). Jesus, the man, did not sin, because He was focused on God and God's plan for His life. This focus on God, allowed Jesus, the man, to live a "sinless" life. Thus, the virgin birth of Jesus, the man, and His sinless life, are the reasons that He is called "the innocent lamb of God" meaning "the 'sinless' lamb of God". We can use the phrase – "the innocent lamb of God", based on several verses. For instance the phrase – "lamb of God", is used in John 1:29 and John 1:36. These verses read:

(John 1:29 NIV) The next day John saw Jesus coming toward him and said, "Look, the Lamb of God, who takes away the sin of the world!

(John 1:36 NIV) When he saw Jesus passing by, he said, "Look, the Lamb of God!"

For the word – "innocent" (or "sinless"), there is Hebrews 4:15. This verse reads:

(Hebrews 4:15 NIV) For we do not have a high priest who is unable to sympathize with our weaknesses, but we have one who has been tempted in every way, just as we are--yet was without sin.

Again, Jesus, the man, was called the "innocent lamb of God", because He was born "innocent" (*because He was born "sinless"*) and He remained innocent, by living a sinless life. These two conditions allowed Him to die as a sacrificial lamb, as God planned it.

Note that the Bible also tells us that as a youth, Jesus, the man, was focus on doing the will of God. See Luke 2:49. Two translations of this verse read:

> (Luke 2:49 KJV) And he said unto them, *How is it that ye sought me? wist ye not that I must be about my Father's business?*

> (Luke 2:49 NIV) "*Why were you searching for me?*" he asked. "*Didn't you know I had to be in my Father's house?*"

Part-4: **A critique**

This critique of the topic question is begun with a reminder that the Bible indicates: "Jesus, God, the Son, would take on human form and then He would fulfill both the 'penalty' and the 'atonement' for our sins." The details on how Jesus, the man, fulfilled God's word reveals the wonder of God's plan. Some of the fulfillment details have already been mentioned. Some of those details may be repeated in this critique, while other details may be mentioned for the first time.

Note that Part-1, Part-2, and Part-3, make it clear that it was Jesus, the man, who died on the cross and then was resurrected, by God, the Father. Now, to develop an answer to the topic question, this critique is organized in two sections. Section-1 presents a brief discussion of the "literal aspect" of the shedding of Jesus' innocent blood. Section-2 presents a discussion of the "symbolic aspect" of the shedding of Jesus' innocent blood.

Section-1: **The "literal aspect"**

For this essay, the "literal aspect" of the shedding of Jesus' innocent blood is taken to mean "the blood of Jesus, the man, actually flowed from His body". This bleeding began when Pontius Pilate, the Roman governor of Judea, had Jesus flogged. This flogging was Pilate's attempt to spare Jesus from a crucifixion and to appease the crowd. Nevertheless, this flogging caused blood to flow from Jesus' body. Later the Roman guards placed a Crown of thorns on Jesus' head. The thorns probably tore into Jesus' skin opening new wounds and providing another way for blood to flow from Jesus' body. Still, later, they nailed Jesus to the cross providing several additional ways for more blood to flow from His body. Finally, to confirm that Jesus was dead on the cross, a Roman soldier thrust a spear through the side of Jesus. This allowed blood, and water, to flow from Jesus' body. Clearly, and literally, blood flowed from Jesus' body before and during His crucifixion. Thus, the flogging, the crowning, the nailing of His limbs to the cross, and the spear thrust in His side, allowed Jesus, the man, to fulfill the literal aspect of the shedding of His innocent blood.

Section-2: **The "symbolic aspect"**

For this essay, the "symbolic aspect" of the shedding of Jesus' innocent blood revolves around the "deaths of Jesus, the man". At first glance, someone might say, "that death is really a 'literal aspect'". However, "death" takes on a "symbolic aspect" with regards to Jesus, the man, because of two of the three types of death. The three types of death are: "physical death", "spiritual death", and the "Second Death (*also called, 'Eternal Death'*)". "Physical death" is "the separation of the body from the soul and the spirit". "Spiritual death" is "a separation in time between man and God's grace". The "Second Death" is "a separation in eternity between man and God's grace". More precisely, the "Second Death" is "an eternal separation from God's grace and an eternal existence under God's judgment." When associated with Jesus and the cross, "physical death" and "spiritual death", take on a "symbolic aspect", because Jesus was representing all humans, past, present, and future, as He died on the cross. However, that representation is only meaningful for those who accept Jesus, as their substitute – as their Lord and Savior.

> *Comment:* This author understands "spiritual death" and "the Second Death", as follows: "'Spiritual death' begins at birth, because all humans, except Jesus, the man, were/are/will be born with Adam's sin-nature. 'Spiritual death' ends at an individual's rebirth in Jesus. More precisely, 'Spiritual death' ends, when an individual accepts the finish work of Jesus on her or his behalf. If an individual reaches the 'age of accountability' (*which is really not a physical age, but a spiritual state when an individual understands* ***their freewill ability to choose good or evil***) and then dies without ever accepting the finish work of Jesus on her or his behalf, that individual will await the final judgment and the 'Second Death'."

> *Comment:* Another way to view "spiritual death", is "as the transition of an individual from an existence under God's grace to an existence under God's judgment". God displayed this transition with Adam and Eve. According to the KJV, God told Adam that "for in the day that thou eatest thereof thou shalt surely die" – (See Genesis 2:17). That is, God told Adam that on the day that he ate the forbidden fruit, would be the day that he would die. However, this "die" was twofold. *First*, and immediately, it was a "spiritual death". *Second*, it was a "physical death", nine hundred and thirty years into Adam's future. Now, God displayed the "spiritual death", by putting Adam and Eve out of the Garden of Eden. God moved Adam and Eve from their existence under His grace in the Garden of Eden to their existence under His judgment in the world, where Eve suffered the pains of childbirth and Adam suffered the toils of getting their – his and his family's – daily bread.

Once more, this discussion of the "symbolic aspect" revolves around the "spiritual death" and the "physical death" of Jesus, the man. But note that it is His "physical death" that most Christians focus on when they think about His death on the cross. Christians say, "Jesus shed His blood for me! Jesus died for me!" Clearly, Jesus, the man, did die physically. However, His "physical death" fulfilled the "atonement part" of the "symbolic aspect". The "penalty part" of the "symbolic aspect" meant that Jesus, the man, also had to die spiritually. For God revealed that "the penalty for sin is death." That is, "the penalty for sin is separation from His grace." Thus, when the sins of man were laid to the account of Jesus, the man, He had to be separated from God's grace. This separation may have only lasted from the moment the sins were laid to Jesus' account until his "physical death". But by whatever means, and for however long, when Jesus, the man, died spiritually, He had to be separated from God's grace. This author makes no claim that he knows exactly how God accomplished this feat. However, this author does claim that only such a separation could satisfy God's word. One possible scenario of how God accomplished this feat can be deduced from basic Christian principles. Thus, a summary of some basic Christian beliefs and this scenario could be worded, as follows:

- Some basic Christianity beliefs:

  Before the cross - before the crucifixion of Jesus, the man:

  Believers: Believers - those who believed God's promises, which included the promise of salvation and a Messiah - looked forward to the cross. When they died, their spirits and souls went to "Abraham's bosom *(a euphemism for the 'abode of the righteous dead, before the cross')*". Their bodies returned to the dust of the earth. But eventually, their bodies will be resurrected and reunited with their spirits and souls to form their glorified-eternal bodies. These individuals will spend eternity in the presence of God's grace, in Paradise - in Heaven.

  Unbelievers: The spirits and souls of unbelievers went to Hades upon their deaths. Hades was separated from "Abraham's bosom", by a wide gulf. Unbelievers went to Hades to await final judgment. After the final judgment, these unbelievers will experience what is called "THE SECOND DEATH". This "Second Death" is their final and eternal separation from the presence of God's grace. These individuals will spend eternity in the presence of God's judgment, in Hell.

  After the cross - after the crucifixion of Jesus, the man

  Believers: Believers look backward to the cross. When they die, their spirits and souls go immediately into the presence of God, the Father, in Paradise. Their bodies return to the dust of the earth. Eventually, their bodies will be resurrected and reunited with their spirits and souls upon the "Second Coming of Christ". These individuals will spend eternity in the presence of God's grace, in Paradise – in Heaven.

Unbelievers: The spirits and souls of unbelievers go to Hades upon their death awaiting the final judgment. After this final judgment these unbelievers will experience "THE SECOND DEATH". These individuals will spend eternity in the presence of God's judgment, in Hell.

- A scenario

While Jesus, the man, was on the cross, God, the Father, laid the sins of all men in His (Jesus') spiritual account. This meant Jesus, the man, had to experience "spiritual death". He had to die spiritually, because it is sin that causes "spiritual death" – that causes "a spiritual separation between man and God's grace". Being that Jesus, the man, had such a close relationship with God, the Father, and God, the Holy Spirit, He sensed the transition of His existence from God's grace to God's judgment. Therefore, according to Matthew 27:46 and Mark 15:34, Jesus, the man, cried out, "Eloi, Eloi, lama sabachthani?", which means, "My God, my God, why have you forsaken me?" With His "spiritual death", He paid the penalty for the sins of men. Then He shed His innocent blood – then Jesus, the man, died physically, His second death, but not THE SECOND DEATH (i.e., not the eternal separation from God). The His second death – His "physical death", satisfied the atonement for the sins of men. Because the two deaths of Jesus, the man, satisfied the penalty and the atonement for sins, He could have gone directly into the presence of God. However, God, the Father, wanted to proclaim to both the spiritual world and the physical world, what Jesus, the man, had done. Therefore, God, the Father, sent Jesus, the man, to "Abraham's bosom (*a euphemism for the 'abode of the righteous dead, before the cross'*)" – the spiritual world, where Jesus preached the good news of His penalty and atonement payments. Sometime after Jesus preached the good news among those in "Abraham's Bosom", He may have led those believers into God's presence in "Paradise". Then God, the Father, resurrected Jesus, the man, to announce to the physical world, His acceptance of the penalty and the atonement payments of Jesus, the man.

Therefore, the "spiritual death" and the "physical death" of Jesus, the man, fulfilled the "symbolic aspect" of the shedding of His innocent blood.

Part-5: **Some concluding comments**

Literally, Jesus' innocent blood flowed from His body before, during, and after, His crucifixion. Symbolically, the "shedding of His innocent blood" occurred on two levels. One level is that symbolically, Jesus, <u>the man</u>, died spiritually and physically for our sins. On another level, the "shedding of His innocent blood" could be considered a euphemism for "His physical death". Thus, once more, God's word that innocent blood must be shed was fulfilled literally and symbolically. But note. The real wonder of the literal shedding is emphasized by the occurrence of crucifixions, where no blood flowed. Thus, all of the events before, during, and after the physical death of Jesus, <u>the man</u>, on the cross: "the beating", "the crucifixion", "the burial", and "the resurrection" of Jesus, <u>the man</u>, displayed the wonder of God's way. Therefore, the answer to the topic question – "What is the real literal and symbolic significance in the shedding of Jesus' innocent blood?", is "God's words were fulfilled literally and symbolically. Jesus, <u>the man</u>, shed His innocent blood for us literally and symbolically. More specifically, Jesus, <u>the man</u>, paid the 'penalty' for our sins and He 'atoned' for our sins (*He was the 'atoning sacrifice' for all of our sins*). But what Jesus did on the cross is meaningless for those individuals, who do not accept His work on the cross on their behalf."

<u>Part-6</u>: **Two relevant comments**

Some relevant comments are presented in two groups, as follows:

<u>Group-1</u>: Some Christians say, "Even if all the believers, who lived before the cross, did not know explicitly about Christ, they trusted and believed in the Word of God. More specifically, they believed whatever God shared with them." However, this author believes that God shared information and concepts with those believers, such that the shared information and concepts explicitly or implicitly, pointed to Christ. And, we know that this was true in the case of Abraham and his son Isaac. See Genesis 22:1-18.

<u>Group-2</u>: When Jesus, <u>the man</u>, died physically, He left this time-dependent physical world of ours. Then when God resurrected Him, Jesus, <u>the man</u>, re-entered this time-dependent world with a glorified body. But any questions about what Jesus, <u>the man</u>, did for three days and nights are meaningless. Perhaps, the easiest way to think of time is this:

> "Visualize a long hollow tube. This tube begins at the beginning of time, and ends at the end of time. The perception of time exists only inside this tube. Our world exists inside this tube. Outside the tube, time does not exist. When Jesus, <u>the man</u>, died, it was like cutting a hole in the side of the tube for Jesus, <u>the man</u>, to step out of the tube (*to step out of this time-dependent world*). Then when He was resurrected three days later (*three days later for those inside the tube*), another hole was cut in the side of the tube. And then Jesus, <u>the man</u>, stepped back into this time-dependent physical world of ours."

Is Jesus the only way to God?

Any statement, which implies that "Jesus is the only way to God", worries some Christians and irritates many non-Christians. The Christians worry about pushing non-Christians away from Christianity, by mentioning that "Jesus is the only way to God." The non-Christians are irritated, by any words that imply "Jesus is the only way to God", because they feel that generally, "only one way" is unfair to all of us. But specifically, it is unfair to those who think that "*they know* a different way", or that "*they know* possibly a better way (*i.e., living a moral life, being kind to others, attending church, and so on*)." Thus, non-Christians rebuff Christians, regarding "Jesus, as the only way to God", with questions. Five sample-rebuff questions are, as follows:

- *Question-1*: "If God allows only one way to Himself, how can He be loving?"

- *Question-2*: "What about the Bushman in Africa, who has never heard about God or heard the Gospel?" Or more specifically, "Is that Bushman condemned to Hell forever, simply because he has never heard about God or heard the Gospel?"

  Comment: Recall that the Christian meaning of the word – "Gospel", is "the good news that we have forgiveness of sins through Jesus"[65]. Another wording for the meaning of the word – "gospel", is "the good news of salvation through the forgiveness of sins that Jesus provides for us."

- *Question-3*: "What about those who were/are/will be born to non-Christian parents?" Some non-Christians are quick to say that children generally remain in the "religion" or "no-religion" of their parents. Thus, "Are non-Christian children condemned to Hell, because their non-Christian parents are condemned to Hell?"

- *Question-4*: "What about those who lived before the death and resurrection of Jesus?"

- *Question-5*: "What about those non-Christians, who lived/live/will live moral lives?" More precisely, "Are moral non-Christians condemned to Hell simply for not accepting Christ?"

Such questions and the concerns that such questions raise, only cloud the truth that "Jesus is the only way to God", because such questions and concerns do not focus on "why Jesus is the only way to God." Such questions and concerns focus on "the potential consequences of not accepting Jesus, as the only way". Furthermore, underlying the questions and concerns are inappropriate notions about God. Three such notions are:

- ✓ *Notion-1*: "God is not loving enough."

✓ *Notion-2*: "God is not powerful enough."

✓ *Notion-3*: "God is not fair."

Such inappropriate notions flow out of some people reasoning that "'if God had enough love, power, or whatever' or 'if God was fair', He would provide more than one way to Himself. Or He would provide everyone with the exact knowledge that they need to accept Jesus." "These inappropriate notions", "questions like the five previously mentioned", and "some of the related issues that such questions raise", will be addressed through the topic question: "Is Jesus the only way to God?"

As some Christians may *need to be reminded* – "Why it is true that Jesus is the only way to God" and as most non-Christians *need to understand* – "Why it is true that Jesus is the only way to God", the rest of this essay is organized around a six-step approach. Step-1 presents "a response to a Christian", which serves to remind Christians about information that they might share with another Christian in response to the topic question. Step-2 presents "a response to a non-Christian", which presents some information that Christians might share with a non-Christian in response to the topic question. Step-3 presents "some relevant comments". Step-4 presents "some concluding comments". Step-5 presents "a response to each of the five sample-rebuff questions", which were mentioned at the beginning of this essay. Step-6 presents "two analogous stories", which are analogies of the concept of "Jesus becoming our human kinsman" and the concept of "God sacrificing His Son".

Step-1: **A response to a Christian**

Whenever possible, a response to a Christian should always be based on the Bible. Basing a response on the Bible may even be possible, when the questions are not specifically about Christianity, but about life. The question – "Why is it true that Jesus is the only way to God?", is answered, by several individual verses and by the Bible, as a whole. Possibly, the best and clearest individual verse, is John 14:6. This verse recorded the fact that Jesus, Himself, said that He is the only way to God. In the NIV, John 14:6 reads:

> "Jesus answered, '*I am the way and the truth and the life. No one comes to the Father except through me.*'"

However, some immature Christians, might want more than an individual verse. Thus, we note that the Bible, as a whole, tells us that "Jesus is the only way to God", because of "Who Jesus is" and "What Jesus did". Consequently, Step-1 is organized in three parts. Part-1 presents a discussion of "Who Jesus is". Part-2 presents a discussion of "What Jesus did". Part-3 presents some concluding comments for this response to a Christian.

Part-1: "**Who Jesus is**"

Jesus is "God, the Son" and a member of the Trinity (*"God, the Father", "God, the Son", and "God, the Holy Spirit"*). Jesus, God, the Son, temporarily veiled His deity to take on human form via a virgin birth. Through this virgin birth, Jesus, God, the Son, became Jesus, the man (the *Messiah*/the *Anointed One*/the *Christ*/the *Son of God*). This means that Jesus has two natures: "God" and "man".

When Jesus, God, the Son, became a man, He also became our "human kinsman". However, unlike other humans, the virgin birth of Jesus, the man, allowed Him to begin His life, as a sinless human being, because He was born without the stain of the original sin of Adam. Furthermore, the sinlessness of Jesus, the man, meant that He was also the "innocent-sacrificial lamb of God". In summary, Jesus is – "God, the Son, a member of the Trinity, who has always existed" and Jesus is – "a man, who was born of a Jewish virgin, becoming the *Messiah*, the *Anointed One*, the *Christ*, the *Son of God*, our human kinsman, and the innocent-sacrificial lamb of God".

Part-2: "**What Jesus did**"

As our "human kinsman", Jesus, the man, exercised a Jewish custom known, as the "Go'el" or "Kinsman-redeemer". Under the "Go'el" or "Kinsman-redeemer" custom, a kinsman could redeem rights, privileges, and properties lost, by a kinsman. Jesus, the man, was redeeming our privilege to exist under God's grace, instead of His judgment. This privilege was lost to us humans, when Adam and Eve sinned. Thus, on the cross, Jesus, the man, "died spiritually (*He was separated from God's grace*)", as the penalty for our sins and then He died physically, as an atoning sacrifice for our sins. Then He was buried. After three days, God, the Father, resurrected Jesus, the man, to show the world that He (*God, the Father*) accepted the penalty payment and the atoning sacrifice of Jesus, the man, on the cross.

Part-3: Conclusion – **A response to a Christian**

Because Jesus, the man, was born sinless, He is the only human, who qualified to be an atoning sacrifice for our sins. Thus, with regards to our sins, the deaths (*the "spiritual death" and the "physical death"*) of Jesus, the man, on the cross are meaningless, unless an individual accepts those deaths on her or his behalf. And those who do accept are "spiritually reborn (*returned to an existence under God's grace*)". Thus, the comments, which make up Step-1, served to remind Christians of information that they can share with other Christians to help them understand that "Jesus is the only way to God", because of "Who Jesus is" and "What Jesus did", as recorded in the Bible.

Step-2: **A response to a non-Christian**

Because non-Christians do not believe in the Bible, a response to a non-Christian will not be centered only on the Bible. Thus, because of the wide variety of issues that need to be presented, this response is organized, as a series of seven presentations in support of the statement: "Jesus is the only way to God." The basis of the seven presentations are, as follows:

- ✎ Presentation-1 *is based on*: "The things of nature".
- ✎ Presentation-2 *is based on*: "Scientific observations of nature".
- ✎ Presentation-3 *is based on*: "An application of logic".
- ✎ Presentation-4 *is based on*: "Historic information".
- ✎ Presentation-5 *is based on*: "The nature of man".
- ✎ Presentation-6 *is based on*: "The Bible".
- ✎ Presentation-7 *is based on*: "Spiritual issues".

Presentation-1: **The things of nature**

The things of nature provide a logical conclusion in support of the belief – "Jesus is the only way to God". This conclusion is independent of whether you believe that the things of nature, including man, came "through an evolutionary process", "through creation by God", "through creation by cosmic forces", or "through creation by something else", because how the things of nature got here, is not the primary point of this presentation. The primary point is that "the things of nature, including man, 'exist'." Thus, when you take a logical look at the existence of the things of nature, you have to reason, as follows:

- ✓ The things of nature, including man, are something.
- ✓ These something's exist.
- ✓ For something to exist now, some entity or thing has to have always existed.
- ✓ For something cannot come out of nothing, by itself.

> *Comment:* See the essay – "How could God create man out of nothing?", which is a sub-essay of the essay: "What is the only meaningful question, about 'God' and 'Christianity'?"

Thus, the logical conclusion is "some entity or something has to have always existed." Now we consider the cause of the existence of the things of nature. And we reason that for this eternal entity or something, to be anything less than God, is illogical. Furthermore, as we are not eternal, God either allowed our existence (*a belief, probably favored by non-Christians*) or caused our existence (*created us, a belief held by Christians*), in either case, God has a right to define His relationship, with us. This includes making "Jesus the only way to Himself (God)".

Presentation-2: **Scientific observations of nature**

Based on scientific observations of nature, a supportive-logical conclusion flows out of both "General scientific observations" and "Specific scientific observations". Thus, Presentation-2 is organized in two sections. Section-1 presents a discussion of "general scientific observations". Section-2 presents a discussion of "specific scientific observations".

Section-1: **General scientific observations**

Under general scientific observations, we note that as the things of nature are examined by us, we should see that God has left His fingerprints everywhere. That is, the universe (*the things of nature, themselves*), tells us that there was a designer. And Christians call this designer, God. Now, some non-Christians like Charles Darwin, have tried to declare other explanations for the things of nature. But most of Darwin's explanations were based on his observations using his naked eye. Consequently, we can give Darwin a little room for not getting it right. But now, with all the modern scientific equipment that allows us to see nature at the molecular level, man has no excuse for not seeing that a designer of the things of nature is the most logical conclusion. For example, scientists have found biological cell mechanisms that are like molecular engines. See the book: "*Darwin's Black Box: The Biochemical Challenge to Evolution*", by Dr. Michael J. Behe. Thus, many scientific observations point to God. And God, as the creator (*as the designer*), has every right to make "Jesus the only way to Himself (God)".

Section-2: **Specific scientific observations**

Under specific scientific observations, we note that the things of nature have been studied under the banners of a variety of sciences, by many individuals. These studies have focused on various aspects of everything from the smallest definable particle of matter to the entire universe. These studies have revealed many complex conditions. For instance, two complex conditions are: "with respect to Biology" and "with respect to Astrophysics". Thus, Section-2 is organized in two segments. *Segment-1* presents a discussion "with respect to Biology". *Segment-2* presents a discussion "with respect to Astrophysics".

Segment-1: ***With respect to Biology***

The complexity of living matter has been revealed. For example, scientists have discovered the existence of **D**eoxyribo**N**ucleic **A**cid (**DNA**) in each cell, and further, discovered that DNA contains the genetic code for each organism. This genetic code is so complex and detailed that statistical probability is against the possibility of DNA developing randomly or by accident.

> *Comment:* According to the website of the "Answers In Genesis Ministry", a couple of years ago, on the fiftieth anniversary of their discovery of DNA, two scientists – Dr. James Watson and Dr. Francis Crick, made statements, which indicated that they did not believe that DNA is the result of a designer (*the result of God*). More

specifically, in an attempt to counter the "design argument", these two scientists said:

> "Some of us think that we humans have a special place in the animal kingdom. However, the human genome is similar to a chimpanzee's, and has a lot in common with the genome of a fruit fly."

Three responses to the comments of Dr. Watson and Dr. Crick, come to mind. These three responses are, as follows:

- *Response-1*: While it is true that there are similarities, between the human genome and the chimpanzee genome and that there are common elements, between the human genome and the fruit fly genome, the similarities and the common elements do not disprove the existence of a designer. In fact, the similarities and the common elements, add credibility to the existence of a designer, in light of the fact that these three distinct organisms exist, and we do not see a human coming from the mating of chimpanzees nor from the mating of fruit flies – or vice versa.

- *Response-2*: While it is true that there are similarities, between the human genome and the chimpanzee genome, and that there are common elements, between the human genome and the fruit fly genome, there are differences and the differences are enough to make a human, a human, to make a chimpanzee, a chimpanzee, and to make a fruit fly, a fruit fly.

- *Response-3*: While *Response-1* and *Response-2* were direct responses to the comments of Dr. Watson and Dr. Crick, *Response-3* is about the two doctors themselves and/or scientists, in general. More specifically, you must remember what scientists are. What are scientists? Well! First and foremost, scientists are human beings. But scientists are also "***interpreters***", because they note the things of nature and/or make scientific observations. Then they try to explain how the things of nature came about, to explain what those things are, and/or to explain how those things work. Thus, for example, Dr. Watson and Dr. Crick did not create DNA. They simply noted the existence of DNA and then they suggested the purpose and function of DNA. However, it is not a logical conclusion that because the two doctors noted the existence of DNA and made suggestions about how it works, their interpretation is totally accurate or complete.

Thus, the complexity of living matter points to the existence of a designer, who is called God, by

Christians and Jews, and who is called Allah, by Muslims.

<u>Segment-2</u>: ***With respect to Astrophysics***

The complexity of this universe has been revealed. For example, a former astronomer, who now heads a ministry, shares his understanding of God and this universe through various means: books, lectures, video tapes, audiotapes, etc. His material suggests a couple of things:

- *First*, "The complexity and the vastness of the universe show the effort and the love that God put into the process of providing a temporary home for us."

- *Second*, "This planet is finely tuned on more than a hundred factors. Change any one of these factors. And life on this planet, as we know it, would cease."

However, even without men of science revealing the complexity of this universe, we can make our own observations of the glory and power of nature. For example:

- ✓ There are the changing seasons.
- ✓ There are ocean tides.
- ✓ There are currents in the oceans.
- ✓ There is the way that water freezes, from top to bottom, compared with all other liquids, which freeze from bottom to top.
- ✓ There are tornadoes, hurricanes, monsoons, waterspouts, and thunderstorms.
- ✓ There are earthquakes and volcanos.
- ✓ There are many "symbiotic relationships (*mutually beneficial relationships*)", in nature, between plants and insects, between plants and animals, between insects, and between various animals.

Thus, we are without excuse. The things of nature cry out to declare the very existence of a designer (*the very existence of God*). And the Bible confirms this with Romans 1:20. In the NIV, this verse reads:

> Romans 1:[20]For since the creation of the world God's invisible qualities--his eternal power and divine nature--have been clearly seen, being understood from what has been made, so that men are without excuse.

Thus, scientific observations of the things of nature declare the existence of God. And God, as the creator (*as the designer*), has every right to make "Jesus the only way to Himself (God)".

<u>Presentation-3</u>: **An application of logic**

Based on an application of logic, we note that the same supportive-logical conclusion flows out of several considerations, which revolve around the logical consistency of "having only one way to God". To address this logical consistency, Presentation-3 is organized in four sections. Section-1 considers the previously mentioned logical consistency through the question: "Why does 'having many ways to God' not make logical sense?" Section-2 considers the previously mentioned logical consistency through the question: "Why does 'having only one way to God' make logical sense?" Section-3 considers the previously mentioned logical consistency through the statement: "A perfect God provided a perfect plan for man's salvation." Section-4 serves, as a logical response to the inappropriate notion: "God does not provide everyone with the knowledge that they need to accept Jesus."

Section-1: **Why does "having many ways to God" not make logical sense?**

This question has to be addressed, because too many individuals, even some immature Christians (*Christians, who really do not understand and/or know all of the essentials of Christianity*), accept the claim: "There are many ways, many roads, and/or paths to God." This claim has been worded in a variety of ways. Three common wordings are, as follows:

- All religions lead to God.
- All roads lead to the mountain top.
- There are many paths to God.

Most "many-ways" statements can be countered logically. For example, the three common wordings of "many-ways" statements, might be countered logically, as follows:

- *Concerning statements like* – "All religions lead to God": With regards to such statements, many Christian apologists say, "Logically, it is impossible for all religions to lead to the same God. The reason is that the different religions present incompatible definitions of God, incompatible philosophies on eternal life, and incompatible purposes for life – just to name a few of the differences. Thus, logically, these different religions cannot lead to the same God."

- *Concerning statements like* – "All roads lead to the mountain top": Such statements are poor religious analogies. For such statements explicitly indicate there is only one mountain top. However, it is not necessarily true that all the roads on a given mountain lead to the mountain top. Whether a road actually leads to the top of the mountain, will depend on, who built the road and the purpose for the road. And remember. The major religions have different definitions of God, different definitions of Jesus, different definitions of how eternal life is obtained, and different definitions of the purpose of life. The various combinations of these differences are analogous to different mountain tops and not to the same mountain top. Consequently, a road analogy would be more correctly expressed, as different roads on different mountains, rather than different roads on the same mountain.

- *Concerning statements like* – "There are many paths to God": Such statements are easy to make, but hard to logically or spiritually support, especially, with respect to Christianity. Logically, if God inspired the writers of the Bible, and if those writers recorded that "there is only one way to God", then "there can only be one way to God." Spiritually, if God uses the Bible to explain why there is only one way, then "there can only be one way to Him."

Thus, "having many ways to God" does not make logical sense. However, what does make logical sense, is God being the One, who defines how people come to Him. And once more according to the Bible, God said that "Jesus is the only way to Him (God)."

Section-2: **Why does "having only one way to God" make logical sense?**

Perhaps, the best way to address this question is through a nonreligious situation. The setup for this nonreligious situation is that you are the sponsor and planner of a fair-like event to be held at "Point A", which is some distance from your normal area of travel. The geographic center of your normal area of travel is designated, as "Point B". Under the proposed situation, you have to provide driving directions to your potential attendees, who live and work around "Point B", so that they can find the site of your fair-like event. For this situation, unlike Christianity, we will start with the explicit condition that there are many roads between "Point A" and "Point B". In summary, for this nonreligious situation, the following five conditions are defined to be true:

- *Condition-1*: You are the sponsor and planner of a fair-like event to be held at "Point A".

- *Condition-2*: All of the people, who may attend your event, live and work around "Point B", which is about a hundred miles from "Point A". And there is a large metropolitan area between "Point A" and "Point B".

- *Condition-3*: There are many ways to get from "Point B" to "Point A" by car. There is a scenic route. There is a toll road. There are several non-toll roads, and so on.

- *Condition-4*: None of the potential attendees of your fair-like event are familiar with the "Point A" area.

- *Condition-5*: Your fair-like event is scheduled for a one-week period, so only an opening day-and-time, the daily hours, and a closing day-and-time will be specified in your announcements for the event. Thus, you have no idea, when any given individual or individuals will leave "Point B" for "Point A".

With respect to these five conditions, there are two views of the driving directions that you must prepare for those who may attend your fair-like event. Obviously, one view is "your view of your driving directions". The other view is "the potential attendee's view of your directions". To discuss these two views, the rest of Section-2 is organized in three segments. *Segment-1* presents a discussion of "your view of your driving directions". *Segment-2* presents a discussion of "the potential attendee's view of your driving directions". *Segment-3* presents "some concluding comments".

Segment-1: "**Your view of your driving directions**"

The easiest way for you to give driving directions would be "to specify, 'the most direct route with the best and most notable landmarks (*to specify one way*)'". Your "one way" should allow for the lightest vehicle, the heaviest vehicle, the smallest vehicle, and the largest vehicle that could be used. And, any special situations like a toll-road should be explicitly indicated in your direction. These considerations would prevent the need for your directions to get complicated, because you tried to give:

- ✓ a route, for those leaving during rush hour;
- ✓ a route, for those with small vehicles;
- ✓ a route, for those with large vehicles;
- ✓ a route, for those with more than two individuals in their vehicle;
- ✓ a route, for those willing to pay a toll;
- ✓ a route, for those not wanting to pay any tolls; and so on.

The additional routes would probably require additional definitions. For example: *to define rush hour*, you need to know the area that the individuals must travel through, the driver's direction through that area, and the time of day that the driver will attempt to drive through that area; *to define a route for small vehicles and/or to define a route for large vehicles*, you might have to specify a definition of a small vehicle versus a large vehicle. Such a definition might use the type of vehicle (*cars versus trucks*), or it might use the actual size or weight of the car or truck to be used. Your definition might even get into specific makes and models of the car or truck. If you specified things about the gross weight of the vehicle, you would have to assume that the owner of a vehicle knows the gross weight of her or his vehicle. The point is:

> "As the author of the driving directions – as the definer of the 'one way', it is your responsibility to consider all the conditions and variables necessary for potential attendees to find 'Point A'. Then you should embed your considerations into the directions for your 'one way', so that the potential attendees, will have as few as possible, options or variables to consider and/or to complicate their decisions. That is, as you decrease the options and variables that need to be considered by your potential attendees,

you decrease the stress and confusion that they will experience in finding 'Point A'. Thus, once more, defining 'one way' with the best and most notable landmarks is logically the best procedure."

<u>*Segment-2*</u>: "**<u>The potential attendee's view of your driving directions</u>**"

If your driving directions included several routes, then those planning to attend your event must sort through the directions to try to decide the best route for them. And as none of your potential attendees are familiar with the "Point A" area, their assessment of the best route is going to be very subjective. Thus, specifying only one way will remove their stress of evaluating several routes.

<u>*Segment-3*</u>: "**<u>Some concluding comments</u>**"

Once more, the knowledge of "many ways", forces individuals into the need to sort through the various ways to decide the best way for them. However, being unfamiliar with the destination or ending conditions, means that these individuals have to make very subjective judgments, as they do their sorting. If providing "only one way" simplifies this physical situation, think how much more "only one way to God" simplifies our spiritual situation. Therefore, it should be obvious that God showed His love and His mercy, by specifying only one way to Himself (God). God kept it simple and direct. Besides, if there were more than one way to God, God would be obligated to ensure that each person knew about each way. However, if it happened that a particular individual knew about all of the ways, except one, and if that particular individual never accepted Jesus, based on all the other ways, then on Judgment Day, this individual might try to say, "God, that one way, which was unknown to me, when I was alive, would have caused me to accept Jesus." How do you think, God would respond, to such a statement? This author believes that God knew of that possibility and that is why He designed and established "Jesus, as the only way to Himself (God)". Furthermore, it is why God <u>informed</u>/<u>informs</u> everyone via the Bible, via the light of nature (*via nature*), or via the light of their conscience, that the only way to Him is through Jesus.

Another way to look at the logical consistency of "one way" is that "*God's main desire is for each individual to come to Him, by accepting the finished work of Jesus on her or his behalf. Thus, it would be illogical for God to do anything that would complicate our attempts to comply with His desire. And the existence of "many ways" to Him would definitely complicate our compliance with His desire.*"

<u>Section-3</u>: **A perfect God provided a perfect plan for man's salvation**

God's perfect plan <u>was</u>/<u>is</u> a simple plan. God's own Son (Jesus, <u>God, the Son</u>) would take on human form, becoming our human kinsman, and then He would die for our sins, becoming our redeemer. More specifically, God's plan included Jesus, <u>the man</u>, being crucified, by the very people that He came to save. On the cross, Jesus, <u>the man</u>, died spiritually to satisfy the penalty for our sins and then He died physically, as an atoning sacrifice for our sins. The deaths of Jesus were required by God, to allow those men, who accept the deaths of Jesus on their behalf, to return to an existence under His grace. Thus, again, God's perfect plan was a simple plan. God's perfect plan provided the only way for man to return to an existence under God's grace. God showed His love for us by providing only one way. Again, one way is a simple plan for simple man. And God offered his plan to man for free. God required nothing of man, except belief in Jesus, the man, as the only way.

Section-4: **The inappropriate notion: "God does not provide everyone with the knowledge that they need to accept Jesus."**

A response to this inappropriate notion is needed, because too many people hold this notion. However, anyone, who makes this accusation, does not understand God, as revealed in the Bible. For the Bible clearly shows that God created us with a "free will". See the first two chapters of the Book of Genesis, and God's interaction with Adam and Eve. The Bible also indicates that God would like everyone to be saved, but as a God of justice, He indicated that the only way to salvation is through the acceptance of Jesus. Thus, God does provide everyone with the knowledge that they need to accept Jesus, but "He does not force anyone to accept that knowledge against their own free will."

Presentation-4: **Historic information**

Based on historical information, we note that several supportive conclusions can be reached. And an interesting factor is that some of the historical information, which is part of this presentation, is from nonbiblical sources. Nevertheless, to present some historical information, Presentation-4, is organized in two sections. Section-1 centers on the fate of ten of the twelve original Apostles of Jesus. Section-2 centers on the fact that many individuals have claimed to be the "Messiah", or "the only way".

Section-1: **The fate of ten of the twelve-original Apostles of Jesus**

Ten of the twelve-original Apostles suffered unpleasant deaths, because of their belief in Jesus. Two others – "the Apostle John" and "the Apostle Judas Iscariot" – did not. John suffered (*may have been boiled in oil, among other things*), for his belief in Jesus, but he is believed to have died of natural causes. Judas betrayed Jesus, which led to the crucifixion of Jesus. But Judas hung himself, before the crucifixion and resurrection of Jesus. However, the other eleven Apostles, including John, had encounters and discussions with the resurrected Jesus. These encounters and discussions changed them. And they openly displayed the evidence of the change in them (*display the evidence of their belief in Jesus*). Thus, the horrible deaths of ten of the twelve original Apostles are possibly the greatest evidence to support "Jesus being the only way to God", because these ten died for their beliefs. Further support comes from modern psychological studies, which shows that men will die for what they believe to be the truth, but there are no documented cases of men dying for what they knew to be lies.

Section-2: **Many individuals have claimed to be the Messiah or "the only way"**

From the time of Jesus through the present time, many individuals have claimed to be the Messiah (*the "anointed one"/the "Christ"*) or "the only way". Two quick responses to such claims are: ***First***, just saying something does not necessarily make it so. ***Second***, the existence of counterfeit Messiahs means that there was/is a genuine Messiah. To reference some individuals, other than Jesus, who claimed to be the Messiah or "the only way", Section-2 is organized in two segments. *Segment-1* presents a discussion of "others, who claimed to be the Messiah". *Segment-2* presents a discussion of "others, who claimed to be 'the only way'".

Segment-1: **Others, who claimed to be the Messiah**

Over the years, several other individuals have claimed to be the Messiah. Such individuals were/are, as follows:

- *Reference-1*: During the life of Jesus, some scholars say, "There may have been as many as fifty others claiming to be the Messiah." However, the existence of one, fifty, or even a million counterfeits does not negate the one and only genuine Messiah, Jesus. Nor does the existence of counterfeits negate the fact that Jesus is the only way to God.

- *Reference-2*: About forty years after the death of Jesus around 70 A.D., a counterfeit Messiah led the Jews in a revolt against Rome. Roman legions came in and crushed this revolt. While crushing the revolt, the legions destroyed the temple. There are *two interesting things* to note about the defeat of the Jews, by these Roman legions.

  ✓ *First*, again, the Jews were led, by a counterfeit Messiah, who fit the Jewish definition of how the Messiah should be. (*Jesus fit God's definition of how the Messiah should be.*)

  ✓ *Second*, in destroying the temple, the Roman legions probably also destroyed all the genealogy records.

    Comment: Over the centuries, the Jews had been very protective of their genealogy records. The defeat of the Jews, and the destruction of those genealogy records, probably meant that Jesus was among the last individuals, who could claim to be of the line of David, and then prove it using those records. Jesus had a claim to the "Throne of David", because of His parents. Mary, His birth mother, carried the "Throne of David", by the word of God and by blood. Joseph, His legal father, carried the "Throne of David", by Jewish Law.

- *Reference-3*: The web document at:

✓ en.wikipedia.org/wiki/List_of_messiahs

presents a more complete list of individuals, who claimed to be a messiah or whose followers made such a claim. This list is divided into four major categories: Jewish Messiah Claimants, Christian Messiah Claimants, Muslim Messiah claimants, and other Messiah Claimants. This web document allows you to click on a name in a list. With that click, a brief description of that particular individual is presented. The presentation, by this web document, is better than anything this author could do, so no additional information about those claimants will be presented in this essay.

The concluding point about all the other individuals, who claimed to be the Messiah, is that none of them were indicated to be virgin born, none of them appeared to have their birth prophesied in advance, and none of them fulfilled the biblical prophecies.

Segment-2: **Others, who claimed to be the only way**

Over the years, other individuals have claimed to be "the only way". Their names will not be listed here. However, anyone can make such a claim. The real task becomes substantiating the claim with some type of proof. To date, the only person that God confirmed, as the way was Jesus, the man. And God made His confirmation, by resurrecting Jesus, the man, from the dead.

Presentation-5: **The nature of man**

Based on the nature of man, we note that a supportive-logical conclusion flows out of the belief that man was created with a "free will" and a "conscience". Here, the phrase – "nature of man", is intended to convey the belief that a "free will" and a "conscience" are part of man's created nature. For Christians, the Bible implies that God created man with a "free will" and a "conscience". "Free will" is implied in the Bible, by a series of events:

- God created Adam from the dust of the ground.
- God created Eve from one of Adam's ribs.
- God told Adam that he could eat any fruit in the Garden of Eden except the fruit of the tree of the knowledge of good and evil.
- God told Adam the consequences of eating the forbidden fruit.
- Adam and Eve chose to eat some of the forbidden fruit anyway.

Thus, Adam and Eve were created with the "free will" to make their own choices, even if their choices meant disobeying God. With regards to man's "conscience", there are thirty-one verses in the KJV that imply the existence of man's "conscience", by using the word: "conscience". However, since non-Christians do not believe the Bible, it will not be used to support the existence of man's "free will" and "conscience". For non-Christians, the "activities of life", can be used to imply the existence of man's "free will" and "conscience". That is, by observing the activities of life, non-Christians can confirm that each of us has the "free will" to choose to turn to the right, to turn to the left, to go forward, to go backward, to stop, to do good, to do evil, to accept Jesus, to reject Jesus, and so on. Such observations should also reveal that "something" aids individuals in assessing their "freewill" choices. Otherwise, given the same choices in the same circumstances, everyone would pick the same choice. But clearly, our observations of life indicate that when put in the same situation, with the same choices, different individuals make different choices. Thus, "something" aids each individual in assessing their "freewill" choices. Christians call this "something", which aids individuals in assessing their "freewill" choices, our "conscience". The word – "conscience", should also be acceptable to non-Christians. Because it does not matter what this "something" is called, as long as, both Christians and non-Christians agree on what this "something" does.

> *Comment:* Many Christians also believe that from birth, we have an "innate knowledge of God" and an "innate sense of good and evil, from God's perspective". With regards to an "innate knowledge of God", this author believes it may be more accurate to say that from conception there is an "innate knowledge of God" in our being, because we are His creations. With regards to an "innate sense of good and evil", this sense may be what Christians call "the light of one's conscience". However, Christians also understand that this "innate sense of good and evil", is countered by and can be overwhelmed by our natural desire to have our own needs, wants, and desires fulfilled, without regards to the needs, wants, and desires of others. Similarly, our "innate knowledge of God" can be deadened by our interaction and reaction to the things of this world. Thus, everyone – but especially, children – need someone to help them keep and develop their "innate knowledge of God" and their "innate sense of good and evil". More specifically, everyone – but especially, children – need someone to guide them toward the realization and understanding that "this world does not revolve around them." Such guidance is the primary responsibility of an individual's parents. Unfortunately, as we grow into maturity, too many of us keep the childish ways of wanting to do our own thing, without regards to the wants, needs, and desires of others. And the more that we continue to do our own thing, the more our consciences are deadened. In fact, some people have managed to deaden their conscience to the point that they can do anything to anyone for any reason. Still, if most of the people with deadened consciences thought about what they were doing, they would realize that they would not want some of the "not right" things, which they were doing to others, done to them. Yet, they do those "not right" things anyway. However, their actions do not negate the fact that they have "the

light of their consciences" to guide them. It is just that they will not accept that light. If they did, it would mean that they understood that each individual has a tendency to be selfish and each individual has a tendency toward evil.

Whether you are a Christian or a non-Christian, you should understand that man's "free will" and "conscience", are implied, by both the Bible and life. Thus, aided by our "conscience", each of us has the "free will" to accept "Jesus, as the only way to God" or to reject "Jesus, as the only way to God".

Presentation-6: **The Bible**

Based on the Bible, we note that the supportive-logical conclusion reached, here, would be the same, as that reached under Step-1: "A response to a Christian". However, here, modifications would have to be made to explain the Bible and its credibility to non-Christians. That explanation could be formed in a detail version and/or in an overview version. A detail version would consist of the presentation of the three essays: "Does God exist?", "Is the Bible the inspired word of God?", and "Did Jesus claim to be God and/or the Son of God?" Here only an overview version will be presented. And to save space under this overview version, the credibility of the Bible is discussed in detail in the essay: "Is the Bible the inspired word of God?" Thus, an overview version is presented, with the following comments:

With the understanding that the Bible is a credible document, it should be read with the intent of trying to understand it. In addition, each reader should try to see the whole picture. That is, each reader should try to develop an overview of the Bible. Hopefully, the whole picture or an overview will reveal the perfect beauty in God's redemption plan for man. In God's plan, we can see His perfect love. God's plan is a "just" and "simple" plan. A "just" plan required God to inform man of His rules, and of any consequences for breaking His rules. For Adam and Eve, there was only one rule: "Do not eat the forbidden fruit!" One rule is about as simple, as such a situation could be. A "simple" plan provides only one way for man to get to God. Many ways would promote a lot of confusion, because God would have to ensure that each of us knew all of the ways. And because of our "free will", many ways would mean each individual has to decide, which way is best suited for them. Or more precisely, and consistent with human nature, most individuals would go for the easiest way for them. After choosing one of many ways, how would anyone know that the chosen way was actually the best way for them? Obviously, again, the existence of "many ways to God" would cause a lot of confusion. And God is not the author of confusion. Thus, having "Jesus, as the only way to Himself (God)" adds to the beauty of His plan. Perhaps, the most beautiful part of God's plan is that He does not force His plan on us. Like Adam and Eve, we have the "free will" to reject or to accept, God's plan. This is why salvation, by grace is so beautiful. In addition, note that God's plan provided Jesus, the man, to take the spiritual consequences of breaking God's rules, if we accept Jesus, the man, as our substitute. And that is why "Jesus, the man, is the only way to God."

Presentation-7: **Spiritual issues**

Based on two spiritual issues, which are "spiritually consistent" with God's redemptive plan for man, we note two supportive-logical conclusions. The two issues are addressed through two statements. Thus, Presentation-7 is organized in two sections. Section-1 addresses an issue, which is represented by the statement: "We do it God's way or we do it our own way." Section-2 addresses an issue, which is represented by the statement: "Over time, believers looked forward and looked backward, to the cross."

Section-1: **We do it God's way or we do it our own way**

This statement has, at least, one implication and a couple of consequences. Comments addressing the implication and two consequences are organized in three segments: *Segment-1* addresses an implication of the Section-1 statement. *Segment-2* addresses a consequence of the Section-1 statement. *Segment-3* addresses a second consequence of the Section-1 statement. The three segments are, as follows:

- *Segment-1*: An implication of the statement is that "If we do things God's way, then He is our God. If we do things our own way, then we are trying to be our own gods. It is one way or the other. And God gave us the "free will" to choose, either way."

- *Segment-2*: A consequence of the statement is that "If you choose not to do it God's way, then you probably do not believe that 'Jesus is the only way to God' or that 'Jesus died for your sins.' If true, then it means that someone besides Jesus must die spiritually, as a penalty for your sins, and then something unblemished must die physically, as an atonement for your sins." There are two reasons for saying this:

  - ✓ *Reason-1*: In God's perfect plan, He said, "The penalty for sin is spiritual death."

  - ✓ *Reason-2*: In God's perfect plan, He said, "The atonement for sin is the physical death of a sacrificial animal." More precisely, the atonement for sin, on a short-term (*yearly*) basis, is the physical death of an unblemished animal. The atonement for sin, on a long-term (*eternal*) basis, is the physical death of the sacrificial lamb of God, Who is Jesus, the man, (*the Messiah/the Christ*).

  While individuals can reject God's way, they are not released from having to satisfy both the "penalty" and the "atonement" for their sins. Thus, such rejections reveal two problems:

✓ *Problem-1*: "You have to pay the penalty for your own sins. This would mean that you will remain separated from God's grace." (*The word – "remain" is used to remind you that we are born separated from God's grace.*)

✓ *Problem-2*: "Your sins must be atoned for, eternally. Thus, you would need another Messiah, other than Jesus, the man, because your atoning sacrifice has to be sinless."

By doing it, God's way, the finished work of Jesus, the man, on the cross, would solve these two problems. Thus, according to God's plan, "Jesus is the only way to God".

➧ *Segment3*: Still, another consequence of the statement is that "If you choose not to do it God's way, then you will spend eternity in 'Hell' or the 'Lake of Fire'." But please note that you will spend eternity in Hell, because you chose not to do it God's way. More specifically, you will spend eternity in Hell, because you reject "Jesus, as the only way to God". You reject Jesus and His payments (*the penalty and the atonement*), for your sins. Put another way, you will be in Hell, because with your sins, you cannot exist eternally in heaven, under God's grace. Your sins are the central obstacle to establishing your existence under God's grace. That is why most Christian apologists say the real issue for people to consider is "Who will die for your sins?" And the only eternal answer is "Jesus". Nothing else works, because whoever dies for your sins, has to be (*had to be*) sinless, according to God's way. Thus, "Jesus is the only way to God."

Consequently, if we want to be with God throughout eternity, then "We do it God's way", which is through "Jesus, who is the only way to Him (God)."

Section-2: **Over time, believers looked forward and looked backward, to the cross**

This statement reflects an important aspect of the Christian belief that "Jesus is the only way to God", because some people ask, "what about the people, who lived before the crucifixion, death, burial, and resurrection of Jesus, the man?" And the answer given by most Christian apologists is that "Believers, who lived/are living/will live, after the crucifixion of Jesus, the man, look 'back to the cross'. Believers, who were alive during the crucifixion of Jesus, the man, looked 'at the cross'. Believers who lived before the crucifixion of Jesus, the man, looked 'forward to the cross'." Thus, it does not matter in which direction we look. It only matters that we look at Jesus, the man, and His finished work on the cross, as the only way to God.

Comment: A belief among many Christians is that "those believers, who died before the cross went to 'Abraham's bosom (*a euphemism for the abode of the righteous dead, before the cross'*)', to await the finished work of Jesus, the man. After Jesus, the man, died on the cross, He may have gone to 'Abraham's bosom' to announce His finished work. Then He may have led the believers there into the presence of God, in "Paradise". Thus, now when a believer dies, her or his body returns to the dust of the ground, while her or his 'soul and spirit' go immediately into the presence of God."

Step-3: **Some relevant comments**

Three groups of relevant comments are, as follows:

- *Group-1*: Some Bible scholars say, "Genesis 3:15 is the first biblical reference to the virgin birth of Jesus and the first reference to Jesus, as the redeemer." In the KJV, Genesis 3:15 reads:

  > And I will put enmity between thee and the woman, and between thy seed and her seed; it shall bruise thy head, and thou shalt bruise his heel.

  More specifically, scholars say, "The phrase – 'her seed', is a reference to the virgin birth of Jesus. The phrase – 'it shall bruise thy head', means 'defeat you', and the phrase – 'thou shalt bruise his heel', means 'Satan would be unsuccessful in his attempt at defeating Jesus.'"

- *Group-2*: Sometime ago, a radio ministry aired the testimony of an old South American minister. As part of his testimony, this minister recounted how he came to Christ, as a young adult. However, as a young lad, he was designated, by his tribe to be the next witch doctor. Therefore, while he was still a young lad, the reigning witch doctor began training him in that art. He learned to use specific drugs to enter trances and communicate with demons. His tribe was in a remote part of his country. Thus, he grew to manhood (*adulthood*) without any exposure to the outside world. He said, "One day, his tribe received word that missionaries were visiting a neighboring tribe." He took drugs to communicate with his demon guides. These demons warned him that the missionaries and Jesus were his enemies. Eventually, the missionaries made it to his tribe. He had several confrontations with them. However, the missionaries did not back down. He watched the way these missionaries interacted with his people. After a time, he became a friendly adversary of the missionaries, as such, the missionaries were better able to witness to him. Eventually, he saw the truth in Jesus and accepted Jesus as the only way to God. This testimony was extremely interesting, especially, when the minister recounted how the demons warned him about Jesus.

- *Group-3*: Some people have the mistaken belief that Jesus, God, the Son, endured humanity to understand how it feels to be human. But we are images of God. Thus, it was not necessary for Jesus, God, the Son, to become human to understand us. No! Jesus, God, the Son, endured humanity (*became Jesus, the man*), for one reason, which was to become our kinsman-redeemer, and by that, Jesus, the man, became the only way to God, the Father.

Step-4: **Some concluding comments**

Hopefully, the previous presentations make it easy to understand why having only one way is the sign of a loving and intelligent God. In addition, everyone must realize that Jesus is the only way, because that is how God designed His relationship with man. Jesus came, as one of us, so that we could recognize Him. Jesus wants us to know Him and to accept Him, as the only way to God, the Father. However,

> "The sad thing is more people search for reasons not to believe, than search for reasons to believe. Or more precisely, more people find it easier to note reasons not to believe, than to believe."

During a religious discussion with a friend, this friend told this author about some things that he read in the book: "The Egyptian Book of the Dead" or "The Book of coming forth by Day or by Night". One thing that this friend mentioned was a reference to the existence of some Hieroglyphic writing that supposedly referred to someone, who claimed to be the only way to God. This friend did not say whether this was a reference to Jesus or someone else. If it referenced someone else, or say that someone today claimed that she or he was the only way to God, a "question" and a "request" would come to my mind. The "question" would be: "On what basis is that claim made?" The "request" would be: "Prove it!" Jesus' answer to the "question" is recorded in the Bible. That is, Jesus based His claim on the fact that God sent Him and that God and He were one. Jesus also stated that "He was the only way to God." Jesus satisfied the "request", when God resurrected Him from the dead. Thus, the answer to the question – "Is Jesus the only way to God?", is "Yes!"

Step-5: **A response to each of the five sample-rebuff questions**

This essay was begun with a reference to questions used by non-Christians to rebuff Christians about "Jesus being the only way to God". In fact, five sample-rebuff questions were listed. The other steps of this essay may have implied answers to some or all of those five sample questions. But this step serves to explicitly respond to each of the five sample-rebuff questions:

- *Question-1*: "If God allows only one way to Himself, how can He be loving?"

  Response-1: Hopefully, this essay has provided a satisfactory response to this question.

However, to summarize, having many ways to most things only creates confusion and delays. Having only one way keeps things simple and direct. And keeping things simple and direct is consistent with a God, who loves us.

➧ Question-2: "What about the Bushman in deepest Africa, who has never heard about God or heard the Gospel?" "Is that Bushman condemned to Hell forever simply, because he has never heard?"

Response-2: Scholars say, "Those who have never heard the 'Gospel' have the 'light of nature' and the 'light of their conscience' to bring them to Jesus." To support this view, scholars point to stories of members of various cultures, who gained knowledge about God, Jesus, and/or about a book, which contained information about God and/or Jesus, before the arrival of missionaries. Some such stories are presented in the book – "Eternity in their Hearts", by author Don Richardson. In this book, author Richardson presents twenty-seven stories of other cultures, which had a belief in the "One True God" and/or in a book, which contained information about Him.

➧ Question-3: "What about those who were/are/will be born to non-Christian parents?" Some non-Christians are quick to say that children generally remain in the "religion" or "no-religion" of their parents. Thus, "Are non-Christian children condemned to Hell, because their non-Christian parents are condemned to Hell?"

Response-3: Individuals, who used the statement – "Children generally remain in the 'religion' or 'no-religion' of their parents", ignore its implications. One implication is "All individuals born to Christian parents are saved." And this is not true, because to be saved each individual must accept Jesus for herself or himself. More precisely, no one else can accept Jesus on your behalf. You must do it yourself. Another implication is that because your parents are Catholics, you will also be a Catholic. But here again, those who use the statement – "Children generally remain in the 'religion' or 'no-religion' of their parents", miss the fact that being Catholic or whatever religion is not what saves you. Only believing in the finished work of Jesus saves you. But implications aside, as mentioned under the response to *question-2*, non-Christians also have the "light of nature" and the "light of their conscience" to bring them to Jesus.

➧ Question-4: "What about those who lived before the death and resurrection of Jesus?"

Response-4: As mentioned before, most Christian apologists say, "Believers, who lived or are living after the crucifixion of Jesus, the man, look back to the cross. Believers, who were alive during the crucifixion of Jesus, the man, looked at the cross. Believers, who lived before the crucifixion of Jesus, the man, looked forward to the cross." And Jesus, the man, and His finished work on the cross provide the only way to God. Thus, it does not matter in which direction we look. It only matters that we look at Jesus, the man, and His finished work on the cross, as the only way to God.

- *Question-5*: "What about those non-Christians, who lived/live/will live moral lives?" "Are moral non-Christians condemned to Hell simply for not accepting Christ?"

  Response-5: How we live is not what our salvation is based on. Our salvation is based on accepting the finished work of Jesus on the cross. How we live reflects our love for God.

Step-6: **Two analogous stories**

Many Christian stories exist that attempt to present in a memorable fashion, the concept of "Jesus becoming our human kinsman" and the concept of "God sacrificing His Son". Some of these stories have several versions. This author's favorite version of the story, which is related to the concept of "Jesus becoming our human kinsman", is titled: "The farmer and the birds". This author's favorite version of the story, which is related to the concept of "God sacrificing His Son", is titled: "The bridge-man and his son". The authors of both stories are not known to me. Nevertheless, paraphrased versions of the two stories are, as follows:

Story-1: **The farmer and the birds**

One Sunday morning, the wife of a non-believing farmer invited her husband to go to church with her and their children. However, the farmer declined his wife's offer. The wife and their children went off to church. Shortly after their departure, it started to snow. It was a sudden and heavy snowfall. When the non-believing farmer looked out a window, which allowed him to see his barnyard, he noticed a flock of small birds struggling against the sudden snowfall. The farmer felt sorry for the birds, so he decided to go out and open the barn door. That would allow the birds to enter the warmth and safety of the barn. The farmer put on his coat and hat, and went outside. The small birds scattered, as the farmer approached them on his way to the barn door. The farmer opened the barn door, turned on a light in the barn, and then went back into his house. Inside the house, the farmer took off his coat and hat, and went to the same window. He was curious to see if the birds would find their way into the barn. To his sorrow, the small birds had returned to the same spot in the middle of the barnyard, ignoring the open barn door. As the snow continued to fall, the small flock of birds continued their struggle against the snow and the cold temperature. The farmer was really becoming concerned about the birds, because they continued to ignore the open barn door. Then he thought, "What if I became a small bird, then I could lead them into the safety and warmth of the barn." With that thought, the farmer fell to his knees and thanked God. For this non-believing farmer had just come to an understanding of why God, the Son, had to take on the nature of a man, as Jesus, so that He could lead us to the Father – so that He could serve as the only way to God.

Story-2: **The bridge-man and his son**

There was a bridge-man, who operated a draw bridge over a river that had a lot of barge traffic. The bridge was used by a variety of trains: passenger, freight, work, etc. One day, the bridge-man decided to take his small son to work. This day was supposed to be his least-busiest work day of the week. At lunch time, the bridge-man and his son went down to the base of the bridge near the motor driven gears that raised and lowered the bridge. This was a perfect spot, because it also afforded the bridge-man and his son a nice view of the river. They had just settled down to eat their lunches when the bridge-man heard the phone ringing in the control tower. He told his son to stay there and then raced to answer the phone. When he picked up the phone, it was the station master of a nearby station. This station master told the bridge-man that a special-passenger train was on the way and would probably be there in less than a minute, so he must bring the bridge down right away to avoid a disaster. Just then the bridge-man heard the whistle of the coming train. He raced to the controls to lower the bridge. Just as the bridge-man started to lower the bridge, he looked out the window to check on his son. To his horror, his small son had disobeyed him, and now, was playing in the gears that would lower the bridge. There was not enough time for the bridge-man to run out to get his son, and then return to lower the bridge. He had time for only one decision. The bridge-man would either lower the bridge or leave it up. If he lowered the bridge, the train passengers would be saved, but his son would be killed. If he did not lower the bridge, the train would crash into the river, but his son would be saved. The bridge-man heard the train whistle again, he knew there was only one thing to do. He lowered the bridge. The train whistle drowned out the cries of his small son, as the big gears crushed him. As the bridge-man looked out a window at the passing train, the passengers waived and smiled at him. They never knew that the bridge-man had sacrificed his son to save them.

(Acts 4:12 NIV) Salvation is found in no one else,
for there is no other name under heaven given to men by which we must be saved."

Does man have a body, a soul, and a spirit?

This question flows from the fact that some people have encountered statements about the Christian concept: "man **has** a body, a soul, and a spirit." This concept is also expressed, as – "man **is** a body, a soul, and a spirit" or possibly, as – "man **is** a body, soul, and spirit". Despite the actual wording, encounters involving this concept may have been through Christian sources and/or through non-Christian sources. Hopefully, most Christians were or will be formally introduced to this concept through Christian sources: the Bible, Christian preachers, Christian teachers, Christian scholars, and/or Christian authors. This is the way it was for this author, as a young Catholic lad taking catechism classes. Now, years later and in spite of leaving the "Catholic Church", my "belief in the concept conveyed by the words" is still strong. However, it has become clear that "believing the concept conveyed by the words" and "understanding the concept conveyed by the words", are two different things. Therefore the time had come to better understand the concept that "man has a body, a soul, and a spirit". More precisely, the time had come to understand the basis for this concept. For Christians, the primary basis – the primary sources for everything should be the original Hebrew/Aramaic[66] version of the Old Testament and the original Koine Greek version of the New Testament. Secondary sources are translations of the Bible in the Christian's native language and/or other Christians. Ternary sources are web documents and/or other publications. Because this author lacks a knowledge of Hebrew, Aramaic, and Koine Greek, secondary and ternary sources will be used. The secondary sources are the NIV, KJV, and statements from various Christians. The ternary sources are several web documents. These sources allow this discussion of the topic question – "Does man have a body, a soul, and a spirit?", to be organized in three parts. Part-1 presents some introductory comments and definitions. Part-2 presents a critique of the topic question. Part-3 presents some concluding comments.

Part-1: **Some introductory comments and definitions**

Introductory comments and definitions are organized in four sections. Section-1 presents some background information. Section-2 presents a related concept about "animals and plants". Section-3 presents a related concept about "the living body". Section-4 presents definitions of the words: "body", "soul", and "spirit".

Section-1: **Some background information**

Background information was developed using the "Yahoo search engine", with a request to find all websites, which included all of the words: "body," "soul," "spirit," "God," and "Jesus". The results of the search produced two surprises for this author. The first surprise was that the "Yahoo search engine" found five hundred and eighteen thousand websites. (*This search was performed more than six years ago. On August 9, 2007, the same search was performed and the "Yahoo Search Engine" found four million nine hundred and fifty thousand websites.*) The second surprise involved web documents and how comments about Christians and the topic question were worded in those web documents. This surprise is better understood by first presenting some definitions. Therefore, in response to the topic question, a consensus of several web documents is that there are three major views or camps: the "monochotomous camp", the "dichotomous camp", and the "trichotomous camp". These camps are defined, as follows:

- The "monochotomous camp" consists of all those individuals, who believe that "Man is just a body." Thus, those in the "monochotomous camp" believe that "man is a 'monochotomous (*one-part*) being'."

- The "dichotomous camp" consists of all those individuals, who believe that "Man is a body and a soul." Or more precisely, "man is a body and a soul/spirit." In the dichotomous camp, the words – "soul" and "spirit", are treated, as synonymous terms. Thus, those in the "dichotomous camp" believe that "man is a 'dichotomous (*two-part*) being'."

- The "trichotomous camp" consists of all those individuals, who believe that "Man is a body, a soul, and a spirit." Thus, those in the "trichotomous camp" believe that "man is a 'trichotomous (*three-part*) being'."

As implied previously, the existence of these three camps was not the second surprise. The second surprise was wording in several web documents, which claimed that "there were individuals in each camp, who call themselves 'Christians'." This claim influenced the wording of the rest of this essay. More specifically, a direct response to this claim is presented in Part-2/Section-1 (*titled: A direct response to the claim: "There are Christians in all three camps."*).

Section-2: **A related concept about "animals and plants"**

Some people believe a related concept about "animals and plants", which seems consistent with the primary concept that "Man is a body, a soul, and a spirit." This related concept is:

"An animal is a body and a soul. And a plant is only a body."

There is a consistent beauty about the above related concept and the primary concept. This beauty makes both concepts worth repeating. Thus, once more, some people believe that:

"A man *is* a body, a soul, and a spirit.
An animal *is* a body and a soul.
A plant *is* only a body."

However, beauty aside, this author is unaware of any biblical support for this "related concept", about animals and plants. But the partial symmetry – complex to simple – between "man, animals, and plants" and "the combinations of body, soul, and spirit that each had", seems consistent with God's way of doing things. And some support for this "related concept", does seem to come through observing nature. More specifically, "man and animals", with their "bodies and souls", appear to "interact", with each other and with plants, or more precisely, with this three dimensional world. "Plants" with only "bodies", appear to "only react" to people, animals, and other plants, or more precisely, to this three dimensional world. Such "interacting" by "people and animals" and such "reacting" by "plants", would seem to support the primary concept and the related concept previously mentioned.

Section-3: **A related concept about the "living body"**

While rewriting this essay, this author realized that there is another concept, which is about the "living body". This concept is:

"The 'living body' is 'three-parts'.
It is 'the shell', 'the matter in the shell', and 'God's breath of life'."

Genesis 2:7 seems to provide some support for this concept, because it indicates that God formed man of the dust of the ground. In the NIV, Genesis 2:7 reads, as follows:

> the LORD God formed the man from the dust of the ground and breathed into his nostrils the breath of life, and the man became a living being.

The word – "formed" in Genesis 2:7, can be taken to mean that God made Adam's "shell" and "the matter inside of his (Adam's) shell". Then God breathed into Adam's nostrils His (God's) "breath of life", which caused Adam to become "a living being". Thus once more, the phrase – "a living being" in the NIV translation of Genesis 2:7 would seem to support this related concept. However, while the NASB and the NRSV translations also use the phrase – "a living being", the KJV translation uses the phrase: "a living soul". But the KJV uses the word – "soul" a lot. In fact, a Bible software program called "QuickVerse" indicates that:

- ✓ The word – "soul" is used 419 times in 396 verses in the KJV.
- ✓ The word – "soul" is used 243 times in 233 verses in the NASB.
- ✓ The word – "soul" is used 139 times in 135 verses in the NRSV.
- ✓ The word – "soul" is used 110 times in 108 verses in the NIV.

Furthermore, Strong's Exhaustive Concordance seems to indicate that the meaning of the word – "soul" in Genesis 2:7, is merely "a breathing creature". Such a meaning is consistent with the word – "being". It almost seems like the phrases – "a living being" and "a living soul" could be replaced with the phrase: "a living body".

Two verses, which seem to imply the final disposition of "God's breath of life", are Job 34:14-15. These read:

(Job 34:14 NIV) If it were his intention and he withdrew his spirit and breath,

(Job 34:15 NIV) all mankind would perish together and man would return to the dust.

These are words that Elihu (*son of Barakel the Buzite, of the family of Ram*) is speaking to Job, as Job and three other friends are incorrectly discussing Job's predicament (*the suffering caused by Satan with God's permission*). Nevertheless, the point is:

"Elihu appears to believe that the 'spirit' and 'breath' are God's – belong to God."

Thus, these two aspects may return to God upon the "physical death" of each individual. Actually, there are other verses, which indicate that the "spirit" does return to God. One such verse is Ecclesiastes 12:7. This verse reads:

(Ecclesiastes 12:7 KJV) Then shall the dust return to the earth as it was: and the spirit shall return unto God who gave it.

Nevertheless, the point is:

"Genesis 2:7 clearly indicates that God's 'breath of life' is in man – is in the 'living body'."

Thus, one could say that the implication of this section can be summarized, as follows:

- Man is a "body", a "soul", and a "spirit".
- A body is a "shell", the "matter in the shell", and "God's breath of life".
- Upon the death of a man, the "spirit" and "God's breath of life" return to God, for whatever He does with them.

Section-4: **Definitions of the words: "body", "soul", and "spirit"**

Many Christian preachers, teachers, scholars, and authors have presented definitions of the three words – "body", "soul", and "spirit". Thus, in conjunction with Section-3, these various Christian definitions are use to form paraphrased-consensus definitions, which in turn form the working definitions, for the words – "body", "soul", and "spirit", for this essay and book. These working definitions are, as follows:

- Our "body" – our "living body" – is "The house containing our 'soul', 'spirit', and "God's breath of life'. It provides the 'means (*eyes, ears, tongue, fingers, hands, toes, feet, skin, etc.*)', for us to contact this three dimensional world. (*In this essay and book, the word – "body", by itself, could mean a "living body" or a "dead body". Hopefully, the context indicates which.*)

- Our "soul" is "An invisible part of us, which contains our intellect, reason, will, emotions, logic, and that kind of thing. It interprets the contact with this three dimensional world provided, by the 'body'.

- Our "spirit" is "An invisible part of us, which contains the God consciousness of man. It is this part through, which God contacts us."

Part-2: **A critique of the topic question**

This critique of the topic question is facilitated by using "a direct response to the claim that 'there are Christians in all three camps.'" Using such a response allows this discussion to refer to Bible verses, which support one of the three camps, and other concepts, which imply that man is a one-part, a two-part, or a three-part being. Thus, to present this critique, Part-2 is organized in one section, which is further divided into four segments. Section-1 begins a direct response to the claim that "there are Christians in all three camps."

Section-1: **A direct response to the claim: "There are Christians in all three camps."**

This direct response to the referenced claim is presented, as it relates to each camp. However, the comments, which form the response for each camp, are presented in an overview format, with the supporting details being presented in *Segment-1* through *Segment-4*. The overview comments about each of the three camps are, as follows:

- "Christians in the 'trichotomous camp'", is totally understandable, because the beliefs of those in this camp are very consistent with our working definitions of the words – "body", "soul", and "spirit". Furthermore, accepting "man, as a 'three-part' being", provides the fullest consistency with the Bible and the most symmetry in a Trinity versus man comparison.

- "Christians in the 'dichotomous camp'", is less understandable, but some understanding is based on "two conditions". One condition is that the minimum requirement on the "nature of man" for a literal consistency with some Bible verses is "man, as a 'two-part' being". The second condition is that the minimum requirement on the "nature of man" for a traditional consistency with some Christian concepts like "death" and "resurrection" and with the biological concept called "death" is also "man, as a two-part" being.

- "Christians in the 'monochotomous camp'", is not understandable at all, because of the minimum requirement of "man, as a 'two-part' being" for consistency with the Bible, with Christian concepts like "death" and "resurrection", and with the biological concept called "death". Thus, we have to wonder how anyone in the 'monochotomous camp' could truly call herself or himself, a Christian, while they are in the 'monochotomous camp'.

The preceding three groups of comments about each of the three camps referenced the Bible and three concepts: the "biological concept of 'death'", the "Christian concept of 'death'", and the "Christian concept of 'resurrection'". Thus, to be thorough, we must now examine the Bible and the three concepts to determine support for man, "as a one-part being", "as a two-part being", or "as a three-part being". To accomplish this task, the rest of Section-1 is organized in four segments. *Segment-1* presents a discussion of the "biological concept of 'death'". *Segment-2* presents a discussion of "some relevant Bible verses". *Segment-3* presents a discussion of the "Christian concept of 'death'". *Segment-4* presents a discussion of the "Christian concept of 'resurrection'".

Segment-1: **The "biological concept of 'death'"**

This concept was researched using the Internet. Several web documents were read. Perhaps, the best definition of "biological death" was from the web document at web address: death-and-dying.org/what-is-death.htm. Paraphrased, this web document defined:

"biological death" as "the separation of the 'mind' and the 'body'".

This definition of "biological death", indicates that "man is a two-part being". However, if a definition of "biological death" was developed from the discussion presented in Part-1/Section-3 (titled: A related concept about the "living body"), that definition would be, as follows:

"Biological death" is "the separation of God's 'breath of life' from 'the shell' and 'the matter (*blood and so on*) in the shell'".

This definition supports "man, as a three-part being". However, since most people would probably favor combining "the shell" and "the matter (*blood and so on*) in the shell", as one component – the "body", this definition would then support "man, as a two-part being". Thus, based on the previous comments, the "biological concept of 'death'":

- ✓ offers no support for the belief that "man is a 'one-part' being",
- ✓ offers strong support for the belief that "man is a 'two-part' being",
- ✓ offers some support for the belief that "man is a 'three-part' being".

Segment-2: **Some relevant Bible verses**

Some relevant Bible verses are Genesis 2:7 and Luke 16:19-31. While it is true that there are several other verses or set of verses that could be presented here, some of the other verses will be presented at a later time. Genesis 2:7 is presented, because it references the creation of man. Luke 16:19-31 are presented, because these verses reference the "Parable of Lazarus and the Rich man", as told by Jesus. In this parable, Jesus tells of a discussion between the Rich man, who has just died, and Father Abraham, who is already dead. Thus, *Segment-2* is organized in two subsegments. *Subsegment-1* presents a discussion of Genesis 2:7. *Subsegment-2* presents a discussion of Luke 16:19-31.

Subsegment-1: **Genesis 2:7**

In the NIV, Genesis 2:7 reads:

> the LORD God formed the man from the dust of the ground and breathed into his nostrils the breath of life, and the man became a living being.

This verse clearly implies that man is, at least, two parts. One part would be the physical body of Adam that God created out of the dust of the earth. The other part would be the "breath of life" that God breathed into Adam, causing Adam to become a "living being". Based on these statements, we can say that "Genesis 2:7":

- ✓ offers no support for the belief that "man is a 'one-part' being",
- ✓ offers strong support for the belief that "man is a 'two-part' being",
- ✓ offers some support for the belief that "man is a 'three-part' being".

Subegment-2: **Luke 16:19-31**

In the KJV, Luke 16:19-31 read:

> Luke 16:[19]There was a certain rich man, which was clothed in purple and fine
> linen, and fared sumptuously every day. [20]And there was a certain beggar named
> Lazarus, which was laid at his gate, full of sores, [21]And desiring to be fed with the
> crumbs which fell from the rich man's table: moreover the dogs came and licked
> his sores. [22]And it came to pass, that the beggar died, and was carried by the
> angels into Abraham's bosom: the rich man also died, and was buried; [23]And in
> hell he lift up his eyes, being in torments, and seeth Abraham afar off, and
> Lazarus in his bosom. [24]And he cried and said, Father Abraham, have mercy on
> me, and send Lazarus, that he may dip the tip of his finger in water, and cool my
> tongue; for I am tormented in this flame. [25]But Abraham said, Son, remember that
> thou in thy lifetime receivedst thy good things, and likewise Lazarus evil things:

> but now he is comforted, and thou art tormented. [26]And beside all this, between
> us and you there is a great gulf fixed: so that they which would pass from hence
> to you cannot; neither can they pass to us, that would come from thence. [27]Then
> he said, I pray thee therefore, father, that thou wouldest send him to my father's
> house: [28]For I have five brethren; that he may testify unto them, lest they also
> come into this place of torment. [29]Abraham saith unto him, They have Moses and
> the prophets; let them hear them. [30]And he said, Nay, father Abraham: but if one
> went unto them from the dead, they will repent. [31]And he said unto him, If they
> hear not Moses and the prophets, neither will they be persuaded, though one rose
> from the dead.

From these verses, at least, three things are apparent. These are, as follows:

- *First*, the wording – "the beggar died, and was carried by the angels into Abraham's bosom", implies that a beggar named – "Lazarus", died and some aspect of him was carried to "Abraham's bosom *(a euphemism for the 'abode of the righteous dead, before the cross', because that where Abraham was)*" – *(a place that angels were aware of)*.

- *Second*, the wording – "rich man also died", obviously implies that a rich man died.

- *Third*, the wording – "And in hell he lift up his eyes, being in torments, and seeth Abraham afar off, and Lazarus in his bosom", implies that the *"part"* of the rich man, which existed in hell, experienced torment and it also had sight, emotions *(concern for his brothers)*, and reasoning. However, the *"part"* of the rich man in hell and the *"part"* of Lazarus in "Abraham's bosom cannot be their physical bodies, because Genesis 3:19, Job 34:15, Psalms 103:14, Psalms 104:29, Ecclesiastes 3:20, and Ecclesiastes 12:7, indicate that our physical bodies will return to the dust of the earth when we die. These verses read, as follows:

  > (Genesis 3:19 KJV) In the sweat of thy face shalt thou eat bread, till thou return unto the ground; for out of it wast thou taken: for dust thou art, and unto dust shalt thou return.

  > (Job 34:15 KJV) All flesh shall perish together, and man shall turn again unto dust.

  > (Psalms 103:14 KJV) For he knoweth our frame; he remembereth that we are dust.

  > (Psalms 104:29 KJV) Thou hidest thy face, they are troubled: thou takest away their breath, they die, and return to their dust.

(Ecclesiastes 3:20 KJV) All go unto one place; all are of the dust, and all turn to dust again.

(Ecclesiastes 12:7 KJV) Then shall the dust return to the earth as it was: and the spirit shall return unto God who gave it.

Therefore, at a minimum, both "Lazarus and the rich man", must have been "two-part" beings. One part of their beings returned to the dust of the earth. Another part of their beings was in "Abraham's bosom" for Lazarus and in hell for the Rich man. Thus, based on the above comments and referenced verses, we can say that Luke 16:19-31:

- ✓ offers no support for the belief that "man is a 'one-part' being",
- ✓ offers strong support for the belief that "man is a 'two-part' being",
- ✓ offers some support for the belief that "man is a 'three-part' being".

Segment-3: **The Christian concept of "death"**

Any discussion of this concept must be preceded by the development of a sense of what the word – "death", means to Christians. Hopefully, most Christians understand that explicitly and/ or implicitly, the Bible references three types of "death": "physical death", "spiritual death", and "the Second Death". Thus, *Segment-3* is organized in four subsegments. *Subsegment-1* presents definitions of the phrase: "physical death". *Subsegment-2* presents definitions of the phrase: "spiritual death". *Subsegment-3* presents definitions of the phrase: "the Second Death". *Subsegment-4* presents some concluding comments about the Christian concept of "death".

Subsegment-1: **Definitions of the phrase: "physical death"**

Unfortunately, the Christian definition of the phrase –"physical death", is different for each of the three camps. Those definitions are, as follows:

- "Physical death" is defined:
  - ✓ in the monochotomous camp, as "the end of life". (*Note that for this camp, death cannot be defined in terms of a separation, because a "separation" explicitly carries the connotation of multiple aspects of something.*)
  - ✓ in the dichotomous camp, as "the separation of the body from the soul/spirit".
  - ✓ in the trichotomous camp, as "the separation of the body from both

the soul and the spirit".

Subsegment-2 **Definitions of the phrase: "spiritual death"**

The phrase –"spiritual death", is defined, as follows:

- "Spiritual death" is defined as *"the separation of man from God's grace"*. More precisely, "spiritual death" is represented by *"the transition of man from an existence under God's grace to an existence under God's judgment, in time"*.

  Comment: For all humans, except Jesus, "spiritual death" occurred, when Adam and Eve sinned. The transition was emphasized by God putting Adam and Eve out of the garden. God moved Adam and Eve from their existence under *His grace* in the garden to their existence under *His judgment* in the world, where Eve suffered the pains of childbirth and Adam suffered the toils of getting their daily bread.

  Jesus was born "spiritually alive", because He was born sinless. Thus, His "spiritual death" occurred on the cross, when God put all of our sins in His (Jesus') spiritual account. (*See the essay: "What is the literal and symbolic significance in the shedding of Jesus' innocent blood?"*) However, Jesus only remained under God's judgment until His "physical death" on the cross. The "physical death" of Jesus, the man, was the atoning sacrifice for all our sins, thus His "physical death" would have reestablished His existence under God's grace. His "physical death" reestablished our existence under God's grace, if we accept His deaths on our behalf.

Subsegment-3 **Definitions of the phrase: "the Second Death"**

The phrase –"the Second Death", is defined, as follows:

- "The Second death", also called "Eternal death", is defined as *"the eternal separation of man from God's* grace". More precisely, regarding eternity, "The Second death" is represented by *"the transition of man from an existence under God's judgment, in time, to an existence under God's judgment, for eternity"*.

  Comment: The wording above is based on some Christian scholars, who try to remind the rest of us that "God is omnipresent - God is everywhere". Thus, "The Second death" or "Eternal death", are more precisely defined, as "the eternal separation of man from God's grace", because those who spend eternity in hell will be "eternally in the presence of God's judgment or God's justice".

Subsegment-4 **Some concluding comments about the Christian concept of "death"**

Concluding comments must begin with the previous definitions of the three types of "death". When those definitions are reviewed, we note that "spiritual death" and "the Second Death" are related to God's grace. Therefore, these two deaths are not relevant to a discussion of the number of parts of man. This means that the focus of this subsegment is "Physical death". However, the definition of "'Physical' death" from *Subsegment-1*, cannot be used in this subsegment, because those definitions are based on each of the three camps (*the "monochotomous camp", the "dichotomous camp", and the "trichotomous camp"*). And our use of these definitions would be a conflict with our goal of determining support for man, as a "one-part", "two-part", and/or "three-part" being. However, the Bible can be used. That usage would allow a repeat of the discussion, which occurred under Part-2/Section-1/*Segment-2* (*titled: Some relevant Bible verses*). In addition, similarities can be drawn between the "biological concept of 'death'" and the "Christian concept of 'Physical death'", by noting two things about each concept:

- *First*,

  by observation,

  under the "Biological concept of 'death'", a dead-human body turns to dust,

  and

  by using the Bible,

  under the "Christian concept of 'Physical death'", a dead-human body turns to dust.

- *Second*,

  by observation,

  under the "biological concept of 'death'", the spark of life leaves a human body turning it into a dead body, but there is no indication of where the spark goes,

  Comment: Even if someone tries to say that the "spark of life" was simply extinguished, it still means that under the "Biological concept of 'death'", man is a two-part being. More precisely, to be alive, man has to have a body and then man has to have the "spark of life".

  and

  by using Bible verses like Ecclesiastes 12:7,

  under the "Christian concept of 'Physical death'", the spirit – a second part of man – returns to God.

Comment: In the KJV, Ecclesiastes 12:7 reads: "Then shall the dust return to the earth as it was: and the spirit shall return unto God who gave it."

Thus, even the discussion, which occurred under Part-2/Section-1/*Segment-1* (*titled: The "Biological concept of 'death'"*), could be repeated here. Based on these considerations, we can say that the "Christian concept of 'death'", or more precisely, the "Christian concept of 'Physical' death":

- ✓ offers no support for the belief that "man is a 'one-part' being",
- ✓ offers strong support for the belief that "man is a 'two-part' being",
- ✓ offers some support for the belief that "man is a 'three-part' being".

Segment-4: **The Christian concept of "resurrection"**

A discussion of the Christian concept of "resurrection", must be preceded by the development of a sense of what the word – "resurrection", means to Christians. One meaning is provided in the "Holman Bible Dictionary", in an article titled – "The Resurrection", by author William L. Hendricks. This article provides some historical and traditional background on the use of the word: "resurrection". It also presented a one sentence definition of the word. Paraphrased, this definition reads:

> "Resurrection" is "the doctrine, event, and act of persons being brought from death to unending life at the close of the age."

Some Christian scholars use John 5:28-29, as support for the word: "resurrection". These verses read:

> (John 5:28 NIV) "Do not be amazed at this, for a time is coming when all who are in their graves will hear his voice
>
> (John 5:29 NIV) and come out--those who have done good will rise to live, and those who have done evil will rise to be condemned.

These Christian scholars say that John 5:28-29 imply that the "death" being referenced is "Physical death". We can say this for two reasons:

- *Reason-1*: John 5:29 indicates that some of those brought back from "Physical death" "will rise to 'live'" with this word – "live", meaning "Spiritual life". Or more precisely, some scholars understand it to mean that those who had accepted Jesus before their death, will "live" with God under His grace through eternity.

➧ *Reason-2*: John 5:29 indicates that some of those brought back from "Physical death" "will rise to 'be condemned'", with this word – "condemned", indicating that these individuals will enter "Eternal death". Or more precisely, some scholars understand it to mean that those who did not accept Jesus before their death, will be separated from God's grace for eternity. These individuals will be under God's judgment for eternity.

There is another way to view the meaning of the word – "resurrection", which is not inconsistent with the statements above. This view is the way those in the "dichotomous camp" and those in the "trichotomous camp" view it. More precisely, the word – "resurrection", is view by those:

in the dichotomous camp, as *"the rejoining of the body with the soul/spirit"*,

and

in the trichotomous camp, as *"the rejoining of the body with both the soul and the spirit"*.

While John 5:28-29 provided some implications about the word – "resurrection", the Bible also records the first resurrection, from the dead with a "glorified body", as that of Jesus, the man (*not Jesus, God, the Son*). More precisely, the resurrection of Jesus, the man occurred after His "spiritual death" on the cross, as the penalty for our sins, and then His "physical death" on the same cross, as an atoning sacrifice for our sins. God "resurrected" Jesus, the man, to show the world that He (God) accepted the finished work of Jesus, the man, on the cross. Thus, the "bodily resurrection of Jesus, the man," provides us with the best opportunity to get a sense of whether the "resurrection" of an individual, supports man, as a "one-part", "two-part", or "three-part" being. To use this opportunity, this portion of *Segment-4* will focus on the attributes displayed by the "resurrected body of Jesus, the man", as recorded in the Bible. To begin this effort, the article – "The Resurrection" by author William L. Hendricks in the "Holman Bible Dictionary", will be referenced, again. For this reference, this author notes that author Hendricks included the following statement in his article:

> "In His post resurrection appearances Jesus had a body that was both spiritual (John 20:19,26) and physical (John 20:20,27; 21:13,15) in nature."

The previously referenced six verses, indicate some of the attributes of the "resurrected body of Jesus, the man". And a seventh verse: John 21:14, confirms that Jesus, the man, displayed these attributes after His "resurrection" from the dead. Therefore, all seven verses will be presented and discussed under either of the two headings: "spiritual body verses" and "physical body verses", which were referenced by author Hendricks. Under the appropriate heading, the seven verses read, as follows:

➧ Spiritual body verses:

✓ (John 20:19 NIV) On the evening of that first day of the week, when the disciples were together, with the doors locked for fear of the Jews, Jesus came and stood among them and said, *"Peace be with you!"*

✏ John 20:19 implies that the resurrected body of Jesus, the man, must have had a spiritual component, because He could suddenly appear in a locked room and then He spoke to His disciples.

✓ (John 20:26 NIV) A week later his disciples were in the house again, and Thomas was with them. Though the doors were locked, Jesus came and stood among them and said, *"Peace be with you!"*

✏ John 20:26 implies that the resurrected body of Jesus, the man, must have had a spiritual component, because He could suddenly appear in a house with locked doors and then He spoke to those present.

- Physical body verses:

✓ (John 20:20 NIV) After he said this, he showed them his hands and side. The disciples were overjoyed when they saw the Lord.

✏ John 20:20 implies that the resurrected body of Jesus, the man, must have had a physical component, because the crucifixion wounds in His hands and side had healed.

✓ (John 20:27 NIV) Then he said to Thomas, *"Put your finger here; see my hands. Reach out your hand and put it into my side. Stop doubting and believe."*

✏ John 20:27 implies that the resurrected body of Jesus, the man, must have had a physical component, because His healed crucifixion wounds are also referenced.

✓ (John 21:13 NIV) Jesus came, took the bread and gave it to them, and did the same with the fish.

✏ John 21:13 implies that the resurrected body of Jesus, the man, must have had a physical component, because He could handle bread and fish.

✓ (John 21:14 NIV) This was now the third time Jesus appeared to his disciples after he was raised from the dead.

✏ John 21:14 confirms that these verses are about the resurrected body of Jesus, the man.

✓ (John 21:15 NIV) When they had finished eating, Jesus said to Simon Peter, *"Simon son of John, do you truly love me more than these?"* "Yes, Lord," he said, "you know that I love you." Jesus said, *"Feed my lambs."*

✏ John 21:15 implies that the resurrected body of Jesus, the man, must have had a physical component, because He could eat and talk.

Some additional verses, which imply that the resurrected body of Jesus, the man, had spiritual and/or physical components, are Luke 24:30, Luke 24:31, Luke 24:36-40, and Luke 24:41-43. In the NIV, these verses read:

> Luke 24:30When he was at the table with them, he took bread, gave thanks, broke it and began to give it to them.
>
> Luke 24:31Then their eyes were opened and they recognized him, and he disappeared from their sight.
>
> Luke 24:36While they were still talking about this, Jesus himself stood among them
> and said to them, *"Peace be with you."* 37They were startled and frightened,
> thinking they saw a ghost. 38He said to them, *"Why are you troubled, and why do*
> *doubts rise in your minds? 39Look at my hands and my feet. It is I myself! Touch me*
> *and see; a ghost does not have flesh and bones, as you see I have."* 40When he had said
> this, he showed them his hands and feet.
>
> Luke 24:41And while they still did not believe it because of joy and amazement,
> he asked them, *"Do you have anything here to eat?"* 42They gave him a piece of
> broiled fish, 43and he took it and ate it in their presence.

Thus, the implication of the statements and verses above is that when God "resurrected" Jesus, the man, from death to life again, after Jesus, the man, had been crucified on the cross, the resurrected body of Jesus, the man, was something more than just the physical body that Jesus, the man, had before the crucifixion. The reason for saying this is that besides the normal activities of walking, talking, and eating, the resurrected body of Jesus, the man, could disappear and appear at His will. And the resurrected body of Jesus, the man, still had the crucifixion wounds, but these wounds had healed. Thus, the point is:

> "'God changing the dead body of Jesus, the man, into a resurrected body' means 'some component or components were reintroduced or were introduced into the dead body of Jesus, the man.'"

Nevertheless, based on these considerations, we can say that the "Christian concept of 'resurrection'":

✓ offers	no	support for the belief that "man is a	'one-part'	being",
✓ offers	strong	support for the belief that "man is a	'two-part'	being",
✓ offers	some	support for the belief that "man is a	'three-part'	being".

Part-3: **Conclusion**

The Bible contains verses, which clearly imply that man is, at the least, a two-part being. Thus, those in the "monochotomous camp" are holding a belief that is not supportable using the Bible. But even worse, this belief is not consistent with the Bible. On the other hand, there are many verses, which explicitly and/or implicitly support both the "dichotomous camp" and the "trichotomous camp". However, in the NIV, there are, at least, four verses, which explicitly support the "trichotomous camp", over the "dichotomous camp". These four verses are Job 7:11, Isaiah 26:9, 1 Thessalonians 5:23, and Hebrews 4:12. These verses read, as follows:

> (Job 7:11 NIV) "Therefore I will not keep silent; I will speak out in the anguish of my spirit, I will complain in the bitterness of my soul.
>
> (Isaiah 26:9 NIV) My soul yearns for you in the night; in the morning my spirit longs for you. When your judgments come upon the earth, the people of the world learn righteousness.
>
> (1 Thessalonians 5:23 NIV) May God himself, the God of peace, sanctify you through and through. May your whole spirit, soul and body be kept blameless at the coming of our Lord Jesus Christ.
>
> (Hebrews 4:12 NIV) For the word of God is living and active. Sharper than any double-edged sword, it penetrates even to dividing soul and spirit, joints and marrow; it judges the thoughts and attitudes of the heart.

Clearly, 1 Thessalonians 5:23 refers to the "body", "soul", and "spirit" in the same verse. The other three verses refer to only the "soul" and "spirit" in the same verse, but this is okay, because of the three parts: (*"body", "soul", and "spirit"*), the "body" is the most obvious and understood, by default. Thus, as stated previously, these four verses support the "trichotomous camp". Therefore, the answer to the question "Does man have a body, a soul, and a spirit?" is "Yes!" And a "yes-answer" is consistent with the Bible.

Did Mary also have to be sinless, since Jesus was born sinless through her?

Most Christians believe that Jesus was born sinless through the Virgin Mary. But too many Christians also believe that "Mary was born sinless." Perhaps, those Christians, who believe this, feel that Mary's sinlessness had some impact on the sinlessness of Jesus. Regardless of the reason, this belief in the sinlessness of Mary has become a point of contention between Christians. It has also become a distraction from the main point of Christianity: "Our salvation through Jesus, the man – (*through Jesus, the Christ*)". Therefore, this belief needs to be examined. Such an examination is the goal of this essay and is accomplished, by organizing this essay in four parts. Part-1 presents some background information, which also serves as the basis for the formation of five more specific questions. Part-2 presents a discussion of the five more specific questions. Part-3 presents some concluding comments. Part-4 presents some relevant comments.

Part-1: **Some background information**

The Bible indicates that Mary was found to be "with child", after "God, the Holy Spirit", overshadowed her. See Luke 1:30-37. In the NIV, these verses read:

> Luke 1:[30]But the angel said to her, "Do not be afraid, Mary, you have found favor with God. [31]You will be with child and give birth to a son, and you are to give him the name Jesus. [32]He will be great and will be called the Son of the Most High. The Lord God will give him the throne of his father David, [33]and he will reign over the house of Jacob forever; his kingdom will never end." [34]"How will this be," Mary asked the angel, "since I am a virgin?" [35]The angel answered, "The Holy Spirit will come upon you, and the power of the Most High will overshadow you. So the holy one to be born will be called the Son of God. [36]Even Elizabeth your relative is going to have a child in her old age, and she who was said to be barren is in her sixth month. [37]For nothing is impossible with God."

These verses tell us that Jesus, the man, did not have a human father. And "no human father" meant that Jesus, the man, was born free of the original sin of Adam. That is, He was born "sinless" – (*He was born "innocent"*) – through the Virgin Mary. But as mentioned before, too many Christians also believe that the Virgin Mary was born sinless. These Christians are divided on exactly how that happened. Some believe that "Mary was also born of a virgin." While others, like Catholics, believe in a doctrine called "the Immaculate Conception of Mary". This doctrine is referenced in the "2003 Grolier Multimedia Encyclopedia", as follows:

The "**Immaculate Conception**" is a Roman Catholic doctrine asserting that Mary, the mother of Jesus, was preserved from the effects of original sin from the first moment of her conception. The doctrine was defined as a "dogma" binding on Catholics by Pope Pius IX in the papal bull Ineffabilis Deus (1854). The doctrine as defined was debated by theologians during the Middle Ages and was rejected by Saint Thomas Aquinas. It is based on the biblical idea of Mary's holiness (*"which some believe is implied by"*[1] Luke 1:28[67]), early church teachings on Mary as the "new Eve," and the belief that Mary is the Mother of God (Theotokos, or "God-bearer"), articulated at the Council of Ephesus (431; see Ephesus, Council of). The feast of the Immaculate Conception is observed on December 8.

Comment: *Wiktionary* defines the word – "dogma", as follows:

> "'Dogma' (*plural* dogmas or dogmata), is a noun: 1. A doctrine or a set of doctrines relating to matters such as morality and faith, set forth in an authoritative manner by a church. 2. An authoritative principle, belief, or statement of opinion, especially one considered to be absolutely true."[68]

Because some formal definitions of the word – "dogma", reference the word – "corpus", *Wiktionary*, defines the word – "corpus", as follows:

> "'Corpus' (plural: corpora or corpuses), is a noun: 1. the body. 2. (linguistics) a collection of writings, often on a specific topic, of a specific genre, from a specific demographic, a single author etc."[69]

To understand the Catholic definition of the doctrine of "the Immaculate Conception of Mary", we will use the previously mentioned "Ineffabilis Deus", which according to *Wikipedia*, is an Apostolic constitution, which was written by Pope Pius IX and formally proclaimed on December 8, 1854.

> Comment: The word – "Apostolic", is generally used to imply "a succession of spiritual authority, which goes back to the twelve Apostles". While the word – "constitution" is used to refer to "a document, which defines, describes, and/or expresses the 'what, why, and/or wherefores' of a system and/or a belief".

The "Ineffabilis Deus" serves to present the historical basis for the doctrine of "the Immaculate Conception of Mary", defines the doctrine, and reminds all that no contrary positions will be

---

1 The phrase – "which some believe is implied by", was added by this author.

accepted by the Catholic church. The entire text is available at several websites. Two such websites are:

- ✎ www.papalencyclicals.net/Pius09/p9ineff.htm.

- ✎ www.newadvent.org/library/docs_pi09id.htm.

According to *Wikipedia*, the phrase – "Ineffabilis Deus", is Latin for "Ineffable God". And then according to *Wiktionary*, the English word – "ineffable", means "'not comparable', 'beyond expression in words', 'unspeakable', 'forbidden to be uttered', and 'taboo'"[70].

Some of the text of the "Ineffabilis Deus", which is important to this essay, is labeled – "The Definition" and reads, as follows:

> Wherefore, in humility and fasting, we unceasingly offered our private prayers as well as the public prayers of the Church to God the Father through his Son, that he would deign to direct and strengthen our mind by the power of the Holy Spirit. In like manner did we implore the help of the entire heavenly host as we ardently invoked the Paraclete[71]. Accordingly, by the inspiration of the Holy Spirit, for the honor of the Holy and undivided Trinity, for the glory and adornment of the Virgin Mother of God, for the exaltation of the Catholic Faith, and for the furtherance of the Catholic religion, by the authority of Jesus Christ our Lord, of the Blessed Apostles Peter and Paul, and by our own:
>
>> We declare, pronounce, and define that the doctrine which holds that the most Blessed Virgin Mary, in the first instance of her conception, by a singular grace and privilege granted by Almighty God, in view of the merits of Jesus Christ, the Savior of the human race, was preserved free from all stain of original sin, is a doctrine revealed by God and therefore to be believed firmly and constantly by all the faithful.
>>
>> [*Declaramus, pronuntiamus et definimus doctrinam quae tenet beatissimam Virginem Mariam in primo instanti suae conceptionis fuisse singulari Omnipotentis Dei gratia et privilegio, intuitu meritorum Christi Jesu Salvatoris humani generis, ab omni originalis culpae labe praeservatam immunem, esse a Deo revelatam, atque idcirco ab omnibus fidelibus firmiter constanterque credendam.*]
>
> Hence, if anyone shall dare – which God forbid! – to think otherwise than as has been defined by us, let him know and understand that he is condemned by his own judgment; that he has suffered shipwreck in the faith; that he has separated from the unity of the Church; and that, furthermore, by his own action he incurs the penalties established by

law if he should dare to express in words or writing or by any other outward means the errors he think in his heart.

With the previous wording in mind, we again note that a little contention has risen between "Christians, who believe in '*the virgin birth of Mary*'", "Christians, who believe in '*the Immaculate Conception of Mary*'", and "Christians, who believe in neither". Thus, another goal of this essay is to remove some of this contention. But more important, with the knowledge that in some "Western Christian Churches", the "sinlessness of Mary", is based on either of two doctrines – "*the virgin birth of Mary*" or "*the Immaculate Conception of Mary*", we can define three tasks for this essay. *First*, we will try to determine, whether these doctrines are biblical (*and thus, true*). *Second*, if biblical (*and thus, true*), what impacts do, these doctrines have on the more precise question: "Did Mary also have to be sinless, since Jesus, the man, was born sinless through her?" *Third*, we will try to answer the question: "What is the importance of these doctrines?" These three tasks can be accomplished by addressing the following five questions:

- *Question-1*: What Bible verses support "the virgin birth of Mary"?
- *Question-2*: What Bible verses support "the Immaculate Conception of Mary"?
- *Question-3*: What impact would "the virgin birth of Mary" have had on the sinless nature of Jesus, if "the virgin birth of Mary" was true, even though it is not biblical?
- *Question-4*: What impact would "the Immaculate Conception of Mary" have had on the sinless nature of Jesus, if "the Immaculate Conception of Mary" was true, even though it is not biblical?
- *Question-5*: What is the importance of the doctrine of "the virgin birth of Mary" or the doctrine of "the Immaculate Conception of Mary"?

Part-2: **A discussion of the five questions**

The five questions from Part-1, will be addressed in the following format. Each question is preceded by a margin-to-margin double line. Then the question is listed followed by comments addressing it.

Question-1: **What Bible verses support "the virgin birth of Mary"?**

This question is easily answered, because the Bible does not contain any information about

Mary's birth. However, literature called – "The Gospel of the birth of Mary", does supposedly record some information about Mary's parents and her birth.

> *Comment:* "The Gospel of the birth of Mary", is one of the so-called lost books of the Bible. It was included in the book: "The Lost books of the Bible and the Forgotten Books of Eden", published by World Bible Publishers, Inc. The title – "The Lost books of the Bible and the Forgotten Books of Eden", reveals that this book is actually two books: the book: "The Lost books of the Bible" (*published in 1926 by Alpha House, Inc.*) and the book: "The Forgotten Books of Eden" (*published in 1927 by Alpha House, Inc.*). Both books are collections of various "apocryphal books"[2] that are *"of questionable authorship or authenticity"*.

In the book – "The Lost books of the Bible and the Forgotten Books of Eden", a portion of a commentary at the beginning of "The Gospel of the birth of Mary", reads:

> "In the primitive ages there was a Gospel extant bearing this name (*'The Gospel of the birth of Mary'*)[3], attributed to St. Matthew, and received as genuine and authentic by several of the ancient Christian sects. It is to be found in the works of Jerome, a Father of the Church, who flourished in the fourth century, from whence the present translation is made. His contemporaries, Epiphanius, Bishop of Salamis, and Austin, also mention a Gospel under this title. The ancient copies differed from Jerome's, for from one of them the learned Faustus, a native of Britain, who became Bishop of Riez, in Provence, endeavored to prove that Christ was not the Son of God till after his baptism; and that he was not of the house of David and tribe of Judah, because, according to the Gospel he cited, the Virgin herself was not of this tribe, but of the tribe of Levi; her father being a priest of the name of Joachim. It was likewise from this Gospel that the sect of the Collyridians, established the worship and offering of manchet bread and cracknels, or fine wafers, as sacrifices to Mary, 'whom they imagined to have been born of a Virgin, as Christ is related in the Canonical Gospel to have been born of her'[4]."

---

[2] The phrase – "apocryphal books", was used on the jacket of the book by World Bible Publishers, Inc.

[3] The wording – "The Gospel of the birth of Mary", was inserted, by this author for clarity. From the placement of the commentary in the book – "The Lost books of the Bible and the Forgotten Books of Eden", a reader would have known that the statement referred to "The Gospel of the birth of Mary", but taken out of context, that knowledge is not obvious, thus the insertion.

[4] The underlinings and apostrophes were added, by this author for emphasis and clarity. The phrase – "Canonical Gospel", is a reference to the four Gospels – Matthew, Mark, Luke, and John.

The implication of this commentary, especially the wording – "whom they imagined to have been born of a Virgin, as Christ is related in the Canonical Gospel to have been born of her", is that "The Gospel of the birth of Mary", indicates that Mary was born of a virgin. However, after reading the Gospel itself, it is clear that, whoever wrote the commentary, is using one definition of the word – "virgin", and whoever wrote "The Gospel of the birth of Mary", is using a different definition. The writer of the commentary is obviously using the word – "virgin", to mean that "she never had sexual relations with a man". We can say this, because the writer of the commentary used the word – "virgin", and the phrase – "the birth of Jesus", in the same sentence. (*Clearly, most Christians understand that the* word – *"virgin", associated with "the birth of Jesus", is understood to mean "a woman, who has never had sexual relations with a man".*) However, in "The Gospel of the birth of Mary", verse 2:5 provides the other definition of the word: "virgin". Using the word – "Mary", as an abbreviation for "The Gospel of the birth of Mary", this verse reads:

> Mary 2:[5]And so when he shuts the womb of any person, he does it for this reason, that he may in a more wonderful manner again open it, and that which is born appearing to be not the product of lust, but the gift of God.

Thus, the definition of the word – "virgin", being used in "The Gospel of the birth of Mary", is that of "a married woman, who has been barren for a long time and then conceives a child". This is reinforced by Mary 1:5, which indicates that Mary's parents had been childless for, at least, twenty years. The definition is also reinforced by Mary 2:6-8 listing other births by women, who had been barren for some period. Then Mary 2:9 specifically references the birth of Mary. Mary 1:5 and Mary 2:6-9 read:

> Mary 1:[5]In this manner they lived for about twenty years chastely, in the favour of God, and the esteem of men, without any children.
>
> > *Comment:* When a proofreader read Mary 1:5 above, he reminded this author that the modern meaning of the word – "chastely", may include "not having experienced sexual intercourse". However, the *Wiktionary* and other verses in "The Gospel of the birth of Mary" support a meaning of "purely" for the word – "chastely". For a detailed discussion of the word – "chastely", see the entry – "The meaning of the word: 'Chastely'" in Appendix A.
>
> Mary 2:[6]For the first mother of your nation Sarah, was she not barren even till her eightieth year: And yet even in the end of her old age brought forth Isaac, in whom the promise was made a blessing to all nations. [7]Rachel also, so much in favour with God, and beloved so much by holy Jacob, continued barren for a long time, yet afterwards was the mother of Joseph, who was not only governor of Egypt, but delivered many nations from perishing with hunger. [8]Who among the judges was more valiant than Samson, or more holy than Samuel? And yet both their mothers were barren. [9]But if reason will not convince you of the truth of my words, that there are frequent conceptions in advanced

> years, and that those who were barren have brought forth to their great surprise; therefore Anna your wife shall bring you a daughter, and you shall call her name Mary;

The Bible also indicates that the women listed in Mary 2:6-8 were barren and then gave birth to a child. In fact, the Bible includes several additional-barren women like Elizabeth, who was both Mary's cousin and the mother of John the Baptist.

> *Comment:* It must be explicitly stated that the inclusion of references, which are consistent with the Bible, in "The Gospel of the birth of Mary" does not in itself validate this gospel. Such inclusions simply increase the possible credibility of this gospel. However, note that the credibility of this gospel is questionable, because of other references like "indicating that Mary was from the tribe of Levi not Judah, because her father was a priest named 'Joachim'". However, "The Gospel of the birth of Mary" does contain the wording – "The blessed and ever glorious Virgin Mary, sprung from the royal race and family of David". This wording is very interesting in light of the fact that family lineage was generally traced through the father and not the mother. Nevertheless, the implication of this wording is that Mary's mother, who was named "Anna" or "Anne", must have been from the tribe of "Judah".

Obviously, conceptions and births after long periods of barrenness are different from the conception and birth of Jesus, because Mary did not have sexual relations with a man until after the birth of Jesus. Thus, without other references to the virgin birth of Mary, we would have to conclude that the supposed virgin birth of Mary was totally different from the virgin birth of Jesus. Because according to "The Gospel of the birth of Mary", Mary was not born of a virgin, but of a woman, who had been barren for, at least, twenty years. Therefore, if "The Gospel of the birth of Mary" is authentic, then at best, Mary's birth was like the births of Isaac (*the son of Abraham and his barren wife, Sarah*), Joseph (*the son of Israel [Jacob] and his barren wife, Rachel*), Samson (*the son of Manoah and his barren wife*), Samuel (*the son of Elkanah and his barren wife, Hannah*), and John the Baptist (*the son of Zacharias and his barren wife, Elizabeth*).

In summary, explicitly or implicitly, there are no Bible verses, which support "the virgin birth of Mary" doctrine. However, "The Gospel of the birth of Mary" contains verses, which indicate that Mary's mother had been barren for twenty years, before she gave birth to Mary. Thus, no Bible verses nor verses from "The Gospel of the birth of Mary" support "the virgin birth of Mary" doctrine, in the same sense, as "the virgin birth of Jesus, the man".

Question-2: **What Bible verses support "the Immaculate Conception of Mary"?**

This question is also easily answered, because the Bible does not contain any verses, which explicitly support "the Immaculate Conception of Mary". More specifically, as previously indicated, there are no Bible verses, which reference anything about the birth of Mary. However, we can use three things:

- *First*, some of the text from the "Ineffabilis Deus";
- *Second*, the three issues upon, which "the Immaculate Conception of Mary" is based;
- *Third*, 'the Gospel of the birth of Mary';

to make a couple of conclusions about the "Bible" and the "Immaculate Conception". To develop these conclusions, *Question-2* is organized in three sections. *Section-1* presents the most relevant text from the "Ineffabilis Deus". *Section-2* presents a discussion of the three issues, upon which the doctrine of "the Immaculate Conception of Mary" is based. *Section-3* addresses the question: "Does 'the Gospel of the birth of Mary', provide any support for 'the Immaculate Conception of Mary'?"

Section-1: **The most relevant text from the "Ineffabilis Deus"**

The definition of the doctrine of "the Immaculate Conception" from the "Ineffabilis Deus" reads, as follows:

> "We declare, pronounce, and define that the doctrine which holds that the most Blessed Virgin Mary, in the first instance of her conception, by a singular grace and privilege granted by Almighty God, in view of the merits of Jesus Christ, the Savior of the human race, was preserved free from all stain of original sin, is a doctrine revealed by God and therefore to be believed firmly and constantly by all the faithful."

The most relevant text is the wording: "preserved free from all stain of original sin".

Section-2: **The three issues, upon which the doctrine of the "Immaculate Conception of Mary" is based**

According to the "2003 Grolier Multimedia Encyclopedia", "the Immaculate Conception of Mary" is based on the following three issues:

- *Issue-1*: *The belief that Mary is the Mother of God,*
- *Issue-2*: *Early church teachings on Mary, as the "new Eve",*

➧ *Issue-3*: *Mary's holiness is implied, by the phrase – "the Lord is with you", which is recorded in Luke 1:28.*

To discuss these three issues, *Section-2* is organized in three segments, which is one segment for each issue.

Segment-1: *Issue-1* – **The belief that Mary is the Mother of God**

According to several web documents and reference sources, the belief that "Mary is the Mother of God" was not formulated or an issue until sometime in the 3rd century. Since that time, various theologians and Christian leaders have expressed their position on the debate over whether Mary is:

the "Mother of God (*'Theotokos', 'God-bearer', or 'Giver of birth to God'*)"

or

the "Mother of Christ (*'Christotokos', 'Christ-bearer', or 'Giver of birth to Christ'*)".

Initially, the prevailing belief appeared to be that "Mary is the 'Mother of God'". Then some individuals (*like Nestorius in the 5th century*) and churches (*like the Assyrian Church of the East, which is sometimes referred to as the Nestorian Church*) started to promote the "Mother of Christ" belief. An article in *Wikipedia*, which is titled – "Nestorians", states that the Nestorians view was that Christ –

> "took only His human nature from His mother, while the divine Logos was pre-existant and external, so calling Mary 'Mother of God' was misleading and potentially wrong."[72]

In 451 A.D., the "Council of Ephesus" convened to condemn the views of Nestorius and reinforce the "Mother of God" belief. Therefore, we will look at this issue from two viewpoints: a "historical" viewpoint (*with the emphasis on the "Ineffabilis Deus" and documents, which formed based on the "Council of Ephesus"*) and a "biblical-logical" viewpoint. With this in mind, the rest of *Segment-1* is presented as three subsegments. *Subsegment-1* will address a "historical" viewpoint, based on the "Council of Ephesus". *Subsegment-2* will address a "historical" viewpoint, based on the "Ineffabilis Deus". *Subsegment-3* will address a "biblical-logical" viewpoint.

Subsegment-1: ***The "Council of Ephesus"***

Several websites present "the text, summaries, and/or extracts of the proceedings from the 'Council of Ephesus'" and/or "historical comments about the council, by various scholars, over the years". In fact, the web documents at website:

✎ www.ccel.org/ccel/schaff/npnf214.toc.html

provide some documents from all seven of the so-called "Ecumenical Councils", of which the "Council of Ephesus" is one. At this particular website, many of the documents were edited with notes gathered from the writings of the great scholars throughout the ages. One web document indicates that prior to the "Council of Ephesus", which was convened to address the views of Nestorius (*who was the Bishop of Constantinople and who viewed the Virgin Mary as the "Mother of Christ" not the "Mother of God", along with several views of Christ*), Cyril (*who was the Bishop of Alexandria*) wrote several letters to Nestorius. These letters were read as part of the proceedings of the "Council of Ephesus". But what is more important, these letters indicate the prevailing view with regards to the "'Mother of God *(Theotokos)*' – 'Mother of Christ (*Christotokos*)'" debate. (*See the referenced web document for the complete letters.*) Meanwhile, five excerpts (*from the text of Bishop Cyril's letters or the documents about the proceedings of the "Council of Ephesus"*) provide us with an understanding of the prevailing view of the Virgin Mary and Christ, during the 5th century. The more important text in these excerpts has been underlined for emphasis. These excerpts read, as follows:

(*Excerpt-1 from page 302, of the referenced document*):

For we do not say that the nature of the Word was changed and became flesh, or that it was converted into a whole man consisting of soul and body; but rather that the Word having personally united to himself flesh animated by a rational soul, did in an ineffable and inconceivable manner become man, and was called the Son of Man, not merely as willing or being pleased to be so called, neither on account of taking to himself a person, but because the two natures being brought together in a true union, there is of both one Christ and one Son; for the difference of the natures is not taken away by the union, but rather the divinity and the humanity make perfect for us the one Lord Jesus Christ by their ineffable and inexpressible union. So then he who had an existence before all ages and was born of the Father, is said to have been born according to the flesh of a woman, not as though his divine nature received its beginning of existence in the holy Virgin, for it needed not any second generation after that of the Father (*for it would be absurd and foolish to say that he who existed before all ages, coeternal with the Father, needed any second beginning of existence*), but since, for us and for our salvation, he personally united to himself an human body, and came forth of a woman, he is in this way said to be born after the flesh; for he was not first born a common man of the holy Virgin, and then the Word came down and entered into him, but the union being made in the womb itself, he is said to endure a birth after the flesh, ascribing to himself the birth of his own flesh.

(*Excerpt-2 from page 303, of the referenced document*):

We, therefore, confess one Christ and Lord, not as worshipping, a man with the Word (*lest this expression "with the Word" should suggest to the mind the idea of division*), but worshipping him as one and the same, forasmuch as the body of the Word, with which he sits with the Father, is not separated from the Word himself, not as if two sons were sitting with him, but one by the union with the flesh. If, however, we reject the personal union as impossible or unbecoming, we fall into the error of speaking of two sons, for it will be necessary to distinguish, and to say, that he who was properly man was honoured with the appellation of Son, and that he who is properly the Word of God, has by nature both the name and the reality of Sonship. We must not, therefore, divide the one Lord Jesus Christ into two Sons. Neither will it at all avail to a sound faith to hold, as some do, an union of persons; for the Scripture has not said that the Word united to himself the person of man, but that he was made flesh. This expression, however, "the Word was made flesh," can mean nothing else but that he partook of flesh and blood like to us; he made our body his own, and came forth man from a woman, not casting off his existence as God, or his generation of God the Father, but even in taking to himself flesh remaining what he was. This the declaration of the correct faith proclaims everywhere. This was the sentiment of the holy Fathers; therefore they ventured to call the holy Virgin, the Mother of God, not as if the nature of the Word or his divinity had its beginning from the holy Virgin, but because of her was born that holy body with a rational soul, to which the Word being personally united is said to be born according to the flesh. These things, therefore, I now write unto you for the love of Christ, beseeching you as a brother, and testifying to you before Christ and the elect angels, that you would both think and teach these things with us, that the peace of the Churches may be preserved and the bond of concord and love continue unbroken amongst the Priests of God.

(Excerpt-3 from page 308, of the referenced document):
Following in all points the confessions of the Holy Fathers which they made (the Holy Ghost speaking in them), and following the scope of their opinions, and going, as it were, in the royal way, we confess that the Only begotten Word of God, begotten of the same substance of the Father, True God from True God, Light from Light, through Whom all things were made, the things in heaven and the things in the earth, coming down for our salvation, making himself of no reputation (καθεὶς ἑαυτὸν εἰς κένωσιν)[5], was incarnate and made man; that is, taking flesh of the holy Virgin, and having made it his own from the womb, he subjected himself to birth for us, and came forth man from a woman, without casting off that which he was; but although he assumed flesh and blood, he remained what he was, God in essence and in truth. Neither do we say that his flesh was changed into the nature of divinity, nor that the ineffable nature of the Word of God was laid aside for the nature of flesh; for he is unchanged and absolutely unchangeable, being the same always, according to the Scriptures. For although visible and a child in swaddling clothes, and even in the bosom of his Virgin Mother, he filled all creation as God, and was a fellow-ruler with him who begat him, for the Godhead is without quantity and dimension, and cannot have limits.

(Excerpt-4 from page 311, of the referenced document):
And since the holy Virgin brought forth corporally God made one with flesh according to nature, for this reason we also call her Mother of God, not as if the nature of the Word had

---

5 This author had to insert each character of these Greek words using the symbol mapping feature of WordPerfect. Hopefully, no errors were made during the mapping process.

the beginning of its existence from the flesh. *(See page 311, of the referenced document.)*

(Excerpt-5 from page 312, of the referenced document):
If anyone will not confess that the Emmanuel is very God, and that therefore the Holy Virgin is the Mother of God (*Theotokos*), inasmuch as in the flesh she bore the Word of God made flesh [*as it is written, "The Word was made flesh"*] let him be anathema.

Clearly, the wording of the previous five excerpts indicates that most theologians of the 5th century understood that the divine nature of Christ had no beginning. This is especially emphasized by *excerpt-2*, which contained the following statements:

> "This was the sentiment of the holy Fathers; therefore they ventured to call the holy Virgin, the Mother of God, **not as if the nature of the Word or his divinity had its beginning from the holy Virgin**, but **because of her was born that holy body** with a rational soul, to which the Word being personally united is said to be born according to the flesh."

The five excerpts also indicate that theologians of the 5th century believed that the divine nature of Christ was with the human nature of Christ in Mary's womb. Thus, the point this author would make is:

> "'God allowed a divine nature and a human nature in Christ somehow' and that somehow appears to be beyond our comprehension, so we should not complicate the issue by assigning words or phrases like 'Mother of God' to what God did. The main reason for saying this is that words carry connotations and some connotations give a false or incomplete impression of a situation and/or relationship. Such a false and an incomplete impression are emphasized by excerpt-5. That excerpt contains the statements – 'therefore the Holy Virgin is the Mother of God (*Theotokos*)' and 'inasmuch as in the flesh she bore the Word of God made flesh'. For these two statements to not present a false or an incomplete impression, a better wording for the first of the two statements might be, as follows:
>
> 'therefore the Holy Virgin is the Mother of the Word of God made flesh'.
>
> Calling the Virgin Mary the 'Mother of God' gives a false impression. Furthermore, note that the fourth excerpt indicates that Cyril understood that the label – 'Mother of God', was used more as a recognition that 'Christ was both divine and human' than as an indication that 'Mary gave birth to God'."

Subsegment-2: ***The "Ineffabilis Deus"***

In writing the "Ineffabilis Deus", Pope Pius IX referenced "tradition", among other things as support for calling "Mary, the Mother of God". Specifically, he referenced the "Council of Trent" and generally, he referenced and presented a vague-overview of church history. In fact, his specific presentation was labeled – "Council of Trent". His general reference to tradition was labeled – "Testimonies of Tradition". Neither presentation, nor for that matter, the entire "Ineffabilis Deus" moved this author from his "Mother of Christ" position. The "Ineffabilis Deus" may make interesting reading for some. However, specific biblical support for calling "Mary, the Mother of God" was lacking. But a *Wikipedia* entry, which is titled "Theotokos", indicated that some theologians may have used Luke 1:43, as their biblical support for their belief that the Virgin Mary was the "Mother of God". The setting for this verse is: Mary *(who is pregnant with Jesus)* has gone to see her cousin, Elizabeth *(who is pregnant [in her sixth-month] with John, the Baptist)*. And Elizabeth greets Mary with the words of Luke 1:43. In the KJV, this verse reads:

> Luke 1:[43]And whence is this to me, that the mother of my Lord should come to me?

If supporters of the "Mother of God" belief, base their belief on this verse, then they have a problem, because the Strong's Concordance, which comes with the QuickVerse Bible Software, indicates that the word – "Lord" or "lord" in Greek is "kurios:G2962". Then it further defines this Greek word, as follows:

> 2962. kurios, koo'-ree-os; from kuros (supremacy); supreme in authority, i.e. (as noun) controller; by impl. Mr. (as a respectful title):--God, Lord, master, Sir.

Furthermore, in the "New Testament", the word – "Lord" or "lord" occurs 711 times in 657 verses in the KJV, 648 times in 603 verses in the NASB, 639 times in 591 verses in the NRSV, and 618 times in 575 verses in the NIV. In the KJV, the words – "Lord" and "lord" are not always a reference to Jesus. In fact, in Matthew 18:23-27, Jesus (*Himself*) is telling a parable and uses the word – "lord". In the KJV, these verses read:

> Matthew 18:[23]Therefore is the kingdom of heaven likened unto a certain king, which would take account of his servants. [24]And when he had begun to reckon, one was brought unto him, which owed him ten thousand talents. [25]But forasmuch as he had not to pay, his lord commanded him to be sold, and his wife, and children, and all that he had, and payment to be made. [26]The servant therefore fell down, and worshipped him, saying, <u>Lord</u>, have patience with me, and I will pay thee all. [27]Then the <u>lord</u> of that servant was moved with compassion, and loosed him, and forgave him the debt.

In this parable, the word – "Lord", means "master". Thus, Luke 1:43 cannot, by itself, be used to say that Elizabeth was acknowledging the baby Jesus, as God. And in this author's read of the "Ineffabilis Deus", there is no substantive-biblical support for believing that literally, "Mary is the Mother of God" or "Mary is the mother of God, <u>the Son</u>." However, there is no doubt that "Mary is the Mother of Jesus, <u>the man</u>, – <u>*the Christ*</u> – Who is fully human. But we have to find another way to indicate that when Jesus, the man, was born, He was also fully God."

Subsegment-3: ***The "biblical-logical" viewpoint***

As previously indicated, this author takes the position that the belief – "the Virgin, Mary was the Mother of God" – is caused by a misapplication of terms and events, because man was trying to find the words to represent the birth of Jesus, who was fully God and fully man. Thus, to this author, the belief that the "Virgin Mary is the 'Mother of God'" is unbiblical and illogical for two reasons:

- *Reason-1*: Without the knowledge of the historical intent of the phrase – "Mother of God", most people would probably take an unbiblical and illogical interpretation of this phrase. One reason for this is that Christians believe in the Trinity – in God, the Father, God, the Son, and God, the Holy Spirit, in One God. Thus, the phrase – "Mother of God", is not precise. Does the phrase – "Mother of God", mean "Mother of God, the Father, God, the Son, and God, the Holy Spirit"? Clearly, no Christian would accept that interpretation. Thus, we are left with the implication that the phrase – "Mother of God" more specifically means "Mother of God, the Son". Therefore, the "concept of the Trinity" makes the phrase – "Mother of God" unbiblical, illogical, and imprecise. Furthermore, the historical intent of the phrase – "Mother of God", was "to merely acknowledge that Jesus was fully human and fully God". (*See the letters to Bishop Nestorius written by Bishop Cyril, which were included with the documents from the "Council of Ephesus".*)

- *Reason-2*: What does the word – "mother" in the phrase – "Mother of God", mean? Clearly, the Virgin Mary was the Mother of Christ – the Mother of Jesus, the man – and Jesus is "fully man" and had a beginning – when God, the Holy Spirit, overshadowed the Virgin Mary. Furthermore, with respect to our current medical knowledge, we can say that Mary gave Jesus part of His humanity. But as indicated by Nestorians, Mary could not have given Jesus any of His divinity. This author would also say that you could not even say that Jesus received His divinity from God, the Holy Spirit, when He (God, the Holy Spirit) overshadowed Mary, because Jesus, God, the Son, has existed forever. Thus, what God, the Holy Spirit, contributed to the birth of Jesus may simply be that He put Jesus (*specifically, the humanity of Jesus*) in Mary's womb. Now, clearly historic documents indicate that most theologians, who used the phrase – "Mother of God", understood that it did not mean that the Virgin Mary was the beginning of the divine nature of Jesus. Therefore, historically, theologians understood that Jesus, God, the Son, was not born through the Virgin Mary. It is just that they did not know what to really say about the divinity of Jesus with respect to the birth of the humanity of Jesus. Once more, the point is:

  "Jesus has two natures: 'God' and 'man'. However, it is biblically and logically inappropriate to say, 'Because Mary gave birth to one nature of Jesus – the human nature, she must have also given birth to the other nature of Jesus – the Divine nature, regardless of whether both natures were present in her womb or not. That is, Mary cannot be the Mother of both Jesus, the man, and Jesus, God, the Son.' In fact, using the words – 'Mother' or 'born', with the word – 'God' or the phrase – 'God, the Son', is biblically and logically inappropriate. We must come to the realization that because God mixed 'His nature' and the 'nature of man', it does not mean that we should attempt explaining it with our words, because words carry too many connotations."

Thus, the belief that Mary is the "Mother of God", should be dismissed, as biblically and logically inappropriate, and as something too complicated for our finite mind to comprehend. This issue should also be dismissed, because it causes dissension between Christians and because it is a distraction from the more important point of Christianity: "Our salvation through Jesus, the man (*through Christ*)".

Segment-2: *Issue-2* – ***Early church teachings on Mary, as the "new Eve"***

This issue can be addressed by using the Bible and by discussing whether it is valid to use tradition, as support for this issue.

- *Biblically*: Clearly, early-church teachings on Mary, as the "new Eve", must have been based on information that was not included in the Bible, because no verse in the KJV, NIV, NASB, or NRSV translations of the Bible, refers to Mary, as the "new Eve". Thus, biblically, this issue can be dismissed, as unsupportable.

- *Traditionally*: Clearly, a view of the Virgin Mary compared with Eve (*before she [Eve] ate the forbidden fruit*) had been established, by the early church. This is confirmed by the "Ineffabilis Deus (1854)", which contains a paragraph titled – "Mary Compared with Eve". This paragraph presents the Churches position on the Virgin Mary, as she is compared with Eve (*before she [Eve] ate the forbidden fruit*). The paragraph reads:

> Hence, it is the clear and unanimous opinion of the Fathers that the most glorious Virgin, for whom "he who is mighty has done great things," was resplendent with such an abundance of heavenly gifts, with such a fullness of grace and with such innocence, that she is an unspeakable miracle of God – indeed, the crown of all miracles and truly the Mother of God; that she approaches as near to God himself as is possible for a created being; and that she is above all men and angels in glory. Hence, to demonstrate the original innocence and sanctity of the Mother of God, not only did they frequently compare her to Eve while yet a virgin, while yet innocence, while yet incorrupt, while not yet deceived by the deadly snares of the most treacherous serpent; but they have also exalted her above Eve with

> a wonderful variety of expressions. Eve listened to the serpent with lamentable consequences; she fell from original innocence and became his slave. The most Blessed Virgin, on the contrary, ever increased her original gift, and not only never lent an ear to the serpent, but by divinely given power she utterly destroyed the force and dominion of the evil one.

The previous paragraph makes interesting reading, but it does not contain anything, which provides biblical support for Mary, as the "New Eve". Therefore, it seems inappropriate and weak to accept "Mary, as the 'New Eve'", based on tradition only. This is especially true when we remember that Jesus rebuked the Pharisees for holding their traditions over the Word of God.

Therefore, viewing the "Virgin Mary" as the "New Eve", might be interesting. But there is no explicit or implicit biblical support for such a view. And once more logically, it is very weak to use only tradition as the basis for anything. That is, because something has traditionally been done one-way, does not mean that way is the best-way, the only-way, or the most appropriate-way.

Segment-3: *Issue-3* – **Mary's holiness is implied, by the phrase – "the Lord is with you", which is recorded in Luke 1:28**

Some early Christians believed: "Mary's holiness is implied, by the phrase – 'the Lord is with you'", which is recorded in Luke 1:28." In the NIV, this verse reads:

> Luke 1:[28]The angel went to her and said, "Greetings, you who are highly favored! The Lord is with you."

However, Luke 1:28 is not the only occurrence of the phrase – "the LORD is with you", in the Bible. In the NIV, this phrase also occurs in three other verses: Judge 6:12, 2 Samuel 7:3, and 2 Chronicles 15:2. In Judge 6:12, an angel of the Lord is speaking these words to Gideon. This verse reads:

> (Judges 6:12 NIV) When the angel of the LORD appeared to Gideon, he said, "The LORD is with you, mighty warrior."

In 2 Samuel 7:3, Nathan the prophet is speaking these words to King David. This verse reads:

> (2 Samuel 7:3 NIV) Nathan replied to the king, "Whatever you have in mind, go ahead and do it, for the LORD is with you."

In 2 Chronicles 15:2, Azariah, son of Oded, is speaking these words to a specific audience. This verse reads:

(2 Chronicles 15:2 NIV) He went out to meet Asa and said to him, "Listen to me, Asa and all Judah and Benjamin. The LORD is with you when you are with him. If you seek him, he will be found by you, but if you forsake him, he will forsake you.

Based on the context for Judge 6:12, 2 Samuel 7:3, and 2 Chronicles 15:2, the phrase – "the LORD is with you", seems to mean exactly what the words imply. Namely, the phrase means "the Lord is with the individual or nation, being addressed" or "the Lord, for His purposes, is going to use and/or protect, the individual or nation, being addressed." Thus, this phrase is not an explicit statement of someone's holiness. Besides the Bible indicates that God used both the unGodly and the Godly, whether nations and individuals, to accomplish His purposes. Therefore, the phrase – "the LORD is with you", does not support the holiness claim. Furthermore, the phrase does not support the doctrine of "the Immaculate Conception of Mary".

Comment: This author is not questioning the holiness of Mary. Rather the question is whether Luke 1:28 proves that holiness. And this author takes the position that Luke 1:28 does not prove the holiness of Mary. Besides based on the customs, which existed around the time that the events of Luke 1:28 occurred, Mary was probably, only a teenager, so time and circumstances had not presented her with the opportunities to become much of a sinner.

Section-3: **Does "The Gospel of the birth of Mary", provide any support for "the Immaculate Conception of Mary"?**

This question can best be answered, by searching "The Gospel of the birth of Mary" for verses, which imply a relationship between God and Mary, at her birth.

Comment: Please note that the word – "Mary", may refer to the "Virgin Mary" or it may be used as the short title for "The Gospel of the birth of Mary". However, the context should indicate which is being refer to; especially since when it is the short title, it may be followed by numbers indicating a chapter and verse or verses.

Such a search reveals that the closest "The Gospel of the birth of Mary", comes to making a statement about a relationship between God and Mary, is Mary 2:9-10, with Mary 2:10 containing the phrase: "be filled with the Holy Ghost from her mother's womb". The verses – Mary 2:9-10 – read:

Mary 2:[9]But if reason will not convince you of the truth of my words, that there are frequent conceptions in advanced years, and that those who were barren have brought forth to their great surprise; therefore Anna your wife shall bring you a daughter, and you shall call her name Mary; [10]She shall, according to your vow, be devoted to the Lord from her infancy, and be filled with the Holy Ghost from her mother's womb;

In the book – "The Lost books of the Bible and the Forgotten Books of Eden", Mary 2:10 is marked with a footnote that cross references Luke 1:15. Four translations of Luke 1:15 read:

> (Luke 1:15 KJV) For he shall be great in the sight of the Lord, and shall drink neither wine nor strong drink; and he shall be filled with the Holy Ghost, even from his mother's womb.

> (Luke 1:15 NIV) for he will be great in the sight of the Lord. He is never to take wine or other fermented drink, and he will be filled with the Holy Spirit even from birth.

> (Luke 1:15 NRSV) for he will be great in the sight of the Lord. He must never drink wine or strong drink; even before his birth he will be filled with the Holy Spirit.

> (Luke 1:15 NASB) "For he will be great in the sight of the Lord, and he will drink no wine or liquor; and he will be filled with the Holy Spirit, while yet in his mother's womb.

Luke 1:15 is referring to John, the Baptist. Obviously, Mary 2:10 is referring to Mary. But the wordings of Luke 1:15 and of Mary 2:10 are similar. Therefore, the possible conditions surrounding the birth of Mary are recorded in the Bible, as happening to John, the Baptist. However, besides Luke 1:15, the NIV has seven additional verses, which contain the phrase: "filled with the Holy Spirit". These verses are all in the New Testament. These verses read:

> (Luke 1:41 NIV) When Elizabeth heard Mary's greeting, the baby leaped in her womb, and Elizabeth was filled with the Holy Spirit.

> (Luke 1:67 NIV) His father Zechariah was filled with the Holy Spirit and prophesied:

> (Acts 2:4 NIV) All of them were filled with the Holy Spirit and began to speak in other tongues as the Spirit enabled them.

> (Acts 4:8 NIV) Then Peter, filled with the Holy Spirit, said to them: "Rulers and elders of the people!

> (Acts 4:31 NIV) After they prayed, the place where they were meeting was shaken. And they were all filled with the Holy Spirit and spoke the word of God boldly.

> (Acts 9:17 NIV) Then Ananias went to the house and entered it. Placing his hands on Saul, he said, "Brother Saul, the Lord--Jesus, who appeared to you on the road as you were coming here--has sent me so that you may see again and be filled with the Holy Spirit."

> (Acts 13:9 NIV) Then Saul, who was also called Paul, filled with the Holy Spirit, looked straight at Elymas and said,

Comment: Please read the verses before and after these seven verses to get the full context of these verses.

These seven additional verses, which include the phrase – "filled with the Holy Spirit", lessen the uniqueness of the phrase. Furthermore, note that Luke 1:15 implies that John, the Baptist, was "filled with the Holy Spirit" from his mother's womb, while Luke 1:41 implies that his mother, Elizabeth, was "filled with the Holy Spirit" upon hearing the greeting of the Virgin Mary. Luke 1:15 and Luke 1:41 would seem to weaken the argument for the "Immaculate Conception of Mary", which revolves around the need to make the Virgin Mary a holy vessel at her own conception, so that she would be a holy vessel before conceiving and giving birth to Jesus, the man. Nevertheless, some might say that two more important questions are:

First, "Are the results of each phrase – 'preserved intact from all stain of original sin' and 'being filled with the Holy Ghost from her mother's womb', valid?"

Second, "regardless of the validity of the results of each phrase, are the results the same?"

Obviously to answer these questions, we must determine three things: *First*, what the end result of each phrase is. *Second*, if the meaning of each phrase yields valid results. *Third*, if the two results are equal. To accomplish these tasks, the rest of *Section-3* is organized as three segments. *Segment-1* presents a discussion of "the result and validity of the phrase: 'preserved intact from all stain of original sin'". *Segment-2* presents a discussion of "the result and validity of the phrase: 'being filled with the Holy Ghost from her mother's womb'". *Segment-3* presents a discussion of the question: "Are the results of the two phrases the same?"

Segment-1: **The result and validity of the phrase: "preserved intact from all stain of original sin"**

Clearly, the phrase - "preserved intact from all stain of original sin", would result in the Virgin Mary being "innocent" – being "sinless" – at her birth, like Jesus at His birth and like Adam and Eve at their creation. And if she never sinned, then she would have been innocent – sinless – all her life and especially as she carried and gave birth to Jesus. However, the Virgin Mary being "sinless" cannot be valid for, at least, four reasons:

Reason-1: One of the central themes running through the Bible is that Jesus is the only "sinless" person to have ever been born. Adam and Eve were created "sinless", and then they sinned. All except Jesus, were in Adam's loins – were in Adam's DNA (*and in Eve's DNA*) – when he (*and Eve*) sinned. Thus, all of us, except Jesus, inherited the stain of original sin from Adam (*and Eve*). Now, someone can say, "The Virgin Mary was preserved intact from all stain of original sin." But why are there no Bible verses to support that position?

Reason-2: We know that Jesus was "sinless", because that is the only thing, which allowed Him to pay the penalty and to serve as a sacrificial lamb (*to serve as the atoning sacrifice*) for our sins. And then God resurrected Jesus to show the world that He (God) accepted the penalty payment and atoning sacrifice of Jesus, by His (Jesus') spiritual and physical deaths on the cross. Now, as far as sin is concerned for the rest of us, see Romans 3:21-24. In the NIV, these verses read:

> Romans 3:[21]But now a righteousness from God, apart from law, has been made
> known, to which the Law and the Prophets testify. [22]This righteousness from God
> comes through faith in Jesus Christ to all who believe. There is no difference,
> [23]for all have sinned and fall short of the glory of God, [24]and are justified freely by
> his grace through the redemption that came by Christ Jesus.

And, see 1 John 1:8-10. In the NIV, these verses read:

> 1 John 1:[8]If we claim to be without sin, we deceive ourselves and the truth is not
> in us. [9]If we confess our sins, he is faithful and just and will forgive us our sins
> and purify us from all unrighteousness. [10]If we claim we have not sinned, we
> make him out to be a liar and his word has no place in our lives.

Reason-3: If the Virgin Mary was "preserved intact from all stain of original sin" from her conception, by God, then she was a "sinless" person. If God made the Virgin Mary a "sinless" person, even though she had a human father, then why did He not use the same method "to preserve Jesus, the man, from all stain of original sin". Or more specifically, why did God create Jesus, the man, as a "sinless" person, by creating Him without a human father? It should be obvious that if God used two different methods to create "sinless" individuals (*Mary and Jesus, the man*), He would become a confused and inconsistent God, which He is not.

Reason-4: From the beginning of creation, God revealed His ways, laws, and customs. He had the Jews record His ways, laws, and customs in the Bible for us. For example, in Genesis 3:15, God revealed the virgin birth of Christ with the phrase: "her seed". See Genesis 3:15 in the KJV or NASB translations of the Bible. God established the shedding of innocent blood as an atonement for sin. God established the pattern of an inheritance being passed from the father to his children. And this pattern included the passing of the stain of the original sin of Adam, from a father to his children. In light of all that God did share in the verses of the Bible, why is it that the "sinless" condition of the Virgin Mary is not clearly predicted and revealed? The virgin birth of Christ is clearly predicted and revealed.

The summation of these reasons is that the Bible does not clearly predict or reveal the "sinless" condition of the Virgin Mary. Therefore, it seems inappropriate to promote such a belief. Furthermore, it seems totally inappropriate to use tradition to override the lack of clear verses to support the "sinless" condition of Mary. For this author, the implied result of the phrase – "preserved intact from all stain of original sin", which is the "sinless" condition of the Virgin Mary from birth, makes that result invalid (*and biblically inappropriate*).

Segment-2: **The result and validity of the phrase: "being filled with the Holy Ghost from her mother's womb"**

The phrase – "being filled with the Holy Ghost from her mother's womb", would result in the Virgin Mary having been filled with God, the Holy Ghost – God, the Holy Spirit – from birth. Now, the question becomes, what does it mean to be filled with the Holy Ghost? A consensus of several web documents about "being filled with the Holy Ghost", along with a little speculation by this author, can be expressed, as follows:

"Before the cross,
Individuals were filled with God, the Holy Ghost, for His purposes.

After the cross,
When an individual –
Admits that she or he is a sinner,
Admits that she or he is in need of a savior,
Accepts the deaths of Jesus on the cross on her or his behalf,
Accepts Jesus, as her or his, Lord and Savior, and
Possibly invites Jesus into her or his life,
Jesus sends God, the Holy Ghost to live within that individual. However, the 'being filled with the Holy Ghost' is over and above the 'indwelling of the Holy Ghost'. This 'being fill with the Holy Ghost' can be the result of the prayers of an individual or it can be the result of the working of the Holy Spirit in an individual's life. And generally, the 'being filled with the Holy Ghost' serves a purpose or is accompanied by a gift – knowledge, faith, tongues, etc. – of the Holy Ghost, so that it is obvious to others."

The Bible clearly indicates that "being filled with the Holy Ghost" is a valid concept.

Segment-3: **Are the results of the two phrases the same?**

In *Segment-1*, we concluded that the result of being – "preserved intact from all stain of original sin" is a "sinless individual". And such a result is invalid, for all except Jesus, based on the implications of the Bible. In *Segment-2*, we concluded that the result of "being filled with the Holy Ghost from her mother's womb", before the cross, is a "being used by the Holy Ghost for His purposes". And such a result is valid based on the implications of the Bible. Thus, we note that the two phrases do not reference the same result. Therefore, even if the Virgin Mary was "filled with the Holy Ghost from conception", this condition provides no explicit support for the doctrine of "the Immaculate Conception of Mary". Besides, note that the wording of the dogma does not explicitly reference "the birth of Mary", rather it references a condition, which is "*Mary, in the first moment of her conception, was preserved intact from all stain of original sin.*" Thus, those who composed the dogma must have had something, other than the "virgin birth of Mary, herself" in mind, because that wording states the result of a process, without clearly defining how the result was accomplished. In a secondary attempt, to understand the phrase - "preserved intact from all stain of original sin", this author performed a web search using the phrase: "*preserved intact from all stain of original sin*". That search found sixteen web documents, at nine websites. Most of the web documents presented a superficial discussion of "the Immaculate Conception of Mary". Nevertheless, a paraphrased-consensus of these web documents is:

> "The Immaculate Conception of Mary" is a doctrine that revolves around a "logical-spiritual process", where this "logical-spiritual process" is defined, as "*the structuring of several spiritual concepts into a logical argument-presentation to imply various things about the relationship between 'God', 'Jesus, the man', and 'the Virgin Mary'*". (*This definition is why the label - "logical-spiritual process", was used. Furthermore, this definition/usage serves to emphasize that the dogma does not seem to involve the "physical process" of the virgin birth of Mary, herself.*) However, this "logical-spiritual process" seems to involve other spiritual concepts like: "the original sin of Adam", "Jesus, as Mary's redeemer and as our redeemer", and "God assigning special rights and privileges to Mary, because she was to be the Mother of Jesus, the man."

Based on the preceding comments, we could say, "Both the 'Bible' and 'The Gospel of the birth of Mary' support the possibility of someone 'being filled with the Holy Spirit from birth'. But 'being filled with the Holy Spirit from birth' may only be relevant to one of the three issues - (the holiness of Mary), upon which "the Immaculate Conception of Mary" is based. Therefore, we cannot say that either the "Bible" or "The Gospel of the birth of Mary" explicitly supports "the Immaculate Conception of Mary".

Question-3: **What impact would "the virgin birth of Mary" have had on the sinless nature of Jesus, if "the virgin birth of Mary" was true, even though it is not biblical?**

This question is addressed better, by answering a more important question: "How did God ensure that 'Jesus was born sinless'?" The answer to the latter question, is provided in the Bible. For it was accomplished explicitly, by God, the Holy Spirit, overshadowing Mary and causing her to be "with child". Read Matthew 1:18, Matthew 1:20, and Luke 1:35. In the NIV, these verses read:

Matthew 1:[18]This is how the birth of Jesus Christ came about: His mother Mary was pledged to be married to Joseph, but before they came together, she was found to be with child through the Holy Spirit.

Matthew 1:[20]But after he had considered this, an angel of the Lord appeared to him in a dream and said, "Joseph son of David, do not be afraid to take Mary home as your wife, because what is conceived in her is from the Holy Spirit.

Luke 1:[35]The angel answered, "The Holy Spirit will come upon you, and the power of the Most High will overshadow you. So the holy one to be born will be called the Son of God.

Therefore, "the virgin birth of Mary" would have absolutely no impact on the sinless nature of Jesus, because God, the Holy Spirit, explicitly ensured that Jesus would be born sinless, that Jesus would be born without Adam's sin-nature, and that Jesus would be born without a human father.

Question-4: **What impact would "the Immaculate Conception of Mary" have had on the sinless nature of Jesus, if "the Immaculate Conception of Mary" was true, even though it is not biblical?**

This question is also addressed better, by answering the more important question: "How did God ensure that 'Jesus was born sinless'?" And the answer would be a repeat of the answer to *Question-3*. More precisely, there is no impact. The sinless nature of Jesus was accomplished by God, the Holy Spirit, separately from anything that may have happened to Mary.

Question-5: **What is the importance of the doctrine of "the virgin birth of Mary" or the doctrine of "the Immaculate Conception of Mary"?**

This question is best answered by reviewing the practices of Christian denominations that promote either doctrine. Take for instance, the Roman Catholic Church, which promotes the doctrine of 'the Immaculate Conception of Mary'. A review of the practices of the Roman Catholic Church reveals things like the practice of "praying 'for and/or to' the dead", "praying to saints", and "praying to Mary".

- The purpose of "praying for the dead" is "to pray that the dead may be loosed from their sins" and "to make it possible for the dead to intercede on behalf of the individual, who is praying."

- The purpose of "praying to saints" is "to ask a saint to intercede with Jesus, on behalf of the individual, who is praying." This carries the implication that the individual, who is praying, is doing so to someone, who is dead, but who was holier than most.

- The purpose of "praying to Mary", is "to ask her to intercede with Jesus, on behalf of the individual, who is praying." This is supposedly taking advantage of the "mother and son" relationship, between "Mary" and "Jesus, the man".

Thus, the importance of the doctrine of "the virgin birth of Mary" or the doctrine of "the Immaculate Conception of Mary", is that the individual, who is praying, is doing so to Mary, who was supposedly, a holier human being." An implication of "a spiritually purer human being" or "a holier human being", is that there are "degrees of spirituality" or "degrees of holiness". A belief in "degrees of spirituality" or "degrees of holiness", is exactly what some denominations promote in the process of defining individuals, who are holier than most, and/or of defining saints. For instance:

- Under the Catholic practice of "defining individuals, who were holier, than most", Mary was defined to be holier, using the doctrine of "the Immaculate Conception of Mary".

- Under the Catholic practice of "defining saints", some individuals were defined to be saints, using external signs, which might include apparent miracles. Furthermore, some individuals are defined as saints with regards to specific aspects of life. For example:

    - ✓ "St. Christopher" was defined to be the "patron saint of travelers". Consequently, if someone was going to embark on a journey, she or he could pray to St. Christopher, asking him to intercede with God on her or his behalf, so the traveler would have a safe journey.

    - ✓ "St. Jude of Thaddaeus" was defined to be the "patron saint of desperate cases". Consequently, if someone was involved in harsh and difficult circumstances, she or he could pray to St. Jude, asking him to intercede with God on behalf of the individual needing help and guidance.

    - ✓ "St. Joan of Arc" was defined to be the "patroness of soldiers and of France". Consequently, soldiers and the people of France, could pray to St. Joan, asking her to intercede with God, on their behalf.

Obviously, we humans can only judge other individuals "to be holier than most" and/or "to be saints", "based on their words and/or deeds", "based on the results of their words and/or deeds", and/or "based on an apparent miracle and/or miracles". More precisely, individuals are judged "to be holier than most" and/or "to be saints", based on external signs, which may include an apparent miracle and/or miracles". God defines individuals to be in Christ, based on internal signs: the condition of their hearts. And God could display a miracle to confirm the condition of an individual's heart. However, care must be exercised, because Satan is able to mimic miracles. In fact, Matthew 24:24 seems to indicate that during the end-times, Satan may come close to deceiving the very elect through false Christ's and false prophets. In the NIV, this verse reads, as follows:

> (Matthew 24:24 NIV) For false Christs and false prophets will appear and perform great signs and miracles to deceive even the elect--if that were possible.

Consequently, while we can – and should – acknowledge the experiences of others (*acknowledge the words and/or deeds of others*), which includes noting any apparent miracles and listening to how some individuals feel that God, the Holy Spirit, has been working in their lives or in the lives of those around them. But we must also weigh everything that we hear, see, feel, and think to confirm "whether God is being glorified" or "whether someone else or something else is being glorified".

The point of this *Question-5* discussion is:

> "neither the doctrine of 'the virgin birth of Mary' nor the doctrine of 'the Immaculate Conception of Mary'?", should have any importance, because God, the Holy Spirit, ensured the "sinlessness" of Jesus, the man, independent of Mary's holiness. Therefore, these two doctrines are a distraction from the main point of Christianity: "Our salvation through Jesus, the man (*the Christ*)".

Furthermore, "praying 'for and/or to' the dead", "praying to saints", and "praying to Mary", are unnecessary, because there is only one mediator between "God" and "man", and that mediator is "Jesus, the man". See 1 Timothy 2:5, which reads:

> (1 Timothy 2:5 KJV) For there is one God, and one mediator between God and men, the man Christ Jesus;

Surely, Jesus must weep when He hears Christians praying to Mary and asking her to intercede on their behalf, because Christians should pray directly to Him.

Before ending this discussion of *Question-5*, two issues must be reiterated and emphasized. These are, as follows:

> *Issue-1*: Those who believe that it is possible for the dead to hear our prayers and then pray on our behalf and/or that it is possible for the dead to intercede with Jesus on our behalf – must reread the Bible. Although the belief that the dead retain all of their mental faculties appears consistent with the Bible. More specifically, it appears consistent with the parable of "the rich man and Lazarus", as told by Christ, Himself and as recorded in Luke 16:19-31. However, this parable also indicates the inability of the dead to communicate with the living and/or to intercede on behalf of the living. This can be stated, because in the referenced parable, the rich man, who was in the abode of the

unrighteous dead, exhibited emotions and the ability to use his mind. But he must have known that he could not communicate with his five living brothers, because he wanted Father Abraham to send someone back from the dead to warn his brothers. If the rich man could have communicated with his living brothers or interceded on their behalf, then there would not have been any reason for him to ask Father Abraham to send someone back from the dead.

Issue-2: The defining of saints was done by the church to acknowledge the words and deeds of my believers in the past. However, currently, the opinion of many scholars is that biblically all believers are saints, not just the group defined as such by the church. This opinion is consistent with an article in the Holman Bible Dictionary titled – "Saints". This article was authored by William Witness. This article addresses the issue of "Saints", from both an Old Testament and a New Testament viewpoint. For this essay only the New Testament viewpoint will be presented and it reads, as follows:

> **New Testament**: One word, hagios, is used for saints in the New Testament. This word, like qadosh, means holy. Consequently, saints are the holy ones. There is only one reference to saints in the Gospels (Matthew 27:52). In this verse, dead saints are resurrected at the Lord's crucifixion. The death of the Holy One provides life for those who believe in God. In Acts, three of the four references occur in chapter 9 (vv. 13,32,41). First Ananias and then Peter talks of the saints as simply believers in Christ. Paul continues this use in his Epistles to the Romans, Corinthians, Ephesians, Philippians, Colossians, Thessalonians, and Philemon. In each case, saints seem simply to be people who name Jesus as Lord. In the Book of Revelation, however, where the word saints, occurs more times than in any other single book (13 times), the meaning is further defined. Saints not only name Jesus as Lord, but they are faithful and true witnesses for Jesus.
>
> Little wonder then that the early church considered witnesses who were martyred for their testimonies to be saints. In fact, soon these saints were accorded special honor and then even worship. Unfortunately, the term saints came to be applied only to such special people.
>
> Biblically, though, the term saint is correctly applied to anyone who believes Jesus Christ is Lord. To believe in Jesus demands obedience and conformity to His will. A saint bears true and faithful witness to Christ in speech and life-style. To be a saint is a present reality when a believer seeks to let the Spirit form Christ within (Romans 8:29; Galatians 4:19; Ephesians 4:13).

Thus, those of you, who "believe in" and/or "practice" prayers to the dead, to the saints, and/or to Mary, please reread the Bible to confirm that your beliefs and prayers are biblical.

Part-3: **Conclusion**

Based on the social, civil, moral, and religious laws that were given to the Jewish people, by God through Moses, there is nothing that requires Mary to be sinless in order to give birth to a sinless Jesus. The sin-nature of Adam was passed by the father. An inheritance was passed from Father to son, unless there were no sons. In addition, the Bible recorded neither "the virgin birth of Mary" nor "The Immaculate Conception of Mary". Therefore, even if either one were true, it was not important to God's plan. Otherwise, He would have had it recorded in the Bible.

Once more, the issue of the sinlessness of Mary through a virgin birth or through the Immaculate Conception only serves as a distraction to the main point of Christianity: "Our salvation through Jesus, the man (*the Christ*)". Furthermore, "the virgin birth of Mary" and "The Immaculate Conception of Mary", are only important to those who believe that she is able to intercede with Jesus on their behalf. And anyone holding such a belief is forgetting that "Jesus is the only way to God". "No other intercessor", "No one else", and/or "Nothing else" are needed. Thus, the answer to both the topic question and the more precise question – "Did Mary also have to be sinless, since Jesus, the man, was born sinless through her?", is "No!"

Part-4: **Some relevant comments**

These comments are presented in three groups, as follows:

Group-1: Members of the "Assyrian Church of the East", the "Oriental Orthodox Church", and the "Eastern Christian Church", may also pray for the dead, to the dead, to the Saints, and to Mary. However, these churches do not accept "the Immaculate Conception of Mary". These churches may base their views of Mary on tradition and Luke 1:46-48. In the NIV, these verses read, as follows:

> Luke 1:[46]And Mary said: "My soul glorifies the Lord [47]and my spirit rejoices in God my Savior, [48]for he has been mindful of the humble state of his servant. From now on all generations will call me **blessed**,

Praying to Saints may also be based on tradition.

Group-2: A proofreader said that the previous version of this essay and especially the statements in the *Question-5* discussion about "praying to Mary", "praying 'for and/or to' the death", "defining Saints", and "praying to Saints", ignored the workings of God outside the Bible, over the past two-thousand years. His comments caused this author to modify this essay by being more specific especially with regards to Saints. An additional response is presented by saying this author is not trying to ignore nor to deny answered prayers. Neither is this author trying to ignore nor to reject experiences, which various individuals have that are attributed to God. In fact, this author might have experienced an angelic visit, several days before my dad crawled under smoke and fire to rescue me – his eight-year-old son, from the back-bedroom of our basement living-quarters, as the house burned. No! This author would never ignore and/or deny miracles and other experiences that occur today. But what this author would say is that everything must be tested to see, who is glorified – "God", "someone else", or "something else". Therefore, this author would summarize this position with the following two points:

- *Point-1*: While God can work in any way that He chooses, we cannot assume every *apparently good* thing is from God and every *apparently bad* thing is from Satan. We must test and examine everything to determine those things, which glorify God and those things, which glorify others instead of God.

- *Point-2*: God has and God can use any individual (*Christian or non-Christian*), any event, or anything else for His divine purposes. Acknowledging those individuals, events, and/or anything else is something that we can and should do. But praying to God through any of those is not biblical. To do so is "**a direct denial of Jesus, as the only mediator between God and man**". Therefore, **"Test everything! If something does not glorify God, it needs to be rejected, as unGodly."**

Group-3: During a final proofread, this author noticed that in *Excerpt-1* on page 304 of this essay. In Bishop Cyril's letter to Bishop Nestorius, which is part of the proceedings of the "Council of Ephesus" in 451 A.D., Bishop Cyril used the wording:

> "So then he *who had an existence before all ages and* ***was born of the Father***, is said to have been born according to the flesh of a woman, ***not as though his divine nature received its beginning of existence*** in the holy Virgin, for ***it*** needed not ***any second generation after that of the Father*** (*for it would be absurd and foolish to say that he who existed before all ages, coeternal with the Father,* ***needed any second beginning of existence***), but since, for us and for our salvation, he personally united to himself an human body, and came forth of a woman, he is in this way said to be born after the flesh; for he was not first born a common man of the holy Virgin, and then the Word came down and entered into him, but the union being made in the womb itself, he is said to endure a birth after the flesh, ascribing to himself the birth of his own flesh."

Unless this author is misreading these statements, Bishop Cyril seems to be implying that God, the Son, had a "***first beginning***" from God, the Father. If true, such an implication is unbiblical.

How do we know that the genealogy of Jesus in the Gospel of Luke is through Mary?

Most Christians know that there are two genealogies of Jesus recorded in the New Testament. One genealogy was recorded, by Matthew in what is called the "Gospel of Matthew" or simply "Matthew". The other genealogy was recorded, by Luke in what is called the "Gospel of Luke" or simply "Luke". While most Christians agree that Matthew's genealogy is through Joseph – the legal father of Jesus, the Christian community disagrees about whether Luke's genealogy is through Mary or Joseph. Some Christian scholars, who believe that Luke's genealogy is through Joseph, try to support their belief, by saying something like – "Luke's genealogy is a non-kingly lineage through Joseph" or "Luke's genealogy is a natural lineage through Joseph." They even say, "The Jews recorded their genealogies through the male members of the family not the female members." Nevertheless, some scholars do believe that Luke's genealogy is through Mary. These scholars remind us that Luke was not Jewish. Obviously, Luke's genealogy cannot be through both Joseph and Mary. Thus, for the moment, we will assume Luke's genealogy is through Mary. With that assumption, the question becomes: "How do we know that the genealogy of Jesus in the Gospel of Luke is through Mary?" To address this question, this essay is organized in six parts. Part-1 presents Matthew's genealogy of Jesus. Part-2 presents Luke's genealogy of Jesus. Part-3 presents some background information. Part-4 presents a critique of the topic question. Part-5 presents a conclusion. Part-6 presents some relevant comments.

Part-1: **Matthew's genealogy of Jesus**

Matthew's genealogy of Jesus is recorded in Matthew 1:1-17. In the NIV, these verses read:

> Matthew 1:[1]A record of the genealogy of Jesus Christ the son of David, the son of Abraham: [2]Abraham was the father of Isaac, Isaac the father of Jacob, Jacob the father of Judah and his brothers, [3]Judah the father of Perez and Zerah, whose mother was Tamar, Perez the father of Hezron, Hezron the father of Ram, [4]Ram the father of Amminadab, Amminadab the father of Nahshon, Nahshon the father of Salmon, [5]Salmon the father of Boaz, whose mother was Rahab, Boaz the father of Obed, whose mother was Ruth, Obed the father of Jesse, [6]and Jesse the father of King David. David was the father of Solomon, whose mother had been Uriah's wife, [7]Solomon the father of Rehoboam, Rehoboam the father of Abijah, Abijah the father of Asa, [8]Asa the father of Jehoshaphat, Jehoshaphat the father of Jehoram, Jehoram the father of Uzziah, [9]Uzziah the father of Jotham, Jotham the father of Ahaz, Ahaz the father of Hezekiah, [10]Hezekiah the father of Manasseh, Manasseh the father of Amon, Amon the father of Josiah, [11]and Josiah the father of Jeconiah and his brothers at the time of the exile to Babylon. [12]After the exile

to Babylon: Jeconiah was the father of Shealtiel, Shealtiel the father of Zerubbabel,
[13]Zerubbabel the father of Abiud, Abiud the father of Eliakim, Eliakim the father of Azor,
[14]Azor the father of Zadok, Zadok the father of Akim, Akim the father of Eliud, [15]Eliud the
father of Eleazar, Eleazar the father of Matthan, Matthan the father of Jacob, [16]and Jacob
the father of Joseph, the husband of Mary, of whom was born Jesus, who is called Christ.
[17]Thus there were fourteen generations in all from Abraham to David, fourteen from
David to the exile to Babylon, and fourteen from the exile to the Christ.

> *Comment:* There are, at least, four interesting things to note about this genealogy. *First*, Matthew 1:1 is like an overview. *Second*, by using the phrase – "Jesus Christ the son of David, the son of Abraham", it is clear that the term – "son", is synonymous with a phrase like: "an ancestor of". *Third*, Matthew 1:17 is like a summary. *Fourth*, this genealogy is from Abraham to Jesus.

Part-2: **Luke's genealogy of Jesus**

Luke's genealogy of Jesus is recorded in Luke 3:23-38. In the NIV, these verses read:

Luke 3:[23]Now Jesus himself was about thirty years old when he began his ministry. He
was the son, so it was thought, of Joseph, the son of Heli, [24]the son of Matthat, the son
of Levi, the son of Melki, the son of Jannai, the son of Joseph, [25]the son of Mattathias, the
son of Amos, the son of Nahum, the son of Esli, the son of Naggai, [26]the son of Maath, the
son of Mattathias, the son of Semein, the son of Josech, the son of Joda, [27]the son of
Joanan, the son of Rhesa, the son of Zerubbabel, the son of Shealtiel, the son of Neri,
[28]the son of Melki, the son of Addi, the son of Cosam, the son of Elmadam, the son of Er,
[29]the son of Joshua, the son of Eliezer, the son of Jorim, the son of Matthat, the son of
Levi, [30]the son of Simeon, the son of Judah, the son of Joseph, the son of Jonam, the son
of Eliakim,[31]the son of Melea, the son of Menna, the son of Mattatha, the son of Nathan,
the son of David, [32]the son of Jesse, the son of Obed, the son of Boaz, the son of Salmon,
the son of Nahshon, [33]the son of Amminadab, the son of Ram, the son of Hezron, the son
of Perez, the son of Judah, [34]the son of Jacob, the son of Isaac, the son of Abraham, the
son of Terah, the son of Nahor, [35]the son of Serug, the son of Reu, the son of Peleg, the
son of Eber, the son of Shelah, [36]the son of Cainan, the son of Arphaxad, the son of Shem,
the son of Noah, the son of Lamech, [37]the son of Methuselah, the son of Enoch, the son
of Jared, the son of Mahalalel, the son of Kenan, [38]the son of Enosh, the son of Seth, the
son of Adam, the son of God.

> *Comment:* There are, at least, two interesting things to note about this genealogy. *First*, this genealogy is from Jesus to God, because of the wording – "Adam, as the son of God". *Second*, the inclusion of Adam in this genealogy confirms his existence, as a real person.

Part-3: **Some background information**

Background information is developed, by doing two things: *First*, Matthew's genealogy for Jesus will be compared with Luke's genealogy for Jesus, because the similarities and differences provide useful information. *Second*, some biblical facts that are explicitly or implicitly indicated in the Bible will be presented. To accomplish these two tasks, Part-3 is organized in two sections. Section-1 presents a comparison of Matthew's genealogy with Luke's genealogy. Section-2 presents some biblical facts.

Section-1: **A comparison of Matthew's genealogy with Luke's genealogy**

A comparison of Matthew's genealogy with Luke's genealogy, by this author produced the following nine-interesting observations:

- *Observation-1*: Both genealogies include King David and references to Joseph, the legal father of Jesus.

- *Observation-2*: Both genealogies involve King David and Bathsheba, who were the parents of both Solomon and Nathan. Solomon is in Matthew's genealogy and Nathan is in Luke's genealogy.

- *Observation-3*: Both genealogies list the same fourteen names, from Abraham to King David.

- *Observation-4*: Four names – "Shealtiel", "Zerubbabel", "Eliakim" and "Joseph", occur in both genealogies. In fact, the name – "Joseph", occurs once in Matthew's genealogy and twice in Luke's genealogy. The names – "Eliakim" and "Joseph", occur in different sequences in the two genealogies. Thus, the names – "Eliakim" and "Joseph", do not present an obvious problem. However, the names – "Shealtiel" and "Zerubbabel", occur consecutively in both genealogies. Therefore, the names – "Shealtiel" and "Zerubbabel", present a problem.

- *Observation-5*: Each genealogy lists a different "set of names" between King David and Joseph, the legal father of Jesus. As a result, each genealogy lists a different name for the father of Joseph. Thus, the different names present a problem. Actually, there are two problems here. One is the more specific problem of the two different names, as the father of Joseph. The other is the more general problem of the two different sets of names, between King David and Joseph.

- *Observation-6*: There are forty-four names from King David to Jesus, in Luke's genealogy, while there are only eighteen names from King David to Jesus, in Matthew's genealogy.

Therefore, the wide variance in the number of names presents a problem.

> Comment: Some might think that the problem of the "wide variance in the number of names" and the "*Observation-5*" problem of two "sets of names", are the same problem. But they are not, because there could have been two "sets of names", but the same number of names, in each set.

- *Observation-7*: The names presented in Matthew's genealogy could be categorized in two groups. "The names from Abraham to Jesse (*the father of King David*)", could be categorized, as the "leaders of Abraham's family group", the "leaders of the Jewish family", and/or the "leaders of the tribe of Judah". "The names from King David to Joseph", could be categorized, as "actual kings of the Jewish nation", "actual Kings of Judah", and/or "could-be-kings of the Jewish nation or the Kingdom of Judah", based on Jewish laws and customs.

- *Observation-8*: In the NIV, Matthew 1:16 uses the phrase – "Jacob the father of Joseph, the husband of Mary, of whom was born Jesus, who is called Christ". (*This is part of the specifics of "Observation-5".*)

- *Observation-9*: In the NIV, Luke 3:23 uses the phrase: "He was the son, so it was thought, of Joseph, the son of Heli". (*This is the other part of the specifics of "Observation-5".*)

The nine interesting-observations above revealed four problems. As previously indicated, these problems are:

- *Problem-1*: Between the two genealogies, there is a "wide variance in the number of names", between King David and Joseph, the legal father of Jesus.

- *Problem-2*: The consecutive occurrence of "the two names: 'Shealtiel' and 'Zerubbabel'", in both genealogies.

- *Problem-3*: The two genealogies list "two 'sets of names' between King David and Joseph".

- *Problem-4*: The two genealogies list "two different names for Joseph's father".

> Comment: To ease the remainder of this discussion, the four problems above will be referenced, by the underlined wording.

Consequently, besides addressing the topic question, we have to address the four problems listed above. However, the problem of the "wide variance in the number of names", and the problem of "the two names 'Shealtiel' and 'Zerubbabel'", are not crucial in addressing the topic question. In fact, these two problems would only serve, as a distraction in this essay. Therefore, the problem of the "wide variance in the number of names", will be discussed in the essay: "Why are there more names in the genealogy listed, by Luke than in the genealogy listed, by Matthew?" The problem of "The two names 'Shealtiel' and 'Zerubbabel'", will be discussed in the essay: "Does it matter, if the two genealogies of Christ converged through Shealtiel and Zerubbabel?" (*Both essays should be in the book: "Last Call!!!"*) With the removal of these two problems from this essay, the remainder of this essay will attempt to address the problem of the "two 'sets of names' between King David and Joseph", the problem of the "two different names for Joseph's father", and the topic question.

Section-2: **Some biblical facts**

Crucial to this essay are six facts that are explicitly or implicitly indicated in the Bible. These facts are, as follows:

- *Fact-1*: Joseph was the legal father of Jesus. He was not the biological father of Jesus.

- *Fact-2*: Matthew's genealogy of Jesus, which is through Joseph, indicates that Joseph came from a line of Kings and could-be Kings of Israel and Judah. (*Therefore, based on Jewish law, Joseph probably had the legal right to claim the throne of King David, if the Roman government had allowed it. Consequently, since Joseph was the legal father of Jesus, Jesus could have claimed the throne of King David, after the death of Joseph. This means that based on Jewish law, Jesus fulfilled the prophecy, which indicated that the Messiah would be "Heir to the throne of David".*)

- *Fact-3*: As the birth Mother of Jesus, the Virgin Mary also had to be a descendant of King David by blood, because of prophecies, which indicated that Jesus, the Messiah, would be "Born of the seed of a woman", "Born of the seed of Abraham", "Born of the seed of Isaac", "Born of the seed of Jacob", "Descended from the tribe of Judah", and based on God's word, He would be "Heir to the throne of David".

- *Fact-4*: Mary was found to be "with child" (*She was found to be pregnant*), after God, the Holy Spirit, overshadowed her. And an Angel told Mary to name her son, Jesus.

- *Fact-5*: Matthew wrote the "Gospel of Matthew" to the Jews and presented Jesus, as the "King of the Jews".

- *Fact-6*: Luke wrote the "Gospel of Luke" to the Greeks and presented Jesus, as the "Son of Man (*as a human being*)".

Part-4: **A critique of the topic question and of related issues**

This critique of the topic question and of related issues, is formed around the background information and other references. In addition to presenting an answer for the topic question, this critique will also propose a solution for the problem of "two different names for Joseph's father" and the problem of "two 'sets of names' between King David and Joseph". To accomplish these tasks, Part-4 is organized in three sections. Section-1 presents a solution for the problem of "two different names for Joseph's father". Section-2 presents a solution for the problem of "two 'sets of names' between King David and Joseph". Section-3 presents an answer for the topic question.

> *Comment:* A margin-to-margin double-line separator was placed before each of the following three sections and at the end of the third section. This separator simply serves, as a visual aid to mark the beginning and end of each section.

Section-1: **A solution for** the problem of "**two different names for Joseph's father**"

As previously indicated, Matthew 1:16 of Matthew's genealogy of Jesus implies that the father of Joseph is Jacob. In the NIV, Matthew 1:16 reads:

> Matthew 1:[16]and Jacob the father of Joseph, the husband of Mary, of whom was born Jesus, who is called Christ.

Luke 3:23 of Luke's genealogy implies that the father of Joseph is Heli. In the NIV, Luke 3:23 reads:

> Luke 3:[23]Now Jesus himself was about thirty years old when he began his ministry. He was the son, so it was thought, of Joseph, the son of Heli,

The listing of the names – "Jacob" and "Heli", as the father of Joseph is an obvious inconsistency. Searching the Bible for other occurrences of both names does not resolve this inconsistency. Several Godly men had the name – "Jacob", but none of the other individuals named – "Jacob", were related to Joseph. And the name – "Heli" does not occur anywhere else in the Bible. This inconsistency has been discussed by many scholars and religious leaders over the years. Perhaps, the best effort was made by Dr. Merrill F. Unger. Using the Bible, as his source, Dr. Unger published the answer in his book: "Unger's Bible Handbook". On page 520, Dr. Unger indicates the term – "son", was traditionally interchangeable with the term: "son-in-law". Thus, according to Dr. Unger, the phrase – "Joseph, the son of Heli" in Luke 3:23 should more precisely read: "Joseph, the son-in-law of Heli". Obviously, this would make Heli the father of Mary. Dr. Unger indicated that he based his interchangeability of "son" and "son-in-law", on 1 Samuel 24:16 and 1 Samuel 18:27. In the NIV, 1 Samuel 24:16 and 1 Samuel 18:27 read:

> 1 Samuel 24:[16]When David finished saying this, Saul asked, "Is that your voice, David my

son?" And he wept aloud.

1 Samuel 18:[27]David and his men went out and killed two hundred Philistines. He brought their foreskins and presented the full number to the king so that he might become the king's son-in-law. Then Saul gave him his daughter Michal in marriage.

From 1 Samuel 18:27, we know that David married Saul's daughter Michal. Therefore, by the time the events recorded in "1 Samuel" reach 1 Samuel 24:16, David is clearly Saul's son-in-law. Thus, when Saul calls David his son, we know that "son" and "son-in-law" are interchangeable. It should also be noted that the use of "son" instead of "son-in-law", by the speaker sounds more personal, more intimate, and more caring. Besides 1 Samuel 18:27, the term – "son-in-law", appears in 1 Samuel 18:21-23, 26. In the NIV, these verses read:

1 Samuel 18:[21]"I will give her to him," he thought, "so that she may be a snare to him and so that the hand of the Philistines may be against him." So Saul said to David, "Now you have a second opportunity to become my son-in-law." [22]Then Saul ordered his attendants: "Speak to David privately and say, 'Look, the king is pleased with you, and his attendants all like you; now become his son-in-law.'" [23]They repeated these words to David. But David said, "Do you think it is a small matter to become the king's son-in-law? I'm only a poor man and little known."

1 Samuel 18:[26]When the attendants told David these things, he was pleased to become the king's son-in-law. So before the allotted time elapsed,

The use of the term – "son", versus the term – "son-in-law", seems to depend on, at least, two things. *<u>First</u>*, it depends on whom the speaker is speaking to. *<u>Second</u>*, as mentioned before, it depends on the closeness of the relationship, that is to be conveyed. Note that, as with the terms – "son" and "son-in-law", a similar situation exists with the terms: "father" and "father-in-law". The reference for this interchangeability is 1 Samuel 24:11. In the NIV, this verse reads:

1 Samuel 24:[11]See, my father, look at this piece of your robe in my hand! I cut off the corner of your robe but did not kill you. Now understand and recognize that I am not guilty of wrongdoing or rebellion. I have not wronged you, but you are hunting me down to take my life.

In this verse, David calls Saul his father. However, David's real father was Jesse. Thus, it is also true that the terms – "father" and "father-in-law", are interchangeable.

Conclusion: <u>A solution for</u> the problem of "**<u>two different names for Joseph's father</u>**"

As previously stated, Dr. Unger's solution to the inconsistency of two different names, for the father of Joseph is that in the NIV, for example, Luke 3:23 should more precisely read:

"Now Jesus himself was about thirty years old when he began his ministry. He was the son, so it was thought, of Joseph, the **son-in-law** of Heli,".

Section-2: **A solution for** the problem of "**two sets of different names between King David and Joseph**"

Besides the "Gospel of Matthew" and the "Gospel of Luke", there are two other books among the sixty-six canonical books of the Bible that are called: "gospels". These are the "Gospel of Mark" and the "Gospel of John". Now, a quick read of the four gospels should make it obvious that the four gospel writers – Matthew, Mark, Luke and John, did not mention all of the same words or events related to the birth, life, ministry, death, burial, and resurrection of Jesus. However, this is not surprising, since each writer emphasized those words or events, which he considered important for his presentation. Each writer presented a different view of Jesus. The presentations according to some Christian apologists could be characterized, as follows:

- ✓ **Matthew** *presented* **Jesus, as King of the Jews**.
- ✓ **Mark** *presented* **Jesus, as a servant of God**.
- ✓ **Luke** *presented* **Jesus, as the Son of Man**.
- ✓ **John** *presented* **Jesus, as the Son of God**.

Each writer directed his presentation to a different audience. The audiences, according to Pastor Jack Hayford of Living Way Ministries, could be characterized as follows:

- ✓ **Matthew** *wrote to the* **Jews**.
- ✓ **Mark** *wrote to the* **Romans**.
- ✓ **Luke** *wrote to the* **Greeks**.
- ✓ **John** *wrote to the* **World**.

With respect to John's gospel, Dr. Merrill F. Unger prefers the wording: "**John** *wrote to the* **Church**". (*See page 467 of Dr. Unger's book: "Unger's Bible Handbook".*) Therefore, it is understandable that only two of the gospels presented genealogies of Jesus and that these two gospels presented two different sets of names, between King David and Joseph.

The issue of only "two genealogies for Jesus in the four gospels", was addressed more precisely, by a Bible scholar, when he said, "When you look at the view of Jesus that each of the four gospel writers presented, you note that:

- In Matthew, the 'King of the Jews', needs a genealogy to support his right by Jewish law to be the 'King of the Jews'.

- In Mark, a 'servant of God', does not need a genealogy to support his existence, as a servant, by the word of God.

- In Luke, the 'Son of Man *(a human being: Jesus, the man)*', needs a genealogy to support his existence, as a human by blood.

- In John, the 'Son of God *(a member of the Trinity: Jesus, God, the Son)*', does not need a genealogy to support his existence, as the 'Son of God', by the word of God."

Conclusion: A solution for the problem of "**two 'sets of names' between King David and Joseph**"

The problem of the "two 'sets of names' between King David and Joseph", resulted from Matthew and Luke presenting two different views of Jesus to two different audiences. As previously indicated, Matthew *presented* Jesus, as King of the Jews and Luke *presented* Jesus, as the Son of Man. Clearly, Matthew's genealogy of Jesus shows that: "Jesus had a legal right to be called 'King of the Jews'". Thus, this genealogy has to be through Joseph, who was the legal father of Jesus. On the other hand, Luke's genealogy of Jesus shows that: "Jesus was the 'Son of Man' (*was a man*) and as such, He had the right to claim the throne of David, by blood and by the word of God." Thus, this genealogy has to be through Mary, who was the birth Mother of Jesus. (*More detailed support for Luke's genealogy being through Mary is presented in Section-3.*) Therefore, both the cause and the solution to this problem are that Jesus was being presented as "King of the Jews" through Joseph in Matthew and as the "Son of Man" through Mary in Luke.

> *Comment:* For anyone, who feels that: "Jesus being the 'king of the Jews', is not relevant", because He said, "His Kingdom was not of this world", two responses are presented. *First*, see Matthew 27:11, which reads:
>
> > (Matthew 27:11 NIV) Meanwhile Jesus stood before the governor, and the governor asked him, "Are you the king of the Jews?" "*Yes, it is as you say,*" Jesus replied.
>
> Therefore, Jesus, Himself, admitted that He was "King of the Jews". *Second*, by the word of God, the Kingdom that Jesus is to rule, is the eternal "Kingdom of King David". This is why He responded with the comment that His kingdom was not of this world. But His statement did not mean that He could not have claimed the earthly "Kingdom of King David". Although to gain the earthly "Kingdom of King David", Jesus would have had to appeal to the Jews, based on His genealogy under Jewish Law, and to the Roman government, neither of whom would have acknowledged, such an appeal by Jesus. These kingdom-comments are also consistent with Luke 1:32-33. In the NIV, these verses read:
>
> > Luke 1:32 He will be great and will be called the Son of the Most High. The
> > Lord God will give him the throne of his father David 33 and he will reign

over the house of Jacob forever; his kingdom will never end."

Section-3: **An answer for** the question: **"How do we know that the genealogy of Jesus in the Gospel of Luke is through Mary?"**

Besides the "Solution for: the problem of the 'two different names for Joseph's father'" and the "Solution for: the problem of the 'two sets of names between King David and Joseph'", at least, four other considerations add credibility, to Luke's genealogy being through Mary. These are:

- *Credibility-consideration-1*: Luke has already recorded in Luke 1:35, his knowledge that God, the Holy Spirit, caused Mary to be "with child". In the NIV, Luke 1:35 reads:

  Luke 1:[35]The angel answered, "The Holy Spirit will come upon you, and the power of the Most High will overshadow you. So the holy one to be born will be called the Son of God.

  Thus, in Luke 3:23 of the NIV, when Luke uses the phrase – "He was the son, so it was thought, of Joseph, the son of Heli", clearly, Luke knows that Joseph is not the biological father of Jesus. With such knowledge, listing a variation of the genealogy of Joseph would be pointless; especially, when Luke's purpose is to show that Jesus is the "Son of Man", where the phrase – "Son of Man", is traditionally understood to be a reference to Jesus, the man, not Jesus, God, the Son. Thus, Luke's genealogy of Jesus has to be a reference to the lineage of Jesus by blood, which must be through Mary, his birth mother.

- *Credibility-consideration-2*: With respect to the two genealogies of Jesus, there are two ways to view them. One way is as God, the Father, might view them. The other way is as man would traditionally view them or any genealogy.

  - ✓ God's view: Christians believe that God inspired Matthew and Luke to record the genealogies of Jesus. Thus, we have to assume that – "In the Gospels of Matthew and Luke, God is conveying whatever He wants us to know." Logically and spiritually, it makes sense that God established the two lineages to Jesus, the man, such that these lineages would be complete by His word, by Jewish law, and/or by blood. Nothing else would matter.

  - ✓ Man's view: If you were going to list someone's lineage (*someone's ancestry*), that lineage would be the most complete, by giving both sides: "the mother's side" and "the father's side". If a kingdom is involved, then there could be two other lineages that would be more important to list. These other two would be – the "legal-lineage" and/or the "blood-lineage", to the throne of that kingdom. In many cases, the "legal-lineage" and/or the "blood-lineage" will be equivalence to one or both "the mother's side" and/or "the father's side". Nevertheless, to provide a complete lineage by whatever name, both "the mother's side" and "the father's side" should be given.

Matthew's genealogy satisfies both views (*God's and man's*), because it is the genealogy of Jesus, by Jewish law, and it is the genealogy of Joseph, the legal father of Jesus. Matthew's genealogy ties Jesus to the "throne of David" by Jewish law. This is one reason why Joseph had to pass from the scene, so Jesus could be legally called: the "King of the Jews". This author firmly believes that Luke's lineage satisfies both views, because it is the genealogy of Jesus, by God's word and by blood and it is the genealogy of Mary, the Mother of Jesus. Luke's genealogy ties Jesus to the "throne of David", by God's word and by blood.

Comment: Actually, to some degree, both genealogies involved all three aspects: "by God's word", "by Jewish law", and "by blood". The reason for saying this is twofold: *First*, Matthew's genealogy was impacted, by God's word and by blood, in a negative fashion, because of a judgment that God placed on, at least, one King of Judah, King Jeconiah (*also called King Coniah, by some sources*). [*See Jeremiah 22:24-30.*] Part of God's judgment on King Jeconiah, was that "none of his heirs would ever again, sit on the throne of King David." And Joseph was from King Jeconiah's blood line. *Second*, part of Jesus' lineage through Mary may have required the enforcement of the "'daughter and inheritance'[73] custom"[1] (*equivalent to by Jewish Law*).

- *Credibility-consideration-3*: It is this author's understanding that until the destruction of the Temple in 70 A. D., genealogies for most Jewish men were available in the Temple. This could mean that when Matthew and Luke were writing their Gospels, they may have had the Temple-genealogies to confirm their listings. If that is true, then the fact that the two listings include different names from King David to Jesus means the two genealogies were intended to serve different purposes.

- *Credibility-consideration-4*: Bible prophecies indicated that the Messiah would fulfill "specific conditions"[74]. Some conditions were specified in more than one verse or set of verses, and its fulfillment was recorded in one or more verses. Crucial to this essays are the following six prophecies and their respective fulfillment's:

---

1 See Appendix A for support for the existence of the "daughter and inheritance" custom.

✓ *Prophecy-1*: "Born of the seed of a woman" (*also understood as* "Born of a virgin"):

✎ *Prophesied by*:

Genesis 3:[15] And I will put enmity between thee and the woman, and between thy seed and her seed; it shall bruise thy head, and thou shalt bruise his heel. (KJV)

Isaiah 7:[14]Therefore the Lord himself will give you a sign: The virgin will be with child and will give birth to a son, and will call him Immanuel. (NIV)

✏ *Fulfilled in*:

Luke 1:[31]You will be with child and give birth to a son, and you are to give
him the name Jesus. [32]He will be great and will be called the Son of the
Most High. The Lord God will give him the throne of his father David,
[33]and he will reign over the house of Jacob forever; his kingdom will never
end." [34]"How will this be," Mary asked the angel, "since I am a virgin?"
[35]The angel answered, "The Holy Spirit will come upon you, and the power
of the Most High will overshadow you. So the holy one to be born will be
called the Son of God. (NIV)

Galatians 4:[4]But when the time had fully come, God sent his Son, born of a woman, born under law, (NIV)

Comment: The phrase – "born of a woman", fits the birth of Jesus, the man, through the virgin, Mary. The phrase – "born under law", could be a reference to Jesus being a legal heir to the throne of David through Joseph, by Jewish law.

✓ *Prophecy-2*: "Born of the seed of Abraham":

✎ *Prophesied by*:

Genesis 12:[2]"I will make you into a great nation and I will bless you; I will
make your name great, and you will be a blessing. [3]I will bless those who
bless you, and whoever curses you I will curse; and all peoples on earth
will be blessed through you." (NIV)

Comment: Some Bible scholars believe that the phrase – "all peoples on earth will be blessed through you", is a reference to Jesus and the free gift of salvation that He offers to all people through His deaths – (*His spiritual death and His physical death*) – and His resurrection.

✏ *Fulfilled in*:

Luke 3:[34]the son of Jacob, the son of Isaac, the son of Abraham, the son of Terah, the son of Nahor, (NIV)

✓ *Prophecy-3*: "Born of the seed of Isaac":

✎ *Prophesied by*:

Genesis 17:[19]Then God said, "Yes, but your wife Sarah will bear you a son, and you will call him Isaac. I will establish my covenant with him as an everlasting covenant for his descendants after him (NIV)

✏ *Fulfilled in*:

Luke 3:[34]the son of Jacob, the son of Isaac, the son of Abraham, the son of Terah, the son of Nahor, (NIV)

✓ *Prophecy-4*: "Born of the seed of Jacob":

✎ *Prophesied by*:

Numbers 24:[17]"I see him, but not now; I behold him, but not near. A star will come out of Jacob; a scepter will rise out of Israel. He will crush the foreheads of Moab, the skulls of all the sons of Sheth. (NIV)

✏ *Fulfilled in*:

Luke 3:[34]the son of Jacob, the son of Isaac, the son of Abraham, the son of Terah, the son of Nahor, (NIV)

✓ *Prophecy-5*: "Descended from the tribe of Judah":

✎ *Prophesied by*:

Genesis 49:[10]The scepter will not depart from Judah, nor the ruler's staff from between his feet, until he comes to whom it belongs and the obedience of the nations is his. (NIV)

✏ *Fulfilled in*:

Luke 3:[33]the son of Amminadab, the son of Ram, the son of Hezron, the son of Perez, the son of Judah, (NIV)

✓ *Prophecy-6*: "Heir to the throne of David":

✎ *Prophesied by*:

Isaiah 9:[7]Of the increase of his government and peace there will be no end. He will reign on David's throne and over his kingdom, establishing and upholding it with justice and righteousness from that time on and forever. The zeal of the LORD Almighty will accomplish this. (NIV)

✏ *Fulfilled in*:

Luke 1:[32]He will be great and will be called the Son of the Most High. The Lord God will give him the throne of his father David [33]and he will reign over the house of Jacob forever; his kingdom will never end." (NIV)

The previous six prophecies and the fulfillment of each, can be condensed into the following summary. For this summary, the fulfillment of each prophecy is expressed in terms of one of Jesus' parents, "Mary" or "Joseph", where the use of the name – "Mary", will also serve to indicate "Luke's genealogy" and the name – "Joseph", will also serve to indicate "Matthew's genealogy". In addition, the phrases – "by God's word", "by Jewish law", and/or "by blood", will be used to indicate the basis for the fulfillment. The summary reads, as follows:

Born of the seed of a woman *was through* Mary and by God's word & by blood.

Born of the seed of Abraham *was through* Mary and by God's word & by blood.

Born of the seed of Isaac *was through* Mary and by God's word & by blood.

Born of the seed of Jacob *was through* Mary and

			by God's word & by blood.
Descended from the tribe of Judah	*was through*	Mary	and by God's word & by blood.
Heir to the [earthly] throne of David	*was through*	Joseph	and by Jewish law.
Heir to the [eternal] throne of David	*was through*	Mary	and by God's word & by blood.

Comment: In this essay, the phrase – "by blood", is being used to convey a sense of individuals, who are related, by what we could call a "chain of births" (*e.g., a generational line or a line consisting of a daughter or son, mother or father, grandparent, great-grandparent, great . . . great-grandparent, and so on*). The reason for emphasizing this usage is, because medically there is no exchange of blood, between a mother and her birth child. The child's blood is created by the child's DNA, as the child grows from an egg inside the mother.

Conclusion: An answer for the question: **"How do we know that the genealogy of Jesus in the Gospel of Luke is through Mary?"**

An answer for the topic question flows from a comparison of the two genealogies and from many of the prophecies about Jesus. However, when it comes to the genealogies of Jesus, as recorded in the Gospels of Matthew and Luke, too many people must implicitly think that God is stupid. Because too many people think that God inspired the recording of two genealogies through Joseph, the legal father of Jesus. But anyone thinking this way, is forgetting, at least, two things:

- *First*, Bible scholars believe that the primary source for the information in the Gospel of Luke was Mary. Many of these same scholars also say that the purpose of Luke's Gospel was to show that Jesus was fully human (*to show Jesus, as the "Son of Man"*). Only a "by blood" lineage would support a fully human claim. Thus, this support would require the lineage through Mary, the birth Mother of Jesus, the man; especially since Joseph was not the biological father of Jesus, the man.

  Comment: After Adam and Eve, when a woman gave birth, there could always be a question of "Who the biological father was?", because the baby did not come out of him. Until the modern medical practice of embryo-implantation began, there was never a question of "Who the biological mother of a child was?", because the baby came out of her. Thus, if proving Jesus was human was the goal, then a genealogy through Mary would make the most sense.

- *Second*, concerning the lineages of Jesus, God would only be concerned with the completeness of those lineages by His word (*by God's word*), by Jewish law, and by blood. Nothing else would have mattered. In more detail, the following comments are presented:

  - ✓ By God's word, the heir to King David's eternal throne had to come through Mary, because Joseph's lineage (*the "by Jewish law" lineage*) included, at least one King, King Jeconiah, who was explicitly rejected by God's word. Furthermore, by God's word, the blood lineage included some of those whom God had put special blessings on.

  - ✓ By Jewish law, Jesus needed a lineage that would allow Him to claim the right to be called the "King of the Jews", by Jewish law. However, this "by Jewish law" lineage made no demands on the "by blood" lineage. More precisely, by Jewish law, the fact that Joseph was from the bloodline of King Jeconiah was not a legal problem.

  - ✓ By blood, Jesus had to be related to Adam, Abraham, Isaac, Jacob, Judah, and King David, through the Virgin Mary.

  Thus, clearly, Matthew's genealogy of Jesus satisfied the by "Jewish law" requirement. And for those who do not make this thing more complicated than it has to be, clearly, Luke's genealogy of Jesus satisfied both the "by God's word" and the "by blood" requirements.

Christians must remember! Our God is not a God of confusion. God keeps most things very simple, because He is dealing with simple men. Yet! There is an eloquent beauty about the way that God does things. Thus, again, the "best answer" for the question – "How do we know that the genealogy of Jesus in the Gospel of Luke is through Mary?", is that "Luke's genealogy has to be a 'by God's word' lineage and a 'by blood' lineage. And these lineages would be through the Virgin Mary, not Joseph." For clearly, Joseph was the legal father of Jesus not the biological father of Jesus. And an angels told Mary that she would be the birth mother of Jesus.

Part-5: **Conclusion**

The "Solution for: for the problem of 'two names for Joseph's father'", is that the phrase – "Joseph, son of Heli", is interchangeable with the phrase: "Joseph, the son-in-law of Heli". This supports Luke's genealogy being through Mary. This knowledge and the other things previously mentioned indicate that Luke's genealogy of Jesus is through Mary. Therefore, we can answer the topic question – "How do we know that the genealogy of Jesus in the Gospel of Luke is through Mary?", by saying, "The Bible supports our belief that Luke's genealogy is through Mary." Thus, this author is very comfortable with the conviction that the genealogy of Jesus given in the Book of Luke is through Mary, "by God's word" <u>and</u> "by blood". This lineage is from Adam through King David to Christ through Mary. And Matthew's genealogy provides the "by Jewish law" lineage from King David to Christ through Joseph.

<u>Part-6</u>: **Some relevant comments**

Some relevant comments are presented in three groups, as follows:

- *<u>Group-1</u>*: During a broadcast of the weekly radio program – "Becoming People of Love", on radio station "WAVA", which is 105.1 FM in the Washington, D.C. area, Pastor Steve King of Cherrydale Baptist Church, Arlington, Virginia, said, "The Gospel of Luke is for women, because this gospel recorded more things about women than the other gospels."

- *<u>Group-2</u>*: As mentioned before, the two genealogies of Jesus involve King David and Bathsheba, who were the parents of both Solomon and Nathan. Solomon is listed in the genealogy given by Matthew. Nathan is listed in the genealogy given by Luke. If the David-Solomon-Joseph-Jesus lineage is true and if the David-Nathan-Mary-Jesus lineage is true, then God showed, at least, two things: "His power (*His control of things*)" and "His mercy".

  ✓ <u>His power</u> was shown by having both lines to Jesus from King David and only one of his wives: Bathsheba. Since King David had many wives, the probability was higher for the two lines coming from King David and two wives, rather than from King David and the same wife: Bathsheba. The fact that King David and Bathsheba were the parents of both Solomon and Nathan was recorded in 1 Chronicles 3:5. In the NIV, it reads:

  > 1 Chronicles 3:[5]and these were the children born to him there: Shammua, Shobab, Nathan and Solomon. These four were by Bathsheba daughter of Ammiel.

  ✓ <u>His mercy</u> was shown in that even though King David sinned "with Bathsheba" and "because of Bathsheba", King David and Bathsheba were allowed to be in both lineages of Jesus. By human standards, King David committed some of his worst sins "with" and "because" of Bathsheba. More specifically, King David committed adultery with Bathsheba, who became pregnant, as a result. Then after several failed attempts to cover up his affair with Bathsheba, King David had Bathsheba's husband, Uriah, murdered, so he (*King David*) could marry her. Thus, King David committed adultery and murder. Yet, God allowed both King David and Bathsheba to be in both the "by Jewish law" lineage of Jesus and the "'by God's word' and 'by blood'" lineage of Jesus.

- *Group-3*: "The New Testament – Recovery Version" published by Living Stream Ministry contains footnotes written by Witness Lee. One of those footnotes is for Matthew 1:16. In the NIV, this verse reads:

  Matthew 1:[16]and Jacob the father of Joseph, the husband of Mary, of whom was born Jesus, who is called Christ.

  This particular footnote also mentions Luke 3:23. In the NIV, this verse reads:

  Luke 3:[23]Now Jesus himself was about thirty years old when he began his ministry. He was the son, so it was thought, of Joseph, the son of Heli,

  In referencing Matthew 1:16 and Luke 3:23, this particular footnote began an attempt to address the problem of "two different names for Joseph's father". However, the footnote incorrectly implies that the phrase – "so it was thought", in Luke 3:23, is a reference to the relationship between Joseph and Heli. When clearly, the reference refers to the relationship between Jesus and Joseph. Nevertheless, the footnote does an excellent job of reminding everyone that God established a "daughters and inheritance" custom. See Appendix A for a discussion of the "daughters and inheritance" custom. From the name "daughters and inheritance", you probably already guessed that this custom allowed for an inheritance to be passed to a daughter or daughters, when there were no sons.

Did God create man through evolution?

Some people, who believe in God, also believe that "God created man through an evolutionary process" or that "God allowed an evolutionary process to take place." Such beliefs mean that to these people, both "creation by evolution (*creation through evolution*)" and "creation by God", are true. These people may link God and evolution, based on reasoning, which involves their interpretation of things like:

- Geology and the Bible (*which resulted in an implied* time-gap between Genesis 1:1 and Genesis 1:2).
- Bible verses *like* Genesis 2:7 (*which indicates that man was created* from the dust of the ground).
- The Bible (*which indicates that* God is all-powerful).

(*These three interpretations – the double underlined wording – will be addressed in more detail later.*) Despite such interpretations by some people, other people, who believe in God, believe that evolution is inconsistent with God and with the Bible. Who is right? And what evidence is there to support or counter either position? Answering these questions by using the topic question – "Did God create man through evolution?", is the explicit objective of this essay. To accomplish this objective, this essay is organized in three parts. Part-1 presents some comments, which serves as "a quick response" to the three interpretations previously mentioned. Part-2 presents some comments, which serves as "a detailed response" to the topic question. Part-3 presents some concluding comments.

Part-1: **A quick response**

To examine and respond to the three interpretations previously mentioned, this quick response is organized in three sections. Section-1 presents a discussion of "a 'time-gap' between Genesis 1:1 and Genesis 1:2". Section-2 presents a discussion of the wording – "from the dust of the ground" in Genesis 2:7. Section-3 presents a discussion of the belief that "God is all-powerful".

Section-1: **A time-gap between Genesis 1:1 and Genesis 1:2**

A discussion of this time-gap must include "a presentation of the wording of Genesis 1:1 and Genesis 1:2", "some background about the 'time-gap'", and "some current scientific data, which refutes the 'time-gap'". Thus, Section-1 is organized in three segments. *Segment-1* presents Genesis 1:1 and Genesis 1:2. *Segment-2* presents some background about the 'time-gap'".

Segment-3 presents some current scientific data, which refutes the "time-gap". *Segment-4* presents some concluding comments.

Segment-1: **Genesis 1:1 and Genesis 1:2**

Genesis 1:1 and Genesis 1:2 read, as follows:

> (Genesis 1:1 NIV) In the beginning God created the heavens and the earth.
>
> (Genesis 1:2 NIV) Now the earth was formless and empty, darkness was over the surface of the deep, and the Spirit of God was hovering over the waters.

Segment-2: **Some background for the "time-gap"**

This discussion of the "time-gap", is begun by noting that over the centuries men have noticed the condition of the surface of the earth. These conditions included noticing the "stratification (*the layers of various types of rock and of other materials [minerals, etc.]*)", in the surface of the earth. Then men further noticed that there were fossils in some of those layers. Based on these two conditions, men reasoned that the "stratification" accumulated vertically and such vertical accumulations would require long time-periods. Then men also reasoned that the organisms, which had died and been fossilized in the various layers, would have required long time-periods to evolve. Thus, the concept that "it took millions of years to get the surface of the earth to appear as it does", slowly became the established geological concept of the eighteenth-century. During this same period, based on the Bible, most Christians held to the belief that this earth was only around five-thousand-years-old. Because of the conflict between the long time-periods required for the geological concept and the short time-period implied by the Bible, some people felt that there needed to be some type of reconciliation between the two.

> "Thus, in 1804, a young Presbyterian pastor named Thomas Chalmers began to preach that Christians should accept the concept of millions of years. Then later in 1814, Pastor Chalmers proposed that the millions of years could fit between Genesis 1:1 and Genesis 1:2. This proposal became known, as the 'Gap Theory'."[75]

Segment-3: **Some current scientific data, which refutes a time-gap**

Current scientific data, which refutes a "time-gap", involves various scientific issues, generally, and at least, one geological event, specifically. Generally, science is showing that the "stratification" of the surface of the earth did not happen vertically, but horizontally. Science has shown that any material collected in moving water is sorted by that water, based on the size and the weight of the material, as the water moves. This results in an appearance of "stratification". Specifically, this was confirmed by one of the most important geological events of our time, the eruption of Mount Saint Helens, on May 18, 1980. After the eruption of Mount Saint Helens, some of its glacial ice melted creating a huge body of water, at a fairly high elevation.

Eventually, this water broke through the material that restrained it. As this large volume of water started to flow, the flowing water collected so much material and moved with such force that it created a miniature "Grand Canyon", as it filled in a valley, among other happenings. This miniature "Grand Canyon" is one-fortieth the size of the actual "Grand Canyon". And even though, this miniature "Grand Canyon" was formed in hours, not millions of years, it still displays features (*layers, canyon walls, etc.*) like the actual "Grand Canyon". Thus, science and the eruption of Mount Saint Helens refute the need for long periods to get the surface of the earth to look like it does. This is supported by an excellent video about the Mount Saint Helens eruption. This video is titled: "Mount St. Helens" and may still be available from the Institute for Creation Research; PO Box 2667; El Cajon, CA 92021.

Segment-4: **Some concluding comments about the "time-gap"**

Besides the scientific evidence against a "time-gap", logically, it would seem that those who believe in a "time-gap" between Genesis 1:1 and Genesis 1:2, have a major inconsistency, between "what they are proposing" and "the wording in Genesis 1:2 indicating that 'Now the earth was formless and empty'". The KJV uses the phrase: "without form and void". QuickVerse (*a bible software package*) indicates that the Hebrew word for "form" is "tohuw" and means:

> 8414. tohuw, to'-hoo; from an unused root mean. to lie waste; a desolation (of surface), i.e. desert; fig. a worthless thing; adv. in vain:--confusion, empty place, without form, nothing, (thing of) nought, vain, vanity, waste, wilderness.

The Hebrew word for "void" is "bohuw" and means:

> 922. bohuw, bo-hoo; from an unused root (mean. to be empty); a vacuity, i.e. (superficially) an undistinguishable ruin:--emptiness, void.

Thus, those who believe in a "time-gap" can put an infinite amount of time between Genesis 1:1 and Genesis 1:2, but at the end of the "time-gap", nothing can be formed or exist. Otherwise, the earth would not be "formless and empty" per Genesis 1:2 in the NIV or "without form and void" per Genesis 1:2 in the KJV. Remember those who believe in a "time-gap" need two things: *First*, they need the "stratification" of the surface of the earth. *Second*, they need the evolution of some organisms, so that their fossils can be formed and then trapped in the various layers. But once more, "stratification" seems inconsistent with "formless" and "fossils" are definitely not consistent with "empty". Once more, the "empty" or "void" would seem to require that any life that might have existed at the beginning of or during the "time-gap", cease to exist at the end of the "time-gap". This creates the question – "Where did all the life come from after the "time-gap". Furthermore, those who believe in a "time-gap" have two additional problems: *First*, there was no light until Genesis 1:3 (*how could organisms grow without light?*) and *second*, there was no dry ground until Genesis 1:9 (*how could the surface of the earth become stratified under water?*).

Section-2: **The wording – "From the dust of the ground" in Genesis 2:7**

In the NIV, Genesis 2:7 reads:

> the LORD God formed the man from the dust of the ground and breathed into his nostrils the breath of life, and the man became a living being.

Some people may interpret the wording – "from the dust of the ground", to mean that God used evolution to create Adam. However, there are, at least, two problems with such an interpretation. *First*, the wording of Genesis 2:7 implies that Adam was formed without life and then God breathed into his nostrils the breath of life, whereas an evolutionary process would require life in Adam, from the start (*during the formation process*). More precisely, evolution would require life in the single cell that evolved into Adam. *Second*, even if someone took the phrase – "from the dust of the ground", to mean "evolution", how is Genesis 2:22 to be interpreted? In the NIV, Genesis 2:22 reads:

> Then the LORD God made a woman from the rib he had taken out of the man, and he brought her to the man.

There is no valid interpretation of Genesis 2:22 that can be twisted to say, "Evolution was used in the creation of Eve." Thus, Genesis 2:7 does not support the position that God used evolution to create man.

> *Comment:* In closing Section-2, "*an interesting aside*" is the fact that Genesis 2:19 references "beasts of the field" and "birds of the air", being created out of the ground by God. In the NIV, Genesis 2:19 reads:
>
> > Now the LORD God had formed out of the ground all the beasts of the field and all the birds of the air. He brought them to the man to see what he would name them; and whatever the man called each living creature, that was its name.
>
> But this verse still does not mean that "God created any creature through evolution". More specifically, this verse does not say, "God created a single celled organism, which mutated into all the beasts of the field and all the birds of the air." It says, "God had formed out of the ground all the beasts of the field and all the birds of the air." Besides note that Genesis 2:19 indicates God formed all the beasts of the fields and all the birds of the air and then brought them to Adam to be named. If "evolution" was used, then Adam must have lived a long time – millions of years – before he was put out of the garden and lived another nine hundred and thirty years. Another verse, which adds credibility against "God using 'evolution'", is Leviticus 19:19. In the NIV, this verse read, as follows:
>
> > (Leviticus 19:19 NIV) "'Keep my decrees. "'Do not mate different kinds of animals. "'Do not plant your field with two kinds of seed. "'Do not wear

clothing woven of two kinds of material.

(*More comments on Leviticus 19:19 are presented later in this essay as part of "Part-2: A detailed response/Section-3: A general view".*)

Section-3: **God is all-powerful**

"God is all-powerful", is a conclusion that many people reach, after reading the Bible. In itself, this interpretation is correct. However, some people use this interpretation to push God into things that He may not have done or cannot do. For instance, some people reason that:

- "God is all-powerful.
- If God is all-powerful, then 'God can do anything'.
- Anything includes creating man through an evolutionary process."

However, note. "God can do anything" is an improper statement, according to the late Dr. Walter Martin, founder of the Christian Research Institute (CRI). Dr. Martin said, "The more precise statement is that 'God can do anything that is consistent with His revealed nature.'[76] Thus, there are 'things that God cannot do'. However, the 'things that God cannot do', are those things, which are inconsistent with His revealed nature." One of several Bible verses that support Dr. Martin's statements is Titus 1:2. Four different translations of this verse read, as follows:

> (Titus 1:2 KJV) In hope of eternal life, which God, that cannot lie, promised before the world began;
>
> (Titus 1:2 NIV) a faith and knowledge resting on the hope of eternal life, which God, who does not lie, promised before the beginning of time,
>
> (Titus 1:2 NRSV) in the hope of eternal life that God, who never lies, promised before the ages began–
>
> (Titus 1:2 NASB) in the hope of eternal life, which God, who cannot lie, promised long ages ago,

Thus, the fact that "God is all-powerful" does not automatically mean that "He can do anything." This forces us to ask, "Is the evolutionary process consistent with God's revealed nature?" And the answer has to be "no", because God is outside of time. He knows everything "that has happened", "that is happening", and "that will happen." Thus, God's knowledge is inconsistent with the evolutionary process, because, by definition, "Evolution is a process within time that revolves around random events with random results". Concerning God's knowledge, God knew that He wanted to create Adam in His (God's) image. Thus, God formed Adam from the dust of the ground, then God breathed the "Breath of Life" into Adam's nostrils and Adam became a living being. Once more, a literal interpretation of the verses about Adam's creation indicates that Adam's body was complete, when God breathed the "Breath of Life" into him. The use of the word – "nostrils", confirms this fact. Thus, the creation of Adam could not have involved evolution. Therefore, evolution cannot be consistent with God's revealed nature, despite the fact that "God is all-powerful."

Part-2: **A detailed response**

This detailed response to the topic question is organized in three sections. Section-1 presents "a literal view", which consists of a discussion of the definitions of "evolution" and "creationism" and of a discussion of whether those definitions allow both to be true simultaneously. Section-2 presents "a biblical view", which consists of an examination of some Bible verses to see whether any are consistent with the evolutionary process. Section-3 presents "a general view", which consists of a discussion of a variety of issues that are inconsistent with the belief that God created man through an evolutionary process.

Section-1: **A literal view**

Under a literal view, we will "define 'evolution' (*biological evolution*)", "define the primary component of the 'evolutionary process' and some related words", "define 'creationism'", and "discuss the question – 'Can evolution and creationism be true simultaneously?'" To accomplish these tasks, Section-1 is organized in five segments. *Segment-1* presents definitions of "evolution". *Segment-2* presents a definition of the primary components of "evolution". *Segment-3* presents definitions of other words important to a discussion of "evolution". *Segment-4* presents definitions of "creationism". *Segment-5* presents a discussion of the question: "Can 'evolution' and 'creationism' be true simultaneously?"

Segment-1: **Definitions of "evolution"**

Definitions of "evolution" are presented from several sources, as an informal definition and a formal definition. The informal definition is a composite of many definitions from web documents and other sources. Thus, a paraphrased-informal definition reads, as follows:

> "Evolution" is "the label placed on a complex process that stresses the impact of environmental changes on pools of related organisms." Each environmental change provided an opportunity for some members of each pool to flourish more than others. The members of each pool that flourished did so, because they possessed traits or characteristics that were more compatible with new environmental conditions. Conversely, those members of each pool, who did not possess traits or characteristics that were compatible with new environmental

conditions diminished. Thus, their traits or characteristics may disappear from the pool. "A pool of related organisms" means "the organisms are of the same species." For sexual organisms, the word – "species", is defined as "a group of organisms that can interbreed (*can mate*), to produce viable offspring". Furthermore, to be a viable offspring, the offspring also must be capable of producing offspring. For asexual organisms, the word – "species", is defined as "a group of organisms that have 'a common origin' or 'many identifiable characteristics' that are similar".

<u>Comment:</u> A better sense of the meaning of "species" for asexual organisms is provided, by author James Trefil in his book: "<u>1001 THINGS EVERYONE SHOULD KNOW ABOUT SCIENCE</u>" published by Doubleday. The ninety-first thing discussed is entitled: "Species of single-celled organisms are not defined in terms of reproduction." In this discussion, author James Trefil says, "In practice, species of single-celled organisms are differentiated from each other by their biological niche, by the way they generate energy, and by the way the cell is put together."

<u>Comment:</u> The meanings of the phrases – "sexual organisms" and "asexual organisms", are implied from the usage of these phrases in the definition of "evolution". But explicitly, the phrase – "sexual organisms", is "a reference to those organisms that reproduce, by interacting with another organism". Therefore, the phrase – "asexual organisms", is "a reference to those organisms that reproduce without interacting with another organism". Once more, as previously mentioned with regards to the statements by author James Trefil, his focus was defining "species" within "asexual organisms", not defining "asexual" versus "sexual" organisms, which <u>IS AN ISSUE</u> of reproduction.

The source of the formal definition of "evolution" is "an article by E. Peter Volpe"[77] in the "<u>2003 Grolier Multimedia Encyclopedia</u>". With some fonts changed to italicized fonts by me for emphasis, a "<u>shortened and modified version of this article</u>" reads:

"Evolution" is the process, by which all living things have *developed from primitive organisms through changes occurring over billions of years, a progression that includes the most advanced animals and plants. Changes occur in living organisms that serve to increase their adaptability, or potential for survival and reproduction, in the face of changing environments. Evolution apparently has no built-in direction or foreordained purpose.* A given kind of organism may evolve only when it occurs in a variety of forms differing in hereditary characteristics, or traits, that are passed from parent to offspring. Purely by chance, some varieties prove to be ill adapted to their current environment and thus disappear, whereas others prove to be adaptive, and their numbers increase. *The elimination of the unfit, or the "<u>survival of the fittest</u>" is known as "NATURAL SELECTION",* *because it is the result of selective pressure. Basically, evolution takes place only when natural selection operates on a population of organisms containing diverse inheritable forms.*

<u>Segment-2</u>: **Definition of the primary components of "evolution"**

The definition of the primary components of "evolution", flows from the informal definition of "evolution", presented in <u>Segment-1</u>. For this essay, this definition reads, as follows:

> "The primary components of 'evolution'" are "'*<u>pools of related organisms, with varying traits and characteristics</u>'. Within a pool, some organisms have traits and characteristics, which are favored by environmental changes over the traits and characteristics of other organisms in the same pool. The favored traits and characteristics occurred by chance, without design or purpose. Nevertheless, those organisms with the favored traits and characteristics, generally, flourish, while those without diminish.*"

<u>Segment-3</u>: **Definitions of other words important to a discussion of "evolution"**

Definitions of other words important to a discussion of "evolution", are necessary, because evolutionists use these to imply how life on this planet developed. That is, evolutionists use such definitions to imply how non-life on this planet evolved into life. Or better, evolutionists use such definitions to imply:

- How non-life evolved into a simple single-celled organism.
- How simple single celled organisms evolved into complex multiple celled organisms, including humans.
- Which species evolved into which other species.

The statement – "Which species evolved into which other species", is reflected in what evolutionists call: the "evolutionary-tree", the "evolutionary-tree of life", <u>and/or</u> the "phylogenetic tree". This is a treelike diagram (*a family-tree diagram*). See the web documents at the following web addresses:

- ✓ www.answers.com/topic/evolutionary-tree.
- ✓ www.phy.auckland.ac.nz/staff/prw/biocomplexity/evolutionary_tree.htm.
- ✓ en.wikipedia.org/wiki/Phylogenetic_tree.

The trunk, branches, and limbs of the tree imply "a sequential flow of one species evolving (*mutating*) into another species" and/or "a sequence of simple organisms evolving into complex organisms". Thus, to complete our definition of "evolution", or more precisely, the "evolutionary process", we must define "mutation", "micromutation", and "macromutation". And then both "micromutation" and "macromutation", must be tied to the definition of "evolution". The task of tying "micromutation" and "macromutation" to the definition of "evolution", results in the definition of "microevolution' and "macroevolution".

An informal-paraphrased definition of "mutation" reads:

> A "mutation" is "physical changes in an organism with an effect on the traits and characteristics of that organism, as expressed by changes in the genetic information of that organism, when compared with its parent organism or organism(s)."

"Micromutation" and "macromutation" will be defined, based on some web documents and several dictionaries. Thus, paraphrased definitions read, as follows:

- A "micromutation" is "a mutation with a small effect on the traits and characteristics of an organism or pool of organisms, as expressed by small changes in the genetic information of the organism(s)."

- A "macromutation" is "a mutation with a large effect on the traits and characteristics of an organism or pool of organisms, as expressed by large changes in the genetic information of the organism(s)."

Based on the definitions of "micromutation" and "macromutation", evolutionists and non-evolutionists say there are two types of evolution. These are, as follows:

- One type is the accumulation of micromutations "over any period", for any pool of related organisms. This type is called: "microevolution". More precisely,

  > "microevolution" consists of "changes within a species".

- Evolutionists imply that the other type results from the occurrence of macromutations, at any moment, for any pool of organisms. This type is called: "macroevolution". More precisely,

  > "macroevolution" consists of "changes from one species into another species".

Some evolutionists try to slip in a second definition of "macroevolution", by saying, that the phrase – "over any period" for "microevolution", should not include "very long periods". This would allow evolutionists to say that the accumulation of "micromutations" "over very long periods", also results in "macroevolution". However, by definition, for either definition of "macroevolution" to be true, a new species would have to exist, at the end of the process. But there is no concrete proof for "macroevolution", under either definition, while there is proof for "microevolution". "Microevolution" is reflected in "micromutations", between parents and their offsprings. "Micromutations" are "changes in skin color, eye color, shape of eyes, etc."; whereas, finding "macromutations" to prove "macroevolution" has always been the problem. Thus, unless otherwise stated, all references to "mutation" in this book mean "macromutation". And unless otherwise stated, all references to "evolution" in this book mean "macroevolution".

> Comment: Note that none of the definitions of "evolution" explicitly address the origin of the organisms in the related pools of organisms. Evolution simply addresses the environmental impact on the pools, once these pools have developed. Therefore, with respect to the creation of life, the underlying assumption of evolution has to be:
>
> > "In the beginning, there was some (*a pool of*) nonliving matter, possibly, in the primordial soup (*the primordial seas*) that supposedly covered portions of the earth. Environmental changes caused "some nonliving matter to become living matter", then this living matter eventually developed into single-celled organisms. In time, a pool of single-celled organisms developed. More environmental changes caused some single-celled organisms to mutate into multiple-celled organisms. Then pools of these multiple-celled organisms developed. The environmental changes and mutations continued until more complex multiple-celled organisms, including man, had developed. All of the mutations occurred by chance (*randomly*) without a purpose or a design."
>
> Comment: Under evolution, if the nonliving matter did not mutate into living matter, then some type of living matter had to always exist. Such an eternal existence would raise all kind of questions, especially since living matter dies. Even nonliving matter mutating into living matter, raises questions, but no further questions based on either consideration will be explicitly addressed in this essay.

Segment-4: **Definitions of "Creationism"**

Definitions of "creationism" are presented from several sources, as an informal definition and two formal definitions. The informal definition reads:

> "Creationism" is "the label placed on the biblical account of how God created this universe, including the life it contains." This biblical account indicates that God created this world and all the life it contains in stages. Specifically, with respect to man, the

indication is that God said, "Let us make man in Our (*God, the Father, God, the Son, and God, the Holy Spirit*) image." It continues with God forming Adam from the dust of the earth, and then with God breathing into Adam's nostrils, and Adam becoming a living being. Later, the biblical account indicates that God caused Adam to sleep. While Adam slept, God took one of Adam's ribs, closed it up, put flesh on it, and thus, God created Eve. God created Adam and Eve with the capacity to reproduce their own kind. Therefore, all subsequent human life through the generations came from Adam and Eve.

Our first formal definition of "creationism", is from an unsigned "article"[78] appearing in the "2003 Grolier Multimedia Encyclopedia". Here, a shortened version of this definition reads:

"Creationism" is the name popularly given to the view of fundamentalist Christians that the biblical account of the origin of LIFE is literally true and that the theory of evolution, first elaborated by Charles DARWIN and basic to modern biology, must therefore be false.

Comment: The above phrase – "the theory of evolution, first elaborated by Charles DARWIN and 'basic to modern biology'", is very disturbing, because it shows the bias of the individual, who composed this definition of creationism. Modern biology does not support evolution in anyway. Currently, there is no scientific data that explicitly indicates the validity of the "evolutionary process".

Our second formal definition of "Creationism" is actually a paraphrased-consensus definition. It reads, as follows:

"Creationism" is "the religious belief in especially, Judaism, Christianity, and Islam, that the creation story given in the Book of Genesis is true".

Segment-5: **Can "evolution" and "creationism" be true simultaneously?**

This question is easily answered, by comparing the previously presented definitions of "evolution" and of "creationism" and then noting that these two concepts cannot be true simultaneously. Major components that make up the definitions of the two concepts are contradictory. These contradictory components are "'the occurrence of mutations by chance', 'a lack of design', and 'a lack of purpose under evolution'" versus "purposeful design under creationism". Thus, the point is:

"If God created a single-celled organism, and then caused it (*or allowed it*) to mutate into Adam over time, Adam was the result God wanted. Clearly, this is indicated by the 'let us make man in Our image' statement of God. There was no chance, no randomness. There was purposeful design. Thus, if God used an evolutionary process to create Adam, the process could not be called 'evolution'. The process would require a different name to convey the fact, that God acted in a PURPOSEFUL manner in creating Adam, the 'intended result'. Therefore, literally, God did not create man through 'evolution'."

Section-2: **A biblical view**

Under a biblical view, we will examine some Bible verses referenced under "Section-1: A literal view", and some other selected verses. All of these verses are presented, as they appear in the NIV. The purpose of these examinations is to see if any of these verses or set of verses are consistent with the evolutionary process. (*Note. The underlining was added by this author to stress some of the text of a given verse.*) This examination is begun with Genesis 1:25-30, Genesis 2:7-8, and Genesis 2:21-23. In the NIV, these verses read, as follows:

Genesis 1:[25]God made the wild animals according to their kinds, the livestock according to their kinds, and all the creatures that move along the ground according to their kinds. And God saw that it was good. [26]Then God said, "Let us make man in our image, in our likeness, and let them rule over the fish of the sea and the birds of the air, over the livestock, over all the earth, and over all the creatures that move along the ground." [27]So God created man in his own image, in the image of God he created him; male and female he created them. [28]God blessed them and said to them, "Be fruitful and increase in number; fill the earth and subdue it. Rule over the fish of the sea and the birds of the air and over every living creature that moves on the ground." [29]Then God said, "I give you every seed-bearing plant on the face of the whole earth and every tree that has fruit with seed in it. They will be yours for food. [30]And to all the beasts of the earth and all the birds of the air and all the creatures that move on the ground – everything that has the breath of life in it – I give every green plant for food." And it was so.

Genesis 2:[7]the LORD God formed the man from the dust of the ground and breathed into his nostrils the breath of life, and the man became a living being. [8]Now the LORD God had planted a garden in the east, in Eden; and there he put the man he had formed.

Genesis 2:[21]So the LORD God caused the man to fall into a deep sleep; and while he was sleeping, he took one of the man's ribs and closed up the place with flesh. [22]Then the LORD God made a woman from the rib he had taken out of the man, and he brought her to the man. [23]The man said, "This is now bone of my bones and flesh of my flesh; she shall be called 'woman', for she was taken out of man."

Collectively, these verses and the rest of the verses from the first two chapters of Genesis show that God did create in stages – in six days. However, creating in stages is not necessarily consistent with evolution. In fact, there is an obvious inconsistency, between the implied stages of "evolution" and the recorded days (*stages*) of "creationism". Thus, when the days recorded in Genesis are noted, there is Genesis 1:1-13, which suggest that the first life forms on Earth were grasses, herbs, and fruit trees. These life forms were created on the third day of creation. In the NIV, these verses read, as follows:

> Genesis 1:1In the beginning God created the heavens and the earth. 2Now the earth was
> formless and empty, darkness was over the surface of the deep, and the Spirit of God was
> hovering over the waters. 3And God said, "Let there be light," and there was light. 4God
> saw that the light was good, and he separated the light from the darkness. 5God called the
> light "day," and the darkness he called "night." And there was evening, and there was
> morning – **the first day**. 6And God said, "Let there be an expanse between the waters
> to separate water from water." 7So God made the expanse and separated the water under
> the expanse from the water above it. And it was so. 8God called the expanse "sky." And
> there was evening, and there was morning – **the second day**. 9And God said, "Let the
> water under the sky be gathered to one place, and let dry ground appear." And it was so.
> 10God called the dry ground "land," and the gathered waters he called "seas." And God saw
> that it was good. 11Then God said, "Let the land produce vegetation: seed-bearing plants
> and trees on the land that bear fruit with seed in it, according to their various kinds." And
> it was so. 12The land produced vegetation: plants bearing seed according to their kinds
> and trees bearing fruit with seed in it according to their kinds. And God saw that it was
> good. 13And there was evening, and there was morning – **the third day**.

Then Genesis 1:20-23 suggest that sea creatures and birds were created next on the fifth day of creation. In the NIV, these verses read, as follows:

> Genesis 1:20And God said, "Let the water teem with living creatures, and let birds fly
> above the earth across the expanse of the sky." 21So God created the great creatures of
> the sea and every living and moving thing with which the water teems, according to their
> kinds, and every winged bird according to its kind. And God saw that it was good. 22God
> blessed them and said, "Be fruitful and increase in number and fill the water in the seas,
> and let the birds increase on the earth." 23And there was evening, and there was morning
> – **the fifth day**.

The appearance of birds and the sea creatures on the fifth day, without any mention of land animals, is inconsistent with the stages implied, by evolutionists (*however, more on that in a moment*). For now, let's review the verses, which recorded the creation of land animals on the sixth day. These verses are Genesis 1:24-31. In the NIV, these verses read, as follows:

> Genesis 1:24And God said, "Let the land produce living creatures according to their kinds:
> livestock, creatures that move along the ground, and wild animals, each according to its
> kind." And it was so. 25God made the wild animals according to their kinds, the livestock
> according to their kinds, and all the creatures that move along the ground according to
> their kinds. And God saw that it was good. 26Then God said, "Let us make man in our
> image, in our likeness, and let them rule over the fish of the sea and the birds of the air,
> over the livestock, over all the earth, and over all the creatures that move along the

ground." [27]So God created man in his own image, in the image of God he created him; male and female he created them. [28]God blessed them and said to them, "Be fruitful and increase in number; fill the earth and subdue it. Rule over the fish of the sea and the birds of the air and over every living creature that moves on the ground." [29]Then God said, "I give you every seed-bearing plant on the face of the whole earth and every tree that has fruit with seed in it. They will be yours for food. [30]And to all the beasts of the earth and all the birds of the air and all the creatures that move on the ground - everything that has the breath of life in it - I give every green plant for food." And it was so. [31]God saw all that he had made, and it was very good. And there was evening, and there was morning - **the sixth day**.

The appearance of birds before land creatures is definitely inconsistent with evolution. Supporters of evolution have always proposed that life developed on this planet in three stages. In the first stage, life began and developed in the primordial soup (*primordial seas*). In the second stage, some creatures crawled out of the seas to evolve on land. In the third stage, some land creatures evolved (*mutated*) into birds, while other creatures evolved (*mutated*) into more advanced land creatures including man. However, as we have already noted, this evolutionary stages (*sequence*) - from the sea to land to air - is inconsistent with the biblical days (*sequence*) of God creating the creatures, which live in water, and the birds of the air, on one day, and then creating land creatures on the next day.

Now, let us address several of the previously listed verses individually:

- Genesis 1:25

> (Genesis 1:25 NIV) God made the wild animals according to their kinds, the livestock according to their kinds, and all the creatures that move along the ground according to their kinds. And God saw that it was good.

is clearly inconsistent with evolution. This verse suggests that creatures only produce after their own kind. Evolution supports the notion of mutations into new species, a different kind.

- Genesis 1:26

> (Genesis 1:26 NIV) Then God said, "Let us make man in our image, in our likeness, and let them rule over the fish of the sea and the birds of the air, over the livestock, over all the earth, and over all the creatures that move along the ground."

is inconsistent with evolution. This verse suggests that God created with a purpose in mind. Evolution is defined as creation by chance and without a purpose.

- Genesis 1:27

> (Genesis 1:27 NIV) So God created man in his own image, in the image of God he created him; male and female he created them.

is inconsistent with evolution. It indicates that God created both male and female in His own image. This is purposeful creation, as opposed to the chance creation under evolution.

> Comment: Males and females have many physiological and psychological similarities. But there are some obvious physiological and psychological differences. For example, this author has heard of research studies that indicate psychologically women are more emotionally attached to events and people, whereas men are more logically attached. Medical research has shown that the female and male brains are wired differently. Noting all of the known differences, between men and women means the image being referenced in Genesis 1:27 is something more than just a physiological or psychological reference. It is possible that this image is a reference to the fact that man (*or mankind, which includes both males and females*) has a spirit, a soul, and a body.

> Comment: In our physical world, an image is trapped in the media used to display it – used to reflect the original. For example, when our image is reflected in a mirror or a stream, that image is trapped in the mirror or in the stream – that image cannot come out of the mirror or stream and stand next to us. God is outside time. He has used the media of space and time, in which to reflect His image, us. Thus, we are the ones trapped in space and time.

- Genesis 2:8

> (Genesis 2:8 NIV) Now the LORD God had planted a garden in the east, in Eden; and there he put the man he had formed.

is inconsistent with evolution. This verse suggests that God formed Adam somewhere other than in the Garden of Eden, then God placed Adam in the garden to care for it. Thus, Adam's environment (*the Garden of Eden*), was created and designed by God, not by chance under evolution.

- Genesis 2:21-23

> Genesis 2:21So the LORD God caused the man to fall into a deep sleep; and while he was sleeping, he took one of the man's ribs and closed up the place with flesh.
> 22Then the LORD God made a woman from the rib he had taken out of the man,

> and he brought her to the man. [23]The man said, "This is now bone of my bones and flesh of my flesh; she shall be called 'woman', for she was taken out of man." (NIV)

are also inconsistent with evolution. For, even if God did create Adam, by an evolutionary process, Genesis 2:21-23 clearly states that "God created Eve from one of Adam's rib." Thus, there is no way anyone could interpret that an evolutionary process was involved in the creation of Eve.

The verses listed here under the "biblical view" were determined to be those most relevant to this discussion. None of these verses are explicitly consistent with an evolutionary process. In fact, most are explicitly inconsistent with an evolutionary process. Thus, biblically, God did not create man through evolution.

Section-3: **A general view**

Under a general view, we will discuss seven issues that are inconsistent with God creating man through an evolutionary process. These issues are, as follows:

- *Issue-1*: Once more, "man defined the concept of 'evolution', as the process, which created life, including man, by chance. Under man's definition of 'evolution', God could not have used evolution to create man, because of the 'chance aspect'. God defined the concept of 'creationism', as His process of creating man, in His image, and in this environment. God had His process recorded in the Bible. Thus, if you believe in the biblical account of creation, then you cannot believe in evolution. If you believe in evolution, then you cannot believe in the biblical account of creation. 'Evolution' and 'creationism (*as recorded in the Bible*)' are mutually exclusive."

- *Issue-2*: All of us are influenced to some extent, by what we see and hear. This is understandable. Most of us do not have the time and/or the talent to do our own in-depth research on every issue and every subject. Thus, lacking time and/or talent for some issues and subjects, we have to take a position, based on what others say. This raises questions like: "Whom do we believe?" and "Why?" After we have chosen whom, we will believe, we still must ask questions like: "Does the person advance a given position for their personal gain?", "Does any evidence support her or his position?", and "Is there any evidence, which supports the opposite position?" Although there may not always be sufficient time or information to address all these questions, we must do our best. Otherwise, we will be led down a dead-end street, which is actually what is happening to those who believe in evolution, because currently there is no scientific data that explicitly validates the "evolutionary process".

  Comment: You will never agree with anyone else on everything. On the flip side, you will never disagree with anyone else on everything.

Issue-3: A friend read a book in which an author proposed the theory that God used both "creationism" and "evolution" to create this universe. Or more precisely, that the author of that book proposed that God filled in the gaps left by the evolutionary process. Creation theories, which combine "creation by God" and "creation through evolution", must reconcile their theory with the biblical implication that there were no deaths before Adam and Eve sinned. The biblical implication comes out of Genesis 3:17-23. In the NIV, these verses read:

> Genesis 3:[17]To Adam he said, "Because you listened to your wife and ate from the tree about which I commanded you, 'You must not eat of it,'" Cursed is the ground because of you; through painful toil you will eat of it all the days of your life. [18]It will produce thorns and thistles for you, and you will eat the plants of the field. **[19]**By the sweat of your brow you will eat your food until you return to the ground, since from it you were taken; for dust you are and to dust you will return." [20]Adam named his wife Eve, because she would become the mother of all the living. **[21]**The LORD God made garments of skin for Adam and his wife and clothed them. [22]And the LORD God said, "The man has now become like one of us, knowing good and evil. He must not be allowed to reach out his hand and take also from the tree of life and eat, and live forever." **[23]**So the LORD God banished him from the Garden of Eden to work the ground from which he had been taken.

Genesis 3:19 appears to be God telling Adam that he is going to die, "physically". More precisely, Genesis 3:19 is a reference to "Adam's physical death". Genesis 3:23 is a reference to "Adam's spiritual death". Adam dies "spiritually", because he and Eve are being banished from the garden, where they existed under God's grace. More specifically, "spiritual death" meant, Adam and Eve went from existing in the garden under God's grace to existing in the world under God's judgment. In the world, Adam's physical death was some nine hundred years in his future. However, many scholars say that Genesis 3:21 is where the first death(s) took place. That is, God had to shed innocent blood to provide the garments of skin to clothe Adam and Eve. If true, it would be hard to believe any evolutionary process occurred before this. The reason is that "The evolutionary process requires the death of the 'unfit (*those not suited to current environmental conditions*)', because the evolutionary process is the survival of the fittest." Other verses, which do not lend credibility to the occurrence of an evolutionary process before Adam and Eve sinned, are Genesis 1:1, Genesis 1:2, and Genesis 1:11. These verses read:

> (Genesis 1:1 NIV) In the beginning God created the heavens and the earth.

> (Genesis 1:2 NIV) Now the earth was formless and empty, darkness was over the surface of the deep, and the Spirit of God was hovering over the waters.

> (Genesis 1:11 NIV) Then God said, "Let the land produce vegetation: seed-bearing plants and trees on the land that bear fruit with seed in it, according to their various kinds." And it was so.

Genesis 1:1 is clearly saying that God created the heavens and the earth and this may have started time. Genesis 1:2 is saying that there was not much to the earth, at this point in time. After some other things were done by God, Genesis 1:11 is saying that the first life was vegetation. And this vegetation reproduced "according to their various kinds". Clearly, any reproduction "*according to their various kinds*" is not the process of one species mutating into another species. That is, vegetation reproducing "according to their various kinds" is "not evolution."

- *Issue-4*: As previously referenced, God told the Jews not to mate different kinds of animals. See Leviticus 19:19, which reads:

> (Leviticus 19:19 NIV) Keep my decrees. Do not mate different kinds of animals. Do not plant your field with two kinds of seed. Do not wear clothing woven of two kinds of material.

This instruction from God, "not to mate different kinds of animals" is inconsistent with the way the "evolutionary process" is supposed to operate. For theoretically, under an "evolutionary process", there would be no limit to the animal-combinations (*the animal variations*) that would have to exist for whatever length of time, to allow for the survival of the fittest new species – to allow for the evolution of the fittest new species. Thus, from this instruction, one could assume that God is against the "evolutionary process".

- *Issue-5*: To dispute "creationism", some people try to say that there are inconsistencies, between "Genesis chapter 1" and "Genesis chapter 2". Yes! There are differences, between "Genesis chapter 1" and "Genesis chapter 2". But Christian scholars say that "Genesis chapter 1" provides an outline and the order of creation, whereas "Genesis chapter 2" gives the details, without regards to the order. Thus, the differences are not inconsistencies. Actually, the differences, between "Genesis chapter 1" and "Genesis chapter 2" may involve one more level than previously stated and some overlap. That is, it may be that:

Genesis 1:1	is the overview of who did the creating and what was created.
Genesis 1:2-2:3	is the outline and order of creation.
Genesis 2:4-25	is a detailed account of the creation, without regards to order.

- *Issue-6*: A friend, who read an early draft of this essay, submitted two questions to this author. The *first question* was: "Do you consider the four major ethnic groups of humans, mutations?" The *second question* was: "If a couple was unable to conceive a child, would you say that this particular man and woman were from different species?"

(Response to the *first question*: My response was to mention an excellent book - "One Blood" and a companion video of the same name. The book - "One Blood", was written by Ken Ham, Carl Wieland, and Don Batten and published by the Answers In Genesis Ministry. The video - "One Blood", is Mr. Ham's presentation of the material from the book. In both the book and the video, these gentlemen define four major ethnic groups: the Caucasoid (European or "white"), the Mongoloid (*which includes the Chinese and the American Indians*), the Negroid (black Africans), and the Australoid (the Australian Aborigines). In addition, these gentlemen stated that these ethnic groups are not based strictly on skin color, because some group like the Caucasoid includes individuals, whose skin color ranges from pale to light brown. They further proposed that all the ethnic groups originated from Adam and Eve. Thus, the four ethnic groups represent "micromutations" from Adam and Eve, because by definition any variations, between the parent and the child are "micromutations".

Response to the *second question*: My response was to say that the fact a couple is unable to conceive a child does not mean the woman and man are from different species. This author is in firm agreement with Mr. Ken Ham, who says that there is only one race of humans. More precisely, all members of the human race are members of the same species. Besides, every sexual intercourse does not result in "conception". "Conception" is a very delicate and complicated process.)

- *Issue-7*: Several years ago, a Christian organization referenced the fields of molecular biology and biochemistry with comments, which are paraphrased, as follows:

> "The new fields of study - Molecular Biology and Biochemistry - are yielding tremendous evidence in support of the design of life at the molecular level. Much of the molecular basis of life exhibits irreducibly complex design, which means the extremely complicated mechanisms of life could not have evolved by chance. The need for simultaneous mechanisms in a given organism supports a designer."

The paraphrased comments above came out just as several books on molecular biology and biochemistry were starting to become known among those who believe in "creationism". One such book on biochemistry was published in 1996 by Michael Behe, Associate Professor of Biochemistry at Lehigh University. Dr. Behe's book is titled: "Darwin's Black Box: The Biochemical Challenge to Evolution".

> "In this book, Dr. Behe argues that the most convincing evidence for design is not to be found in the stars or the fossils, but in biochemical systems. In this very readable layman's guide to biochemistry, Behe uses examples such as vision, blood-clotting, and cellular transport, to demonstrate that life comprises an astonishing array of chemical machines, made up of finely calibrated, interdependent parts, that defy current naturalistic explanations. Behe surveys professional science literature and shows, that it is completely silent on the subject, stymied by the elegance of the foundation of life."[79]

Part-3: **Some concluding comments**

These concluding comments serve to summarize this essay and to present an answer to the topic question based on both the quick and the detailed responses. Thus, under "Section-1: **A literal view**" of "Part-2: **A detailed response**", a literal interpretation of the definitions of "evolution" and of "creationism" means both concepts cannot be used to explain the origins of life, simultaneously. Their definitions contain features that are incompatible. This means, if God did use a process similar to evolution to create Adam, that process must be called, by a different name to clearly indicate that God created with purpose and design, as stated in the Bible. But definitions aside, clearly the Bible indicates that God did not use an evolutionary process in creating life on this planet, because the living things created by God reproduced **according to their kinds**. And, this is definitely not evolution. Under "Section-2: **A biblical view**" of "Part-2: **A detailed response**", it was mentioned that there are no verses in the Bible, especially, the Book of Genesis, that are "**explicitly consistent**" with an evolutionary process. However, there are Bible verses that are "**explicitly inconsistent**" with evolution. Under "Section-3: **A general view**" of "Part-2: **A detailed response**", a variety of issues that appear to be inconsistent with God creating man through an evolutionary process were presented. Thus, literally, biblically, and generally, God did not create man through an evolutionary process. Or more precisely, the answer to the topic question – "Did God create man through evolution?", is "No!"

Does the union of a sperm and an egg create human life?

Most people believe that "the union of a sperm and an egg creates human life." The more precise medical wording of this belief is "human life begins at conception." This belief has become the traditional view of the human reproductive process. However, is this belief really true? Does the union of a sperm and an egg "create human life"? To develop an answer for this question, one must first address the air of ambiguity, which surround the question, because of the phrase: "create human life". This phrase is ambiguous, because it could mean "create life (*change nonliving into living*)", "create a life (*create a life form*)", or both. The traditional view of the human reproductive process seems to implicitly assume both meanings, while ignoring the difference between the two meanings. Furthermore, one meaning – "create life", raises the more fundamental question: "What is life?" And obviously, the phrase – "human life begins at conception", implies that "human life begins at conception". But the truth of this phrase is dependent on the meaning of the word: "life". Thus, the phrase – "human life begins at conception", raises the topic question more directly, as the question: "When does human life begin?" With all of this in mind, for this essay the tasks become:

1) Addressing the more fundamental question: "What is life?"

2) Addressing the more direct question: "When does human life begin?"

3) Defining the phrases – "create life" and "create a life", more precisely.

4) Addressing the topic question: "Does the union of a sperm and an egg create human life?"

To accomplish these four tasks, this essay is organized in six parts. Part-1 presents a discussion of the more fundamental question: "What is life?" Part-2 presents a discussion of the more direct question: "When does human life begin?" Part-3 presents a more detailed discussion of the definitions of the phrases: "create life" and "create a life". Part-4 presents a critique of the topic question. Part-5 presents some concluding comments. Part-6 presents a relevant comment.

Part-1: **The more fundamental question: "What is life?"**

This more fundamental question requires a definition of "life". However, "life" or the "essence of life" cannot and will not be defined directly, by this essay nor by this author. Nevertheless, we must admit that the "presence of 'life'" or the "essence of 'life'" in matter is usually "marked by something", which we can note by using our five senses, with or without the aid of devices, like a microscope, a stethoscope, etc. Thus, to ease further discussions, these "[marked by something]'s" will be called: "observable qualities". Any matter exhibiting any of the "observable qualities", we label: "living matter". Any matter not exhibiting any of the "observable qualities", we label: "nonliving matter". However, it is important to note that even though the "observable qualities" tell us whether any matter is living or nonliving, the "observable qualities" are not the "life" itself. The "observable qualities" are merely an evidence of the presence of "life".

Part-2: **The more direct question: "When does human life begin?"**

This more direct question and the topic question – "Does the union of a sperm and an egg create human life?", address some of the same issues. But the more direct question has a more religious overtone. Thus, the more direct question will be addressed in a separate essay, which is naturally titled: "When does human life begin?"

Part-3: **A discussion of the definitions of the phrases: "create life" and "create a life"**

The process of defining the phrases – "create life" and "create a life", is complicated by the religious beliefs of this world. However, to keep this essay from getting too complicated, we will generalize those beliefs into the Christian view and the non-Christian view. Under these two views, the two phrases will be defined, as follows:

- Under the Christian view, the phrase – "Create life", or any of its variations, like "creating life", is defined as "what God did when He created living matter like plants, animals, and then Adam out of the dust of the ground. More specifically, God created living matter out of nonliving matter."

- Under the non-Christian view, the phrase – "Create life", or any of its variations, like "creating life", is defined, as "nonliving matter evolving into living matter through the evolutionary process or some other process."

- Under both views, the phrase – "Create a life", or any of its variations, like "creating a life", is defined, as "the process of creating offspring via sexual or asexual reproduction". More precisely, for human sexual reproduction, "Creating a life" is defined, as "offspring coming from the union of a sperm and an egg."

> *Comment:* The previous definitions hint at the answer to the topic question. And that is okay! However, the rest of this essay is used to explicitly develop an answer and the justification for it.

Part-4: **A critique of the topic question**

This critique of the topic question must include a discussion of, at least, three issues. *First*, generally, it must discuss some "observable qualities" of living matter. *Second*, specifically, it must discuss some "observable qualities" of human sperms and eggs. *Third*, it must discuss some biblical creation issues. These three issues are addressed using references to medical research and to the Bible. Consequently, the topic question has two answers: "a medical answer" and "a biblical answer". Thus, Part-4 is organized in two sections: "Section-1: A medical answer" and "Section-2: A biblical answer".

Section-1: **A medical answer**

A medical answer to the topic question flows out of various medical research projects. Some projects have focused on various aspects of human sperms and/or human eggs. These projects have shown sperms and eggs possess some of the "observable qualities" that indicate the presence of "life". On a microscopic level, some "observable qualities" are that sperms exhibit the ability to move under their own power and eggs exhibit the ability to interact with a sperm. Other "observable qualities" revealed under the microscope are both sperms and eggs display the biological structure of living matter [i.e., complex structures based on organic molecules, the presence of a nucleus with DeoxyriboNucleic Acid (DNA)]. In addition, medical research has also revealed seven additional facts that are useful to this discussion. These seven facts are, as follows:

- *Fact-1*: Depending on conditions, mature human sperms may live up to seventy-two hours after being released from a man's reproductive system. However, the ability of the sperm to penetrate an egg diminishes after about forty-eight hours.

- *Fact-2*: Human sperms exist as two types: a "male" or a "female". And reference sources indicate that the head of a sperm containing genetic information for a "female" is larger.

- *Fact-3*: Depending on the conditions, mature human eggs may live up to twenty-four hours after being released from a woman's ovaries.

- *Fact-4*: Ten weeks after conception, female fetuses have their ovaries and all of the eggs that their reproductive systems will ever release.

  > *Comment:* The fact that "ten weeks after conception, a female fetus has her ovaries and all her eggs" means "the DNA of each female fetus contains the information to create both her ovaries and her eggs." And then projecting this "ovaries-eggs" situation back to Adam, the first man, and Eve, the first woman, we could reason that the DNA of Adam and Eve contained the information for all the ovaries and all the eggs for all subsequent generations of females, or more precisely, female fetuses.

- *Fact-5*: Human sperms and eggs are grown from an immature state to a mature state in their respective human reproductive organs.

- *Fact-6*: Mature human sperms and eggs are single celled organisms *released by* the human reproductive organs.

- *Fact-7*: Human sperms and eggs appear to differ from most of the single celled organisms created directly by God in two ways.

  - ✓ *First*, when mature and while separate, sperms and eggs do not appear to have a means to feed themselves. Rather, with the appropriate stimulation (*more of a situational-process for males, and more of a biological-process for females*), sperms and eggs are released from the respective male and female reproductive organs with a limited amount of food (*with a limited amount of energy resources*). If a sperm and an egg join, and they can plant roots in the female's uterus, they establish the means to take in food and to expel internal waste. If a sperm and an egg join, but they cannot plant roots, then they die after their combined energy resources have been exhausted or their internal waste overwhelms them. If they do not join, they do die, as each of their energy resources is depleted or their internal waste overwhelms them.

  - ✓ *Second*, although "mature sperms appear to have a means to expel internal waste", mature eggs may not have such a means. However, a mature sperm having a means to expel "internal waste" makes sense, because a mature sperm is a container of genetic information attached to an engine (*attached to a propulsion device*). An engine generates a lot of waste, as it converts energy into some type of motion. A mature egg is a container of genetic information inside a container of food (*a container of energy*). Nevertheless, despite whether a cell converts energy into motion or converts energy for any other purpose, all living cells produce "internal waste", as a natural byproduct of the conversion process. More specifically, "internal waste" is created, as a cell reacts to or interacts with its environment – as it goes about the business of living.

Based on the medical facts like the previous six facts, the point is:

> "Mature sperms and eggs can survive separately for sometime without joining. This ability to survive for a while "*outside the organs that released them*"[80] confirms that there is "life" within each."

Therefore, the union of a sperm and an egg merely combines the genetic information contained in each to create a new physical body (*to create offspring*). More specifically, the union of a sperm and an egg merely combines the "life" in the sperm with the "life" in the egg. Thus, the union of a sperm and an egg is "creating a life", rather than "creating life". Before we could say that "life" was created in the "create life" sense, we would need offspring coming from the union of a dead sperm and a dead egg. However, such an occurrence would contradict current medical knowledge that indicates a sperm and an egg can only join, if both are alive. Once more, if separately the sperm and the egg are already alive, then we cannot say, "The union of a sperm and an egg is 'creating life'." Therefore, the medical answer to the question – "Does the union of a sperm and an egg create human life?" is "No!", because the union of a sperm and an egg "creates a life form" or "creates offspring".

Section-2: **A biblical answer**

A biblical answer to the topic question flows out of Genesis 2:7. This verse indicates two things: *First*, God formed Adam from the dust of the ground. *Second*, God breathed into Adam's nostril, causing him to come alive. In the NIV, Genesis 2:7 reads:

> the LORD God formed the man from the dust of the ground and breathed into his nostrils the breath of life, and the man became a living being.

Whether you take this verse, as a literal statement of fact or as a symbolic statement, the results are the same. God created Adam and then He gave Adam the "Breath of 'Life'". That is, God created Adam and then He gave Adam the "essence of 'life'". As a result, Adam would have exhibited "observable qualities" that are the evidence of the "presence of 'life'". Adam's human form was probably like ours. It was made up of living cells and "dead cells"[81]. Consequently, God must have caused the "essence of 'life'" to permeate all the cells of Adam's body. Then when God created Eve from one of Adam's ribs, that rib already had the "breath of 'life'" or the "essence of 'life'" in it. Thus, Eve received the "breath of 'life'" from God through Adam. Adam passed the "breath of 'life'" to all subsequent generations through his sperms. Eve passed the "breath of 'life'" to all subsequent generations through her eggs.

> *Comment:* This author's belief regarding the passing of "life" by Adam through his sperms, is based on Hebrews 7:10. Three translations of this verse read:
>
> > (Hebrews 7:10 KJV) For he was yet in the loins of his father, when Melchisedec met him.
> >
> > (Hebrews 7:10 NIV) because when Melchizedek met Abraham, Levi was still in the body of his ancestor.
> >
> > (Hebrews 7:10 NRSV) for he was still in the loins of his ancestor when Melchizedek met him.
>
> Hebrew 7:10 seems to support the existence of future generations in the loins of their male ancestors. Thus, Hebrew 7:10 would support "the passing of 'life'" by Adam through his sperms. However, "the passing of 'life' by Eve through her eggs" is supported by the previously mentioned medical research. And recall that some of that research indicated that ten weeks after conception, a female fetus has her ovaries and all her eggs.

Therefore, a union of Adam's sperm and Eve's egg merely passed on the "breath of 'life'" that was in each, as an offspring was created. This means that the union of a sperm from Adam and an egg from Eve merely served to "create a life", rather than to "create life". Therefore, the biblical answer to the question – "Does the union of a sperm and an egg create human life?", is also "No!", because the union of a sperm and an egg "creates a life form"/"creates offspring".

Part-5: **Some concluding comments**

Concluding comments flow out of both a medical answer and a biblical answer to the topic question. Both answers are "No!" "No" is the medical answer, because the union of a sperm and an egg does not "create life". "Life" already exist in each, before their union. "No" is the biblical answer, because the Bible tells us that God created Adam and Eve. God "created life" in Adam and Eve, who passed that "life" to all the members of subsequent generations, except Jesus. Therefore, the union of a sperm and an egg merely serves to "create a life" – to "create an offspring".

Part-6: **Some relevant comments**

Some relevant comments, which represent some speculation by this author, are presented in two groups, as follows:

- *Speculation-1*: The existence of DNA seems to imply that God "created life (*created the 'essence of 'life'*)" only once, "*in Adam*" and "*in each parent organism for each plant and animal species*", when He created Adam and the first members of each plant or animal species. For example, while God was creating Adam, He (God) placed "*in Adam*", the seeds for all the members of subsequent generations, except Jesus. This means that the DNA of Adam and Eve contained the information for all the members of subsequent generations, except Jesus, because God knew which sperm would join with which egg to produce each individual throughout time. Therefore, God put that information in the DNA of Adam and Eve. (*See the essay: "When does human life begin?"*) Likewise, God placed "*in those first members of all other species*", the seeds for all subsequent generations of each species.

- *Speculation-2*: Originally, before Eve existed, all of the human DNA was probably in Adam. However, as God created Eve from one of Adam's ribs, He (God) may have pulled half the chromosomes from Adam's seeds (*from Adam's sperms*) and put them in Eve's eggs. This might be why a human sperm has half the necessary chromosomes for a human form and a human egg has the other half. Nevertheless, again, the DNA of Adam and Eve had to contain the information for all the members of subsequent generations, except Jesus.

When does human life begin?

This question was briefly touched on in the essay: "Does the union of a sperm and an egg create human life?" Or more precisely, that essay briefly touched on the more specific question: "When did human life begin?" That briefness was due to the purpose of that essay. Its purpose was not to address when human life began/begins. Rather, its purpose was to reject the traditional notion that "human life is created by the union of a sperm and an egg." That rejection revolved around the following three conditions:

- *Condition-1*: There is a difference between "creating life" and "creating a life". For Christians, "Creating life" is what God did when He created living matter like plants, animals, and then Adam out of the dust of the earth. God created living matter out of nonliving matter. For non-Christians, "Creating life" is what happened, because of evolution or something else. For Christians and non-Christians, "Creating a life" is the process of creating offspring via sexual or asexual reproduction.

- *Condition-2*: "Life" in matter is evidenced by "observable qualities". For human sperms and human eggs, such "observable qualities" are revealed under the microscope where both display the biological structure of living matter [i.e., complex structures based on organic molecules, the presence of a nucleus with DeoxyriboNucleic Acid (DNA)].

- *Condition-3*: "Life" in the "creating life" sense (*in the "nonliving into living" sense*) is not created by the union of a sperm and an egg, because each separately already displays the evidence of "life" – (*because each separately already contains the "essence of 'life'"*). Thus, two entities, which each contains "life", do not "create life" by joining, rather by joining they "create a life", which is different from creating living matter from nonliving matter, which is "creating life".

The purpose of this essay is to present a more detailed discussion of the topic question – "When does human life begin?", and the more specific question: "When did human life begin?" Obviously, this essay will focus on the two questions, more from the "creating life" sense (*the "nonliving into living" sense*), than the "creating a life" sense (*the creation of offspring sense*).

Like the question – "Does the union of a sperm and an egg create human life?", the two questions – "When does human life begin?" and "When did human life begin?", raise the more fundamental question: "What is life?" However, once again, "life or the essence of life" cannot and will not be defined in this essay nor by this author. Nevertheless, we still must acknowledge that the "presence of 'life'"or the "essence of 'life'" in matter is usually marked by "observable qualities". Therefore, any matter exhibiting any of the "observable qualities", we label: "living matter". Any matter not exhibiting any of the "observable qualities", we label: "nonliving matter".

Furthermore, it is important to emphasize that even though the "observable qualities" tell us whether any matter is living or nonliving, the "observable qualities" are not the "life" itself. The "observable qualities" are only an evidence of the presence of "life".

To develop an answer for the two questions – "When does human life begin?" and "When did human life begin?", in the "creating life" sense, we will refer to some medical issues and some Bible verses. Thus, we will develop two answers to these questions. One answer is labeled – "a medical answer", even though it includes references to several Bible verses. The other answer is labeled: "a biblical answer". Therefore, this essay is organized in four parts. Part-1 presents "a medical answer". Part-2 presents "a biblical answer". Part-3 presents some concluding comments. Part-4 presents some relevant comments.

Part-1: **A medical answer**

This medical answer is based on two issues. Thus, Part-1 is organized in two sections. Section-1 presents a discussion, which revolves around "medical information about human eggs and sperms". Section-2 presents a discussion, which revolves around the phrase – "the 'life', is in the blood."

Section-1: **Medical information about human eggs and sperms**

The medical information about human eggs and sperms is presented separately in two segments. *Segment-1* covers "human eggs". *Segment-2* covers "human sperms".

Segment-1: **Human eggs**

Medical information about human eggs must begin with comments about the female reproductive system. Therefore, two facts about the female reproductive system are: *First*, a human female is born with all the eggs that will ever be released, by her reproductive system. *Second*, the female reproductive system takes an immature egg and causes it to grow into a mature egg, at the appropriate time.

Support for the first fact was presented, during a broadcast of a Christian radio program, when a guest, said, "A female fetus has her ovaries and 'all of her eggs at about ten weeks'." This statement means that science is able to confirm the existence of the ovaries and the eggs at ten weeks into the growth cycle of a female fetus. It also means that "the genetic information needed to create the ovaries and the eggs, are present when a sperm and an egg join to create that particular female." Or more precisely, it means that "the genetic information needed to create the ovaries and the eggs, are in the DNA for that female fetus."

Segment-2: **Human sperms**

Medical information about human sperms is begun with a speculative statement by this author. This speculative statement is actually, based on the simplicity and symmetry that God appears to love. Nevertheless, it is speculative, because to date, this author has never heard any medical statements to support it. The speculative statement is:

> "If it is true that 'females are born with all the eggs that they will ever release', then it is probably also true that 'males are born with all the sperms that they will ever release.'"

However, establishing the presence of immature sperms in a male fetus is probably extremely difficult, due to the size of immature sperms. A mature human sperm is about one-thousandth the size of a mature human egg. A mature "human egg is only about 100 microns (0.004 in) in diameter."[82] Consequently, only God knows the size and the location of immature human sperms in a ten-week-old male fetus. When sperms are confirmed in a ten-week-old male fetus, it will mean that "the genetic information needed to create sperms is present when a sperm and an egg join to create that particular male." Or more precisely, it will mean that "the genetic information needed to create sperms is in the DNA for that particular male fetus." However, it is already a confirmed medical fact that sperms must grow to maturity, before they are released by the male reproductive system.

Please forgive the repetition. But this is important! With all of the previous statements in mind, the problem for this author is simply that "if males are not born with all the sperms that they will ever release, then it would mean that men could possibly be in the business of 'creating life', as their reproductive system '*creates sperms*'." More precisely, if males are not born with all the sperms already existing in some immature form, then it would mean that males have to create sperms. Creating sperms would require either of two options:

- *Option-1*: The cells in the male's testicles share the "life" in them with the sperms created by the male's testicles. Thus, the sperms would also contain "life".

- *Option-2*: The male's testicles creates the "life" in the sperms from some nonliving substance(s) in the male's body, as the sperms are created. Thus, the sperms would also contain "life".

In reviewing both options, *Option-1* is consistent with God's providence, because "life" is passed from one cell to another. Whereas, *Option-2* violates God's providence (*only God can create the living from the nonliving*), because "life" must be created in the "something come out of nothing" sense or the "living from the nonliving" sense. For those who do not believe in God's providence, then the logical argument of "something coming out of nothing" could be applied. Under such an application, *Option-1* does not require that "something come out of nothing", because again, "something is passed to something else". Whereas, *Option-2* does require that "something come out of nothing". Thus, in addition to being inconsistent with God's province, *Option-2* is logically unsupportable.

Section-2: **The "life" is in the blood**

The "'life' is in the blood", is referenced in Genesis 9:4, Leviticus 17:11, Leviticus 17:14, and Deuteronomy 12:23. Two different translations of each of these verses read, as follows:

(Genesis 9:4 NIV) "But you must not eat meat that has its lifeblood still in it.

(Genesis 9:4 NASB) "Only you shall not eat flesh with its life, that is, its blood.

(Leviticus 17:11 NIV) For the life of a creature is in the blood, and I have given it to you to make atonement for yourselves on the altar; it is the blood that makes atonement for one's life.

(Leviticus 17:11 NASB) 'For the life of the flesh is in the blood, and I have given it to you on the altar to make atonement for your souls; for it is the blood by reason of the life that makes atonement.'

(Leviticus 17:14 NIV) because the life of every creature is its blood. That is why I have said to the Israelites, "You must not eat the blood of any creature, because the life of every creature is its blood; anyone who eats it must be cut off."

(Leviticus 17:14 NASB) "For as for the life of all flesh, its blood is identified with its life. Therefore I said to the sons of Israel, 'You are not to eat the blood of any flesh, for the life of all flesh is its blood; whoever eats it shall be cut off.'

(Deuteronomy 12:23 NIV) But be sure you do not eat the blood, because the blood is the life, and you must not eat the life with the meat.

(Deuteronomy 12:23 NASB) "Only be sure not to eat the blood, for the blood is the life, and you shall not eat the life with the flesh.

Both issues – "Medical information about human sperms and eggs" and "The 'life' is in the blood", add credibility to the Christian belief that "'life' was created, by God when He created the first members of each species." Thus, even though this is called the "medical answer", the point is:

> "Living matter had to have a beginning. Something had to cause living matter to come into existence. And God is the most logical source. The two issues above simply add credibility to God being the source."

Therefore, a medical answer to the topic question – "When does human life begin?" and the more specific question – "When did human life begin?", is that "human life began, when God breathed into Adam."

Part-2: **A biblical answer**

A biblical answer is based on six issues. However, some of the six issues are the same issue viewed from a different vantage point. But that is okay! Thus, Part-2 is organized in six sections. Section-1 presents a discussion of "God's creation of Adam". Section-2 presents a discussion of "the words: 'life' and 'lives'". Section-3 presents a discussion about only "the word: 'lives'". Section-4 presents a discussion of "Life developing from a seed". Section-5 presents a discussion of "the sovereignty of God".

Section-1: **God's creation of Adam**

The creation of Adam was recorded in Genesis 2:7. This verse records that God formed Adam from the dust of the ground, then God breathed into his nostrils, and with that act Adam became a living being. Two different translations of Genesis 2:7 read, as follows:

> (Genesis 2:7 NIV) the LORD God formed the man from the dust of the ground and breathed into his nostrils the breath of life, and the man became a living being.
>
> (Genesis 2:7 KJV) And the LORD God formed man of the dust of the ground, and breathed into his nostrils the breath of life; and man became a living soul.

Now, someone might say that Genesis 2:7 could be taken literally or figuratively. Taking Genesis 2:7 literally means that:

"*First*, God formed Adam from the dust of the ground.

Second, God breathed into Adam's nostrils. Note: 'The breathed into Adam's nostrils' statement confirms the 'formed' statement, because God could not breathe into Adam's nostrils unless Adam had nostrils. However, care has to be exercised here, because while we want to show Adam, as a real (*physical*) being, we do not want to put physical constraints on God. Actually, the wording of the verse does not put constraints on the nature of God, because God is the 'active' member of the events and Adam is the 'passive' member of those same events. Logically, the constraints are on the 'passive' members of an event not the 'active' members. [*It is like saying, 'Bill poured a glass of water.' The 'glass' is the 'passive' member of the event and has physical constraints on it. However, 'Bill' is the 'active' member. And whatever he did or used to do the pouring is unconstrained, by the wording of the statement. Bill could have used a larger glass, a pitcher, a bucket, a barrel, or the likes.*] Thus, God is not required to have a mouth to do the breathing. God could have caused a flow of air like breath to enter Adam's body through his (*Adam's*) nostrils. Remember the Bible uses words that will make us comfortable and will convey images that are meaningful to us. A nonbiblical example of this occurred when this author encountered the statement: 'The wind was like the breath of God.' This statement conveyed an image to this author that was meaningful. But it does not mean that God has a mouth.

Third, Adam became a living being."

Taking Genesis 2:7 figuratively is illogical, because Adam is listed in the genealogy of Jesus, which means someone understood that he was a real person. In addition, Jesus made several references to Adam. The point is:

"Adam was the first human and God gave him 'life'."

Section-2: The words: "life" and "lives"

The words – "life" and "lives", are important, because of the "fact" that "females are born with all of the eggs they will ever release", and because of the "probability" that "males are born with all of the sperms they will ever release". With this "fact" and "probability" in mind, a statement by Pastor Jack Hayford of Living Way Ministries, becomes more meaningful. In discussing Genesis 2:7, Pastor Hayford said:

"'The Hebrew word used for 'life' is actually plural.'[83] Thus, Genesis 2:7 should read:

> the LORD God formed the man from the dust of the ground and breathed into his nostrils the breath of lives, and the man became a living being.

This means that "God breathed into Adam, more than one 'life'". Some people interpret the word – "*lives*", as two lives: Adam's life and Eve's life, since God created Eve from one of Adam's ribs. At a minimum, this is a fair and logical interpretation. However, there are other people, who take a more liberal interpretation of the word – "lives", in Genesis 2:7. These individuals interpret the word – "*lives*", as the seeds for every individual, who would ever be conceived. Also under this more liberal interpretation, it would be easy to understand why God would frown on all sexual activities outside marriage, where a male released some of his sperm. In all such instances, God would label those activities, as a waste of the male's seed. But because of His foreknowledge, God would have accounted for any wasted seeds. But more important, the point is:

"Adam must have contained in his loins the seeds (*in his sperms, the DNA*) for all of the individuals, who would ever be conceived, except Jesus. Similarly, Eve could have contained in her loins the seeds (*in her eggs, the DNA*) for all of the individuals, who would ever be conceived. Eve may have even contained the seed for Jesus, the man, even though Jesus, the man, was not conceived, in the normal way. God, the Holy Spirit, overshadowed Mary and then she was found to be 'with child'."

> *Comment:* Forgive what may be a nontraditional use of the word – "loins", with respect to Eve (*to the female gender*). But this usage allows for a symmetry to be made, between Adam and Eve, with respect to all subsequent generations. Actually, the use of the word – "loins", with Eve, is not really inappropriate. Because the definition of the word – "loins" in both "The New Unger's Dictionary" and the "Holman Bible Dictionary" indicate that "loins" is a euphemism for "reproductive power" or "procreative powers", which could be used with a male or a female

Therefore, in creating Adam and the first members of all the other species, God "created life". Furthermore, this is speculation, but God may have created Adam with all of the lives of every human being, except Jesus. More specifically, God may have created Adam with both male and female characteristics and with paired sperm-egg combinations, which represented every human, who would ever be conceived, except Jesus. Then when God took one of Adam's ribs to create Eve, He may have also taken all of the female characteristics and all of the eggs from Adam. After Adam and Eve were created, God allowed them and all other species to "create offspring", who contained "God's breath of life" that He breathed into Adam and the first members of all the other species.

Section-3: **The word: "lives"**

The word – "lives", as used in the "concept of God breathing '**LIVES**' into Adam" may be implied by Jeremiah 1:5. In this verse, God is telling Jeremiah that He (the Lord) knew Jeremiah, before he (Jeremiah) was formed in his mother's womb. Four different translations of Jeremiah 1:5 read, as follows:

> (Jeremiah 1:5 KJV) Before I formed thee in the belly I knew thee; and before thou camest forth out of the womb I sanctified thee, and I ordained thee a prophet unto the nations.
>
> (Jeremiah 1:5 NIV) "Before I formed you in the womb I knew you, before you were born I set you apart; I appointed you as a prophet to the nations."
>
> (Jeremiah 1:5 NASB) "Before I formed you in the womb I knew you, And before you were born I consecrated you; I have appointed you a prophet to the nations."
>
> (Jeremiah 1:5 NRSV) "Before I formed you in the womb I knew you, and before you were born I consecrated you; I appointed you a prophet to the nations."

This author is not going to pretend to know exactly "how God created man", "how God breathed 'lives' into Adam", and/or "how God designed the human reproductive system." However, it does seem apparent to this author that "our traditional views of human life beginning at conception in the 'create life' sense is not consistent with the Bible." Hebrews 7:10 also seems to not support our traditional view. In Hebrews 7:1-10, the author of Hebrews is recounting an Old Testament encounter between Melchizedek, who was the "King of Salem and a priest of God", and Abraham. In this particular encounter, Abraham paid a tithe to the Priest Melchizedek. Then the author of Hebrew makes the point that "the act of Abraham paying the tithe, was like Levi (*who was a great-grandson of Abraham*) paying that tithe, because Levi was in Abraham's loins, when he (*Abraham*) paid the tithe to the Priest Melchizedek." Also note that the priests came from the tribe of Levi. Anyway four translations of Hebrews 7:10 read, as follows:

> (Hebrews 7:10 KJV) For he was yet in the loins of his father, when Melchisedec met him.
>
> (Hebrews 7:10 NIV) because when Melchizedek met Abraham, Levi was still in the body of his ancestor.
>
> (Hebrews 7:10 NASB) for he was still in the loins of his father when Melchizedek met him.
>
> (Hebrews 7:10 NRSV) for he was still in the loins of his ancestor when Melchizedek met him.

The point is:

> "The 'concept of all humans being in Adam's loins', is consistent with several Bible verses." The implication of "being in Adam's loins'" is that "All of us, except Jesus, were in Adam, when he sinned."

Section-4: **"Life" developing from a seed**

"Life" developing from a seed is usually automatically associated with the process of dying. That is, the seed must die, so that new life can spring forth. This is discussed from two viewpoints: "*a practical viewpoint*" and "*a biblical viewpoint*". Thus, Section-4 is organized in two segments. *Segment-1* presents "*a practical viewpoint*". *Segment-2* presents "*a biblical viewpoint*"

Segment-1: ***A practical viewpoint***

This viewpoint flows from the fact that some people believe that "Plant seeds are examples of 'life' developing from something that is not alive." However, this is not true. The Bible does not tell us exactly how God put the "breath of life" into plants or animals. Nevertheless, a seed is the way that a plant passes on the "breath of life" created in it by God. Once a seed has been produced, by the parent plant or plants, it will only begin to grow, if it is alive. Therefore, a seed is not an example of life coming from something that is dead. A seed is really an encasement that contains the "breath of life" (*that the plant is passing on to subsequent generations*), genetic information, and nourishment, just like an egg.

Segment-2: ***A biblical viewpoint***

This viewpoint flows from the Bible, because it contains some imagery of a "seed dying". However, a "seed dying" to develop into something else is really "figurative language". See John 12:24. Four translations of this verse read, as follows:

> (John 12:24 KJV) Verily, verily, I say unto you, Except a corn of wheat fall into the ground and die, it abideth alone: but if it die, it bringeth forth much fruit.
>
> (John 12:24 NIV) I tell you the truth, unless a kernel of wheat falls to the ground and dies, it remains only a single seed. But if it dies, it produces many seeds.
>
> (John 12:24 NASB) "Truly, truly, I say to you, unless a grain of wheat falls into the earth and dies, it remains by itself alone; but if it dies, it bears much fruit.
>
> (John 12:24 NRSV) Very truly, I tell you, unless a grain of wheat falls into the earth and dies, it remains just a single grain; but if it dies, it bears much fruit.

In John 12:24, the word – "dies", is used to mean "give up its selfish focus on itself and its current state". More precisely, the word – "dies", means "dies to its current state". It does not mean physical death.

> *Comment:* As a plant is "only a body", for a plant "physical death" is "the separation of God's 'breath of life' from 'the body and the matter in the body'". (*See the essay: "Does man have a body, a soul, and a spirit?"*)

Thus, the point of Section-4 is:

> "From a practical viewpoint and from a biblical viewpoint, 'life' can only come out of that which is already alive. While it may be true that something may die to feed 'something else', it is also true that the 'something else' has to be alive in order to feed. Thus, it is still true that 'life' only comes from 'life', unless you are God."

Section-5: **The sovereignty of God**

The sovereignty of God is such that He knows, which sperm will join with which egg to produce each "new life form" throughout time. This is true for humans, animals, and plants. And it is true for asexual and sexual reproduction. God's knowledge is confirmed by Psalms 139:13. This verse reads, as follows:

> (Psalms 139:13 NIV) For you created my inmost being; you knit me together in my mother's womb.

The point of Section-5 is:

> "God is sovereign and in control."

The Part-2 issues add credibility to the belief that "God created life and placed the seeds for all future generations in the first members of each species whether human, animals, or plants." More precisely, based on the Part-2 issues, a biblical answer to the topic question – "When does human life begin?" and the more specific question – "When did human life begin?", is that "human life began when God breathed into Adam."

Part-3: **Conclusion**

With our little minds, we are unable to even partially comprehend the full beauty of God's ways. And we might not have the knowledge or the scientific expertise to conclusively prove that God created all "life". However, we do have the scientific expertise and the appropriate reasoning skills to determine that "life" in the "create life" sense (*in the "nonliving into living" sense*) is not what is taking place, when a sperm and an egg join. When this is understood, or more precisely, when we understand the difference, between "creating life" and "creating a life", we will be on our way toward understanding that "all 'life' being created by God", is consistent with the Bible and with our reasoning skills. Nevertheless, again, a medical answer and a biblical answer to the topic question – "When does human life begin?" and the more specific question – "When did human life begin?", is that "human life began when God breathed into Adam."

> *Comment:* Both this essay and the essay – "Does the union of a sperm and an egg create human life?", indirectly address the sloppy use of the English language, by most of us. Our sloppy use has caused us to overlook the fact that there is a difference, between "creating life" and "creating a life". In these two phrases, the word – "life", is being used in two difference senses. And that difference is the real sloppiness. In one sense, the word – "life", is used to refer to that special something, which distinguishes living matter from nonliving matter. In the other sense, the word – "life", is used to refer to the offspring resulting from the union of two living entities like "a sperm" and "an egg".

Part-4: **Some relevant comments**

Some relevant comments are presented, as speculations by this author. The reason for submitting these speculations is to suggest how much beauty and symmetry there is in the ways that God has appeared to have done things and the way that God does things. Our little minds cannot begin to comprehend the "who", "what", "when", "why", "where", and "how" of God's ways of accomplishing His plan for us. These speculations cannot even begin to hint at God's ways. In addition, some of the following speculations have been explicitly or implicitly presented before. In such cases, the repetition here is for emphasis. Furthermore, some speculations flow from other speculations. Nevertheless, the speculations are, as follows:

- *Speculation-1*: Initially, God may have created Adam, as a complete human being with both "male" and "female" physiological aspects, sexual aspects, and mental aspects.

- *Speculation-2*: If God created Eve by pulling all of the "female" physiological, sexual, and mental aspects out of Adam with his (*Adam's*) rib, then "the Adam before the creation of Eve", was different from "the Adam after the creation of Eve".

- *Speculation-3*: If God separated different physiological, sexual, and mental aspects (*separated male and female aspects*) into Adam and Eve, as He took one of Adam's ribs to create Eve, this adds a greater beauty and truth to the "biblical concept that a man and a woman, become one under marriage" and to the "psychological concept that man and woman complement each other".

- *Speculation-4*: If there were "lives" in Adam before the creation of Eve, then these were probably complete "lives". That is, the DNA information for a sperm was paired with the DNA information for an egg, in Adam's original DNA. More precisely, the DNA-creation scenario might have been something like the following:

  - ✓ God created Adam from the dust of the ground.

  - ✓ God created Adam with DNA. In creating the DNA information in Adam, God could have paired the DNA information for an egg with the DNA information for a sperm, such that every individual, who would ever be conceived was accounted for, except Jesus.

  - ✓ God created Eve from one of Adam's ribs. As God removed one of Adam's ribs to create Eve, God could have removed all of the DNA information for the eggs for all the members of subsequent generations. And based on our current understanding of the female physiology, God placed the DNA information for the eggs for all subsequent generations in Eve. Obviously, this would have left all the DNA information for the sperms for all subsequent generations in Adam. That is, this would have left all the seeds for all subsequent generations in Adam's loins (*in Adam's body*). Then DNA information from Adam and Eve would have unraveled through subsequent generations to produce each member of those generations according to God's design.

Comment: The speculations above could have been composed in terms of paired and unpaired chromosomes, because the chromosomes contain the DNA information. This would have allowed the use of the medical fact that the man's sperm contains half the chromosomes needed to "create a life" and the woman's egg contains the other half. However, composing *Speculation-4* in terms of paired and unpaired chromosomes might have complicated this discussion without changing the final implications of these speculations.

Comment: The question of whether Eve's DNA had the DNA information for the egg for Jesus, the man, will not be addressed here. God knows. This author does not know and will not speculate on that question.

- *Speculation-5*: The possibility of humans "creating life", as offspring are created, makes almost no sense. The possibility of animals "creating life", as offspring are created, makes less sense. And the possibility of plants "creating life", as offspring are created, makes absolutely no sense. The reason for saying, these possibilities make no sense is, because obviously to "create life" humans, animals, and plants would have to have abilities that are reserved for God.

- *Speculation-6*: Two interesting asides – *First*, "asexual reproduction" involves the "passing of life" – involves the "sharing of life". More specifically, there is absolutely no question that "asexual reproduction" does not involve the "creating of life out of nothing". *Second*, under sexual reproduction for humans, animals, and plants, a variation of asexual reproduction also occurs. For instance, for humans, once the sperm and the egg have joined. The result of the joining, grows into a recognizable human being via cell divisions, which is basically, asexual reproduction.

Is variety the spice of life?

In the United States, the statement – "Variety is the spice of life", is becoming less popular, but once, it was often used with respect to various realities of life. For instance, one person used it, during a discussion of foods. Another person used it, during a discussion of her or his leisure activities (*knitting, sewing, fishing, hunting, boating, hiking, skiing, etc.*). A third person used it, during a discussion of her or his sexual activities. This third usage could have been a reference to "one sexual partner and a variety of sexual activities". However, a "variety of sexual partners (*many different sexual partners over some period*) and essentially the same sexual activity", were understood by most Christians and non-Christians in the U.S., to be the more common usage. This common usage is the focus of this essay and means that for this essay, the topic question should be more precisely worded – "Is sexual variety really the spice of life?"

The use of the word – "spice", gives the topic question, the more precise question, and the statement – "Variety is the spice of life", a positive inference. More specifically, the positive inference is that "just as 'spices' enrich the flavor of your foods", "variety will enrich your life." But remember, even with a good flavor, a food item could still cause an upset stomach.

To address the more precise question, this essay discusses the realities of life from three different viewpoints: a "medical viewpoint", a "biblical viewpoint", and a "physical-psychological viewpoint". Such an examination allows this essay to be organized in four parts. Part-1 presents the medical answer. Part-2 presents the biblical answer. Part-3 presents the physical-psychological answer. Part-4 presents some concluding comments.

Part-1: **The medical answer**

The medical answer to the more precise question, flows easily from current medical information. Such information makes it obvious that being sexually intimate with a variety of partners (*with many different individuals*) is dangerous, because there are so many nonsexual and sexual diseases that can be transmitted from one individual to another via various means (*via their sex organs, via their hands, via their mouths, via various parts of their bodies touching, via a shared items, and/or via any combination of these*). Currently, some of the transmitted diseases are not curable. Thus, medically, having a variety of sexual partners is like playing Russian roulette with one's health. Therefore, the medical answer to the more precise question – "Is sexual variety really the spice of life?", is "No!"

> *Comment:* Being sexually intimate with one person can also be dangerous, if that person has had other sexual partners. More specifically, the medical community is saying that when you kiss, touch, and/or have sexual relations with another person, you are kissing, touching, and having sex with every other individual that

person has kissed, touched, and/or had sexual relations with.

Part-2: **The biblical answer**

The biblical answer to the more precise question, is based on God's wisdom, as indicated by the Bible. Several Bible verses address the issue of a "one man and one woman" relationship. Such a relationship is implied by the following verses:

(Genesis 2:24 NIV) For this reason a man will leave his father and mother and be united to his wife, and they will become one flesh.

(Matthew 19:4 NIV) "Haven't you read," he replied, "that at the beginning the Creator 'made them male and female,'

(Matthew 19:5 NIV) and said, 'For this reason a man will leave his father and mother and be united to his wife, and the two will become one flesh'?

(Matthew 19:6 NIV) So they are no longer two, but one. Therefore what God has joined together, let man not separate."

(Ephesians 5:31 NIV) "For this reason a man will leave his father and mother and be united to his wife, and the two will become one flesh."

(Hebrews 13:4 NIV) Marriage should be honored by all, and **the marriage bed kept pure**, for God will judge the adulterer and all the sexually immoral.

In general, these verses and the Bible, as a whole, imply that the best situation (*the best relationship*) is one man and one woman, especially, when the relationship is consummated under the bonds of marriage. While it is true that God allowed (*that God did not forcibly prevent*) polygamy or multiple-partner relationships among His chosen people, it is also true that God did not shield His chosen people from the consequences of such activities. The Bible clearly shows that polygamy or multiple-partner relationships only created headaches, directly for those involved in such activities and indirectly for the rest of us. For example, the current "Arab – Jewish" conflict is basically two half-brothers fighting. More precisely, the Arabs and the Jews came out of a multiple-partner relationship involving Abraham and two women. One woman was his wife, Sarah. And the other woman was Sarah's hand maiden, Hagar. Abraham and Hagar had a son, Ishmael, who is considered the forebear of most of the Arab people. Abraham and Sarah had a son, Isaac, who can be considered the forebear of the Jewish people. In addition, the Bible clearly shows that sexual activities outside of marriage are considered sin. Therefore, the biblical answer to the more precise question – "Is sexual variety really the spice of life?", is "No!"

Part-3: **The physical-psychological answer**

The physical-psychological answer to the more precise question, is based on the way humans appear to be built physically and psychologically. That is, when an individual's physical and psychological health is taken into account, a "one-on-one" relationship is better. The reasoning for this could be expressed, as follows:

> Clearly, human beings of the same sex are very different. They differ physically by taste (*of their exterior shell - skin, etc.*), by smell (*the natural body scent - the non-perfumed body scent*), by the shape and size of their whole bodies, by the shape and size of their individual body parts, by the color and texture of their skin, by the sound of their voices, and so on. They differ psychologically by the thoughts that they express, by their mannerisms, by their personalities, and so on. Consequently, as you associate or have intimate[84] relationships with more and more members of the opposite sex, the best physical or mental features of each are taken consciously or unconsciously to mentally form what becomes your ideal partner. Your ideal partner is also affected by the worse features of your intimate partners and of others with whom you associate. Obviously, the worse features are something that you do not want in your ideal partner; whereas, the best features are something that you do want in your ideal partner. The result is that as the number of different partners increases, it becomes more and more unlikely that your ideal partner will match a real person.

The real impact of a best physical feature was revealed by a friend, who shared his encounter with a "best physical feature". His story goes, as follows:

> While attending a West Coast university, my friend worked, as a student-employee at its computer center. More specifically, he worked in a room filled with "keypunch machines"[85]. (*Mentioning a keypunch machine really dates my friend, because these days most people probably have no idea what a keypunch is.*) Anyway, this room was called the "keypunch room". It was open twenty-four hours a day during the week, and eight hours a day on Saturday and Sunday. My friend worked the Saturday and Sunday hours. His job was to instruct others (*students, staff, faculty, and so on*) in the use of the equipment, clear jams, and keep needed supplies, mostly blank computer cards, available to the users. The room had a small, one-person office in one corner, opposite the only door into the room. The office was where the staff member on duty sat until she or he was needed by someone. The office had large glass windows, which extended from about waist-high to the ceiling. This allowed the staff member to see all areas of the room. At the time, my friend's boss was a twenty-five-year-old man, who had dropped out of classes at the university to take the full-time staff position (*the eight-to-five-weekday shift*) in the "keypunch room".
>
> One year, about five days before Christmas, my friend went to the keypunch

room to visit his boss. As my friend entered the keypunch room, he saw his boss in the office. But of greater interest, he saw a young-female student, who was a student-employee of the computer center library. She was seated at a keypunch machine doing some work for her boss. It was common knowledge that this young lady was in a platonic relationship with my friend's boss. Anyway, my friend said that he was in a good mood, so he decided to give the young lady a Christmas kiss. Even though there was not a mistletoe in the room, my friend walked up to the young lady and said something that caused her to turn her head toward him. Then he bent down and planted his lips on hers. As soon as his lips touched her lips. Bam! Cannons went off in his head. Flashes of light danced around inside his head. He forgot who he was, where he was, and what he was doing. He temporarily lost his mental connection to reality. The entire focus of his being was concentrated at the union of his lips with the lips of this young lady. Now, this kiss was not a movie kiss, where the parties twisted their heads and lips during the kiss. It was supposed to be just a simple touching-of-the-lips kiss. But this kiss was nothing like anything my friend had experienced before. My friend said that the shape and texture of this young lady's lips provided an unbelievably pleasurable stimulus, with mere contact. He would still be kissing her today except for her muffled call of his name, which brought him back to reality.

Now, anytime my friend kisses any woman. The feel of her lips is compared with the feel of the young student's lips, so many years ago. And, to date, no other lips have come close. Worded differently, every time that my friend kisses another woman, his mind will flash back to the young student's lips. This is not a healthy situation emotionally or spiritually for him nor for whomever he is kissing. But more to the point, similar feelings could occur with any feature of the human body, regardless of the degree of intimacy. In fact, this same friend also told me about three other young ladies that he knew, who had a specific physical feature, which was unforgettable. Two of the features were favorable, but the third sickened my friend. Thus, it should be obvious that having intimate relationships with many different individuals leads to comparisons. Comparisons produce evaluations. Evaluations produce discontentment. Therefore, as revealed in the Bible, God's wisdom in calling for the avoidance of sexual variety, via a lifelong monogamous relationship, is understandable.

Besides sharing the previous story, this friend also shared a potential problem that could accompany experiences, with members of the opposite sex, who possess unforgettable features. As stated by this friend, the problem is sometimes, he felt that he loved the unforgettable feature more than the young lady possessing the feature. It was like loving a part (*the unforgettable feature*), but not necessarily the whole person. And if the focus stayed on the unforgettable feature, then the relationship could turn ugly and dishonest. This is exactly what happened to my friend and the young student with the pleasurable lips. Their relationship ended with her hating him.

As we move toward a conclusion, we will focus for a moment on the female and male genitals. Both the female and the male genitals differ somewhat among individuals. The differences can easily be confirmed by a quick surf of X-Rated websites. For example, female's genitals differ in the size of the vaginal opening, shape and length of the clitoris, the color, shape, and size of both the outer and inner lips. Male genitals differ in the length and diameter of both the erect and non-erect penis, the length of time that various men are able to maintain an erection, and the force and volume of semen and sperms released, by the male organ. And then some men are circumcised and some are not. The point is:

> "The variety in human bodies impacts the physical and psychological experience of any sexual intercourse. And the fact that an experience can be evaluated against another such experience, means that variety can produce discontentment or dissatisfaction."

Physically and psychologically, most variety does not add spice, because variety only increases one's knowledge of physical-psychological differences between members of the opposite sex. Physical differences are sensed through our five senses, when we notice that this individual has prettier eyes, has prettier teeth, has a prettier smile, has a prettier skin texture, has a more pleasant body aroma, is a better sexual partner, etc. Psychological differences are sensed through our minds and our emotions, when we notice that this individual understands me better, makes me laugh all the time, is smarter, has a nicer personality, etc. Then if we focus on the physical differences related to sexual activities, we note that not all sexual encounters leave us with the same feelings, because of differences in our partners (*because of the variety within the opposite sex*). These differences impact our ideal partner. As our ideal partner becomes less and less like a real person, we will become more and more discontent.

If those individuals, who have had more than one sexual partner, were asked about their enjoyment of all of their sexual encounters. This author would guess that many would admit that they did not enjoy every one of those encounters, regardless of how much they were focused on themselves. Thus, the physical-psychological answer to the more precise question – "Is sexual variety really the spice of life?", is "No!"

Part-4: **Some concluding comments**

Some concluding comments flow out of the first three parts of this essay. Under "Part-1: The medical answer", comments were presented, which indicate that "sexual variety" is "medically" dangerous, because of an increasing number of sexually-transmitted diseases (*STD's*) and nonsexually-transmitted diseases (*non-STD's*). Under "Part-2: The biblical answer", comments were presented, which indicate that "sexual variety" is "biblically" dangerous, because God calls sexual relations, between a married person and another individual, other than the spouse, "adultery", and God calls sexual relations, between unmarried individuals, "fornication". Both "adultery" and "fornication" are called sin, by God. Under "Part-3: The physical-psychological answer", comments were presented, which indicate that "sexual variety" is "physically-psychologically" dangerous, because sexual variety causes a psychological itch that is hard to soothe or satisfy. Sexual variety is more like the poison ivy of life. Thus, the answer to the more precise question – "Is <u>sexual</u> variety <u>really</u> the spice of life?", is "No!"

You cannot miss what you do not know about!

If you only have one of something,
then you have nothing to compare it to!
And thus, you have less, or nothing, to be dissatisfied about!

If you only have one of something,
then you can enjoy that something on its own merit!

Is there such a thing, as safe sex?

This question flows out of two situations:

- *Situation-1*: Some individuals and groups are promoting a concept, which they called – "safe sex".

- *Situation-2*: Just because someone defines a concept and promotes that concept, does not mean that the concept is valid.

Thus, the purpose of this essay is to address the validity of the concept of "safe sex" through the question – "Is there such a thing, as safe sex?" To accomplish this purpose, this essay is organized in six parts. Part-1 presents a discussion of the question: "What is safe sex?" Part-2 presents a discussion of two facts generally not mentioned, by promoters of "safe sex". Part-3 presents some general comments about "safe sex". Part-4 presents some concluding comments. Part-5 presents some relevant comments. Part-6 presents a four-page summary of some "sexually transmitted diseases".

Part-1: **What is "safe sex"?**

Generally, the word – "sex", when not referring to the gender of an individual, is equated with "sexual intercourse". The word – "foreplay", is generally used to refer to all of the "physical, emotional, and/or mental" activities, which may precede an actual "sexual intercourse" or a potential "sexual intercourse". However, the question – "What is 'safe sex'?", is best answered by noting, how the phrase – "safe sex", is used. Many people use the phrase – "safe sex", to imply that there are techniques or procedures, which those involved in sexual intercourse can follow to "prevent the spread of 'sexually transmitted diseases'". The technique or procedure suggested, by most promoters of "safe sex" is "using a condom". An obvious side benefit of "using a condom" is the possible "prevention of pregnancies". However, the "prevention of pregnancies" is not the main focus of the "safe sex" concept. Thus, the answer to the question – "What is 'safe sex'?", is "the use of a condom during intercourse to prevent the spread of 'sexually transmitted diseases'".

Part-2: **Two facts generally not mentioned, by promoters of "safe sex"**

Most promoters of "safe sex", do not mention two facts:

- *Fact-1*, we know that a condom can come off, by itself during the heat of intercourse.

- *Fact-2*, using a condom will not necessarily prevent the spread of "sexually transmitted diseases (STD's)".

To discuss these two facts and present six examples of other ways that diseases are spread, Part-2 is organized in three sections. Section-1 presents a discussion of *Fact-1*. Section-2 presents a discussion of *Fact-2*. Section-3 presents six examples of how some diseases are transmitted.

Section-1: *Fact-1*: **We know that a condom can come off, by itself during the heat of intercourse**

A condom can come off, by itself during the heat of intercourse (*during the interaction of female and male organs*). This can happen even though neither participant may want the condom to come off. In addition, we know that some condoms are defective, because they have small holes in them. These are things that the promoters of "**safe sex**" through the use of a condom rarely mention.

Section-2: *Fact-2*: **Using a condom will not necessarily prevent the spread of "sexually transmitted diseases (STD's)"**

Using a condom might prevent the spread of a disease, if the only physical contact between the sexual partners was through a condom, and the condom was not defective. However, everyone not thinking with their genitals, should realize that such limited contact is unrealistic. Generally, during those sexually related activities prior to, during, and after an intercourse or a potential intercourse, the participants can have physical contact in many ways, using various parts of their bodies. Thus, promoters of "**safe sex**" through the use of a condom are indirectly pushing the concept that diseases; especially "'sexually transmitted diseases', can only be transmitted, by direct contact between sexual organs." However, the realities of life should make it clear that some diseases, including some of those labeled – "sexually transmitted diseases", can be passed from one individual to another, by a variety of interactions. Such interactions are, as follows: "hand to hand", "hand to body",

> *Comment:* For example, lets say that Zed has a STD. If Zed scratched his genitals with his bare hand, and then before washing his hands, he touched another individual in some way. It might be possible for Zed to pass his STD to the other individual. This is especially true, if the other individual had open wounds of some type that came into contact with Zed's hand.

> *Comment:* A radio ministry aired a program during which a guest stated that the most common transmittal medium between humans is the "**hand**".

"body to hand", "body to body", "hand to a sexual organ", "a sexual organ to hand", "mouth to body", "body to mouth", "mouth to a sexual organ", "a sexual organ to mouth", and **the interaction most often overlooked: "mouth to mouth** (especially, when fluids are passed)". The transmission of sexual diseases by means other than intercourse (*other than "a sexual organ to a sexual organ" contact*) is another fact that the promoters of "using a condom" rarely mention. Surely, no promoter of "safe sex" would be foolish enough to try to deny that "hand to a sexual organ" interactions are common during sexual activities.

Section-3: **Six examples of how some diseases are transmitted**

These examples present different ways that diseases, both STD's and non-STD's, might be transmitted other than by sexual intercourse. The first two examples are situations reported, by the print and televison news media. The remaining four examples are situations shared with this author, by friends. The six examples are, as follows:

- *Example-1* **(Body to hand to mouth):** A variety of news agencies have reported incidences, where food handlers (*cooks, waitresses, waiters, etc.*) have passed some disease to those who consumed the handled food. However, please note that many of these same diseases could be passed to another individual, by direct contact. That is, the food is not essential to the spread of some diseases. In some cases, the food is just one of many convenient vehicles that could help spread some diseases.

- *Example-2* **(Body to hand to body)**: A television network news program showed a segment about a young boy, who went blind in one eye. The blindness occurred, when the boy picked up microorganisms from his dog. More specifically, the boy had been playing with his dog, and managed to get microorganisms from his dog on his hands. Then the boy rubbed one of his eyes. This transferred the microorganisms from his hand to the rubbed eye. Eventually, some microorganisms entered the rubbed eye, causing the boy to go blind in that eye.

- *Example-3* **(Mouth to mouth)**: A friend dated a particular young lady a couple of times. One evening, this young lady French-kissed him (*the young lady stuck her tongue in his mouth*). My friend was not into French-kissing, but this young lady had French-kissed him, before he could stop her or pull away. While brushing his teeth a couple of days later, my friend noticed that there appeared to be a difference in the lining of his mouth. He thought the color of his lining had changed a little. Later, circumstances revealed to him that the young lady was involved in lesbian sexual activities. This did not make my friend feel good about that French-kiss, or more specifically, about the lining of his mouth.

- *Example-4* **(Body to mouth)**: Another friend dated several young ladies. This friend enjoyed playing the role of a baby, by nursing at his dates' chest. However, he dated one young lady, who had scaly nipples. Pieces of skin from this young lady's nipples would come off during his nursing. This skin got into my friend's mouth and made him physically ill, so he never played a baby with this particular young lady, again.

- *Example-5* **(A sexual organ to hand to body)**: Another friend dated a particular young lady a couple of times. One evening, circumstances allowed this friend to directly massage this young lady's genital area. During the massaging, this friend developed an itch near one of his elbows, so he scratched it using the same hand he used in doing the massage. A couple of days later, he noticed a rash had developed where he had scratched himself.

- *Example-6* **(A sexual organ to mouth)**: The wife of a friend is a nurse. One day my friend's wife told him that she had encountered a patient, who had gonorrhea of the throat. It is probably safe to assume that this patient got the gonorrhea by performing oral sex on someone else, who had the disease in their genitals. Or this patient got the gonorrhea, by kissing someone else, who had gonorrhea of the throat or who had gonorrhea in her or his mouth.

Part-3: **Some general comments about "safe sex"**

Some general comments about "safe sex" are, as follows:

We acknowledge that some bacteria, fungi, microorganisms, viruses, etc., can be passed from animals to humans. We acknowledge that some nonsexual diseases can be passed between humans. We even acknowledge that some sexual diseases can be passed between humans, during sexual intercourse. But we seem to ignore the fact that some "sexually transmitted diseases" are transmitted between individuals, without the explicit act of sexual intercourse. More specifically, we seem to ignore that:

"**'Sexually transmitted diseases' can be transmitted between individuals by contacts other than sexual intercourse – (other than the interaction of their sexual organs).**"

But the real impact of this is that:

"**Whenever you interact with anyone else on any level – (physical, emotional, mental, and/or religious), there is a very high probability that you are interacting with every individual with whom that person has interacted with on all levels.**"

Thus, with respect to diseases, when you kiss someone on the mouth, you are probably not only kissing every person that individual has kissed. You are possibly interacting with almost everything that individual has ever had on and/or in their mouth. You are also possibly interacting with everyone else and everything else that individual has interacted with. Once more, the reason for saying this is that the individual, whom you kissed, could have developed a disease from any source. Then if the disease agent made its way to the individual's mouth. There is a chance of it being passed to you during the kiss. Similarly, when you have sex with someone, you are probably also having sex with every person that individual has had sex with, in the sense that anything your partner picked up from any of her or his other partners will possibly be shared with you.

The problem with the phrase – "**sexually transmitted disease**", is that it conveys the false impression that a disease can only be transmitted during sexual activities, or more specifically, during intercourse. True, sexual intercourse might be the most common way for some diseases to be transmitted, but we must be conscious of the fact that "**it is not the only way**." At the end of this essay, there is a four-page summary of the most prevalent "sexually transmitted diseases". Please pay special attention to the ways that these diseases are transmitted, as indicated by the medical community.

Part-4: **Some concluding comments**

Some concluding comments flow out of the first three parts of this essay. The conclusion indicated by those comments is that:

"**There is no such thing, as 'safe sex', between any individuals**."

In addition to the supporting comments presented in the first three parts of this essay, additional support for the previously mentioned conclusion is provided by noting:

> "For even a virgin, whether female or male, could have picked up a 'sexually transmitted disease' from her or his birth mother, during the pregnancy or during the birth process. For instance, there are babies, who are born with HIV/AIDS, Syphilis, etc. Or a virgin could have picked up a 'sexually transmitted disease', by kissing someone, who has one."

Thus, the answer to the question – "Is there such a thing as safe sex?", is "No!" "**Safe sex**" **is an illusion. It is a lie!** However, there is such a thing, as "safe**r personal habits**", where the phrase – "safe**r personal habits**", would involve the concept of doing things to reduce the "likelihood of contacting a disease". Obviously, the word – "sex", has been replaced, because of the fact that not even "sexual abstinence before marriage" could reduce the "likelihood of getting an STD" to zero. The latter comment flows from the situations previously mentioned with regards to virgins. For that matter, "total sexual abstinence" would not reduce the "likelihood of getting a sexually transmitted disease" to zero, because an individual could contact a "sexually transmitted disease" from an inanimate object like towels, sheets, and so forth. (*See the four-page summary at the end of this essay.*) Thus, the phrase – "safe**r personal habits**", involves doing things like:

- Entering a monogamous relationship, as early as possible in life.

- Having both partners abstaining from sex activities – foreplay and/or sexual intercourse – with anyone other than their lifelong partner.

- Having both partners follow good private and public personal hygiene practices, like:

  - ✓ Avoiding unnecessary and unwarranted direct contact with personal items used by individuals other than their lifelong partner.

  - ✓ Using good sanitary practices when using private and public restrooms.

- Having both partners avoid mouth-to-mouth kisses with anyone other than their lifelong partner (*an additional benefit of this practice is emphasized, by the story of a "best physical feature", which was really a "kissing-story", presented in the essay: "Is variety the spice of life?"*).

Part-5: **Some relevant comments**

Some relevant comments are presented in two groups:

- *Group-1*: Since the mouth and the vagina are both cavity-like components of the human body, logic seems to dictate that most bacteria, viruses, etc., that can survive in one could also probably survive in the other. However, this author also recalls reading the comment that:

  "The mouth is the dirtiest cavity of the human body, because the vagina may contain enzymes and/or other substances to fight some types of bacteria and viruses."

- *Group-2*: A Christian radio personality, said,

  "**Condoms do not protect your conscience**."

Part-6:

SUMMARY OF SOME SEXUALLY TRANSMITTED DISEASES - (Sheet 1 of 4)

Name	Description	Transmitted	Symptom
Chlamydia	Chlamydia is the number one bacterial sexually transmitted disease (STD) in the United States today. Four million new cases of chlamydia occur each year. It's particularly common among teens and young adults. Pelvic inflammatory disease (PID), which can be caused by chlamydia, is a leading cause of infertility when left untreated.	**Through unprotected vaginal and anal sex**	Chlamydia is known as the "silent epidemic", because three quarters of the women and half of the men with the disease have no symptoms. Possible symptoms include discharge from the penis or vagina and a burning sensation when urinating. Additional symptoms for women include lower abdominal pain or pain during intercourse and bleeding between menstrual periods. Men may experience burning and itching around the opening of the penis and/or pain and swelling in the testicles.
Genital Warts	Genital warts are caused by the Human Papilloma Virus (HPV), one of the most common sexually transmitted diseases (STD's). HPV is the name of a group of viruses that includes more than 60 different types.	**Through sexual activities, which permit the HPV virus to be passed from one person to another**	Most HPV infections are subclinical--that means that there are no visible signs. Subclinical HPV infections can cause abnormal cell growth (dysplasia) on the female cervix. Visible signs of the disease include condylomata, which range from soft, pink, cauliflower-like warts to hard, smooth, yellow-gray warts. In women, they may develop inside the vagina, where they are hard to detect. They may also appear on the lips of the vagina or around the anus. In men, they usually appear on the penis, but are sometimes found on the scrotum (the sac that holds the testicles) or around the anus. If there are visible signs, you will notice them within 3 weeks to 6 months after having sex with someone who is infected. This time period makes it difficult to track the infection as it is passed from partner to partner.

SUMMARY OF SOME SEXUALLY TRANSMITTED DISEASES - (Sheet 2 of 4)

Name	Description	Transmitted	Symptom
Gonorrhea	Gonorrhea is caused by Gram-negative bacterium "Neisseria gonorrheae". This bacterium may infect the columnar epithelium of the urethra and endocervix. Non-genital sites in which it thrives are in the rectum, the oropharynx and the conjunctivae of the eyes.	**Through oral, anal, and vaginal sex**	It's possible to have gonorrhea without any symptoms. If symptoms do appear, they may include discharge from the penis or vagina, the need to urinate often, burning or pain when urinating, and in women, bleeding between monthly periods. About half of the women with gonorrhea have no symptoms.
Hepatitis B	Hepatitis B is an infection of the liver caused by a virus. It's 100 times more infectious than HIV. About 300,000 Americans get hepatitis B each year. Most people recover, but a few become chronic carriers with increased risk of serious problems later, such as permanent liver disease and cancer of the liver	**Through contact with infected blood or body fluids**	Symptoms usually appear within 2 to 6 weeks after contact. They can include poor appetite; nausea; vomiting; headaches; general malaise; jaundice (yellowing of eyes and skin); dark, tea-colored urine; and light-colored stools. Even without symptoms, you can pass the virus to others. Chronic carriers carry the hepatitis B virus for the rest of their lives and unknowingly pass it to their sex partners.
Herpes	Genital herpes is a chronic, lifelong viral infection. An estimated 40 million people have it.	**Through oral, anal, and vaginal sex**	Symptoms vary. Most people have no noticeable symptoms. If you do get symptoms, you'll probably notice them 2 to 20 days after having sex with someone who is infected. Early symptoms may include a burning sensation in the genitals, lower back pain, pain when urinating, and flu-like symptoms. A few days later, small red bumps may appear in the genital area. Later, these bumps can develop into painful blisters, which then crust over, form a scab, and heal.

SUMMARY OF SOME SEXUALLY TRANSMITTED DISEASES - (Sheet 3 of 4)

Name	Description	Transmitted	Symptom
HIV/AIDS	AIDS stands for Acquired Immunodeficiency Syndrome. AIDS is caused by HIV, the Human Immunodeficiency Virus, which attacks the body's immune system. Without immunologic protection, people with AIDS suffer from fatal infections and cancers.	**Through contact with infected blood or body fluids [can be passed from mother to child during pregnancy or birth]**	You can be infected with HIV, the virus that causes AIDS, and have no symptoms at all. On average, it takes about 7 to 9 years for symptoms to develop. Most symptoms of AIDS are not caused directly by the HIV virus, but by an infection or other condition acquired due to the weakened immune system. Symptoms can include severe weight loss, fevers, headaches, drenching night sweats, fatigue, severe diarrhea, shortness of breath, and difficulty swallowing. The symptoms tend to last for weeks or months at a time and do not go away without treatment. Since these symptoms are commonly seen in other diseases, you can't assume any symptom is HIV/AIDS-related until you get laboratory tests. See a doctor if you think you may be at risk or if you have symptoms.
Pubic lice (*often called "crabs"*) and Scabies (*itch mites*)	Pubic lice and Scabies are tiny insects that live on the skin. They are sometimes spread sexually, but you can also pick them up by using the same bed linen, clothes, or towels as an infected person. Scabies, an itchy rash, is the result of a female mite burrowing into a person's skin to lay her eggs. Pubic lice infect hairy parts of the body, especially around the groin and under the arms. Their eggs can be seen on the hair close to the skin, where they hatch in 5 to 10 days	**Through contact with an infected area on another person or through contact with infested materials such as sheets and towels**	Although some people infected with pubic lice have no symptoms, you may experience considerable itching around the genitals. You may see light-brown insects the size of a pinhead moving on the skin or oval eggs attached to your body hair. The main symptom of scabies is itching, especially at night. A rash may appear in the folds of skin between the fingers or on the wrists, elbows, abdomen, or genitals.

SUMMARY OF SOME SEXUALLY TRANSMITTED DISEASES - (Sheet 4 of 4)

Name	Description	Transmitted	Symptom
Syphilis	Syphilis is a curable sexually transmitted disease caused by the Treponema pallidum pirochete. The route of transmission of syphilis is almost always by sexual contact. However, there are examples of congenital syphilis via transmission from mother to child in womb. If not treated, syphilis can cause serious effects such as damage to the heart, aorta, brain, eyes, and bones. In some cases these effects can be fatal.	**Through oral, anal, and vaginal sex [can be passed from mother to child in uterus]**	Syphilis has three stages. During the first stage, a painless sore may appear at the spot where the bacteria first entered the body (usually from 10 to 90 days after sexual contact with an infected person). This sore may appear around or in the vagina, on the penis, or inside the mouth or anus. Sores inside the vagina or anus are often unnoticed and may disappear on their own if not treated, but the bacterial infection remains. The second stage occurs from 3 weeks to 3 months after the primary stage and includes flu-like symptoms and possible hair loss. Some people experience a rash on the palms of the hands and soles of the feet, as well as over the entire body. Although extremely rare, tertiary syphilis can appear 3 to 10 years or more after the first and second stages. Symptoms of this stage may include skin lesions, mental deterioration, loss of balance and vision, loss of sensation, shooting pains in the legs, and heart disease.
Tricho-moniasis	Trichomoniasis ("trich") is a common sexually transmitted disease (STD), attacking 2 to 3 million Americans every year. It is caused by infection with a flagellated protozoan, Trichomonas vaginalis.	**Through sexual contact and infected objects such as sheets and towels**	Many people with trichomonias experience no symptoms. Women may experience itching, burning, vaginal or vulval redness, unusual vaginal discharge, frequent and/or painful urination, discomfort during intercourse, and abdominal pain. Symptoms tend to worsen after menstruation. Men are usually asymptomatic, but symptoms can include unusual penile discharge, painful urination, and tingling inside the penis.

Should Christians worship God, under the leadership of a homosexual?

Over the past thirty years or so, in the United States and in many other places around this world, some people have been pushing for the acceptance of homosexuals and their lifestyle. Because of this push, people from various walks of life have admitted being homosexuals. In the United States, avowed homosexuals have been elected to various local, state, and federal political offices. Even more crucial to Christians, avowed homosexuals have been ordained, as ministers or priests, or elevated to high leadership positions in several Christian denominations. For Christians, these events should raise the question: "Should Christians worship God, under the leadership of a homosexual?" After raising this question and developing an answer, Christians must confirm that their answer is consistent with the Bible. These are the objectives of this essay. However, the first task is to prepare a foundation upon which an answer can be develop. This foundation will use two things: *First*, "a definition of a 'homosexual religious leader'" and *second*, "two crucial Christian beliefs". Thus, to address the topic question, this essay is organized in four parts. Part-1 presents a definition of a "homosexual religious leader". Part-2 presents two important Christian beliefs. Part-3 presents a critique of the topic question. Part-4 presents some concluding comments.

Part-1: **A definition of a "homosexual religious leader"**

A definition of a "homosexual religious leader" is "a religious leader for whom either or both of two conditions are true.

- *Condition-1* is 'the leader is actively participating in homosexual sex acts (*is actively participating in sexual interactions with someone of the same gender*).'

- *Condition-2* is 'the leader may not be participating in homosexual sex acts, but he or she actively supports individuals, who are.'

For *Condition-2*, the most crucial part is indicated by the word: 'support'. Here, the word – 'support', is intended to convey the fact that 'the religious leader does not attempt to encourage homosexuals to leave the homosexual lifestyle.'"

Part-2: **Two crucial Christian beliefs**

Two crucial Christian beliefs are: *First*, "except for Adam, Eve, and Jesus, all humans were born/are born/will be born sinners" and *second*, "Christians are to hate the sin, but love the sinner." Some background comments about these two beliefs are, as follows:

➧ *Belief-1*: "Except for Adam, Eve, and Jesus, all humans (*Christians and non-Christians*) were born/are born/will be born sinners." But Christians are supposed to be repentant sinners, while non-Christians are unrepentant sinners. Or worded differently, individuals become Christians by accepting Jesus, as their Lord and Savior. Yet, even after accepting Jesus, Christians still sin. However, Christians are repentant sinners, rather than being unrepentant sinners. Repentant sinners should not be sinning willfully with planning and forethought. And God, the Holy Spirit, easily convicts repentant sinners of their sins. Consequently, repentant sinners acknowledge their sinful nature, and pray to God for forgiveness and for the strength to resist future temptations. On the other hand, unrepentant sinners have no problem committing any sin or continually committing the same sins. Unrepentant sinners are not concerned about what God may think of their activities. In fact, many unrepentant sinners reject the notion that they sin. Therefore, they have no problem flaunting their sinful activities.

> *Comment:* The Bible implies that all humans are sinners, with 1 John 1:8 and Romans 3:23. These verses read.
>
> > (1 John 1:8 NIV) If we claim to be without sin, we deceive ourselves and the truth is not in us.
> >
> > (Romans 3:23 NIV) for all have sinned and fall short of the glory of God,

➧ *Belief-2*: "Christians are to hate the sin, but love the sinner." As the model for all Christians, explicitly or implicitly, by deeds or with words, Jesus indicated that He hated sin, but loved the sinner. Two examples – perhaps not the best, but examples anyway – are Luke 5:31-32 and John 8:1-11. The setting for Luke 5:31-32 is provided by Luke 5:27-30. Thus, in the NIV, Luke 5:27-32 read, as follows:

> Luke 5:27After this, Jesus went out and saw a tax collector by the name of Levi
> sitting at his tax booth. *"Follow me,"* Jesus said to him, 28and Levi got up, left
> everything and followed him. 29Then Levi held a great banquet for Jesus at his
> house, and a large crowd of tax collectors and others were eating with them. 30But
> the Pharisees and the teachers of the law who belonged to their sect complained
> to his disciples, "Why do you eat and drink with tax collectors and 'sinners'?"
> 31Jesus answered them, *"It is not the healthy who need a doctor, but the sick. 32I have
> not come to call the righteous, but sinners to repentance."*
>
> > Comment: Many sources indicate that during the time of Jesus, the Jews hated the tax collectors, many of whom were Jewish, because the tax collectors were considered traitors, who preyed on their own people.

The setting for John 8:1-11 is provided in these verses. In the NIV, John 8:1-11 read, as follows:

> John 8:[1]But Jesus went to the Mount of Olives. [2]At dawn he appeared again in the
> temple courts, where all the people gathered around him, and he sat down to
> teach them. [3]The teachers of the law and the Pharisees brought in a woman
> caught in adultery. They made her stand before the group [4]and said to Jesus,
> "Teacher, this woman was caught in the act of adultery. [5]In the Law Moses
> commanded us to stone such women. Now what do you say?" [6]They were using
> this question as a trap, in order to have a basis for accusing him. But Jesus bent
> down and started to write on the ground with his finger. [7]When they kept on
> questioning him, he straightened up and said to them, *"If any one of you is without
> sin, let him be the first to throw a stone at her."* [8]Again he stooped down and wrote
> on the ground. [9]At this, those who heard began to go away one at a time, the
> older ones first, until only Jesus was left, with the woman still standing there.
> [10]Jesus straightened up and asked her, *"Woman, where are they? Has no one
> condemned you?"* [11]"No one, sir," she said. *"Then neither do I condemn you,"* Jesus
> declared. *"Go now and leave your life of sin."*

Once more, Jesus was the model for all Christians. Therefore, we should hate the sin, but love the sinner.

Part-3: **A critique of the topic question**

Implicitly, this critique of the topic question, uses the definition of a "homosexual religious leader" and the "two Christian beliefs". Explicitly, this critique approaches the topic question from the "biblical viewpoint", that homosexuality is a sin. However, to be thorough with this presentation, we will broaden its sin aspect by including four other acts labeled, as sin in the Bible. These four sins are: "murder", "stealing", "adultery", and "lying". By including these four sins, with the sin of "homosexuality", in this discussion, hopefully, two things may become apparent. *First*, too many Christians believe that some sins are worse than others. (*While it is true that the physical consequences of some sins are worse than others, the spiritual consequences are the same.*) *Second*, the spiritual state of the religious leader's heart is what should determine, whether we should be worshiping under his guidance. Unfortunately, because we are not God, we can only judge the state of a religious leader's heart, by external signs, which are the leader's words and deeds. More specifically, we only have external signs to judge whether the religious leader is a "repentant sinner" or an "unrepentant sinner". Under such considerations, the actual sin that the religious leader is committing, becomes less important, while the external signs become more important. This should lead us to asking questions like: "Is this religious leader flaunting his sins?" (*One way, a leader may flaunt her or his sins, is when her or his sins become known to others, and she or he knows that others know, this leader does not stop her or his sinful activities. Such a leader may even try to justify her or his sinful activities.*)

Now, this critique is begun in earnest, using the five sins, in the following observation:

If a religious leader is actively murdering people, then it would be easy for most Christians to say, "Christians should not worship God under the leadership of this murderer." This is especially true, if the murders were committed without any moral justification, such as in the defense of the innocent.

Now, change the sin from murder to stealing, and then ask, "Should Christians worship God, under the leadership of a thief?" Unfortunately, before responding, too many Christians would say that they needed to ask several questions. Their first question would most likely be: "What is the leader stealing?" Their next questions might be: "What method is the leader using to accomplish the thefts?", "Is a gun being used?", or "Is any type of force being used?" Some Christians might even ask, "What is the purpose of the thefts?" Once such questions, as these were answered, most responders would probably feel qualified to answer the question: "Should Christians worship God, under the leadership of this thief?" Thus, their answer would not be based on the fact that the sin of stealing is being committed. On the contrary, their answer would be based on the circumstances and the facts (*the "who", "what", "when", "why", "where", and "how"*) surrounding the thefts. Fewer Christians are likely to say, "Christians should not worship God under the leadership of a thief" than would say, "Christians should not worship God under the leadership of a murderer."

Now, change the sin from stealing to adultery, and then ask, "Should Christians worship God, under the leadership of someone committing adultery?" You would probably find still fewer Christians saying, "Christians should not worship God under the leadership of an adulterer", than those who would say the same thing for a murderer or for a thief.

Now, change the sin from adultery to lying. And you would probably find even fewer Christians saying, "Christians should not worship God under the leadership of a liar." Most Christians would probably order the so-called severity (*most sinful to least sinful*) of the five sins, as murder, stealing, homosexuality, adultery, and lying. Thus, the number of Christians, who would have a problem worshiping under the leadership of a homosexual, is somewhere between the "number of those who would have a problem worshiping under a thief" and the "number of those who would have a problem worshiping under an adulterer".

In the above observation, it was assumed that the religious leader was still actively involved in the particular sin being discussed. Thus, in that observation, the religious leader was an unrepentant murderer, unrepentant thief, unrepentant homosexual, unrepentant adulterer, and/or unrepentant liar. This author believes that you could confirm the observation above for yourself, by performing your own test. You can discuss these issues with other Christians. However, if you do, do so in stages, and in the same order, as the observation above, or in "murder-stealing-homosexuality-adultery-lying" order. Nevertheless, based on the observation above, the topic question – "Should Christians worship God, under the leadership of a homosexual?", should be reworded, as the more precise question: "Should Christians worship God, under the leadership of 'an **unrepentant** homosexual'?" Or even better, the topic question could be reworded, as the more generic question: "Should Christians worship God, under the leadership of an '**unrepentant sinner**'?"

Part-4: **Some concluding comments**

The observation of Part-3 served to remind us that too few Christians are focused on the issue of repentance. Even though, repentance is an important factor in reflecting the spiritual state of our heart. But the most important thing to flow out of Part-3, hopefully was the reminder that our religious leaders are all sinners. Each has committed the sin of murder, of thievery, of homosexuality, of adultery, of lying, and/or so on. Therefore, each is either a "repentant sinner" or an "unrepentant[86] sinner". And once more, with the help of the Holy Spirit, "repentant sinners" are trying to change their sinful behavior (*whether they are successful is a separate issue*). "Unrepentant sinners" are not trying to change their sinful behavior. In fact, as previously mentioned, most "unrepentant sinners" do not even admit that they are sinners. Regardless of the sin being committed by "Unrepentant sinners", they should be put out of our fellowship groups, despite whether they are the leaders or members. Putting them out does not mean that we do not love them. On the contrary, it shows sinners that we do love them. Especially, since our purpose in putting them out of our fellowship groups is to get them to reflect on their sinful activities and their relationship with Christ. We must always keep in mind that "Christians are to hate the sin, but love the sinner." Therefore, we should not worship God, under the leadership of "an unrepentant murderer". We should not worship God, under the leadership of "an unrepentant thief". We should not worship God, under the leadership of "an unrepentant adulterer". We should not worship God, under the leadership of "an unrepentant liar". Therefore, when the topic question is reworded as: "Should Christians worship God, under the leadership of 'an unrepentant homosexual'?", clearly, the answer is "No!" More precisely, we should not worship God, under the leadership of anyone, who is involved in unrepentant sinning! How can someone lead the flock, if they are not willing to submit to God's Will? How can someone lead the flock, if they are not willing to follow the Bible? However, worshiping God, under the leadership of "a repentant murderer", "a repentant thief", "a repentant homosexual", "a repentant adulterer", and/or "a repentant liar" is acceptable, because, by definition, such individuals are submitting to God's Will.

On Judgment Day, how will God probably respond to nonbelievers, who say, "They never had a chance to know Him"?

Worded one way or another, this question has been pondered, over the years, by some Christians. Consistent with this pondering, this essay serves to develop an answer to the topic question. But first, a pleasant opening for this essay is a comment made by Mr. Stephen Morin, a murderer and a rapist, to Mrs. Margy Mayfield, months after their initial encounter. At the time of their initial encounter, Mr. Morin had abducted Mrs. Mayfield, a Christian, and her vehicle. During this initial encounter, Mrs. Mayfield witnessed (*presented Christ*) to Mr. Morin, who did finally accept Jesus, as his Lord and Savior. Months later Mr. Morin asked to see Mrs. Mayfield, who went to the prison, where Mr. Morin was. During this visit, Mr. Morin revealed to Mrs. Mayfield that as she was witnessing to him, he heard another voice say, "**This is the last time that I am going to call you!**"

> Comment: The audiotape: "**SPIRITUAL WARFARE: THE STORY OF STEPHEN MORIN by Mrs. Margy Mayfield**", contains the testimony of Mrs. Mayfield, a Christian, and her encounter with Mr. Morin. At the time of their initial encounter, Mr. Morin was on the run from the law, after having committed a murder. Law enforcement agencies from several states were seeking Mr. Morin for several rapes and several other murders. When Mr. Morin encountered Mrs. Mayfield, he abducted her along with her vehicle. However, during this encounter, God used Mrs. Mayfield to get Mr. Morin to accept Jesus, as his Lord and Savior. Mrs. Mayfield describes how Mr. Morin was later captured, tried, and sentenced to death. Mrs. Mayfield also mentions that while Mr. Morin was waiting for his execution, he brought others to Christ. This audiotape may still be available from the Focus on the Family Ministry. [*The toll-free telephone number for Focus on the Family is (800) 232-6459.*]

The conversion of Mr. Morin may have been more dramatic than many others, but the statement that he heard is consistent with a desire of God, as revealed in the Bible. This desire is that "All are saved, through the finished work of Jesus, on the cross." (*But remember God's character will not allow Him to force salvation on anyone.*) Nevertheless, the statement heard by Mr. Morin, made this author wonder, about those who choose not to accept Christ; especially, those who say, "They do not have enough evidence for them to believe. Or there is not enough evidence for them to know God!" Thus, we ponder the question: "On Judgment Day, how will God probably respond to nonbelievers, who say, 'They never had a chance to know Him'?"

Implicit in any discussion of this question are some basic Christian beliefs. Paraphrased, three such beliefs are, as follows:

- *Belief-1*: Christ died for the sins of all men, throughout time.

- *Belief-2*: Christ **freely offers** His spiritual death, as the penalty payment, and His physical death, as the atoning sacrifice, for the sins of all men throughout time.

- *Belief-3*: The deaths of Jesus are only meaningful to those who accept His offer of salvation through His deaths (*through His finished work, on the cross*). By accepting His offer of salvation, we allow Him to become our substitute. Those who do not accept His offer, commit the one "unpardonable sin", which is also called the "sin of unbelief" or the "sin of the blasphemy of the Holy Spirit".

The salvation offer made by Christ is like someone offering to be your substitute. However, no matter how badly someone might want to be your substitute. That individual can only be your substitute, if you accept her or him, as your substitute. The more traditional way that this is worded, is: "A '**gift**' is not a gift, unless it is accepted, by the one to whom it is offered!"

Another way to view Jesus wanting to be our substitute is:

> "'All of our sins are pardonable', 'if we allow the finished work of Jesus, to cover them, by accepting Him, as our substitute.' The 'unpardonable sin' is 'the sin of not allowing Jesus to be our substitute'. It is 'the sin of not allowing the finish work of Jesus, to cover all of our other sins.' The 'unpardonable sin' is also called the 'sin of unbelief', because someone is committing the 'sin of not believing in Jesus nor His finished work on the cross'. Therefore, this individual is also committing the 'sin of not allowing Jesus to be her or his substitute'. The 'unpardonable sin' is also called the 'sin of the blasphemy of the Holy Spirit', because the primary work of the Holy Spirit is 'to promote and strengthen our belief in Jesus and His finished work". Consequently, an individual, who blasphemes the Holy Spirit, is doubting the miracles of Jesus and His work.' Therefore, such an individual is also committing the 'sin of not allowing Jesus to be her or his substitute'."

Nevertheless, whether you believe in God or not, this author believes that a loving and just God will show nonbelievers on Judgment Day, how He worked in their life, to draw them to Himself. He will show each nonbeliever, how and when, she or he rejected His efforts and Jesus. Thus, on Judgment Day, the conversation between God and each nonbeliever might go, as follows:

The nonbeliever may say to God, "You did not give me enough information to believe in You! I never had a chance to know You!" Then God will say, "You had the light of your own conscience, but you ignored it, so that you could do your own thing. You had the light of nature, but you ignored it, as nonsense, so that you could do your own thing. You had the light of my Son, Jesus, but you rejected him, as a mere myth, so that you could do your own thing. However, let us get specific. Let us review some events in your life:

- "Do you remember when such and such happened? I was watching you. When your free will choices, and the freewill choices of others got you into that particular mess, I approached you to comfort you and to help you. That mess gave Me an opportunity to draw you to Me, so that you could know Me (*so that I could comfort you and share with you, My desire for your eternal salvation*). Yes! That was a low point in your life. However, had you asked Me, then I would have carried you through that rough time. But instead of calling on Me for help and comfort, do you remember how you reacted? Do you remember how you cursed Me?

- Later, do you remember when such and such happened? I was still watching you. Again, your choices, and the choices of others got you into a mess. Again, I approached you to comfort you and to help you. That mess gave Me another opportunity to draw you to Me, so that you could know Me (*so that I could comfort you and share with you, My desire for your eternal salvation*). Yes! That was another low point in your life. And again, had you asked Me, then I would have carried you through that rough time. But instead of calling on Me for help and comfort, again, you cursed Me!

- Later, do you remember when such and such happened? I was still watching. However, this time, your choices and the choices of others brought you good fortune. I approached you to share your joy, and to share My happiness for your good fortune. Thus, your good fortune also gave Me an opportunity to draw you to Me, so that you could know Me (*so that I could share with you, My happiness with your good fortune and My desire for your eternal salvation*). Yes! That good fortune was a high point in your life. Nevertheless, had you asked Me, then I would have shown you My happiness with the good fortune that you experienced. But instead of allowing Me to display My happiness, you cursed Me. And then you told others, 'See, I do not need God!'

- Low points and high points continued to occur in your life. Each of those points gave Me an opportunity to draw you to Me. But you never called on Me that I might bear your sorrow or share your happiness. You rejected the knowledge of Me that you were born with. You rejected the knowledge of Me in nature. And you rejected the "**gift of salvation**" that my Son, Jesus, offered you. Thus again, out of your own "free will", you rejected "the light of your own conscience", "the light of nature (*including the signs that I put in the heavens*)", and "the light of My Son, Jesus". Now, you must depart and leave the presence of My grace forever! You will dwell forever in the presence of My judgment!"

This is how God might respond to nonbelievers, on Judgment Day, when they say, "I never had a chance to get to know you!"

Conclusion

This author firmly believes that on Judgment Day, God will somehow prove to each nonbeliever that he or she willfully rejected Him (*that he or she had more than enough information, but refused to recognize it* and/or *to accept it*). Thus, get to know His Son, Jesus, now! God loves you. And if you, but ask, **He will reveal Himself to you in a more personal way, so that you may believe**. God wants everyone to be saved, but His justice will not allow Him to save those who willfully reject Jesus [*who is the only way to Him (God)*]. Therefore, again, the answer to the question – "On Judgment Day, how will God probably respond to nonbelievers, who say, 'They never had a chance to know Him?'", is "**God will probably show each nonbeliever that she or he had enough information to accept Jesus and His finished work on the cross, but she or he willfully rejected Him (Jesus)**."

Some appropriate closing verses

(Romans 1:20 NIV)

Romans 1:[20]For since the creation of the world God's invisible qualities--his eternal power and divine nature--have been clearly seen, being understood from what has been made, so that men are without excuse

(John 3:16-21 NIV)

John 3:[16]"For God so loved the world that he gave his one and only Son, that whoever believes in him shall not perish but have eternal life. [17]For God did not send his Son into the world to condemn the world, but to save the world through him. [18]Whoever believes in him is not condemned, but whoever does not believe stands condemned already because he has not believed in the name of God's one and only Son. [19]This is the verdict: Light has come into the world, but men loved darkness instead of light because their deeds were evil. [20]Everyone who does evil hates the light, and will not come into the light for fear that his deeds will be exposed. [21]But whoever lives by the truth comes into the light, so that it may be seen plainly that what he has done has been done through God."

(Matthew 7:7-11 NIV)

Matthew 7:[7]"Ask and it will be given to you; seek and you will find; knock and the door will be opened to you. [8]For everyone who asks receives; he who seeks finds; and to him who knocks, the door will be opened. [9]"Which of you, if his son asks for bread, will give him a stone? [10]Or if he asks for a fish, will give him a snake? [11]If you, then, though you are evil, know how to give good gifts to your children, how much more will your Father in heaven give good gifts to those who ask him!

(Proverbs 18:2 NIV)

Proverbs 18:[2]A fool finds no pleasure in understanding but delights in airing his own opinions.

(Ezekiel 18:32 NIV)

Ezekiel 18:[32]For I take no pleasure in the death of anyone, declares the Sovereign LORD. Repent and live!

(Ezekiel 33:11 NIV)

Ezekiel 33:[11]Say to them, 'As surely as I live, declares the Sovereign LORD, I take no pleasure in the death of the wicked, but rather that they turn from their ways and live. Turn! Turn from your evil ways! Why will you die, O house of Israel?'

(Jeremiah 29:13 NIV)

Jeremiah 29:[13]You will seek me and find me when you seek me with all your heart.

Did God lose ownership of the earth, when Adam sinned, as some preachers claim?

Some preachers claim that "God lost ownership of the earth, when Adam sinned, and only regained ownership with the help and faithfulness of Abraham." More specifically, these preachers claim that "God gave Adam ownership of this earth. When Adam sinned, ownership was passed to Satan. Then God regained ownership through Abraham." Despite the wording of any claim that God lost ownership of this earth, too many Christians accept such a claim, without testing it against the Bible or without considering the evidence.

The process of developing an answer to the topic question begins with two tasks:

- *Task-1*: We must establish a definition of the word: "ownership". Or better, we must develop a sense of what "ownership" involves.

- *Task-2*: We must examine a major piece of evidence that contradicts any claim implying God lost ownership of this earth.

With these two tasks and the topic question in mind, this essay is organized in four parts. Part-1 presents a discussion of the word: "ownership". Part-2 presents some evidence, which contradicts the claim that God lost ownership of the earth. Part-3 presents some concluding comments. Part-4 presents some relevant comments.

Part-1: **A definition of the word: "ownership"**

Defining the word – "ownership", is not easy, especially, if we try to describe the state of ownership. An easier approach is to develop a sense of "ownership", based on an examination of "'what ownership allows the owner to do to her or his property' versus 'what ownership allows the nonowner to do to that same property'". However, before discussing this ownership issue, we must say a few things about the word: "property". Depending on the society and the context, property could be a person, place, thing, or a process. The moral correctness of calling a "**person**" property will not be addressed in this essay. Please understand that the historical sense of the word – "property", is being used. Also, in some countries today, people are still bought and sold as property. It is just not done in the open.

Now, as ownership relates to "the privileges of the owner" of a property versus "the privileges of the nonowner", a discussion of ownership might go, as follows:

- Clearly, the owner of a property is entitled to do more things to that property than any nonowner. In fact, a nonowner should ask the owner of the property for permission, before doing anything to that property. Consequently, it should be obvious that, if what the nonowner wants to do to the property is not in the best interest of the owner, then the owner will not give her or his permission to that nonowner.

This view of "what ownership allows the owner to do" versus "what ownership allows the nonowner to do", is the view of "ownership" that will be useful for this discussion.

Part-2: **Some evidence, which contradicts the claim that God lost ownership of the earth**

Implicitly, the Bible contradicts the claim that Satan gained ownership of this world, when Adam sinned. The contradictory evidence is "the universal flood (*which occurred during Noah's lifetime*)". This universal flood is recorded in the Book of Genesis. This universal flood occurred a long time after Adam sinned and about one hundred and twenty years after the birth of Noah. But more important, this universal flood occurred before the birth of Abraham. Thus, if Satan gained the ownership of the earth, when Adam sinned, a holy God would have been required to ask Satan for permission, before He (God) could cause a universal flood. Under such circumstances, why would Satan allow God to destroy the evil people of Noah's generation? The people of Noah's generation were doing what Satan, wanted them to do. They were ignoring God and doing what was pleasing to their wicked minds. Obviously Satan had a strong influence over the people of Noah's day, but he did not have ownership of the earth. The fact that God caused a universal flood meant He (God) had ownership of this earth, not Satan. The universal flood also proved that God was in control, not Satan.

Part-3: **Conclusion**

The Bible clearly shows that God's authority is greater than Satan's. Obviously, Satan can exert an influence upon the inhabitants of this earth, but anyone saying, "Satan owned the earth", is implying that Satan has more power and authority than he actually does. Yes! The Bible seems to imply that Satan rules the earth, but "ruling it" is different from "owning it". Furthermore, the sense of the word – "rule", probably means that the number of people, who will freely listen to Satan and do his bidding is greater than those people, who will freely listen to God and do His bidding. This is also why the Bible suggests that Satan is the "prince of this world".

If we look at the Biblical evidence, we must conclude that God never lost ownership of this earth. God allows everyone, including Satan, to make choices, then God works all of our choices out for His glory, and for the good of those who love Him. Thus, the answer to the question – "Did God lose ownership of the earth, when Adam sinned, as some preachers claim?", is "No!"

Part-4: **Some relevant comments**

Some relevant comments are presented, here in two groups, as follows:

➧ *Group-1*: When Satan tempted Jesus, the man, he (*Satan*) offered Jesus all the kingdoms of this world. This could imply that "Satan owns this earth." Or it could imply that "Satan 'rules' this earth." This author believes the intended meaning is "Satan 'rules' this earth." Here as previously mentioned, "rule" means that Satan is able to get a lot of people to do those things that he wants them to do and in the manner that he wants those things done. The word – "rule", does not necessarily mean that Satan has absolute power or authority over us, because biblically, Satan appears to rule more by persuasion and by trickery than by force. Furthermore, Satan is a liar. He is willing to promise what he knows that he cannot fulfil, just to accomplish his purpose.

➧ *Group-2*: Before Satan could test Job, he had to get God's permission. See Job 1:6-12 and Job 2:1-7.

✓ Job 1:6-12 reads:

(Job 1:6 NIV) One day the angels came to present themselves before the LORD, and Satan also came with them.

(Job 1:7 NIV) The LORD said to Satan, "Where have you come from?" Satan answered the LORD, "From roaming through the earth and going back and forth in it."

(Job 1:8 NIV) Then the LORD said to Satan, "Have you considered my servant Job? There is no one on earth like him; he is blameless and upright, a man who fears God and shuns evil."

(Job 1:9 NIV) "Does Job fear God for nothing?" Satan replied.

(Job 1:10 NIV) "Have you not put a hedge around him and his household and everything he has? You have blessed the work of his hands, so that his flocks and herds are spread throughout the land.

(Job 1:11 NIV) But stretch out your hand and strike everything he has, and he will surely curse you to your face."

(Job 1:12 NIV) The LORD said to Satan, "Very well, then, everything he has is in your hands, but on the man himself do not lay a finger." Then Satan went out from the presence of the LORD.

✓ Job 2:1-7 reads:

(Job 2:1 NIV) On another day the angels came to present themselves before the

LORD, and Satan also came with them to present himself before him.

(Job 2:2 NIV) And the LORD said to Satan, "Where have you come from?" Satan answered the LORD, "From roaming through the earth and going back and forth in it."

(Job 2:3 NIV) Then the LORD said to Satan, "Have you considered my servant Job? There is no one on earth like him; he is blameless and upright, a man who fears God and shuns evil. And he still maintains his integrity, though you incited me against him to ruin him without any reason."

(Job 2:4 NIV) "Skin for skin!" Satan replied. "A man will give all he has for his own life.

(Job 2:5 NIV) But stretch out your hand and strike his flesh and bones, and he will surely curse you to your face."

(Job 2:6 NIV) The LORD said to Satan, "Very well, then, he is in your hands; but you must spare his life."

(Job 2:7 NIV) So Satan went out from the presence of the LORD and afflicted Job with painful sores from the soles of his feet to the top of his head.

Therefore, it should be obvious that God, and not Satan, is in control. Thus, once more, the answer to the question – "Did God lose ownership of the earth, when Adam sinned, as some preachers claim?", is "No!"

If God knows where each individual will spend eternity, then how can each individual have free will?

Some Christians and many non-Christians ask, "If God knows where each individual will spend eternity, then how can each individual have free will?" Over the years, this question has generated two standard responses. These two responses are not a problem for most Christians. However, most non-Christians are very uncomfortable with one of the responses, because it stresses the difference between "knowing something" and "causing something". Non-Christians have fewer problems with the second response, because it revolves around "God knowing" and "each individual not knowing". To present these two responses and discuss the validity of the topic question, this essay is organized in five parts. Part-1 presents a discussion of the response, which involves "God knowing" and "each individual not knowing". Part-2 presents a discussion of the response, which involves the difference between "knowing something" and "causing something". Part-3 presents a discussion of the question: "Is the topic question a valid question?" Part-4 presents some concluding comments. Part-5 presents some relevant comments.

Part-1: "**God knowing**" and "**each individual not knowing**"

Discussing "God knowing" and "each individual not knowing", is best done by addressing each component separately. The "God knowing" component, flows out of the wording of the topic question, because that wording concedes that "God knows where each of us will spend eternity." However, we will delay a discussion of the "God knowing" component until Part-2 (*titled: "Knowing something" and "causing something"*). Here, we will begin a discussion of the "each individual not knowing" component with the following observation:

> "Clearly, the Bible indicates that the eternal destiny of all, who accept Jesus, as their Lord and Savior, is heaven, and that the eternal destiny of all, who reject Jesus, as their Lord and Savior, is the Lake of Fire or Hell."

However, non-Christians do not believe in the Bible. Thus, a nonbiblical approach to a discussion of the "each individual not knowing" component, will be used. Under such an approach, we will accept the premise that "each individual does not know where they will spend eternity". This means that we must examine the impact of "each individual not knowing" on their lives. This examination would produce the following observation:

> "'Not knowing' where you will spend eternity does not stop you from living your life. On the contrary, your daily survival requires that you make choices almost every moment of each day of your brief life. For that matter, even babies make choices, although babies make their choices in response to their environment and their physical conditions, rather than making choices based on some combination of their environment and their spiritual,

mental, emotional, and physical circumstances. The point is:

> 'Regardless, of whether you are a baby, an infant, a child, a teenager, or an adult, your very survival requires that you make choices, while you are waiting for your own death and eternal destiny. However, especially as you grow into maturity, your daily freewill choices affect your eternal destiny, whether you like it or not.'

This point does not mean that you work your way into heaven. Rather, it means that your daily freewill choices are spiritually, physically, and mentally in line 'with the way God wants us to do things', or 'with the way you want to do things'. And the main thing that God wants us to do is 'To accept the finish work of His Son, Jesus Christ (*to accept what Christ did on the cross for us*)'. Thus, even though God knows where you will spend eternity and you do not, you still have freewill choices. And your freewill choices affect where you will spend eternity. Worded differently, God knowing, your eternal destiny does not negate your 'free will' to make choices, which affect your eternal destiny."

Part-2: "**Knowing something**" and "**causing something**"

"Knowing something" and "causing something", are two different conditions. Furthermore, there are two viewpoints: "God's viewpoint" and "man's viewpoint", which support the difference. The two viewpoints are discussed by making "God" or "man" the subject of both phrases. Thus, Part-2 is organized in two sections. Section-1 presents a discussion of the phrases: "God knowing something" and "God causing something". Section-2 presents a discussion of the phrases: "Man knowing something" and "Man causing something".

Section-1: **"God knowing something"** and **"God causing something"**

"God knowing something" and "God causing something", are two different conditions, as previously mentioned. "God knowing something", flows out of two of God's attributes: "God is a personal God" and "God is outside of time." (*Thus, He knows all of the details of everything. He knows everything past, present, and future, because He created everything including time. [Also note that because God created time, He is not affected by time.]*) However, "God knowing something" does not mean that "God caused something". Besides, if God caused everything, then He could NOT hold us accountable for our own actions. He would have to hold Himself accountable for our actions. However, if God knows everything, but does not cause everything, then He must allow some things. Thus, we have three situations: "God knowing something", "God causing something", and "God allowing something". With these three situations in mind, two responses to the question – "If God knows where we will spend eternity, then how can we have free will?", might go, as follows:

- *Response-1*: "God is outside of time, so He knows the beginning, the end, and everything in between, because everything has already occurred in His timeless dimension. While it is true that God knows everything, 'God knowing something', 'God allowing something', and 'God causing something', are clearly three different things. That is,

- ✓ 'God knowing something' *is the result of His* being outside of time.
- ✓ 'God allowing something' *is the result of His* having the power to make us do His will, but His not exercising such power.
- ✓ 'God causing something' *is the result of His* having the power to make us do His will and His exercising such power."

- *Response-2*: "If God caused everything – that is, if we did not have 'free will', then our creation would be pointless. Worded differently, if we could only execute those thoughts, words, and/or deeds, that God planned and nothing else – if God totally controlled all of our thoughts, words, and/or deeds, then our creation would be pointless."

Thus, "God knowing something" does not necessarily result from "God causing something". Yes! God knows everything and God caused some things. However, everything that God knows is not caused by Him. Rather some things are simply allowed by Him, because He created beings with "free will". Once more, "God knowing something" and "God causing something", are two different conditions, which are not necessarily dependent on each other.

Section-2: **"Man knowing something"** and **"Man causing something"**

"Man knowing something" and "Man causing something", are also two different conditions. With regards to man, there is a nice analogy to "God knowing something and yet, God not causing it". The analogy is:

- "Man knowing something" *is equated to* "You knowing that your loved ones will eventually die".
- "Man not causing something *is equated to* "Your loved ones dying of natural causes".

Whereas,

- "Man causing something" *is equated to* "You causing the death of a loved one".

"Man knowing something", is the result of man's interaction with and/or the observation of the individuals and things in this world. "Man causing something" would simply be the result of man's free will choices. That is, it would be the result of man selecting a choice and then executing the thoughts, words, and/or deeds related to that particular choice. Thus, "man knowing something" and "man causing something" are two different conditions, which are not automatically related to each other.

Part-3: **Is the topic question a valid question?**

This question flows from the fact that the topic question – "If God knows where each individual will spend eternity, then how can each individual have free will?", is an "If-Then-question". And an "If-Then-question", is only valid if the following three conditions are true:

- *First*, the "IF – part" must be valid and logical.

- *Second*, the "Then – part" must be valid and logical.

- *Third,* there must be a valid and logical relationship between the "IF – part" and the "Then – part".

Thus, the validity of the topic question can be determined, by using a three-step process: *Step-1*, determine the validity and logical consistency of the "If – part". *Step-2*, determine the validity and logical consistency of the "Then – part". *Step-3*, determine the validity and logical consistency of the relationship between the two parts. Performing this three-step process on the topic question yields the following results:

- *Step-1*: When the "If – part – 'God knows where each individual will spend eternity'", is examined, we should note that based on the definition of God and the Bible. God exists in a timeless environment. However, He created us in this space-time environment in His image. Now the beginning, the middle, and the end of all the happenings in our space-time environment have already occurred in the timeless environment of God. Consequently, God knows which individuals will accept Jesus as their Lord and Savior and which individuals will not. Thus, God knows where each individual will spend eternity. Therefore, based on the definition of God and the Bible, this "If – part" is valid and logically consistent.

- *Step-2*: When the "Then – part – 'how can each individual have free will?'", is examined, we should note that it is obviously a question. Thus, to confirm the validity of this "Then – part, we just need to provide a valid and logical answer to this question. And the answer is "Each individual can have "free will", because that is the way God created us in this space-time environment. Our "free will" is supported by both "the Bible" and "the observations of daily life". More specifically:

  - ✓ "The Bible" supports the existence of our "free will", because it recorded many examples of individuals, groups, and/or nations, exercising their "free will" to choose good or evil. Possibly, the best biblical example is "Adam and Eve choosing to eat the forbidden fruit, after God asked them not to". More specifically, the Bible recorded how God created Adam and Eve. Then it recorded how Adam and Eve sinned against God by eating the forbidden fruit, after God asked them not to. Thus, we know that God created us with "free will". If you read the details surrounding this example, another aspect of our God given "free will", is confirmed. This aspect is "even though God has given us the 'free will' to choose, He is not obligated to ignore our bad choices or to prevent the consequences of those bad choices."

✓ "The observations of daily life" support the concept that "Man was/is created with 'free will'", because everyone can observe that we have the "free will" to think, to say, and to do, a large variety of things within our own physical, spiritual, social, economical, emotional, and mental limits. Therefore, the existence of man's "free will" is beyond question.

Thus, being that this "Then – part" is a valid question with a realistic and supportable answer, this "Then – part" is valid and logically consistent.

➧ *Step-3*: When we analyze the logical consistency of the relationship of the "If – part" to the "Then – part", we should look for a possible "cause-and-effect" relationship, an "action-and-reaction" relationship, or some other logical relationship. In the case of the topic question, there does not appear to be any obvious relationship between its two parts. More specifically, there is no relationship between "God knowing our eternal destiny" and "our 'free will'". Thus, this question is determined to be invalid and logically inconsistent.

Another way to look at the validity of the topic question is that the topic question is an invalid question, because "God knowing" what our "freewill choices" will be does not change those choices. We make our own "freewill" choices. Therefore, based on both validity issues, the answer to the Part-3 question – "Is the topic question a valid question?", is "No!"

Part-4: **Some concluding comments**

Based on Part-3, the topic question – "If God knows where each individual will spend eternity, then how can each individual have free will?", is an invalid question. Thus, in responding to the individual, who asked the topic question, our first duty is to tell her or him, that "the question is invalid" and "why it is invalid." *(See the essay: "Are all questions valid and/or contextually appropriate?")* After that, the comments under Part-1 and Part-2, could be shared with that individual. This is how this author would respond to the topic question.

A last minute inspiration on this issue is:

"People focus only on the fact that **God knows our eternal destiny**. They fail to remember that He also knows '**<u>How</u> we will reach our eternal destiny**.' And that '**<u>How</u>**' involves our choices – what we do (*accepting or rejecting Jesus as our Lord and Savior*) and what we do not do (*not accepting Jesus as our Lord and Savior*). And once more, even though He knows and we do not know, we must make choices as we go about the process of living."

<u>Part-5</u>: **Some relevant comments**

Some relevant comments are, as follows: "Because of our 'free will', most of us stray from God's plan for us. However, the Bible shows that many times, when people strayed from God's plan for them, He put '***individuals***', '***things***', <u>and/or</u> '***events***' in their paths, in an attempt, to draw them back to His plan for their lives. Biblical examples of '***individuals***', are '***Joseph** (who was one of Jacob's twelve sons), **Moses, God's prophets, Jesus, <u>and</u> the Apostles***'. Biblical examples of '***things***', are '***Noah's Ark, the Manna** (grainlike substance, considered to be food from heaven, which sustained the Israelites in the wilderness)*[1]***, the Ark of the Covenant, <u>and</u> a big fish***'. Biblical examples of '***events***', are '***the Passover, the exile of the Jewish people from the promised land, the Babylonian captivity of some of the Jewish people, and the crucifixion of Jesus***'. Furthermore, the Bible shows that when some individuals exercised their "free will", it prevented them from responding to those '***individuals***', '***things***', <u>and/or</u> '***events***' that God put in their paths. A biblical example of someone, whose 'free will' prevented him from responding to an '***individual*** (*in this case, Moses*)', who was put in his path, is 'the Pharaoh of Egypt (*who initially would not let the Jews leave Egypt*)'. Thus, once more, man's 'free will' is clearly a biblical concept. In addition to confirming the previously mentioned, 'straying from God's plan' comment, the Bible also confirms the fact that **God does not force anyone to respond** to the '***individuals***', '***things***', <u>and/or</u> '***events***', that He may put in their path, in a manner, which is inconsistent with their 'free will'. More specifically, the Bible clearly shows that **God does not force us against our 'free will'**."

---

1 The source of this definition is the "<u>Holman Bible Dictionary</u>".

Who is a "born-again" Christian?

Sometime ago, while introducing himself to me, an individual declared himself to be a "born-again" Christian. Upon hearing this declaration, the first question that popped into my mind was "Who is a 'born-again' Christian?" Or more precisely, "What does it mean to be a 'born-again' Christian?" Then recalling my high school English classes, one thing became clear. Basic English grammar indicates that anytime a modifier is placed in front of a noun. Such placements of a modifier automatically imply that there is some type of variation involving that particular noun. The most common variations implied would be the modifier and its "antonym" (*or "the opposite in meaning" of the modifier*). Thus, the phrase – "'born-again' Christian", implies that there must be "'**born-again**' Christians" and "'**not-born-again**' Christians", where the phrase – "not-born-again", is the obvious antonym of the phrase: "born-again". However, "Christianity 101" implies that all Christians are by definition "born-again" in the sense that, at least, the first three of four things are supposed to happen, when someone becomes a Christian. These four things are, as follows:

- *First,* the individual must understand that she or he is a sinner in need of a savior.
- *Second,* the individual must die to her or his old life.
- *Third,* the individual must accept the finished work of Christ on the cross on her or his behalf. (*The individual must be reborn in Christ, by accepting the deaths and resurrection of Christ, on her or his behalf.*)
- *Fourth,* the individual must invite Christ to sit on the throne of her or his life.

Once again, when an individual accepts Christ, "she or he is reborn spiritually." Other wordings of this process are:

- ✓ "An individual goes from being 'spiritually dead' to being 'spiritually alive'",
- ✓ "an individual goes from existing under God's judgment to existing under God's grace", or
- ✓ "an individual goes from being separated from God's grace to being separated from God's judgment."

A more common wording is "All who accept Christ must die to themselves and '**be born again in Christ**'." When we accept Christ, He sends the Holy Spirit to guide (*or to aid*) us in living a

Christ-centered life and becoming more Christlike. Thus, the point is:

"Everyone, who accepts Christ, is by definition, a "**born-again Christian**".

Conclusion

Like too many other questions and issues, the topic question points to the sloppy use of language. Consequently, we must be careful whenever we put any type of modifier in front of a word like "Christian", because as previously indicated, such occurrences explicitly indicate categories of Christians. While it is appropriate to use the word – "mature" and its antonym – "immature", to modify the word – "Christian", using the phrase – "born-again", is sloppy and inappropriate, because by definition, there is no such thing, as a "not-born-again" Christian. Thus, the obvious answer to the topic question – "Who is a 'born-again' Christian?", would appear to be:

"Everyone, who accepts Christ, as their Lord and Savior".

However, because the phrase – "born-again", is modifying the word – "Christian", the question is really invalid.

Are all questions valid and/or contextually appropriate?[87]

Questions – especially "spiritual"[88] and/or "religious"[89] questions – inspired many of the essays in this book. Regardless of their form – written, verbal, or whatever, questions are an important part of most discussions or exchanges of thought on any subject. However, during religious discussions or exchanges between Christians and non-Christians, often some of the questions asked by non-Christians are unfair or inappropriate, because the questions are designed to embarrass or to stump, careless Christians, rather than being designed to seek an answer or to seek information. In reality, many of these unfair and inappropriate questions cannot truly be answered directly, because they are invalid and/or contextually inappropriate questions. For example, my favorite invalid question is the philosophical-religious question:

"Can God make a rock, so large that He cannot handle it?"

The best response to this question that this author has heard was presented by Dr. Walter Martin, founder of the Christian Research Institute (CRI). On Dr. Martin's audiotape, "Evil and Human Suffering", he opens his response by reminding the listener that "**God cannot do anything that would violate His revealed nature**." (*Please note the Bible reveals many things about God and His nature, but not everything.*) Based on Dr. Martin's presentation, a "yes–answer" to this question implies that God is not all-powerful, because He could not HANDLE such a rock. A "no–answer" to this question implies that God is not all-powerful, because He could not MAKE such a rock. But the truth according to Dr. Martin is that if God made a rock, so big that He could not handle it, He would have to violate His revealed nature. Consequently, this question is invalid, because it requires God to be physically, logically, and spiritually inconsistent. More specifically, this question requires God to violate His revealed nature. And God is not going to do that.

Thus, it should be obvious that words can easily be put together to form "valid and contextually appropriate", "valid and contextually inappropriate", "invalid and contextually appropriate", or "invalid and contextually inappropriate" questions in the physical arena, the logical arena, or the religious arena. With this understanding, we have actually answered the topic question with an obvious, No! However, we need to do more. We need to take a moment to examine the nature of questions and then develop a framework to aid us in determining the validity of a question and its contextual appropriateness. That is, we need to answer two questions:

- *First*, "How can we test the validity and/or the contextual appropriateness of a question?"

- *Second*, "How should we respond to invalid and/or contextually inappropriate questions?"

Some might say that these two questions reference a trivial issue. But understanding the nature of questions and the validity or contextual appropriateness of a specific question, will ease your search for an appropriate response. However, before going any further, two things need to be expressed.

- *First*, there is no such thing, as a dumb question, if you honestly do not know something.

- *Second*, there are questions, which violate the definition of a valid question and/or violate the conditions of contextual appropriateness.

These two statements can be made for three reasons:

- *Reason-1*: We are not trying to deny anyone the right to ask whatever question they wish.

- *Reason-2*: Whenever someone forms a question about a particular subject, they have to make underlying assumptions about that subject. Then planned or unplanned, the formed question automatically carries underlying implications about the subject and/or related things. This is true, despite the amount of knowledge that the author of the question has on the particular subject.

- *Reason-3*: Questions are inserted into some context. Furthermore, the wording of the question implies a context.

With these reasons in mind, we will discuss the two questions – "How can we test the validity and/or the contextual appropriateness of a question?" and "How should we respond to invalid and/or contextually inappropriate questions?", in more detail through "**four more fundamental questions**" and "**a brief critique**". The four fundamental questions are, as follows:

- ✓ What is a question?
- ✓ What is the purpose of a question?
- ✓ What makes a question valid or invalid?
- ✓ What makes a question contextually appropriate or contextually inappropriate?

Thus, this essay is organized in seven parts. Part-1 through Part-4 address one of the four questions above, in the order presented. Part-5 presents a brief critique of the topic question. Part-6 presents some concluding comments. Part-7 presents some relevant comments.

Part-1: **What is a question?**

"A question" is "a word or a group of words that one individual directs to someone else, herself, or himself in an effort to request some type of response. The response is usually, but not necessarily, a verbal one."

Part-2: **What is the purpose of a question?**

The purpose of a question is really only an expansion of its definition. More specifically, in general, the word or the group of words forming the question is chosen to indicate that some type of response is requested from the individual to whom the question is directed.

> *Comment:* The word – "requested", is used because there are words that "'command' a response". Under the rules of English grammar, these "'command' responses" are called: "exclamations (*abrupt and/or forceful utterances*)". Examples of exclamations are: "Look!", "Stop!", "Wait!", and "Now!".

Thus, the purpose of a question is to request some type of response. This means there is a reason why the question was formed. There are, at least, seven obvious reasons for asking questions. Note that some of these seven reasons are variations of each other. Nevertheless, it is important to state them explicitly. The seven reasons are, as follows:

- *Reason-1*: To find out something – to increase one's knowledge base, to satisfy one's curiosity, etc.,
- *Reason-2*: To try to get someone to review an issue from a different viewpoint,
- *Reason-3*: To rebut someone's position,
- *Reason-4*: To avoid answering someone else's question,
- *Reason-5*: To make someone else feel important/accepted,
- *Reason-6*: To embarrass someone,
- *Reason-7*: To control or steer the direction of the conversation.

And once more, for any reason, there are definitely valid and invalid questions.

Part-3: **What makes a question valid or invalid?**

To be a "**valid question**", a question must:

have valid underlying assumptions[90]

and

have valid underlying implications[91].

As part of the definition of a valid question above, the two phrases – "underlying assumptions" and "underlying implications", have the word – "valid", in front of them. Here, the word – "valid", is intended to mean that any "underlying assumptions" or "underlying implications", can each be supported by a logically valid argument. The word – "underlying", in front of the words – "assumptions" and "implications", is intended to mean that some "assumptions" or "implications", are always present, but not necessarily explicitly stated.

To be an "**invalid question**", a question must:

have invalid underlying assumptions

or

have invalid underlying implications.

As part of the definition of an invalid question above, the two phrases – "underlying assumptions" and "underlying implications", have the word – "invalid", in front of them. Here, the word – "invalid", is intended to mean that the "underlying assumptions" or the "underlying implications", cannot be supported by a logically valid argument.

Part-4: **What makes a question contextually appropriate or contextually inappropriate?**

This question flows out of the fact that a question is not inserted into a vacuum. Questions are inserted into some context[92] (*into "a setting of a subject or a specific view of a subject" and "any statements and/or questions that may have preceded it"*). The setting may even include such things, as a process or the deeds of one or more individuals. The process and the deeds may have occurred before or occurred during the time that the question is asked. Nevertheless, the point is:

> "A question must be contextually appropriate, for the setting into which it is inserted."

One way to verify the contextual appropriateness of a question, is by applying a three-step process:

- *Step-1*: Define the contextual setting implied by the wording of the question.
- *Step-2*: Define the contextual setting into which the question is inserted.
- *Step-3*: Compare the two defined contexts for logical consistency.

Thus, the question is contextually appropriate, if its implied contextual setting is consistent with the setting into which it was inserted. Otherwise, it is contextually inappropriate.

Part-5: **A brief critique**

As previously implied, it should be obvious that simply putting some words together to form a question, does not mean the resulting question is automatically valid and contextually appropriate. This tells us, before you address any question, you should try to understand the question, including a consideration of "How was the question framed?"[93] And you should also try to determine the context (*the setting*) of the question and the context into which the question is being inserted. Determining the validity and the contextual appropriateness of a question, can be accomplished through the following five tasks:

- *Task-1*: Confirm that you understand the question.

  Comment: Reverend Eugene Burrell, a minister with "The Navigators Ministry", said, "A good procedure is to restate the question, as part of your effort to understand it." Restate the question, as asked or restate the question, using your own (*different*) words, if necessary.

- *Task-2*: Determine what the underlying assumptions are.

  - ✓ If you are unsure of the underlying assumptions, then discuss the assumptions with the author of the question, if possible.

  - ✓ Determine if these assumptions are valid.

- *Task-3*: Determine what the underlying implications are.

  - ✓ If you are unsure of the underlying implications, then discuss the implications with the author of the question, if possible.

  - ✓ Determine if these implications are valid.

- *Task-4*: Define both the context implied by the question and the context into which the question was inserted.

  - ✓ Determine if the context implied by the question is logically consistent with the context into which the question was inserted?

- *Task-5*: Try to determine why the question was asked.

  Comment: With regards to understanding why the question is being asked, Reverend Burrell said, "Sometimes when he is engaged in philosophical-religious discussions, people will ask him an invalid religious question." His first response is to ask them, "If I answer your question to your satisfaction, then would you accept my Jesus?" If they say, "Yes!", then he will give them his best response. If they say, "No!", then he will tell them that they are just playing the "'I-don't-care-what-the-answer-is–I-just-want-to-stump-you' game" with him.

  Furthermore, understanding why the question is being asked, can reveal other situations. For example, a very young child asks a question about specific sexual activities. Such a question should tell the parents that this child is being inappropriately exposed to something either by her or his peers, by some adult, by a television program, by some type of literature, etc. Thus, the parents need to determine why the question is being asked, to reveal, to assess, and to counter the source of the exposure.

To ease the application of the previously mentioned five tasks, these tasks are converted into the following seven questions:

1) Do I (*the one to whom the question is directed*) understand the question?
2) What are the underlying assumptions of the question?
3) Are the underlying assumptions valid?
4) What are the underlying implications of the question?
5) Are the underlying implications valid?
6) Is the context implied, by the question consistent, with the context into which the question was inserted?
7) Why is the question being asked?

If you apply these seven questions, then hopefully you will not be pulled into the "'I-don't-care-what-the-answer-is–I-just-want-to-stump-you' game". Furthermore, if you apply these seven questions and determine that a question is an invalid and/or a contextually inappropriate question, then you should share that evaluation with the author of the question. If you determine that a question is valid and contextually appropriate, then you should do your best to provide an appropriate answer. In either case, but more appropriately for the valid and contextually appropriate question, you should never be ashamed or embarrassed to say, "I don't know!" However, when you don't know, a better response is "I don't know, but I will try to find out for you!"

Part-6: **Some concluding comments**

Many words can be chosen to form a question. However, forming a grammatically correct question does not automatically make the resulting question a "valid question" and/or "a contextually appropriate question". Therefore, as previously mentioned, this should tell us that before rushing to respond to any question, we need to take a moment to analyze it. We should do something like applying the seven questions given in Part-5 to the question. Then we can respond to the question accordingly. Thus, as also previously mentioned, the answer to the topic question – "Are all questions valid and/or contextually appropriate?", is "No!"

A final concluding comment is required here. More specifically, it needs to be explicitly expressed that there may be times, when you know that a question is invalid and/or contextually inappropriate, but you decide to present an answer anyway. And that is okay! The main point to this essay is that you should not let someone misdirect or stump you with an invalid and/or contextually inappropriate question.

Part-7: **Some relevant comments**

Relevant comments are organized in four groups, as follows:

- *Group-1*: This essay was directed toward questions introduced within discussions in any arena: the physical arena, the logical arena, or the religious arena. However, immediately behind the essay – "Are all statements (*non-questions*) valid and/or contextually appropriate?", which follows this essay, there are three essays, each of which addresses a question framed in the religious arena. These three essays provide us with an opportunity to apply the seven previously mentioned questions. The three essays are titled:

  a) How can I have "free will", if I did not choose to be born?

  b) If God is all-powerful and loving, then why doesn't He end all evil and human suffering?

  c) If you were going to have a son and you knew that he would become a mass murderer, would you still have him?

  In applying the seven previously mentioned questions to the three essays above, this author had to determine the underlying assumptions, the underlying implications, and then assume the context in which the question might be inserted. This process exposes this author to a charge of "putting up straw men in order to knock them down". However, as you read those essays, if you feel that this author misapplied the seven questions in anyway, then please send your comments to the author via the publisher. Thank you.

Comment: The author and publisher hope to improve the next edition of this book, based on your feedback.

- *Group-2*: There are questions for which the underlying assumptions, the underlying implications, and/or the context may be muddied. This can make the process of assessing the validity of the question or its contextual appropriateness more difficult. Still, this difficulty is eased somewhat, because rarely are all three muddied for the same question.

- *Group-3*: In analyzing some invalid questions or contextually inappropriate questions, it may be clear from the start that

  an underlying assumption is invalid,

  or

  an underlying implication is invalid,

  or

  the context implied by the question is inconsistent with the context into which the question was inserted.

  In such cases, if time or circumstances do not lend themselves to a full discussion of all three aspects – "the underlying assumptions", "the underlying implications", and "the context", of the question, then focus on the one aspect, which seems to be the clearest indicator of a problem with the question.

- *Group-4*: Some invalid and/or contextually inappropriate questions are formed, when someone takes known facts about a person, a thing, an event, or a process, and then forms a question, based on these facts, while excluding other known facts about the same person, thing, event, or process.

Are all statements (*non-questions*) valid and/or contextually appropriate?

This question flows out of the fact that the essay – "Are all questions valid and/or contextually appropriate?", obviously focused on questions. An obvious follow-up question to that essay is the question: "Should the validity and contextual appropriateness of '**statements**' also be checked?" The obvious answer is "Yes!", because every issue raised, in the previously mentioned essay with respect to questions, is also true of statements. The basis for saying this is that in the English language, a question can easily be turned into a statement or vice versa, in most cases, by changing the order of the main verb and subject. For example, the essay – "Are all questions valid and/or contextually appropriate?", referenced my favorite invalid-philosophical-religious question:

"Can God make a rock, so large that He cannot handle it?"

This question can be turned into the statements:

"God can make a rock, so large that He cannot handle it."

or

"God cannot make a rock, so large that He cannot handle it."

Just as the above question was shown to be invalid in the essay – "Are all questions valid and/or contextually appropriate?", the two statements above can be shown to be valid or invalid. Additionally, when the contextual setting that each statement was inserted into is known, the contextual appropriateness or inappropriateness of each statement can be determined. Therefore, just as all questions should be evaluated for their validity and contextual appropriateness, all statements or non-questions should also be evaluated. And the method defined for questions, in the essay – "Are all questions valid and/or contextually appropriate?", is applicable for statements. Thus, the obvious answer to the topic question – "Are all statements (*non-questions*) valid and/or contextually appropriate?", is also "No!"

How can I have "free will", if I did not choose to be born?

During a religious discussion, a friend (*let us call him, Zed*) asked, "How can I have 'free will', if I did not choose to be born?" Zed's words formed what seems to be a valid and contextually appropriate question. But is it? Before trying to respond to Zed's question, we must determine its validity and contextual appropriateness. To make such a determination, we must answer the seven questions defined in the essay – "Are all questions valid and/or contextually appropriate?", as these seven questions apply to Zed's question. The seven questions are, as follows:

1) Do I (*the one to whom the question is directed*) understand the question?
2) What are the underlying assumptions of the question?
3) Are the underlying assumptions valid?
4) What are the underlying implications of the question?
5) Are the underlying implications valid?
6) Is the context implied, by the question consistent with the context into which the question was inserted?
7) Why is the question being asked?

To apply the previous seven questions to Zed's question and then to respond to his question, this essay is organized in eight parts. Part-1 through Part-7 address one of the seven questions above, in the order indicated by the number of the question. Part-8 presents a response to the topic question, based on the answers to the seven questions.

Part-1: **Do I (*the one to whom the question is directed*) understand the question?**

During the process of confirming your understanding of any question, you should confirm the definition of questionable terms or phrases. Thus, for the question – "How can I have 'free will', if I did not choose to be born?", you could confirm the definition of the phrase: "free will". The definition of "free will" in *Wiktionary*, reads:

> "'Free will', as a noun: 1. (philosophy) The ability to choose one's actions, or determine what reasons are acceptable motivation for actions. 2. (philosophy) The doctrine that humans (and possibly other entities) are able to choose their actions without being caused to do so by external forces."[94]

> *Comment:* Note. When the phrase – "free will", is used, as a *noun*, it is two words (*a phrase*). However, when it is used, as an *adjective*, it is one word: "freewill". Thus, the definition of "freewill", as an adjective in *Wiktionary*, reads:
>
> "'Freewill', as an adjective: 1. voluntary."[95]

Comment: Why do we complicate our language, by mixing the form of words and/or phrases like "free will" and "freewill"?

With the previously referenced definition of "free will" in mind, this author understands the question – "How can I have 'free will', if I did not choose to be born?", to be, as follows:

> "Free will" means "being able to freely choose, between two or more options ".
> I did not choose, between "being born" and "not being born".
> Therefore, how can I have "free will"?

Part-2: **What are the underlying assumptions of the question?**

The topic question appears to have, at least, three underlying assumptions: *First*, the question assumes that "we did not choose to be born (*or 'we did not choose to be created'*)". *Second*, according to Reverend Eugene Burrell, a minister with "The Navigators Ministry", the question assumes that "'free will' is total (*or 'free will' should be total*)". *Third*, the question assumes that "because we did not choose to be born, we do not have 'free will'".

Part-3: **Are the underlying assumptions valid?**

Is the *first* assumption – "we did not choose to be born (*or 'we did not choose to be created'*)", valid? This assumption reflects the reality of life that most of us have no recollection of being given the choice to be born or not. The Bible is consistent with our recollection, because it does not include any indication that God gave Adam or Eve, the choice of being created or not. Thus, based on the Bible and the apparent realities of life, this *first* assumption – "we did not choose to be born (*or 'we did not choose to be created'*)", is valid.

Is the *second* assumption – "'free will' is total (*or 'free will' should be total*)", valid? If "free will" was total, there would be infinite choices and eternal possibilities. More specifically, for us to be created under "total-free-will", there would seem to be only two possible options: *Option-1*: God would have to create us in some nonhuman form and then give us the "free will" to choose to be born a human or not. *Option-2*: We would have to preexist, as God's equal, and then we could choose to be born, as humans. However, clearly *Option-2* is not realistic. This leaves just *Option-1*. But if *Option-1* is taken to its "absurd limit", it clearly becomes a logical absurdity. This is true, because under "total-free-will", the "absurd limit" is that in each prior nonhuman form back to infinity, we would require the "free will" to choose to come forward to the next form. Obviously, becoming a human would be the final limit at this end. But the problem is at the beginning end – in infinity, where the process of choosing to go to the next form requires a "first choice". But there is no form in which one could exist to exercise this "first choice" that would not require a prior form. Consequently, there could never be a "first choice", which pushes this situation into a logical absurdity. Therefore, we could never exist under "total-free-will". Consequently, *Option-1* is not realistic. Then putting both options aside, daily survival clearly proves that we do not have "total-free-will", because our choices are limited within this space-time environment, by the realities of the circumstances around our very existence. For example, your "free will" alone will not allow you to violate the Laws of Gravity. Thus, it should be clear that "free will" is not total. Therefore, the second assumption – "free will is total (*or 'free will should be total'*)", is invalid.

Is the *third* assumption – "because we did not choose to be born, we do not have 'free will'", valid? Daily life clearly reveals that we do have some "free will" within this space-time environment. That is, we do have some "free will" within the realities of the circumstances around our very existence. Thus, our "free will" is limited to a specific framework, which is this space-time environment and the realities of our circumstances. More specifically, within this framework, we note the "freewill" choices, which revolve around the thoughts, words, and deeds that we perform on a daily basis. For example on a daily basis, barring physical obstacles or limitations (*barring the limitations of the realities of your circumstances*), you have the "free will" to choose to turn to the right or the left. You have the "free will" to choose to accept or reject Jesus, as the only way to God. You have the "free will" to choose between doing good and doing evil. Thus, we obviously have some "free will" within the framework, in which we exist. Therefore, the *third* assumption – "because we did not choose to be born, we do not have 'free will'", is invalid.

Part-4: **What are the underlying implications of the question?**

Based on the underlying assumptions and other considerations, the topic question appears to have, at least, two underlying implications: *First*, the question implies that "because we have no memory of choosing to be born, we did not have such a choice." *Second*, the question implies that "if God gave us 'free will', then He should have also given us the 'free will' to choose to be born."

Part-5: **Are the underlying implications valid?**

Is the *first* implication – "because we have no memory of choosing to be born, we did not have such a choice", valid? The best responses to this implication are practical examples. For example, this author has no memory of his mother giving birth to him. He has no memory of learning to walk (*of those first steps*). He has no memory of the first time that he drove a vehicle. Does that automatically mean these three events did not happen? Obviously, not! Having no memory of some event, does not automatically mean that the event did not happen. It may mean we cannot remember the event. Thus, the *first* implication – "because we have no memory of choosing to be born, we did not have such a choice", is invalid.

Comment: The point is:

> "If possible, the truth about the occurrence of an event should not be based only on whether we remember the event or not. We should also seek

other corroborating evidence to prove or disprove the occurrence of that event."

Is the *second* implication – "if God gave us 'free will', then He should have also given us the 'free will' to choose to be born", valid? (*Anyone promoting the point of view that "God should have also given us the 'free will' to choose to be born", would have to believe that she or he could design creation and the "God and man" relationship better than God.*). As indicated under several of the responses to underlying assumptions of the topic question, for us to exercise a "freewill choice" to be born human, would mean our existence in some nonhuman form. Such an existence when compared to the realities of our human existence, yields a couple of problems and/or issues. The problems and/or issues revolve around the fact that as humans, our "freewill choices" appear to be based on our needs, our wants, our desires, our lust (*if applicable*), and/or our past experiences. This raises the issue: "If we existed in a nonhuman form prior to choosing to be born human, what would our choice to become human (*or to stay nonhuman*) be based on." Especially, if as "nonhuman's", we did not have the ability or opportunity to observe humans. And, if as "nonhuman's", we did have the ability or opportunity to observe humans, who did Adam (*the first human male*) and Eve (*the first human female*) observe? This implication generates so many illogical and unrealistic situations and conditions, that it can be dismissed. More precisely, the *second* implication – "if God gave us 'free will', then He should have also given us the 'free will' to choose to be born", is invalid.

Part-6: **Is the context implied, by the question consistent with the context into which the question was inserted?**

This question is addressed using a three-step process. Step-1 presents a discussion of "the context implied, by the topic question". Step-2 presents a discussion of "the religious context into which the topic question was inserted". Step-3 presents a discussion of "the contextual consistency of the question".

Step-1: The context implied, by the topic question

Zed (*the author of the topic question*) is allowing for the existence of God, because of the way that his question was worded. Furthermore, Zed knows that most Christians believe God created us with "free will". However, Zed is saying, "We cannot have 'free will', because we were not given the choice to be born." More precisely, Zed is saying, "'free will' should be 'total-free-will'." That is, not only should we have "free will" within a framework, but we should have the "free will" to enter that framework. (*Hopefully, you noted the previously mentioned, "absurd-limit argument" and you know that if God gave us "total-free-will", He would have to give us some of His sovereignty, and that is inconsistent with His revealed nature.*) The point is:

"The context of Zed's question implies 'total-free-will' or 'free will should be total.'"

Step-2: The religious context into which the topic question was inserted

Once more, most Christians believe that God created us with "free will". Our "free will" is implied in the Bible. In fact, in the very first book of the Bible – the Book of Genesis, we have God telling Adam not to eat the fruit from the tree of the knowledge of good and evil. God also told Adam that he could eat the fruit of any other tree in the garden. But Adam and Eve chose to disobey God, based on comments made by Satan. Likewise, our "free will" allows us to accept God or to reject Him. More specifically, on a daily basis, we have the "free will" to choose from a variety of options available to us at the time. Some options cause us to sin (*to violate God's plan for our lives*) and other options are consistent with God's plans.

In summary, God gave us "free will" within a specific framework. This "free will" allows us to obey God's commandments or not. More precisely, this "free will" allows us to choose to be under God's grace throughout eternity, or choose to be under His judgment throughout eternity. However, God did not give us the "free will" to choose to be born or not. Thus, the religious context into which the topic question was inserted, implies "partial-free-will". This "partial-free-will" is even more obvious, when you note that our "free will" does not allow us to violate the laws of nature, for example the Law of Gravity.

Step-3: The contextual consistency of the question

The context implied by the topic question and the context into which the topic question was inserted, are not consistent, because the "total free will" implied, by the question is incompatible with the "partial free will" in the context that the question was inserted. Thus, the topic question is contextually inappropriate.

Part-7: **Why is the question being asked?**

It is this author's opinion that Zed thinks that he has formed an unanswerable question and/or a question that will stump Christians.

Part-8: **A response to the question: "How can I have 'free will', if I did not choose to be born?"**

This question is invalid and contextually inappropriate. It is invalid, because it has invalid underlying assumptions and invalid underlying implications. This question is contextually inappropriate, because the context implied by the topic question is inconsistent with the context into which the topic question was inserted. Furthermore, while conceding the validity of the statement – "We did not choose to be born", this author emphatically rejects the notion that it is logically valid to discuss "free will (*being able to freely choose, between two or more options*)" and "choosing to existing or not existing (*choosing to be born or not*)" in the same context. Again, these two issues: "having choices" and "choosing to be born or not", are logically incompatible for the following two reasons:

- *Reason-1*: "Free will" is only meaningful in a framework where choices exist.

- *Reason-2*: Choosing to exist or not to exist is only meaningful in a framework, where such a choice is possible. More specifically, such a choice requires some form of existence at the beginning of the process. Thus, the need for some beginning form of existence creates an illogical situation. It would almost be like existing, at some point, in order to choose whether to exist or to not exist, which is obviously a logical absurdity.

If God is all-powerful and loving, then why doesn't He end all evil and human suffering?

During one of many religious discussions with a friend (*once more, let us call him, Zed*), Zed asked, "If God is all-powerful and loving, then why doesn't He end all evil and human suffering?" Zed's words formed what seems to be a valid and contextually appropriate question. But is it? Before trying to respond to Zed's question, we must determine its validity and contextual appropriateness. To make such a determination, we must answer the seven questions defined in the essay – "Are all questions valid and/or contextually appropriate?", as these seven questions apply to Zed's question. The seven questions are, as follows:

1) Do I (*the one to whom the question is directed*) understand the question?
2) What are the underlying assumptions of the question?
3) Are the underlying assumptions valid?
4) What are the underlying implications of the question?
5) Are the underlying implications valid?
6) Is the context implied, by the question consistent with the context into which the question was inserted?
7) Why is the question being asked?

To apply the previous seven questions to Zed's question and then to respond to his question, this essay is organized in eight parts. Part-1 through Part-7 address one of the seven questions above, in the order indicated by the number of the question. Part-8 presents three responses to the topic question, based on the answers to the seven questions and other considerations.

Part-1: **Do I (*the one to whom the question is directed*) understand the question?**

This author understands the question – "If God is all-powerful and loving, then why doesn't He end all evil and human suffering?", to be, as follows:

> If God is all-powerful and loving,
> why doesn't He end all evil and human suffering?

Or a more respectful wording of the topic question would be, as follows:

> If God is all-powerful and loving,
> what are His reasons for not ending all evil and human suffering?

Part-2: **What are the underlying assumptions of the question?**

The topic question appears to have, at least, one underlying assumption. This question assumes that "God exists."

Part-3: **Are the underlying assumptions valid?**

Is the assumption – "God exists", valid? Based on the standard definitions and concepts under Christianity, this is a valid assumption. Furthermore, Zed directed the question to me and he knows that my beliefs are consistent with the essential concepts of Christianity. See the essay – "What are the essential concepts of Christianity?", in the book: "Last Call!!!" The framing of the topic question concedes the existence of God. Thus, this assumption – "God exists", is valid.

Part-4: **What are the underlying implications of the question?**

Based on the underlying assumptions and other considerations, the topic question appears to have, at least, two underlying implications: *First*, the question implies that "God could end all evil and human suffering." *Second*, the question implies that (*if God is all-powerful and loving, and evil and suffering exist, then*) "God is not in control."

Part-5: **Are the underlying implications valid?**

Is the *first* implication – "God could end all evil and human suffering", valid? This implication is consistent with the essential concepts of Christianity. More specifically, the Bible indicates that God will end all evil and human suffering. But He will do so His way and in His timing. Thus, the fact that God will end all evil and human suffering, means that He could. Therefore, the *first* implication – "God could end all evil and human suffering", is valid.

Is the *second* implication – "God is not in control", valid? This implication is inconsistent with the implication of the essential concepts of Christianity, which is "God is in control." Based on the essential concepts of Christianity, if "God is not in control", then everything else about Christianity becomes meaningless. Thus, based on the implication of the essential concepts of Christianity, the *second* implication – "God is not in control", is invalid.

Part-6: **Is the context implied, by the question consistent with the context into which the question was inserted?**

This question is addressed using a three-step process. Step-1 presents a discussion of "the context implied, by the topic question". Step-2 presents a discussion of "the religious context into which the topic question was inserted". Step-3 presents a discussion of "the contextual consistency of the question".

Step-1: The context implied, by the topic question

The topic question was formed in light of the evil and suffering that obviously exist in this space and time environment called earth. The existence of evil and suffering, by some is taken to mean that "God is not in control" or that "God is not all-powerful and loving." Thus, the context of the topic question implies that "God is not in control" or "God is not all-powerful and loving."

Step-2: The religious context into which the topic question was inserted

The Bible clearly tells us that "God is in control" and that "God is all-powerful and loving". The Bible also indicates that "God will end all evil and suffering, at the end of this age". Thus, the context that the topic question was inserted is "God is in control" and "God is all-powerful and loving."

Step-3: The contextual consistency of the question

The context of the topic question implies "God is not all-powerful and loving" and "God is not in control." The context into which the topic question was inserted, is "God is all-powerful and loving" and "God is in control." The two contexts differ over "God's power and love" and "whether God is in control". A second contextual difference is the timing of the end of "evil and human suffering". The timing implied, by the way Zed worded the topic question, is right now. That is, Zed wants God to end all evil and human suffering right now. Whereas the Bible indicates that God will end all evil and human suffering at the end of this age. This author would say that neither of these contextual differences is enough to declare this question contextually inappropriate. (*Some contextual differences must be accepted. Otherwise, many questions could never be addressed.*)

Part-7: **Why is the question being asked?**

People, who ask questions like the topic question, have not been able to reconcile "God's power and love" and "the existence of evil and human suffering". Most of these individuals will not accept the Christian explanation for the existence of evil and human suffering. As previously indicated, the Christian explanation is "God created this space-time framework for us to temporarily live in and He created us with 'free will'. Then God gave us the option of exercising our own 'free will' or of allowing Him to exercise His 'free will'. Adam and Eve chose to exercise their own 'free will' and we inherited that bend from them. And although God allows us to exercise our own 'free will', He is not obligated to prevent us from suffering the consequences of our own 'free will' or the consequences of the 'free will' of others." Thus, Zed asked the topic question, because he refuses to accept the fact that evil and human suffering are the results of the "free will" of beings (angels and men) created by God.

Part-8: **Three responses to the question: "If God is all-powerful and loving, then why doesn't He end that whatever?"**

Although the topic question has an invalid implication and appears to be contextually inappropriate, both of these center on acceptable differences. Thus, before responding to the topic question, this author would share his thoughts on the invalid implication and the contextual inappropriateness with the individual, who asked the question. Then this author would present three responses. Response-2 is rejected offhand, by many non-Christians, because they refuse to see its logical beauty. Thus, Response-1 is presented not only, as a stand alone response, but also as logical support for Response-2. Response-3 is how some Christian scholars respond to the topic question. The three responses, which are separated by a double-margin-to-margin line, are as follows:

Response-1: Because of all the evil and suffering that obviously exist in this world, many non-Christians say, "There is no God; God is powerless; God is unloving; and/or God is not in control." These individuals say this, by making direct statements to that effect or by asking questions like, "If God is all-powerful and loving, then why doesn't He —

end that famine,
end that disease,
end that war,
end all evil and human suffering,
end that whatever?"

Individuals, who make direct statements or ask questions like those above, ignore the fact that God has other attributes besides being all-powerful and loving. Three other attributes of God are – He is just, He is merciful, and He is patient. Some of the ways that God has shown these five attributes are, as follows:

- God showed His **Power**: By creating a vast universe just so that we could live on this tiny planet called: "earth". (*Some scientists consider the size and vastness of this universe, as one of possibly thousands of parameters, which make life on the earth possible.*)

- God showed His **Love**: By creating us with "free will" and by sending His only begotten Son to die on a cross to redeem us, after Adam and Eve exercised their "free will", by sinning.

- God showed His **Justice**: By telling Adam and Eve that there was only **one thing**, which He did not want them to do (*God kept it simple for them*), by telling Adam and Eve what the consequences would be, if they chose to disobey Him, and by sending Jesus to pay the penalty for Adam and Eve's decision to disobey Him and for our decisions.

- God showed His **Mercy**: By not killing Adam and Eve immediately, after their decision to sin, by not destroying all humans, during the flood, and by setting a plan in motion to redeem man through the finished work of Jesus, since the finished work of Jesus serves to reestablish man's existence under God's grace.

- <u>God showed His **Patience**</u>: By not having Jesus return (*His second coming*) immediately, after His crucifixion. Jesus will return to rapture His church. He is coming as a King and as a Judge. In the meantime, the delayed return of Jesus is giving more people the chance to accept Him, as their "Lord and Savior" and by that be saved.

In addition to ignoring God's other attributes, people want Him to forget His plans for us. People want God to intervene here or there in human affairs, but not in their own lives. More precisely, people want God to intervene on their terms, not His. But note that God is not obligated to respond to the desires, needs, and wants of those who do not believe in Him (*of those who reject what Jesus did on the cross*). Also, note that "evil and human suffering: famine, disease, war, and so on", flow out of the freewill choices of man. For example:

- Many **famine**s have and do occur even though there may be ample supplies of food else where in the world. It may be that those with the power and resources may not be concerned enough to make the freewill choices to get the food where it is needed.

- Many **disease**s, especially sexually transmitted diseases, continue to spread, because of the lust of man and our "free will" choices to indulge in sexual activities outside marriage and because of man's freewill rejection of God's suggestion that monogamous relationships are the best way for man.

- Many **war**s have and do occur, because of man's freewill to defend his pride, because of man's freewill to lust after the resources of others, or because of man's freewill to hate others.

Again, to summarize the relationship of man's "free will" and three of God's attributes, we have, the following comments:

- Because of God's **love**, we were created with the "free will" to make choices.

- Because of God's **justice**, once Adam and Eve chose to do things their own way, God was obligated to respect our "free will" choices. And we inherited the bent of choosing to do things our own way from Adam and Eve, along with an existence under God's judgment. God is not obligated to shield us from the consequences of our freewill choices or the freewill choices of others. But because of God's holiness, He is obligated to hold us accountable for our freewill choices.

- Because of God's **mercy**, He presented Jesus, whom we can choose to accept of our own "free will" and by that return to an existence under God's grace.

Thus, once more, the point is:

> "Evil and human suffering flow out of our freewill choices. Among those choices, which add to the evil and our suffering, are the 'rejection of God' and the 'rejection of Jesus, as the only way to God'."

Response-2: God created man with "free will". Evil and human suffering flow out of the freewill choices of man. More precisely, evil and human suffering flow out of the consequences of not only our own freewill choices, but also the freewill choices of others. Thus, the existence of evil and human suffering does not mean that "God is powerless or unloving" or "God is not in control." Rather, "God is all-powerful and loving" or "God is in control" means that He created us with "free will", then He allows us to exercise that "free will" within the framework, which He created for us. "God is all-powerful and loving" or "God is in control" means that He allows us to decide whether to do things His way or to do things our own way (*to decide whether to do good or evil*). However, once we decide, God does not shield us from the consequences of our decisions – from the consequences of our own freewill choices. "God is all-powerful and loving" or "God is in control" also means that, at times, He places people, events, or things in our paths to motivate us to make good choices – to make Godly choices. The prophet Jonah is an example of this that ended with Jonah doing it God's way. The Pharaoh of Egypt, who interacted with Moses over the Jewish people, is an example of this that ended with the Pharaoh doing it his way. Thus, again, evil and human suffering flow out of our own ways, not God's way.

Response-3: Many Christian scholars say something like:

> "To end all evil and human suffering, God would have to overrule our freewill choices, which would make us robots, or He would have to end our lives."

If you were going to have a son and you knew that he would become a mass murderer, would you still have him?

During a friendly religious discussion, a friend asked, "If you were going to have a son and you knew that he would become a mass murderer, would you still have him?" This friend's question may appear to be a valid and contextually appropriate question. But is it? Before responding to my friend's question, we must determine its validity and contextual appropriateness. To make such a determination, we must answer the seven questions defined in the essay – "Are all questions valid and/or contextually appropriate?", as these seven questions apply to my friend's question. The seven questions are, as follows:

1) Do I (*the one to whom the question is directed*) understand the question?
2) What are the underlying assumptions of the question?
3) Are the underlying assumptions valid?
4) What are the underlying implications of the question?
5) Are the underlying implications valid?
6) Is the context implied, by the question consistent with the context into which the question was inserted?
7) Why is the question being asked?

To apply the previous seven questions to my friend's question and then to respond to his question, this essay is organized in nine parts. Part-1 through Part-7 address one of the seven questions above, in the order indicated by the number of the question. Part-8 presents a response to my friend's question, based on the answers to the seven questions. Part-9 presents a response to the relevant question: "Why would God create man knowing that man was going to sin?"

Part-1: **Do I (*the one to whom the question is directed*) understand the question?**

This author understands the question – "If you were going to have a son and you knew that he would become a mass murderer, would you still have him?", to be one that sets up a hypothetical scenario and then poses a question.

The scenario is:

> You and your spouse are going to have a son. Through some sort of premonition, you discover that your unborn son will become a mass murderer, at some point in his life.

The question is:

"Knowing this, would you still allow this son to be born?"

Part-2: **What are the underlying assumptions of the question?**

The question – "If you were going to have a son and you knew that he would become a mass murderer, would you still have him?", appears to have, at least, three underlying assumptions: *First*, the question assumes that "we have sufficient knowledge to weigh this son's destructive actions against all the good he might also do, or against all the people that he may influence for good." *Second*, the question assumes that "the phrase – 'mass murderer', has negative connotations. Therefore, this scenario is automatically indicated to be a negative situation." *Third*, the question assumes that "God could not use the impact of the activities of a mass murderer to witness to others."

Part-3: **Are the underlying assumptions valid?**

Is the *first* assumption – "we have sufficient knowledge to weigh this son's destructive actions against all the good he might also do, or against all the people that he may influence for good", valid? Obviously, this assumption must be examined under the wording of the topic question. And the wording only implies that we know the son will become a "mass murderer". The wording of the question tells us nothing about other aspects of this son's life. And no one could answer the question fairly without more details on the son's "whole-life". Actually, the information process is further complicated by the fact that details would be needed about everyone whose sphere of awareness the son entered. For instance, the reality of life might dictate that as a mass murderer, this son may have been responsible for say, ten deaths. But what if he were also a famous surgeon, who was directly responsible for saving a thousand lives. Or what if this son saved the life of just one person, who then went on to save thousands. No! Without reading a book about this son and about everyone whose sphere of awareness he entered, a simple question could never provide enough information for us to properly answer the topic question. Thus, the *first* assumption – "we have sufficient knowledge to weigh this son's destructive actions against all the good he might also do, or against all the people that he may influence for good", is invalid.

Is the *second* assumption – "the phrase – 'mass murderer', has negative connotations. Therefore, this scenario is automatically indicated to be a negative situation", valid?

> *Comment:* Obviously, the phrase – "mass murder", literally, takes its meaning from the word – "mass", which conveys a sense of number, with that number probably being more than three, and the word – "murder", which conveys the sense of "taking the life of an 'innocent' individual", with the word – "innocent", conveying the sense that "individual did not deserve to die." More specifically, we can say, "'taking the life of anyone without due process or without any legal justification'

is 'murder'". That is why when a state takes a life after due process, it is called an "execution" – an execution by lethal injection, an execution by hanging, an execution by the electric chair, etc. When a homeowner takes the life of an intruder, it is said, "the homeowner killed an intruder." The intruder is not assumed to be innocent, because, first of all, she or he is somewhere that she or he had no legal right to be. Thus, the negative connotations of the phrase – "mass murderer" are, at least, twofold: *first*, the "taking of innocent life", and *second*, the taking of many of those lives. And this is why a negative situation is assumed.

As the wording of the topic question implies a negative situation, we must assume that my friend wants us to believe that the individuals, who were murdered did not deserve to die. Consequently, we have to admit that the phrase – "mass murderer", does indicate a negative situation. Thus, the *second* assumption – "the phrase – 'mass murderer', has negative connotations. Therefore, this scenario is automatically indicated to be a negative situation", is valid.

Is the *third* assumption – "God could not use the impact of the activities of a mass murderer to witness to others", valid? To understand the full impact of those activities, my friend seems to want us to play God, because only God could know the full impact. However, the Bible indicates that, for those who love Him, God does work "evil and suffering" into something good. Thus, God can even use the impact of the activities of a mass murderer to witness to others. An example of this was one of the impacts of the shootings at Columbine High School on April 20, 1999. More precisely, an impact was that many teenagers throughout the nation deepened their faith, and some teenagers even came to know the Lord for the first time. The mass murders at Columbine have motivated more Christian young people to witness and share their faith with classmates and friends. Consequently, it is invalid to assume that God cannot use the impact of a mass murderer for some good. Thus, the *third* assumption – "God could not use the impact of the activities of a mass murderer to witness to others", is invalid.

Comment: One individual, who reviewed an early draft of this essay, challenged this author to find some good in the Holocaust, because history has recorded only one greater mass-murder event than what occurred during the Holocaust. The one greater mass-murder event was those murdered, by Joseph Stalin during and after his rise to power in Russia. Nevertheless, the task of finding some good in the Holocaust is easier than this individual thought, because this author has heard several Christian radio programs, which detailed events in the death camps of Nazi Germany. Some of these programs told of how Bible studies were conducted in possibly a flea-infested area of the barracks. Flea-infested areas were selected, because the prison guards avoided those areas. Anyway, the Bible studies gave prisoners, including Jewish prisoners, the opportunity to accept Jesus, as their Lord and Savior. Still, the two most significant events, from a Christian viewpoint, to come out of the Holocaust, were: *first*, the return of many Jews to their promised land and *second*, the reestablishment of the Jewish nation. (*Both of these events were prophesied in the Bible.*)

Part-4: **What are the underlying implications of the question?**

Based on the underlying assumptions and other considerations, the question – "If you were going to have a son and you knew that he would become a mass murderer, would you still have him?", appears to have one underlying implication. The *one* implication is that "Because you know that your unborn son will become a 'mass murderer', you have a reason to abort him."

Part-5: **Are the underlying implications valid?**

Is the *one* implication – "Because you know that your unborn son will become a 'mass murderer', you have a reason to abort him", valid? Now, the realities of life indicate that there is no way for one person to assess the life or the impact of another person's life no matter how evil the other individual may appear. Thus, knowing about some evil acts performed, by some individual does not tell us anything about the possible good that may come out of their existence. To properly weigh the good and evil in someone's life would require that the one doing the weighing be God. For only God could look down all the lines of influence of a given individual to know how others were effected, by her or his life. Thus, the *one* implication – "Because you know that your unborn son will become a 'mass murderer', you have a reason to abort him", is invalid.

Part-6: **Is the context implied, by the question consistent with the context into which the question was inserted?**

This question is addressed using a three-step process. Step-1 presents a discussion of "the context implied, by the topic question". Step-2 presents a discussion of "the religious context into which the topic question was inserted". Step-3 presents a discussion of "the contextual consistency of the question".

Step-1: The context implied, by the topic question

This context is "the individual, to whom the question is directed, must play God or be God." For only God would have enough knowledge to know the value of this son's existence, even though this son becomes a mass murderer. As we are only human, we do not have sufficient information to properly answer the topic question.

Step-2: The religious context into which the question was inserted

The religious context is "God is God. We are not God. We are only human."

Step-3: The contextual consistency of the question

The context implied by the topic question is inconsistent with the religious context into which the question was inserted. Therefore, the question – "If you were going to have a son and you knew that he would become a mass murderer, would you still have him?", is contextually inappropriate.

Part-7: **Why is the question being asked?**

The topic question is being asked, because my friend does not understand why God created man knowing that man was going to sin. (*Part-9 includes an explicit response to the question: "Why would God create man knowing that man was going to sin?"*) In forming the topic question, my friend has tried to create a scenario that he feels is analogous to God's creating man, knowing that man would sin. Then he wants the individual, to whom the question is directed to play God. My friend has assumed that the only reply to his question is "No!" More precisely, my friend is hoping that the individual, to whom the question is directed, will agree with him, by replying with "No!" However, my friend's analogy fails, because God has infinite knowledge and we – humans – do not.

Part-8: **A response to the question: "If you were going to have a son and you knew that he would become a mass murderer, would you still have him?"**

The topic question is invalid and contextually inappropriate. It is invalid, because it has two invalid underlying assumptions and an invalid underlying implication. This question is contextually inappropriate, because the context implied by the topic question is inconsistent with the context into which the topic question was inserted. More precisely, there is no way for us to have sufficient information to make a fair assessment of the impact of this son's life. Furthermore, the past twenty years, or so, have shown that most mass murderers focused on a specific group of people or a specific setting. Thus, again, if this son became a mass murderer of babies, there would be a major outcry from others. However, if this son became a mass murderer of individuals, who were on the verge of becoming the mass murderer of babies and this could be proven, there would probably not be much of an outcry.

My friend is focusing on the sins of men. Thus, he is ignoring those who willfully accept Christ. More precisely, my friend is ignoring those who willfully seek the help of the Holy Spirit to overcome their sinful nature. Also being ignored is a basic Christian concept that "every individual has until the moment of their death to accept, what Christ did on the cross for them. And to God, whatever someone did during their life is less important than whether they accept Christ before they die."

Part-9: **A response to the relevant question: "Why would God create man knowing that man was going to sin?"**

This response to the relevant question, has a two-part answer: *First*, God created beings (angels, man, and others) PERFECTLY, which is confirmed by their ability to rebel or sin against Him. Second, created beings (angels, man, and others) having the ability to rebel or to sin against God provides Him with the opportunity to deal with rebellion and sin forever. Thus, Part-9 is organized in two sections. Section-1 presents a discussion of the fact that "God created beings (angels, man, and others) PERFECTLY, which is confirmed by their ability to rebel or sin against Him". Section-2 presents a discussion of the fact that "created beings (angels, man, and others) having the ability to rebel or to sin against God provides Him with the opportunity to deal with rebellion and sin forever".

Section-1: **God created beings (angels, man, and others) PERFECTLY, which is confirmed by their ability to rebel or sin against Him**

The fact that God created beings PERFECTLY is confirmed by the ability of His created beings to rebel against Him and to sin against Him, because He created beings with "free will". More specifically, God's created beings were not robots. And the ability of God's created beings to exercise their "free will" is recorded by two facts: *first*, the Book of Revelations and other verses of the Bible, indicate that with one-third of the angels, Satan led a rebellion against God and *second*, the Book of Genesis indicates that after being tempted by Satan, Adam and Eve chose to sin against God. Nevertheless, once more, the ability of God's created beings to rebel against Him and to sin against Him shows how much "free will" that He created in them. Besides, with "free will", God's created beings can love Him by choice. And a love relationship is only meaningful if both parties give their love of their own "free will".

Section-2: **Created beings (angels, man, and others) having the ability to rebel or to sin against God provides Him with the opportunity to deal with rebellion and sin forever**

God's created beings having "free will" and thus, the ability to rebel against Him or to sin against Him, provided Him with the opportunity to deal with rebellion and sin forever. Therefore, God created the "Lake of Fire" for Satan and the one-third of the angels, who followed Satan in his rebellion against God. Then God banished Satan and his followers from heaven. (*Revelation 12:9 seems to indicate that Satan and his followers were cast down to the earth.*) Later Satan tempted Adam and Eve. And because of that tempting, Adam and Eve sinned against God. (*Then God banished Adam and Eve from the Garden of Eden.*) However, God created a redemption plan for humans. Under this plan, those humans, who choose to accept the finish work of Jesus on the cross, on their behalf, will spend eternity with God in paradise. On Judgment Day, those humans, who rejected Jesus, along with Satan and his demons, will be condemned to an eternal existence in the "Lake of Fire", which is the Second Death (See Revelation 20:14) - an eternal existence under God's judgment or an eternal existence separated from God's grace. This is how God will deal with rebellion and sin forever.

How should Christians respond to a "We-don't-know!" statement?

This author has found that during religious discussions with non-Christians, the statement – "We don't know!", is one of their favorite replies. However, is it a valid reply? Or more important, "How should Christians respond to a 'We-don't-know!' statement?" To discuss a possible response to such a statement, this essay is organized in two parts. Part-1 presents a critique of the topic question. Part-2 presents some concluding comments.

Part-1: **A critique of the topic question**

Many of those using a "We-don't-know!" statement, have not thought about its implications. The primary implication of this statement is "if we do not know, then we cannot take any action (*we cannot take a stand*). Or possibly, we cannot make a decision." However, the reality of life is there are many religious-and-nonreligious things and/or conditions that we do not know with certainty. However, daily life requires that we make many assumptions and then continue our activities based on those assumptions. For example, you do not know if the chair you are about to sit in will support your weight. Naturally, you hope and pray it will. Under the assumption that the chair will, indeed, hold you, you sit on it. If things go your way, the chair will support your weight. If things do not go your way, the chair will collapse under your weight. Similarly, you do not know if the food that you are about to eat will poison you or not. You continue on the assumption, and the hope that the food is good. We could go on and on. But the point is:

> "We don't know many things with certainty, so we make many assumptions just to continue with our daily lives. If we do not allow 'not knowing' to stop us with our daily living, then why is it appropriate to allow 'not knowing' to stop us from making religious decisions on religious issues."

Part-2: **Conclusion**

Under the religious contextual setting of the topic question, the response to a "We-don't-know!", could be twofold, as follows:

> "*First*, confirm that a "we-don't-know" reply is valid. That is, do not let someone get away with using a "we-don't-know" reply in response to some issue, which has historical, biblical, logical, or physical support.
>
> *Second*, if a "we-don't-know" reply is valid, you could say something like – 'You are right. Whether we are dealing with the physical arena, the logical arena, or the religious arena, there are many things that we do not know for sure.

Consequently, many times we must make assumptions, based on the available information, and then continue with our life. More specifically, in the religious arena, using the Bible, we take our best interpretation and make whatever-religious decision seems appropriate. But 'whatever we do', should never be contrary to the concepts presented in the Bible, as a whole."

How should Christians respond to an "It-is-possible-that-such-and-such-happened" statement?

During a religious discussion with a friend, this author used some supportable-logical arguments to counter his position on the religious issues being discussed. However, this friend responded with an "It-is-possible-that-such-and-such-happened" statement. This was the first use of such a statement that this author really noticed. The statement left this author momentarily speechless, numb, and wondering – "How should Christians respond to an 'It-is-possible-that-such-and-such-happened' statement?" After recovering, this author ignored this friend's statement and continued the discussion with more supportable arguments. Months later, another use of an "It-is-possible-that-such-and-such-happened" statement occurred, during a discussion with another friend. This particular discussion started around the question: "How was life created?" During this discussion, this author commented that – "Life was created by God." This friend responded with the statement: "It is possible that life came here from another planet!" This second use of an "It-is-possible-that-such-and-such-happened" statement, was the final straw. At that moment, this author decided to think about how to respond to such statements. Then after weeks of praying and thinking, a method of responding to an "It-is-possible-that-such-and-such-happened" statement came to mind. This method is presented here by responding to the statement: "It is possible that life came here from another planet!" Thus, this essay is organized in three parts. Part-1 presents some general comments. Part-2 presents a response to the statement: "It is possible that life came here from another planet!" Part-3 presents some concluding comments.

Part-1: **Some general comments**

It is easy for someone to say, "It is possible that such and such happened." Or someone could say, "It is possible that such and such could happen." Or someone could express any of the many variations of these statements. All one has to do is to open her or his mouth and let the words flow out. However those individuals, who just let words flow out of their mouth without some consideration for the physical, logical, spiritual, and/or scientific basis for their words, are being unfair to themselves and to those who hear their words. And those who hear these words are also unfair to themselves, if they do not make sure that they understand whatever is being said. Or more precisely, they should try to understand the implication of whatever is being said. Based on the previous statements, it should be clear that those who hear an "It-is-possible-that-such-and-such-happened" statement, need to ask questions like: "Is there any physical, logical, spiritual, and/or scientific evidence that support the possibility of such and such happening?" Or "Is there any physical, logical, spiritual, and/or scientific evidence that support the impossibility of such and such happening?" These questions need to be asked, because associating the word – "possible", with some event, process, or something else in a sentence does not automatically make that event, process, or something else truly "possible". Even though, that is precisely the connotation, which is conveyed by using the word: "possible". The point is:

> "It is logically weak and inappropriate to make any possibility statement, without the knowledge of some clear and valid evidence to support that possibility."

Part-2: **A response to the statement: "It is possible that life came here from another planet!"**

As indicated in Part-1 before responding to any "It-is-possible-that-such-and-such-happened" statement, we should perform, at least, two tasks:

- *Task-1*: Think about the meaning of the specific "It-is-possible-that-such-and-such-happened" statement and think about its implications.

- *Task-2*: Ask yourself, "Is there any physical, logical, spiritual, and/or scientific evidence that support the possibility of such and such happening?" or "Is there any physical, logical, spiritual, and/or scientific evidence that support the impossibility of such and such happening?" You could even ask the individual, who made the statement, these two questions.

An application of these two tasks to the statement – "It is possible that life came here from another planet!", might produce, the following comments:

It is possible that life came here from another planet!

Introduction

When my friend used the statement – "It is possible that life came here from another planet!", she meant this statement liberally. Thus, some people believe that life came here from another planet. Those who hold this belief differ on exactly how that life arrived here, and on the form of that life. More specifically, most of the individuals holding this belief are divided into two major camps. Those in one camp think that space aliens brought life to this planet. Those in the other camp think that life landed here after traveling through space on its own. The beliefs of those in both camps imply that God did not create life on this planet. With these comments in mind, we will discuss the statement – "It is possible that life came here from another planet!", by discussing two questions:

- *First*, what evidence supports the belief that space aliens brought life to this planet?

- *Second*, what evidence supports the belief that life landed here after traveling through space on its own?

Thus, the rest of this discussion is organized in three sections. Section-1 presents a discussion of the first question: "What evidence supports the belief that space aliens brought life to this planet?" Section-2 presents a discussion of the second question: "What evidence supports the belief that life landed here after traveling through space on its own?" Section-3 presents some concluding comments, which form an explicit response to the statement: "It is possible that life came here from another planet!".

Section-1: **What evidence supports the belief that space aliens brought life to this planet?**

This question flows out of a logical reflection of the statement – "It is possible that life came here from another planet!" Furthermore, if space aliens brought life to this planet, then all of the questions that people ask of their gods would have to be redirected to these space aliens. Examples of such questions are, as follows:

> Did you create us or just put us here? If you did not create us, then who did? Why did you create us? Or why did you put us here? Why didn't you leave us some explicit knowledge of your existence? Why haven't you come back and made yourselves known?

Other questions revolve around the form of the life that the space aliens brought here. Such questions might be worded, as follows:

> Did the space aliens just bring substances, which evolved into life, as we now know it?,
> Did the space aliens bring a single cell, which evolved into life, as we now know it?,
> Did the space aliens bring two of every kind of organism (*which would have been something akin to a "space Ark"*)?

If the form of life that arrived here required evolution, then the need for "evolution" would also require a discussion like that in the essay: "Is evolution a matter of facts or of faith?", which is in the book: "Last Call!!!) However, returning to the main issue of Section-1, which is the question – "What evidence supports the belief that space aliens brought life to this planet?", the only supposed physical evidence that this author is aware of is several objects and a specific landscape. More specifically, the supposed physical evidences include things like:

- A small ancient statue found in South America that resembles a being, who could be wearing something akin to a space suit.

- There are markings around a large plateau in South America that are best viewed from a plane at a high altitude. The markings surround what appears from high altitudes, as a landing field on that plateau.

Both of the above-mentioned items were reported by a television program about strange things. This particular program was aired many years ago. Unfortunately, this author cannot recall the name of the program. Nevertheless, both of the previously mentioned items are the result of someone's interpretation. There may be other things that some might try to use to support the possibility of space aliens bringing life to this planet, but those things are probably, as scientifically weak as the two items previously mentioned.

> Comment: For sometime now, many individuals have assumed that we - modern man - are more technologically intelligent than ancient man - especially, more than those who lived between the time of Adam and the flood. Consequently, when markings that only make sense when viewed from an airplane are encountered, modern man would rather attribute the creation of these markings to space aliens than to ancient man. Because surely, ancient man did not have the ability or the technology to be able to fly. Modern man was able to get away with this until several finds: first, a battery-like device was found in a bed of coal - some believe this battery device is pre-flood, and second, HIEROGLYPHICS of ancient Egypt show devices being used that some think are batteries or electrical capacitors.

Thus, this author would say, "There does not appear to be any good scientific evidence to support space aliens bringing life here, that is convincing and testable."

Section-2: **What evidence supports the belief that life landed here after traveling through space on its own?**

If life arrived on this planet, as a result of one or more organisms traveling through space, then that was something akin to a miracle on its own. The reason that we can say this is based on the implications of our knowledge of the conditions in space and of the requirements to get a man from here to the moon. Four implications of this knowledge are, as follows:

- *Implication-1*: The organism had to be encased in some protective material. This material had to be of a sufficient size, shape, etc. that it kept the organism from being destroyed in space. (*If the organism was not encased in some protective material, it would require a biological makeup that would allow the conditions in space to suspend its life-sustaining activities without destroying it. Whether that is possible is unknown to this author.*)

- *Implication-2*: Space travel takes time. Travel time means that the encasement the organism was in also had to contain a food supply, or the organism had to have most or all of its life-sustaining requirements suspended, while it was in the encasement.

- *Implication-3*: Once the organism and its encasement reached earth, conditions on earth would have been such that the encasement was opened releasing the organism. Then the environment had to be conducive to the survival of the organism.

- *Implication-4*: Once on this earth, the organism had to evolve into all the other creatures on this planet, unless the ancestors of other organisms also traveled through space to reach this planet.

Several scientists claimed that a fragment of a meteorite found in Antarctica supposedly contained traces of something that might have been alive, or contained traces of something that represented one of the building blocks of life.

> *Comment: Update!* The material in the meteorite found in Antarctica has been declared to be something else – not related to living matter from Mars. (*After the claim about material in the meteorite was withdrawn, some felt that the initial announcement of the claim was a funding ploy.*)

Thus, this author would say that there does not appear to be any good scientific evidence to support the arrival of life here from another planet, that is convincing and testable.

Section-3: **Some concluding comments** (*for the response to the statement*: "It is possible that life came here from another planet!")

The concept that life came from another planet merely muddies the creation waters by adding the "space travel" variable, and possibly, the "space alien" variable to the equation. But we can cut through the mud by asking, "How did life start on the planet from which the life came?" And we keep asking this question until we get to the very first planet on which there was life. On this first planet with life, we ask, "What created the life?", because neither "space travel" or "space aliens" could have been involved on this first planet.

Part-3: **Some concluding comments** (*for this essay:* "How should Christian respond to the 'It-is-possible-that-such-and-such-happened' statement?")

Hopefully, the response above to the statement – "It is possible that life came here from another planet!", serves as the answer to the topic question: "How should Christians respond to an 'It-is-possible-that-such-and-such-happened' statement?" Nevertheless, remember that science is the art of looking at all the possibilities, and then tying reality to those possibilities with a best-fit effort. Also remember not everything that we can think of is really possible, so we need to watch our use of the word: "possible". And a second way to look at these "possible" statements is:

> "We need to request evidence for 'possible' statements, because if we do not, we leave open an infinite number of 'possible' statements with some 'having incompatible components', 'having contradictory components', and/or 'having illogical or unrealistic conditions or requirements'."

What is the only meaningful question, about "God" and "Christianity"?

This question flows out of the fact that both non-Christians and Christians ask many questions about "God" and "Christianity". But not all of these questions are valid, contextually appropriate, and/or meaningful. Nevertheless, seven examples of questions about "God" and "Christianity" are, as follows:

1) How could a virgin (*Mary*) conceive a child without sexually knowing a man?

2) How could men accurately record words, supposedly inspired by God, and then pass these words accurately down through time?

3) How could God create man out of nothing?

4) Who created God?

5) How can there be three Gods (*God, the Father, God, the Son, and God, the Holy Spirit*) in One?

   Comment: Christians use the word – "Trinity", for the concept of "three Gods in One".

6) What if a believer sins and then dies, before she or he can repent?

7) How could two of every kind of animal fit on Noah's Ark?

To address the seven questions above (*as they apply to the topic question*) and the topic question, this essay is organized in three parts. Part-1 presents a critique of the topic question. Part-2 presents some concluding comments. Part-3 presents a direct response to each of the seven questions above.

Part-1: **A critique of the topic question**

Sometimes asking questions like the seven questions above, can be good, because questions can cause us to think. And thinking could result in intellectual and/or spiritual growth, especially when we are not trying "**to be God**" (*when we are not trying "**to out think God**"*). However, when we are trying "**to be God**" (*when we are trying "**to out think God**"*), our thinking creates problems for us, because our human nature causes too many of us to ask detailed questions, about "**how**" God did this or that. Or even more problematic, too many of us ask questions about "**why**" God did this or that. Clearly, because most of us cannot even begin to understand the "**how**" and "**why**" of God, too many of us look at this world and then assume that there are limits to God's grace, mercy, power, knowledge, justice, love, etc. Furthermore, some people feel that they could do many things better than how God does (*did*) those things. Most Christians understand that we humans are the ones with limits, because we are merely images of God that He created in the media of space and time. Thus, our inability to find satisfactory answers for many of our questions, does not negate the grace, mercy, power, knowledge, justice, love, etc. of God. God has His reasons for everything. Our inability to understand the "**how**" and "**why**" of God's reasons or of our physical world, does not change God. Yes! Our inability may change our "perception of God", but not God, Himself. Besides, most of those with questions about "God" and "Christianity" have forgotten the definition of "God". Or more precisely, these individuals have forgotten or never knew the nature of "God", as revealed in the "whole Bible".

> *Comment:* The phrase – "whole Bible", was used, because some individuals reference verses like 1 Samuel 15:3, where God told the Jews to kill the men, women, children, infants, and the animals of Amalekites, to imply that "The God of the Old Testament is a mean-vengeful God." These same individuals make no attempt to understand why God told the Jews to kill whomever. In the NIV, 1 Samuel 15:1-3 reads:
>
>> 1 Samuel 15:[1]Samuel said to Saul, "I am the one the LORD sent to anoint you king over his people Israel; so listen now to the message from the LORD. [2]This is what the LORD Almighty says: 'I will punish the Amalekites for what they did to Israel when they waylaid them as they came up from Egypt. [3]Now go, attack the Amalekites and totally destroy everything that belongs to them. Do not spare them; put to death men and women, children and infants, cattle and sheep, camels and donkeys.'"

If the "whole Bible" is studied, people should see that the Bible presents God, as One with unlimited grace, mercy, power, knowledge, justice, love, etc. People, who read the Bible, should also see that the Bible presents God, as One, Who has always had our best interest in mind, if we would only listen. Under such a presentation, all the religious questions about "God" and "Christianity", can be reduced to the most meaningful question: "Does God exist?", or some variation of it. Thus, the answer to the question – "What is the only meaningful question about 'God' and 'Christianity'?", is the question – "Does God exist?", for two reasons:

- *First*, as previously stated, if God does exist, everything else flows out of His attributes, despite whether we understand His attributes, the "how", and/or the "why", or not.

- *Second*, all other religious questions about "God" and "Christianity" – all religious questions other than "Does God exist?", may impose limits on God's attributes (*may impose limits on God's grace, mercy, power, knowledge, justice, love, etc.*). When by definition only the attributes of God, Himself, can impose any limitations on Him. For example, the limitation that "God cannot lie" comes out of His attribute of "Holiness".

Part-2: **Some concluding comments**

Concluding comments flow out of Part-1 and the Bible. Part-1 presented the question – "Does God exist?", as the answer to the topic question. The Bible presents verses, which reference "God" and "our thoughts". For instance, see Isaiah 55:8-9, which reads:

(Isaiah 55:8 NIV) "For my thoughts are not your thoughts, neither are your ways my ways," declares the LORD.

(Isaiah 55:9 NIV) "As the heavens are higher than the earth, so are my ways higher than your ways and my thoughts than your thoughts.

These two verses imply that we will never fully understand most of the things about God. More precisely, these verses imply that we will never "***out think*** **God**" nor "***out do*** **God**". However, this does not mean that we cannot ask questions, even questions about "God" and "Christianity". Asking questions is a part of our human nature. But we must understand that our questions are formed based on explicit or implicit, underlying assumptions. Then once formed (*once we have decided on the wording of our questions*), our questions carry underlying implications. If we examine the underlying assumptions and implications, of most of our questions about "God" and "Christianity", our questions are really asking some variation of the question: "Does God exist?" Thus, once more, the answer to the question – "What is the only meaningful question, about 'God' and 'Christianity'?", is the question: "Does God exist?"

> *Comment:* With regards to the question – "Does God exist?", if your answer is "No!", then perhaps the essay – "Does God exist?", may provide some additional information, for you to consider. If your answer is "Yes!", then you must allow God to exercise the grace, mercy, power, knowledge, justice, love, and so on, that are His, as revealed by the Bible. You must allow God to exercise His attributes on His schedule. You must not try to impose unrealistic limits on God's attributes nor try to suggest that He should change His schedule. If you do either one, then you will have an improper perception of God. Besides scholars, like the late Dr. Walter Martin, tell us that God can do anything that is consistent with His revealed nature. Therefore, as previously mentioned, there are some things that God cannot do. But once more, the "things that God cannot do", are imposed by His own nature, rather than by conditions or limits imposed on Him, by some other more powerful entity. Consequently, the qualities imposed by God's nature, make Him consistent, without altering His grace, mercy, power, knowledge, love, and so on.

Part-3: **A response to each of the seven example questions**

Each of the seven questions is restated, then immediately after the restatement, the response to that particular question is presented. Thus, the questions and responses are, as follow:

---

1) **How could a virgin (*Mary*) conceive a child without sexually knowing a man?**

Response: Some non-Christians respond to the virgin birth of Jesus with questions like:

"Today, if a woman had a baby,
and if you were told that she was a virgin,
would you believe it?"

Today, the obvious answer to this question, is "Yes!", based on the existence of artificial fertilization. Perhaps, a "yes-answer" more than thirty years ago, might not have seemed appropriate. However, any discussion of a "yes-answer" or a "no-answer" clouds the more appropriate Christian response, because questions like – "Today, if a woman had a baby, and if you were told that she was a virgin, would you believe it?", need to be filtered through the seven questions indicated in the essay: "Are all questions valid and/or contextually appropriate?" If that filtering is performed, then it should become clear that questions like – "If a woman had a baby today, and if you were told that she was a virgin, would you believe it?", are contextually inappropriate with respect to the virgin birth of Jesus. One reason that we can say this is the virgin birth of Jesus was prophesied (*announced before hand*). And even the existence of others, who claimed to be the "Messiah", during the same time that Jesus lived cannot discredit the existence of the original (*the existence of Jesus, who fulfilled all the prophecies about the "Messiah"*). However, putting aside the contextual inappropriateness of the question – "Today, if a woman had a baby, and if you were told that she was a virgin, would you believe it?", another Christian response to the virgin birth of Jesus is, as follows:

> "Christians believe that God created everything. Thus, 'having a virgin conceive a child without a man', is a trivial feat compared to the feat of creating the universe from nothing. 'Having a virgin conceive a child without a man', is a trivial feat compared to the feat of creating the first man, Adam, from the dust of the ground. 'Having a virgin conceive a child without a man', is a trivial feat compared to the feat of creating the first woman, Eve, from a rib of the first man, Adam."

Thus, while this question does not explicitly question the existence of God, it does question His attributes, which are part of His existence.

---

2) **How could men accurately record words, supposedly inspired by God, and then pass these words accurately down through time?**

Response: With some understanding of human nature, many people believe, it is impossible for men to have passed the recorded words of God through time, without messing them up. To support this belief, some people often refer to games or psychology-experiments, where a simple story is passed down a line of people. By the time the story reaches the end of the line, the final version is totally different from the beginning version. People say these games or experiments show that man is incapable of passing stories, without messing them up. However, many of us ignore the fact that most of the participants in these games or psychology-experiments are not trained storytellers. In ancient times, many cultures had storytellers, who passed stories verbally from generation to generation. These storytellers were selected or volunteered to be the storyteller of a tribe or group. Often, these storytellers devoted their entire lives to this effort and may have learned their art, from whomever they may have replaced. After the written word was devised, individuals, who served as religious scribes, devised methods to increase the accuracy of the copies written by them. Several such methods are detailed in historical documents. Obviously, this does not mean their copies were perfect. However, it does mean that these religious scribes incorporated into their process of making copies, procedures, which served to minimize errors. This is viewing the process, without the intervention of God. If God does become involved in the process, then because He is God and He created us, anything consistent with His revealed nature is possible.

Archeologists and others have discovered ancient copies of various portions of the Bible written in Hebrew, Aramaic, and Greek. When these copies are compared with our modern Hebrew/Aramaic and Greek versions, there are no substantive differences.

In the past, many cultures had more group tasks, such as hunting, fishing, harvesting, cooking, childbirths, weddings, building structures, and so forth, than we have today. During some of these group events, stories were probably repeated and songs sung, to deaden the drudgery of whatever they were doing. Generally, their stories and songs referred to past events. A very few may have referred to future hopes. Nevertheless, their stories and songs helped to pass information from one generation to another.

God using men to record His words and then to pass these words down through time, is a trivial feat, compared to the feat of creating this universe. Thus, if you question God's ability to have men record His words and then pass those words through thousands of years, you are really questioning His attributes, which are part of His existence.

---

3) **How could God create man out of nothing?**

Response: One response to this question is a "**mathematical analogy**" that is too beautiful to ignore. It is obvious that God could create anything, in any way that is consistent with His revealed nature. Nevertheless, a mathematical representation of God creating something out of nothing could be characterized, by the following equations:

nothing = nothing;

0 = 0;
0 = 1 - 1;
0 = 2 - 2; . . . etc.;
0 = one million - one million; . . . etc.;
0 = infinity - infinity.

The physical representation of the previous equations can be summarized, as follows:

nothing = nothing,
nothing = pure-energy - pure-energy,
nothing = (pure-energy) + (- pure-energy),
or nothing = (positive pure-energy) + (negative pure-energy).

> Comment: The "dash" between the words – "pure" and "energy", does not serve to indicate the "subtraction process". That "dash" serves to allow the formation of the label – "pure-energy", from the two words. (*This may have been obvious to many, but this author decided to explicitly state this, to remove all doubt.*)

However, possibly, an even better physical representation would be expressed, as follows:

nothing = (pure-energy) + (antipure-energy).

In this equation, obviously the "pure-energy" is the "positive pure-energy" and the "antipure-energy" is the "negative pure-energy". But what is more important is that this equation is the best representation of God creating out of nothing. More specifically, this equation is a physical representation of the "Big Bang", which the latter equation proposes was God separating the "pure-energy" from the "antipure-energy". However, this author would admit that the equation:

nothing = pure-energy - pure-energy

is probably the clearest equation of God creating out of nothing. And then to get to an even better equation, which represents our physical universe, we will use the interpretations of a scientist, whose name escapes this author, because the literature from this particular scientist was remembered from five decades ago. That is why this author cannot recall her or his name nor the title of her or his material. Nevertheless, this particular scientist proposed several things: First, "at the moment of the 'Big Bang' each component – the positive pure-energy and the negative pure-energy – would have experienced, at least, three conditions: 1) the greatest accelerations – more specifically, an instantaneous acceleration in opposite directions from the point of the bang; 2) the "second highest temperatures"[1] in this universe; and 3) the greatest density." Second, "after the explosion – after the separation of the two energies, the positive component would have started to implode upon itself and the negative pure-energy would have started to slow, to cooled, and to become less dense as it moved away from the point of the 'Big Bang'". Third, "as the negative pure-energy slowed, cooled, and became less dense, it developed into matter and antimatter." Fourth, "God caused the matter and antimatter to clump in various places throughout the universe. And then God created things like stars, planets, and living organisms (*plants, animals, and man*) out of the matter and He created things like 'black holes' out of the antimatter." Fifth, "some of the pure-energy turning into matter and antimatter is probably only applicable to the negative pure-energy side of the equation, because the positive pure-energy is imploding upon itself and this probably creates an entirely different set of physical conditions, which the scientist did not speculate on."

Now, perhaps the best way to visualize the "positive pure-energy" and the "negative pure-energy" a short time after the "Big Bang", is to imagine three concentric spheres. In short, imagine a small sphere inside of a larger sphere and then those two spheres inside of a still larger sphere, with all three spheres sharing the same center point. Or better, imagine a large sphere, a medium sphere, and a small sphere, which have a common center point. The large sphere would be the "negative pure-energy" and it would be moving outward away from the medium sphere and from the common center point. The medium sphere would be constant and represents where the positive and negative pure-energies separated. The smallest sphere would be the "positive pure-energy" and it would be moving inward away from the medium sphere and toward the common center point.

A simplified mathematical expression of the previously stated *third* and *fourth* proposals could be expressed, as follows:

$$\text{Pure-energy} \Rightarrow \text{matter - matter}$$
$$\text{Pure-energy} \Rightarrow \text{matter + antimatter}$$

Then substituting this relationship for the "negative pure-energy" in the "Big Bang" equation:

$$\text{nothing} = (\text{pure-energy}) + (\text{antipure-energy}).$$

$$\text{nothing} = \text{positive pure-energy} + \text{negative pure-energy}.$$

$$\text{nothing} = \text{pure-energy} - \text{pure-energy}.$$

---

1 After the "Big Bang", the highest temperatures may exist in the "positive pure-energy" component of the equation, because the "positive pure-energy" began imploding upon itself.

nothing ⇒ pure-energy - (matter + antimatter).

nothing ⇒ pure-energy - matter - antimatter.

The last equation is an uncomplicated-unencumbered representation of our universe. This presentation is a speculative way of how God created out of nothing. But the point is:

> "Creating out of nothing is easy for God, because He is God. Thus, if you question God's ability to create anything out of nothing, you are really questioning His attributes, which are part of His existence."

Note: "Creating out of nothing", is also discussed in the essay – "Was the 'Big Bang' an exploding 'Point of Singularity'?", which is one of the essays in the book: "Last Call!!!"

---

4) **Who created God?**

Response: If God were created, then He cannot be God. If God were created, then whatever created Him would be "God". Therefore, God has always existed. Furthermore, whether you are an "evolutionist", a "creationist", or something else, pure logic dictates that some entity has to have always existed, because pure logic tells us that "something cannot come from nothing, by itself". And, for the eternal entity to be something less than God, is illogical. Once more, this question does not explicitly question the existence of God. But it does question His attributes, which are part of His existence.

---

5) **How can there be three Gods (God, the Father, God, the Son, and God, the Holy Spirit) in One?**

Response: Some say that having the concept of "the Trinity" (*the concept of "three Gods in One"*) in the Bible, adds to the credibility of the Bible, because the Trinity is foreign to the nature of man. That is, the Trinity is not something men would have dreamed up on their own. What is meant, by saying that "the concept of 'the Trinity' is in the Bible", is "there are Bible verses which explicitly, reference each member of the Trinity, as God." (*See the web document at: www.biblehelp.org/reference_1.htm. This web document list sixteen verses, which indicate that Jesus is God; two verses, which indicate that the Father is God; three verses, which indicate that the Holy Spirit is God; and sixteen verses, which indicate that there is only one God.*) However, Matthew 3:13-17 references all three members of the Trinity, during the baptism of Jesus, by John the Baptist. In the NIV, Matthew 3:13-17 reads:

> Matthew 3:[13]Then Jesus came from Galilee to the Jordan to be baptized by John.
> [14]But John tried to deter him, saying, "I need to be baptized by you, and do you come

to me?" [15]**Jesus** replied, "Let it be so now; it is proper for us to do this to fulfill all righteousness." Then John consented. [16]As soon as Jesus was baptized, he went up out of the water. At that moment heaven was opened, and he saw the Spirit of God descending like a dove and lighting on him. [17]And a voice from heaven said, "This is my Son, whom I love; with him I am well pleased."

A well-known evangelist says, "Man explaining the Trinity is like a two-dimensional object explaining four dimensional man." A well-known minister says, "Read the Bible from cover to cover and you will see the Trinity."

The concept of "the Trinity" is explained, by some using "man". Under such an explanation, we note that many Bible scholars and Christians believe in the Christian concept: "Man has a soul, a body, and a spirit." With this Christian concept in mind, recall that the Bible declares: "Man was created in the 'image of God'". Then note that an image is a reflection of the original. But an image is less than the original, because as a reflection, the image is in another medium (*is in an inferior medium compared to the original*). More specifically, the original exists in one medium and the image exists in another medium (*exists in an inferior medium, by definition*). Therefore, as "PURE SPECULATION", by some people including this author, an explanation of Trinity is presented, as follows:

> "The 'Trinity' is 'God, the Father', 'God, the Son', and 'God, the Holy Spirit'. The Trinity created man in their image. The 'Trinity' created 'man' with a '*soul*', a '*body*', and a '*spirit*'. Thus, the expression of the 'Trinity' in terms of 'man', might be worded, as follows:
>
> | | | |
> |---|---|---|
> | 'God, **the Father**' | *would be equivalent to* | 'God, **the soul**'. |
> | 'God, **the Son**' | *would be equivalent to* | 'God, **the body**'. |
> | 'God, **the Holy Spirit**' | *would be equivalent to* | 'God, **the spirit**'. |
>
> But unlike man, the three members of the 'Trinity' are able to communicate with each other."

However the Trinity is explained, those who reject the concept of "the Trinity", are really questioning the attributes of God, which are part of His existence.

---

6) **What if a believer sins and then dies, before she or he can repent?**

Comment: For those of you, who have read sequentially through this book, this question would have been a good candidate to discuss in or after the essay: "Are all questions valid and/or contextually appropriate?" And hopefully, those who read that essay, know the perfect response to the question: "What if a believer sins and then dies before she or he can repent?" However, for your convenience, and for those who have not read the essay – "Are all questions valid and/or contextually appropriate?", this author's response follows.

Response: Of all the various questions that can be asked, by Christians and non-Christians, the "believer-sins-and-then-dies-before-repenting" series, is among "the most direct attacks on the character of God". For more than most of the other category of religious questions, this series of questions denies the revealed attributes of God: His grace, mercy, power, knowledge, justice, love, etc. Furthermore, individuals, who ask such questions forget that if God is in control, then He controls the timing of each death. Thus, "God controlling the timing of each death" means "the death implied, by this series of questions, would not happen unless God allowed it." Furthermore, God appears to be more concerned about the condition of our hearts, than the deeds that come out of our minds. Thus, the point is:

> "These 'believer-sins-and-then-dies-before-repenting' questions are invalid in the context of the revealed attributes and character of God." Furthermore, such questions explicitly question the attributes of God, which again are part of His existence.

---

7) **How could two of every kind of animal fit on Noah's Ark?**

Comment: A proofreader reminded this author that this question was not formed consistent with Genesis 7:2-3. This proofreader is correct, because Genesis 7:2-3 indicates that "God made a distinction, between clean and unclean animals", and that "God made a special provision for the birds of the air". Thus, there were more than just two of some kinds of animals on Noah's Ark. However, most people, who question issues related to the animals on Noah's Ark, do not know the Bible well enough to be aware of Genesis 7:2-3. Thus, the question – "How could two of every kind of animal fit on Noah's Ark?", is reflective of most of the questions, asked about the animals on Noah's Ark. Nevertheless, for your convenience, in the NIV, Genesis 7:2-3 read:

> Genesis 7:[2]Take with you seven of every kind of clean animal, a male and its mate, and two of every kind of unclean animal, a male and its mate, [3]and also seven of every kind of bird, male and female, to keep their various kinds alive throughout the earth.

Response: Please forgive this author, if this seems unkind, but it is just illogical for anyone to think that Noah's Ark was too small, after God gave specific instructions to Noah, about how to build the Ark. It is far more logical for someone to question whether the Ark existed at all, than to question whether it was large enough. The Bible records, at least, four statements, which support the Ark being large enough. These statements reference the Ark and its builder, Noah, and are, as follows:

- *Statement-1*: "God told Noah that there would be a flood." See Genesis 6:17. In the NIV, this verse reads:

  Genesis 6:[17]I am going to bring floodwaters on the earth to destroy all life under the heavens, every creature that has the breath of life in it. Everything on earth will perish.

- *Statement-2*: "God told Noah to build an Ark out of specific material and with specific dimensions." See Genesis 6:14-16. In the NIV, these verses read:

  Genesis 6:[14]So make yourself an **ark of cypress wood**; make rooms in it and coat it with pitch inside and out. [15]This is how you are to build it: The ark is to be **450 feet long**, **75 feet wide** and **45 feet high**. [16]Make a roof for it and finish the ark to within 18 inches of the top. Put a door in the side of the ark and make lower, middle and upper decks.

- *Statement-3*: "God gave more instructions to Noah and then God drew the animals to the Ark." See Genesis 6:18-21. In the NIV, these verses read:

  Genesis 6:[18]But I will establish my covenant with you, and **you will enter the ark--you and your sons and your wife and your sons' wives with you**. [19]You are to bring into the ark two of all living creatures, male and female, to keep them alive with you. [20]**Two of every kind of bird, of every kind of animal and of every kind of creature that moves along the ground will come to you to be kept alive**. [21]You are to **take every kind of food that is to be eaten and store it away as food for you and for them**."

- *Statement-4*: "We are told that Noah followed God's instructions." See Genesis 6:22. In the NIV, this verse reads:

  Genesis 6:[22]Noah did everything just as God commanded him.

With respect to the previously indicated four statements, if God knew:

a) How and when He would cause the flood,
b) Who would build the Ark,
c) How large the Ark was going to be,
d) How many animals He would draw to the Ark,
e) How long the flood would last,

f) How much food would be required for those in the Ark,

how could He miscalculate the size that the Ark needed to be? Such a miscalculation is logically inconsistent with the information recorded in Genesis. Furthermore, there is nothing in the Bible to tell us whether the animals that God drew to the Ark were fully grown or not. Some or all of these animals may have been young for their particular species. That is, these animals may have included a female and male elephants that were only a year old, a female and male deer that were six months old, and so forth. It should be obvious that the young of a species would be much easier to care for, but again, the Bible says nothing about whether the animals on the Ark were young or old (*were fully grown or not*). Nevertheless, all variations of the question – "How could two of every kind of animal fit on the Ark?", are invalid questions in light of the details recorded in Genesis.

Before ending our discussion about the number of animals on the Ark, some excellent comments made by Mr. Ken Ham of the Answers In Genesis Ministry, must be mentioned. Mr. Ham's comments were included in his video presentation entitled: "One Blood"[96]. In this video, Mr. Ham explained, how the many ethnic groups came from one set of great . . . great grandparents, Adam and Eve. He also explained that this same principle held true for all animals. Thus, according to Mr. Ham, even though there are more than four hundred and fifty breeds of dogs existing today, only one pair of dog-like creatures was needed on the Ark to produce all of these different breeds.

Was the flood local or universal (*worldwide*)?

If the flood was local and not universal (*not worldwide*), then the Ark was not needed. God could have told Noah to simply take his family and the animals to a place that would not be affected by the flood. After all, God told Noah about the flood more than one-hundred years before it occurred. Thus, saying, "The flood was not universal (*not worldwide*)", is logically weak, in light of the statements recorded in the Book of Genesis, especially, Genesis 6:17. In that verse, God said, "I am going to bring floodwaters on the earth to destroy all life under the heavens, every creature that has the breath of life in it. Everything on earth will perish." Furthermore, the Ark and the flood served both a physical purpose (*a practical purpose*) and a spiritual purpose, for God. Physically, the flood served to wipe out a sinful generation. Spiritually, the flood served, as a model for how God saves by grace, because He saved Noah, Noah's family, and some animals.

What is biblical justice?

The best discussion on "biblical justice" that this author ever heard, was given by Reverend Eugene Burrell of the Navigators, which is a Christian ministry based in Colorado Springs, Colorado. Over the years, as a minister and a member of the Navigators, Reverend Burrell has been invited to talk at various gatherings and churches around the world. His audiences have been mixed socially, economically, politically, and racially. When he is not traveling, Reverend Burrell conducts Bible studies with a variety of individuals and groups in his home city. In response to a question from a member of a Bible study group, Reverend Burrell shared his thoughts on "biblical justice". This was the first time that Reverend Burrell presented his thoughts on "biblical justice" to that particular Bible study group. However, several members were not present, during that presentation. Consequently, Reverend Burrell was asked to give his "biblical justice" presentation on two additional occasions. The second and third presentations by Reverend Burrell were recorded, by a member of that particular Bible study group, and shared with this author. As Reverend Burrell's presentations flowed from his heart, none of the three presentations were exactly the same. Therefore, for this essay, the two recorded presentations have been combined into one written version.

What is biblical justice?
by Reverend Eugene Burrell

I want to share some thoughts on biblical justice. And I pray that some of what is shared will be a blessing to all of our hearts. Let me start by giving you a little background.

Background

One of the problems that we have today is we do not spend enough time communicating with God. That is why there is so much anxiety in this world. Recently, I had the opportunity to spend four days at a prayer retreat with some intercessors. These intercessors are people from around the country. They came to this prayer retreat to seek the face of God for three, four, or five days. These people spent most of their time in prayer from early in the morning to late at night. As a consequence, we definitely saw the spirit of God moving in a mighty, mighty way. However, it is not all just talking to God. Sometimes what we need to do, is listen to God. For example, I think it was Tom Brokaw, who once asked Mother Theresa, "Mother Theresa, when you pray, what do you say to God?" And Mother Theresa replied, "I don't say anything. I listen." From a short pause, it was obvious that Mr. Brokaw did not understand what that meant spiritually, so he said, "Okay, you don't say anything when you pray. You just listen, so when you are listening to God, what does He say to you, Mother Theresa?" And Mother Theresa said, "He doesn't say anything. He listens." You see a message from the heart will speak to the heart of God. I have found that the biggest tragedy is that people have learned to engage God in a conversation, without being quiet long enough to listen to what God's trying to say to them. A lot of us come to God with a "God, give me this or give me that" attitude or with a "God, I need this or I need that" attitude, as if God is some big sugar daddy. I think that is why the scriptures speak from time to time saying "**Be STILL and know that I am God**" (Psalms 46:10). God wants our hearts to be still before Him. Thus, when intercessors gather at a prayer retreat, a lot of barriers come down, because we see that we are one in Christ. At this particular prayer retreat, there were Asian Americans present. There were White Americans present. There were Native Americans present. There were Black Americans present. But we were just a group of about forty people from around the country who were serious about prayer. With our focus on God, our differences did not matter. But when we get outside such retreats and forget about the presence of God, our differences show up again. You have some whites that don't like African Americans, some African Americans that don't like Asians, some Asians don't like Hispanics, some Hispanics who don't like whomever, and so on. And when we have problems, what do we do in our society? We say, "let's take it before a court of law to take care of things."

An Urban Missiologist (*which means that he is a missionary, who studies the facts of mission in an urban context [in a major city context]*) named Dr. Raymond J. Bakke, wrote a book with Jim Hart. Their book is titled: "The Urban Christian". In this book, Dr. Bakke stated the purpose of his book. As a White American, his purpose was to share with his fellow White Americans, his knowledge of the devastation that exists in the communities of people of color. In this book, Dr. Bakke shared how it is almost, as if we are at the bottom of a great ravine with high cliffs on either side. At the bottom of the ravine are all these people, who have broken up from having fallen off the cliff and hit the rocks at the bottom. What we do, is we put together ministerial groups. These ministerial groups visit the homeless, the sick, the poor, the shut-in, and so on. These groups try to gather clothing, obtain housing and other stuff. They say that we have to heal these people, who have fallen off the cliff. These groups are able to patch up some of the people who have fallen off the cliff, but people keep falling off. Two recent examples of people who have fallen off the cliff came to mind. One example was presented by Native Americans at the prayer retreat. The other example is a young girl who is currently staying with my family.

Example-1: "Native Americans"

At this prayer retreat, there were about fourteen Native Americans from different Indian nations. There were Choctaw, Navaho, and Apaches, to name several. These Native Americans began to share, what many Native American reservations are going through. Some Native American reservations make the black community look good. In terms of alcoholism and drugs, their rates are much higher than many black communities. A female Native American, who is twenty-eight-years-old and lives on a reservation, shared how it is very difficult to find a young girl under eighteen who has not been raped. The level of violence, not on all native American reservations, but on too many, is high. These Native Americans also shared that the level of hope is very low, while despair is very high.

Example-2: "Young girl"

A young eight-year-old girl is staying with my family. She has been with us for the last couple of days. She was staying with her aunt, who is a friend of my wife. Several weeks ago, the aunt and her grown daughter went to a funeral in Richmond, Virginia. While in the Richmond area, the aunt encountered the young girl and the young girl's father, who is her (*the aunt's*) brother. This brother has a number of children by different women. Even though he is over fifty-years-old, he has not learned a lot of things. He recently got married again to a lady, who already had a child. Then they had another child after their marriage. The real mother of this eight-year-old girl did not want to take care of her any longer, so she gave her back to the father (*the brother*). But the brother did not want to bring his eight-year-old daughter into his new family, because it might mess up that relationship. This little girl is eight-years-old going on nine-years-old and is still in the second grade. I have never seen a child so starved for affection. She has been bounced around. When the aunt and her daughter picked up the little girl, she was wearing a size two shoe. She kept saying her feet hurt. They found out that she wears a size three-and-a-half. Yesterday, my wife sat down to read to our son. When my wife started reading, this young girl just curled up under my wife's arm and laid her head on my wife's chest. She just wanted to hug my wife. When my wife went to take a nap, the young girl lay in the bed right beside her. The young girl is just a sweet little girl. Anyway, how the young girl got to this area is. When the aunt and her daughter went to the funeral, the family members in the Richmond area told her, "by the way, when you go back, you have to take the young girl with you, because nobody here wants her anymore." They just gave the young girl away. That is, the situation with so many of our kids, because our community is in such bad shape.

Now, returning to Dr. Bakke's imagery, we have the people, who have fallen off the cliff. Our knowledge of God's "grace" and "mercy" tells us that these people are hurting or are oppressed. And we should heal them. The words – "grace" and "mercy", occur many times in the Bible. Remember how we defined "grace" and "mercy". In a nut shell, "grace" is "me getting what I do not deserve, which is the goodness of God". And "mercy" is "me not getting what I do deserve, which is the wrath of God". Consequently, we go to the bottom of the ravine and we try to heal people. We pick them up and try to bind their lives back together. Based on God's "grace" and "mercy", this is the just thing to do.

Biblical Justice

The word – "justice", is mentioned many times in scriptures. The word – "justice"[97], is identical to the word: "righteousness"[98]. Therefore, you can take each occurrence of the word – "righteousness" and substitute the word: "justice". When you do this, you begin to see verses differently. For example, take Matthew 6:33. In the KJV, it reads:

> Matthew 6:[33]But seek ye first the kingdom of God, and his **righteousness**; and all these things shall be added unto you.

Now, replace the word – "**righteousness**", with the word: "**justice**". And Matthew 6:33 would read:

> But seek ye first the kingdom of God, and his **justice**; and all these things shall be added unto you.

God wants things done justly and rightly. In our society in America, we call justice this sister (*this woman*) standing with a rag tied around her eyes and holding up a scale. This image is called "blind justice". If the bad out weighs the good, then the appropriate legal action is taken. But this is not necessarily God's justice. It is the American sense of justice. An example of American justice, was shared by Dr. Bakke. He went to court for some people, who were evicted, because they were not able to pay their rent. The landlord of their building wanted to sell the land that the building was on to some developers. Therefore, he raised everyone's rent, by two-hundred percent in one month. Most of the people could not pay it, so that is when he evicted them. Dr. Bakke said that one time, after hearing such stories over and over, he stood up in a court room. Then he asked a judge, "Your honor, where is justice in this court room?" Dr. Bakke said that the judge replied, by saying, "This is not a court of justice. It is a court of law." The rule of law takes precedence over justice. We know that is what the American society is built on. We are not built on justice, but the rule of law. When you see the rule of law, you need to know that the word – "justice", literally means "rectification". And the word – "**rectification**", means **"making wrong things right**". If we are really going to be a part of the Kingdom of God, then we have to realize that God wants us, here, as people committed to justice (*to making the wrong things right*).

How in the world, can we live in a society that enjoys all the immense wealth of this world? A society where one man, Microsoft Chairman Bill Gates, is worth sixty billion dollars. At the rate he's going by the year 2005, he will be worth in excess of a hundred billion. Look folks! I am not against people making money. And please do not call me a socialist or a communist. I am neither. You can make whatever you want. But something is fundamentally wrong in our society. When we have one person headed toward one hundred billion dollars and someone else starving in the same society. Something is wrong. When the Chief Executive of the wealthiest nation in the history of civilization lives in the White House and across the street is Lafayette Park, where you find people begging for nickels. Yes! Something is fundamentally wrong. Again, does that mean that you cannot make, as much money as you want? No! It does not. But scriptures speak about taking care of the widow, the poor, the orphans, and the strangers. Who were these four categories? In the scriptures, there were most often people, who were on the bottom rung of society that everyone else stepped over. The Bible says not only give your tithes to the Lord. (*Today, I do not have time to go into tithes, but the tithes really were about 23 percent, when you look at all the tithes.*) But the Bible also tells us to give alms to the poor. In fact, the Bible gives examples of biblical justice. Two such examples are with regards to "harvesting" and "the Gibeonites".

Example-1: "Harvesting"

During harvesting, God told the Jews that they were not to glean everything. They were to leave some for the widows, the poor, and others. Remember in the case of Ruth and Naomi. How Boaz had his farm workers leave parts of the crop in the fields, where Ruth could pick up some. What Boaz told his servants to leave for the poor was biblical. Our modern philosophy is "**get all you can, can all you get, and burn all the rest, so nobody else can get it**."

Example-2: "The Gibeonites"

Another example of biblical justice was recorded in the Book of 2 Samuel, chapter 21. This is where the Gibeonites were given justice. But the story starts when Saul first became king, he oppressed the Gibeonites. He even killed some of them. In spite of the oppression, the Gibeonites only tried to please Israel. Later, Saul died and David became King. Then later yet, there was a three-year famine that took place in the land of Israel. King David inquired of the Lord to learn why there was a famine. The Lord told David: "The famine came, because of what Saul had done to the Gibeonites many years ago." David said, "how do I take care of this?" God said, "why don't you go and ask the Gibeonites?" David did that. He asked the Gibeonites. They said, "We don't have the right to put to death in Israel or require money from Saul's family. But we do feel that it is right, because Saul shed our blood, some of his family's blood should be shed, so give us seven of Saul's male descendants and we will hang them." In response to their request, King David sought seven of Saul's male descendants and found them. Three of the seven were Saul's direct sons. Who were the other four? They were Saul's grandsons. And note that God basically approved that plan. All seven were given to the Gibeonites and hung by them. Then God lifted the famine off the land. Can you imagine Saul's grandson saying, "I had nothing to do with what my granddaddy did. Why are you punishing me?" We need to learn to take a fresh look at the Bible. I do not want it to sound like the Bible is cruel, because it's not. What I am trying to do is answer some problems, today, from the Bible. Yes! The Bible has the answers, but we have to be willing to look for them. I am not talking about twisting scripture to make it fit your philosophy. What I am saying is "When we talk about the principle of what happened, the Bible is very clear and straight forward. Please read 2 Samuel chapter 21 for yourself. Justice is biblical rectification (*making wrong things right*). The only way that we are going to make wrong things right, is to go back and do the healing. This is biblical justice, as defined by God."

My intent today was to share a few thoughts on biblical justice. In closing, I would like to add a few thoughts on racial justice. These thoughts on racial justice are a natural extension of biblical justice.

Racial Justice

These thoughts on racial justice are being recalled from a presentation that I made to a group of White Christians. They had asked me to speak on what I felt was one of the fundamental issues of our society. That is racial justice. I told them that I was not making an excuse for the black community. There are things that blacks have to straighten up for ourselves. But there are also things that are systemic. Things set in society to prevent us from getting to the next level. Women call it the "glass ceiling". Whatever you want to call it, there are things set up that we can't get to the next level. You got to be a superman to break through these barriers and most of us are not. And so the hope is "When we talk about race relations, we will talk about justice or rectification. I say that there should be a sharing of the resources." The reason is best shown through an example:

"Let us say that twin boys were born to you and your spouse. One of the boys, you loved and encouraged. You affirmed him. You brought this one twin everything that he wanted. As a child, you read to him. You took him to private classes. He grew up and you prepared him for the SAT (Scholastic Aptitude Test). Then he went to an Ivy League College. During school breaks, you sent him around the world. He was exposed to everything. Meanwhile, from birth, you had placed the other boy in a closet. Once in a while, you threw him some food. He grows while living in this closet. He is ignorant, because he cannot read. Normally, he is not allowed out of the closet, to even go to the bathroom. And when he does relieve himself in the closet, he is forced to clean it up. Not wanting to be totally cruel, you take the boy out for few minutes of sunshine every week and then you put him back in the closet. When the twins reach the age of twenty-seven, you have a change of heart. You say, 'Okay, maybe I wasn't totally correct on this thing.' You take both boys (*the boy, who has been in the closet all of his life, and the boy, who has been around the world and is highly educated with a Ph.D.*). You say, 'All right, now I am going to give both of you an equal chance at life starting from here. Go for it. Which one of the twins is going to make it? Obviously, it will be the educated one. The other one is going to be afraid of people. He has been handicapped mentally and emotionally."

I say that this is our community (*the Black community*). Most of us keep forgetting that the slaves were not even allowed to benefit from the things that they had to do. There are many students of history. Recall the Oklahoma land rush. You probably saw it in an old western movie. People got these little carriages and horses. And at the appropriate signal, people rushed in and planted a marker to claim a parcel of land ("forty acres and a mule"). At the end of the Civil War, blacks were promised "forty acres and a mule". Of course, we never got the forty acres and a mule. It was promised, but never delivered. Again, the Oklahoma land rush, allowed people to grab all this land free, after the Native Americans were kicked off. Now, landowners there may say, "Well, you know this land has been in my family for one hundred and ten years." I say, "Blacks were there, but the system would not let us even get into the running for the land." Some say that many people need to grow up and stop complaining about what happened during slavery. Everyone must understand that what happened in slavery has precedence today. Even though some land has been in your family for one hundred and ten years, it is so, because that land was given to you, at the expense of Native Americans, or at the expense of African Americans, who were not allowed to get into the rush for the land. That is why your family owns five hundred acres of prime Oklahoma farm land. You got it free. And if we say, "Give us a little bit of it", then you say, "This is not a welfare state." But you got it free.

Now, today, one of the questions is "Why should I have to suffer, because of what my great-grandfather did back in slavery?" I should not have to suffer. Has anybody ever heard that question before? In response, the principle that I use is of the "Gibeonites" in 2 Samuel chapter 21, as mentioned before. One of the biggest tragedies of today occurred in 1997, when President Clinton suggested apologizing to the African Americans for what took place in slavery. Most White Americans said, "You are crazy!" But Christianity 101 says, "If you offend your brother, then go to your brother and say, 'I am sorry'." Imagine this "I offended my wife, by saying something really dumb. She says, 'You hurt my feelings.' And I say, 'get over it.'" Now, I got trouble, deep trouble, in my home. I need to go back and say, "Baby! I am sorry. I blew it. Will you forgive me?" Now, that heals. Yes! Those words can heal and we know that. We teach our kids that when they are growing up. But we must not fall into a cheap "grace" or "apology" from whites. Some whites want to go to a conference and grab a black and then apologize for all their ancestors may have done. And that's it. This is done to relieve their guilt. There is no redistribution of resources to minorities. It is just saying, "I am sorry." But there is no justice (*no making wrong things right*).

One of the reasons why blacks were not apologized to, was because Africa was not recognized, as a strong nation. It is also why Afro-Americans got put in slavery. But when Japan got really strong again, what did the American government do in response to the internment of Japanese Americans during World War II? The American government gave those Japanese Americans, twenty thousand dollars, a piece and apologized to them. What about the Japanese? Did they ever apologize for what they did to the Chinese, to the Filipinos, or to Americans during the same war? **There will never be total healing, until we put wrong things right.**

Reverend Eugene Burrell

Closing Comment

Although Reverend Burrell will talk to anyone about God, he is an Afro-American whose passion is witnessing to people, who live in the inner cities of this nation. Reverend Burrell and his wife, Diane, have eight children. Their children are learning about God, because Reverend and Mrs. Burrell try to model God's love for others.

Should Christians be angry with Jews, because they crucified Jesus?

This question flows out of the fact that over the years, as non-Jews started to outnumber Jews in the Christian church, an air of hostility toward Jews developed and grew. This hostility was based on the feeling of many non-Jewish Christians that the Jews were responsible for the crucifixion of Jesus. But is this hostility an appropriate response to the crucifixion? Or more specifically, "Should Christians be angry with Jews, because they crucified Jesus?" To develop an answer, this essay is organized in four parts. Part-1 presents an answer based on the Old Testament. Part-2 presents an answer based on the New Testament. Part-3 presents some concluding comments. Part-4 presents some relevant comments.

Part-1: **An answer based on the Old Testament**

The Old Testament reveals the plan of God, the Father, for the redemption of man. Under this plan, God, the Son, was to take on human form, as Jesus, and then the spiritual and physical deaths of Jesus would serve as a penalty and an atoning sacrifice for our sins. More specifically, God's plan was revealed through Old Testament prophecies. These prophecies indicated that:

- God, the Son, would take on human form, as the Messiah (*which means "Anointed one" in Hebrew and was translated into Greek, as "Christos" and into English, as "Christ"*).

- The Jews would reject Jesus, as their Messiah and have Him crucified.

- Jesus would die spiritually, as a penalty for the sins of all men, and then he would die physically, as an atoning sacrifice for the sins of all men. (*But the deaths of Jesus are only meaningful to those who accept His deaths on their behalf.*)

Thus, as it was clearly God's plan for Jesus to be crucified, if Christians want to be angry with someone over the crucifixion of Jesus, their anger should be directed at God, the Father. However, such anger would be silly. On the other hand, if the Jews had not crucified Jesus, we would still be lost, because of our sins, and there would be no Christianity. Thus, based on the Old Testament, there is absolutely no justification for any Christian to be angry with the Jews over the crucifixion of Jesus.

Part-2: **An answer based on the New Testament**

The New Testament reveals how Jesus told his followers to treat both their friends and their enemies – not that Jews are the enemies of Christians. Clearly, the New Testament contains verses, which implicitly or explicitly indicate that Jesus wanted His followers to "love their neighbors, as themselves", to "love their enemies", and to "love the sinner, but not the sin". Thus, based on the New Testament, being angry with the Jews, because they crucified Jesus is totally inappropriate for anyone calling herself or himself, a Christian.

Part-3: **Some concluding comments**

According to the Old Testament, God, the Father, planned the crucifixion of Jesus. According to the New Testament, Jesus accepted God's plan for His crucifixion. Thus, based on the Old and New Testaments, the answer to the question – "Should Christians be angry with Jews, because they crucified Jesus?", is "No!"

Part-4: **Some relevant comments**

Relevant comments from this author and from Mr. Nicolas Criticos (*who wrote the Foreword and who proofread two editions of this book*) are, as follows:

Comments from the author:

Some Christian leaders take the position that each of us caused the crucifixion of Jesus, because each of us is a sinner! And it was sin that required Jesus to be crucified. Therefore, based on this position, being angry with the Jews would also be inappropriate. Based on this position, it would be more appropriate for each of us to be angry with herself or himself.

Comments from Mr. Nicolas Criticos:

It is absurd to blame all the Jews for the crime of a few. For it was the spiritual blindness of the priests, the lawyers, Pharisees, etc., that killed Jesus. These were theoretically, the spiritual and religious leaders of the nation. Religious they were. Spiritual they were not. They were blind, with no spiritual discernment to know the difference, between a man of God and a man from the devil.

Jesus exposed the wretchedness of their soul. He tore the Pharisees apart. Proud men like them could not tolerate such a humiliation. In addition, Jesus was shaking the fundamental status quo, everything they got their worth from. He had to be eliminated.

Let us remember that all Jesus' disciples and the apostles, were Jews and so was He. His mother was a Jew. Almost all the one-hundred-and-twenty people, who were gathered together praying on Pentecost (*which was the day that the Holy Spirit descended upon the disciples*), must have been Jewish. Nicodemus, a Pharisee, a hidden disciple was a Jew. The apostle Paul was a Jew. Jews spread Christianity all over the known world in its beginning, so how can we justify any ill feeling against all the Jews under such circumstances.

What did the author hope to accomplish with this book?

The author believes that there are some essential concepts, facts, and beliefs of Christianity. In fact, these essential concepts, facts, and beliefs define Christianity. Nevertheless, too many Christians appear to be just glossing over too many of these essential concepts, facts, and beliefs, because it is easier to accept and profess the doctrinal line of their denomination than to read the Bible for themselves and then test the doctrines promoted by their denomination against what the Bible says. Consequently, in creating this book, the author hoped to accomplish two things: *first*, to get Christians to read the Bible and pray for the discernment of the Holy Spirit, and then to reflect on their beliefs and Christian observances to determine if they "are really serving God" and *second*, to get non-Christians to "check out God for themselves". That is, the author is hoping to get non-Christians to confirm for themselves that God does exist and that God's existence is the only thing, which gives meaning to life.

For this author, the essential concepts, facts, and beliefs of Christianity, are as follows:

- The Trinity – (God, the Father, God, the Son, and God, the Holy Spirit, as One).
- God is a personal God.
- Creation was accomplished by God only. That is, there was no "macroevolution (*which is one species evolving into another species*)" nor "theistic evolution (*which is God using evolution in His creative process*)".
- God created Adam, who was the first human being, out of the dust of the ground and then breathed into his nostrils the breath of life, and the man became a living being.
- God created Eve, who was the first woman, out of one of Adam's ribs.
- Adam and Eve were created sinless. They were also created with "free will". Unfortunately, they exercised their "free will", by choosing to sin.
- There was no death before Adam and Eve sinned.
- All humans, except Adam, Eve, and Jesus, were/are/will be born sinners, because we were in Adam's loins when he sinned (*i.e., in Adam's DNA when he sinned*). As sinners, we are in need of a savior – a redeemer – to reestablish our existence under God's grace.
- God, the Son, veiled His deity and was born of a virgin to also become Christ, our "kinsman-redeemer".
- Jesus, the man, is the *Messiah*/the *Anointed One*/the *Christ*/the *Son of God*, Who will save His people from their sins.
- Jesus is fully God and He is fully man.
- Salvation is a gift from God through the finished work of Jesus. Salvation is through the spiritual and physical deaths of Jesus, on the cross. Thus, there is only "ONE WAY" to God – there is only "ONE WAY" for our existence under God's grace to be reestablished – and that is through the finished work of Jesus.

- The "spiritual death" of Jesus on the cross served, as the penalty for our sins.
- The "physical death" of Jesus on the cross served, as the atoning sacrifice for our sins.
- The bodily resurrection of Jesus, after His deaths on the cross.
- The Second Coming of Jesus.
- The Bible is the Word of God.
- In the original languages of Hebrew, Aramaic, and Koine Greek, the Bible is inerrant. (*However, this inerrancy does not include Bibles, which may have been translated into some other language and then that translation used to translate back into the original languages.*) Many translations are not inerrant, because of language differences.
- Most of the revelations of God are through Nature and through the Bible.
- The Jews are God's chosen people.
- Both Jews and non-Jews can exercise their "free will" and accept the free gift of salvation offered, by the finished work of Jesus.

Thus, Christians!

"Are You Really Serving God?"

Non-Christians!

Obviously, you probably do not believe any of the essential concepts, facts, and beliefs of Christianity listed in this essay. Therefore, for you the question is:

"Have You Checked out God for Yourself?"

ENDNOTES

Obviously, endnotes are listed in numerical order. However, the title of the essay that the endnotes are in, is listed before the endnotes. Thus, the format is, as follows: 1) Preceding the essay title is a thick margin-to-margin line. 2) The title of the essay for which the endnotes are applicable. If an essay does not have any endnotes, then it is not listed. 3) A double margin-to-margin line. 4) All of the endnotes applicable to that essay.

ACKNOWLEDGMENTS

1.
The name – "George Jones", was made-up and inserted in place of the real name of an acquaintance, who was originally helping with the process of publishing this book. But at some point, this acquaintance became confused, over the objective of this book. Therefore, he withdrew his support and permission to use his name. This author's objective in publishing this book is stated in the Preface. Nevertheless, to reiterate, "This author is not saying that every word from him or anyone else is true and accurate. This author is saying that the subjects of these essays are things, which we, Christians, must discuss, in order to confirm, whether 'we are really serving God'."

Essay: **What is life all about?**

2.
This author is not aware of any creation view that cannot be included in one of the four-subgroups. However, if you feel that there is such a creation view, then please send your comments and details to the publisher. Write the phrase – "Creation view", on the envelope. Time permitting, you will receive a reply.

3.
In the KJV, Matthew 15:1-3 reads:

> Matthew 15:[1]Then came to Jesus scribes and Pharisees, which were of Jerusalem, saying, [2]Why do thy disciples transgress the tradition of the elders? for they wash not their hands when they eat bread. [3]But he answered and said unto them, Why do **ye also transgress the commandment of God by your tradition?**

Essay: **Does God exist?**

4.
The rest of the non-Christian texts are being excluded, based on the studies of several well-known evangelists, who took the time to read all of the texts of the major non-Christian religions. They concluded that the other non-Christian texts included physical, scientific, and/or logical inaccuracies or inconsistencies, that were unworthy of a supreme being. Therefore, they dismissed these non-Christian texts from any further consideration. And this author will do likewise. As the non-Christian concepts should be supported and defined by the non-Christian texts, they will also be dismissed from any further consideration.

5.
(Source: Deductive reasoning. [Version before 2007, November 8]. In *Wikipedia, The Free Encyclopedia.* Retrieved 16:33, October 28, 2007, from http://en.wikipedia.org/w/index.php?title=Deductive_reasoning&oldid=170207997)

6.
(Source: Inductive reasoning. [2007, October 29]. In *Wikipedia, The Free Encyclopedia.* Retrieved 16:27, November 13, 2007, from http://en.wikipedia.org/w/index.php?title=Inductive_reasoning&oldid=167823111)

7.
(Source: Abductive reasoning. [2007, November 11]. In *Wikipedia, The Free Encyclopedia.* Retrieved 16:22, November 13, 2007, from http://en.wikipedia.org/w/index.php?title=Abductive_reasoning&oldid=170832256)

8.
(Source: Retroduction. [Version prior to 2007, October 31]. In *Wikipedia, The Free Encyclopedia.* Retrieved 20:20, September 23, 2007, from http://en.wikipedia.org/w/index.php?title=Retroduction &oldid=168361386)

9.
(Source: Logical reasoning. [2007, June 18]. In *Wikipedia, The Free Encyclopedia.* Retrieved 23:52, November 13, 2007, from http://en.wikipedia.org/w/index.php?title=Logical_reasoning&oldid =138988212)

10.
(Primary source: Logical reasoning. [2007, June 18]. In *Wikipedia, The Free Encyclopedia.* Retrieved 23:52, November 13, 2007, from http://en.wikipedia.org/w/index.php?title=Logical_reasoning&oldid =138988212) & (Secondary source: "T. Menzies. Applications of Abduction: Knowledge-Level Modeling. November 1996")

Essay: **What are some names, terms, and phrases, which are useful to a discussion of the formation of the Christian Bible?**

11.
The **Semitic languages** are a family of languages spoken by more than 300 million people across

much of the Middle East, North Africa, and the Horn of Africa. They constitute the northeastern subfamily of the Afro-Asiatic languages, and the only branch of this group spoken in Asia.

The most widely spoken Semitic language today is Arabic[1] (206 million first language speakers),[2] followed by Amharic (27 million first language speakers),[3][4] Tigrinya (about 6.7 million total speakers[5]), and Hebrew (5 million first language speakers[6]). Semitic languages were among the earliest to attain a written form, with Akkadian writing beginning in the middle of the third millennium BC. Maltese is the only Semitic Language written in Roman script. The term "Semitic" for these languages, after Shem, the son of Noah in the Bible, is etymologically a misnomer in some ways (see Semitic), but is nonetheless standard.

(Source: Semitic languages. [2008, January 2]. In *Wikipedia, The Free Encyclopedia*. Retrieved 22:38, January 6, 2008, from http://en.wikipedia.org/w/index.php?title=Semitic_languages&oldid=181548797)

Source footnotes:

[1] Including all varieties.
[2] http://www.ethnologue.com/show_language.asp?code=arb
[3] 1994 Ethiopian census
[4] http://www.omniglot.com/writing/amharic.htm
[5] In 2005, Ethnologue estimated a total of 4.45 million Tigrinya speakers ranging over all countries; 3.2 million in Ethiopia, 1.2 million in Eritrea, 10,000 Beta Israels in Israel (the remaining 15,000 are unaccounted for).[1] The Tigrinya ethnic group, almost entirely Tigrinya speaking is estimated at 3.3 million by Ethnologue, whereas other estimates indicate 4.3 million in Ethiopia (CSA 2005 National Statistics, Table B.3.), 2.4 million in Eritrea (July 2006).[2]
[6] [a] [b] Gordon, Raymond G., Jr. (ed.), 2005. Ethnologue: Languages of the World, Fifteenth edition. Dallas, Tex.: SIL International. Online version: http://www.ethnologue.com/. (Hebrew->Population total all countries,[3])

12.
(Source: "Aramaic language". [2007, December 29]. In *Wikipedia, The Free Encyclopedia.* Retrieved 22:37, January 5, 2008, from http://en.wikipedia.org/w/index.php?title=Aramaic_language&oldid=180813034)

13.
(Source: "Biblical Aramaic". [2008, February 14]. In *Wikipedia, The Free Encyclopedia.* Retrieved 18:59, February 14, 2008, from http://en.wikipedia.org/w/index.php?title=Biblical_Aramaic&oldid=191402027)

14.
John Wycliffe (also Wyclif, Wycliff, or Wickliffe, Czech Jan Viklef) (mid-1320s – 31 December 1384) was an English theologian and an early dissident in the Roman Catholic Church during the 14th century. He founded the Lollard movement, a precursor to the Protestant Reformation (thus he became known as "The Morning Star of the Reformation"). He was one of the earliest antagonists of the papal encroachments on secular power.[1] Wycliffe felt that all Christians should have access to the Bible in the vernacular. He is credited as the force behind the first

complete translation of the Bible into English (called Wycliff's Bible). It is believed that he translated at least the four Gospels of Matthew, Mark, Luke, and John. It is possible he could have translated the entire New Testament, while his associates translated the Old Testament.[2] Wycliff's Bible first appeared over a period from approximately 1382 to 1384,[3] with additional updated versions being done by Wycliffe's assistant John Purvey and others in 1388 and 1395.[4]

(Source: John Wycliffe. (2007, November 11). In *Wikipedia, The Free Encyclopedia.* Retrieved 21:43, November 14, 2007, from http://en.wikipedia.org/w/index.php?title=John_Wycliffe &oldid=170651999)

Source footnotes:

[1] The Reader's Encyclopedia, Volume Two - page 1105, Thomas Y. Crowell Company publisher, New York 1965, Second Edition, Library of Congress Card No. 65-12510.

[2] Sir Frederic G. Kenyon in the article "English Versions" from the Dictionary of the Bible edited by James Hastings, published by Charles Scribner's Sons of New York in 1909. Sir Frederic G. Kenyon says: "Exactly how much of it was done by his own hand is uncertain."

[3] English versions of the Bible

[4] Catholic Encyclopedia Versions of the Bible

15.
(Source: "*Easton's Bible Dictionary*", by M. G. Easton) – In this definition, author M. G. Easton uses the statement – "The Bible consists of sixty-six different books". This statement means that he was thinking about the "Protestant Bible" and not the "Peshitta Bible", the "Orthodox Bible", nor the "Catholic Bible".

16.
(Source: "Attic Greek". *Wikipedia, The Free Encyclopedia.* 22 Jan 2008, 16:37 UTC. Wikimedia Foundation, Inc. 11 Feb 2008 <http://en.wikipedia.org/w/index.php?title=Attic_Greek&oldid=186137817>)

17.
Matres lectionis (Latin "mothers of reading", singular form: *mater lectionis*) is used for certain Hebrew consonants that can sometimes fill the position of a vowel. More specifically:

> The letters hei, vav and yud can represent consonantal sounds (/h/, /v/ and /j/, respectively) or serve as a markers for vowels. In the latter case, these letters are called "emot q'ria" (*"matres lectionis" in Latin, "mothers of reading" in English*).
>
> The letter hei at the end of a word usually indicates a final /a/, which usually indicates of feminine gender or /e/, which usually indicates masculine gender. In rare cases it may also indicate /o/, such as in שְׁלֹמֹה (Shlomo, Solomon). It may also indicate a possessive suffix for 3rd person feminine singular (סִפְרָהּ, her book), but in that case the hei is not a mater lectionis, but the consonant /h/, although in spoken Hebrew the distinction is rarely made. In texts with niqqud, the hei is written with a mappiq in the latter case. Correct pronunciation must be guessed according to context and niqqud may be used for disambiguation.

Vav may represent /o/ or /u/, and yod may represent /i/ or /e/. Sometimes a double yud is used for /ej/. In some modern Israeli texts, the letter alef is used to indicate long /a/ sounds in foreign names, particularly those of Arabic origin.

18.
(Source: Hebrew language. [2008, January 2]. In *Wikipedia, The Free Encyclopedia*. Retrieved 02:48, January 3, 2008, from http://en.wikipedia.org/w/index.php?title=Hebrew_language&oldid=181673416)

19.
"The 'Paleo-Hebrew alphabet' also know as 'Ktav Ivri' is an offshoot of the Phoenician alphabet, used to write the Hebrew language from about the 10th century BCE until it began to fall out of use in the 5th century BCE with the adoption of the 'square-script' Aramaic alphabet as a writing system for Hebrew and the subsequent emergence of the Hebrew alphabet.

Decline of use: After the Babylonian capture of Judah, when most of the nobles were taken into exile, the Paleo-Hebrew alphabet continued to be used by the people who remained to work the fields. One example of such writings are the 6th century BCE jar handles from Gibeon, on which the names of winegrowers are inscribed. Beginning from the 5th century BCE onward, when the Aramaic language and script became an official means of communication, the Paleo-Hebrew alphabet was preserved mainly for writing the Tanakh by a coterie of erudite scribes, who most likely belonged to the sect of the Sadducees. The Paleo-Hebrew fragments of the Torah were found among the Dead Sea Scrolls. The vast majority of the Hasmonean coinage, as well as the coins of the First Jewish-Roman War and Bar Kokhba's revolt, bears Paleo-Hebrew legends. The Paleo-Hebrew alphabet fell completely out of use only after 135 CE.

Use of Paleo-Hebrew by Samaritans: The divergence of the Samaritan alphabet began sometime in the last two centuries of the first millennium BCE. Unlike the Jews, the Samaritans continued to use this script for writing both Hebrew and Aramaic texts well into the Middle Ages. A comparison of the earliest Samaritan inscriptions and the medieval and modern Samaritan manuscripts clearly indicates that the Samaritan script is a static script which was used mainly as a book hand."

(Source: Paleo-Hebrew alphabet. [2008, January 22]. In *Wikipedia, The Free Encyclopedia*. Retrieved 13:19, January 25, 2008, from http://en.wikipedia.org/w/index.php?title=Paleo-Hebrew_alphabet&oldid =186184673)

20.
(Source: "Protocanonical books". [2007, December 14]. In *Wikipedia, The Free Encyclopedia*. Retrieved 02:12, March 24, 2008, from http://en.wikipedia.org/w/index.php?title=Proto canonical_books&oldid=177787316)

21.
(Source: "Biblical apocrypha" (2008, August 1). In *Wikipedia, The Free Encyclopedia*. Retrieved 02:27, August 7, 2008, from http://en.wikipedia.org/w/index.php?title=Biblical_apocrypha&oldid=229232502)

22.
(Source: Biblical canon. (2007, November 6). In *Wikipedia, The Free Encyclopedia*. Retrieved 23:15, November 14, 2007, from http://en.wikipedia.org/w/index.php?title=Biblical_canon& oldid=169508439)

23.
MALACHI (Mal' uh ki) is a personal name or common noun meaning, "my messenger", or "my angel". He is believed to be the writer of the last book in the English Old Testament which bears his name. (Source: Article by author Ralph L. Smith from the "Holman Bible Dictionary")

24.
The Council of Trent was the 19th Ecumenical Council of the Catholic Church. It was convened three times between December 13, 1545 and December 4, 1563 in the city of Trent (modern Trento, Trentino) as a response to the theological and ecclesiological challenges of the Protestant Reformation. It is considered one of the most important councils in the history of the Catholic Church, clearly specifying current Catholic doctrines on salvation, the sacraments, and the Biblical canon. The council standardized the Mass throughout the church, largely by abolishing local variations. This became known as the "Tridentine Mass", from the city's Latin name *Tridentum*. The council also commissioned the first Catholic catechism, the Roman Catechism. The Council of Trent was a major first step in the Counter-Reformation. (Source: Council of Trent. [2007, November 3]. In *Wikipedia, The Free Encyclopedia*. Retrieved 00:31, November 14, 2007, from http://en.wikipedia.org/w/index. php? title=Council_of_Trent&oldid=168884577)

25.
(Source: Pseudepigrapha. (2007, November 7). In *Wikipedia, The Free Encyclopedia*. Retrieved 19:31, November 14, 2007, from http://en.wikipedia.org/w/index.php? title=Pseudepigrapha& oldid=169868441)

Source footnotes:

[1] Bauckham, Richard; "Pseudo-Apostolic Letters", Journal of Biblical Literature, Vo. 107, No. 3, September 1988, pp.469–494

[2] It is written by a man who identifies himself only as "the presbyteros".

[3] Bauckham 1988, op. cit., pp. 469: "New Testament scholars are now nearly unanimous in the opinion that at least one NT letter, 2 Peter, is pseudepigraphical."

[4] Colossians as Pseudepigraphy (Bible Seminar, 4 Sheffield:JSOT Press) 1986, p 12.[not specific enough to verify]

[5] [a] [b] Harris, Stephen L., Understanding the Bible. Palo Alto: Mayfield. 1985.

26.
(Source: "Book of Ezra" entry in the "Holman Bible Dictionary", authored by D. C. Martin)

27.
(Source: Vulgate. [2007, December 23]. In *Wikipedia, The Free Encyclopedia*. Retrieved 01:43, January 2, 2008, from http://en.wikipedia.org/w/index.php?title=Vulgate& oldid=179710950)

28.
(Source: "Common Era". In *Wikipedia, The Free Encyclopedia*. Retrieved before 15:23, August 7,

2008, from http://en.wikipedia.org/w/index.php?title= Common_Era)

29.
(Source: Masoretic Text. (2007, November 4). In *Wikipedia, The Free Encyclopedia*. Retrieved 19:45, November 14, 2007, from http://en.wikipedia.org/w/index.php? title=Masoretic_Text&oldid=169255181)

Source footnotes:
[1] A seventh century fragment containing the Song of the Sea (Exodus 13:19-16:1) is one of the few surviving texts from the "silent era" of Hebrew biblical texts between the Dead Sea Scrolls and the Aleppo Codex. See "Rare scroll fragment to be unveiled," Jerusalem Post, May 21, 2007.

30.
Reference source was website cor.cua.edu.

31.
(Source: Targum. (2007, September 3). In *Wikipedia, The Free Encyclopedia*. Retrieved 19:42, November 14, 2007, from en.wikipedia.org/w/index.php?title=Targum&oldid=155495048)

Source footnotes:
[1] Oesterley, W. O. E. & Box, G. H. (1920) A Short Survey of the Literature of Rabbinical and Mediæval Judaism, Burt Franklin:New York.

Essay: **What do biblical scholars, Christian historians, and others say, about the formation of the Christian Bible?**

32.
This translation of the Peshitta by George M. Lamsa contains the thirty-nine books of the Protestant Old Testament and the twenty-seven books of the Protestant New Testament. However, officially and traditionally, the Assyrian Church of the East does not recognize as canon five books of the New Testament. These are: 2 Peter, 2 John, 3 John, Jude, and Revelation. Furthermore, officially and traditionally, the Assyrian Church includes some of the Old Testament Apocrypha and Pseudepigrapha in the official version of the Peshitta. Or more specifically, the official version of the Peshitta includes more than thirty-nine books in its Old Testament and only twenty-two books in its New Testament.

33.
(Source: The "Holman Bible Dictionary", by an unspecified author.)

34.
polity - noun (plural polities)
1. An organizational structure of the government of a state, church etc. 2. Politically organized unit, a nation. (Source: "polity". In *Wiktionary, The Open Dictionary*. Retrieved 22:08, November 12, 2007, from http://en.wiktionary.org/wiki/polity)

35.
(Source: "Holman Bible Dictionary", article by author Mike Mitchell)

36.
(Source: "Attic Greek". *Wikipedia, The Free Encyclopedia.* 22 Jan 2008, 16:37 UTC. Wikimedia Foundation, Inc. 11 Feb 2008 <http://en.wikipedia.org/w/index.php?title=Attic_Greek&oldid=186137817>).

37.
B. Metzger, *The Text of the New Testament*. Tr. by P Ackroyd (Oxford University Press, 1963), p. 27.

38.
Qumran is located on a dry plateau about a mile inland from the northwestern shore of the Dead Sea in the West Bank, just next to the Israeli Kibbutz of Kalia. The site was most likely constructed sometime during or before the reign of John Hyrcanus, 134-104 BCE and saw various phases of occupation until, probably after the fall of Jerusalem in 70 CE, Titus and his X *Fretensis* destroyed it. It is best known as the settlement nearest to the hiding place of the Dead Sea Scrolls in the caves of the sheer desert cliffs. (Source: Qumran. [2007, November 7]. In *Wikipedia, The Free Encyclopedia*. Retrieved 22:10, November 12, 2007, from http://en.wikipedia.org/w/index.php?title=Qumran&oldid=169904347)

39.
R. Pfeiffer, *Introduction to the Old Testament,* rev. ed. (New York: Harper and Row, 1948), p. 80.

40.
H. von Soden, *Die Schriften des Neuen Testamentes* (Goettingen: Vandenhoeck, 1912), I, 484.

41.
For material on the history of the modern chapter and verse divisions see the article in *Die Religion in der Geschichte und der Gegenwart* (3rd ed.), III, 1141 f., and the literature cited there.

42.
von Soden, ibid., p. 482.

43.
R. Tasker, *The Greek New Testament* (New York: Oxford University Press), 1964.

44.
K. Aland, M. Black, B. Metzger, A. Wikren, eds., *The Greek New Testament* (New York: American Bible Society, 1966).

45.
A. Robertson, *An Introduction to the Textual Criticism of the New Testament* (Nashville: Broadman Press, 1925), p. 101.

46.
In the NIV, 1 Samuel 3:1-18 reads: 1 Samuel 3:[1]The boy Samuel ministered before the LORD under Eli. In those days the word of the LORD was rare; there were not many visions. [2]One night Eli, whose eyes were becoming so weak that he could barely see, was lying down in his usual place. [3]The lamp of God had not yet gone out, and Samuel was lying down in the temple of the LORD, where the ark of God was. [4]Then the LORD called Samuel. Samuel answered, "Here I am." [5]And he ran to Eli and said, "Here I am; you called me." But Eli said, "I did not call; go back and lie down." So he went and lay down. [6]Again the LORD called, "Samuel!" And Samuel got up and went to Eli and said, "Here I am; you called me." "My son," Eli said, "I did not call; go back and lie down." [7]Now Samuel did not yet know the LORD: The word of the LORD had not yet been revealed to him. [8]The LORD called Samuel a third time, and Samuel got up and went to Eli and said, "Here I am; you called me." Then Eli realized that the LORD was calling the boy. [9]So Eli told Samuel, "Go and lie down, and if he calls you, say, 'Speak, LORD, for your servant is listening.'" So Samuel went and lay down in his place. [10]The LORD came and stood there, calling as at the other times, "Samuel! Samuel!" Then Samuel said, "Speak, for your servant is listening." [11]And the LORD said to Samuel: "See, I am about to do something in Israel that will make the ears of everyone who hears of it tingle. [12]At that time I will carry out against Eli everything I spoke against his family--from beginning to end. [13]For I told him that I would judge his family forever because of the sin he knew about; his sons made themselves contemptible, and he failed to restrain them. [14]Therefore, I swore to the house of Eli, 'The guilt of Eli's house will never be atoned for by sacrifice or offering.'" [15]Samuel lay down until morning and then opened the doors of the house of the LORD. He was afraid to tell Eli the vision, [16]but Eli called him and said, "Samuel, my son." Samuel answered, "Here I am." [17]"What was it he said to you?" Eli asked. "Do not hide it from me. May God deal with you, be it ever so severely, if you hide from me anything he told you." [18]So Samuel told him everything, hiding nothing from him. Then Eli said, "He is the LORD; let him do what is good in his eyes."

47.
See Appendix A, for an expanded definition of three variations of "Female Circumcisions".

48.
Origen (also called "Origen of Alexandria" or "Origen Adamantius", ca. 185–ca. 254) was an early Christian scholar, theologian, and one of the most distinguished of the early fathers of the Christian Church. According to tradition, he is held to have been an Egyptian[1] who taught in Alexandria, reviving the Catechetical School of Alexandria where Clement had taught. The patriarch of Alexandria at first supported Origen but later expelled him for being ordained without the patriarch's permission. He relocated to Caesarea Maritima and died there[2][3] after being tortured during a persecution.

His writings are important as one of the first intellectual attempts to describe Christianity. He espoused a Platonic view of eternal souls achieving perfection while escaping the temporary, imperfect material world. He imagined even demons being reunited with God. His views of a hierarchical structure in the Trinity, the temporality of matter, "the fabulous preexistence of souls", and "the monstrous restoration which follows from it" were declared anathema in the 6th century.[4]

(Source: Origen. (2007, November 10). In *Wikipedia, The Free Encyclopedia*. Retrieved 22:02, November 14, 2007, from http://en.wikipedia.org/w/index.php?title=Origen&oldid=170557946)

Source footnotes:

[1] George Sarton (1936). "The Unity and Diversity of the Mediterranean World", Osiris 2, p. 406-463 [430].
[2] http://www.caesarea.landscape.cornell.edu/about.html
[3] Another source [1] says "Tyre."
[4] http://www.ccel.org/ccel/schaff/npnf214.xii.ix.htm

Essay: **Does the Bible contradict itself?**

49.
Web document was at www.ugcs.caltech.edu/cgi-bin/webnews/read/contradictions/0.

50.
The wording of this sentence was changed to fit the context of this discussion. The original wording was – "I encourage the reader to keep these points in mind as we go through the purported contradictions." In addition, the wording – "*(Dr. Bumbulis)*", was inserted, by this author for clarity.

Essay: **How is it possible for different believers to get different interpretations of the same verses of the Bible?**

51.
This has possibly a double meaning: "His body stayed in the tomb for three days and three nights" and "His soul and spirit went to Abraham's bosom to preach the good news of His finished work on the cross to the righteous dead. Then He probably lead them into the present of God, the Father, in paradise."

Essay: **What does the phrase – "ability to sin", mean? (Is the phrase – "ability to not sin", meaningful or is it inappropriate?)**

52.
(Soruce: "ability". *Wiktionary, The Open Dictionary*, Retrieved 22:08, November 16, 2007, from http://en.wiktionary.org/w/index.php?title=ability&oldid=3239297)

53.
A proofreader responded to *Reason-1*, with the comment that there is clearly a difference between the phrase – "to not freely choose" and the phrase – "to freely not choose". He further proposed that while the phrase – "to not freely choose", does imply "being inhibited from freely choosing (*which is a robotic situation*)", the phrase – "to freely not choose" implies "the choice is 'freely choosing not to choose'". This author appreciated the proofreader's comments, because those comments forced a review of the wording of this essay. But clearly, the proofreader is conceding the validity of the first phrase. Thus, only the validity of the phrase – "to freely not choose", needs to be determined. And if the literal meaning of this phrase is "freely choosing not to choose", then clearly this is inappropriate and illogical wording, because "not choosing" is itself a choice or a choosing. That is, the choices are "choosing" and "not choosing", with "not choosing" being the final choice. Therefore, this author would totally dismiss the phrase – "to freely not choose", for being invalid and inappropriate.

Essay: **What do the three phrases – "knowledge of good and evil", "knowledge of good", and "knowledge of evil", mean? and** What is "the age of accountability"?

54.
When the sense of "touch" is mentioned, most of us immediately focus only on the hands. However, for most of us, our whole bodies – from our heads to our feet – are tactile receptors.

55.
In the NIV, Genesis 3:2-3 read, as follows:

Genesis 3:[2]The woman said to the serpent, "We may eat fruit from the trees in the garden, [3]but God did say, 'You must not eat fruit from the tree that is in the middle of the garden, and you must not touch it, or you will die.'"

56.
Dr. Dick L. Temple's sermon was titled – "WHAT YOU NEED TO KNOW ABOUT TEMPTATION". A PDF version of the sermon is available at: www.bethelchristiancenter.org/sermon_ notes/temptation/734dt01_temptation.pdf. In this sermon, Dr. Temple discussed the three categories of temptation – the "lust of the flesh", the "lust of the eyes", and the "pride of life" and how these categories were related to the tempting of Eve and the tempting of Jesus.

Essay: **Did Jesus, the man, have the "ability to sin" like Adam and Eve?**

57.
One of the definitions of the word – "nature" is "The essential characteristics". (Source: "nature". *Wiktionary, The Open Dictionary*, Retrieved 22:08, November 16, 2007, from http://en.wiktionary.org/w/index.php?title=nature&oldid=3301404)

58.
[Source: The essay: "What does the phrase – 'ability to sin', mean? (Is the phrase – 'ability to **not** sin', meaningful or is it inappropriate?)"]

59.
(Source: "desire". *Wiktionary, The Open Dictionary*, Retrieved 22:08, November 16, 2007, from http://en.wiktionary.org/w/index.php?title=desire&oldid=3212803)

60.
(Source: "lust". *Wiktionary, The Open Dictionary*, Retrieved 22:08, November 16, 2007, from http://en.wiktionary.org/w/index.php?title=lust&oldid=3232976)

61.
(Source: "entice". *Wiktionary, The Open Dictionary*, Retrieved 22:08, November 16, 2007, from http://en.wiktionary.org/w/index.php?title=entice&oldid=3080925)

62.
(Source: "lure". *Wiktionary, The Open Dictionary*, Retrieved 22:08, November 16, 2007, from http://en.wiktionary.org/w/index.php?title=lure&oldid=3221175)

63.
This author firmly believes that Jesus, the man, had some "self-awareness". But He would not have had total "self-awareness", because He was still totally focused on God not on himself. Worded differently, this author believes that "self-awareness" under God's grace is different from "self-awareness" under God's judgment. The difference may be a matter of degrees or it might be something more substantial, like "a matter of focus" or "a matter of not being concerned about oneself (*trusting in God's care*)" or "being concerned about oneself (*trusting in one's own care*)".

Essay: **What is the literal and symbolic significance in the shedding of Jesus' innocent blood?**

64.
One might interpret this wording to imply that Eve, the first woman, was sinless, because she did not have a father. Eve was created, by God from one of Adam's ribs. However, while it is true that God created Eve sinless, it is also true that she chose to sin. Clearly, statements in Genesis 3:2-3 indicate in Eve's own words, she knew that she and Adam were not suppose to eat the fruit from the "tree of the knowledge of good and evil". Thus, when she ate the fruit, she knowingly sinned. Now, it is possible that Eve was told not to eat the fruit by Adam, instead of being told directly by God. However, the source of Eve's information did not negate the fact that she sinned.

Essay: **Is Jesus the only way to God?**

65.
(Source: "Gospel" by Matthew Slick, http://www.carm.org/dictionary/dic_g-h.htm#"Gospel")

The entire definitions reads, as follows:

The Gospel is the good news that we have forgiveness of sins through Jesus. Specifically, the gospel is defined by Paul in 1 Corinthians 15:1-4: "Now I make known to you, brethren, the gospel which I preached to you, which also you received, in which also you stand, by which also you are saved, if you hold fast the word which I preached to you, unless you believed in vain. For I delivered to you as of first importance what I also received, that Christ died for our sins according to the Scriptures, and that He was buried, and that He was raised on the third day according to the Scriptures."

The gospel comes from God (Galatians 1:10-12), is the power of God for salvation (Romans 1:16), is a mystery (Ephesians 6:19), and is a source of hope (Colossians 1:23), faith (Acts 15:7), life (1 Corinthians 4:15), and peace (Ephesians 6:15).

Essay: **Does man have a body, a soul, and a spirit?**

66.
In an article included in the "Holman Bible Dictionary", author Tom Smothers states "Parts of the Old Testament were written in Aramaic: Ezra 4:8-6:18; 7:12-26; Daniel 2:4b-7:28; Jeremiah 10:11. Two words in Genesis 31:47, Jegar-sahadutha (heap of witness) are in Aramaic. A number of Aramaic words came into common Hebrew usage, and several passages in the Hebrew Bible show Aramaic influence."

Essay: **Did Mary also have to be sinless, since Jesus was born sinless through her?**

67.
From four translations – KJV, NIV, NASB, and NRSV, Luke 1:28 reads:

(Luke 1:28 KJV) And the angel came in unto her, and said, Hail, thou that art highly favoured, the Lord is with thee: blessed art thou among women.

(Luke 1:28 NIV) The angel went to her and said, "Greetings, you who are highly favored! The Lord is with you."

(Luke 1:28 NASB) And coming in, he said to her, "Hail, favored one! The Lord is with you."

(Luke 1:28 NRSV) And he came to her and said, "Greetings, favored one! The Lord is with you."

68.
(Source: "dogma". *Wiktionary, The Open Dictionary*, Retrieved 22:08, November 16, 2007, from http://en.wiktionary.org/w/index.php?title=dogma&oldid=3063054)

69.
(Source: "corpus". *Wiktionary, The Open Dictionary*, Retrieved 22:08, November 16, 2007, from http://en.wiktionary.org/w/index.php?title=corpus&oldid=3043727)

70.
(Source: "ineffable" at en.wiktionary.org/w/index.php?title=ineffable&oldid=3681038)

71.
The word – "paraclete (*plural* paracletes)", means "an advocate, especially the Holy Spirit". (Source: "paraclete" en.wiktionary.org/w/index.php?title=paraclete&oldid=4088387)

72.
(Source: Nestorianism. [2008, April 21]. In *Wikipedia, The Free Encyclopedia*. Retrieved 16:15, April 25, 2008, from http://en.wikipedia.org/w/index.php?title=Nestorianism&oldid= 207214036)

Essay: **How do we know that the genealogy of Jesus in the Gospel of Luke is through Mary?**

73.
The "daughter and inheritance" custom, was established by God to cover those situations, where there were no male heirs for an inheritance. In such situations, an inheritance could be passed to a daughter(*s*), who was (*were*) then required to marry within her (*their*) own tribe (*one of the twelve tribes of Israel*), so that the inheritance would stay within that particular tribe. "Witness Lee" indicates in his footnotes in the "The New Testament – Recovery Version" that the "daughter and inheritance" law is referenced by Numbers 27:1-8 and Numbers 36:1-12. (*See the closing comments, at the end of this essay.*)

Comment: Nothing in the Bible tells us whether the "daughter and inheritance custom" was used by the "Virgin Mary". For that matter, we cannot know for sure whether the "daughter and inheritance custom" was used, at any point in the blood lineage of Jesus from King David to Mary. Nevertheless, some speculation by this author is based on the way God appears to accomplish things, as revealed by the Bible. For upon reading the Bible, it becomes apparent that God established the "Jewish people", the "Jewish language", and "many of the Jewish laws and customs", which facilitated the explanation, the definition, and the implementation of issues related to the birth, life, works, death, burial, and resurrection of Jesus, the man. Thus, when you understand that using the "daughter and inheritance" custom, allowed a daughter to inherit rights, privileges, and properties normally reserved for the male members of the family, you understand that this would have been consistent with the birth of Jesus via the "seed of a woman". Consequently, this author strongly suspects that the "daughter and inheritance" law, was probably used by the "Virgin Mary". This may have contributed to her marrying Joseph, who was also of the tribe of Judah. However, these comments are only speculations, by this author.

74.
Several sources present this information. However, most used the Gospel of Matthew for some of the conditions. This author replaced a "Matthew reference" with a "Luke reference" whenever possible. The reason for this is that this author felt "Luke references" are more consistent with the purpose of the essay, because Luke's genealogy is "by God's word" and "by blood", whereas Matthew's genealogy is "by Jewish law". Furthermore, this author used verses from the NIV instead of the KJV.

Essay: **Did God create man through evolution?**

75.
Source: "Millions of Years & the Downfall of the Christian West", by Terry Mortenson, Ph.D. and published by the Answers In Genesis Ministry.

76.
The statement – "God can do anything that is consistent with His revealed nature", is quoted from Dr. Walter Martin's audiotape, "Evil and Human Suffering". Dr. Martin has gone home to be with the Lord. But he left us some excellent audiotapes. This particular audiotape is the best presentation on "evil and human suffering" that this author has ever heard and it includes an excellent discussion of "our free will and God's sovereignty". Order this tape using www.waltermartin.org. Click on "Purchases Tapes/CDs". Then execute the "find-feature" to find the word – "Suffering".

77.
The following bibliography is for the article titled – "Evolution" by E. Peter Volpe.

Bibliography: Bowler, Peter J., *Life's Splendid Drama: Evolutionary Biology and the Reconstruction of Life's Ancestry, 1860–1940* (1996); Burkhardt, R. W., Jr., *The Spirit of System: Lamarck and Evolutionary Biology* (1990; repr. 1995); Depew, D. J., and Weber, B. H., eds., *Darwinism Evolving* (1994); Edey, M. A., and Johanson, D. C., *Blueprints* (1989); Eldredge, Niles, *The Pattern of Evolution* (1998) and *Reinventing Darwin* (1995); Futuyma, Douglas J., *Evolutionary Biology*, 3d ed. (1998); Gould, Stephen J., *Wonderful Life* (1989); Nielsen, Claus, *Animal Evolution* (1995); Osawa, Syozo, *Evolution of the Genetic Code* (1995); Raff, R. A., *The Shape of Life: Genes, Development, and the Evolution of Animal Form* (1996); Ruse, Michael, *The Darwinian Revolution: Science Red in Tooth and Claw*, 2d ed. (1999); Schopf, J. W., *Evolution and the Molecular Revolution* (1996); Slatkin, Mongtomery, *Exploring Evolutionary Biology* (1995); Smith, J. M., and Szathmary, Eors, *The Major Transitions in Evolution* (1995); Volpe, E. P., *Understanding Evolution*, 5th ed. (1985); Wallace, D. R., *The Monkey's Bridge: Mysteries of Evolution in Central America* (1997); Williams, G. C., *The Pony Fish's Glow: And Other Clues to Plan and Purpose in Nature* (1997); Willis, D., *The Hominid Gang* (1989); Young, D. G., *The Discovery of Evolution* (1993); Zimmer, Carl, *At the Water's Edge: Macroevolution and the Transformation of Life* (1998).

78.
The following bibliography is for the article titled – "creationism" (*the author's name was not given*):

Bibliography: Numbers, Ronald L., *The Creationists* (1992) and *Darwinism Comes to America* (1998); Pennock, Robert T., *Tower of Babel: The Evidence against the New Creationism* (1999); Sonder, Ben, *Evolutionism and Creationism* (1999).

79.
The source for these comments, was a web document, which no longer exist.

Essay: **Does the union of a sperm and an egg create human life?**

80.
The author wants it understood that the phrase – *"outside the organ that released them"*, has a specific reference with respect to the word – "outside", which is intended to mean outside the ovaries or testicles, but generally, still inside a human body. Yes! Sperms and eggs can live outside the human body. But they would survive for a much shorter period, unless they were placed in an artificially created and controlled environment.

81.
Note that all dead cells were alive at sometime in the individual's life. How God accomplished this in Adam and Eve is a side issue. Obvious examples of dead cells are one's hair, finger nails, and the outermost layer of skin. Clearly, continued life requires more living cells than dead cells. Furthermore, it is important which cells are living, and which ones are dead. In closing, note for example. Hair grows, but the growth is at the end that is alive, not at the dead end.

> *Comment:* A proofreader of this essay brought up the issue of "the continued growth of hair and nails after an individual has died". And even though, this issue is not crucial for this essay. According to my understanding, different parts of the human body cease to function at different times during the death process. Furthermore, recently this author heard comments to the fact that "the continued growth of hair and nails after an individual has died" is **an illusion**. What is actually happening is "the skin and muscles near the hair and nails are shrinking giving the illusion that the hair and nails are growing. Or worded differently, as the skin and muscles near the hair and nails shrink, more of the hair and nails are exposed."

Essay: **When does human life begin?**

82.
Source: An article entitled – "Egg", by Peter L. Petrakis in the "2003 Grolier Multimedia Encyclopedia". His bibliography is "Board, R. G., and Fuller, R., eds., *Microbiology of the Avian Egg* (1993); Burton, Robert, *Eggs* (1987)".

83.
Pastor Hayford's statement was on his audiotape entitled – "Abortion and Adoption", which is tape number 01521. This tape may still be available from the Living Way Ministries for a nominal fee. The toll-free telephone number for Living Way Ministries is (800) 776-8180.

Essay: **Is variety the spice of life?**

84.
The "degree of intimacy" could range from "being nonsexual (*one end of the intimacy spectrum*)" to "being sexual (*with intercourse being the opposite end of the intimacy spectrum*)". But in reality, the "degree of intimacy", is not the important factor. For this essay, the important factor is the actual physical and/or mental interaction between individuals, regardless of the degree.

A well-known evangelist has stated something to the effect that "the bonding process between a man and a woman, has a natural progression of stages. Paraphrased, these stages are: 'eye to body', 'eye to eye', 'voice to voice', 'hand to hand', 'hand to shoulder', 'hand to waist', 'face to face (*touch/kiss*)', 'hand to head', 'hand to body', 'mouth to body', 'touching below the waist', and then 'intercourse'." These "bonding stages" could also be considered "degrees of intimacy".

85.
For those who are unfamiliar with keypunch machines (*keypunches*), at one point in the history of computer technology, a keypunch was one of several components used to get computer programming instructions and data into computers. Two other input components were – "computer cards" and a "card reader". A brief description of each component follows:

Computer cards were about the thickness of index cards (*three-inch by five-inch cards*), but a computer card was a bit larger, measuring something like 3.25 inches by 7.375 inches. The computer card was designed, with 960 possible punch positions, which is twelve rows of possible punches by eighty columns of possible punches (*think of a spreadsheet, which is twelve rows by eighty columns, each cell could be punched or not punched*).

A **keypunch** was like a "manual typewriter" and a "paper punch", combined into one machine. The keypunch consisted of three primary stations: a "blank card hopper", a "punch station", and a "punched card holder". A computer card was fed from the "blank card hopper" into the "punch station". The "punch station" consisted of a column of twelve punches. The card was pulled through the "punch station" one column at a time, moving from right to left, as various keys of the keyboard were pressed, by the keypunch operator. Thus, in addition to punching various hole patterns (*punch patterns*), in various columns of the card, the character that the hole pattern represented was generally printed on the top row of the card in the same column. The hole patterns (*punch patterns*) were defined, as follows: The numbers (0 - 9) were represented, by a single punch in the appropriate row of a given column. The letters (A - Z) were represented, by two row punches in a given column. Special characters – the "plus sign", the "minus sign", the "ampersand", the "number symbol", the "period" or "decimal point", etc., were generally from one to three punches in a given column. A space was represented, by no punch in that column. If every potential position was punched, there would have been 960 punches (*12 rows in each column, by 80 columns*) on a single card. After each of the eighty columns had been punched or skipped, the card was released from the "punch station" and moved to the "punched card holder". Once the keypunch operator was done punching, the punched cards were removed from the "punched card holder", organized in the appropriate sequence, bundled or boxed, and then passed to someone to be processed, by a "card reader".

A **card reader** consisted of two primary stations: a "card hopper" and a "read station". Punched cards were unbundled or removed from their boxes and placed in the "card hopper". Then one card, at a time, was fed through the "read station", which consisted of a light source on one side and a light detector on the other side. As a computer card moved from right to left between the light source and the light detector, light shone through those positions that had been punched out, by the keypunch. The light detector determined the hole pattern in each of the eighty columns of the card, and then the logic in the circuitry of the "read station", converted the hole patterns into binary representations. The binary data represented computer instructions and/or data. This binary data was fed into a mainframe computer, so that it could be used, by various software packages: a "COBOL compiler", a "Fortran compiler", and so forth, which were loaded in a mainframe computer, along with an operating system. The mainframe computer was much like a Personal Computer today. The operating system was loaded when the computer was turned on or rebooted.

Essay: **Should Christians worship God, under the leadership of a homosexual?**

86.
Prideful (*unrepentant*) sinning is intended to mean that an individual is consistently sinning without remorse.

Essay: **Are all questions valid and/or contextually appropriate?**

87.
An opportunity presented itself for this author to discuss this question with Reverend Eugene Burrell of "The Navigators Ministry". In addition, several other individuals read drafts of this essay. Consequently, their comments had a major impact on the final contents of this essay.

88.
"Spiritual", as an adjective: 1. Of or pertaining to the spirit or the soul. 2. Of or pertaining to the God or a Church; sacred. 3. Of or pertaining to spirits; supernatural. "Spiritual (*plural* spirituals)", as an noun: 1. An African-American folk song, or a song in that style. (Source: "spiritual". *Wiktionary, The Open Dictionary*, Retrieved 22:08, November 16, 2007, from http://en.wiktionary.org/w/index.php?title=spiritual&oldid=3082183)

89.
"Religious", is an adjective: 1. Concerning religion. 2. Committed to the practice of religion. 3. Highly dedicated, as one would be to a religion. (Source: "religious". *Wiktionary, The Open Dictionary*, Retrieved 22:08, November 16, 2007, from http://en.wiktionary.org/w/index.php?title=religious&oldid=3223923)

90.
Wiktionary, The Open Dictionary, (Wiktionary 2007), defines the word – "assumption (*plural* assumptions)", as a noun meaning: 1. The act of assuming, or taking to or upon one's self; the act of taking up or adopting. 2. The act of taking for granted, or supposing a thing without proof; supposition; unwarrantable claim. 3. The thing supposed; a postulate, or proposition assumed; a supposition. 4. The minor or second proposition in a categorical syllogism. 5. The taking of a person up into heaven. 6. A festival in honor of the ascent of the Virgin Mary into heaven. (Source: assumption. In *Wiktionary, The Open Dictionary*. Retrieved 22:08, November 12, 2007, from http://en.wiktionary.org/wiki/assumption)

91.
Wiktionary, The Open Dictionary, (Wiktionary 2007), defines the word – "implication (*countable and uncountable; plural* implications)", as a noun meaning: 1. (uncountable) The act of implicating. 2. (uncountable) The state of being implicated. 3. (countable) An implying, or that which is implied, but not expressed; an inference, or something which may fairly be understood, though not expressed in words. 4. (logic) (*countable*) The connective in propositional calculus that, when joining two predicates A and B in that order, has the meaning "if A is true, then B is true". (Source: implication. In *Wiktionary, The Open Dictionary*. Retrieved 22:08, November 12, 2007, from http://en.wiktionary.org/wiki/implication)

92.
Wiktionary, The Open Dictionary, (Wiktionary 2007), defines the word – "context", as a noun meaning: 1. the text in which a word or passage appears and which helps ascertain its meaning. 2. the surroundings, circumstances, environment, background or settings which determine, specify, or clarify the meaning of an event. (Source: context. In *Wiktionary, The Open Dictionary*. Retrieved 22:08, November 12, 2007, from http://en.wiktionary.org/wiki/context)

93.
Reverend Burrell prefers the phrase – "How was the question framed?", which serves to emphasize the fact that in forming the question, the author of the question generally takes a specific, and perhaps, a narrow view of a subject, a relationship, an event, a process, etc. Using the word – "framed", is a more visual way of saying four things: First, the question is based on specific assumptions. Second, the question will have implicit or explicit implications. Third, the question is inserted into some context. Fourth, the question is being asked for a reason (*is being asked to accomplish something*).

Essay: **How can I have "free will", if I did not choose to be born?**

94.
(Source: "free will". *Wiktionary, The Open Dictionary*, Retrieved 22:08, November 16, 2007, from http://en.wiktionary.org/w/index.php?title=free_will&oldid=2743555)

95.
(Source: "freewill". *Wiktionary, The Open Dictionary*, Retrieved 22:08, November 16, 2007, from

http://en.wiktionary.org/w/index.php?title=freewill&oldid=3099291)

Essay: **What is the only meaningful question, about "God" and "Christianity"?**
Sub-essay: How could two of every kind of animal fit on Noah's Ark?

96.
This excellent video may be ordered from the Answers In Genesis Ministry. The toll-free telephone number for "The Answers In Genesis Ministry", is (800) 778-3390.

Essay: **What is biblical justice?**

97.
The word – "justice", occurs "*twenty-eight times in twenty-eight verses*", in the KJV, "*one hundred-thirty-four times in one hundred-thirty-two verses*", in the NIV, "*one hundred-thirty-eight times in one hundred-thirty-five verses*", in the NASB, and "*one hundred-thirty-one times in one hundred-twenty-nine verses*", in the NRSV.

98.
The word – "righteousness", occurs "*three hundred-six times in two hundred-eighty-nine verses*", in the KJV, "*two hundred-thirty-nine times in two hundred-thirty verses*", in the NIV, "*three hundred-nine times in two hundred-ninety-six verses*", in the NASB, and "*two hundred-thirty-two times in two hundred-twenty-three verses*", in the NRSV.

APPENDIX A

Every entry in this Appendix has, at least, four main components: 1) Every entry is preceded by a thick margin-to-margin line. 2) The entry title, which occurs in alphabetical order. 3) A double margin-to-margin line. 4) The comments, which comprise the entry.

Basis for the inclusion of the "Thinking view" and the "Eternal view"

The "Thinking view" and the "Eternal view" have been included in one of the four-subgroups: the "non-Religious views", the "non-Jewish/non-Islamic views", the "Jewish/Islamic views", and the "Christian views". The basis for the inclusion of each is, as follows:

- **The basis for the inclusion of the "Thinking view"**

The "Thinking view" has been included in one of the four-subgroups, as the result of any one of three lines of reasoning. These lines are, as follows:

1) If "We only think that we exist", then we should ask ourselves, at least, two questions. *First*, "What gave us the ability to think?" And *second*, "Where were we before we thought?" Answering the first question forces us to consider how we were created. Such a consideration will reveal what we think may have created us. "Whatever we think may have created us", will fit into one of the four-subgroups. Answering the second question forces us to consider issues around when and how we began to think. Such considerations will also reveal "What we think may have created us." And again, "Whatever we think may have created us", will fit into one of the four-subgroups.

2) If it is true that "We only think that we exist", then we are in this environment as a result of the thinking process. While we may not be able to prove that "the thinking got us into this environment", we can prove that we are **in this environment** (*our world*). Then in noting the things about our environment, an obvious question becomes "What created our environment?" That is, while we were thinking ourselves into existence, did we also think our environment into existence? Or was our environment created by something else? Thinking is both an involuntary act and a voluntary act. Also, the subjects of our thoughts are both involuntary and voluntary. Generally, when we are conscious, or better, not sleeping, our thinking is more voluntary. Consequently, we should voluntarily think up a better environment. We should voluntarily think up an environment with no obvious human suffering. Since we are not able to think up a better environment, it should be obvious that this environment was created by "something else" not our thinking. If this "something

else" created our environment, then it is probably safe to assume that this same "something else" created us, especially since we are part of the environment. We cannot exist without this environment. And again, this "something else" will fit into one of the **four-subgroups**.

3) The statement – "We only think that we exist", brings up so many contradictory issues that it shows itself to be a logically weak statement. Three examples of such issues are, as follows:

Issue-1: Like many others, a friend tried to use the statement – "I think, therefore I am!", to support his belief that "We only think that we exist." The statement – "I think, therefore I am!", was made by the famous French philosopher Rene Descartes. This author believes that "when Descartes made that statement, he was not concerned about how he came to exist. His statement – 'I think, therefore I am!', was focused on his actual existence. Descartes was really saying 'I think therefore I know that I exist.' Thus, the statement – 'I think, therefore I am!', is not the same, as saying, 'I thought myself into existence!', which is implied by the statement: 'We only think that we exist.'" Therefore, it is logically improper to stretch Mr. Descartes' statement into something it is not saying.

Issue-2: We see a baby being born. At what point does that particular baby begin to think that she or he exists? Obviously, that particular baby will exist in the minds of others before that baby begins to think she or he exists. Or more precisely, that particular baby will exist in the minds of others before that baby is fully conscious of her or his own existence. This should motivate each of us to ask, "Does the existence of everyone else depend on my thinking?" If we think about this question under the premise that "We only think that we exist", then it should be obvious that there are only two possible answers. For each of us, either "the existence of others is dependent on our thoughts" or "the existence of others is not dependent on our thoughts". If "the existence of others is dependent on your thoughts", then why is it that your thoughts cannot change or control their actions? If "the existence of others is not dependent on your thoughts", then how did others become part of the environment that you think you exist in? Both questions show the logical weakness of the statement: "We only think that we exist."

Issue-3: If you say, "We only think that we exist", then someone else could seriously or jokingly ask, "How do you know that 'We only think that we exist'? Perhaps, we *only think* that we are thinking we exist." This individual could further ask, "Could we stop thinking to see if we would cease to exist?" But without the thinking process, how would we know that we did indeed cease to exist? This is obviously logically weak.

If the statement – "We only think that we exist", is indeed logically weak, then it can be dismissed. But even if it could not be dismissed, based on the three reasons previously stated, "the act of 'thinking that we exist'", would fit into one of the four-subgroups on its own merit, because "thinking is a biological process" and "biologically something had to create us".

In concluding our discussion of the "Thinking view", we must note that the statement – "We only think that we exist", unnecessarily muddies the waters out of which we are trying to fish an answer to the question: "How were we and this world created?" The water is muddied, because our focus is shifted from the "*question*" to the "*act of thinking*". However, with regards to the topic question – "What is life about?", we can remove the mud from the waters, by saying that "the act of thinking" is not the important issue. Rather, "the result of the thinking", is the important issue. The issue is "How is an individual living her or his life in response to what she or he thinks may have created us (*in response to her or his creation view*)?" If you are going to allow an individual to think, then you may not put limits on her or his thinking. If an individual only thinks that she or he exists, then her or his life should reflect that. If an individual **thinks** that cosmic forces created us, then her or his life should reflect that. If an individual **thinks** that evolutionary forces created us, then her or his life should reflect that. If an individual **thinks** that God created us, then her or his life should reflect that. Therefore, creation "by thinking", "by cosmic forces", "by evolutionary forces", or "by God", all fit into one of the four-subgroups: the "non-Religious views", the "non-Jewish/non-Islamic views", the "Jewish/Islamic views", or the "Christian views".

➧ The basis for the inclusion of the "Eternal view"

The "Eternal view" has been included in one of the **four-subgroups**, as the result of the following line of reasoning:

For something to be eternal that something must "be self-sufficient and unchangeable" or must "be refreshed, by some eternal entity, which is 'self-sufficient and unchangeable'". Clearly, realistic observations of this world and modern science show that this world changes. This world is running down (*is wearing out*). For example, many of the natural resources of this planet have been or are being depleted (*including the extinction of many plants and animals*), while the environment is being polluted. Thus, the declining conditions of this environment mean two things: *First*, this environment is not "self-sufficient". *Second*, this environment is "changeable". Therefore, if this world is eternal, then at some point in time, some eternal entity must refresh our environment or life, as we know it will cease. Clearly, the "refreshing entity" has to be outside the world (*has to be an external entity*). Otherwise, this "refreshing something" would also be running down. This refreshing entity will fit into one of the four-subgroups: the "non-Religious views", the "non-Jewish/non-Islamic views", the "Jewish/Islamic views", and the "Christian views".

In concluding our discussion of the "Eternal view", it is easy to say, "Something is eternal." However, consistent with the above reasoning, if that "something" is not "self-sufficient and unchangeable", then it cannot be eternal. To appear eternal, this "something" would have to be refreshed by some entity that was "self-sufficient and unchangeable". Again, such an "eternal refreshing entity", will fit into one of the four-subgroups. More precisely, those who believe in the "Eternal view", must make assumptions about the "eternal refreshing entity". Actually or practically, those assumptions define the entity. And that definition will put the "eternal refreshing entity" in one of the four-subgroups.

In summary, based on the previously stated reasoning, both the "Thinking view" and the "Eternal view" can be (*and have been*) included in one of the four-subgroups: the "non-Religious views", the "non-Jewish/non-Islamic views", the "Jewish/Islamic views", or the "Christian views".

Daughters and inheritance custom

Under this custom, if daughters were the only heirs to an inheritance, then they were to receive that inheritance with the stipulation that they had to marry a man within their own tribe. Obviously, marrying within their own tribe served to keep the inheritance within that tribe. In his footnote, Witness Lee used Numbers 27:1-8 and Numbers 36:1-12, as his source for the "daughters and inheritance" custom. In the NIV, Numbers 27:1-8 reads:

> Numbers 27:[1]The daughters of Zelophehad son of Hepher, the son of Gilead, the son of Makir, the son of Manasseh, belonged to the clans of Manasseh son of Joseph. The names of the daughters were Mahlah, Noah, Hoglah, Milcah and Tirzah. They approached [2]the entrance to the Tent of Meeting and stood before Moses, Eleazar the priest, the leaders and the whole assembly, and said, [3]"Our father died in the desert. He was not among Korah's followers, who banded together against the LORD, but he died for his own sin and left no sons. [4]Why should our father's name disappear from his clan because he had no son? Give us property among our father's relatives." [5]So Moses brought their case before the LORD [6]and the LORD said to him, [7]"What Zelophehad's daughters are saying is right. You must certainly give them property as an inheritance among their father's relatives and turn their father's inheritance over to them. [8]"Say to the Israelites, 'If a man dies and leaves no son, turn his inheritance over to his daughter.

And also in the NIV, Number 36:1-12 reads:

> Number 36:[1]The family heads of the clan of Gilead son of Makir, the son of Manasseh, who
> were from the clans of the descendants of Joseph, came and spoke before Moses and the
> leaders, the heads of the Israelite families. [2]They said, "When the LORD commanded my
> lord to give the land as an inheritance to the Israelites by lot, he ordered you to give the
> inheritance of our brother Zelophehad to his daughters. [3]Now suppose they marry men
> from other Israelite tribes; then their inheritance will be taken from our ancestral
> inheritance and added to that of the tribe they marry into. And so part of the inheritance
> allotted to us will be taken away. [4]When the Year of Jubilee for the Israelites comes, their
> inheritance will be added to that of the tribe into which they marry, and their property will
> be taken from the tribal inheritance of our forefathers." [5]Then at the Lord's command
> Moses gave this order to the Israelites: "What the tribe of the descendants of Joseph is
> saying is right. [6]This is what the LORD commands for Zelophehad's daughters: They may
> marry anyone they please as long as they marry within the tribal clan of their father. [7]No
> inheritance in Israel is to pass from tribe to tribe, for every Israelite shall keep the tribal
> land inherited from his forefathers. [8]Every daughter who inherits land in any Israelite
> tribe must marry someone in her father's tribal clan, so that every Israelite will possess the
> inheritance of his fathers. [9]No inheritance may pass from tribe to tribe, for each Israelite
> tribe is to keep the land it inherits." [10]So Zelophehad's daughters did as the LORD
> commanded Moses. [11]Zelophehad's daughters--Mahlah, Tirzah, Hoglah, Milcah and
> Noah--married their cousins on their father's side. [12]They married within the clans of the
> descendants of Manasseh son of Joseph, and their inheritance remained in their father's
> clan and tribe.

If the Bible told us that Mary, the birth mother of Jesus, had no brothers, the "daughters and inheritance" custom, would add more credibility to both Mary and Joseph being from the tribe of Judah. Still, here, the interesting thing to note is the existence of the "daughters and inheritance" custom.

Female circumcisions

Some sources refer to "Female circumcisions (FC)" with the phrases: "Female genital cutting (FGC)" or "Female genital mutilation (FGM)". One such source is the *Wikipedia*. Its entry on "Female circumcisions" is very detailed and includes discussions of the types of FC; the "debate over the various terms – "FC", "FGC", and "FGM"; of its "prevalence", of its "cultural and religious aspects"; its "medical consequences"; its "sexual consequences", and "attempts to end the practice of FGC". However, only the types of FC are presented here. That portion of the entry reads, as follows:

Female genital cutting (FGC), female genital mutilation (FGM), or female circumcision (FC), is the excision or tissue removal of any part of the female genitalia for cultural, religious or other non-medical reasons. It is not the same as the procedures used in gender reassignment surgery or the genital modification of intersexuals.

Different types:

There are several distinct practices of FGC that range in severity, depending on how much genital tissue is cut away. Four major types have been categorized by the WHO[7] (see source for Diagram 1), although there is some debate as to whether all common forms of FGC fit into these four categories, as well as issues with the reliability of reported data.[8]

Type I: Clitoridectomy

Clitoridectomy involves the removal or splitting of the clitoral hood, termed "hoodectomy" (or "clitorodotomy"), with or without excision of the clitoris.[4] (*see source for Diagram 1B*) The clitoral hood is the female prepuce, homologous to the foreskin of the male. This term was devised in The Sudan by the Anglo-Sudanese administration in 1946 in an attempt to promote this "milder" form of FGC instead of the more severe Type III, infibulation or pharaonic circumcision, that was widely practiced. Removal of the clitoral hood may be performed in order to increase sexual response.

Type II: Excision

Excision refers to clitoridectomy (removal of the prepuce and the clitoris) plus the partial or total removal of the labia minora, the inner lips of the vulva (*see source for Diagram 1C*). Type II circumcision is a more extensive form of FGC compared to Type I and due to the sewing together of the leftover labia minora epidermis, which contains sweat glands, a buildup of sweat and urine in the closed off space beneath this closure can lead to local or urinary infection, septicemia, hemorrhaging and cyst formation.[9] This type of FGC is also called *khafd*, meaning reduction in Arabic.

Type III: Infibulation

Type III is the most severe form of FGC and is called infibulation or *pharaonic circumcision* (referring to the Pharaohs who were thought to practice this form). Infibulation involves extensive tissue removal of the external genitalia, including all of the labia minora and the inside of the labia majora, leaving a raw open wound. The labia majora are then held together using thorns or stitching and the girl's legs are tied together for two to six weeks, to prevent her from moving and allow the healing of the two sides of the vulva. Nothing remains of the normal anatomy of the genitalia, except for a wall of flesh from the pubis down to the anus, with the exception of a pencil-size opening at the inferior portion of the vulva to allow urine and menstrual blood to pass through (*see source for Diagram 1D*). Generally, a male nurse deemed to have the necessary skill carries out this procedure, and a local anesthetic is used. However, when carried out "in the bush", infibulation is often performed by an elderly matron or midwife of the village, with no anesthesia used.[10]

A reverse infibulation can be performed to allow for sexual intercourse (often by the husband using a knife on the wedding night) or when undergoing labor, or by female relatives, whose responsibility it is to inspect the wound every few weeks and open it some more if necessary. During childbirth, the enlargement is too small to allow vaginal delivery, and so the infibulation must be opened completely and restored after delivery. Once again, the legs are tied together to allow the wound to heal, and the procedure is repeated for each subsequent act of intercourse or childbirth. When childbirth takes place in a hospital, the surgeons may preserve the infibulation by enlarging the vagina with deep episiotomies. Afterwards, the patient may insist that her vulva be closed again so that her husband does not reject her.[10]

This practice is reported to cause the disappearance of sexual pleasure for the women affected, as well as major medical complications. However, a five-year study of 300 women and 100 men in Sudan found indications that "sexual desire, pleasure, and orgasm are experienced by the majority of women who have been subjected to this extreme sexual mutilation, in spite of their being culturally [bound] to hide these experiences."[11]

Most advocates of the practice continue to perform the procedure in adherence to standards of beauty that are very different from those in the west. Many infibulated women will contend that the pleasure their partners receive due to this procedure is a definitive part of a successful marriage.

Type IV: Other types

There are other forms that are collectively referred to as Type IV and usually do not involve any tissue removal at all, but rather the "cutting" is simulated with a knife as part of a ceremony. This includes a diverse range of practices, including pricking the clitoris with needles, burning or scarring the genitals as well as ripping or tearing of the vagina or introducing herbs into the vagina to cause bleeding and a narrowed vaginal opening (ref). Type IV is found primarily among isolated ethnic groups as well as in combination with other types.

(Source: Female genital cutting. (2007, November 13). In *Wikipedia, The Free Encyclopedia*. Retrieved 16:48, November 13, 2007, from http://en.wikipedia.org/w/index.php? title=Female_genital_cutting&oldid=171111367)

[4] Female genital mutilation, World Health Organization, June 2000, http://www.who.int/mediacentre/factsheets/fs241/en/>. Retrieved on 2007-03-10.

[7] *Female Genital mutilation - A joint WHO/UNICEF/UNFPA statement, Department of Reproductive Health and Research (RHR), World Health Organization, <http://www.who.int/*

reproductive-health/publications/fgm/fgm_statement.html>

[8] S Elmusharaf; N Elhadi, L Almroth (2006-07-15). "Reliability of self reported form of female genital mutilation and WHO classification: cross sectional study". *BMJ* **333** (7559): pp. 124. doi:10.1136/bmj.38873.649074.55. PMID 16803943. Retrieved on 2007-03-03.

[9] http://www.cirp.org/pages/female/diriel/

[10] [a] [b] Pieters, Guy, M.D.; Albert B. Lowenfels, M.D., F.A.C.S. (April 1977). "Infibulation in the Horn of Africa". *New York State Journal of Medicine* 77 (6): 729-731.

[11] Lightfoot-Klein, Hanny, M.A. (August 1989). "The Sexual Experience and Marital Adjustment of Genitally Circumcised and Infibulated Females in The Sudan". *The Journal of Sex Research* 26 (3): 375-392. The Society for the Scientific Study of Sexuality.

The meaning of each of the phrases – "lust of the flesh", "lust of the eyes", and "pride of life"

Paraphrased, this author's understanding of the three phrases is, as follows:

The "**lust of the flesh**" encompasses "all those things, which raise the flame of an evil desire and/or covetousness within an individual and which seem to imply a promise to gratify the craving of the flesh" – or worded differently, "all those things, which raise the flame of an evil desire and/or covetousness within an individual and which seem to imply a promise to gratify our senses, our sexual desires, physical desires (*non-sexual physical desires*), and/or our mental desires".

The "**lust of the eyes**" encompasses "all those things, which raise the flame of an evil desire and/or covetousness within an individual, when she or he sees those things".

The "**pride of life**" encompasses "all those things and/or conditions associated with our physical world and/or our spiritual world, which when associated with a particular individual, are a source of pride for that individual". (Note: *The spiritual world was included, because someone could, for example, become prideful of the fact that he was the Pope. And such pride might prevent that individual from doing things God's way.*)

The meaning of the word: "Chastely"

The essay – "Did Mary also have to be sinless, since Jesus was born sinless through her?" referenced a verse from Mary 1:5. Where the word – "Mary", stands for "The Gospel of the birth of Mary". Mary 1:5 reads:

> Mary 1:[5]In this manner they lived for about twenty years chastely, in the favour of God, and the esteem of men, without any children.

Today, the use of the word – "chastely" might be taken by some to mean "not having experienced sexual intercourse". However, the definition of the word – "chaste" in *Wiktionary*, reads:

> "'Chaste', is an *adjective*: 1. maintaining the integrity of the powers of life and love placed within the person and opposing any behavior that would violate one's personal dignity or the dignity of another. 2. (*sometimes considered incorrect*) abstaining from sexual intercourse. Note: chaste is often confused with *abstinence. Strictly speaking, chaste* means 'pure' and not 'abstaining from sex', because married couples are often exhorted to have 'chaste sex' – cf. the Vatican encyclical *Casti Connubii* (Of Chaste Wedlock)." (Source: "chaste". *Wiktionary, The Open Dictionary*, Retrieved 22:08, November 16, 2007, from http://en.wiktionary.org/w/index.php?title=chaste&oldid=3033910)

Thus, in spite of the modern usage of the word – "chaste" and consistent with the previous definition, the meaning – "not having experienced sexual intercourse", seems inappropriate because other verses in "The Gospel of the birth of Mary" imply that Mary's parents must have engaged in sexual intercourse. For instance, Mary 2:5 is part of a conversation between Mary's father and an angel. This conversation occurs after Mary's father has been rebuked by a higher-ranking priest for having no children. In Mary 2:5, the angel indicates that God shuts the wombs of some women, so He might open it later to display a special birth. And the evidence of a shut womb cannot be confirmed without sexual intercourse occurring. Thus, once more, the context of "The Gospel of the birth of Mary" adds credibility to the word – "chastely", meaning "'morally pure in thought or conduct' and 'decent and modest'", which would allow sexual intercourse under a marriage covenant.

BIBLIOGRAPHY

The sources for this discussion are too numerous to list individually. Those that can be listed individually will be. The rest will be listed by the source media or organization.

Groups: My Immediate Family

Individuals:
Herbert & Ted Armstrong
Pastor Alistair Begg
Dr. James M. Boice
Pastor Tom Brock
Diane Burrell
Rev. Eugene Burrell
Nicolas Criticos
Dr. James Dobson
Dr. Tony Evans
Bob Fraley
Bob George
Dr. Jack Graham
Pastor Jack Hayford
Dr. June Hunt
Dr. D. James Kennedy
Pastor Steve King
Bob Lepine
Crawford W. Loritts, Jr.
Rev. James MacDonald
Dr. Walter Martin
Josh McDowell
Dr. J. Vernon McGee
Dr. David Moore
John P. Newport
Pastor Bob Phillips
Dennis & Barbara Rainey
Henriette Rankine
Travette Scroggins
Dr. Charles F. Stanley
Lee Strobel
Phillip A. Succarotte
Dr. Merrill F. Unger
Stu Weber
Dr. Ravi Zacharias

Radio Programs: Discover the Word

Family Life Today
Focus on the Family
Grace to You
In Touch Ministries
Leading the Way
Let My People Think
Listen to Jesus
Love Worth Finding
People to People
So What
The Bible Answer Man
The Pastor's Study
Thru the Bible
Truth for Life
Walk in The Word

Literature: Campus Crusade for Christ
Radio Programs listed above
Reasons To Believe
The Navigators
Worldwide Church of Christ

Audiotapes: Radio **Programs** listed above
Reasons To Believe
The Navigators

VHS Tapes: Answers In Genesis
Creation Museum
Creation Science Evangelism
Focus on the Family
Grace to You
Ravi Zacharias International Ministries
Reasons To Believe

Television Programs: It Is Written
World Tomorrow

Other Organizations: Campus Crusade for Christ
Coral Ridge Ministries

INDEX

Appendix A
- Basis for the inclusion of the "Thinking view" and the "Eternal view" 499
- Daughters and inheritance custom 502
- Female circumcisions 503
- The meaning of each of the phrases – "lust of the flesh", "lust of the eyes", and "pride of life" 506
- The meaning of the word: "Chastely" 506

Charts, Summaries, and Tables
- Believe it or not - six views 40
- Comparison of Jewish Bible, Septuagint, Catholic O.T., and Protestant O.T. 96
- Four classical arguments for the existence of God 38-39

Computer Software
- 2003 Grolier Multimedia Encyclopedia xviii
- Holman Bible Dictionary xvii
- QuickVerse . . . . xviii, 116, 281, 307, 343

Definitions - phrases
- Abductive reasoning 24
- Argument from Being 38
- Argument from Design 39
- Argument from First Cause 38
- Argument from Man 39
- Biblical Aramaic 44
- Biblical canon 53
- Biblical Hebrew 47
- Catholic Bible 58
- Christian views 7
- Classical Hebrew 47
- Council of Trent 57
- Deductive reasoning 23
- Eternal view 4
- Free will 429
- Gravitationally bound cluster of stars 127
- Greek Old Testament 59
- Hebrew Old Testament 59
- Hebrew Text 60
- Immaculate Conception 296
- Inductive reasoning 24
- Involuntary learning 16
- Jewish Bible 60
- Jewish Canon 61

Jewish/Islamic views. 6
Koine Greek. 47
Latin Vulgate. 62
Library of Divine Revelation. 45
Massoretic text. 63
Nestorian Bible. 64
New Testament Apocrypha. 54
New Testament Canon. 55
New Testament – tests of canonicity. 88
Non-Jewish/non-Islamic views. 6
Non-Religious views. 3, 5
Old Testament Apocrypha. 55
Old Testament Canon. 57
Old Testament – tests of Canonicity. 83
Orthodox Bible. 64
Physical death. 251
Protestant Bible. 66
Religious views. 3
Retroductive reasoning. 24
Safe sex. 385
Semitic language. 43
Spiritual death. 251
Syriac Bible. 66
Thinking view. 4
Two horns. 127
Voluntary learning. 16
Definitions - words
Agnosticism. 40
Anagignoskomena. 53
Antilegomena. 52
Antilogomena. 52
Apocrypha. 53
Aramaic. 43
Atheism. 40
Atonement. 247
Autograph. 44
Bible. 45
Book. 45
Canon. 45
Canonicity. 46
Chastely. 300, 507
Codex. 46
Context. 422

Copy. 46
Creationism. 350, 351
Deism. 40
Deuterocanonical. 46
Evolution. 346, 347
Extant. 47
Freewill. 429
Greek. 47
Hebrew. 47
Homologomena. 54
Innocent. 247
LXX. 63
Macromutation. 349
Messiah. 162
Micromutation. 349
MSS., MSS, mss., mss. 48
Notha. 55
Panentheism. 40
Pantheism. 40
Penalty. 247
Pentateuch. 49
Peshitta. 65
Peshitto. 65
Polity. 78
Premise. 26
Protocanonical. 49
Pseudepigrapha. 57
Pseudopigrapha. 57
Question. 421
Scriptures 49
Septuagint. 66
Standard. 13
Syriac. 50
Tanakh. 66
Targum. 67
Temptation. 206
Testament. 50
Theism. 40
Torah. 50
Translation. 51
Version. 52
Organizations - Ministries
Answers-In-Genesis Ministry. 141, 259, 342, 359, 466, 510

Christian Research Institute (CRI). . . . 172, 345, 419
Coral Ridge Ministries. . . . 28, 119, 510
Eternal Productions. . . . 119, 120
Focus on the Family. . . . 107, 401
Living Stream Ministry. . . . 340
Living Way Ministries. . . . 153, 330, 372
The Navigators. . . . 419, 423, 430, 467, 510

Organizations - non-Ministries
B-F Enterprises. . . . xvi
Public Broadcasting System (PBS). . . . 36

People
Bailey, Edward V.. . . . vii
Bakke, Dr. Raymond J.. . . . 468-470
Barabbas. . . . 106, 116, 117, 145
Batten, Don.. . . . 359
Begg, Pastor Alistair. . . . 213, 509
Behe, Dr. Michael J.. . . . 259, 359
Brown, Ronald W.. . . . vii
Bumbulis, Dr. Michael J. . . . 135, 138
Burrell, Rev. Eugene.. . . . 419, 423, 424, 430, 467, 473, 474, 509
Criticos, Nicolas. . . . v, viii, xix, 476, 509
Darwin, Charles. . . . 259, 351
Descartes, Rene. . . . 500
Fraley, Bob. . . . 119, 127, 128, 509
Ham, Ken. . . . 141, 359, 466
Hayford, Pastor Jack.. . . . 153, 330, 372, 509
Josephus, Flavius. . . . 27, 28, 61, 78, 84, 85
Kennedy, Dr. D. James.. . . . 27, 28, 47, 79, 119, 509
King, Pastor Steve.. . . . 97, 108, 109, 339, 509
Lee, Witness. . . . 333, 340, 502
Lewis, C. S.. . . . 160, 161
Lindsey, Hal. . . . 119, 125
Madoo, Robert A.. . . . vii
Marin, Dr. Walter. . . . 172, 173, 345, 419, 457, 509
Mayfield, Margy. . . . 97, 107, 108, 401
McDowell, Josh. . . . 134, 509
Moore, Dr. David. . . . 106, 107, 509
Morin, Stephen. . . . 97, 107, 401
Mortenson, Dr. Terry. . . . 342
Nestorius.. . . . 48
Papania, Tom. . . . 97, 107, 108
Pilate, Pontius.. . . . 27, 102, 117, 159, 250
Richardson, Don. . . . 275

Rickford, John. vii
Russell, Dr. Rex. 113
Strobel, Lee.. . . . . 134, 509
Tacelli, Ronald. 36
Temple, Dr. Dick L.. . . . . 184, 185, 214
Unger, Dr. Merrill F... . . . . 153, 154, 328-330, 509
Wickliffe, John. 45
Wieland, Carl. 359
Programs - radio
Becoming People of Love. 339
Focus on the Family. 107
Moore on Life. 106, 107
References - Books
1001 Things Everyone Should Know About Science. 347
Darwin's Black Box: The Biochemical Challenge to Evolution. 259, 359
Eternity in their Hearts. 275
God Reveals the identity of the 'Beast'. 119, 127
Last Call!!!. . . . . vii, xvi, xvii, 28, 36, 105, 107, 143, 238, 327, 436, 451, 462
Mere Christianity. 160
Millions of Years & the Downfall of the Christian West. 342
One Blood. 359
The Lost books of the Bible and the Forgotten Books of Eden. 299, 312
The New Testament – Recovery Version. 333, 340
The Urban Christian. 468
Unger's Bible Handbook. 154, 328, 330
What the Bible Says About Healthy Living. 113
References - Essays
Are all questions valid and/or contextually appropriate?. . . . 415, 427, 429, 435, 441, 458, 463, 464
Are deathbed conversions to Christianity fair?. vii
Did God create man through evolution?. vii
Did Jesus claim to be God and/or the Son of God?. 270
Do the four Gospels present . . .He died on the cross?. vii
Does God exist?. 270, 456, 457
Does it matter, if the two genealogies . . . Zerubbabel?. 327
Does the Bible contain . . . Jewish nation in 1948?. 28, 105, 107
Does the Bible contradict itself?. xiii
Does the union of a sperm and an egg create human life?. 367, 376
How do we know that the genealogy of Jesus in the Gospel of Luke is through Mary?. 106
How should Christians respond to a "We-don't-know" statement?. vii
Is evolution a matter of facts or of faith?. . . . . vii, 451
Is it proper to use the Bible to prove the Bible?. vii

Is Jesus the only way to God?.. vii
Is the Bible the inspired word of God?. 19, 27, 70, 131, 270
Is variety the spice of life?. 390
Was the 'Big Bang' an exploding 'Point of Singularity'?. 462
What are the essential concepts of Christianity?. 436
What do biblical scholars, Christian historians, and others say, about the formation of the Christian Bible?. xiii, 61, 67
What is biblical Justice?. xiii
What is life all about?. vii
What is the only meaningful question, about "God" and "Christianity"?. vii, 30, 258
Why are there more names in . . . listed by Matthew?. 327
References - from computer software
2003 Grolier Multimedia Encyclopedia.. 295, 302, 347, 351, 369
Holman Bible Dictionary. 47, 48, 55, 58, 61, 65, 77, 79, 116, 162, 164, 204-206, 279, 290, 291, 373, 416
References - On-line
Webster's Revised Unabridged Dictionary. 52, 54, 57
Scientific concepts referenced in the Bible
Electricity. 127
Helicopter.. 125
How some things hold together. 124
Innumerable Stars. 123, 126
Matter is composed of things that we cannot see.. 123
The Earth is floating in space. 122
The Earth is spherical.. 126
The gravitationally bound Pleiades star cluster. 126
Tapes - audio
Abortion and Adoption. 372
Evil and Human Suffering. 173, 345, 419
From Mafia to Ministry.. 107
Spiritual Warfare: The Story of Stephen Morin. 107, 401
Tapes - video
A Question of Origins. 120
Creation Mini-series. 141
Mount St. Helens. 343
One Blood.. 359, 466
Toll-free telephone numbers
Answers In Genesis Ministry is (800) 778-3390. 466
Coral Ridge Ministries (800) 229-WORD. 28
Eternal Productions is (877) 370-7770 120
Focus on the Family is (800) 232-6459. 107, 401
Living Way Ministries is (800) 776-8180. 372